NATIONAL
TREASURE

NATIONAL TREASURE

The History of Trans Canada Airlines

PETER PIGOTT

HARBOUR PUBLISHING

Harbour Publishing
P.O. Box 219, Madeira Park, BC Canada V0N 2H0
www.harbourpublishing.com

Harbour Publishing acknowledges the financial support of the Government of Canada through the Book Publishing Industry Development Program (BPIDP) and the Canada Council for the Arts, and the Province of British Columbia through the British Columbia Arts Council, for its publishing activities.

THE CANADA COUNCIL | LE CONSEIL DES ARTS
FOR THE ARTS | DU CANADA
SINCE 1957 | DEPUIS 1957

Printed in Canada

Cover and page design by Martin Nichols
Front cover illustration from a 1948 Trans Canada Airlines flight schedule
Back cover photos (clockwise from top left): Significant airplanes in the history of TCA: the DC3, the North Star, the Lancaster, and the Constellation, all courtesy Air Canada Archives.

Acronyms used in photo credits: BCA: British Columbia Archives; DND: Government of Canada, Department of National Defence; DOT: Government of Canada, Department of Transportation; LBPIA: Lester B. Pearson International Airport; NAC: National Archives of Canada; SML: Science Museum London; UAA: United Airlines Archives.

All photographs not otherwise credited are courtesy Air Canada Archives.

National Library of Canada Cataloguing in Publication Data

Pigott, Peter.
  National treasure

  Includes bibliographical references and index.
  ISBN 1-55017-268-9

  1. Trans-Canada Airlines—History. I. Title.
HE9815.T72P54 2001   387.7'06'571   C2001-910908-3

for
John Charles Pigott

Preface

National Treasure, the history of Trans Canada Airlines, is the story of Canada itself or, more precisely, of this nation between 1937 and 1964. Though I did not consciously set out to write a social history, by the fourth chapter I could no longer ignore the ghosts that intruded on my computer screen. Everyone, it seemed, who had ever been part of TCA in its twenty-seven-year existence wanted to tell their stories, thus my narrative line weaves back and forth through the lives of these people, especially those who joined the company in 1937 and were still working there when it became Air Canada on June 1, 1964. Another common theme is the progression of technology, as each of them climbed the corporate ladder—from radio operator to dispatcher, accounts clerk to vice-president of finance. Often I lifted their stories directly from the employee newsletter, *Between Ourselves*, and these accounts themselves became an exercise in social history. For this reason, I included employees' poems, jokes, complaints, letters, obituaries and personal stories and gave them equal place with aircraft specifications, fleet purchases and annual reports. If today we find many of these offerings naive, politically incorrect and even silly, we must remember that none of the writers ever supposed that they were composing great literary works or that they would be read far in the future. Conversely, passengers' gripes about lost luggage and rude counter staff and questions in the House of Commons concerning the airline's monopoly or the confrontational relations between management and pilots could have been taken out of the *Globe and Mail* this morning.

Slashed across the pages are the jarring death notices written after aircraft crashes, supplemented during the war with the casualty lists of TCA staff who had enlisted. An excerpt from a poem by stewardess Mary Wright after a company aircraft disappeared over the Atlantic is a sonata in defiance:

> Pity us, you of the common lot?
> Life's sweeter if short to us of the brave.
> You stumble your way to a well-planned grave,
> But sudden and true,
> To ours we flew.

The two generations that formed the airline, post-World War I and post-World War II, could not help but be influenced by those monumental conflicts. Whether they went over the top at the Somme (or more likely knew someone who had) or were part of the RCAF's 6 Group in Yorkshire or bought Victory Bonds at home, every TCA employee, like every Canadian of the day, was conditioned by those world wars. A passenger flying TCA to Vancouver on Christmas Eve, 1944, put it eloquently in "Night Flight": "Looking at his fellow travellers, he was struck by the wealth of human sorrow, joy and consolation within the Lodestar cabin. The country had been at war for five years..."

Few Canadians today are aware of how much TCA contributed to the war effort, either through the Canadian Government Trans Atlantic Air Service (CGTAS) or on the home front. Far more than just providing transportation, the airline was a symbol of the nation's coming of age, especially when its aircraft began crossing the Atlantic. Repeatedly employees of that era would write, "I wanted to do something for Canada so I joined TCA."

I could not resist bringing Gordon Roy McGregor into this story long before he joined TCA, his destiny is so linked with that of the airline. But it was characteristic of the man that when asked what he thought his place in TCA's history would be, he replied, "It would have to be a very detailed history if I go down in it." While C.D. Howe's bulldozer-like drive protected the company through its first twenty-two years, it was "GRM" who had the harder part. Both men consistently put the welfare of the airline ahead of their own careers, but by the time of McGregor's presidency, publicly owned airlines were less in fashion and the strings that came attached to them longer and more byzantine. Tasked by the government with running TCA—"on sound business principles," as he used to say—he suffered "milk runs," money-losing show-the-flag routes and aircraft so uncompetitive that their only virtue was that they were locally built and thus provided employment for Canadians. Most perfidious of all were his immediate bosses, the ministers of transport who bent with every prevailing wind. It was expected that the Conservative era would be the worst of times for McGregor, but when the returning Liberals under Lester Pearson abetted competition even on the main transcontinental artery, McGregor, a Battle of Britain hero, must have found it harder than when the Luftwaffe was the only enemy. With regard to airline competition, *National Treasure* should be read as a companion piece to *Wingwalkers,* my history of Canadian Airlines. As McGregor predicted, one day the CPR shareholders would get tired of supporting Grant McConachie's schemes and the two airlines would be merged.

The scenes in the book move constantly with the expansion of the airline. Beginning with Stevenson Airport, Winnipeg, and moving to the camaraderie of the original employees, to the lonely bachelors of Armstrong, Ontario, to bomb-shattered London immediately after the war, to idyllic Bermuda and "Bowker's Airline," the story culminates at the airline's headquarters at Place Ville Marie in downtown Montreal. The single, immutable reference to all of this is Ottawa and the House of Commons, where the airline's birth was debated, its monopoly was endlessly questioned, and it was eventually transformed into Air Canada.

My single personal experience with Trans Canada Airlines took place at its sales office at Regent Street in London. It was this office to which my parents brought our family directly (I think) from the immigration section at Canada House, to purchase tickets for the journey to our new home. I remember seeing in the office a display of models of aircraft that the airline then flew. Through researching this book, I now know a few more details about that office: that the advertising posters would have proclaimed "Canada In Only a Day by TCA" and "More Time for Play, Fly TCA," and that the panelling behind the desks of the passenger agents was knotty pine—brought over from Canada. I know too that the aircraft models had actually been made locally by a young Englishman in Reading, Berks. One of the planes, either a Constellation or North Star, was a "cutaway," and we could peer in at the little passengers, all contentedly waiting to be served by a stewardess who stood in the galley. The flight crew were at their stations, supremely confident in the power and reliability of the Curtiss-Wrights or Merlins (with plastic discs for propellers) that powered their aircraft. That one could travel in such elegance amazed us, and it was this TCA model that became our family's first impression of the country we were going to—all those well-dressed, smiling Canadians in miniature, flying—what else but TCA. Family lore has it that on our own flight over, the stewardess allowed us to sit anywhere we liked "because we were immigrating to Canada." Thus when we landed at Dorval Airport on a luminously clear winter night and crowded into a taxi—a big American car—we knew we were in Canada. Just outside the airport was a giant, heart-stopping neon sign that proclaimed "Dominion." The airline, the country, our new-found patriotism— it was all interconnected.

Only later did the culture shock set in. It wasn't that the streets of Canada were not paved in gold or that "Dominion" turned out to be the name of a grocery chain, but to our chagrin Trans Canada Airlines, the airline that we had thought of as the soul of the country, disappeared into history. It was time for Act Two.

Acknowledgements

Many people helped in their own ways in the preparation of this manuscript, but pride of place goes to three:

Clayton Glenn supplied not only personal memories of TCA but his own studies on aviation as well—and provided updated lists of addresses of other retirees. Both he and Ken Leigh, the son of TCA's Dick Leigh, read my manuscript with great thoroughness, correcting me (gently) at gross errors in engineering, economics and aviation history. Ken also generously selected photos from his own extensive collection for the book.

Air Canada's photographer Brian J. Losito, also excelled in generosity of photos and time and giving up his weekend to accommodate my schedule, as he has done with my other efforts.

National Treasure has many other godparents who entrusted me with family photos, diaries, newsletters and brochures. Ron Peel, Alan Bain, Tim Hollick-Kenyon, Lindy Rood, John W. Reid, Heather Chetwynd and the Lothian family all helped. My gratitude to Janet Proudfoot with her notes on decorating the North Star and explaining the legend of the rabbits on the Airways maps, to Ross Smyth for excerpts from his diaries (his youthful enthusiasm evident six decades later), to Kathleen Torell (nee Stewart) for her account of first seeing her future husband while taking the Post Office truck to Malton, to Philip G. Johnson, the son of one of aviation's greatest figures, for his reminiscences about his father and what it was to be a Yankee when Canada still basked in the British imperial sun, to Dud Taylor for unravelling the mysteries of radio antennae and reading my manuscript, to Joanne Peck, who believed in this project before I typed the first word, to George Brien for his details of the TCA radio operator's profession in the 1950s, and finally to the late Jack Dyment.

Besides supplying me with accounts of his early training and Lodestar/DC-3 days, Max Church found me Murray Wallace, whose perceptive comments on the Bristol Freighter and Vickers Vanguard are entertainment themselves. Speaking for many TCA pilots, Wallace summed up his career thus: "My wife claims I have never done a day's work in my life, and it was all so enjoyable that I have to agree with her!"

The dashing George Lothian, featured in my previous book *Flying Canucks III*, might have stepped out of a novel. Ferry pilot, CGTAS pioneer, author and Viscount enthusiast, he was not only witness to much of our national aviation history but, with Lindy Rood, a central character in it. Trans Canada Airlines was fortunate to count both men as early employees.

Lockheed Martin's Eric Schulzinger and United Airlines' Barbara Hanson furnished the photos and Sean Smith of the Canadian Auto Workers and Peter Foster of the Air Canada Pilots Association the material on labour relations. I am grateful for the support I received from Doug Port and Priscille Leblanc of

Air Canada, Ian Wilson of the National Archives, Wayne Ramsay of Commemorations Division, and to Second Lieutenant C.L. Robertson, Heritage and History, 1 Canadian Air Division, Winnipeg. As always, my admiration and thanks to the Lester B. Pearson Library's Rejean Tremblay, from whose hands hard-to-find reference sources appeared as if by magic.

For a whole year, log books, newspaper clippings, aircraft models and photographs of Trans Canada Airlines camped out in the Pigott dining and living rooms, filling our family's lives even to the point of detestation. Belated kisses to my wife and two daughters, who endured (and sometimes got me out of) my writer's black moods. This book could never have been written without their support.

National Treasure is dedicated to my father, John Charles Pigott. It was he who imbued me with this madness for aviation, which through my writing I have tried to explain to others. Of the same generation of many who founded TCA, my father grew up during the Depression, fought a war on the other side of the world, came home, raised a family and saw me through university. He died in 1987 and is buried in the Field of Honour not far from Dorval Airport. I miss him every day.

Donald MacLaren (right) and Herbert Hollick-Kenyon (centre) posing with Lt. Col. Jimmy Doolittle when picking up the Lockheed Electra CF-AZY in Burbank, California, July 6, 1936.

C H A P T E R   1

O n April 10, 1937, when "His Majesty King George VI, by and with the advice and consent of the Senate and the House of Commons," gave his assent for the Trans Canada Airlines Act to be enacted, commercial air travel was born in Canada. There had been a host of air companies before, mainly in the bush, but as a result of the country's size, none had been economically viable. Now the federal government was stepping into the breach.

Evidence might suggest that the country lurched into this public monopoly of transcontinental air services in a fit of absent-mindedness. It was, however, the result of a policy carefully orchestrated by the Liberal government. Its chief architect, the minister of railways and canals, Clarence Decatur Howe, later summed up that policy thus: "It had been contemplated that Trans Canada Air Lines would be a non-competitive, non-profit system of transportation by air, planned to avoid the duplication of services that were the outgrowth of competitive building for profit in the field of surface transportation. The reason for this is not hard to explain. Canada, having one twelfth the population of the United States, could support only one service . . . and to have a second coast to coast service would be wasteful and unjustified."[1]

The truth is that airlines have always been ruinously expensive, and heavy political and financial investment in airports, airways and aircraft fleets have made them ideal candidates for public ownership, an option that Australia and Britain also took up in the 1930s.

Not since November 7, 1885, when Lord Strathcona hammered in the last spike for the Canadian Pacific Railway (CPR) at Craigellachie, British Columbia, had there been anything like it in the Dominion. The CPR's east–west lifeline had brought the concept of Canada as a nation into reality—although how a privately owned railway, its shares held mostly by foreign nationals, became an instrument of national policy is a convoluted story. From the earliest days of settlement in Canada the central government had spent public monies, extended public credits and made grants of publicly owned land to assist in providing transportation. The promise of railway construction had even formed an integral part of agreements for Confederation, from building the Intercolonial

Railway for the Maritimes entirely at public cost to connecting British Columbia by rail to the East. It was only after failing to interest venture capital in the latter that Sir John A. Macdonald and successive Conservative prime ministers entered into their arrangement with the CPR, giving it a virtual monopoly in western Canada in order to satisfy the terms of Confederation.

Now the federal government was once again going to embark on a venture that it hoped would, in one decisive move, overcome this country's vast geographical barriers, thwart the Americans, reassure the British and unite the country. The prime minister of the day, the Liberal William Lyon Mackenzie King, would have taken exception to being compared with Conservative Prime Minister Macdonald, but each man recognized the opportunity with which technology had presented him: as Macdonald took to the steam engine and the telegraph, so King to the aircraft and radio beam. Given the country's minuscule tax base, both men were forced to guarantee their chosen means of transport a monopoly, ensuring decades of political resentment and economic discontent. But whatever the criticism, until almost the last decade of the twentieth century, both railway and airline admirably served the cause of Canada's unity.

No other airline in this hemisphere and few elsewhere has been launched with such pomp and circumstance, but Trans Canada Airlines: Canada's National Air Service—the very name denoted its purpose—was baptized at birth to be more than just a means of commercial transport. Other air companies may provide transportation; this one was to be a flying symbol of national identity—a maple leaf with wings. To it would be entrusted the privilege and responsibility of flying the major artery of a sparsely populated country. And if in the end the volume of traffic did not warrant the government's investment of personnel and planes, then—and only then—would private enterprise be permitted to pick up the service.

Canada's earliest experiment with public ownership had actually begun at the provincial level, when in 1906 the government of Ontario established its own power company. Ottawa's direct entry into the transport sector came a decade later, when Conservative Prime Minister Sir Robert Borden refused to permit the CPR to purchase majority shares in the Canadian Northern Railway. Consequently, to prevent the economic and social hardship that would take place if the railway went into receivership, on September 30, 1917, his government was reluctantly forced into buying the railway. Later they consolidated it with other equally bankrupt lines into the sickly giant, the Canadian National Railway (CNR). When the Liberals, led by William Lyon Mackenzie King, came to power in 1921, the public ownership of railways, maritime services and hotels began in earnest. To keep faltering ventures out of the CPR's clutches, they voted to spend money freely to buy up unprofitable railways in the East and build steamships for Pacific coastal routes, which were abandoned soon afterwards. Thus, no matter which party was in power, the coherent policy in national transportation was to keep the CPR and the CNR empires in a delicate balance, each serving as a financial yardstick for and political check on the other. It was, in fact, the hope for democracy in Canada that both railroad empires would continue to strive earnestly but that neither would succeed. As in Australia, there emerged a dual public–private system in railways and steamship lines. And into this system was born commercial aviation.

Canadians were slow to recognize the potential of air transport, and the first airmail flight in Canada, between Seattle and Victoria, was flown by two Americans, Eddie Hubbard and William E. Boeing, on March 3, 1919. The previous month the Canadian Pacific Railway had applied to extend its charter to include operating an air company, but when granted this had not pursued it further. However, the company's initiative sufficiently alarmed the government that it passed the Air Board Act to regulate civil aviation in the Dominion; this legislation was all that Ottawa would do for aviation for almost a decade.

In contrast, governments elsewhere were deeply involved, both financially and politically. On April 1, 1924, the British government consolidated four money-losing, private local airlines to form Imperial Airways, a single international carrier that it then subsidized to carry the Royal Mail and colonial administrators throughout the Empire. On the continent, commercial aviation was so far advanced that it was possible to purchase a collection of air tickets and travel from Helsingfors in Norway to Casablanca in North Africa completely by air. In September 1920 the US Congress appropriated $1,250,000 for the construction of lighted "airways," and within four years a coast-to-coast airmail service was in operation with aerial beacons and landing strips (called "crack-up fields" by the aviators) at 25-mile intervals from New York to San Francisco. The US Post Office stopped flying the mail itself in 1925 and instead awarded mail contracts to private air companies, jump-starting that country's commercial aviation industry. With such incentives, aircraft manufacturers like Bill Boeing could pool resources with Pratt & Whitney, the aero-engine makers, to build aircraft that would one day carry cargo and passengers for a profit, thus freeing airlines from reliance on mail subsidies.

In Canada, however, the prospects for commercial aviation were not as promising. The country was impoverished by the Great War and the railroad crisis, its population centres were too few and too far apart, and there was neither venture capital nor a local aircraft industry. And although by 1926 there were twenty-nine registered air companies in Canada, aviation was still considered a fringe means of transport. Used by surveyors, mining engineers, foresters and the Post Office, aircraft were an adjunct rather than a rival to the railways, most useful as connectors between railheads and ocean-going ships, mining camps or remote settlements. As for administration, the only point on which both prime ministers, W.L. Mackenzie King and R.B. Bennett, were in agreement was that civil aviation should be sloughed off to the Department of National Defence for administration. It was, therefore, left by the government "to fly by itself ... as in no other country."[2]

By the onset of the Depression, 80 percent of commercial air transport in Canada was in the hands of the Winnipeg grain entrepreneur James Richardson.

Within three years of buying his first aircraft in 1926, Richardson had success-fully expanded his air company, Western Canada Airways (WCA)—later renamed Canadian Airways Ltd. (CAL)—so that its network along with the routes of its subsidiaries stretched from Moncton to Edmonton and north to Aklavik. There were, however, large gaps in Richardson's network. There were no flights through the Rockies, and the Canadian cities of Vancouver and Victoria received their airmail via Seattle. And there was no air route between Windsor and Winnipeg because the pre-Cambrian Shield that had almost stymied railroad building sixty years earlier made the cost of constructing airports north of Lake Superior prohibitive for private enterprisers. Canadian airmail destined for the West crossed the border to Detroit; then, using the American airmail system, it was taken to Pembina, North Dakota, for delivery to Winnipeg.

On February 22, 1929, the federal government moved to close these gaps in east–west air communication by funding the Trans Canada Airway. An ambitious undertaking built partly for purposes of defence, it rivals the build-ing of the first railway across Canada. Its foundation was a system of stations that transmitted radio waves radiating in a circular pattern from antennas called loops. Each station had two such loops, one transmitting Morse signals in the form of "dit da" (As) and the other "da dit" (Ns). When a pilot listened to the signals on his low or medium frequency radio receiver, he knew he was to the right or the left of the beam by the A or N signals he was hearing, and that he was "on the beam" if he heard a steady hum. When he flew directly over or very near the station, no signal was heard; this was called the "cone of silence." The A and N signals were interrupted every half minute to transmit two other letters identifying the station—for example, UL for Montreal, FC for Fredericton, HZ for Halifax (these later became YUL, YFC and YHZ on luggage tags)—and three letters for American stations. Stretching 3,314 miles from Vancouver to Toronto with a side line north from Lethbridge to Calgary and Edmonton, the Airway joined eight public airports, eleven municipal airports and seventy-nine intermediate airports together with thirty-five radio range stations, the whole allowing for the reliable delivery of airmail and eventually passengers across the country.

Until Charles Lindbergh made his historic crossing from New York to Paris non-stop in 1927, it was generally agreed that as a means of mass transport, aviation would never pay its own way. Afterwards, most Canadians were will-ing to concede that it had "potential." The boards of the CNR and the CPR cer-tainly thought so. Never missing an opportunity to countercheck one other, each invested $250,000 in James Richardson's company. Of CAL's 127,088 shares, each took 10,000, and Sir Edward Beatty, president of the CPR, and Sir Henry Thornton, president of the CNR, accepted positions on CAL's board. But being dependent for the most part on the uncertainty of mining, even in pros-perous years CAL was never far from bankruptcy, and its only salvation lay in being appointed by the federal government to officially ply the Trans Canada Airway on its completion. Richardson understood that the national market could not support more than one transcontinental air venture, and he lobbied hard to prevent the government from considering potential rivals. The owners of other air companies protested to their members of parliament, but their pleas fell on deaf ears. Meanwhile, both Liberals and Conservatives shared the fear that the CPR would take up its 1919 option and start its own airline. Neither party wanted to see the competition between the privately owned CPR and the publicly owned CNR spread to aviation as well.

However, Canadian Airways' dominance in commercial aviation was objected to by Post Office officials, who considered it their duty to get the mail carried as cheaply as possible without concerning themselves about the effect on aviation companies. The situation was made even worse when on March 31, 1932, Prime Minister Bennett cancelled all federal airmail contracts. This was an entirely political move: Bennett represented the agricultural region around Calgary where the railway policies of previous

Prime Minister R.B. Bennett, who cancelled all airmail contracts in 1932, pushing Canadian Airways closer to insolvency.

ous governments had been disastrous to farmers, and he decided that it was cruel (and politically unwise) to subsidize airmail flights while the farmers were suffering the effects of the Depression. Unfortunately, the cancellation pushed CAL further toward insolvency. When Richardson complained, Bennett told him that if his company couldn't manage its own finances, it should fold. As the CAL figures below demonstrate, there was a market for mail, freight and passengers in Canada, but it was never large enough to give sufficient return on investment. Even in 1933, the worst year of the Depression, Richardson's airline business almost doubled, but his company still lost money.

Year	Passengers	Freight (lbs)	Mail (lbs)
1929	8,607	1,314,847	264,764
1930	4,659	601,661	111,155
1931	5,676	763,023	78,537
1932	8,583	1,869,336	162,977
1933	16,105	2,521,357	183,018

Source: Public Archives, Manitoba. CALP Box 9, File: "Brief on Northern Air Transport."

Bennett did promise, however, that in more prosperous times the airmail service would be resumed and CAL would receive first consideration. As he also implied this would include a monopoly to fly the Trans Canada Airway, Richardson determined to hang on, believing that the inauguration of the Airway, slated for 1936, would prevent his airline from closing down. To be fair, Bennett did understand the gravity of CAL's situation, but he also knew that no matter which company was chosen for the transcontinental air system, someone was going to be dissatisfied. He delayed the decision by appointing a Trans Canada Airway Committee to select the best candidate. To no one's surprise they recommended in 1933 that CAL be made the sole Airway operator. Had their recommendation been implemented immediately, Trans Canada Airlines would never have been born and the history of commercial aviation in Canada would have taken another course. But still unwilling to make a decision, Bennett returned the report to the committee for further study.

Bennett's secondary purpose in appointing an Airway committee had been to blunt international criticism. Without a national airline or even a department of commercial aviation, Canada was not equipped to participate in future British or American transatlantic air service schemes. For their part, the British would have been quite pleased for Imperial Airways to take over all airmail services within Canada on a subsidized basis, and they offered to invest up to 50 percent, as they had done in Australia, in a local airline of Ottawa's choice. But 1935 was an election year, and criticism in the press that Canada could barely muster a feeder service for US airlines received enough attention that both parties began calling for the creation of a national air service to use the Airway. As a result, Bennett underwent a political rebirth and introduced a series of new initiatives in the House, one of them being a conference on a transatlantic air service to be held that November in Ottawa. By the time it came off, however, he was out of office.

Below the border, meanwhile, airlines were thriving because the smaller ones had been merged to form four strong ones, while at the same time airframe and aero-engine technology had been developing. The three largest American airlines—American Airways, Transcontinental Air Transport and United Airlines—reported a total of 270 million revenue passenger miles that year. All three offered transcontinental services and the comfort of multi-engined, all-metal Ford or Boeing aircraft. Canada, with its Depression-years economic policies and US encroachment, was losing what little aviation infrastructure it had. In fact, the number of commercial pilots in the country declined from 474 in 1932 to 370 in 1936, and only five Canadian cities had any air connections at all, three of them being on a direct north–south axis. While these gave Canadian mail essential access to the postal systems of the United States, the Caribbean and South America, they did nothing for transportation across the country.

Montreal–Albany–New York was served by Canadian Colonial Airways, an American Airways company. Its flights went three times a day except Sunday, with a fare of $50 each way. For the majority of Canadians this was the closest they would come to flying on a commercial aircraft. The Winnipeg–Pembina, North Dakota, route had been inaugurated by Northwest Airlines on December 2, 1931. Vancouver–Seattle was served by United Airlines. In operation since July 1, 1934, this route was the result of the persuasiveness of Bill Templeton, the airport manager at Vancouver's Sea Island Airport. Moncton–Charlottetown was the only internal mail connection. Run by CAL, its existence had little to do with economics and everything to do with politics. Since 1931 Pan American Airways had been flying between Boston and Halifax as a preliminary step to eventually crossing the Atlantic. To prevent further American incursions into the Maritimes, even when other mail contracts were cut, the Bennett government allowed the Moncton–Charlottetown mail flight to continue. Passengers were carried on a "space available" basis.

In the rest of the country, there was little in the way of landing fields. The best equipped was Montreal's St. Hubert airport, which had been established in 1927 for the use of airships rather than aircraft. Vancouver's Sea Island Airport dated from 1931 and was little more than a flying school and repair shed. The country's second largest city, Toronto, to the vocal indignation of its mayor, had no international air connection at all because none of its many airfields was suitable. When in February 1935 the federal government offered to help build an airport either at the Toronto Flying Club, where the airfield was owned by CAL, or at Barker Field, eleven of the city's twenty councillors, the members of the Board of Trade and the Harbour Commissioners objected. They wanted it on Toronto Island—despite the disadvantage of fog—with either a bridge or a tunnel to connect it to the mainland. In spite of opposition from the federal government and the island's residents, city council approved the tunnel site in August 1935, the contract was given to Dominion Construction Corporation for $976,264 and digging began on October 15. But the Liberals under Mackenzie King had just been elected by a landslide, and King stopped work on the tunnel just two weeks later. The city sued, and it was December 14, 1936, before the suit was settled and the federal government made the city's options clear: if Toronto wanted a grant to build its airport it would have to accept the location chosen by the new Department of Transport; that was to be north of the city near the village of Malton. Everyone from the local RCAF squadron commander to the de Havilland Aircraft Company and the *Globe* newspaper opposed this choice, but fearful of being left off the Airway, the mayor gave in. In July 1937, twenty-four farms and a cemetery were bought up in the Malton area, and surveying for the airport began. The provincial government even promised to lay down a four-lane highway to it.

The Trans Canada Airway Committee had accomplished nothing by the time it was disbanded in 1935, but the minutes of its last meetings indicate that its members were undergoing a change of heart that did not augur well for CAL, even though Richardson had proved himself amenable to each new federal demand. When CAL had been underbid on the Winnipeg–Pembina

The Canadian Airways Stearman, based at Sea Island Airport for the mail contract. It would later be bought by TCA but never used for that purpose.

The Canadian Airways Dragon Rapide CF-AVJ at Sea Island Airport, Vancouver. The aircraft was flown by pilots E.P. "Billy" Wells, Maurice McGregor, Harry Winnie and junior pilot George Lothian, and maintained by Sam Reid. It was used to fly the first Canadian scheduled international airmail services between Vancouver and Seattle in 1935. It would later serve on the Vancouver–Victoria run.

mail contract by Northwest Airlines, the Post Office had offered the company Vancouver–Seattle as compensation. Richardson knew there would be more prestige than profit on this route, but rather than look the proverbial gift horse in the mouth, he accepted. Then judging his company's Stearman biplane *CF-ASF* to be adequate for the amount of mail expected, he ordered it taken out of storage and based at Sea Island Airport, but the Post Office insisted CAL use a de Havilland Rapide, a British-made plane that was assembled and serviced by de Havilland Canada in Toronto. Eager to please, Richardson complied, and on October 1, 1935, the first Canadian-owned, scheduled international airmail service began with the Rapide *CF-AVJ*. The Stearman was maintained at Sea Island as insurance against the Rapide's mechanical failure.

The committee, however, now doubted that Richardson could simultaneously manage a bush network and the mainline service. There was also a feeling that as the government had invested $7 million in the construction of the Airway, the contract should go to a public company. Two other recommendations also reflected committee members' growing support for the Liberals' position: all the principal officers of the airline chosen must be not only British subjects (as all Canadians were at that time), but resident in Canada. The first would keep Americans from bidding to fly the Airway and the second the British. As an added bonus, the second requirement would also prevent the CPR from bidding, because the majority of its shareholders lived in Britain.

The Westbound Mail

The drizzling rain was falling,
A nearby clock tolled eight;
They watched the sky with an eager eye
For the Westbound Mail was late.
The rain beat down on the old tin roof;
The hangar chief stood by.
When the drumming tone of a motor's drone
Came from the misty sky.

The beacon sent its welcome beam
To the flyer of the night;
He brought her down to the soggy ground
Down to the guiding light.
They swap the mail and shout, Okay,
And she roars and lifts her tail!
She's up again in the rain and hail;
On with the Westbound Mail!

The crystals stick on the windshield
And form a silvery veil;
The icy struts, a man with guts
And a sack of westbound mail.
Over the peaks of the mountains now,
Clear of their treacherous rim;
Away up there in the cold night air,
Just God, the Mail and him.

His thoughts turn back to a summer night
And a girl, not so long ago
Who shook her head and firmly said,
"While you're flying, No!"
He tried to quit the blooming job
And stick to the concrete trail;
But his wish came back to the canvas sack
And the feel of the Westbound Mail.

———————————— Trans Canada Air Lines Newsletter, 1939. Author unknown

The election of a Liberal government in 1935 gave James Richardson fresh hope, especially since as soon as Mackenzie King assumed power, he appointed a subcommittee of council to examine the Airway and prepare a briefing report to bring him up to date. Richardson took this as his cue to press his case to the new prime minister, his postmaster general, J.C. Elliott, and the neophyte minister for railways and canals, C.D. Howe. To each, Richardson presented a summary of CAL's achievements in pioneering the North without government support and asked that his company now be rewarded with the monopoly on the Airway. Both railway presidents, Sir Edward Beatty and S.J. Hungerford (who had replaced Sir Henry Thornton as president of the CNR), assured him they would lobby King on his behalf. The railways were keenly aware that if CAL went bankrupt they would lose their $250,000 investment. Meanwhile, Richardson's letters to the prime minister had been passed on to Howe, and in February 1936 the new minister wrote to him and to Beatty. It was essential, he told them, that both national railways be part of any future airline and, because both were already represented on CAL's board, Richardson was "fortunately situated."

Unfortunately, in the prime minister's opinion, Richardson's fatal error was that he alternately whined and curried favour to whatever the government was in power, much as he remembered the promoters of the Grand Trunk Railway behaving to the Conservatives during the railway construction boom.

He was very clear on two things. First, the development of commercial aviation was not going to be a repeat of the political corruption that had accompanied the overbuilding of the railways—a crime for which he blamed the Conservatives. Second, the two abominations of his life—Sir Edward Beatty and the Canadian Pacific Railway—were going to be kept as far from the Trans Canada Airway as possible. Despite its name and place in the national consciousness, the CPR was a foreign company, and as late as 1945 British shareholders still owned 62 percent of its voting stock, compared to 10 percent owned by Canadians. King is reported to have felt that "when he was at [#10] Downing Street he was really dealing with the CPR there because its policies were directed from London and aimed at carrying out Imperial designs rather than leaving Canada free to carry out its own."[3]

But only a fool would turn down the opportunity to make some political capital out of Bennett's two legacies to civil aviation—the almost completed Airway and the impending transatlantic air conference—and King embraced them both as his own. On November 22, 1935, British, Newfoundland, Irish and Canadian delegates met in Ottawa to discuss the means by which they could pool resources and co-operate in commercial aviation across the Atlantic. Canada, like Newfoundland and the Irish Free State, had little to offer in the way of technology, but their strategic locations on either side of the Atlantic made them essential as refuelling stops for the Imperial Airways seaplanes that London hoped would ultimately circumnavigate the globe. To encourage its Canadian hosts, the British put forward a tripartite plan called the Joint Operating Company (JOC), which made Montreal the North American terminal for all British transatlantic flights. Ottawa's contribution would be to provide landing rights for Imperial Airways seaplanes at Shediac, New Brunswick—just as it had already extended such rights to Pan American Airways—and the promise of meteorological information from Botwood, Nova Scotia. But more important, at this conference the Canadian government committed itself to establishing a national airline to fly between Montreal and Vancouver within the near future.

Clarence Decatur Howe, the minister who was expected to deliver on this promise, was just beginning his long and amazing career in the government. Although one of his forebears was Joseph Howe of Nova Scotia, "C.D." was born in Waltham, Massachusetts, in 1886 and came to Canada as a professor of civil engineering to teach at Dalhousie University in Halifax. In 1913 he became a naturalized Canadian and in the same year he was appointed chief engineer to the Board of Grain Commissioners at Fort William, Ontario. Widely travelled and fluent in Spanish and Italian, Howe also ran his own engineering firm; when elected by the local constituency in 1935, he was one of the wealthiest men in the House. When King made him minister of railways and canals and minister of marine, one of Howe's first priorities was to reorganize the CNR by replacing its trustee management with a directorate of seven.

Apolitical before 1935, Howe was as neutral toward the doctrines of both the Conservatives and Liberals as he was to public and private enterprise. There was, he said, only one test of the strength and weakness of each—parties and philosophies—namely, which one best served the needs of the Canadian public, and it wasn't the elixir of competition that made a business flourish but good management and relentless drive. A self-made millionaire, he was certainly no socialist but is remembered for building more public enterprises, from the National Harbours Board to the St. Lawrence Seaway, than any other minister before or since. On a personal level, the minister was described as "good-natured, affable and with a ready sense of humour, but with a mind that is razor-edged and a character that is not deficient in determination."[4] As the nation was to discover, Howe was all of that and more.

In the spring of 1936, anxious to begin talks on the Airway monopoly, Richardson sent the superintendent of his Pacific lines, former World War I air ace Don MacLaren, to Ottawa to lobby for him with the new minister. MacLaren's rival for Howe's attention, British North America Airways, had been organized by the financier Percy Parker in 1920, but by 1935 when Howe dealt with them, the members were all based in Toronto, all powerful businessmen, and, with a single exception, all prominent Liberals. They included Frank Common, president of Hydroelectric Securities; James Henry Gundy, chairman of Wood, Gundy & Co; Ray Lawson, director of the Royal Bank; C.G. McCullagh, financial editor and owner of the Toronto *Globe*; and Brigadier-General Victor W. Odlum. A year later E.P. Taylor, president of Brewing Corporation, and the Honourable J.L. Ralston apparently became members as well. However, in spite of their high profiles in the financial community, their airline still only existed on paper.

CAL, on the other hand, was the largest, most experienced air company in Canada, enjoying the support of both railways and now, to judge by his statements, the support of the new minister as well. Richardson was fully aware that he still had enemies in the Post Office but, as buying the Rapide for the Vancouver–Seattle run had demonstrated, he was willing to do whatever it took to placate them. About this time, his general manager, G.A. "Tommy" Thompson, persuaded him that the best way to do this was to demonstrate that his pilots were training to use the radio ranges of the Airway where flying by radio beam would be mandatory, and Richardson chose the Vancouver–Seattle route for instrument flying practice with the intention of eventually implementing passenger service there. The Rapide was fitted with a radio, and uniforms were introduced for the crew, although as yet they were unable to fly by instruments into Vancouver, as the DOT had not installed radio range facilities at the airport. CAL staff at Sea Island Airport at this time were pilots E.P. "Billy" Wells, Maurice McGregor and Harry Winnie, and the maintenance engineer was Sam Reid. There was also a young junior pilot named George Lothian who hoped to make first officer; his break came filling in on the Rapide when McGregor had the mumps.

A 1937 view of the terminal complex at Vancouver Sea Island airport. The control tower and administration building are in the background, right, and the new radio station monitoring the airway is on the left. In the foreground is TCA's first Lockheed 10A, CF-AZY, used on the Vancouver–Seattle international air services.

Wells and McGregor flew the first scheduled CAL passenger flight on March 7, 1936, but while summer is traditionally an airline's busiest season, between June 1 and 15 of that year the Rapide only carried 30 passengers over the route, while its competitor, United Airlines (UAL), carried 256. The success of UAL, which had already captured the lead in transcontinental flying throughout the United States, was largely due to the Boeing 247s that had been built exclusively for the company by its affiliate, the Boeing Airplane Company. The first 247 was launched on February 8, 1933, and entered service exclusively with UAL on March 30; such was Boeing's capacity for production that a year later there were thirty 247s in United's fleet. The aircraft made it possible to cross the United States in 19 hours and 30 minutes—eight hours faster than the Ford Trimotors of its closest competitor, Transcontinental & Western Air Transport. The 247 carried four fewer passengers than the Trimotor and its main wing spar passed through the cabin, but these drawbacks were far outweighed by its technical improvements: its streamlined shape, retractable landing gear, radio, flaps and automatic pilot. It was roomy enough that its ten passengers could be provided with the attentions of a stewardess, who served meals kept hot in vacuum flasks. Other airlines discovered when they tried to buy the 247, however, that it was only available to UAL, which was to have the first 60 aircraft off the Boeing assembly line.

As Douglas was then retooling to build DC-2s, Northwest Airlines and some of the small air companies opted to equip themselves with the smaller Lockheed airliners. Consequently, on June 20, Thompson urged Richardson to replace the Rapide with a Lockheed 10A Electra, justifying the $60,000 purchase price with the prospect of being awarded the Trans Canada Airway contract, but by this time CAL's credit rating was so poor that Richardson had to

Lockheed's response to the Boeing 247: the compact Lockheed 10A Electra. It could carry the same crew/passenger load at higher speed using smaller engines. To celebrate Air Canada's 50th anniversary in 1986, this aircraft, CF-TCC, was revitalized at Air Canada's Winnipeg shop.
Chuck Sloat photo

guarantee the loan personally. The Electra was ordered from Lockheed on July 6, 1936, and CAL's most senior pilots, Donald MacLaren and Herbert Hollick-Kenyon, went to the factory in Burbank, California, to get it. The first modern airliner in Canadian aviation was registered *CF-AZY*, and while Thompson's choice of aircraft changed CAL's history, it was to have even more far-reaching effects on the yet-to-be-born Trans Canada Air Lines.

Meanwhile, Howe was using the summer parliamentary recess of 1936 to investigate at first hand the state of commercial aviation in North America and to tour the Airway. He flew on several airlines in the United States and consulted with the men who were responsible for the major US companies—Juan Trippe of Pan American Airway and Eddie Rickenbacker of Eastern Airlines. Then on July 13 the minister arrived with J.A. Wilson, the Controller of Civil Aviation, at CAL's head office in Winnipeg to commandeer the imminent Electra, complete with a crew, for three months in order to calibrate the Airway's radio ranges. Richardson was on holiday in Europe, having been assured that no decision was going to be made regarding the Airway until

Parliament reconvened in the fall, but Howe told Thompson that he expected an answer within twenty-four hours. "This was typical of Howe's handling of the trans-Canada question," historian Shirley Render wrote later. "More than once he rashly decided upon a course of action and then tried to ram it through without fully considering the consequences."[5] Richardson had planned to send the Rapide *CF-AVJ* to the company's subsidiary, Quebec Airways, as soon as the new Electra, *CF-AZY*, arrived; taking it off the Vancouver–Seattle run with nothing to replace it most probably meant losing the passenger market to UAL permanently. But under pressure from Howe, Thompson cabled Richardson, encouraging him to agree to Howe's demands. Hoping that his acquiescence would influence the minister to give his company the monopoly on the Airway, Richardson gave in and on the following day ordered the purchase of a second Lockheed Electra.

Smaller than either Douglas or Boeing, the Lockheed company had been created by the Loughead brothers, Allan and Malcolm (their accountant suggested simplifying the spelling to "Lockheed" for the company's name), who had carved out a niche for themselves with their family of single-engined "feeder" aircraft named after the stars: Sirius, Altair, Orion and Vega. In 1929 the Lougheads were bought out by the Detroit Aircraft Corporation, which then so mismanaged the company that in 1932 its assets were acquired at a bargain price by Robert Gross, who reigned as chairman and treasurer of the company for the next thirty years. Gross had the singular and very profitable talent throughout most of his career of knowing exactly the type of aircraft that airlines and air forces would want next. A year earlier a TWA Fokker F10A had crashed, and among those killed was Notre Dame's football coach, Knute Rockne. Amid the outpouring of grief that followed, investigations by the US Bureau of Air Commerce revealed structural weakness in the Fokker's wooden main spars and ribs. All airlines were therefore instructed to inspect them regularly for flaws in future. As this would cost dollars and time, Gross knew that the domestic and foreign airlines would rush to replace their Trimotors with all-metal monoplanes that could be "stretched" into larger models. By 1934 he also knew that the next Lockheed would have to be twin-engined because the US government had brought down legislation forbidding the use of single-engined aircraft to carry passengers at night on scheduled services.

Bob Gross of Lockheed, who had the profitable talent of knowing exactly what aircraft airlines would next want. In 1934, when the US government forbade single-engined aircraft from carrying passengers at night on scheduled services, Gross developed a succession of all metal, twin-engined monoplanes starting with the Lockheed 10

S.J. Hungerford. As president of the Canadian National Railway, he would become the first president of Trans Canada Airlines, from 1937 to 1941.

The Electra was designed by the team of Hall Hibberd, Richard Von Hake, and Lloyd Stearman, and the first designs were for a cantilever, low-wing monoplane powered by two Pratt & Whitney Wasp Jr. radial engines enclosed by cowlings. It had a retractable undercarriage for its main wheels, and its cabin seated ten passengers with a crew of two. However, its single vertical fin and rudder failed in wind tunnel tests at the University of Michigan, and it was twenty-three-year-old Clarence "Kelly" Johnson, a true aeronautical genius, who came up with the solution. He discovered that each rudder put behind an engine increased control and pitch stability, and he redesigned the tail into what was to become the familiar Lockheed configuration: the oval twin-fin rudder. The 10A was first flown on February 23, 1934, and after the chief test pilot, Marshall Headle, put it through a series of tests, it was awarded its Approved Type Certificate on August 11.

As the first modern aircraft in Canada, the Electra's statistics are worth noting:

Span:	55 ft (16.76 m)
Length:	38 ft (11.76 m)
Height:	10 ft 1 inch (3.07 m)
Wing area:	458.5 sq ft (42.6 sq m)
Empty weight:	6,454 lbs (2,927 kg)
Loaded weight:	10,300 lbs (4,672 kg)
Wing loading:	22 lbs per sq ft (109.7 kg/sq m)
Power loading:	11.4 lbs per hp (5.2 kg/hp)
Maximum speed:	202 mph at 5,000 ft (325 km/h at 1,525 m)
Cruising speed:	190 mph (306 km/h)
Rate of climb:	1,140 ft/min (347 m/min)
Service ceiling:	19,400 ft (5,915 m)
Normal range:	810 sq m (1,296 km)
Propellers:	Hamilton Standard, constant speed, non-feathering

A total of 148 Electras were built, 101 of the Model 10A with two Pratt & Whitney 400 hp Wasp Jr. engines; five of these would fly for Trans Canada Airlines. While one 10A—British Airways *G-AEPR*—would fly Prime Minister Neville

Aerial photograph of the airport in Toronto, 1939. The new Department of Transport chose the location for the airport: near the village of Malton, and in July 1937 twenty-four farms and a cemetery in the area were bought up and survey work began. LBPIA Archives.

Chamberlain to meet Adolf Hitler in September 1938, undoubtedly the most famous of the series was the later Model 10E with its two 600 hp Pratt & Whitney 53-H-1s. Of the 15 built, *NR 16020* would become the best known, as it was used by the aviatrix Amelia Earhart on her ill-fated flight around the world.

Though smaller than the Boeing 247 and the DC-2, the Electra was faster, and MacLaren and Hollick-Kenyon set a speed record flying *CF-AZY* from Burbank to Vancouver on August 4 in 6 hours and 23 minutes. It was put on the Vancouver–Seattle route, where it was initially flown by Harry Winnie; when he left the company to return to the Arctic, George Lothian took his place in the cockpit as well as in his uniform.

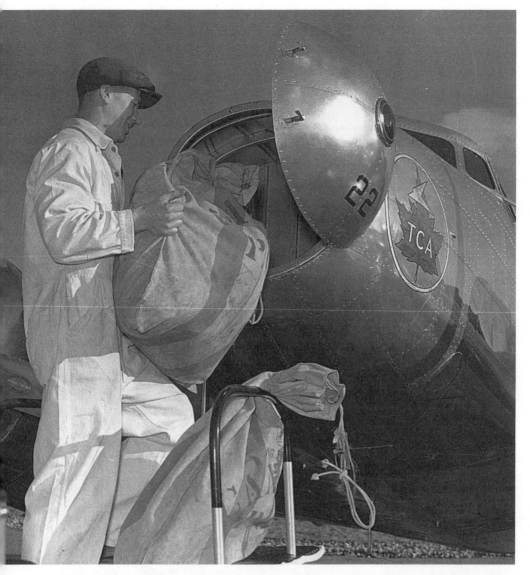

R.J. Bulger loading mail into CF-BAF's nose compartment. In 1938 a radio technician was also expected to sell tickets, perform airport passenger manifests, make out the customs and immigration forms, check the cabin, test the radio, help with the engine run-up, load passengers and sometimes even fly to Seattle with the crew.

The second Electra, *CF-BAF*, was picked up by Hollick-Kenyon and Zebulon Lewis Leigh on August 21 and flown to Lethbridge, both men remaining with it for the testing of the Airway's radio ranges. Richardson was pleased that Howe seemed to favour Lockheed Electras over other aircraft. On his return from Europe in August, he proposed setting up a wholly new company equipped with twelve Electras, which would be used exclusively for the Trans Canada Airway. But Howe showed no interest in meeting with him to discuss this plan.

That September the Cabinet discussed the structure of the company that would use the Airway, and at the prime minister's insistence, it was decided that the government would no longer have only a minority representation in it. Events moved quickly after that. On November 2, Howe transferred civil aviation from the Department of National Defence (DND) to his newly created Department of Transport (DOT), giving him wide powers over all areas in aviation, including the determination of air routes. The inner Cabinet, meeting in camera on November 26, discussed the framework of an air transportation bill to be presented to the next session of Parliament and agreed that only public enterprise would be permitted to fly the major air routes in Canada. If the volume of traffic proved not to warrant public investment of personnel and planes, then—and only then—could private enterprise be allowed to pick up the service. No minutes were kept of the meeting and, as no Cabinet documents produced prior to 1940 exist, the only record is Howe's summary of it to the prime minister a fortnight later. This was the conception of Trans Canada Airlines.

Dick Leigh loading the mail at Vancouver for the Seattle run, 1938. Ken Leigh collection

CHAPTER 2

By December 1936, $8 million had gone into radio beacon equipment and ground service facilities for the Trans Canada Airway, and by the end of 1937 it would be ready for use; it was becoming urgent that the Cabinet designate which airline was to be given the right to fly it. There was no shortage of applicants for that honour, all of them presupposing a very substantial mail contract from the government. Canadian Airways (CAL), which by this time was carrying 90 percent of all His Majesty's mail, led the pack, but while both the Canadian National (CNR) and the Canadian Pacific (CPR) held shares in CAL, they had also made a separate joint application to take on the trans-Canada service. The Toronto group had also made a formal application, though C.D. Howe noted that although each member had sub-scribed $5,000 for promotion purposes, their company had done no actual fly-ing. Canadian Colonial Airways of Montreal, a subsidiary of American Airlines Inc.—the largest airline in the US—operated a service from Albany, New York, to Ottawa. Its application was submitted by the Honourable J.L. Ralston and Frank Common. Another aspiring airline magnate was MP Ross Gray, who represented a combination of three western Canadian air transport companies that were still in the process of establishing federal incorporation. A newly incorporated company in the Maritime provinces was seeking public subscription to be in time to take over the service, while informal applications were submitted by practically every small company then engaged in air trans-port work.

In the meantime, international pressure was also mounting for Canada to make a decision. Mackenzie King had signed the agreement with the United Kingdom and Ireland to participate in a North Atlantic service, and the Cabinet would soon have to nominate an airline to hold Canada's 24.5 percent share of the stocks in the transatlantic company. Howe was convinced that the air-line flying the Airway should also be the one to hold these stocks, but he had changed his mind about which airline that would be. In a secret memo to the prime minister, dated December 7, 1936, he wrote:

The United States, over the past ten years, has permitted aviation to be conducted by competitive private enterprises backed by promotions using funds of the small investor. At the commencement, very large mail subsidies were given and the public was led to make its investment accordingly. The multiplicity of companies entering the flying field finally created a condition approaching a scandal, with the result that the Government canceled all mail contracts for a time, and finally re-issued contracts to the more efficient operators on a basis requiring only a small fraction of the earlier cost. Loss to private investors has been enormous even though the more substantial companies have developed to a high state of efficiency. Nevertheless, the experience of privately operated aviation in the United States to date clearly indicates that it is unwise for Canada to permit participation by the small investor. Care must be taken to make sure that the operating company is amply provided with funds without recourse to that form of financing.

Having regard to the above, and after giving the whole situation a great deal of study, I recommend that the trans-Canada aviation service be entrusted to the Canadian Pacific and the Canadian National Railways jointly, with the provision that the Railways may obtain from existing aviation companies in Canada useful assets in the way of aviation equipment and personnel at fair market valuations in exchange for the stock of the aviation company.

The railway companies' proposal provided for the establishment of a company with an authorized capital of $5 million, of which an estimated $2.15 million would be required for equipment and another $1.25 million for the acquisition of Canada's portion of the transatlantic company, with the balance to be available for extending services and as a reserve to cover losses during the startup phase of operations. Its board of directors would include representatives of both railways and "present Canadian aviation interests." Operating personnel would be drawn from Canadian and American officers familiar with the latest developments in aviation.

Howe's memo continued:

The proposed company will be entitled to an air mail contract on a space mile basis from the Canadian Post Office. Similar agreements in the United States provide that the Interstate Commerce Commission shall determine rates for mail contracts. Pending the setting up of a Board of Transport to replace the present Board of Railway Commissioners in Canada, I suggest that fixing of the mail rates be left to a committee which will include the Minister of Finance, the Postmaster General and the Minister of Transport. Rates should be based on the cost of the service, as determined by audit of aviation company accounts, until such time as mail contracts can be brought down to parity for a similar service on competing United States lines. The Trans-Canada company will perform a national service, and should be protected against loss in its initial stage.

Howe justified his recommendations by saying:

I believe the described set-up is the most efficient way to develop the service from the viewpoint of Canada as a whole, and at the same time, will be the best guarantee of a safe and adequate aviation service. Private aviation interests will have no basis for objection as their present operations will not be disturbed in any way. Participation by the Railways will make for economy as well, in that railway service can be used for the sale of passenger tickets and handling of air express. It will also be more readily possible to co-ordinate air services with rail services, so that the air service can be protected against interruption by weather by an alternative rail service.

A choice of any of the private operating companies now applying for operation of the service could be made only by competitive tender, which would result in the abuses that have been evident in the United States' experience. With a private company chosen by competitive tender, it would be difficult to protect the government in the matter of a safe and adequate service. Assignment of the service to the Railways will cause disappointment to private applicants but less so than the choice of one of the applicants. The nature of the service is such that one company must necessarily handle the service, thus precluding the possibility of dividing the work among several private companies.

The abdication of King Edward VIII pushed the national airline bill out of the parliamentary spotlight in December 1936, as members struggled with Bill No. 1 concerning alteration to the succession to the throne. As a result, the February 1937 session was well underway before a draft of a national airline bill was drawn up, and it was March 4 before Howe presented it as Bill 74 in the House. In this version, the two railways were to be equal partners in the airline with four directors elected from each and a single director appointed by the minister of transport. Beatty and Richardson received copies and were in agreement on the board's makeup.

Howe's motion that the House go into committee at the next sitting to consider the bill was passed, but on March 10 he amended it so that there would still be a total of nine directors on the board but three would now come from each railway and three would be appointed by the minister. The shares would be equally divided between the railways and, if they turned them down, would be issued to other aviation interests approved by the minister. This time Beatty and Richardson were not happy; they did not like other aviation interests being involved, and since the three directors from the CNR could be counted upon to vote with the ministers' three, the CPR would always be in a minority position. Beatty wrote Howe acidly suggesting that the CNR was "to all intents and purposes a department of the Government." Howe was prepared for this; on March 15 he replied that "on the contrary the Government maintains only a very slight contact with the Railway." It was useless, he added, to attempt at this time any fundamental change in the Bill. Two days later Beatty withdrew the CPR from the scheme, ending his letter with "I should appreciate it if, in the Bill as introduced, you would omit any reference to this Company. I hope the new company will realize your highest hopes."[1] Why the CPR withdrew so hastily is still a matter for speculation. The suggestion that Howe laid a trap for Beatty and Richardson by appealing to their vanity may have some truth, but a more likely explanation is that the CPR's board of directors knew there were other ways to get into the airline business, that is, by simply buying up small companies as they had done with railways. Within three years the CPR did have its own airline.

The first reading of Bill 74 took place at 8:00 p.m. on March 22. Only R.B. Bennett, the former prime minister, now opposition leader, had any questions for Howe. "Perhaps the minister will give us a reasonable explanation," he said. "By reasonable I mean reasonably long so that we can understand the purpose of this resolution."

Howe obliged him with a lengthy speech in which he pointed out that Canada was one of the few countries in the world that did not yet have national scheduled air service and that Canadians were demanding one be established. He explained how Britain and the US had developed their airlines and how Canada's national carrier would differ. It was not, he said, the government's intention to own any stock in the new company.

> The government's existing agency for the conduct of the transportation business, the Canadian National Railway, will underwrite the stock and distribute it among firms at present engaged in aviation in Canada that wish to participate. The government has decided that the proper course is to determine the form that the company shall take, place the underwriting in the hands of the national railway, ask those who desire to participate to signify the degree to which they are interested after the terms of the arrangement are known.

> The company will fly only the main artery of traffic across the country, and such other arteries of traffic as designated by the government as being of national importance... It will not undertake inter-urban services of any kind. It will be given an exclusive contract to carry mails, passengers and express over the specified routes... The company's... deficits will be paid by the government for two years, during which period we anticipate the personnel will be perfected. The setting up is such that the company will be protected against loss, but its profits will be very strictly limited. In other words, it is organized to perform a certain national service and it is expected that the service will be performed at or near cost... The cost of operation of the coast to coast service is estimated at about $1,000,000 a year.

Bennett's response was to ask to have the bill "introduced without prejudice, for discussion in detail." Then he surprised his Conservative colleagues by announcing that the trouble with the Bill was that it did not create a completely public enterprise monopoly. "I plead with the Minister to reverse the process, to own the whole enterprise now, and sell it later if he so desires... "[2] This must have been exactly what Howe (and Mackenzie King) wanted to hear. With the leader of the opposition advocating outright public ownership, who could argue against the new company becoming a government monopoly? The Conservatives must have been too confused at their leader's last-minute conversion to mount any effective offensive against the Bill. But Howe's reply was canny; he said that the experience of other countries hardly indicated that this would be wise. "As a minister of the government I shudder over the possibility of being responsible for the crash of a plane-load of passengers traveling on a wholly owned government airline."[3]

On March 25 when Bill 74 was read the second time, there were two inquiries. The first came from Howard C. Green (Vancouver South), the Conservatives' transportation critic, who was worried that the Bill was being rushed through the House. "Once such a policy has been adopted," he said, "it will be hard to change, and we do not want to make any mistake from the start." Green wanted the federal government to run the airline, rather than have the CNR do it.

J.S. Woodsworth, leader of the Co-operative Commonwealth Federation (CCF) (Winnipeg South), who was still basking in the fame of his "Regina Manifesto," asked that the Liberals commit themselves to public ownership of all essential services. "Mr. Speaker, it does seem a very awkward arrangement to ask an already overburdened railway to carry out the organization...I cannot see why the government could not undertake a service of this kind through the formation of a commission. It is a new kind of service, one which covers the whole country and in connection with which there must be...a monopoly. It must in the long run necessarily come under government control."

Howe could have done no better had he written Woodsworth's script himself. In fact, TCA would become exactly what the leader of the CCF wanted: a monopoly that covered the whole country and was under government control. But Howe had good reason to make the new company a subsidiary of the CNR. "I think we are getting the best features of government ownership without the obligation of direct government operation which in the past has been troublesome."[4]

Of the $5 million capital provided for TCA, $1.25 million was for a transatlantic service to be operated jointly with Imperial Airways, $1.75 million for trans-Canada service and $2 million for future expansion. The capital stock was to be divided into shares of $100 each, and the CNR was authorized to buy these to hold or sell. But it could not sell more than 24,900 of the shares, half of the capital, without the approval of Parliament. The minister of transport was authorized by the governor-in-council to enter into a contract with the corporation to provide for the operation of services both inside and outside the country. An annual subsidy was to be paid to the corporation equal to the deficit on its operations, but the rates charged, types of aircraft bought, buildings and equipment used were all to be regulated by the government.

The contract also specified that the rates to be paid until the end of 1939 for carrying airmail was 60 cents per airplane-mile. At a meeting of the Standing Committee on Railways and Shipping held on April 27, 1938, the minister enlarged on this by saying that if there was a surplus on the whole organization, the Post Office was to pay only the net cost of carrying the mail. From 1940 on, the rates were to be set each year by the governor-in-council on the joint recommendation of the minister and the postmaster general at a level that would eliminate the corporation's deficit for the previous year. Should it earn a surplus, the rates would be reduced to a level that would cut the surplus in half. While these arrangements guaranteed against losses, they also provided no incentive to operate efficiently and make a profit. "The mail contract was both the crux and the major enigma of the Act. An element of asymmetry was present, for although there was to be no ceiling on mail rates, there was to be no floor."[5]

The House's only major amendment to Bill 74 was to change the number of directors from nine to seven with an executive council of three. With the withdrawal of the CPR, the CNR was allowed to subscribe to 51 percent of the stock with the remaining 49 percent offered by the minister to other aviation interests. At the same time the CNR disposed of its shares in Canadian Airways.

The new company was to operate an all-weather, year-round daily service using aircraft on wheels only. Fares charged for transporting passengers and goods were to be set on a competitive basis with US airlines, which charged 6 cents a mile. It was given the exclusive right to fly the mail, passengers and freight—in that order—over the Trans Canada Airway. This was east from

Vancouver through the Crowsnest Pass to Lethbridge, from where a branch of the Airway went north to Calgary and Edmonton. The main line continued east to Regina and Winnipeg, then north almost exactly above the main CNR line to Armstrong, Kapuskasing, North Bay then southeast to Ottawa and Montreal. The Maritime route was extended from Montreal across the state of Maine to Moncton and Halifax. As Toronto was off the Airway, the Toronto–Ottawa and Toronto–Montreal flights were viewed as feeder lines. The government stressed that the new corporation would only be subsidized and responsible for this transcontinental main line; all supplementary routes were to be left to private enterprise, but for national reasons only Trans Canada Airlines could operate international flights. For its part the DOT would be responsible for the operations and maintenance of all landing fields, lights and radio beams, and provide weather reports—without charge to the corporation—until in the minister's opinion the company's finances permitted such charges to be imposed.

On one level, Bill 74 is a mishmash of the ideologies of capitalism and socialism that served, perhaps intentionally, to confuse listeners in the House. In one sentence Howe extols private enterprise, in another public ownership. In hindsight it is obvious that he had fully expected the CPR to refuse to participate and looked forward to running the airline as a public enterprise. Now, like the CNR, the airline could be run as a business, but in return for government guarantees regarding its annual deficits, the minister of transport and the postmaster general would nominate its directors and protect it from competition, foreign and domestic. Howe defended this by saying that the government was entitled to choose the directors by virtue of its investment not only in the airline but in the Trans Canada Airway itself.

When the Senate met on April 5 to consider Bill 74, the only objection to it came from the Honourable Lynch Staunton, who asked why they were in such a hurry to deliver mail across the continent, "when most of the mail matter... consisted of patent medicine advertising, election circulars... and love letters." However, there were three amendments from the Senate, the most important being the number of directors changing once more, this time from nine to seven, three of whom would be appointed by the government and four by the shareholders. This time there were no questions from the opposition or even curiosity from the media as to why the makeup of the board was weighted so heavily in the government's favour. The airline was completely subject to the control of the triumvirate of the minister of transport, the postmaster general and the governor-in-council, though only the minister could decide if the company's revenues were sufficient for it to pay for use of airports and meteorological information. He also had the power to acquire TCA shares from the CNR or from any other shareholder. Under the Companies Act, were he to do so, he would then be able to exercise all the powers of a shareholder.

Bill 74 received royal assent at 9:00 p.m. on April 10, 1937, as Parliament was prorogued, but the birth of Canada's national airline, buried as it was between a bill providing for cancellation of "certain indebtedness of the

Canadian National Railway" and one calling for federal protection of the Dionne quintuplets, passed unnoticed in the media. The second session of the eighteenth parliament ended with its members, like most other Canadians, looking forward to the next day when radio and newspaper coverage of the coronation of King George VI, the man who had signed Bill 74 into force, would begin.

As with the institution of Parliament itself, a lot of the details in the TCA Act were unwritten and left to evolve over time. Under the Companies Act the airline was required to report annually to its shareholders, but in spite of the amount of federal investment involved, there was no mention of reporting annually to the minister or to Parliament. Directors' salaries, their qualifications and termination of their appointments were also unspecified. In the years immediately following, the Act was amended twice. In 1938 it was amended to allow TCA to co-operate with Britain and Ireland and buy shares in a transatlantic air service as part of the Joint Operating Company (JOC); nothing came of this and it was repealed in 1945. The 1940 amendment was more relevant: it extended for a year the period during which the government would pay a subsidy to the airline equivalent to its annual deficit. A year later that period was extended by a further fifteen months, but the price the airline paid was that the minister was now given the power to name the corporation's auditors and receive their reports.

The prime minister had been absent from the House during the whole debate, having embarked for the UK to attend the coronation ceremonies and participate in the annual Imperial Conference. He had about as much interest in aviation, military or civil, as his predecessor, Bennett, but with Europe edging toward war, he knew that some clear direction in policy was necessary. On the other hand, British Prime Minister Neville Chamberlain, faced with US neutrality, was anxious to have closer co-operation among the senior members of the Commonwealth, in particular a round-the-world route for Imperial Airways that would bind the Empire together from Britain to India (with a side trip to South Africa), Australia, and Canada. He hoped that an air service across Canada would be an integral part of this scheme, but although Mackenzie King was pleased to return to London on May 28 to attend the Conference on Civil Air Communications, he would not commit Canada to imperial entanglements. However, for the first time the Canadian delegates could speak with some authority on civil aviation; the country now had—though only just—the makings of a national airline.

Meanwhile, six days after Parliament ended, Howe met with Richardson in Montreal. The minister proposed that if Richardson would accept a seat on the board of the new company, CAL would be permitted to subscribe for shares in it, and its aircraft would be allowed to feed off the main line for passengers going on to bush destinations. But Richardson, making one last attempt to redefine the relationship, proposed that Canadian Airways organize and operate the air route for TCA between Winnipeg and Vancouver, the most hazardous part, with the remainder of the trans-Canada service to be discussed later. When Howe told him this was not possible, Richardson refused Howe's offer of a seat on the board, knowing that he would be powerless as the only director unconnected with the government.

Accepting the inevitability of it all, he turned over the Vancouver–Seattle route to TCA and recouped some of his losses with the sale of the three CAL aircraft at Sea Island. The route was no loss to CAL; had it not been for representations from the Vancouver Board of Trade, Richardson would have terminated it long before. But as soon as he relinquished it, many CAL employees, realizing that their careers would be more secure with a government-sponsored airline, jumped ship and applied for jobs with TCA.

Howe met with the CNR board of directors on April 23 to inform them that the railway would be required to provide TCA with "startup" services such as accounting, advertising and publicity, legal, medical and purchasing as well as all secretarial help. As a businessman himself, he was fully aware of the advantages to TCA of not having to start "cold," hiring unproven staff and suffering through a corporate puberty. While Winnipeg was to be the operating headquarters of the airline, Montreal—because it was the CNR's head office—would also serve as the airline's base. Two experienced clerks from the CNR, W.F. "Bill" English and F.T. "Fred" Wood, were immediately sent to the airline's Montreal office to help with the bureaucracy. On May 5, three of the TCA directors were appointed by Order-in-Council. When shareholders met four days later, the other four directors were elected, and when they all met on May 11, they proposed the company's officers. Since all six were already officers of the CNR, the new corporation did not have to pay for their services. The seven-man board of directors—three government-appointed civil servants and four CNR officers—would remain in place until 1953, when the board would be increased to nine—five CNR and four government-appointed. But everyone knew that ultimate power rested with Howe.

TCA Directors and Officers—1937

1. Appointed by Order-in-Council:
   Chief of Air Services: C.P. Edwards (Department of Transport)
   Controller of Civil Aviation: J.A. Wilson (Department of Transport)
   Chief Superintendent of the Air and Land Mail Services:
      G. Herring (Post Office)

2. Elected by Shareholders:
   S.J. Hungerford: chairman and president of the CNR
   J.Y. Murdoch, K.C.: barrister, and a director of several mining
      companies
   H.J. Symington, K.C.: barrister, and a director of railway and
      power companies
   Wilfrid Gagnon: a former Quebec cabinet minister

3. Officers:
   President: S.J. Hungerford*
   Secretary: W.H. Hobbs*
   Treasurer: C.D. Cowie*
   Comptroller: T.H. Cooper*
   Counsel: F.E. Fairweather*
   Director of Publicity: W.S. Thompson*

*All were CNR officers, and no fees were to be paid to them by the new corporation.

Once the board of directors and officers was in place, employees could be taken on payroll. The first was Don MacLaren, who was personally selected by Howe on May 15 to be assistant to the vice-president of operations. Being TCA's first employee was a distinction that Don MacLaren was extremely proud of all his life. An aviation icon long before Howe met him, Donald Roderick "D.R." MacLaren, Distinguished Service Order, Military Cross, Distinguished Flying Cross, Croix de Guerre, was born in 1883 in Ottawa but did not grow up with a compulsion to fly. As a youth, he had accompanied his father to Keg River in northern Alberta to open a fur trading post, but a recruiting advertisement for the Royal Flying Corps in a 1917 newspaper changed his aspirations. He left immediately for Vancouver, ultimately becoming a fighter pilot in 46 Squadron on the Western Front. Less than eight months later, D.R. had downed forty-eight enemy aircraft and six observation balloons, becoming the fourth-ranking Canadian fighter ace of the war. In 1919 he assisted in the formation of the Canadian Air Force on the Pacific Coast and chose Jericho Beach at the south entrance to False Creek as a flying boat base. He was also responsible for choosing the location of the Vancouver airport.

MacLaren decided to strike out on his own in 1924 and set up his company, Pacific Airways Ltd., at Swanson Bay near Princess Royal Island, living off whatever fisheries patrol contracts he could get. After James Richardson bought him out in 1928, he worked for CAL, flying the first airmail on the prairies in 1929, the year he was made assistant general manager for British Columbia. It was MacLaren whom Richardson sent to Ottawa in 1936 to plead his case with the federal government, and while MacLaren failed to save CAL, he impressed Howe so much that the following April the minister of transport offered him the first job with the new airline.

Howe's candidate for the man who was to be MacLaren's boss, the vice-president of operations, was made known on June 24, and it certainly raised eyebrows in government circles in both Ottawa and Washington. He was an American, P.G. Johnson, who had been implicated in the 1935 US airmail scandal and forced to resign the presidency of United Airlines—all of which was unprecedented good fortune for Howe, TCA and Canada. "The directors," the minister said later, "chose the man best qualified by ability and experience to

TCA employee No. 1, Don MacLaren, 1918. He already had considerable previous flying experience when Howe recruited him in 1937. A multiple ace and celebrated war hero with forty-eight victories on the Western Front, he is shown here with his Sopwith Camel.

plan the new system. He came to Canada at what was for him a very nominal salary... his ambition was to make Trans Canada Airlines the finest air transportation system in North America."[6]

Born in Seattle of immigrant Swedish parents, Philip Gustav Johnson worked his way through the engineering school at the University of Washington by driving a laundry truck and, after graduating in 1917, went to work for William E. Boeing, a local aircraft manufacturer. More than just a good engineer and administrator, P.G., as he was known, was an aviation industry phenomenon and by 1925 had risen to be president of the Boeing Airplane Company. Two years later he secured the transcontinental mail contract from the United States Post Office for the company's in-house airline, United Airlines (UAL), which, along with Boeing and Pratt & Whitney, was part of the monster holding company of United Aircraft and Transport Corporation (UATC). P.G. became the airline's president in 1931 just as it entered its boom period, which was caused in part by Boeing's development of the 40A mail plane, powered by Pratt & Whitney Wasp engines and capable of squeezing four passengers into its

Boeing 247. Innovations to this model, introduced in 1933, became the benchmark for airliner construction in the following decades. Featuring all-metal construction and twin engines for safety and reliability, and streamlined shape and retractable landing gear for speed and comfort, this aircraft meant that United Airlines could now cross the United States in 19$^{1/2}$ hours, cutting 8 hours off the previous best services offered by Ford Trimotors. UAA

United Airlines' fleet of Boeing 247s, which established new standards in airline travel. Ten passengers, two pilots and a stewardess travelled in speed and comfort on daily services between Seattle and Vancouver—something TCA had to consider in the reciprocal services they were establishing. UAA

cockpit. Two years later, just as Boeing unveiled its Model 247 airliner, Johnson was appointed the president of the whole UATC conglomerate. By this time media people were calling him "The King of the Air," and the aviation author Frank Taylor wrote of him that "Johnson collected presidencies the way other men collect neckties."[7] With United taking the first sixty 247s off the assembly line, Johnson, Boeing and UATC had effectively captured the whole North American commercial aviation market.

However, the outcry from the other airlines caused President Franklin D. Roosevelt to launch an investigation into the industry, and suddenly Postmaster General Walter F. Brown's meeting with airmail carriers in 1930 to persuade them to consolidate and divide up the available routes was vilified by the new administration as the "Spoils Conference." Roosevelt's own postmaster general, James A. Farley, initiated an industry-wide witch hunt, accusing all participants at that conference of collusion. When Farley ruled that no airline could bid for a mail contract until it had rid itself of "collusionists," Johnson, who had unfortunately been a spectator at the conference, was forced to resign on December 31, 1934. UATC's troubles came in legions after that. A pariah in Washington, it lost 60 percent of its routes to American Airlines and Trans World Airlines (formerly Transcontinental & Western Air Transport) just as those carriers were putting the new Douglas Commercial-2 and 3 into service, making the Boeing 247 obsolete. Roosevelt then moved to break up all the aircraft conglomerates, with special emphasis on UATC. In January 1937 UAL, freshly separated from Boeing and Pratt & Whitney and facing bankruptcy, bought its first ten DC-3As at exorbitant prices and then publicly disassociated itself from everyone connected with its former successes. A year later Congress passed the Civil Aeronautics Act which, in complete contrast to Canadian practices, stipulated that no aircraft manufacturer or common carrier (that is, surface transportation company) be allowed to own, manage or operate an airline.

Exiled from the industry that he had played such a large part in developing, Johnson took over Seattle's Kenworth truck company and immediately revitalized it. The company was already well known for putting together buses and light trucks, but under Johnson it expanded to manufacturing airport fire engines, heavy off-road logging trucks and specially designed haul-trucks for the sugar cane industry in Hawaii. But steering Kenworth to substantial growth was not enough to satisfy Johnson, and when Howe toured the United States in the summer of 1936, it was either Juan Trippe of Pan American Airways or C.R. Smith of American Airlines who recommended P.G. to him as the man who could midwife the birth of the Canadian national air service. Already wealthy, Johnson had little need of the annual salary of $17,500 that Howe offered him, but the idea of creating a transcontinental airline from nothing greatly appealed to him. He took up the challenge, and in the summer of 1937 the Johnson family moved to Montreal. They stayed at the Ritz Carlton Hotel on Sherbrooke Street until they found a house in Mount Royal to lease.

In July, P.G. and MacLaren left on a tour of the Airway in the DOT's new Lockheed 12A *CF-CCT*, piloted by J.H. "Tuddy" Tudhope, and on their return Johnson set about organizing the airline into an Eastern Division (Montreal–Winnipeg) and a Western Division (Winnipeg–Vancouver). The airline's administrative base would of necessity be in Montreal with the parent CNR, but all operational requirements would be met in Winnipeg because it is the geographical centre of the country. It was also, because of James Richardson's efforts, at that time the aviation capital of Canada. Rather than contract it out or send candidates to an airline school in the US, it had been decided that TCA would do its own technical training in Winnipeg, using a learn-as-you-go program. First priority was the operational training of pilots, air engineers, meteorologists and dispatchers. According to P.G.'s son Philip Jr., his father emphasized that "Fuel, parts, mechanics, service personnel must all be in place before a single passenger was carried. Navigation equipment, communications and dependable weather information had to be available from the start. This is what my father and his coworkers understood and undertook."[8]

Johnson asked that he be allowed to bring in four Americans with the experience that TCA needed. They were to be hired on two-year contracts while Canadians were trained to take their places. Three were friends from UAL—D.B. Colyer, O.T. Larson and H.T. "Slim" Lewis—and the fourth—Steve Stevens—was a Canadian who had been working for Eastern Airlines. All were hired on August 1, 1937; later Johnson recruited one more UAL colleague, Oliver West, to be his chief of maintenance. Except for himself, all of these UAL exiles were stationed in Winnipeg, but whenever they visited Montreal, P.G.'s son remembers his dad showing off his adopted city, taking them out to all the night spots.

Harold Turner "Slim" Lewis, Johnson's best friend, was a tall, taciturn, Gary Cooper figure who looked like the rancher he had become rather than the World War I test pilot that he had been. Slim was forty-six when he came to TCA as assistant general manager. "Before reaching the age of 20 he had developed a distaste for work after several associations with it on cattle ranches and in the oil fields," the editor of the TCA newsletter later wrote. Becoming a pilot, therefore, had a strong appeal. Slim trained at the first flight school established in California in 1915 and was one of the first half-dozen licensed pilots in the United States and one of the early flying instructors and test pilots for the US Army.

He entered the Air Mail Service of the US Post Office in 1919, "in the days when lion tamers, high divers, human flies, and others with equally hazardous professions still regarded the boys who flew the mail with considerable awe." Once when Slim was flying the mail over Pennsylvania, "the wind took a piece of the aircraft's tail off." Because he was too low to bail out, he kept on flying until the engine stopped. Seeing a baseball diamond below, he made for that, but when the aircraft landed, it rolled into a teahouse on the edge of the park. "Where am I?" Lewis asked when rescuers pulled him unhurt from the wreckage. "Tyrone, Pennsylvania," was the reply. "What will you take for this place?" he asked, looking around. The post office later rebuilt the teahouse.

What fascinated the Canadians about Slim, apart from his making a ritual of rolling his own cigarettes, was the large diamond he had acquired during his early days in aviation and which served in lieu of a bank account. All too frequently it had been deposited in what Lewis called "one of those places" to re-establish a temporary cash flow. But one time while the stone was temporarily in his possession, he persuaded the future Mrs. Lewis to accept it and share his name; now, to the wonder of the Canadians, she sported this massive, storied jewel.

Young Lowell Dunsmore remembered the first time he met Lewis. "Slim was hiring pilots then in Winnipeg. He asked me a few questions, then went on reading his newspaper. It sort of took the wind out of my sails. I finally screwed up the courage to ask, 'Well, what do you want me to do?' Slim looked up and said, 'Oh, see Stan, the office boy. He'll give you a slip of paper to get a medical. If the medical's okay, you can come out and work any time you like.'" Dunsmore later discovered that the company had already done "quite a bit of research on him."

Lewis had seen most of his early colleagues—called "the Flying Postmen" by the media but "the Suicide Club" amongst themselves—killed in flaming crashes, so it was little wonder that when he wrote the operations manual around which the airline would be formed, his axioms were:

- The first principle is Safety.
- Always have an ace in the hole. "Never go into a situation unless there is some clear way of extracting yourself if the original plan does not work out."
- Never take out a flight under duress from management, company personnel, or the public.

While flying for the Post Office, Slim had crashed near Cheyenne, Wyoming, and killed a local farmer's prize bull. Years later, as chief pilot for UAL, he bought a large ranch close to that crash site, and in 1940 when he had completed his contract with TCA, that is where he retired. When he left, the editor of the employee newsletter bade him farewell with "Undoubtedly, the patience Slim has acquired through the years teaching the pilots in Trans Canada Air Lines will stand him in good stead handling the 'dogies'." But George Lothian summed Lewis up best when he wrote, "There was no pilot in the new airline who did not respect and like him. We were lucky to have Slim Lewis with us for the few short years he was in Canada."[9]

The son of Swedish immigrants, Oscar Theodore "O.T." Larson grew up on a farm in Minnesota. His first job was with the Meteorological Service of the US Department of Agriculture, but in 1929 he joined Boeing Air Transport at Cheyenne, Wyoming, as a meteorologist. He was assistant to the general superintendent of UAL in charge of meteorology and dispatch when in 1937 he accepted P.G. Johnson's offer to help organize TCA. O.T. held several positions with TCA, starting as technical advisor, meteorology and dispatch, then moving on to assistant general superintendent, before becoming general superintendent of operations.

Larson is credited with beginning TCA's flight dispatch system. In 1934 when the United States Bureau of Air Commerce had imposed regulations on commercial operators, one of the most important was that "Each aircraft operation of a scheduled airline shall be authorized by an aircraft dispatcher through the issuance of a clearance form properly executed bearing his signature." This was followed in 1938 by the establishment of aircraft dispatchers' certificates and the licensing of the first dispatchers. Larson imported this system to TCA but called his dispatchers Flight Control Officers. "On the rare occasions when he allows himself to forget the tribulations of the job," the employee newsletter said of Larson, "he is not averse to discussing at some length and on little provocation his prowess as a fisherman."

Duard Browing "D.B." Colyer was a former Illinois schoolteacher and another veteran from the US Post Office airmail days, having risen to the job of superintendent of the US Air Mail Service. After he joined Boeing Air Transport in 1929, Colyer persuaded the Post Office to replace their old de Havilland death traps with Boeing 40As as mail planes. This coup backfired on him, however, because when Postmaster General James Farley began his witch hunt in 1934, Colyer, now vice-president of UAL, was accused of profiteering from his previous employment with the Post Office. Colyer followed Johnson to Canada to become chief technical advisor for TCA. Rene Giguere, a railway employee, recalled D.B. coming over to the CNR office that summer of 1937 looking for a private secretary. "Are you any good?" he asked the young Rene, who held a pilot's licence as well as a stenographer's diploma. "I might not be the fastest in the world, but I am accurate," he replied. But Giguere's career as a secretary for Colyer was short; by January 1, 1938, he was a First Officer.[10] (When P.G. Johnson returned to Boeing in August 1939, Colyer was appointed to the position of vice-president.)

Not part of the United Airlines expatriate group, Steve S. Stevens was also younger than the Americans Johnson imported. Born in Vancouver in 1910, he was educated at the University of Southern California in electrical engineering. Stevens entered the airline world in 1932 as an engineer for TWA, and while stationed in Kansas City he taught the aviatrix Amelia Earhart the radio code. In 1935 he was made assistant chief of radio communications for Eastern Airlines of Miami. When he began working for TCA on October 1, 1937, he was the entire communications department: in a colleague's words, he "found himself confronted with a void of long Canadian miles empty of radio, teletype and trained personnel." He set about interviewing staff from a downtown Winnipeg office and later from the old CAL hangar at the airport. Stevens remained with TCA to run its communications division as departmental superintendent when the Americans returned home.

The first radio technician Stevens hired was Tommy Hall, the first radio operator Bob Williamson. The radio operators could trace their professional status to the CNR and CPR railway telegraphers and had long ago been organized as the Commercial Telegraph Union (CTU) by their American brothers. Radio telephone was used for everything then—point-to-point communication and aircraft-to-ground work—and it was not until the spring of 1939 when the airline began to carry passengers that radio telegraphy or "CW" was brought in to handle reservations. With the spanning of the continent, high frequencies were installed; in July 1940, as passenger lists grew, "CW" was retired and the first teletype circuit introduced.

While P.G.'s friends were organizing the company, on July 30 C.D. Howe's epic "Dawn to Dusk" flight took place. Well documented in the annals of aviation history as a quantum leap in air travel in Canada, the flight, though technically unconnected to TCA, followed the flight route from Montreal to Vancouver along the Airway that the new airline would soon fly. For the first time, "civilians" dressed as they would be to catch a train—and not leather-coated, goggled and gloved professional aviators risking life and limb—flew safely in relative comfort across Canada—within a day. Justifying the flight as a survey of the Airway, Howe had outfitted the little DOT Lockheed 12A *CF-CCT* with an auxiliary fuel tank and, with TCA directors C.P. Edwards and H.J. Symington accompanying him, took off from Montreal's St. Hubert Airport in the early morning. The RCAF crew were pilot J.H. "Tuddy" Tudhope—a McKee Trophy winner and the man who made the first air survey of the Rockies—co-pilot Jack Hunter, and engineer Lou Parmenter. (Tudhope left the RCAF in 1938 to work in aviation insurance, then joined TCA as executive assistant to the vice-president in 1943.)

The flight was not without drama. They refuelled first at Gillies, an emergency strip near North Bay, Ontario, but because the Airway radio beacons were not properly calibrated, they missed Kapuskasing, which should have been their next stop. The aircraft was almost out of fuel when, quite by chance, they found Sioux Lookout, Ontario. *CF-CCT* landed at Sea Island Airport 17 hours later, in an actual flying time of 14 hours and 30 minutes. When Howe had promised the prime minister the previous December that the Airway would be complete by July 1, 1937, he had been optimistic, but with this flight

Arrival in Vancouver of the DOT Lockheed 12A at the end of the "dawn-to-dusk flight" along the new Trans Canada Airway, July 30, 1937. After a seventeen-hour trip, C.D. Howe (centre) has a public word with pilots H.J. Tudhope (left) and Jack Hunter (right) as the sun sets. DOT

he proved dramatically not only that the Trans Canada Airway functioned but also that a commercial airliner could now cross the country by day or night within twenty-four hours.

James Richardson, who heard all about the flight from its crew, was not the only one amazed at what he considered Howe's grandstanding. He wrote to Beatty that P.G. Johnson had been in Winnipeg when *CF-CCT* refuelled there and that the American was very annoyed. "The Minister told him it was not a stunt, and [Johnson] wanted to know if it wasn't a stunt, what was it?"[11] The other Americans were appalled as well. The deaths of all on board would have set the program back years, and professional that he was, Johnson knew that this was no way to begin an airline. Unperturbed, on August 20 Howe was in Toronto, inspecting farmland at Malton and giving his approval for Toronto's airport.

Perhaps as a reward for taking their lives in their hands to accompany him on the flight, Edwards was made Deputy Minister of Transport in 1941 and Symington the second president of TCA. Few in the world were more qualified in air transport and wireless communication than Edwards. Born in Dodleston on the Welsh border near Chester on December 11, 1885, Charles Peter Edwards came by his interest in radio by good fortune: he had been studying at Arnold Technical School to be an electrical engineer when the great Guglielmo Marconi built a temporary wireless station for demonstration purposes at Chester. When Marconi's technicians' batteries ran low, the boy came to the rescue by recharging them at the school. On Edwards's graduation, Marconi asked him to join his staff. In 1906 Edwards came to Canada to take charge of the wireless stations at Camperdown and Sable Island in Nova Scotia. During World War I he held the rank of lieutenant commander in the RCNVR and was awarded the Order of the British Empire for his detection of German wireless code messages. He served as deputy minister of transport from 1941 to 1951—all the while on the TCA board.

MacLaren hired the first sales staff on July 31, 1937. He phoned Wallace George Courtney, a former Alaska-Washington Airways employee now living in Victoria, and told him to be at the CNR ticket office in Vancouver the next day. At forty-three, Wally was older than MacLaren and, at a time when everyone else in the airline was young, he would be for many years one of the company's "old men." He and D.H. Bunch were TCA's complete sales department until George Wakeman joined them a year later.

Meanwhile, TCA was acquiring aircraft. Johnson had recommended that the aircraft used for training pilots and engineers be the most modern ones available in Canada, that is, CAL's two Electras. On August 28 *CF-BAF* was sold to TCA, followed by *CF-AZY* on September 10. The first cost $55,234, the second $63,618 because it was less used. As an afterthought, $5,000 was paid out for the Stearman *CF-ASF* that had been used on CAL's prairie mail route. CAL's records show that it would be another ten days before TCA actually owned *CF-AZY*, but on September 1 the company took over both Electras, the Stearman and all the CAL property at Vancouver. Included in the changeover were two trucks and some tools, as well as some of CAL's staff at Sea Island: Billy Wells, Maurice McGregor and air engineer Sam Reid. Wells recommended that MacLaren also hire young George Lothian, and when Wells became the TCA station manager, Lothian took his place flying *CF-AZY*, which continued to be used for the Vancouver–Seattle run, this time wearing TCA insignia. *CF-BAF*, which had spent part of the winter on skis as Richardson tried to adapt it for bush flying conditions, was sent to Winnipeg to train pilots. As it had with CAL, the Stearman served as a backup mail plane. Some of the pilots were checked out on it, but it never did any official flying. It was sold to Northern Airways, a bush operator, in 1939.

The first TCA flight took off at 5:00 p.m. on September 1, 1937, the very day that TCA took over CAL's aircraft and personnel. Passengers were Don MacLaren; Percy W. Baldwin, a seconded CNR employee and the airline's first auditor; W.T. Moodie, another CNR officer; and George C. Miller, the mayor of Vancouver. "Canadian Airways" had been removed from above the Electra's passenger door and "Trans Canada Airlines" painted in its place. As Maurice McGregor remembered, TCA didn't have its own tickets ready so "Canadian Airways" was stroked out on the tickets that were on hand and "TCA" written in. The aircraft followed the familiar route it had taken in Canadian Airways' livery an hour before; fifty-five minutes after takeoff it landed at Seattle. The omens were good for the whole venture, MacLaren recalled, as the flight took place in brilliantly clear weather, but until June 20, 1938, when a second daily flight was added, this was to be the sole revenue-producing route for the airline.

Two days after that Vancouver–Seattle flight, on the other side of the country the Imperial Airways Short "C" Class flying boat *Cumbria* splashed down majestically on the river at Ottawa at the start of a survey tour of North America. The flight was actually just a publicity stunt to blunt the British Parliament's criticism of Imperial Airways for its conservatism and general "stodginess" and to forestall moves to amalgamate the airline with the privately owned British Airways. However, the massive flying boat, moored at the RCAF Rockliffe air station almost within sight of the Parliament buildings, vividly demonstrated the British commitment to the Joint Operating Company and eventual round-the-world flights. Naturally, Howe made sure he got to inspect the aircraft and have his photo taken with the crew.

Don MacLaren was now in charge of hiring air crew. "I drew up a list of pilots and had them report to this advisor on pilot training [Slim Lewis] in Winnipeg. He said, 'We want only men who've got 1,000 hours of flying as pilots and who are not over 28 years of age. We'll build our system on that.' Well, he got quite a boxful... and was really impressed with the fact that these people were so easily adjusted to instrument flying and were so reliable, because they'd had to find their own way around the country. There were two or three of them, though, who were really old—not old in years but old in hours of flying—who couldn't master instrument flying. Quite simply, their nerves couldn't take it. So they went back to the bush."[12]

Like many other TCA pilots, the company's first pilot, Zebulon Lewis Leigh, had been a barnstormer in his youth. "Lewie" was born in 1906, learned instrument flying at the RCAF school at Camp Borden and joined CAL in 1934. He made the first postal flight from Fort Chipewyan to Goldfields on September 2, 1935, and earned a commendation from the RCMP for his flying skills while they were searching for a wanted criminal. In January 1936 Richardson had sent him to the Boeing School of Aeronautics in Oakland for advanced instrument flight training, and when he returned as one of Canada's first instrument-rated pilots, he was put in charge of the CAL instrument flight school. While at the Boeing school, Leigh had met P.G. Johnson, and on August 17, 1937, while he was flying for CAL in northern Saskatchewan, Johnson phoned from Ottawa to ask if he would like to be the new airline's senior pilot. Leigh discussed this with Tommy Thompson, CAL's general manager, who told him that as CAL was now relegated to purely bush flying, this might be his best opportunity to get into commercial aviation. Leigh accepted Johnson's offer and was sent to Vancouver to liaise with the DOT concerning radio ranges.

E.P. Wells, who was christened Edward but nicknamed Billy, was one of the pilots acquired by TCA when the company bought out CAL's west coast operation in mid-August 1937. He was born in Sussex, England, in 1901 and joined the RAF shortly after the Armistice; his natural flying skill soon put him into its No. 1 Squadron, where he and two other pilots were selected to perform with the RAF's aerobatic team. One of their routines at the annual Hendon Air Display was to fly in formation with their wings actually tied together. In 1925 No. 1 Squadron was sent to the British Protectorate of Iraq to co-operate with the army in restoring peace among warring native tribes. One day as Wells was flying patrol, the control wires on his Sopwith Snipe were cut by a bullet from a tribesman's rifle, jamming the rudder hard right while the torque of the rotary engine pulled the Snipe to the left. "By alternately zooming the ship up to the right and then gliding down to the left," Wells explained, he managed to stay in the air above his pursuers, but crashed finally in front of a lonely army outpost, where he joined the soldiers in beating off the attack until reinforcements arrived. Wells was awarded the Distinguished Flying Medal for his Middle East tour of duty. He came to Canada in 1924, transferred to the RCAF, and in the late 1920s found himself stationed at Jericho Beach in Vancouver as an instructor. In 1932 CAL offered him a five-year contract to fly fishery patrols and do charter work, then put him on the Seattle mail run in 1936. His colleagues at TCA knew nothing of his former aerobatic career until the summer of 1939, when the RCAF's No. 1 Squadron was based at Vancouver Airport to practise formation flying. Every time their Hurricanes went up, Billy Wells was at the window, going through the manoeuvres with them. Only after several days of watching him direct the planes overhead with "That's it . . . close in now . . . watch out for his slipstream . . . over, over . . . look out!" did they question him about his past.

George Lothian, who was hired by TCA on Billy Wells's recommendation, was a Vancouverite who had learned to fly in 1929 with the Aero Club of BC and started working for CAL in 1936. Pilots W.A. "Bill" Straith, D.P. Glen and M.B. "Jock" Barclay were all hired on October 1. Straith, who already had a reputation as one of the best pilots in the country, had built his own aircraft and actually taught himself to fly. He was hired away from Northwest Airlines, where he had been a pilot and later an instructor, to become TCA's chief flying instructor. The other TCA pilots said that he knew the height of every rock and crag between Vancouver and Lethbridge, how to get the last knot out of an aircraft teetering under a load of ice, and how to pick up the faintest signal of a radio through a roar of snow static.

Herbert "Bertie" Hollick-Kenyon was famous before he joined TCA in October 1937. He had been one of the Western Canada Airways pilots who had scoured the North in 1929 for the lost MacAlpine Expedition, pioneered the Edmonton–Great Bear Lake flights for CAL in 1933, and flown the first airmail from Winnipeg to Berens River in February 1935. Later that same year he piloted the American explorer Lincoln Ellsworth across Antarctica, and then in 1937 provided the same service for the Australian explorer Sir Hubert Wilkins, who was searching for downed Soviet pilots in the Arctic. He was made an honorary Air Commodore by the RCAF in 1936 in recognition for his work in mapping the North. Because of Hollick-Kenyon's skill in navigation and his stature in the international aviation community, TCA soon transferred him to Lethbridge and made him operations superintendent.

Robert Bruce Middleton, who had already obtained both his private pilot's licence and his commercial licence in Canada in 1932, graduated from the RAF's pilot's course eighteen months later and served with 22 Flying Boat squadron in Malta. After a stint with Imperial Airways as a navigator on the London–Paris flights, he returned to Canada in March 1937 and worked briefly for CAL before joining TCA. He later became one of the founders of the Canadian Air Line Pilots Association (CALPA).

Art Rankin had flown for United Air Transport, but after losing out in a shady deal flying in the Yukon for an American expedition, he was quite pleased to join TCA. Walter Warren Fowler earned his pilot's licence in 1928 at the famous Jack Elliott flying school in Hamilton, Ontario. He worked his way up through the ranks at CAL as pilot-mechanic and instructor before being made superintendent of the Maritime region in 1930. He was destined to captain many of TCA's "firsts": the first to fly the Montreal–Toronto airmail (1938), Montreal–Moncton (1940), Toronto–New York (1941), and the first to pilot a passenger flight from Moncton to St. John's (May 1, 1942).

Herbert W. Seagrim and Lindsay "Lindy" Rood, both pilots, joined the company on December 6. Seagrim had learned to fly at the Winnipeg Flying Club in 1931 and worked for F. Roy Brown's Wings Ltd. at Lac du Bonnet,

Manitoba, until 1937.[13] Lindy Rood was hired by British Airways in 1935 to fly de Havilland 86s, four-engined biplanes, on the London–Amsterdam–Hamburg–Copenhagen–Malmo–Stockholm route. He moved on to the Electra when the airline purchased four of them in February 1937 and was checked out on it by Lockheed's chief test pilot, Marshall Headle. Though smaller than the 86, the 10A for Lindy was more comfortable and faster. It was also the first unpressurized aircraft that did not leak. "Being all-metal, it was nice to get away from the wires, struts and fabric," he said.[14]

He was pleased to see the familiar contours of the Electra again when he arrived in Winnipeg, although he discovered the plane did have drawbacks when flying through the mountains. Since it did not have variable pitch propellers which could be "feathered" or maintain the minimum safe altitude over the mountains, the Crowsnest Pass section could only be flown in weather conditions that allowed a visual approach to the airfields at Cranbrook and Oliver. However, the Pratt & Whitney Wasp Jr. was a very reliable engine, and he only had one engine failure: on a training flight he and Bob Smith were approaching the "Steeples," the highest point on the Vancouver–Lethbridge route, when they lost all oil pressure on the right engine. They shut it down but it continued to windmill until the final approach at Lethbridge—when the engine seized. This happened before the new airport was opened so they landed beside a grain elevator on the old grass airfield just east of the town.

Ted Allan of Winnipeg first tried his hand at law, then at insurance, before attending the Boeing School at Oakland, California. He came to TCA three months after graduating at the top of his class as a commercial pilot in December 1937. He was promoted to captain by 1940 and transferred to Toronto. C.L. "Ches" Rickard had been with the Royal Canadian Signals in 1936 when Howe commandeered CAL's Electra *CF-BAF*, and he had been selected to fly the Airway choosing the radio station sites. He was hired by TCA as a radio operator, but he was training to become a pilot; he achieved this on July 18, 1941, and was promoted to captain in 1944. Alf Westergaard had fought with the Royal Flying Corps in World War I, then flown for Western Canada Airways out of Sioux Lookout and in the Northwest Territories before signing on to fly for TCA. Like Walt Fowler, Frank Ingle Young took flying lessons at the Jack Elliott school in Hamilton, earning his private pilot's licence in 1927 and his commercial two years later. In 1932 he attended the RCAF instrument flying course at Camp Borden, all the while surviving by barnstorming. He was hired by TCA in January 1938 along with Jack Wright, who had started his working life as a lawyer. He took his pilot's test at the Aero Club of BC in 1930, became an instructor at Fort William and later in Toronto before working as a bush pilot. Harry Marlowe Kennedy had flown for the Canadian Air Board, surveying much of northern Ontario and Manitoba. During the 1930s he flew for Western Canada Airways and Mackenzie Air Service and in 1937 flew the Governor General Lord Tweedsmuir on a tour of the Canadian Arctic. Bob Bowker got his pilot's training with the RCAF in Camp Borden and his seaplane training in Vancouver, where his instructor was Billy Wells. He left the air force in 1936 for a job with Canadian Colonial Airways flying a three-passenger Stinson Junior between Montreal and Ottawa. Barney Rawson had flown for the US Weather Bureau and later for American Airlines as a captain before returning to Canada in 1938 to join TCA. James D. Storie graduated from the Ryan School of Aeronautics at San Diego in December 1937 and was chosen by Ryan to be check pilot for his trainees' flights across the Tahachapi mountains. Storie returned to Canada and joined TCA as first officer based in Toronto.

TCA's engineering division was headed up by John Talbot "Jack" Dyment, a University of Toronto mechanical science graduate, who had worked in the Ford Motor Company's "Aeroplane Division" in Dearborn on the Ford Trimotor before returning to Canada to become an aeronautical engineer with the DND and the DOT in Ottawa. When he joined TCA in 1938, the engineering division consisted of four recently graduated engineers from McGill and one from Manitoba, plus one old-time draftsman; he was the only member of the department with any aviation experience.

Fortunately for the airline, the maintenance personnel were all experienced and, having learned their trade with CAL and the other bush companies, knew how to look after aircraft in climates as cold as Winnipeg's. And TCA had one great advantage over the bush companies in that, wherever the Lockheeds remained for the night, electricity was always available to operate the heaters that kept the engines and lubricating oil warm. Until then in Canada the usual procedure when stopping in the winter was to laboriously drain the oil from the engine and take it indoors to reheat and pour back into the engine the next morning. "But even with its equipment," Dyment recalled, "TCA still suffered when Winnipeg's ground temperatures dropped to –65 degrees F, and one night we lost four engines as a result of lack of oil and the failure of the hose in the engine oil system. The manufacturers quickly shipped us the specially designed, flexible hose made for the United States Air Force in Alaska, but when we left a sample of it on a windowsill overnight, the next morning when the hose was bent, it broke in two like a carrot! So it was 'back to the drawing boards' until we had solved it. It was essential that all the equipment we used had the capability of operating after a cold soaking at –70 degrees F for twelve or more hours."

Merlin "Mac" MacLeod joined TCA as one of the brotherhood of "Metal Bashers," which was exactly what their name implied. An almost mystical figure in TCA history who could fix anything to do with aircraft, he had spent a decade with CAL as an air engineer. Stories about his improvisations in the bush, of dogsled expeditions to salvage damaged aircraft, were the stuff of legend. In one of them, after a crash in the wilds in which the aircraft's wooden propeller was splintered beyond repair, Mac carved a propeller out of a handy tree trunk. (In another version of the story, he used a fence post.) At TCA he was soon foreman of the metal shop and set about improving the Lockheed's braking system and developing a cowl flap to regulate engine temperatures, both inventions soon to be in use around the world.

Until its own hangar was built, the airline took over the CAL hangar at Stevenson Airport (which still housed a disused Junkers) for a radio room and weather office. This is where young Dudley Taylor, who had worked his way through McGill by installing radios in fire towers for a Maniwaki paper company, started work in April 1938. Most of his attention was focussed on the Lockheeds' radios; they were made by Bendix and he thought them "really state of the art for their day." A radio compass was a very new item then, as was the high frequency (HF) transmitter and companion receiver. An emergency receiver located under the pilot's seat could be tuned to the radio range frequencies. As well as being responsible for communications with aircraft, the communications department took care of communications throughout the whole airline. This included the HF ground radio stations at each airport as well as the teletype machines that brought in the weather reports.

By December 1938 TCA had 332 employees, many of whom had already carved their names into Canadian aviation history, and several who were about to, though at times TCA must have seemed like a CAL alumni reunion, so many had trained at that company. This was made more evident by the fact that until November 13, 1937, the flight crew on the Vancouver–Seattle run had continued to wear their CAL uniforms. The new TCA uniforms introduced on that date for flight crews consisted of a blue, single-breasted blazer, a belt and a cap with a white top. A captain wore two gold rings on the sleeve and a first officer wore one. Uniforms were also a "first" for maintenance crew: from now on white coveralls and cap were required for ramp duty and all personnel were provided with enough uniforms for rotation through the laundry cycle.

Meanwhile, TCA's new employees had begun organizing. On December 13 Captain "Jock" Barclay brought together nine pilots and one supervisor in a Winnipeg hotel room to discuss the idea of creating a professional body that would consolidate pilot views on airline problems and that would possess the legal authority to voice them when necessary.[15] Present were pilots Walt Fowler, R.F. George, P.M. Howard, D. Imrie, R.B. Middleton, A. Rankin, J.L. Rood, J.H. Sandgathe and H.W. Seagrim. The superintendent was W.A. Straith, who as an American pilot was a member of the Air Line Pilots Association (ALPA), which allowed him to advise his Canadian colleagues on union rules. Grievances with TCA focussed on clarification of working conditions; for example, at that time to get a salary increase it was necessary to pass an examination. TCA's contracts also provided that any pilot who was ill or injured would be kept on full pay until he recovered.

> This was not as generous as it sounds. They did not replace the unserviceable man. His flying duties were merely taken over by his mates, and if his illness was short ... he made up his lost flying when he returned. The contract called for a maximum

85 hours flying a month or 255 hours in a three-month period. Thus a pilot could, through illness, lose 50 or so hours in the first month of that quarter, and wind up over-projected by flying more than 100 hours in each of the remaining two months. The system protected a man's pay at minimum cost to the company but imposed heavily on both the pilots who had to cover and the sick man who had to make up for his lost time. At the first meeting Barclay was elected chairman and Sandgathe secretary-treasurer; a name was chosen: the Canadian Air Line Pilots Association (CALPA); dues of $1.00 were collected from each person present; and the drafting of a constitution was begun for the next annual meeting.[16]

The airline's first timetable was a simple affair. A single sheet of paper, folded twice, it was intended to entice the public away from the comforts of UAL's Boeing 247D and instead squeeze themselves into the TCA Electra, sans stewardess service. Three more Lockheed 10As had been purchased on October 1, 1937, from Fairchild Aircraft, Longueuil, Quebec, Lockheed's Canadian agents—CF-TCA, CF-TCB and CF-TCC. Each cost $73,000. With the two originals from CAL, these became known in TCA lore as the "Five Sisters." CF-TCA was first put on pilot training before starting its commercial career on the Vancouver–Seattle, Winnipeg–Regina, Lethbridge–Vancouver, Lethbridge–Calgary–Edmonton routes.

However, on the cover of the new timetable the company disdained the valiant little Electra or perhaps passed it over because of its Canadian Airway's associations and chose instead to feature—against a gold background—its next purchase, the Lockheed 14H "as selected by Howard Hughes for his globe-encircling flight as the world's fastest transport plane." According to the brochure, the 14H had "luxurious, fully reclining seats" and flew "at normal speeds of 180 mph," and was provided with two-way radio contact. "Fly with His Majesty's Mail" the timetable proclaimed, promising that if enough customers did so, their future (both company and the customers) would be brighter.

More travelogue than business planner, as there was only one route—Vancouver–Seattle–Vancouver—the brochure was filled out with a map and aerial photos of the San Juan Islands, Mount Baker and downtown Seattle. "It is no exaggeration to say that this is one of the most scenic flights to be found anywhere in the world. Snow-capped mountains, green islands dotting the Gulf of Georgia, pleasing hills and fertile farmlands provide attractions that are not found in the arid districts further south." Tickets could be purchased in Vancouver at 527 Granville Street (phone reservations Marpole 111 or Seneca 4040) or in Seattle at 1329 - 4th Avenue (phone Main 2553). Passengers were warned that "Each person is allowed 35 lbs. baggage free. Animals, birds and reptiles will not be carried. Children under two years of age carried free. Children between two and under twelve at half fare."

The TCA logo, for which the company chose to reconcile the past and future. With the Canadian National Railway handling TCA affairs, including sales and advertising, it was expedient to be identified by a maple leaf similar to that of the railway's with the initials "TCA" within it. The futuristic "speedbird" motif (placed above the letters) was unauthorized as Imperial Airways had already chosen it for its own crest. TCA dropped the speedbird in 1943.

Trip 7	Trip 3	ALL DAY TRIPS	Trip 8	Trip 4
Northbound	Northbound		Southbound	Southbound
1:00 p.m.	9:40 a.m.	**LV SEATTLE**	12:25 a.m.	7:55 p.m.
1:55 p.m.	10:35 a.m.	**ARR VANCOUVER**	11:30 a.m.	7:00 p.m.

The brochures were printed in Vancouver in what was considered a large quantity—8,000. After that, all company printing was moved to Winnipeg, where Bulman Brothers took over the contract, using TCA's colours of Moira grey and Pekin red to background the company crest on the front cover. An airline's insignia must have all the symbolic import of a family coat of arms, with the company's origins and ambitions so identifiable within it as to make further explanation unnecessary. The first airlines, because they had generally originated as mail carriers, usually included a version of their nation's postal logo—an eagle, a falcon, some mythical winged creature or a lightning bolt. Delta Airlines' "triangle" told of its crop-dusting origin on the Mississippi delta. Other liveries prophesied their companies' futures: when Pan American Airways adopted its familiar blue and white world logo, all it had was a Caribbean island-hopping route and Juan Trippe's determination to circumnavigate the globe. Trans Canada Airlines chose to reconcile both past and future. With the parent Canadian National Railway handling its affairs, including sales and advertising, it was expedient to simply insert the initials "TCA" within a maple leaf similar to that used by the railway. Not only was this patriotic, it was in the style of official airmail cachets, and at a time when the national flag was more colonial than Canadian, the maple leaf was the closest the country came to having a national symbol. But perhaps it was the fact that the only other readily recognizable symbol, the Canada goose, had already been taken by James Richardson's Canadian Airways Ltd. as its emblem; this prompted TCA to add the futuristic "Speedbird" motif above the maple leaf, although Imperial Airways had chosen the Speedbird for its own crest years before.

The twin rudders on the Electra already had the Lockheed "star" insignia on them, preventing TCA from emblazoning their new logo there; instead the maple leaf was painted high on the aircraft's nose. When the company got its Lockheed 14s with their Plexiglas noses, the logo was put above the front cabin window. It was only in 1943 when the first transatlantic flights to Britain took place, that TCA quietly and diplomatically dropped the Speedbird from the airline's logo.

In the birth of every great enterprise, the first years are remembered by those who were there as a heady cocktail of hard work, youthful enthusiasm, euphoria and sense of purpose. TCA's "Class of 1937" cherished forever being part of a great crusade, that of binding the country together. In more practical terms, because it was the Depression, they also appreciated being paid regularly. "Paydays were great and glorious events," wrote Fred Wood, "and called for celebrations of one form or another." Everyone from the most junior employee to the vice-president attended the dances at the Marlborough Hotel, danced the Lambeth Walk at the Cave cabaret and gathered for picnics at Grand Beach. There was roller skating at the local "palace," where in the evening the men from maintenance, accounting and communications could be seen "whirling around, making three-point landings" with more finesse, some said, than the pilots were accomplishing with their 10As during the day. The company's first official social event, a supper dance in the Marlborough's Blue Room, took place on February 8, 1938.

As the hangar at Winnipeg's Stevenson Airport was filled with young, single people who were far from friends and family, there was a tendency for them to form social groups within the ranks. The Sherburn Ice Rink was the scene of memorable clashes between the accounting office's hockey teams—the Revenue Rats and the Disbursement Dogs. In summer TCA softball teams—the Radio Ramblers, the Metal Bashers, and the Office Pen Pushers—played in the CNR league, and to the surprise of all, in 1938 it was the Pen Pushers who won the softball trophy donated by Bill Straith. There were ongoing dice and card games as well. In Lethbridge's Marquis Hotel, the flight crews' card games were almost continuous, with pilots coming and going, as there was always a plane waiting there for the weather in the mountains to clear. And everyone, it seemed, sat around after work or while they played cards or dice, discussing how the airline could be "organized, disorganized and reorganized."

TCA's Class of '37

TCA employees hired in 1937 and spring 1938:

Date hired	Name	Job
1937		
May 15	Donald Roderick MacLaren	assistant to vice-president of operations
July 22	Fred T. Wood	accounts
July 31	Wallace George Courtney	sales
August 20	Zebulon Lewis Leigh	pilot
September 1	Sam Reid	engineer
September 1	George Roper	engineer
September 6	Russel J. Bulger	radio technician
September 9	George Lothian	pilot
October 1	W.A. Straith	chief flying instructor
October 1	D.P. Glen	pilot
October 1	Malcolm B. Barclay	pilot
October 4	Stan Knight	air engineer
October 6	Herbert Hollick-Kenyon	station manager
October 15	Arnold Thomas Gilmour	engineer
October 20	Allan R. Hunt	air engineer
October 23	Robert Bruce Middleton	pilot
October 27	Robert D. Williamson	radio operator
October 27	Merlin MacLeod	foreman of the metal shop
October 28	Arthur Rankin	pilot
November 3	Richard Leigh	air engineer
November 3	Casey Van der Linden	engineer
November 4	Walter Warren Fowler	pilot
November 9	John Leslie Scott	technical assistant, stores
November 13	V.J. Hatton	pilot
November 15	Bruce M. Saunders	air engineer
December 1	René C. Baudru	clerk
December 6	Lindsay Rood	pilot
December 6	Herbert W. Seagrim	pilot
December 10	Al Took	radio operator
December 15	Chester L. Rickard	radio operator
December 15	Charles M. Adams	maintenance
December 15	Ted Allan	pilot
December 15	Alf Westergaard	pilot
December 15	Bert Mottishaw	driver

Also hired as pilots before December 13, 1937, were R.F. George, P.M. Howard, D. Imrie and J.H. Sandgathe.

1938

January 3	Frank Ingle Young	pilot
January	Jack Wright	pilot
January 10	Harry Marlowe Kennedy	pilot
February 5	D. Weir	
March 9	Bob Bowker	pilot
April 1	Charlie Proudfoot	engineer
April 21	Dudley Taylor	communications
April 25	Barney Rawson	pilot
April 27	James D. Storie	pilot
April 27	John Talbot Dyment	chief engineer

Also hired sometime before February 8, 1938 were David Tennant, George Featherstone, and Morris Mallet.

Also hired in the spring of 1938 were:

Herbert Harling	Toronto office manager
James H. McMaster	foreman of instrument shop
Jack Stewart	engineer
Charlie Wilson	engineer
Jack Hughes	assistant to chief of instrument shop
Frank Kelly	engineer
George Taylor	driver
D.S. McLeod	air engineer

(Duncan Dingwall MacLaren, who would later become president of Pacific Western Airlines, was hired by TCA in August 1938 as an air engineer.)

Trans Canada Airlines' first Annual Report covered the period up to December 31, 1937, and while the company did show a deficit, it was certainly not unexpected. Only nine months had passed since C.D. Howe had introduced Bill 74, the Trans Canada Airlines Act, in the House of Commons. It was all ahead of them.

TRANS CANADA AIRLINES FIRST ANNUAL REPORT

For the Year ending December 31, 1937

INCOME ACCOUNT
For the Initial Development and Operating Period 1st June, 1937 to 31st December, 1937

Three aircraft types of different sizes, all operating on the Vancouver–Seattle run in the late 1930s. It is not immediately apparent that they are all of the same vintage. The late model Boeing 247D in the foreground, Lockheed 10A and de Havilland Rapide (right) all flew for the first time in 1934. SML

Operating Revenue

Passenger $3,610.22
Mail 12,627.00
Express 10.00
Excess Baggage. 31.06

Total Revenue **$16,278.68**

Operating Expenses

Aircraft Operation and Maintenance $20,098.74
Ground Operation and Maintenance 1,582.88
Traffic and General Administration 3,664.62
General Taxes. 84.52

Total Expenses **$25,430.76**

Net Deficit Vancouver–Seattle
Service (From Sept. 1). $9,152.08
Organization and
Development Expense $93,798.20
Interest on Capital Investment 8,054.79

**DEFICIT TO BE REIMBURSED
BY DOMINION** **$111,005.07**

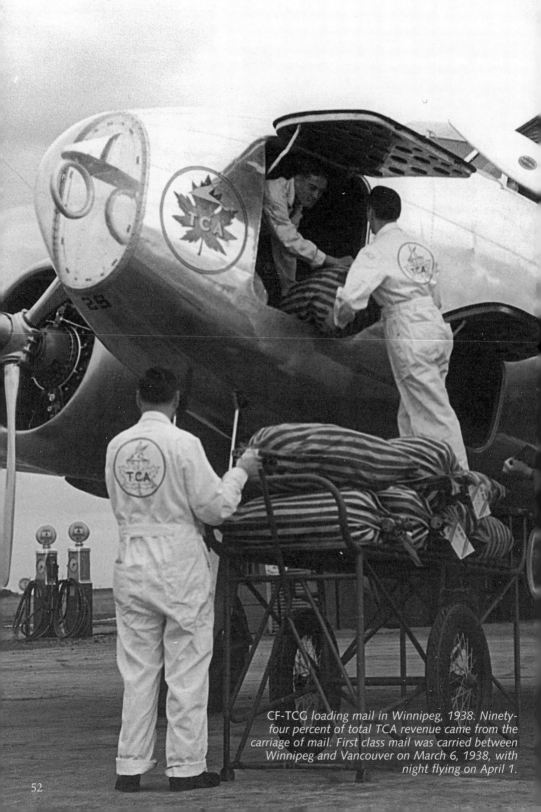

CF-TCG loading mail in Winnipeg, 1938. Ninety-four percent of total TCA revenue came from the carriage of mail. First class mail was carried between Winnipeg and Vancouver on March 6, 1938, with night flying on April 1.

C H A P T E R   3

Although TCA already flew between Vancouver and Seattle, Washington, a legacy from the CAL purchase, the original Trans Canada Airlines Act lacked the blanket permission that the company needed to carry passengers outside of the Dominion. Given that it was then struggling to maintain training flights over the Rockies, international operations must have seemed a long way off, but the Act was amended in February 1938, a necessary first step so that international flights could at least be planned. However, on July 28 of that same year, after an exchange of diplomatic notes, a reciprocal air navigation agreement came into effect with the United States, and because of the amendment the airline was able to apply immediately for a licence to operate a direct service between Toronto and New York.

For TCA's newly established flight operations department, the company's four Lockheed 10As were ideal for instrument and radio range flying, and on February 1, 1938, daylight training flights started between Winnipeg and Vancouver. The aircraft were manned by two captains with the one in the right seat acting as the "safety" pilot while the one on the left flew "under the hood," which meant that he could not see the outside world and he had to rely entirely on the cockpit instruments. As if this weren't difficult enough, at liftoff the instructor would shut down one of the engines by cutting the ignition. The trainee then had to counteract the yaw, feather the propeller blades and climb up to a safe altitude. Still under the hood, the trainee no longer knew where he was in relation to the airport. Using the radio beam he would make some pre-calculated manoeuvres to identify one of the four beam legs of the airport's radio station before making a single-engine approach. At 500 feet the hood was removed. It was a tough regimen that produced a high standard of pilots. TCA's purchase of a Link trainer in March 1938 allowed the company to do all its pilot training in-house. Young Ed Link had built his first model in a corner of his father's organ factory and perfected it by 1928. Mounted on a universal joint and cradled in a chamber of compressed air controlled by bellows, the machine did everything an aircraft could do except fly, but there had been no market for it in the Depression, and Link had supported himself by giving rides in it at carnivals. It wasn't until Europe started re-arming in 1937 and the British placed a large order for trainers that Link was able to open a factory in Gananoque, Ontario.

At TCA, under the scrutiny of Percy T. Cole, everyone from the most experienced pilots like Don MacLaren and Herbert Hollick-Kenyon to the dispatchers and engineers to the medical examiners were required to undergo Link training. "It was," Cole said, "to be one of the greatest bits of apparatus for revealing the character of said victims, and I have seen it change contempt to respect via determination." The Link acquired a few nicknames over the years, such as "the Torture Chamber" and "the Sweat Box," but the one that remained, at least until the war was "Jeep," probably from a cartoon series called "Jeepers Creepers." Cole's own preference was "the Thought Eliminator."

"Early in the game it became apparent that the 10A lacked the range required for use on many of the routes that TCA had in mind," pilot Herb Seagrim wrote later. "Sometimes, for example, while flying the route from Lethbridge to Vancouver, we had to land at Cranbrook or Oliver, BC."[1] Their single-engined performance for the mountains was also of concern, and the 10s were always regarded as a stopgap measure until Lockheed's model 14—the Super Electra—came out.

Jack Dyment once asked management why TCA had bought the Lockheed Super Electra instead of the Douglas DC-3. He was told that the Electra had a better "one-engine service ceiling" than the Douglas aircraft, an advantage essential for flights over the Rockies. Dyment later discovered that this was false and that the Electra, with its high wing loading, was dangerously unsuited for what was expected of it. "Some maintained that the DC-3 was too slow or too big or simply not available," Herb Seagrim wrote. "Each of these factors may have had some credibility, but the fact remains that the Rt. Hon. C.D. Howe, fired with enthusiasm over what he regarded as 'his' airline, had a tentative order placed for four Lockheed 14s and three 10As by the spring of 1937...It is doubtful if any of the management group subsequently hired had any inclination to argue with Howe's selection."[2]

In 1946, when questioned in the House as to why TCA was still flying Lodestars on its transcontinental routes when it now had DC-3s, Howe replied that the DC-3 "has not a good single-engined performance at high altitude. Trans Canada Airlines has some twenty-five DC-3s and operates them everywhere in Canada except across the Rockies, for it does not believe it is safe to operate them over mountainous country at altitudes above 11,000 feet. That is a technical opinion and for that reason TCA uses Lockheeds which have a satisfactory single-engine performance at high altitude."[3] However, it may have been a simple matter of supply and demand: as United Airlines (UAL) had once monopolized Boeing's output of 247s, American Airlines and Trans World Airlines (TWA) now had a hammerlock on the Douglas production line while they equipped their own fleets.

Clayton Glenn, who joined the airline in 1943, wrote:

By modern standards the Lockheeds were poorly built, and it took a flock of mechanics to keep them flying. The noise and vibration were terrific and one would wonder why any airline in its right mind would purchase such an airplane. When I asked the question as to why TCA did not have DC-3s, I got a number of answers, depending on who answered the question. One was that the DC-3 was too big—"It has 21 seats and we only need one with 12 or 14." Or it could not fly high enough. In the United States, the Rockies have wide passes and it was possible even under instrument conditions to operate through them and not fly over the top. In Canada there are no wide passes and it was necessary for TCA to fly over the mountains. The Lockheeds 14 and 18, with the same power as the DC-3, were considerably lighter so could reach higher altitudes. I am sure that this was the correct answer to my question.[4]

However maligned, the Lockheeds were the lesser of two evils. The Department of Transport had actually recommended the airline buy the single-engined Northrop Delta for the mountain run because of its higher ceiling (23,400 feet compared with 18,000 feet). However, influenced by the performance of the four 10s already in use, TCA's management decided to stay with the Lockheed family of aircraft in the hope that the high cruise capacity of the Super would get it over the mountains.

The prototype of the Super Electra was still being built when Howe announced to the airline's board of directors that he had ordered it. Officially it was known by Lockheed as the Model 14H2, the "H2" meaning two 875 hp Pratt & Whitney engines. Designed by the team of Hall Hibbard and Clarence "Kelly" Johnson, it featured the familiar low-wing and twin-tail form of its predecessors, the 10 and the 12. It made its debut at Burbank on July 29, 1937, with the manufacturer's chief pilot, Marshall Headle, at the controls and received its Approved Type Certificate in November. Smaller than the DC-2, the Super was sold on its high cruising speed—faster than either the Boeing 247 or the Douglas DC-2—achieved by its small wingspan and overly powerful engines. The fuselage was deeper than the 10E, and there was now no wing truss to step over, as had been the case with Lockheed's Models 10 and 12 and Boeing's 247.

On the basis of discussions with US airline presidents and aircraft manufacturers, Howe bought four of the new Lockheed 14s at $99,000 each. There was no question of looking for locally made aircraft; the largest, latest Canadian-built plane was the Fleet 50 Freighter, which that month was just completing its testing at Fort Erie, Ontario. For sales tax reasons, TCA's first Model 14, registered as *CF-TCD*, was accepted in Reno, Nevada, on May 10, 1938, followed by *TCE*, *TCF* and *TCG* in June, and flown to Vancouver by Slim Lewis, Lewis Leigh, Lindy Rood and Maurice McGregor. But while at Burbank the TCA pilots discovered that the Lockheed test pilots were wary of the aircraft's handling characteristics, especially in landing and in the stall, and they refused to check out the Canadians on the latter, having tried stalling the 14 a couple of times and almost losing control as it turned over on its back. That, they said, was about as far as they wanted to go. When landing *CF-TCD* at Vancouver on May 12, Rood and Lewis Leigh also found out that the test pilot's advice on 75-percent use of flaps was also wrong. Watched by a welcoming crowd, the pair bounced down the runway, damaging a fuel tank before making a second circuit and "bleeding" the flaps up slowly. Before flying passengers, the airline would also have to work out how to control the 14's stalls.

The Electra

The most famous aircraft in the Electra series was the one used in the 1942 Warner Brothers film *Casablanca*, a 12A borrowed from Lockheed. Filming was underway, and the scene in which the Nazi Major Strasser lands at Casablanca (actually Van Nuys Airport in California) had already been shot, when the Japanese attacked Pearl Harbor, and all subsequent outdoor shooting was cancelled. Thus, the whole farewell scene between Humphrey Bogart and Ingrid Bergman had to be filmed on Stage 1 at the Warner Brothers studios in front of a mock-up of the 12A made of plywood and balsa with liberal amounts of fog to cover up the deception. It is possible that the original 12A used for the Strasser scene is now part of the *Casablanca* set at Walt Disney World in Orlando, Florida.

While TCA was taking delivery of its four Super Electras, the millionaire aviator Howard Hughes, who had been negotiating to buy a DC-3, changed his mind and bought a Lockheed Model 14(N) powered by Wright Cyclone engines (Lockheed offered its Electras to customers with a variety of engines), and on July 10 he flew it around the world in 91 hours and 14 minutes. The Lockheed company couldn't have hoped to buy publicity like that, and export orders poured in. KLM (Dutch), LOT (Polish), Aer Lingus (Irish), Guinea Airways and British Airways bought enough to keep the aircraft in production. Of the 112 Super Electras that Lockheed built, TCA bought sixteen 14Hs to become the manufacturer's best customer, and these were delivered from June 1938 to August 1939. The TCA fleet numbers were 26 to 41, their Canadian registrations beginning with *TCD* and continuing alphabetically to *TCS*. Aircraft delivered later were equipped with the more powerful Pratt & Whitney Twin Wasp engines, and the fuselage was stretched by $5\frac{1}{2}$ feet to accommodate four more seats. These were known as the Lockheed 18 Lodestars. Because of the modifications, the price per aircraft had risen to $127,000.

The 14s were regarded at "hot aircraft " by the TCA pilots who had trained on the 10s, but they proved from the outset that they could not be taken lightly. Their several design flaws would today have been discovered after extensive testing, but in 1938 there was no time to do it. Every airline that did not have a DC-3 in service wanted their Electras immediately, and the British, French, Japanese and Dutch airliness were buying as many aircraft as they could.

One of the Super Electra's problems was that although it was a "tail dragger," it had to be flown like a "nose wheel" aircraft. Landing it in the conventional "3-point" manner—that is, main wheels and tail wheel down—caused it to ground loop or swing. Through painstaking trials, flight instructors learned to land with the tail up; not until the main wheels were securely planted on the runway did they allow the tail to drop slowly. At takeoff, to guard against the 14's vicious stall characteristics, the main wheels had to be held firmly on the runway until single engine-controllability was sure.

Lockheed had attempted to compete with the DC-3's better seat–mile economics by including a number of advanced design features in the Electra series to increase performance. Because its stubby wings led to takeoff and landing speeds in excess of the generally accepted norms of the time, Lockheed adapted the flap by cutting slots into each wing tip leading upward and back through the wing, so that on approach and landing the air would flow through the slot and over the wing, smoothing out turbulence. Fowler flaps were used for the first time in production aircraft at the trailing edges of the wings to direct the air flow over the top of the wings, keeping it smooth across the lifting surface and hopefully preventing stalls. Thus they not only performed the function of conventional flaps but also augmented the wing area for takeoff and landing. Even today the Fowler flap is considered to offer the most advantages and fewest disadvantages of all flaps; the use of the slot and Fowler flap together is a powerful combination. Selection of the flap gave an ever-increasing change of wing surface curvature. Full flap actually made a very high-lift wing out of the normal high-speed low-lift wing, and since early airport runways were only 3,000 to 4,000 feet long, this low landing speed feature was very desirable.

However, what had looked good in California didn't work in the Canadian climate. After some near-crashes, TCA pilots realized that the inlets of the slots iced up and aggravated the stall. Worse, the ice buildup could not be observed from the cockpit windows. "It was equivalent," one pilot said, "of having a two-by-four nailed under the first three feet of each wing tip."[5] The airflow through the slots left a deposit of ice on the lower side that would cause the aircraft to quit flying. In modern aircraft the stall starts at the wing root and goes outward, giving the pilot enough time to react, but with the 14 and later the 18, the reverse was true. The outer wing stalled first, leaving the pilot little warning and no control as the ailerons were also stalled.

A clear view of the flaps deployed in landing the Lockheed 14 CF-TCF. The aircraft was more than adequate aerodynamically, but Canadian winters posed unforeseen hazards by snagging the mechanisms during TCA service.

For Herb Seagrim it was an awesome experience to be sitting at the controls of a 14 for the first time and to have the infamous stall demonstrated. "With the flaps and gear tucked up and power off, a pregnant silence would prevail. Then, abruptly and without warning, the wheel would almost be snatched from one's hands as the airplane dropped its left wing and started into the makings of a spin. This was accompanied by feverish activity in the cockpit."[6] He recalled one such flight out of Winnipeg in late 1938.

> To meet the standards of the TCA training curriculum required that 45-degree banked turns be performed with one engine throttled back. During one such training flight in *CF-TCE* with instructor Howard "Sandy" Sandgathe and a pupil at the controls, the aircraft suddenly stalled at 7,000 feet and commenced a tight spin to the right. The spin, actually a power dive, continued with increasing speed. Recovery was made at 3,000 feet above the ground by the cool-headed Sandgathe with the differential use of engines and centring the rudder trim tab. The violence of the manoeuvre can be judged by the fact that when they landed, the left wing tip was bent upwards to the vertical—like a fighter aircraft on an aircraft carrier. Sandgathe later estimated that the speed was in excess of the allowable 284 mph and that the aircraft was on the verge of structural disintegration.

Resolving this problem provided TCA with its most difficult post-delivery modification. Lockheed sent its engineers to Winnipeg to assist Oliver West's maintenance team in fitting pneumatic rubber de-icing shoes in the slots, but when tests showed that these were unreliable, the slots were permanently sealed over.

Prolonged service in winter conditions, it seemed, had not been priorities for the designers at Lockheed, and maintaining scheduled flights between December and April was especially hard on West and his assistant, Jim Bain. The 14 had externally mounted navigation lights in the wing tips and a large, externally mounted warning light in the left wing tip; both collected ice and precipitated stall conditions toward the left. After a few harrowing flights, TCA modified its aircraft by removing the warning light and burying the navigation ones in the wing tips.

Fortunately there was one Lockheed 14 design flaw that TCA did not encounter: the one that killed the crew of a Northwest Airlines aircraft between Spokane and Seattle in 1938. The aircraft's tail planes had come off in flight because of a frequency vibration (tail flutter). After that, all Lockheeds had lead counterbalances installed inside the rudders. Northwest suffered three Super Electra crashes in rapid succession and in 1939 sold its entire Electra fleet, replacing them with DC-3s. As a result of these accidents, the US government withdrew the Lockheed 14's certificate of airworthiness. To a major degree, it was because of TCA's tail modifications and the company's demonstration that the aircraft was safe that the US government later reinstated the certificate and assured the future of the aircraft—and the Lockheed company.

TCA had to redesign the pitot masts and equip the fleet with de-icing vanes in front of the masts, feeding them with alcohol to eliminate the false air speed and altitude readings that resulted from ice buildup. When the recommended aviation oil for lubrication of aircraft parts froze, the maintenance staff discovered that one of the better reasons for being part of the CNR was the ready availability of railroad semaphore oil, which they used instead. As well, the water systems on the 14s were useless in the winter. All the plumbing had to be insulated from the structure because the cold of the fuselage skin would freeze the water in the lines. TCA maintenance crews also redesigned the system with a single drain cock so that the entire water system could be drained quickly if the aircraft had to be parked outdoors during the winter. And as soon as polyethylene tubing came on the market, TCA replaced all of its metal plumbing with plastic.

Lindy Rood would never forget the 14H flight from Lethbridge to Winnipeg that he captained on New Year's Eve 1938. "We were at 16,000 feet when I was suddenly slapped with severe icing over Grand Forks. The air intakes were iced up badly, making the fuel air mixture overly rich and the cloud around the aircraft looked as if the whole aircraft was on fire. I regained control at 9,000 feet and went back to Lethbridge." Had he been using oxygen—that is, had oxygen been available—he would never have ventured into the frontal area at that altitude, and he has always thought that the lack of it affected his reasoning.

Cabin heating in the Lockheeds was also poor, as it was derived from the hot exhaust gases in the tail pipe through which a scoop pipe took in cold air as the aircraft moved forward. The amount of heated air was controlled by a valve operated by a handle mounted on the rear bulkhead of the passenger cabin. Two heat ducts extended the length of the cabin under the floor and entered the cabin directly below the passenger seats. At least, this is how it worked in theory. Radioman Dudley Taylor recalled a Winnipeg–Montreal flight that left Winnipeg when the temperature was –40 degrees F. "It was the custom to load the passengers into the aircraft in the hangar so that both men and machines would get a warm start. It was really cold in the air and we all kept our overcoats on as well as covering ourselves with the blankets that the stewardesses provided. When we landed at Kapuskasing, the ground crew opened the door, and a passenger called out, 'What's the temperature here?' The crew man answered, 'Ten below, sir.' The passenger yelled back, 'Leave the bloody door open and let some heat in.'"

The pilots' standard complaint was the "Lockheed shoulder," a stiffening in the shoulder caused by sub-zero air seeping in through the cockpit's side windows just an inch away from the pilot's body. Once more Jack Dyment's department came to the rescue with the use of a rectangular box called a mixing chamber, which mixed hot air with the cold brought in via a scoop facing forward on the lower side of the wing. "The air still did not pick up enough heat by this method until we 'dimpled' the intensifier tube and this improved the heat transfer with only the cost of the dimpling involved."[7] Pilots could also roast in the Electra's cockpit. On one flight between Regina and Lethbridge in early 1940, the heating system went haywire and the cockpit's heat lever became stuck in the open position. The station manager recorded that "The boys arrived in Lethbridge minus tunics, ties and shoes and in a somewhat parboiled state. But they said they hated to complain to maintenance after freezing the previous trip."[8]

Insufficient lubrication of the Electras' engines, which inevitably caused them to seize up, was first encountered by Northwest Airlines, the "launch" customer for the Super Electra. But when Dyment learned that they were also experiencing foaming in the engine oil, he went to work on the problem. "We installed a clear plastic line in an oil system so we could see the oil with the engine running... and found that our oil was foaming coming in and going out. Not really knowing how to stop the foaming, maintenance redesigned the aircraft's oil tanks by installing a gently sloping wide ramp inside the tank so that the foamed oil from the engine could flow down it. This caused most of the trapped air to escape and the oil returning to the engine was free of foam."[9]

The extreme cold was the cause of many of the aircraft's teething problems, both in flight and on the ground. Some were easily overcome: if the aircraft became covered with freezing rain while on the ground, it was towed to a warm hangar until this melted clear. But although most weather-related problems could be corrected in-house with the addition of electrically heated propeller shoes and anti-static loops, the persistent fuel-tank leaks taxed even the ingenuity of Jim Bain. The seepage from the tanks between each engine nacelle and the cabin wall was almost impossible to trace and, if found, to seal with Thiokol sealant, which was supposed to be impervious to aviation fuel. Because they were so close to the flaming engine exhausts, these leaks could have grounded the fleet before the airline could carry passengers. This time Lockheed sent their expert Adolph Merta to Winnipeg. Cheerful and always optimistic, Merta put on protective breathing gear and worked for long hours inside the tanks, stripping off the old sealing compound down to the bare metal, then coating the inside of the tank with Thiokol sealant followed by zinc chromate paste and a second coating of Thiokol.

Lockheed did equip their aircraft with the latest pneumatic inflatable rubber boots on the wing's leading edges and tail plane. With any buildup of rime ice, the wing boots were pulsated, and the resulting broken chunks disappeared into the slipstream. And because the propeller could become unbalanced with ice buildup, a "Slinger Ring," a metal ring around the propeller base, had been installed to direct alcohol fluid along the blades. To loosen up any rime ice, the pilot increased the revolutions per minute, relying on centrifugal force to fling it off, and this hit the fuselage with a satisfying clatter. What the pilots could not do was remove the ice adhering to the radio masts, tail wheel and nose.

The Electra's Hornet engines failed with embarrassing frequency. This was the result of the screen in the engine oil system becoming blocked with sludge because the de-icing fluid used on the propellers was entering the engine air intake. This acted as a solvent that cleaned the carbon off the inside of the engine so quickly that it blocked the screen. The solution? "We changed the de-icing fluid to methyl alcohol," Dyment wrote, "and incidentally had to add a little gasoline to the alcohol to prevent people from stealing and drinking it."

In fairness to Pratt & Whitney, the Hornets were being strained beyond their 750 hp specifications. Heavy ice created drag, the extra weight causing the airspeed to slowly drop back, and the captain would counter this by adding full engine power to maintain altitude and speed. This was especially true of flights over the Rockies, where encountering heavy ice meant that because of the Electra's high wing loading, the aircraft remained in the air on the strength of its engines alone—or so it seemed to the crew. The excessive power used to escape icing caused the engine's cylinders to crack from the front spark plug port to rear spark plug port, and TCA's mechanics held that you could trace the company's route across the country by following the trail of Hornet cylinders on the ground! To minimize the chances of complete rupture and engine shutdown, maintenance adopted a shorter operating life for the top three cylinders of each engine because they were subject to the most heat, and the mechanics became very efficient at changing these three even if the aircraft was undergoing a minor service check.

The most distinguishing feature of the 14s and 18s was the Plexiglas noses in which were housed the radio compass loops. Less noticeable were the two "T" antennas supported between a pair of masts on the aircraft's belly, one of them feeding the radio compass and the other the emergency receiver located under the co-pilot's chair. (Crew members always said that this was a good location because if it failed, all you had to do was kick it with the heel of your shoe to get it working again.) This system had been designed by Lockheed engineers who had figured that an antenna running from a mast above the cockpit to one of the twin rudders would create drag and icing problems. Instead they had used a length of rubber-covered stainless steel wire with a fitting at the end that plugged into a mated fitting under the tail of the aircraft. This could be paid out to improve reception. The rubber covering was to minimize wear on the wire when the aircraft was taxiing, but in order to protect the wire when the aircraft was being manoeuvred by maintenance staff, as soon as the aircraft arrived at its destination, a radioman wound up the antenna and put it onto brackets built in the tail. It was unwound again before the aircraft taxied out. Few aircraft ever took off with the antenna still wound up, as communications would cease a few hundred yards out onto the runway and be noticed immediately.

However, ingenious though it was, this trailing antenna was one of the communications department's major problems at TCA. Wear and tear on the antennae was very high and making spare ones in the shop was drudgery. They were also very prone to lightning strikes on aircraft in flight: they would simply evaporate and leave the pilot without radio contact. Dudley Taylor, who worked in the Winnipeg radio shop, remembers an aircraft landing with no communications at all, but when it taxied in, the antenna was right there behind it. Close examination revealed that what looked like the antenna was only its rubber coating. The lightning had evaporated the steel wire and left the rubber intact!

The Complete Record of Lightning Strikes on the Lockheeds

A/C No.	Type	Date	Altitude	Location	Damage
28	14	28/9/38	10,000 ft	Pagawa, ON	antenna burned off
34	14	11/5/43	8,000 ft	Maple Ridge, ON	antenna, prop blade burned
31	14	7/6/43	-	no information	antenna burned off
37	14	19/3/44	5,000 ft	BC	antenna burned off, prop blade seared
33	14	20/7/44	12,000 ft	BC	antenna burned off
35	14	19/8/44	-	Porquois, ON	HF radio burned up

29	14	1944	-	Porquois, ON	prop blade burned
56	18	22/7/47	-	BC	large holes burned in trailing edge of wing
49	18	16/8/47	-	BC	one prop blade burned

D.R. Taylor, "Lightning Strikes as Experienced by Trans Canada Airlines," CATC (49) 124, November 3, 1948.

Though lightning strikes continued to plague the airline, the introduction of the Lockheed 18 ended the use of the trailing antenna. Because it was really a stretched version of the 14—it carried four passengers more than the 14—its tail section was squeezed, so the radio equipment had been moved from there to the forward baggage compartment. Two antenna masts were added, one above the cockpit and the other on top of the fuselage between the two fins. An insulator was installed just above the forward baggage compartment, and the antenna ran from it to the forward mast and then parallel to the fuselage to the rear mast. Besides getting rid of the trailing antenna, these changes also provided for better weight distribution for the longer aircraft.

While antenna problems were overcome by design changes on the 18s, tubes remained a problem on radio equipment. Transistors hadn't been invented yet and aircraft vibrations were hard on the tubes. "Someone in the industry," Taylor figures, "discovered that tubes are like people—if they last a certain length of time, the chances are that they would last very much longer. The company picked up this idea and tried vibrating tubes before using them. In this way they were able to weed out the weak ones and the balance had a much longer life. The tube manufacturers heard about this and began doing their own vibration tests and made an effort to build stronger structures within the tubes themselves. The new line of 'rugged' tubes cost more but went a long way in improving the reliability of radios on the aircraft."[10]

When automatic radio compasses were installed in the Lodestars at an expense of $65,484, the Sperry automatic pilots were sold off for $73,710, making TCA a neat profit. The outcome of the co-operation between the Bendix radio corporation and the Sperry Gyroscope Company, the automatic radio compass was one of the most critical radio aids to air navigation. As soon as it was tuned in, it was capable of automatically indicating the bearing of a station in relation to the aircraft's flight direction. In addition, it would operate not only on radio range stations but other types of broadcast stations in different frequency ranges, thus increasing the number of stations on which bearings could be taken. The compass loop was mounted in a streamlined housing and automatically rotated toward the station to which it was tuned. Best of all, severe static had no effect on it.

As time went on, reliability problems with the Hornet engines on the Lockheed 14s, the shortage of parts during the war years and the need for commonality with the Lockheed 18 Lodestars on order pushed the airline to replace the 875 hp Hornets with 1,200 hp S1C3-G Pratt & Whitney Twin-Row Wasp engines. The upgraded aircraft were renamed 18-08s. Replacing the engines was a joint program between TCA and Pratt & Whitney, with Boeing of Canada doing the conversion at its new Vancouver plant between January 1942 and February 1943. As the new engines were heavier and had considerably more power, TCA had to increase the aircraft's gross weight in order to maintain the same payload/range capability. A new certificate of airworthiness was therefore necessary; this meant that the modified aircraft had to be stress-analyzed and a complete schedule of flight testing drawn up. The flutter and vibration tests were conducted by Eddie Allen, Boeing's chief test pilot, and the performance capability tests were done by that company's chief pilot, Ron George.

Lockheed 14 & 18 Specifications:

	14H2 (Super Electra)	18-08 (Lodestar)
Wingspan	65 ft 6 inches	65 ft 6 inches
Wing area	551 sq ft	551 sq ft
Wing loading	31.8 lbs/sq ft	33.57 lbs/sq ft
Overall length	44 ft 3$7/8$"	49 ft 9$7/8$"
Gross weight	17,500 lbs	18,500 lbs
Empty weight	12,000 lbs	12,075 lbs
Useful load	5,500 lbs	6,425 lbs
Power plants	P&W Hornets	P&W Twin Wasps
Max power	900 hp at 2,300 rpm	1,200 hp at 2,325 rpm
Cruise power	520 hp at 1,950 rpm	700 hp at 2,325 rpm
Top speed	244 mph	263 mph
Cruising speed at 12,000 ft	207 mph	236 mph
Cruising range	1,550 miles	1,250 miles
Ceiling, two-engine	23,000 ft	25,000 ft
Ceiling, one-engine	11,000 ft	13,000 ft
Passengers	10	14
Crew	3	3

There was also a version of the 18-08 called the 2200, the difference being that it was produced under the controls of the US Wartime Production Board.

By the time all the "bugs" were eliminated from the 14s, the Second World War was raging, and in June 1940 they were effectively orphaned when Lockheed ended production in order to concentrate on its military orders. Douglas, meanwhile, continued to build DC-3s, thereby ensuring that aircraft's immortality, but the Super Electra deserves its place in history as well. Though the

DC-3 had a wider cabin and a 50 percent larger payload capacity, making it more popular with passengers—and airline accountants—the Super Electra was more than the DC-3's match in speed as its powerful engines gave it a higher cruise performance, and possibly this is what those who chose it for TCA had in mind. History, however, knows the basic Electra model better in its military versions—the A-28 and A-29, the Hudson and the Harpoon, all of which were built in various Marks to serve in every theatre of war with the Allied air forces. During the war the Super Electra actually flew for both sides. After buying 30 of them in 1938, the Japanese aeronautical company Kawasaki Kokuki K.K. acquired the rights to build it. Early in the war Kawasaki manufactured 121 of them, designating them as military transports; the Allies codenamed them "Thelma."

On April 13, 1938, P.G. Johnson and G.E. Bellerose, the CNR's general manager, met to finalize plans for a TCA Air Express Service, patterned on the air courier industry already well developed in the United States. Effective from that date, Canadian companies could ship by air such items as flowers, currency, perishable foods, X-ray tubes, diamonds, electrotype plates and mats for newspapers. These goods were carried by air between Winnipeg, Regina and Vancouver and, as the airline grew, from all other TCA stations as well. As they had done for TCA's early mail and passenger services, the CNR took responsibility for ground operations and furnished personnel, equipment, advertising, receipts, waybills and other stationery for the air express service, though all communications were printed on TCA Express Services letterhead. For its part, when full service began in October, the airline loaded and unloaded the express freight, transporting it to and from the aircraft, transferring it at airports to connecting flights and/or delivering it directly to the consignees. At some points the express shipments were carried by TCA's own trucks.

For a "start-up" operation like TCA to plug into a company that had fifty-five years of experience and operated a network of 1,700 offices with collection points in 592 cities across North America, Mexico and the West Indies was propitious, for financial reasons as well as for publicity. If CNR management ever felt worried that TCA would take away potential passengers, freight and mail, there is no sign of it in official correspondence. As the federal government's agency for transcontinental transportation, the railway was not only underwriting the shares of an enterprise that gave poor return on its investment, but in doing so it was competing against itself. Yet there exists no record of the railway being other than co-operative, perhaps because no one from its directors to its porters could conceive of TCA ever being a threat.

The delivery of more Electras to TCA in the early months of 1938 allowed for added training flights. The crews referred to these as "ghost flights" because of their unofficial status, but sometimes they did carry mail between cities—which must have mystified the recipients. Captain R.M. Smith flew the first experimental mail flight on March 1, 1938, from Winnipeg to Vancouver

A beehive of activity in front of the terminal at Vancouver Airport, summer 1939. A newly arrived TCA Lockheed 14 on the left faces off with United Airlines late model Boeing 247D.

via Regina and Lethbridge, but because of weather problems the aircraft did not arrive in Vancouver until March 3. Regular service was launched on October 1 from Winnipeg to Vancouver with stops in Regina and Lethbridge and a spur to Edmonton.

Further expansion of service suffered a setback on November 18 when the airline had its first crash: pilots D. Imrie and J.W. Herald were killed while taking off from Regina in *CF-TCL* on a regularly scheduled flight to Vancouver. There was not enough wreckage left to determine what had caused the crash. At first it was supposed that Imrie had become disoriented and, instead of climbing out after takeoff, had allowed the aircraft to descend into the ground. It was only after a Northwest Airlines Electra 14 crashed soon after and enough of that aircraft was left intact, that the chain of events could be pieced together. It was discovered that the vapour from the gasoline-feed valve between the pilots' seats had been ignited by a faulty electric light switch.

By the end of 1938 transcontinental flights were at last in effect between Vancouver and Montreal (November 30) and from Winnipeg to North Bay, Toronto, Ottawa and Montreal (December 1). Three other significant events took place that last month of 1938. With war looming in Europe, the Non-Permanent Active Air Force (NPAAF) of the RCAF was put on a more belligerent footing and renamed the Auxiliary Air Force. The Trans Canada or McKee Trophy was awarded to the personnel of Trans Canada Airlines for their work in setting up the airline. And for the third time a Bell Telephone Company manager named Gordon R. McGregor won the John C. Webster trophy for best amateur pilot. A year earlier he had piloted the D.H. Tiger Moth *CF-CBU* from Kingston to Moose Jaw along the Airway and back, but when he went on to earn his commercial licence in 1938 and wrote to TCA for a job as a pilot, he received only a polite acknowledgement.

SECOND ANNUAL REPORT FOR THE
YEAR ENDING DECEMBER 31ST, 1938

Correlated with the repair base and overhaul shop at Winnipeg were the opening of stations with complete radio facilities:

Montreal (St. Hubert), Que.
Ottawa, Ont.
Toronto (Malton), Ont.
North Bay, Ont.
Kapuskasing, Ont
Wagaming, Ont.
Regina, Sask.
Lethbridge, Alta.
Edmonton, Alta.

Property and Equipment
At December 31, there were 9 Lockheed 14H, each with two Pratt & Whitney S1E2G Hornet engines 850 hp, hydrometric full feathering propellers and Bendix radio.
5 Lockheed 10A; each equipped with two Pratt & Whitney S.B. Wasp Junior engines of 450 hp, controllable pitch propellers and Western Electric radios.
The Stearman was sold to Northern Airways.

Personnel:

The staff totaled 332, an increase of 261 comprised of:
Administrative	14
Flight Personnel	37
Maintenance	178
Communication and Dispatch	55
Station, clerical and other	48

It has become the recognized practice of air transport companies on this continent to employ stewardesses to care for the comfort of passengers. In the month of July stewardesses were engaged for the Vancouver–Seattle service and will be employed on other runs when the passenger service is inaugurated. In anticipation of this a traffic department was organized and Mr. G.G. Wakeman was appointed General Traffic Manager and district offices were opened at Winnipeg and Vancouver.

It is with the deepest regret that the loss of the lives of two valued pilots Captain D. Imrie and First Officer J.W. Herald is recorded. They were killed when aircraft "CF-TCL" crashed and was destroyed in the early morning hours of November 18 just after takeoff from Regina on a regularly scheduled flight to Vancouver. Full investigation by the company's officers and also by a Board of Enquiry constituted by the Minister of Transport failed to determine the cause of the crash.

Mail Carried:

	Pounds	Total per Route
Winnipeg–Vancouver: West	5,801	
(October and November) East	5,837	11,638
Montreal–Vancouver: West	9,829	
(December only) East	10,067	19,896
Lethbridge–Edmonton: North	3,715	
(October–December): South	4,164	7,879
Vancouver–Seattle: North	23,671	
(Year 1938): South	39,333	63,004
Total airmail:		**102,417**

In addition, 265,317 pounds of regular first class mail were carried in scheduled training flights Winnipeg–Vancouver from March 6th to September 30. The first leg of a proposed airmail service was made on March 1, 1938, from Vancouver to Winnipeg. On October 1, the Vancouver to Edmonton airmail route began. On November 30 an experimental airmail flight was made between Vancouver and Montreal, arriving in that city on December 1, 1938.

Financial

$3,200,000 capital has now been raised by the issue of capital stock, an increase of $2,350,000 during the year. $2,779,314 has been invested in aircraft, aircraft engines, communications equipment. The income account for the year, after providing for all operating costs including depreciation and interest of capital shows a deficit of $818,025, which is slightly under the amount of $830,000 appropriated by Parliament. Ninety-four percent of the total revenue was from the carriage of mail. First class mail was carried between Winnipeg and Vancouver on March 6, 1938, with night flying on April 1. On August 15 the flights east of Winnipeg began, reaching Montreal on September 7, and on October 1, regular mail service was started between Winnipeg and Vancouver, and this was extended to Montreal on December 1. The rate of mail was fixed at 60 cents per mile from mid-1938 until the end of 1939, when the provisions of the Act would determine changes. The rate of 60 cents was per plane-mile flown with mail and did not depend on the weight.

Passenger service was operated between Vancouver–Seattle only. The amount in reserve on December 31 was $87,921.30. To provide for the loss of *CF-TCL* destroyed in the Regina accident the amount in reserve was utilized in full and the deficiency of $35,652.18 charged to aircraft operation. The report did draw attention to the high proportion of depreciation charges to the total operating expenses as a result of so much flying being for training purposes.

TCA was well represented on the historic"Dawn to Dusk" flight by two of its directors C. P. Edwards (far left) and H.J. Symington (far right) and C. D. Howe next to him.

Trans-Atlantic Trial Flights:

The plans of Imperial Airways Limited for a number of trial flights across the north Atlantic were curtailed and only one crossing was made: "The Mercury," the upper component of the composite aircraft developed in England, left Foynes, Irish Free State, at 1900 GMT on July 20th and flew non-stop to Montreal, arriving at 15:19 GMT on July 21st. A payload of approximately 1,000 lbs was carried. The return journey was made from New York on July 25th, via Montreal, Newfoundland, the Azores and Lisbon. The present indications are that there will be considerably greater activity in this connection during 1939.

A Lockheed 14 at the Malton
terminal, taking on a full load.
From a TCA postcard series 1939
via Hugh A. Reid

W hen the first scheduled "through" train for Vancouver puffed out of Montreal's old Dalhousie station on June 28, 1886, it was seen off by many hundreds of flag-waving well-wishers, a full military band and a fifteen-gun salute. But on March 1, 1939, when the first scheduled Montreal–Vancouver passenger flights by TCA took place, there was no such pageantry. The Post Office alone acknowledged the event by furnishing cachets for dispatch. The nation's attention, like that of the government, was on the disturbing events in Europe, but in their own way the flights were as significant to the national consciousness as the first CPR train had been. For thanks to Trans Canada Airlines, for the first time mail and passengers could be flown from Montreal to Vancouver without going through the United States. All of the crews and some of those intrepid passengers were recorded for posterity.

Passengers and Crew on the first Montreal– Vancouver Flights

Westbound:

Montreal–Ottawa–Kapuskasing (used as the crew change point)
Captain B.A. Rawson, first officer D.R. MacLaren, stewardess Annette Brunelle. C.D. Howe, H.J. Symington and Wilfrid Gagnon officially opened the service. They had embarked from St. Hubert Airport on the "Dawn to Dusk" flight two years before. Of the eight passengers, three were female. The first Montrealer to buy a ticket was H.W. Johnson, a Montreal grain broker, who flew to Winnipeg. The baggage limit was 40 lbs each.

Toronto–Kapuskasing–Winnipeg
Captain K. Edmison, first officer F.I. Young, stewardess P.A. McNamara.
Passengers: J.A.B. Riley of Regina; H.H. Bishop, T.G. Phillips, R.R.
Day, W.J. Addison, Geo. E. Scott, all of Toronto; H. Hilliard,
Vancouver; E.W. McQuay, Owen Sound; L. Grover and C.A. Stuart,
Toronto.

Winnipeg–Regina–Lethbridge–Vancouver
Captain Z.L. Leigh, first officer G.W. McLaren, stewardess M.M.
Wilson.

Vancouver–Seattle
Captain J.R. Bowker, first officer G. Rivers, stewardess P. Eccleston.

Eastbound

Seattle–Vancouver
Captain G.B. Lothian, first officer B.S. Macklin, stewardess R. Crispin.
Vancouver–Lethbridge–Regina–Winnipeg
Captain B. Middleton, first officer W.E. Barnes, stewardess N.T.
Wallace.
Bruce Middleton left TCA the following month to rejoin Imperial
Airways, flying their London–Frankfurt–Budapest route. On the very
day that World War II was declared, he was on that flight and landed
in Frankfurt, which was now "enemy territory." Though he was near-
ly incarcerated there, Bruce was allowed to return to London and eventually to Canada, where he flew for the RCAF.

Winnipeg–Kapuskasing–Ottawa–Toronto
Captain R.M. Smith, first officer D.B. Stevens, stewardess D.J. Price.
Passengers: T.P. Brown of Toronto; E.B. Brown of Robert Simpson Co.,
Saskatchewan; Mrs. M. Baillie of T. Eaton Co., Toronto.

Toronto–Montreal
Captain W.W. Fowler, first officer H. Umphrey, stewardess G. Brunelle.
Northbound (connecting at Lethbridge) and Southbound
Captain A. Rankin, first officer R. Giguere, stewardess M.J. Brass.

Lethbridge–Calgary–Edmonton
Captain R. Giguere, first officer A. Rankin, stewardess M.J. Brass.

Lethbridge–Calgary–Edmonton, April 2, 1939
Captain J.G. Haslett, first officer J. Bradley, stewardess E. Allen.

Members of the press had been invited to enjoy the pre-inaugural flight, and
one reporter filed a story describing how he had left Montreal on Wednesday
and arrived in Vancouver in time for lunch on Thursday, "of being whisked

high above the Pacific Coast city," and arriving back at St. Hubert Airport "all in only 15 hours. Now that we are back on earth we realize how fast we really traveled. Up there, it did not seem unusual to us that cities like Winnipeg and Regina were only two hours apart, that we had spanned the giant ranges of the Canadian Rockies in less than three hours, or that we dozed off to sleep somewhere in Ontario and woke up halfway across the Prairies." His final observation: "We spanned a continent in 15 hours. We were carried in big, modern planes by an organization that is so efficient its service operates with clock-like precision. On the way back we left Vancouver late because of a delay in mail delivery to the airport. We arrived in Montreal the next morning ahead of schedule."[1]

That was the press's version of the jaunt. Fred Wood, TCA's future vice-president of corporate services, was the steward on that flight, and his recollections were somewhat different.

> It would seem that some sort of bar must have been in operation prior to the arrival of these passengers at the airport, and while no liquor was served on-board the aircraft, it now seems reasonable to assume that all of our guests were in possession of private stocks, for there was no lessening in the feeling of joy throughout the entire trip—at least until we arrived over Vancouver at an altitude of 6,000 feet. At this point we encountered the customary Vancouver weather conditions and descended by circling until we broke through at 500 feet. By this time a few of our friends resembled the colour usually associated with St. Patrick's Day and tottered off the aircraft in a state of collapse. One was so overcome at having made it safely that he immediately arranged for his return trip—by train. A real tribute to air travel. Following a "lost weekend" in Vancouver, the group reassembled for the return flight to Montreal which was uneventful until one of the two engines ceased to function in the vicinity of Swift Current.[2]

The flight landed at Regina for repairs.

Bruce West, a reporter for the Toronto *Globe and Mail*, took the Toronto–Vancouver flight on March 15, 1939. In his research before the flight took off from Malton, West discovered that exactly ninety-eight years before, another traveller had started out for the Pacific coast from Montreal. The governor of the Hudson's Bay Company, Sir George Simpson, crossed the country by canoe, oxcart and on foot, taking six weeks to do so. West also recalled the hoopla fourteen years earlier when the CNR's oil-electric train broke three world records by racing from Montreal to Vancouver in seventy hours. That he was about to cross the same distance in fifteen hours was to him "startling in its casualness." TCA, he concluded, "doesn't have to lift its hat to anyone."[3]

The expanded schedules meant that more pilots were hired in 1939, and Herbert Hopson was one of them. He was familiar with instrument flying, having taken the course at Camp Borden and received his Instructor's Certificate in 1937 before joining Mackenzie Air Services. His rapid promotions through TCA were justified by his superior technical skills, and by July he had made captain, in good time to be posted to the new routes between Moncton and Toronto on November 1, initially on a daylight schedule. By 1943 he was the airline's check pilot and became chief pilot the following year. Jack F. Crosby from Darlingford, Manitoba, also joined TCA that year. He had flown for Northwest Aero-Marine, the Winnipeg Flying Club and Canadian Airways. He was promoted to captain in March 1940.

On November 1 a second flight began operating on the Montreal– Ottawa– Toronto triangle, marking the start of the future intercity shuttle service and future "gravy train" for TCA and its successor, Air Canada. The Montreal–Ottawa corridor was the original intercity and interprovincial commercial air route in Canada, dating back to October 8, 1913, when William Robinson delivered the Montreal *Daily Mail* from Snowdon, Montreal, to Slattery's Field, Ottawa.

TCA's flight crews kept track of each other across the country by listening to position reports being made to the ground stations below, and there were soon fifteen such stations on the "hookup" between Vancouver and Montreal. They varied in size. Kenora, Nakina, Pagwa, Sioux Lookout (Soo) and Porquois Junction (Porky) were alternate or emergency landing strips, each with only a windsock and a radio operator. Some of these stations never saw an aircraft at all. The only recorded instance of a TCA Lodestar ever landing at Pagwa (which can be vaguely described as east of Nakina and west of Kapuskasing) was on January 12, 1945, when Captain Don McArthur and First Officer Doug Haddon put Flight 3 down on the emergency strip there because of a defective oil tank. By the time another aircraft could drop off a tank with Jim Kenyon, the Winnipeg crew chief, and Frank Hughes, a North Bay mechanic, to install it, the Lodestar and crew had been there two and a half long days. Pagwa Airport Manager Bill Savoie was delighted with the company, but by then McArthur and Haddon were prepared to push the aircraft all the way to Winnipeg, if necessary.

Higher up the comfort scale were "one-flag stops" like North Bay (The Bay), Kapuskasing (Kap) and Wagaming, Ontario—all regular refuelling stations on the transcontinental artery and where, it seemed, the Hornet engines always chose to break down. Kap, which had been an unemployment relief project during the Depression, was taken over by the airline because it was better situated than the previous temporary station at Porquois Junction. It saw its first TCA aircraft on February 27, 1938. Kap had a reputation for mosquitoes said to be so huge that when one landed, the ground crew had put fifty gallons of 87 octane into it before they realized that it wasn't a 14.

Except for Montreal's long established St. Hubert airport, all the other airfields, rural and urban, had only recently been carved out of the wilderness or

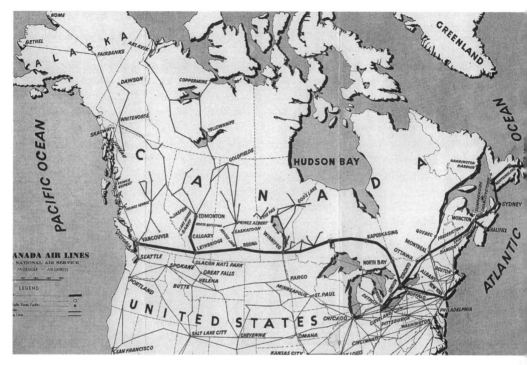

TCA route map, 1937–40.

farmland and sported little more than the prerequisite hangar, windsock and a generator for the radio range. If the post was large enough, there would also be a gas truck, a luxury for engineers who were used to using wobble pumps in the bush. Sometimes there was even a four-wheeled, rubber-tired tractor called a doodlebug for manoeuvring the Lodestar or bringing fuel barrels and luggage to the aircraft.

To the most isolated stations the airline assigned a minimum of two men: a radio operator and an experienced engineer, who soon discovered that accommodations and amusements at such places were minimal. They boarded at nearby farms, and if flights were grounded overnight because of mechanical difficulties or the weather, the passengers were put up at the local hospital. Keeping the runways clear of snow in such places with the use of snowplows was beyond the staff's capability; rather than move the drifts, they used large rollers to flatten them. If visibility was severely reduced, the pilot asked the ground crew to set out flares to mark the runway. Before the days of spraying the wings and tail surfaces of aircraft with a de-icing solution, ground crews installed lightweight fabric covers on the aircraft's wings. They would then accompany the aircraft as it taxied out onto the runway and remove the covers just before it took off.

Each of the TCA bases had their raison d'être. Because Montreal was administrative headquarters for the CNR, it also became the airline's administrative headquarters, and in April 1939 the TCA office was located downtown at 1465 Peel Street, next to the Mount Royal Hotel. It had the distinction of being the only three-storey traffic office in the system. The basement housed the teletype machines, reservation charts, six telephone lines and attendant staff. The public traffic counter was on the ground floor, where the ticket agent, Maurice "Joe" Gagnier, presided. On the top floor were the offices of Gord Wilson, traffic manager, and Gerry Gray, traffic representative. Wilson was a transportation veteran who from 1927 to 1937 had worked for the CNR. Gray had done his apprenticeship with the Canadian Pacific Steamships and the Chicago-Burlington-Quincy Railroad before coming to TCA. Communication between them and the floors below was simple: gravity going down and a very squeaky dumbwaiter coming up. In 1943, with eight trips a day coming through Montreal—from 6:30 a.m. to 10:00 p.m.—roomier quarters were found at 1478, directly across the street.

Though Toronto was only a feeder line to the Airway, it was the heart of the Central Division and responsible for service from Armstrong, Ontario, to Montreal. In 1938 the airline's Toronto staff were housed in the CNR building at Yonge and King streets, but plans were afoot to move them into the CNR's Royal York Hotel. Meanwhile, the city's new airport was under construction 18

A wintry view of the TCA offices on Peel Street in downtown Montreal, late 1950s. The office opened April 1939.

The airline's first airport terminal at Malton was "the Chapman House," an old two-storey red brick farmhouse near Sixth Line, later called Airport Road. Note the steps, used when it was necessary to "go remote." The terminal was remembered for the framed motto "Industry–Intelligence–Integrity" left by the original occupants on one of the walls.

miles out of Toronto within sight of the village of Malton, although even before the two hard-surfaced runways were completed on April 15, 1938, an experimental TCA flight from Winnipeg landed there. The airline's first airport terminal was also at the new airfield: the "Chapman House" was an old two-storey red brick farmhouse near Sixth Line, later called Airport Road. Officially renamed Malton House, it was remembered by those who laboured in it for the framed motto on one of the walls—Industry–Intelligence–Integrity—left there by the original occupants. By January 1939 as the country began rearming for war, TCA was joined at Malton by Canadian Associated Aircraft, which set up an assembly plant to build Lysander Mk IIs. Shortly afterwards, TCA's own hangar, "H12," was completed southeast of the Chapman farmhouse.

On May 15, 1939, tenders were called for the construction of an administration building about a mile north of the present day Terminal One at a cost of $22,000. Designed by the architect J.C. Hedges, the two-storey wooden building was the twin of one that was later erected (and still can be seen) at Toronto Island Airport. It was equipped with a control tower and its ground floor housed the check-in counter and baggage area, its second floor the operations, radio, weather and airport manager's offices. The airline moved in on September 1, 1939, and its public address system was inaugurated two days later to proclaim the sombre news that a state of hostilities now existed between Britain and Germany. The framed "Industry" motto followed the company from the Chapman farmhouse to the new building and was sunk into the blue linoleum floor of its lobby. Here, flanked by the crescent curve of glass, were the counters that TCA shared after 1941 with American Airlines. The Chapman house itself was taken over by the kitchen staff of Canadian Railway News Co., the airline's first caterers. Until then all the food had been trucked in from the CNR kitchens at Sunnyside.

On December 26, 1939, the minister of munitions appropriated the airport for the British Commonwealth Air Training Plan (BCATP), leasing it for a dollar a year despite opposition from the city's mayor, who had wanted Ottawa to choose the Island Airport for that purpose. However, the airline continued to operate Malton Airport on behalf of the Toronto Harbour Commission until the spring of 1940, when a DOT airport manager from St. Hubert was sent to take it over. Federal financing soon brought improvements such as a traffic control system that was run from the control tower, which until then had remained empty. DOT controllers were installed with "instruments that would allow them to illuminate the correct runway to be used and set off distant smoke pots as indicators." Now TCA's Lockheeds had to share Malton's runways with locally built Lysanders and Hampdens and swarms of pesky Tiger Moths from the elementary flying training school.

Under Bob Williamson, the station manager, and his assistant Dave Clark, the company's Toronto station was handling 480 trips a month by the spring of 1940, and the new terminal building was already crowded. Immigration, Toronto Airways Traffic Control, a radio office, the pilot's room, teletype machines and a lunch counter (also run by Canadian Railway News) were crammed in, along with a growing number of TCA offices. On the first floor were Maurice McGregor, now operations superintendent, chief pilot Frank Young, supervisory stewardess Betty Halstead and flight control officer Noel Humphrys. Only one thing at Malton had not changed, and that was Brown's Line, the road to the airport. While three levels of government argued over who was responsible for it, a permanent fleet of tow trucks hauled cars out of the roadside ditches. Because the airport was so far from downtown, there was no public transport, and with the increase in TCA staff to 80 and rationing of gasoline, the situation had become critical. But it was not until 1941, when Victory Aircraft Ltd. moved to Malton, that special buses began running there.

In the west, Lethbridge had been chosen over Calgary as a TCA station because the route through the Rockies was narrowest at that point, and the town became the main transfer point for crews. New pilots were put on the easier prairie flights, while the more experienced ones flew through the mountains to Vancouver. Lethbridge's Marquis Hotel became the airline's unofficial home, a circumstance that led to the day when the bellhop's pants were in jeopardy. First officer J.K. Lewis had just been elevated to the exalted rank of captain, which entitled him to two stripes of gold braid on each arm. "Being far from the salt sea breezes, admirals and things, gold braid is a scarce commodity in these parts. The whole TCA staff rallied to the cause, our stewardesses contributing their time and best efforts, spending one whole afternoon stalking the bellhop at the hotel who sported two stripes of the coveted braid down each trouser leg...but in the nick of time word was

Maurice McGregor.

received from a local clothing store that...a sufficient quantity of braid had been found to decorate both arms of our worthy captain as befitted his rank. Thus, the day and the pants of the bellhop were saved."[4] Early in the war a TCA city office, which was opened on the Marquis Hotel's mezzanine floor, employed an all-female staff of ten passenger agents under the direction of Doris Forbes with Margaret Jaynes and Mary D'Arcy assisting.

The new Lethbridge airport was opened on July 7, 1939, and named after Herbert Hollick-Kenyon, regional manager for the Western Zone and the TCA's superintendent at Lethbridge Airport. But Hollick-Kenyon missed flying enough to resign in 1942 to go to work for the competition, Canadian Pacific Airlines (CPA), and organize their pilot training, and Ted Stull took his place at Lethbridge.

Walkerville Airport at Windsor, Ontario, was billed in 1938 as the "Gateway to the United States," but it was no more than a radio shack in a farmer's field, and the next year it lost its licence to operate as an airport. Named for the generous farm family who had leased the land without charge to the Border Cities Aero Club and also built them a hangar, Walkerville Airport, not being part of the Trans Canada Airway, had been given over to the city of Windsor to maintain and was consequently starved of funds for improvements. When the DOT bought it from the city in 1939 to establish a BCATP flying school it was in primitive condition, the most modern piece of equipment being an old "nose" hangar, and things had hardly improved when TCA began services to Windsor on August 1, 1940.

Perhaps because of its location next door to Detroit, Windsor had its full share of "first flighters." When Neil Hepburn became station manager soon after it opened, he had a difficult encounter with a pair of hunters who wanted to tote their explosives aboard the plane. Neil naturally objected, and then they started objecting. Neil won and "with a sweeping bow ushered them aboard sans shells."

Of vital importance to TCA for refuelling and radio services was Wagaming, in the wilderness 8 miles east of the railroad town of Armstrong, Ontario, and, like Kapuskasing, built in 1936 as an unemployment relief project. It was staffed by TCA in April 1939 and, given the range of the aircraft available then, quickly became essential to the airline. As TCA employees preferred to call it (among other things) "Armstrong," this became its official name in 1940. It was used by the airline to train (and test the endurance) of generations of radio operators who in later years said with pride that they had graduated from "the Armstrong College of Knowledge." Many who served their time there defended the little post with the maxim "Without Armstrong, we'd be hamstrung," which had some truth to it.

Al Took was posted to Armstrong and remembers it as one of the most interesting and harrowing in his years with the airline. "The job of radio operator was one thing—what we did during our workday was often quite another." He remembers refuelling planes with wobble pumps, assisting mechanics to change an engine cylinder in sub-zero weather, living in barracks-style accommodation and "going remote." To keep the pilot informed of weather and airfield conditions and any other traffic in the vicinity, ground-to-air communications would be broken for a few frantic seconds to allow the operator to dash up to the roof of his radio shack for a quick visual check, then scramble back downstairs, earphone and microphone in hand, in time for the final approach and landing. "We had to move pretty fast when we went remote and often went up top in shirt sleeves with the winter wind biting through us. There was no such thing as a canceled flight. If you got held up by the weather or mechanical problems in the Ontario bush, that was it. You just had to wait until the skies cleared or the problem was fixed. Sometimes it took two and three days to get between Winnipeg and Vancouver." Fortunately, along with the town of Armstrong, the tiny airport "went electric" in 1940 so that the gas pump no longer had to be started to draw water for drinking and bathing or to power the generators for the radio and lights.

Took wasn't alone in his trials as a radio operator. Others found their breath freezing to their microphones, and Bill Lucas at Kapuskasing actually fell off the roof. Another operator on remote at that same station never forgot the snowy morning at 3:00 a.m. when Captain Ron Baker made three instrument approaches off the radio range before landing. By then the radio operator was nearly frozen lifeless on the roof; a few hours later he rushed into town to buy the warmest parka he could find.

By 1940 the radio operator's job had become too complicated for one man alone, though many of his duties had little to do with radio. In fact, one long-suffering radioman wrote that if he had a hat for every different job he did at the station, he could run a haberdashery. Taking weather observations, doing load sheets, figuring out fuel requirements and maximum allowable takeoff weights, and somewhere in between talking to pilots on the radio was only part of it. And so on January 1, 1940, radio operators Noel Humphrys and Dick Williams became the company's first flight control officers, later to be called flight dispatchers. The profession had originated in the US in 1936, when the government had legislated that all airlines must employ federally licensed flight dispatchers. These American dispatchers were fond of saying that Wilbur Wright became the first flight dispatcher when he ran alongside his brother in the *Flyer* shouting instructions; TCA control engineers said that Alexander Graham Bell was the first of their profession in Canada when he granted J.A.D. McCurdy clearance to take off at Baddeck.

For its Armstrong staff TCA operated a boarding house, which was run by two locals, Mr. and Mrs. Reeve (and later by Andy and Mrs. Potter), with Miss Marion Lang helping feed and clear up after the normal consignment of six bachelors. Between eight-hour shifts of radio range coverage and teletype operation, the men filled in as cargo clerks, dispatchers, passenger agents, janitors, control tower operators and, during the war, as unpaid RCAF traffic forecasters. "The company was good enough to provide free transportation to our respective homes for the overtime 'periodics' that we earned every three months," Ernie W. Lawson said, "and we also had our regular two weeks' annual leave." These poor souls must have counted down the days until their next leave, as the only major local attraction was a bar known with good cause as the Leaky Roof. There were no theatres, bowling alleys or single young women. The ten minutes between flights when they actually saw stewardesses was, they complained, hardly sufficient for romance to bloom.

The airport at Regina was not much better equipped than Armstrong. Stan Knight was the manager of the Regina station in 1938 and never forgot the elementary landing aids there. As the flush-type runway lights were often covered with snow, to guide aircraft in after sunset or in poor visibility, kerosene flare pots were put out to mark the edge of the runway. The maintenance crew had to do this job quickly after it had been decided which runway was to be used and this information had been radioed to the incoming aircraft. "We used to run contests to see how fast we could leave the terminal with the flare pots in an old cab, place them, light them and get back. But one night we were in a bit too much of a rush to get back after dousing and loading the flares in the car. It seems that one of them was not out. The whole cab went up in flames."

Airport administration building, Regina.

The TCA staff in Regina were at that time operating out of a cramped shack and looking forward to the completion of the new administration building, which they would share with the DOT range and meteorological services and Prairie Airways. The topmost of its three storeys, distinguished by its large windows, was the air traffic control room, an innovation that would end the need for the radio operator to go "remote" when an aircraft was on final approach. It was ready for occupancy by February 1940.

The TCA station at North Bay was opened in the summer of 1938, the city having received the airport as a gift from the DOT the year before. Other municipalities struggled to pay for their airports, but so important was North Bay to the Trans Canada Airway that over the winter of 1938–39 the DOT built the country's first airport terminal there, installed obstruction and contact lights and threw in a hangar for TCA as well. This last was particularly welcome to the airline's mechanical department, who had been using their own unique method of warming engines that had been sitting outdoors all night. "From what could be observed, it consisted of 10 percent electric heaters and 90 percent profanity," the office manager reported.

The northernmost outpost of the TCA network was Blatchford Airport in Edmonton. As early as 1920 Edmontonians, led by the mayor after whom the airport was named, had been enthusiastic supporters of commercial aviation. Blatchford Airport was the gateway to the Mackenzie and Peace River territories, and on July 22, 1933, the city had basked in worldwide attention when Wiley Post had landed there on his round-the-world flight. As part of the CNR, the TCA city office was in the MacDonald Hotel, known to locals as "the Mac," a big grey structure perched on the edge of the North Saskatchewan valley. Here a single TCA employee, D'Arcy S. McLeod, sat in what he termed the Cave of the Winds, a box under the main staircase just off the lobby, dealing with traffic and operations.

In 1936, when CAL had sent Zebulon Lewis Leigh to brush up on his instrument flying skills at the Boeing school in California, he had caught a UAL flight from Vancouver to Los Angeles. The journey took place in rough weather that would have grounded a CAL aircraft, but the UAL pilots were flying on instruments and could keep on schedule. Yet what had impressed Leigh, besides the comforts of the enclosed, heated Boeing 247, was the smartly dressed young woman on board who served him chicken and coffee, leaving the co-pilot free to concentrate on his duties. When he returned to Winnipeg, Leigh told Thompson that UAL's in-flight service was something that CAL should emulate.

Air hostess, flight attendant, stewardess—whatever the name, the profession had been invented by UAL on May 15, 1930. That year, Steve Stimpson, the airline's San Francisco manager, was on a company flight that encountered turbulence. The twelve passengers on-board were frightened and hungry, and as the co-pilot could not leave the cockpit to hand out the sandwiches, Stimpson took over the job, reassuring the passengers while doing so. Back on the ground again, he wired his superiors in Seattle for permission to employ stewards immediately; he was about to hire three himself when a young woman walked into his office. Ellen Church was a nurse at San Francisco's French Hospital who had taken flying lessons and desperately wanted to become a pilot, but had realized there was little chance of being so employed during the Depression, when it was almost impossible for experienced male pilots to find work. So she approached Stimpson with the idea of adding a third crew member, a "flying nurse" who would keep the passengers comfortable, serve them food and make their experience in the air a pleasant one. This was exactly what Stimpson wanted to hear. "Imagine the psychology of having young women as regular members of the crew," he wired his headquarters. UAL was cool to the idea of Stimpson's "skygirls." He was told, "We don't want any flappers or usherettes in pantaloons." However, sense prevailed and Stimpson hired Ellen Church and seven other nurses as stewardesses, none of them weighing more than 115 pounds and all of them willing to fly 100 hours per month for $125 plus expenses on layovers. Besides feeding and caring for the passengers, the duties of those first UAL stewardesses included winding the clocks and altimeters in the passenger cabin, checking the floor bolts on the seats, saluting the captain and co-pilot as they came aboard and deplaned, and swatting the flies in the cabin after takeoff. UAL's experiment was such a success that other US airlines followed suit, with the exception of Pan American Airways, which employed only stewards until 1943.

As tiny as TCA's Electras were—five seats on either side of the aisle—they did allow room for a toilet, and a stewardess's seat could be attached to its

The first female employees with TCA and the first Canadian airline stewardesses, who were required to have a background in nursing. Lucille Garner (left) and Pat Eccleston pose in front of a Lockheed 14 in 1938.

door. Billy Wells began looking for stewardesses. It so happened that when the Vancouver–Seattle service was expanded to twice daily in June 1938, TCA posted Bob Bowker, a former American Airlines pilot, from Montreal to Sea Island to help out. In the east Bowker had met Kilby Harding, a nurse at Royal Victoria Hospital in Montreal, who had given him a social introduction to Lucille Garner, a fellow graduate now in Vancouver. Bowker took Garner out to dinner and suggested that she ask for an interview with Wells. Garner did so, and Wells was so taken by her good humour, wit and common sense that he hired her along with Pat Eccleston, a nurse who had trained at St. Paul's Hospital in Vancouver. They were both put on payroll on July 1, 1938, to work the Vancouver–Seattle run and have the distinction of being not only the first Canadian stewardesses but also the first female employees of TCA as well.

They never encountered the condescension and sometimes outright hatred that many of their American sisters did from the pilots they flew with. Rather than having to salute their captains as required on some American airlines, the stewardesses in TCA were made to feel part of the team from the start, walking out to the aircraft with the flight crew. As the only stewardesses Garner or Eccleston had ever seen were those on the UAL flights into Vancouver, they borrowed a stewardess manual from UAL to set up the TCA program. That fall Garner went to Winnipeg to organize the first class of TCA stewardesses, and was replaced by another St. Paul's graduate, Rose Crispin.

"I had already been nursing five and a half years and here was an exciting new challenge. My salary was $125 per month, $50 more than my wages as a nurse," Eccleston remembered. "And when I became a supervisor in 1939, I started earning $150."[5] To become a TCA stewardess the applicant had to be a registered nurse between age twenty-one and twenty-five, no taller than 5 feet 5 inches, enthusiastic, personable, in good health (no eyeglasses), and single. As soon as she married, she was to leave the airline. "That's why so many girls left within a year and a half. The casualty rate was very high," Eccleston said.

An article in the June 1939 issue of *Chatelaine* magazine titled "On Duty in the Skies" described exactly what stewardesses did in those days.

> What tiptoeing little probationer wouldn't dream about it? To be suddenly transported from the rigid routine of the hushed, white hospital corridor to a job aboard a great luxury air liner ten thousand feet above the earth! Such has been the good luck of eighteen smart young Canadian graduate nurses. And today if you happen over to your nearest Trans Canada airport to see one of the ten glittering Lockheeds that make up the Dominion's new passenger flight take off, you'll notice a smiling, efficient young woman looking after the passengers. She's one of Canada's newly appointed Air Stewardesses (please don't call them hostesses, says the company). And if you think she's there for decoration, you don't know a thing about the busy life she leads, flying through the air at more than two hundred miles an hour.
>
> Three of the nurses selected have been on the long established Vancouver–Seattle run. One is Lucille Garner, a Regina girl, who has been appointed TCA's Chief Stewardess. Stationed at Winnipeg, she helps oversee the six week course through which her young brigade was put before going on duty in March. On the whole the new feminine flying corps has had little previous experience in the air. But they did have the basic qualities that go to make a good air stewardess. For instance, a graduate nurse has been trained to meet the public. She's adept at handling people and situations. She can judge character accurately and knows when to take a friendly, informal attitude, and when to leave people strictly alone. She ought to. Because the most difficult people she will encounter in the air are much like her former patients. There are always those who want to break the rules...to follow their own devices regardless of the convenience and comfort of others...to be too palsy-walsy with everyone including stewardesses.
>
> And these are just the people who imagine that when they bought tickets, they purchased a good-sized portion of the whole line for their own personal pleasure. Of course, they are in the minority. But a nurse has been trained to cope with difficulties of all sorts.

Then there is the question of children. She's learned to look after them from infancy. It is to such tender and valuable citizens that the stewardess is ready to pay special attention. She's equipped with a baby kit, and can supply everything from a much-needed safety pin to a special bottle of formula. When running at full strength, her kit will include baby foods, pureed vegetables, cereals, sterilized milk, spoon, bowl, disposable diapers, cream, powder and even a doll. She's also great at feeding time and can be counted on to give mother a hand when necessary.

It is not for her actual medical training that the nurse is chosen. While she can administer simple first aid, she is not prepared to look after any major illness or accident. Doesn't need to be. Less than one per cent of people traveling by air get ill. It is true that chewing gum and swallowing help keep the ears clear, as in a fast elevator, for ascents and descents, but there's no real health hazard for anyone. "If he's fit to be walking around, he is fit to fly" is the dictum of most medical men on the subject. And that's that. So the stewardess's duties have to do chiefly with keeping the passengers informed, entertained and fed. Whether the altitude's responsible or air travel just naturally attracts the curious, every stewardess finds herself barraged with questions throughout the flight.

"How high are we?" "What's that down there?" "What's the weather like below?" are favorites. That's why she's learned about geography, meteorology and navigation on that six-week course. Once the motors start, the doors are locked and the plane takes off, she is the only link her passengers have with civilization. So there they are—ten passengers and their stewardess. Every half hour the pilot reports by telephone to her. [This was journalistic licence: TCA didn't install telephones between cockpit and cabin until 1946.] Meanwhile she's plugged up on Canadian geography. She knows where the plane is, and why, how high up, what the weather conditions are, and unless one is too detailed about the whole business, "What's down there?"

You've probably heard that there is a definite weight limit for stewardesses. That's incorrect. But there is a height deadline. She can range from five feet to five feet four inches. And the reason is a psychological rather than a physical one. If you stand up in one of the beige and red upholstered aisles, you'll find rather to your surprise that you don't need to stoop. If you're sitting down and watching an individual walk up and down, lean over your chair, move quietly and smoothly among the passengers, she'll look bigger than she really is. That's why it's necessary to have petite stewardesses.

Naturally, in order to be trim and well proportioned, the girl of five feet or so can't weigh a hundred and fifty. Therefore her weight must conform to her height, which would put her in the neighborhood of 115 to 120 pounds.

You can't miss the stewardess when you see her. She wears a well tailored, double-breasted, navy blue serge suit with a spanking white blouse, oxfords and a Glengarry bonnet type of a little pointed cap.

She is expected to be meticulous about her appearance (girdles and deodorants are indicated!), not to use cheap perfumes or sensational hose, to keep her hair smart but inconspicuous (long hanging bobs are frowned upon!) and to steer clear of jewelry. Passengers should be treated, according to her code, like guests in a home. She may make up a hand of bridge or help with a crossword puzzle or one of the magnetized games which will be added onboard later. But by the same token, she doesn't have to put up with "propositioning." Or any kind of unpleasantness. She has a knack of handling such things simply and charmingly. Going out with passengers as a

High above the Rockies in 1939, a candid view of Rose Crispin taking time out with passengers. Dud Taylor

regular thing is discouraged. She has an array of sick aunts and aged mothers to forestall undesirable bids. While marriage among stewardesses has been the highest of any profession for women in the United States during the seven years of service, very few alliances are with travelers.

If the general rate of romance in other parts of the world is any criterion, there'll be something like a one-third turnover every year, and therefore a steady flow of opportunity in the direction of young graduating nurses. Incredible as it may seem, the average US stewardess spends only 1.6 years in the service before resigning. And she usually marries someone in the business.

Canadian applicants must be under twenty-five years of age and unmarried. The salary, as those of business girls go, is excellent. The longest flight will be that of between Toronto and Winnipeg, a matter of little over seven hours. Each stewardess serves one meal on board, and at present time it is hot coffee and sandwich lunches. Eventually the elaborate meal prepared in many air lines may be introduced—the menu, which takes in everything from soup to nuts, all ready in thermos containers brought aboard at the time of taking off. There is no cooking on the ship, and lap trays are used for serving. The little housekeeper in the clouds will chalk up a maximum of 100 flying hours a month.

From the moment she fastens the seat belt around a passenger's waist at the take-off (to be removed when flying level is reached) the stewardess is "at your service." She will not allow smoking going up or coming down, but it is permissible to light up once aloft. If it's a first flight, she helps the passenger get properly adjusted. She'll spend approximately one-third of her time on women, for that's the proportion of flyers of the feminine sex. She'll help get a camera, typewriter or briefcase down from the rack. The other forty pounds of luggage allowance are carried elsewhere. She'll help adjust individual air and heat control, which gives the exact temperature desired at every seat. She'll pass out especially light-bound magazines, and even look at pictures of wives and babies.

And whatever part of Canada the passenger comes from, he's apt to meet up with a home towner, because dark stewardess Pat McNamara was born in Sault Ste. Marie and Dorothy Price and Norah Wallace, dainty brunette and blonde respectively, come from Orillia, Ontario. Fair Marcelle Lovec and the sisters Brunelle, Geralde and Annette, are natives of Quebec. From the prairies hail fair, brown-eyed Margaret

Beeber of Bassano, Alberta, and Constance Hairbeck, a Lethbridge, Alberta, brunette, dark Kilby Harding of Regina, Sask, and Margaret Brass of Yorkton, Sask. Sheila Neill is a native of St. Agathe, Manitoba, and from the Winnipeg head-quarters are dark Margaret Wilson, Ruth Leslie, a blonde, and Florence Shanahan, the only copper-haired member of the staff. Rose Crispin and dark-haired Pat Eccleston are Vancouverites. Dark, petite Mary Mussen isn't a stewardess, but as a veteran of US airlines she does important ground work in Toronto. She was born in China of Canadian parents and educated in Toronto. All are graduates of first-rate Canadian hospitals, and keen sportswomen and outdoor girls.

Perhaps this will give you an idea that there's nothing soft about air stewardessing on Trans Canada airlines. On the other hand, it isn't the kind of job at which a bright young graduate nurse would turn up her nose. Or what do you think?[6]

A lot of women must have agreed with the author, for in 1939 more than a thousand of them applied to be stewardesses with TCA. For the first stew-ardesses, in-flight catering was elementary. On the fifty-five-minute Vancouver–Seattle flight, they poured coffee from a thermos fixed by the door, passed out chewing gum to cope with the noise and cigarettes for the nerves. With flights above three hours' duration, box lunches containing sandwiches, an apple and a slice of fruitcake were served, to be washed down with coffee. For all this, a tray was balanced on a pillow placed on the passenger's knees. As there was no refrigeration on board, the box lunches were kept in the tail of the aircraft, which was always cold. At first drinking water was also carried on-board in large flasks, but after the airline was reprimanded by the govern-ment because the spout of the thermos could become contaminated after use, a water tank system was put in and the water kept potable with filters and chlorine tablets.

On short flights the stewardess rarely had the chance to do more than pour herself a cup of coffee. She was too busy answering questions about the weath-er and the scenery below and attending to her charges' comfort.[7] In 1939, 85 percent of the passengers were males travelling on business, and it was safe to say that none had flown before entering that very aircraft. All must have been intrigued and somewhat frightened by the new experience. One stewardess remembers a definite "first flighter" getting on at Windsor. "A large, portly gen-tleman was the last passenger, and as I stepped into the plane behind him, I discovered him attempting to hang his coat on the cup handles. Result—two broken cup handles and one embarrassed passenger." Used to crossing the country by train and walking about a Pullman railway car, passengers found the tiny Electra dangerously claustrophobic and, except when they squeezed down the aisle to the toilet in the rear, they had to sit in their seats and endure the rollercoaster flight.

One of the modifications made by TCA to the Lockheeds did not prove popular with the passengers. Because the aircraft going in opposite directions on the transcontinental route passed one another at a distance of 1,000 feet above or below, the airline installed flashing warning lights on the top and bottom of their fuselages. Unfortunately, their combined red glow, especially in a cloud, so illuminated the whole cabin that it scared the passengers into thinking that the aircraft was on fire. The stewardesses found there was little point in reassuring them that TCA was the first airline in North America to equip its aircraft with smoke detectors in the cargo compartment and the first to put oxygen masks in the cockpit long before government regulations required them. The lights were removed within a year.

The stewardess was on duty for as long as it took to get to the destination—hours or days—regardless of delays due to the weather. The passengers were her responsibility, both on and off the plane. "Sometimes I would go off on a flight not knowing when I would be coming back," said Pat Eccleston. "I could be gone anywhere from two to five days." If the flight was grounded in Lethbridge for several days, she shepherded her charges to and from the hotel, ate with them, played cards and made sure that they were ready to get to the airport at a moment's notice. If a passenger got fed up with waiting for the weather to clear and decided to take the train, the stewardess was ready with a refund and the train schedule.

Eccleston had to know the geography of the terrain as well because passengers would want to know about what they could see below. "In 1938 it was considered daring to fly to Seattle rather than to take the train. The flight was beautiful on a clear day. We flew only 2,000 feet above the water and you could see the schools of fish. I would point out certain houses to the passengers and tell them who lived there."[8] When the airline began flying between Lethbridge and Vancouver, the aircraft climbed to 10,000 feet, about 1,000 feet above the peaks. If they hit bad weather, the unpressurized plane had to cruise below it or barrel through it, which made for very rough trips. "Occasionally passengers would panic when they noticed chunks of ice flying off the wings and hitting the windows. I would assure them that there was no danger."

The lack of pressurization caused passengers deafness for days afterwards, and if they had colds, the consequences could be severe ear problems. With the combination of pain and fear of flying, it is perhaps understandable that some of these frightened souls sought refuge in liquor, although none was served on TCA (or on US airlines, with the exception of the transoceanic Pan American Airways), and the airline staff from the ticket counter to the flight crew were vigilant about forbidding anyone even slightly tipsy to get on-board. "At the check-in desk," Pat Eccleston recalled, "I could spot inebriated passengers and explain that we couldn't take them . . . the minute we are up in the mountains, they are going to be air sick, difficult to handle and a hazard to our other passengers. Occasionally a passenger would bring a flask on board and dig it out of his briefcase. I wasn't a head nurse for nothing. I was used to having a few smart patients, so I knew how to handle smart passengers without hurting their feelings...I would say, 'I'm terribly sorry, sir, but one should not drink because there is a lack of oxygen in this aircraft.'"⁹

"It was no easy task getting over the Rocky Mountains," Al Took said when interviewed years later. "Captains got an extra $50 a month bonus for flying the Rockies." Then he added that passengers didn't have it too easy either. "They had to start drawing on the old oxygen tube at 11,000 feet, which they kept on doing right on into Vancouver. The crews began taking oxygen at 9,000 feet [this was mandatory]; that was, of course, if big winds out the Crowsnest Pass didn't hold the plane up altogether." It was this oxygen that allowed the pilot to fly above dangerous weather and icing conditions. The main oxygen tank was in the rear of the cabin with a long tube running to the cockpit and a plug-in at each seat. Although their use by passengers was entirely optional, each had an oxygen mask that the stewardess had to personally strap around his head. At first the oxygen regulator was kept in the cabin under the stewardess's control, but she was usually too busy attending to the passengers to notice that the crew might be suffering from oxygen deprivation. After stewardess Rose Crispin fainted and was revived when one of the passengers put his own mask on her face, the oxygen regulator was moved to the cockpit. The smell of the masks, one stewardess recalled, was "atrocious." One of the stewardess's jobs was to wash them all in disinfectant on landing, then repackage them in cellophane for the next flight.

Because TCA terminated at Montreal and there was no passenger service to the Maritimes until 1940, a unique air/rail connection developed between TCA and the CNR: the air/rail timetables were coordinated so that the Ocean Limited, the CNR express from Moncton, stopped at St. Hubert Airport daily to discharge passengers for the Ottawa–North Bay–Toronto flight. The proximity of St. Hubert Airport to the railway line was, however, sometimes a problem. Bob Bowker, flying into St. Hubert in 1939, received this message from the control tower: "Okay, TCA. Have you in sight. No...correction. It's a railroad train." And it was indeed the CN train coming into the station.

While Moncton continued to be an important part of the CNR's system, it was soon obvious that it was also the right choice for an air transportation centre east of Montreal. Unlike other Canadian municipalities, the city had always been "air-minded" and traced its aviation beginnings to 1928, when the city fathers built an airport and held the first Maritime Provinces Air Pageant on it the following year. Their airport had, however, been overshadowed by the flying boat base at Shediac, 9 miles from Moncton, after the Italian general Italo Balbo had landed there in 1933 with twenty-four Savoia Marchetti flying boats. Since then Pan American's transatlantic clippers alighted there. But Moncton Airport's day was yet to come.

Though the CNR continued its unique co-operation with TCA, what the CNR brass really thought of Trans Canada Airlines and commercial aviation was clearly illustrated after a speech that P.G. Johnson gave to the Canadian Railway Club on April 17, 1939. At its conclusion, the senior railway officer who had been delegated to thank Johnson rose and said, "It has been an extreme pleasure to have you come and speak to us on airplanes, and I compliment you, considering the fact that this is a Railway Club. However, there is one thing you omitted in your speech, and I think it is important, and that is this: it is advisable to be close to a railway line when flying in an airplane, because on four different occasions I have found it necessary to complete my trip that way when it had started in the air, and I am sure these gentlemen present would be interested in knowing this."[10]

The airline's use of the CNR's facilities at downtown hotels and stations might have been designed to avoid duplication, but company loyalty being what it was, it was sometimes difficult for a customer actually to obtain an air ticket from a partisan CNR agent. TCA's future president, Gordon McGregor, later wrote that "a potential traveler could only obtain an airline ticket from a dedicated railway passenger agent at the price of an argument; in fact this situation became such that in self-defence the airline at one time paid sales commissions to each individual railway passenger agent who had lost his argument with the customer and allowed him to take an airline ticket."[11]

In fact, the staid railway men of the CNR must have hardly known what to make of their johnny-come-lately airline cousins and were often bemused by the cavalier approach they had to business. Company procedures were a little loose, Russ Bulger admits. Manning the Vancouver Airport ticket office one day, he was approached by Bill Harvey, who had been seconded from the CNR to become the airline's senior accounts clerk with his headquarters in Winnipeg. After inspecting the ticket stock, he asked Russ where the petty cash was. Russ replied that he had it in his pocket. "After he recovered, he asked me how much it was, and I said $10, whereupon he asked to see it. Luckily I had $15. I gathered from him that this was no way to run an airline because first thing we knew, a nice new safe arrived by CN Express."

One of the benefits of being part of the CNR was, as the airline brochure below shows, that the railway provided TCA with office accommodation at its downtown hotels in every large city.

From the 1939 Passenger Brochure of Trans Canada Airlines:

TRANSPORTATION TO AND FROM AIRPORTS:

When making a reservation between airports and urban centers, passengers should request TCA agent to arrange for cab at destination if desired, or this may be arranged through Stewardess en route.

CITY	AIRPORT	CAB OPERATOR	FARE PER PASSENGER	CITY TERMINAL FOR PICK UP
Montreal	St. Hubert	Murray-Hill	$1.00	TCA City Office, Mount Royal Hotel
Ottawa	Ottawa	Red Line Taxi	0.75	Chateau Laurier
Toronto	Malton	Cadillac Livery	1.00	Royal York Hotel & TCA City Office, King and Yonge
North Bay	North Bay	De Luxe Transport Co.	0.50	De Luxe Transport Office
Winnipeg	Stevenson Field	Moore's Taxi	0.50	TCA City Office, Portage/Main
Regina	Regina	Moore's Taxi	0.50	Saskatchewan Hotel
Lethbridge	Kenyon Field	Marquis Taxi	0.75	Marquis Hotel
Calgary	Municipal	Brewster Taxi	0.75	TCA City Office, 218-8th Ave.
Edmonton	Edmonton	McNeill's Taxi	.90-1/ .45-2/ .30-3	MacDonald Hotel
Vancouver	Vancouver	MacLure's Taxi	0.75	Vancouver Hotel
Seattle, WA	Boeing Field	Yellow Cab	0.75	TCA City Office, 1329-4th Ave.

Baggage: The term baggage means personal belongings necessary and appropriate for the comfort and convenience of the passenger for the purpose of the journey and may include brief cases, typewriters and portfolios. Individual books, magazines, binoculars, pocket size cameras and coats will not be considered as baggage when carried by passengers. Forty (40) pounds of baggage will be carried free on any ticket. Maximum dimensions for any single piece of baggage acceptable are 15"x20"x36".*

Fountain Pens: The change in atmospheric pressure at certain altitudes may cause some types of fountain pens to leak. It is advisable to wrap the pen in cloth to avoid damage to clothes or contents of baggage or hand bags.

Gratuities: Passengers are respectfully requested to refrain from offering gratuities to personnel of Trans Canada Air Lines as Company regulations prohibit their acceptance.

Refreshments: Refreshments served aloft are complimentary.

* Carry-on baggage was not allowed as there was no place for it under the seat. The aircraft did have net baskets above the seats, but these were only large or strong enough to accommodate pillows and the occasional book or binoculars.

Regularly scheduled trans-Canada flights had come none too soon for TCA, as the Americans were already asserting themselves across the Atlantic. Pan American Airways inaugurated the first regular passenger and air mail service over the north Atlantic on June 26, 1939, when the company's *Yankee Clipper*, a Boeing 314 flying boat, refuelled at Shediac before taking off for Foynes, Ireland. They had beaten out the competition, Imperial Airways, by forty days. The *Yankee Clipper* carried twenty paying passengers and 2,543 pounds of mail, just twelve years after a Ryan monoplane had carried Charles Lindbergh over the same ocean.

James Richardson.

On the same day that the *Yankee Clipper* set down in Shediac, James Richardson died in Winnipeg of a heart attack. Whether he died of despair or accepted his fate with quiet resignation will never be known. *Maclean's* magazine described him as "rugged, simple and genuine."[12] His place in history as the "Father of Commercial Aviation in Canada" remains secure; because of Western Canada Airways and Canadian Airways, a whole generation of pilots, radio operators and engineers were trained and kept employed during the Depression, and this was a legacy from which Trans Canada Airlines profited.

Although Richardson's Canadian Airways Limited was still the largest air company in Canada (and still losing money), he had left the stage of commercial aviation long before his death. The truth is that by the 1930s the business of commercial aviation had become too expensive even for such a wealthy man. Now only a government—

or a railway—could afford its own airline because they could afford to subsidize it. For example, neither the flying boats of Imperial Airways nor those of Pan American Airways were ever designed to show a profit. In fact, in 1939 the load factor for Imperial Airways—that is, the percentage of seats the company had to sell to make any money on each flight—was 130 percent!

On September 1, 1939, P.G. Johnson asked that he be allowed to relinquish his appointment as vice-president of operations and return to Seattle to run Boeing Aircraft. The company was expanding to mass produce B-17 *Flying Fortress* bombers, and Johnson's organizational skills were needed as never before. Understandably, the TCA directors regretted losing him, but with tensions mounting in Europe, they acceded to his wishes. In return, Johnson agreed to devote a certain amount of time to the affairs of the company and accepted the position of consultant to the airline. His son Philip Jr. wrote: "a very happy time now came to an abrupt end with the war and the rescinding of the U.S. government's decree against my father's involvement in the Collusion scandal." The pragmatic reason, he concluded, was that Washington needed someone like his father to get Boeing geared up for the coming war. "But in contrast to his Canadian experience where he had been honored and loved, my father had much of the heart taken out of him by having been vilified and then called back by his own government." This, he has always believed, was a contributing factor to his father's early death.

When Oliver West completed his two-year contract with TCA and left his position as superintendent of maintenance and overhaul in September 1939, James "Jim" Tocher Bain took his place. A native of Edinburgh, Bain had enrolled at age fourteen in the Royal Air Force Technical College at Cranwell, then served with the RAF in the Mediterranean and Near East. In 1931 he joined Hillman Airways as chief ground engineer, and he moved next to the Scottish Motor Traction Co. (aviation department) and Spartan Aircraft. When these companies were merged in 1935 to form British Airways, Bain was promoted to chief inspector and made responsible for the maintenance of some fifty assorted aircraft that ranked in size from complex Armstrong Whitworth Argosies to de Havilland Tiger Moths. When BA modernized by buying Lockheed 10As, Bain was

"P.G" Johnson. He was already wealthy when he took on the challenge of setting up TCA, and he was the first of the Americans to whom the company (and later Air Canada) owed much. UAA

A young, eager J.T. Bain, graduate of RAF Cranwell, participant in the RAF high speed flight at the Schneider Cup contest in Venice, 1927, and recruited from British Airways to join TCA in 1937. Hugh A. Reid photo

sent to Burbank for training and there wrote an operating manual for the aircraft that Lockheed published. He had come to TCA in 1937 to work under Wells in maintenance and overhaul.

Bob Williamson first encountered Jim Bain one stormy night in Armstrong, Ontario. "Winnipeg and Kapuskasing were closed in so the aircraft [in which Bain was a passenger] turned around and landed at Armstrong in a foot of snow. It had to taxi at full power to get to the hangar. "We opened the hangar door and the pilot just drove the aircraft in. And that's when I met Jim. 'Do you realize what you've done?' he bellowed. 'If the brakes had slipped, the airplane would have gone right through the hangar!'" Williamson concluded his story by saying that Bain was most unhappy, though "not quite as unhappy as we were since we had to shove the thing out the next morning. In those days, four of us ran the airport."[13]

Insisting on perfection from both himself and those who worked for him, Bain was not above giving recognition to his staff. "It is a great credit to the foremen in those shops that they learned and then taught to their staffs the high degree of perfection which must always characterize the whole operation."[14] But Bain also held classes in the boiler room for his mechanics during the lunch hour, though neither he nor his students received any financial consideration from the company for doing it. It was just typical of the spirit of the day.

Canadians had been expecting a war in Europe since the failure of the League of Nations to intervene in the Ethiopian crisis, but it was still a grim surprise when it actually came. The shock was made worse by the speed at which Hitler's forces swept through everything in their path. With every disheartening radio broadcast, emotions ran high at all TCA posts. Older employees like pilots Don MacLaren and Herbert Hollick-Kenyon had fought the Germans in the Great War. Bill English had served in France for four years with the 49th Battalion, Edmonton Regiment. Pilot Bill Coulson had only recently immigrated from England, where he had been in the Royal Air Force. Harry Kennedy and Jack Dyment had trained in the RCAF cadet program. So when

Britain declared war on September 3, 1939, many in the airline were prepared to resign and rush over to defend the country that for most was the motherland. There was even greater urgency when the news spread down the line that if Canada followed Britain into the war, TCA would be made an essential service and its pilots would be prohibited from leaving.

But the Prime Minister, aware that there were many who did not want the country involved in another European conflict, played a cautious role. The House met in an emotionally charged special session, and not until Sunday, September 10, one week after the British declaration, did it approve a declaration of war against Germany and its allies. By then a few TCA pilots, radio operators and engineers had already taken a leave of absence or resigned outright to join the air force—either the RCAF or the RAF. The first of the many to do so were A.L. Anderson, A.J. Gurney, D.D.G. Carmichael, H.C. Cotterell, W.G.A. Coulson, G.S. Gibson, B.A. Hanbury, F. Klaponski, J.E. MacLaughlin, W.R. Ramsay, J.J. Solenski and G. Vadboncoeur. Those left at home sometimes caught a glimpse in newsreels of former TCA colleagues in uniform coming down a gangplank "somewhere overseas."

Still in its delicate "puberty" phase, the airline was not only in danger of losing trained employees but was also restricted in the purchase of aircraft, fuel and tires. Blackout curtains were fitted to aircraft windows, and weather reports were broadcast in code. On the other hand, there were some positive changes. All major airports and some minor but strategically placed ones like Kapuskasing were transferred for the war's duration from their local municipalities to federal control, allowing for the financing of long overdue improvements to their facilities. A wartime cost-of-living bonus was paid to TCA employees up to the rank of foreman. And the war also provided an opportunity for TCA to sell off four of the Lockheed 10s it had outgrown—not to potential competitors but to the RCAF, which needed them for its expanded pilot training program. The fifth 10A went to the DOT.

As the United States was neutral, border regulations were tightened on July 1, 1940. Crew passports had not come into general use yet, so all TCA crews on the Seattle run were made to carry some kind of identification. As they all had to be photographed and fingerprinted, pilot Billy Wells was sent on a special course at the Vancouver police station. He then "mugged" and fingerprinted the pilots and stewardesses at his desk, so that it looked like (in his words) "a crime scene." Apparently one pilot's wife, after seeing her husband's blackened hands, exclaimed, "What? Back in the bush again?"

Without doubt the farthest-reaching effect of the war on TCA, although not obvious at the time, was the social and gender revolution in the workplace. Apart from stewardesses, the pre-war aviation industry had gloried in being an exclusively male profession. But now, with its men released for military duties, the airline actively sought out women to replace them, initially as telephonists, office and counter staff, later as machinists. In the Annual Report for December 1940, the board of directors accepted the fact that the hiring of females to replace men was necessary, but it also emphasized that the women must understand that their employment was only for the duration of the war. The expected flood of women employees was slow in coming, and that month, apart from the stewardesses, there were still only eighteen women working for TCA, and all of them were in accounting. But by December 31 the following year this figure had jumped to 101.

A year before the outbreak of war, negotiations had started between Britain and her senior dominions for a massive air crew training program to be carried out in Canada, and on December 16, 1939, an agreement to undertake the British Commonwealth Air Training Plan (BCATP) was signed in Ottawa. When C.D. Howe put the operation of nine air observer schools out to tender, seven were awarded to bush air companies that were soon to be bought up by Canadian Pacific Airlines. Given the patriotic fervor of the day, there was some chagrin at this development among TCA's rank and file, but Howe was not eager to have his airline expend resources training air crew instead of concentrating on its domestic expansion.

As a background to all the airline's adjustments, a never-ending torrent of bad news came from Europe. Stalin's troops invaded Finland, the Germans overran Norway and Denmark, the French surrendered and the British Army retreated across the Channel. Perhaps because it looked as if the Nazi armies were invincible, those remaining in TCA sought comfort in each other and in the normalcy of the home front. One means was by compiling an unofficial employee newsletter. With employees now numbering 400, vice-president O.T. Larson thought some means of personal communication with and among employees was necessary, and in December 1939 the first issue of *TCA News* appeared. It was edited and collated in his spare time by René Baudru at operations headquarters in Winnipeg, and he solicited contributions from all stations. The result was a fifteen-page mimeographed newsletter, the only artwork a cartoon of a rather plump, smiling Electra on the cover sailing above a TCA Maple Leaf. It was crammed with local gossip, bad poetry, the odd drawing and a few statistics thrown in for bulk, but more effectively than any annual company report, it provides an informal window into the company.

As the newsletter's editors observed, with expansion across the country, employee communication was becoming difficult, and because of this, in late 1939 TCA was faced with the threat of its first strike. Discontent among its pilots was focussed on a former Canadian Air Line Pilots Association (CALPA) member. R.F. George had been one of CALPA's founders in April 1938, and when he had become a company executive, he had resigned from the association. However, rather than being sympathetic to the pilots' aspirations, "he apparently saw no reason to resolve pilot grievances on remuneration, hours of service, vacations, examinations, seniority, investigation or discipline."[15] CALPA's demand for his resignation drove the airline and the association into its first labour crisis. On November 3, accompanied by a solicitor, CALPA chairman Captain Malcolm "Jock" Barclay met with airline management, but they emerged from the meeting convinced that their complaints about George and other grievances had received short shrift. On November 7 CALPA called on its members to refuse to fly until he was removed from his position. The pilots had other gripes such as flight time limitations and basing privileges, but because of the war they were hesitant to press the airline on them, and as the deadline approached, many of them had a change of heart. Shutting down the national airline suddenly seemed like sabotaging the war effort, and the majority of the pilots notified CALPA that they no longer supported its action. The strike collapsed before the first flight had been refused. Barclay lost heart after the strike's failure, and the following spring Captain G.W. McLaren was appointed president. He succeeded in ridding the pilots of promotion examinations and he forced TCA to deal with the perennial issue of seniority.

The second group of TCA employees to organize were the machinists in the Winnipeg maintenance shop. Most had worked for the CNR and had railway affiliations, but at TCA they worked in the machine shop, metal shop, engine overhaul and propeller shop, though later cargo and ground equipment handlers would join them. Like the pilots, they looked for guidance to the labour movement in the United States, where airline employees were protected under the National

DECEMBER, 1939.

Top: The first cover for the TCA News, *a fifteen-page mimeographed newsletter put together by René Baudru in his spare time. The cover cartoons—the only illustrations in the issue—show a stylized TCA bird and maple leaf over a rather chubby Electra punching its way through cloud. Bottom: René Baudru on his retirement, receiving a dummy front page of* Between Ourselves, *the TCA newsletter, from Norm Garwood, the editor.*

Railway Labor Act. In the face of crippling rail strikes in 1924, President Calvin Coolidge had brought the railroads and their unions together to make peace. The Railway Labor Act, passed in 1926, forced management to recognize the rights of unions but restricted unions from interrupting service before a federal mediator had been called in. The Air Line Pilots Association had lobbied successfully to have the whole airline industry covered by this act as well. The first Canadian airline employees admired the act because it committed management and labour to a process of collective bargaining, something that would not have come into effect in Canada until after World War II.

Union affiliation was hotly debated among TCA's machinists because of their varied backgrounds, but in the end the consensus was to follow in the footsteps of the organized machinists working for United Airlines and join the International Association of Machinists (IAM). In December 1939 the Winnipeg machinists signed their charter in the IAM as Lodge 714. The founding members were William Cook, Roy Parsons, Ed Kiely, Les Armstrong, Fred Pink, A. Hawkins, Jack Davey, Harry Pickering, Gord Fanstone, Art Trotter, Bob Ferguson, Stan Tardiff, "Perc" Scarr and Mike Serada. Unlike the pilots, passenger agents and stewardesses, Lodge 714 would be part of the brotherhood of American machinists from the very start, giving them international status. Their first formal agreement with the airline was signed on February 26, 1941, with D.B. Colyer and W.F. English representing TCA.

EXCERPT FROM THE ANNUAL REPORT FOR 1939

Route Miles Operated

December 31, 1938		December 31, 1939	
Toronto–Vancouver	2,291	Moncton–Vancouver	2,839
Montreal–North Bay	307	Ottawa–Toronto	288
Lethbridge–Edmonton	288	Toronto–North Bay	187
Seattle–Vancouver	122	Lethbridge–Edmonton	288
		Seattle–Vancouver	122
Totals	**3,008**		**3,664**

Mail (pounds) carried in the various services during the year 1939 was as follows:

Transcontinental:	
West or North	169,866
East or South	189,866
Total	359,732
Lethbridge–Edmonton	8,390
Montreal–Toronto	11,297
Vancouver–Seattle	73,480
Total mail carried	**452,899**

In addition 71,007 pounds of regular first class mail was carried in scheduled flights between Moncton and Montreal during November and December.

Passenger Service:

Passenger service was inaugurated between Montreal, Toronto and Vancouver and between Lethbridge and Edmonton on April 1. A direct Montreal–Ottawa–Toronto Service was established July 18. The patronage of the service has considerably exceeded expectations, particularly on the transcontinental route. A total of 21,569 revenue passengers was carried, the average journey being 559 miles. The following shows the percentage of passenger occupancy (passengers carried in relation to seat capacity) on the various schedules during the year:

Transcontinental	69%
Lethbridge–Edmonton	31.2%
Montreal–Toronto	53.5%
Montreal–Toronto (2nd Schedule)	54.5%
Montreal–Toronto–North Bay	40%
Toronto–North Bay	48%
Vancouver–Seattle	26%
All schedules	56%

(The lack of radio coverage is expected to delay the inauguration of a passenger service to Moncton until February, 1940)

Air Express Service:

This was inaugurated between Montreal–Toronto–Vancouver on October 17 1938, and was extended in 1939 to cover Montreal–Ottawa–Toronto and to Moncton on November 1. Total number of shipments: 10,897 Weighed 45,819 pounds

Property & Equipment:

As of December 31st, the flight equipment consisted of:
    15 Lockheed 14H aircraft. Six acquired during the year to replace an equal number of Lockheed 10As which were sold at their depreciated book value to the Inspection Division, Dept of Civil Aviation (one), the Royal Canadian Air Force (four).

Ground Equipment:

Construction of the hangar at Malton Airport (Toronto) was commenced in the fall of 1938 and completed in February 1939. A hangar of similar design was erected at St. Hubert (Montreal) and work was commenced on one at Moncton for completion in 1940.

Airway Facilities:

Radio range facilities furnished by the DOT are now in operation at all stations along the company's route from Vancouver to Moncton and at the intermediate 100 mile landing fields. Improved type of range equipment was installed at Carmi and Crescent Valley ranges in the mountain section and a high frequency range marker installed at Maple Ridge, BC, the approximate point at which the westbound flight commences its descent after crossing the mountains. New ranges were installed in Megantic, Que. Blissville, NB and Moncton, NB. The new range at Sterling, Ont. (20 miles north of Trenton, Ont.) reduces the mileage and flying time between Ottawa and Toronto by 48 miles and 15 minutes. A radio range installed by the United States authorities at Millinocket, Maine, for use by the airline is to be completed by the end of January, 1940.

Personnel:

Personnel on December 31, 1939, totaled 497, an increase of 165, and comprised of:

Administrative officers and technical advisors	12
Captains and first officers	54
Stewardesses	28
Maintenance and overhaul	233
Communications and dispatch	81
Station, clerical and others	89
Total	**497**

Of this, 270 were stationed at Winnipeg.

Financial:

Operating Revenue

Passenger	$643,915.48*
Mail	1,632,873.00
Express	23,613.01
Excess Baggage	3,940.78
Other Transportation	13,347.56
Incidental Services	32,748.14
Total Revenue	**$2,350,473.97**

Operating Expenses:

Aircraft Operations and Maintenance	$1,724,153.00
Ground Operations	636,256.94
Incidental Services	20,537.94
Traffic and General Administration	195,031.97
General Taxes	10,763.33

The Lockheed 10A (at top left) and two larger Lockheed 14H-Z Super Electras at the Winnipeg maintenance base. Throughout the war years, TCA domestic services were still maintained using the Lockheed series of airliners.

Total Expenses **$2,586,743.68**

Net Operating Loss. **$236,269.71**

Misc. Income 517.65
Interest On Capital Invested 175,904.53

**DEFICIT PROVIDED BY
DOMINION SUBSIDY** **$411,656.59**

*The cost of an airline ticket in 1939 was:

	One-way	Round Trip
Seattle–Vancouver	$7.90	$14.25
Lethbridge–Vancouver	30.05	50.65
Calgary–Lethbridge	6.80	12.25
Edmonton–Calgary	10.50	18.90
Regina–Vancouver	50.15	90.25
Winnipeg–Vancouver	70.15	126.25
Toronto–Winnipeg	67.30	121.15
Toronto–Vancouver	130.90	228.50
Ottawa–Toronto	13.55	24.40
Ottawa–Winnipeg	67.90	122.25
Montreal–Vancouver	144.65	255.10
Montreal–Toronto	20.15	36.25
Montreal–Ottawa	6.60	11.90

The Lockheed Super Electra,
erroneously thought to be
better suited to flying over the
Rockies than the DC-3

CHAPTER 5

"Lift Up Your Hearts. All will come right. Out of the depths of sorrow and sacrifice will be born again the glory of mankind." These stirring words from Britain's new prime minister, the Right Honourable Winston Churchill, were reprinted in Trans Canada Airlines' newsletter.

In spite of Canada's formal declaration of war, Mackenzie King did not nationalize the country's airlines as TCA employees had feared, but Trans Canada Airlines was designated "of maximum value to the Post Office, the armed forces, and those firms and individuals engaged in war production." This meant that TCA personnel would now need an Order-in-Council to leave the company and join the armed forces; by December 1941, sixty-six had done so. Harry Marlowe Kennedy and Zebulon Lewis Leigh resigned to join the RCAF as flight lieutenants, and both men became instrumental in beginning the RCAF's long-range transport capabilities to England, North Africa and Italy. Bob Williamson, station manager at Malton, joined as an operations officer and was attached to 164 and 168 squadrons at Moncton and later Prestwick, Scotland. According to Williamson, the RCAF's "operations plans were copied from the TCA operations manual, and that's what helped win the war."

Other TCA employees took leaves of absence; these included Al Ramsay (operator, Winnipeg), Pat Roy (passenger agent, Lethbridge), Alex Reid (accounting, Winnipeg), James Ames (passenger agent, Calgary) and Greg Loney (maintenance, Edmonton). Jack Ross, TCA's first station manager in Moncton, became an RCAF squadron leader in North Africa. It wasn't only men that heeded the call, either. Edna Louise Belden, a stewardess, joined the Royal Canadian Navy as a nurse and, before being posted overseas in September 1943, was decorated for her bravery during a fire that occurred while she was on duty in Newfoundland.

But for one of TCA's former captains, the war ended almost as soon as it began. William G.A. Coulson had learned to fly at the Regina Flying Club in 1928 and became a pilot instructor for Northwest Aero-Marine in Winnipeg a year later. He had taken a commission in the Royal Air Force and spent the next five years in England, India, Burma and the Far East, then found a job as a pilot with Imperial Airways. He came back to Canada when he heard TCA was hiring pilots and was made a captain on February 22, 1938. Coulson, who returned to the RAF at the outbreak of war, was the first former TCA employee to die in the line of duty.

Coulson, William George Allen S/L(P) 29237 – Royal Air Force. From Winnipeg, Manitoba. Killed Aug. 15, 1940, age 37. #220 Squadron (We Observe Unseen). Hudson aircraft lost. He is buried in the Elmwood Cemetery, Winnipeg, Manitoba.

If they couldn't fly Spitfires against the Luftwaffe or, like their Canadian Airways (CAL) colleagues, train BCATP crews to do so, TCA personnel found other ways to volunteer their expertise: delivering training aircraft purchased in the United States, ferrying military aircraft between training depots and providing radio coverage and servicing for RCAF flights. None of this was done on company time, and in April 1940 the RCAF commended the airline's pilots with the following:

Shortly after war was declared last fall, the RCAF purchased four TCA Electras. Arrangements were made to give RCAF pilots special flight training on these machines prior to delivery. At the time TCA had underway a heavy pilot training program, and the captains at Winnipeg observed that there were insufficient instructors available to properly handle the RCAF pilots in addition to their own candidates. A number of TCA captains volunteered to assist in the special training of the RCAF pilots during their layover in Winnipeg between regular flights. During February 1940 the RCAF requested that the company give similar training to an additional group of five RCAF pilots. The pilot group flew one of the Electras to Winnipeg early in March and once more the captains are giving flight training to the military flyers in addition to making their regular trips.

While this was going on, the airline's own guardian angel, C.D. Howe, had been made responsible for the War Purchasing Board, a bureaucracy which by April 9, 1940, had evolved into the Department of Munitions and Supply. He held the post of minister of this new department along with his transportation portfolio until July 7, 1940, when shipping, rail and road were given to Pierre-Joseph Cardin (and later in the war to Joseph Enoil Michaud). No one in Cabinet or the House questioned the fact that Howe retained the Air Services Branch of the DOT in his new position as minister of munitions and supply, a peculiar arrangement legalized through the Ministerial Transfer of Duties Act.

Air Mail Gives
Wings to Business

It's easy to use. Simply mark your envelopes "Via Air Mail." You do not need special envelopes or special stamps. Costs you only 3 cents more.

————————————————— TCA advertisement, September 1940

New Year's Day 1940 was chosen to inaugurate the airmail service to Moncton, followed by passenger flights on February 15. Then in preparation for a second daily transcontinental passenger service scheduled to begin on April 1 and the imminent arrival of more Lodestars with their accommodation for four passengers more than the Electra, the airline recruited eighteen new stewardesses. They graduated just in time as passenger loads jumped from 21,569 in 1939 to 53,180 in 1940, a rise of 150 percent.

TCA's stewardess class in the spring of 1940:

Frances Smith
Phyllis Margaret McIvor
Elsie Mills Dunnet
Mary Ellen Ward
Wilma Maxwell Struthers
Ruth Jennie Alm
Lois Margaret Wright
Winifred Anderson
Irene Pearl Lewis
Helen Brown
Pauline M. Betson
Geraldine May Cullen
Mary Aileen Halstead
Constance Elizabeth Stanley
Blanche Winnifred Mitchell
Patricia Grace Rand
Mary Irene Graves

Before they could be snapped up by the air force, more pilots were also recruited by the airline in the spring of 1940. According to *Between Ourselves*, when they were asked why they wanted to be pilots, the intrepid airmen replied, "A pilot is a lazy man whose life is punctuated by moments of intense fear." All admitted to having been aviation crazy as children, "when Wallace Reid was the Clark Gable of the silent screen—in a helmet and goggles and always flew with a devilish grin on his face." After an adolescence of practising that devilish grin in front of the mirror, they grew up and paid $30 per hour to get private pilot's licences. With that piece of paper they could now go around scaring the hell out of their parents and telling girls, "Shucks, 'tweren't nothin'!" But after achieving the ultimate—the Commercial Licence—came their rude awakening: there were no jobs for pilots. Years followed of picking fruit, working in wallpaper factories, slaving for road contractors and selling everything from vacuum cleaners to vegetables, interspersed with weekend flying, for which they didn't get paid. "We were lucky they loaned us the aeroplane, to carry their passengers in and to instruct."

Some had escaped starvation by barnstorming. This meant that they slept under the aircraft's wing in summer and cadged free meals from farmers "until the farmer chased you with a pitchfork because the noise of the motor had killed two of his prize pigs!" All in all, the new recruits were ecstatic to be part of TCA and had only one question: Why couldn't they wear a helmet and goggles like Wallace Reid?

Where TCA's new pilots had trained is indicative of the wide variety of activity in Canadian aviation during the 1930s:

Robert C. Wingfield:	St. Catharines Flying Club
Chas. E. Lloyd:	Toronto Air Transport and Toronto Flying Club
Don Lawson:	Ginger Coote Airways
Dal Woodward:	Winnipeg Flying Club
Spencer Dutton:	Winnipeg Flying Club
Lowell Dunsmore:	Prairie Airways
Art Hollinsworth:	Prospectors Airways
I.K. "Bing" Davis:	Imperial Airways
Robert C. Ramsay:	Flying Associates, Winnipeg
Bud M. Jones:	Manitoba Provincial Air Services
Paul E. Jensen:	Manitoba Provincial Air Services
Don H. McArthur:	Winnipeg Flying Club
John Holley:	Toronto Flying Club
Rene Bussiere:	RCAF
Nelson Norquist:	Boeing Aircraft, Vancouver
Frank Syme:	Canadian Airways
Dan Driscoll:	Yukon Southern Air Transport
A.G.K. "Gath" Edwards:	McIntyre Mines Exploration

Alex H. Palmer:	Hudson's Bay Company
John T. Noble:	Vancouver Airport
Gordon Brown:	Maintenance, Winnipeg
Gerard Ste. Marie:	Gatineau
John Laskoski:	MacKenzie Air Services
Gerry Avison:	Toronto
A.F. Madore:	Saskatoon Flying Club

Lowell Leonard Dunsmore was typical of the new pilots recruited in the spring of 1940. A farm boy from Rockyford, Alberta, he had abandoned an agricultural course at the University of Alberta in 1929 for the opportunity to be trained by the great World War I air ace Fred R. McCall. Once when he and McCall were flying Moths together, Lowell got cocky enough to try to evade his instructor by sharply pulling into a loop and levelling out again. When he had accomplished the manoeuvre and almost taken the Moth's wings off, to his shock there was McCall, "right on his tail, imaginary guns spitting tracers." When they landed, McCall growled, "Listen kid, don't pull off any more stunts like that. I can follow you all the way through them and knock you right out of the sky." The lanky, flight-crazy Dunsmore graduated to flying a Moth for Great Western Airways at Calgary. Subsequently he barnstormed in the province, then moved to Vernon, BC, where he flew a Gipsy Moth through the mountain passes. The Depression forced him to return to farming and ranching, and years later his TCA colleagues said that if you wanted a bronco broken, Lowell Dunsmore could do it. He returned to aviation after a special commercial pilot's course at RCAF Camp Borden and joined the ranks of the fabled bush pilots, working for M & C Aviation Company of Prince Albert, hauling mail, prospectors, dogs, traders, fish and fur. This was followed by a stint with Prairie Airways on Beechcrafts and instructing RCAF pilots when war came. At TCA Dunsmore was soon made captain on the Winnipeg–Lethbridge route and later the Winnipeg–Toronto service. It was here that he picked up the nickname "Doc" because of the little satchel in which he carried his toothbrush.

Another recruit was "Bing" Davis, who had apprenticed at the Toronto Flying Club in 1934 and obtained his commercial licence three years later. With no jobs available, he went barnstorming in an old Avro Avian owned by a local farmer. One afternoon a friend of the farmer accepted a dare to go up with Davis for a couple of loops. On the first loop the pilot couldn't see his passenger at all because his head was apparently tucked so far down in the cockpit. On the second loop, however, Davis did see his head come up and at the same time, while the plane was in an inverted position, he was suddenly blinded by oil—windshield, goggles and face all splattered. Davis throttled back, straightened out and landed, then jumped out to look for the oil leak. Just then he heard his passenger say to the plane's owner, "Well, I enjoyed the first loop all right, but in the middle of the second one, I opened my mouth and my chaw of tobacco fell out!"

After barnstorming and hauling fish for Norcan Fisheries at Nakina, Davis gave up looking for an airline pilot's job in Canada and went to England, where he flew for Imperial Airways out of Croydon. When war broke out, he came home to join TCA and in two years was made captain.

A.G.K. "Gath" Edwards, whose career in aviation stretched from World War I "Jennies" to DC-8s, was another of the graduates of the Jack Elliot school in Hamilton, Ontario. As a teenager, Edwards barnstormed with his instructor Len Tripp, his duties being "gas pourer and ticket-seller." Throughout the Depression years Edwards flew for a variety of bush outfits—Commercial Airways, Harry McLean's Dominion Construction and General Airways—before joining TCA. In May 1964 he had the privilege of ferrying a CH300 Pacemaker from Prince Rupert, BC, to the National Aeronautical Collection in Ottawa; this was the same type as that flown by Errol Boyd when he made the first Canadian crossing of the Atlantic.

"I was crazy about aviation as a boy," said Max Church. Born in 1920, the son of a Royal Flying Corps instructor, he recalls that "the talk at home was about air aces and fighter planes." He was just eight when his father took him to the airport for a ride in an open cockpit Waco, and he was hooked for life. When the aviator Jimmy Mattern flew a Lockheed Super Electra around the globe in 1938, the teenager was "enamored by the looks of the plane" and followed the formation of TCA closely; in 1940, when he learned that the company was looking for pilots, he immediately began lessons at Leavens Brothers at Barker Field under the chief instructor, Len Tripp. In May 1941 Church was accepted by TCA and flown to Winnipeg Ground School. "The Link trainer instructor there was Jim Meekin," Max remembers, "and on his desk was a large chart of the Winnipeg Airport. On the chart a mechanical 'crab' received electronic signals from the trainee pilot under the hood in the Link Trainer—his course charted by a telltale red line. At the end of the lesson the trainee had to look at what the crab had drawn and explain the lines, good or bad. The whole class had a good chuckle one day when Meekin accused the trainee of making a good approach but descending below the height of the airport. Tense and a bit flustered, the poor student said, 'Yes, but I pulled up as soon as I noticed it.'"

Art Hollinsworth had worked as a brakeman for the CPR and as a hockey player in Toronto before he earned enough to train for his commercial licence, granted on May 6, 1929. While flying in northern Ontario, he was marooned for three days beside the Albany River until, like Robinson Crusoe, his footprints were discovered by prospectors; a Toronto newspaper reported that by then his condition was "half-crazed." Jobs for pilots being scarce during the Depression, Hollinsworth attended the RCAF instrument flying course at Camp Borden. "In 1940, after seeing TCA pilots placidly landing and taking off in Armstrong in low weather conditions," said his friend, captain Rube Hadfield, "Art joined TCA."

All the new recruits began their careers as co-pilots, their lowly status reflected in one man's experience when "holding over" at Kapuskasing later that year. While dining with the radio operators at the "Kap Inn," he was asked by a waitress whether he could really fly "or was he just the co-pilot?"

The Co-Pilot

by Ken Murray, CCA

I am the co-pilot, I sit on the right,
It's up to me to be quick and bright.
I never talk back, for I have regrets,
But I have to remember what the Captain forgets.

I make out the flight plans and study the weather,
Pull up the gear and stand by to feather,
Check the tanks and do the reporting,
And fly the old crate while the captain is courting.

I call for my Captain and buy him cokes,
I always laugh at his corny jokes;
And once in a while when his landings are rusty,
I always come through with "By gosh, it's gusty."

All in all, I'm a general stooge
As I sit on the right of the man I call "Scrooge."
I guess you think that is past understanding
But maybe some day he will give me a landing.

The Chateau Laurier in Ottawa has always been more than just the hotel across from the Union railway station. From the hotel's earliest days, the thickly carpeted lobby and cigar smoke-filled Grill Room had been the gathering place for Cabinet ministers and captains of industry, and because of the history that unfolded within its walls, the press had dubbed it "the Third Parliament."

"The Transportation Room," adjacent to the spiral staircase in the southwest corner of the hotel's main lobby, had been conceived as a museum to progress, its walls adorned with murals of robust Canadian scenery. But in 1937, this imposing room had been divided into a pair of offices to become the CNR and TCA ticket counters, the latter under Gordon Wood, the airline's first manager in Ottawa. Trans Canada Airlines flight departures from Ottawa's Uplands Airport were announced throughout the main floor. Passengers would gather in the lobby for the aged bellmen (pageboys would not appear until after the war) to take their luggage and escort them to the Red Line taxi, which was on permanent call under the stone canopy outside. TCA's importance to essential war work meant that the number of personnel in the airline doubled in 1940 and the former Transportation Room was now crowded and busy. An experimental teletype circuit had been set up earlier that year connecting the office to Malton, the Royal York Hotel, St. Hubert, Uplands and Mount Royal Hotel in Montreal, and now the machines churned out endless messages while telephones rang continuously as the transportation industry coped with the exigencies of the war.

Many of the teletype messages emanated from TCA's Central Reservations Control Office—generally known as CC, the airline's nerve centre. Born on July 1, 1940, in a tiny corner in the passenger agent's room at Malton Airport, CC had graduated to 347 Bay Street, Toronto, where fifty-eight staff members worked in Room 408, an air-conditioned and soundproofed room with walls painted a restful dull grey-blue to minimize light reflection. From here teletype circuits went out to Windsor, Winnipeg, Montreal and Halifax. Whenever a customer stepped up to the ticket counter of a city traffic office to reserve a seat, he unknowingly set into motion the experts at CC. The ticket clerk contacted the reservations control supervisor on a direct line; he channelled it to the chart clerk in charge of that flight. The availability of space was then passed back up the line to the counter clerk and the anxious customer. At the same time the reservation control operator opened a file in the passenger's name so that he could be advised about changes in the flight schedule. Supervisor Charlie Woolley and his assistant, Ted Moore, admitted that with 4,000 messages on the teletype daily and continuous telephone calls, CC was "organized bedlam"—there were quieter places in the world to inhabit. TCA had other Control Centres with fewer employees: Atlantic Control Halifax (thirteen), Secondary Control Winnipeg (ten) and New York Reservations (five).

As more and more men signed up, the airline began taking on women employees for the duration, but by late 1940, apart from the stewardesses, what female employees there were worked mainly in accounting at the Winnipeg main office. Counter staff remained exclusively male until May 9, 1940, when Grace Humphrys of Winnipeg became the first female passenger agent in Canada, but two young women, Dorothy M. Pearson and Jane Irwin, were among the first counter staff hired for the Chateau office in Ottawa. Both were fingerprinted, required to swear allegiance to the Crown, and assigned to shift work so that the counter was manned twenty-four hours a day.

Working at TCA's counter in wartime Ottawa was a heady business. In the CBC radio studios above them, Lorne Greene, the "Voice of Doom," told the nation of battles in Tobruk and the Coral Sea, of the heroic city of Stalingrad and of the RCAF squadrons hunting for the German warships *Scharnhorst* and *Prinz Eugen*. (He had just completed the narration for a movie on TCA, *Wings of the Continent*, part of the wartime *Canada Carries On* series by the National Film Board.) Soldiers in uniforms of every shade and rank strode though the hotel lobby; here and there among them were the civilian suits of Howe's "Dollar a Year" men. General Motors, Ford, A.V. Roe and de Havilland kept permanent suites at the Chateau and their directors had standing reservations with TCA to be flown from their hometowns to Ottawa on Sunday night or

Monday morning and back home every Friday evening. The famous were there, too. The movie star Jimmy Cagney stayed at the hotel in the summer of 1941 while he starred in *Captains of the Clouds*, then being filmed at Uplands Airport. Winston Churchill came with his huge cigar and his "V for Victory" salute, as did the tall, imperious Charles de Gaulle, and the grinning General Dwight Eisenhower.

"Ottawa before the war was notoriously short of unmarried young men. The figures were supposed to be around thirteen women to one man. The war changed all of that to surplus of men."[1] TCA's women employees were invited to embassy parties, dated foreign military attachés, and moved in social circles that before and after the war were out of their reach. Dorothy Pearson even had her portrait photograph taken by the famous "Karsh of Ottawa" whose studio was in the Chateau lobby. A newspaper society column reported that the Mexican ambassador to Canada, a Dr. Del Rio, said the TCA secretary at the Chateau, Miss Nellie Alberding, was to be his choice next winter for the "Good Neighbour Rhumba Sweeps." Of Dutch descent, Nellie was at that time more pleased to hear that her cousin, Captain Jan Alberding of the Netherlands East Indian Air Force, had escaped from Java just ahead of the Japanese. Not all the attention was welcome. "At times we would have a particular man come to the office in the evening looking for a young woman to go out with," wrote Joan Keogh Rankin, TCA passenger agent at the Chateau during those years. "Whenever we saw him coming, we would hide in the back of the office; then if a real passenger came along, we would have to go out. The hanger-on was a real pest."[2]

C.D. Howe, as minister for the airline and practically everything else in those days, visited the TCA office daily and on his way to and from seeing the airline manager in his inner sanctum, he always had a cheery greeting for the counter staff. "The work was exciting," Rankin remembered.

> We were a dedicated but wacky group...TCA executives were a friendly bunch. Mr. [Herbert] Symington [soon to be TCA president] was a businessman of high repute. A modest man who never threw his weight around. W.F. (Bill) English, the vice-president, was a big teddy bear of a man, with ruddy cheeks, grey hair and a hearty laugh...He was always open to suggestions of how to improve certain procedures or change any aspect of our work and would encourage us to speak up.
>
> A system of priorities had to be set up for travel in wartime. It often became necessary to deplane passengers concerned in non-essential business. That was not a pleasant task for employees, especially if a passenger who was trying to get to a point at some distance for a funeral of a loved one had to be removed. Occasionally someone tried to throw his

weight around by demanding a priority to which he was not entitled. In order to overcome that type of situation, government travellers were issued a priority passenger form duly signed by an authorized person in each department."[3]

The Blanket Theory
Applied to Vacations

Once upon a time, a man cut a piece from one end of his blanket and sewed it to the opposite end, in order to lengthen it. Of course, he was wrong. He ended up with a shorter blanket!

Today you would be right if you applied his theory to your vacation. If on your holiday trip you go by air you will save days both going and returning—and have more time at your destination for fun and relaxation. TCA enables you to get farther, stay longer and do more. For your business as well as vacation trip, we'll gladly prove the "blanket theory."

— TCA advertisement, January 1941

Prior to 1940 all air negotiations between Canada and the US had been handled by the postal authorities of the two countries, but as few Americans flew north of the border, Canadian routes had not been coveted by the major American airlines. However, in the face of a growing Japanese threat to Alaska, on September 9 and 10, 1940, air transport authorities from the United States and Canada met in Ottawa to hammer out the first allocation of bilateral air routes. As well, even as the diplomats met in Ottawa, Canadian and American engineers were in Vancouver drawing up plans for a northern airway between the state of Montana and the territory of Alaska. For a change, Canada had the upper hand in these plans because to get to Alaska, American aircraft would have to fly by instrument flight regulations (IFR) via Lethbridge, Calgary and Edmonton with suitable refuelling stops along the way. Meanwhile, on the Atlantic coast where land planes were in more frequent use, Moncton and Gander had become increasingly important for US transatlantic flights. The resulting payoff for Canada in these negotiations was the allocation of two of the six bilateral services authorized in the agreement going to Trans Canada Airlines. One was the monopoly Toronto–New York route, a prize also sought by American Airlines. The other route was from any point in Canada to the city of Detroit. Northeast Airlines took up the Montreal–Boston and Boston–Moncton options, while Western Air Express flew between Great Falls, Montana, and Lethbridge. In addition, in the first arrangement of its kind, the agreement stipulated that TCA would provide radio coverage and servicing for both of these US airlines. The sixth route was that from Vancouver to Seattle, and on May 11, 1941, TCA terminated its money-losing service between these two cities, leaving the field once more to United Airlines. (TCA did not return to Seattle until 1946, and then only via Victoria.) As co-operation in continental defence grew, there was also the first tentative discussion concerning an air service between the two capital cities, Washington and Ottawa. This first commercial air agreement between the two countries was designed to expire on December 31, 1942, but by then the United States was in the war and it was extended to 1945.

Lockheed had meanwhile been redesigning the Super Electra in 1940, after its launch customer, Northwest Airlines, had sold off its whole fleet and switched to DC-3s. The tail plane of the redesigned aircraft, now called the Lodestar, had been modified with a trailing edge extension, which cured it of the "flutter," and the fuselage was stretched to accommodate four more passengers for better seat-mile economy. By this time it was too late to compete with the DC-3 domestically as

Herbert J. Symington, 1944. When TCA was judged stable enough to have a president of its own, Symington—a board member and a Winnipeg lawyer—was elected on July 24, 1941.

every US airline of note had already equipped itself with Douglas Commercials. But the requirements of overseas airlines were another matter. The Netherlands East Indies branch of KLM bought twenty-nine Lodestars as did South African Airways. Trans Canada Airlines followed with an order for twelve Lodestars, registering them from *CF-TCT* to *CF-TCY*, then from *CF-TDA* to *CF-TDF*. The cost of each of these last six aircraft, which were the Wartime Production Board version of the Lodestar, was $154,219.

A year before the war began, the British Purchasing Commission had toured the United States, looking to buy several types of aircraft, one of which was an armed reconnaissance/light bomber. Spearheaded once more by Robert Gross, the Lockheed design team hurriedly adapted its Super Electra to seat a crew of four, added a nose gun and dorsal turret and—where the cargo hold had been—a bomb bay. The British liked the new version, which Lockheed named the B14, but asked that the nose gun be eliminated and the nose be made transparent so that the navigator's seat could be shifted into it and he could double as the bombardier. Lockheed agreed to these modifications and

*The distinctive Lockheed design features in wing plan and the twin tail fins mask the
subtle differences between the Lockheed model 14 Super Electra (above) and the model
18 Lodestar (opposite). Visual reference shows that the Lodestar had a 5-foot fuselage
extension and a slight bulge at the tail. The trailing edge of the wing was extended and
no longer straight-lined. The cooling gills on the engines were a feature of the more
powerful Pratt & Whitney Twin Wasp engines, which provided a considerable increase
in cruise speed and payload, two very important factors in airline operation.*
Ken Leigh collection

the British ordered 200 B14s, known as the "Hudson" by the RAF—all to be
delivered before December 1939. (Not all of the Hudsons purchased by the
British left Canada, however; twenty-eight were assigned to the RCAF, and one
of them from 31 OTU sank a German submarine off Nova Scotia on July 4,
1943.)

The first batch of Hudsons arrived in Britain by sea, shipped from either
Long Beach, California, or flown to Floyd Bennett Airfield, New York, taken
apart and put on-board ship to Liverpool, where they were reassembled at
Speke Airport near the docks. The scheme worked well enough until Congress
passed the Neutrality Act, which forbade the delivery of aircraft directly to the
combatants. At the same time, German submarines kept sinking the Hudson-
carrying ships at an alarming rate, making the sea route too dangerous.

Lockheed, however, continued to fulfill its side of the contract by having factory crews fly the Hudsons to Canadian soil either at St. Hubert, Montreal, or to Pembina, North Dakota, where the runway extends from the US into Canada. To keep within the letter of the Act, the Hudsons were landed at the US end of the field where the paperwork was done, then towed to the Canadian side and flown off. As a collection point for all the British aircraft purchases, St. Hubert Airport was overflowing with aircraft by the summer of 1940 and staggering under its traffic load.

At this point the CNR's old nemesis stepped into the airline picture. The war had provided the Canadian Pacific Railway with unprecedented good fortune, allowing it to accumulate a vast cash reserve; this, combined with its administrative, legal and purchasing powers, allowed the company to enter the aviation business via the back door. On Richardson's death, Sir Edward Beatty, as Canadian Airways' principal shareholder, had assumed control of his company, and beginning in the fall of 1940 he—or more precisely his vice-president of finances, Laurence Unwin—engineered the purchase of the major private bush carriers in the country. This was a move that had been made relatively easy because fuel rationing and the lack of replacement parts or aircraft had driven the bush air companies—never far from insolvency in the best of times—to the brink of closing down.

It wasn't so much the motley collection of bush planes that Unwin wanted, but the licences that each company had. In 1937 the Liberal government, desiring (it said) to undo the injustices of the Bennett years that had driven many bush companies into bankruptcy, introduced an amendment to the Railway Act. When it became law the next year, it ended the unrestricted warfare for postal subsidies by allocating all such routes to the sixteen air companies then in operation. No longer would newly formed competitors be able to challenge the initial carrier and undercut their rates. As well, it not only ensured a regular postal delivery for regions that TCA had at that time no ambitions to serve, but gave many of the bush airlines their greatest asset: a mail contract on a specific route or routes. Therefore, when Unwin purchased Edmonton-based Mackenzie Air Services in November 1940, the routes to Aklavik, Coppermine and Stoney Rapids came under CPR control. Adding Quebec Airways in December 1941 meant obtaining the right to operate from Montreal and Quebec City up the Saguenay and through eastern Quebec. After melding these two into the Canadian Airways system, the CPR then purchased controlling interests in Starrat Airways, Wings Ltd., Prairie Airways, Arrow Airways and Dominion Skyways.

The purchase of Grant McConachie's Yukon Southern Air Transport (YSAT) in January 1941 not only brought with it modern Barkley-Grow airliners and a workforce of seventy, but licences to operate between Vancouver and Whitehorse and the increasingly vital airfields along the Alaska Highway. As well, the purchase enlisted the services of its visionary founder. In the same month that Philip Johnson was inspecting the Trans Canada Airway in 1937, McConachie had been piloting his Ford 6 AT on an inaugural flight between Edmonton and Whitehorse to begin the Yukon's first regular air service. His energy was surpassed only by his luck. Through sheer bravado and recurring bankruptcies, McConachie had put together a potential rival to TCA by 1941.

Even before Unwin's acquisitions were complete, on June 14, 1940, Beatty proposed to Mackenzie King that the Canadian Pacific Railway's new Air Services division at St. Hubert be allowed to organize the ferrying of the Lockheed Hudsons to the beleaguered British. King's Cabinet dismissed the idea out of hand, with Howe grumbling that it would be preferable if Canadian Airways concentrated on aiding the domestic war effort, as TCA was doing, rather than floating such fanciful schemes. But the audacity of Beatty's proposal appealed to Britain's minister of aircraft production, Lord Beaverbrook, the former Canadian millionaire Max Aitken. As Bennett's friend and mentor, he must have also seen an opportunity to score over the Liberal government, and ignoring the DOT and Howe, he approached Beatty directly. Under Beaverbrook's wing and with the blessing of Prime Minister Winston Churchill, Beatty then organized a group of well-connected Montreal businessmen to help Canadian Pacific Air Services (CPAS) run the Atlantic Ferry

Organisation (ATFERO). However, Beaverbrook apart, the British really did not have any faith in the "old boy" network which had produced ATFERO, and the US government was critical of its unofficial status and the growing log-jam of aircraft that embarrassed the Roosevelt policy of neutrality. But Beatty "made do" with BOAC air crews and volunteer pilots garnered from recruiting drives held by the Clayton Knight Committee in the US, and despite a barrage of criticism from all sides, the ferrying of the Hudsons from St. Hubert to Belfast, Northern Ireland, was successful.

In Ottawa, anything that either Beatty or the CPR was involved in had an effect on the prime minister similar to that of taunting a bull with a red flag. Howe's views were not much better, with the minister saying publicly that the CPR's air service was run by amateurs, "cast-off personnel without adequate ground facilities." In his opinion only D.B. Colyer, the current TCA vice-president of operations, was qualified to run the ferrying. But Colyer thought otherwise. To him "all the civil transport organizations in the United States and Canada combined would not now have personnel enough to do the ferrying job as it will develop."[4]

In the midst of all these negotiations, in December 1940 C.D. Howe set off for Britain to discuss aircraft production when his ship, *Western Prince*, was torpedoed off Iceland. As the lifeboats were pulling away, the U-boat surfaced. The correspondent for the *Manchester Guardian* was in one of the boats and remembers seeing an old man with craggy eyebrows shaking his fist at the looming conning tower. Fortunately, the survivors were rescued shortly after this encounter. As his parliamentary opponents had discovered, Mr. Howe was unsinkable.

With the succession of Axis victories in 1940–41 and the desperate air battles taking place over Britain, considerable pressure was brought on Howe to turn over the resources of TCA to ATFERO, and he told Beaverbrook that he would not hesitate to break up Trans Canada Airlines if he thought it would solve the ferrying problem, "but not under the present management." Now if Howe were responsible for the ferrying, he continued, he would get Phil Johnson, then in Seattle as president of Boeing, back to Canada to do the job. "I have already sounded out the principal shareholders of the Boeing Company in this regard," Howe told anyone who would listen, "and know we can get Johnson if the way is clear. Johnson is a driver and a most careful operator and with him in charge our troubles would be over."

When in March 1941 the Roosevelt Administration passed the Lend-Lease Act, which allowed American military personnel to deliver aircraft to Montreal, the urgency to rationalize the whole ferry process could not be ignored. Just as the number of aircraft to be delivered was going to triple, ATFERO was running out of pilots and navigators, and while the former could be obtained from the neutral United States, navigators were almost non-existent in North America because use of the radio beam on this side of the Atlantic had made their profession obsolete. As aircraft could not be flown across the ocean on a radio beam because the distances were too great, for a time radio bearings were taken on coastal stations. But these were only good for about 200 miles, and the original method of navigation—that of flying by dead reckoning and astro observations—was revisited. With its far-flung colonial routes, Imperial Airways had been a good school for pilots and navigators, and ATFERO had been fortunate that Imperial's most experienced pilot, D.C.T. Bennett, had been available to lead the first formation of Hudsons across.

St. Hubert Airport too was woefully unqualified for its new role. As ranks of Hudsons gathered on its tarmac, the DOT looked for an alternative and found it in a BCATP airfield being built on a disused race track at Dorval on Montreal's West Island as an air observer school. This was given over to ATFERO and the airlines to use, all of whom moved there on September 1, 1941, with St. Hubert Airport ending all civil operations the day before. The distinctive sweeping terminal building at Dorval was modelled on that of Washington's National Airport, its wide lobby reminiscent of a luxury hotel. Of the six hangars built, one was for the DOT and leased to TCA, which also built its own; three were for the RAF Ferry Command which replaced ATFERO; and the last was for the RCAF. TCA had fifty-five staff at the new airport, excluding those who worked on the BOAC program.

Reflecting the modern contemporary architecture of the 1930s, Montreal's new terminal was more than adequate for the time and was still in use in the early 1960s, relatively unchanged. The cobweb of radio aerials contrasts nicely above a newly arrived Lockheed 18 Lodestar. Max Church photo

The first TCA station manager at Dorval was the celebrated Romeo Vachon. Awarded the McKee Trophy when operations manager for Quebec Airways from 1934–38, Vachon was already a historic figure in Canadian aviation. One of the original "Flying Postmen" on Quebec's north shore, he was known to the public for having piloted the first aircraft to reach the crashed "Bremen" in 1928 and for flying a Saro-Cloud (a twin-engined amphibian aircraft) from coast to coast in the 1931 Canadian Air Pageant. His son Pierre Vachon recalled that his father was very unsure about leaving a well-paid management position at Quebec Airways to join TCA. "Eventually he decided that the future would be brighter with TCA as Canadian Airways did not appear to have the political wind in its sails."[5] The company hired him as a pilot in 1938, and Vachon was sent to Winnipeg to be put through the instrument course, but being already forty years old, he declined the position of regular line pilot and was pleased when he was made station manager at St. Hubert, where there was a single daily flight. At Dorval, however, he oversaw eight daily flights.

That the TCA Lodestars did not thunder over downtown Montreal any more to land at St. Hubert came as a relief to the city's classical music lovers. A letter addressed to Captain Barney Rawson from station manager Bob Williamson at St. Hubert explains why.

> We received a phone call yesterday from the Chairman of the Montreal Symphony Orchestra regarding annoyance caused by our trips six and three flying above the mountain. Each Thursday night during the summer, when weather is CAVU, music lovers from Montreal and the suburbs gather at the Chalet atop Mount Royal, overlooking the city, to harken to the symphony concert. As you are a musically minded man, you will realise that to have a couple of "Hornets" lustily roaring their heads off 200 feet above you whilst you are rapt in ecstasy listening to Brahms' Fifth Concerto or Beethoven's Unfinished Symphony, you would no doubt be a little displeased.
>
> So we ask you kindly if it would be possible to have the boys fly about half a mile either side of the Chalet on concert night, when weather permits. A small thing, no doubt you say, but to the music lovers who have toiled their hearts out climbing to the mountain top just to listen to sweet music, this annoyance reaches the magnitude of a slap in the face, and TCA receives much unfavourable comment as saboteurs of fine music and an enemy of culture in this time of trial.

TCA suffered its second fatal accident on February 6, 1941, when Lockheed 14, *CF-TCP* crashed while landing at Armstrong, Ontario, killing all the crew and passengers. The Winnipeg-bound aircraft had left Malton the previous day, refuelled at North Bay and Kapuskasing and was about to make a routine landing at Armstrong. According to the Dominion Law Reports, "Light snow was falling and there was nothing said by the pilot to the radio operator at Armstrong to suggest any trouble. A witness heard and saw the aircraft fly over the airport and then turn to make its landing. The red and green wing tip lights were visible as it did so. Then he suddenly saw a white light (which he correctly took to be the taillight of the aircraft) fall rapidly. After close investigation of the wreckage, no ice was found on the wings and there was evidence that the engines were still running and propellers revolving up to the time of the crash. The trailing antenna was found on a treetop and further on, one of the wings had been torn off. The Lockheed's barograph (which recorded altitude) indicated that at some point from 800 to 1,000 ft above the ground the aircraft had gone into a precipitous descent as if it had dived or fallen." Crew members killed were Captain William Edward Twiss, First Officer Charles Edward Lloyd and stewardess Mary Gertrude Mayne. Just before it hit, the pilots had struggled to level the aircraft over and through some trees. It was deduced that the plane was travelling in a horizontal position in its final seconds, and some semblance of recovery had been made. But as the investigators saw, it was then aimed away from the runway and deeper into the woods. The company cited "pilot error" as the cause of the crash, making it vulnerable to its first lawsuit. Agnes Malone and Florence Moss, whose husbands had been on that plane, took TCA to the Ontario Court of Appeal on a charge of negligence. The judgement handed down on June 29, 1942, was that the pilot had brought the Lockheed in too low in his approach to the runway. Damages awarded to Agnes Malone were $10,000, her children Aileen Malone $2,100 and Ernest Malone $3,300. Florence Moss was awarded $4,000.

The court's ruling and the company's explanation of the cause of the crash as "pilot error" created a furor among CALPA members, and a ballot was also sent out to all members asking pilots whether the association should accept or contest the company's judgement. The case further highlighted the need for some sort of an agreement between CALPA and the airline to protect pilots in trouble.

More far reaching was the judge's ruling in the case. "Travel by aeroplane must now be regarded as a common means of transport, extensively used, not only in North America, but throughout the world. With experienced and careful pilots and proper equipment, a passenger has the right to expect that he will be carried safely to his destination."[6] The judgement set a legal precedent for all future air travel and would be cited in several other "negligence" cases.

Defence of Canada regulations prohibits passengers from carrying cameras on board TCA aircraft. Cameras may be included with checked baggage or surrendered to the custody of the stewardess.

———————————————— TCA notice on all tickets, June 1941

The company must have thought it would have a friend in high places when D.B. Colyer resigned on August 31, 1941, to become controller, United States Steel Division, Department of Munitions and Supply in Washington, D.C. At his farewell dinner in Winnipeg, besides a silver tray with their names inscribed on it, staff presented him with a silk hat, cane and a pair of yellow gloves in keeping with his new "diplomatic status." His place as vice-president of operations was taken by O.T. Larson.

In 1941 it still hadn't been decided whether the company's newsletter was to be published monthly or quarterly, but René Baudru, who had been promoted to chief clerk and a year later to office manager of the operations department, now had less time (but no less interest) in editing it. In any case, he was having great difficulty recruiting volunteer station correspondents, and in the fall of 1941 he included this sad plaint in the newsletter.

Pome—In Season

Ten correspondents, heart o' mine
RAF called one, then there were nine.

Nine correspondents—hand of fate!
Along came a stewardess, then there were eight.

Eight correspondents took off toward Heaven.
One in a rocket ship, then there were seven.

Seven correspondents, hangar made of bricks,
Remote control dropped one, then there were six.

Six correspondents, *Transcanews* pride.
Gossiped via teletype then there were five.

Five correspondents, who would want more?
Waybills got mixed up, then there were four.

Four correspondents, just as you and me.
Forgot about the whirling prop, then there were three.

Three correspondents feeling kinda blue
Drank some de-icer fluid...

Two correspondents, desperate for fun,
Wouldn't fasten seat belts, then there was one

One correspondent—what the hell,
Who reads *Transcanews* anyway!

Management certainly did, and O.T. Larson, the new vice-president of operations, decided to make the publication official by allocating a budget and assigning a permanent staff to the job of producing it. Renamed *Between Ourselves*, the newsletter's first two issues were personally blue pencilled by Bill English, who had been seconded from the CNR to run TCA's offices. The cover photo on the first one showed a Lockheed 14H, but while it contained only eleven pages of news—possibly because of paper rationing—it did include the historic newswire photo of a Parisian gentleman with tears trickling down his anguished face as he watched the German Army enter his city. The accompanying article began: "Two years ago this man was as free as you and I. Today he humbly steps into the gutter to let his conquerors swagger past... What does he think of today? It is probably something like this: I wish that I had been less greedy for myself and more anxious for my country. I wish that I had known that Patriotism is work, not talk—giving, not getting. It is this thought that TCA employees, among others, should ponder on. We should have a full realization that whatever we do is not too much because this is Total War. We have with us the cause of freedom and it is up to us to fight with all the merit that cause deserves."

At first, the newsletter appeared intermittently. It was not until March 1943, when Don McLeod, who would later become assistant director of publications, formally took over from English under the banner headline "We are here to stay!" that it appeared monthly. There was less gossip now about who was blushing when she heard a certain captain's name, and more articles reflecting the great events unfolding overseas. Between the poetry and announcements of promotions, births, deaths and marriages, there were now photos, pleas to write to former TCA employees serving in the military and exhortations to buy more Victory Bonds. Caricatures drawn by D.F. Mathias mixed realism and whimsy and have become historical reminders of airline personalities.

The magazine's vocabulary reflected each and every writer's enthusiasm at being part of the airline and the war effort. It is vivid with slang—military and political, Allied and enemy—that two years before would have been alien to Canadians. Terms such as jerry can, concentration camp (although few could imagine the horrors that this word signified), radar (S.S. Stevens initially called it "radio phonics"), the office pin-up girl (said to be Mary Quelch, counter clerk at Vancouver), our Calgary blonde bombshell, Uncle Joe (for Josef Stalin) and cover girl were used regularly. The word "Jeep" underwent a change in meaning: in use with TCA since 1938 to mean the Link trainer, by 1943 with the American invasion underway, it had come to mean the familiar four-wheel-drive vehicle, as used in the newsletter's description of "Miss Edna Gamblin of general traffic (Edmonton) who may be seen around town escorted by a US Army captain, no less, complete with jeep."

Though the war was never out of the newsletter's pages, in a feature called "Meet the Gang," readers learned of the after-work activities of their colleagues.

For example, the female TCA counter staff (passenger agents) at the Royal York Hotel in Toronto danced the rhumba on Friday nights and did "a mean Xavier Cougat conga." They shopped at Eaton's and curled for the airline recreation association, but also found time to donate blood for the Red Cross and contribute to the Milk for Britain Fund from their salaries. Dr. K.E. Dowd, the airline's medical officer at Dorval, sternly advised personnel that "Food is Our Weapon while the Axis scours the earth for their needs. The efficiency of the company's personnel stand in direct relation to the sanity of their food habits. Instead of meat and sugar, a daily ration of six slices of whole wheat or 'Canada Approved' bread will help us out-think, out-produce and out-last the enemy."

As the contributors to *Between Ourselves*—invariably male—were posted around the airline network and as more women invaded all-male professions, they lost their inhibitions and provincial attitudes and succumbed to current Hollywood slang. In the newsletter's pages, men became "real guys" and one was described as "a real smoother-over." Women, on the other hand, were "those flashing, dark-eyed brunettes in Accounting" or "the little rays of sunshine in Sales" or "those chic little things with expressive blue eyes." The description of Elsie Spencer, the clerk stenographer at Vancouver station, as (using a quote from Tennyson) "tall and willowy—a daughter of the gods...divinely fair" must be read in the context of the innocence of the time. When interviewed, the women claimed that all they wanted were "up-sweep" hairdos and figures "designed by Maxine." One TCA "gal"—women didn't mind being called that in 1943—was said to have a weakness for blond paratroopers.

The war also provided comic relief, especially at the stations that shared facilities with the RCAF squadrons and BCATP schools. Here the runways—many of which had seen no more than two aircraft movements a day before the war—were overrun by Tiger Moths and Ansons, and pilots frequently found themselves jostling for taxi and runway space with these erratically flown or weaving "Yellow Perils." The newsletter reflected the comedy of these situations.

Winnipeg

Recently the Air Force (God bless 'em) has been our primary source of amusement. Stories of an anti-militaristic nature might send our Editor-in-Chief to prison for the duration of the war, but we still like the one about the guard on the Lockheed bomber which was housed in Winnipeg for a few days. Said guard was standing around under the wing when the sergeant-major approached. He snapped to attention, shouldered arms, and stuck the bayonet through the wing!

Edmonton

The big event at the airport was the arrival of Gracie Fields on Trip 21. A host of civic, military and police officials covered with gold braid did the honours, to the consternation of Jack Pitt, the local commissionaire. Escorted by Herb Harling, Gracie got off the aircraft humming her signature tune and won all hearts by walking across the apron to greet the large crowd outside the surrounding fence.

The second big event which no doubt could be termed "earthshaking" was the arrival of a number of Lockheed 10As and Avro Ansons for No. 2 Observer School. Those in the Western Division who were with TCA when the 10As were in use will appreciate why the term "earthshaking" is used and will also possibly understand the condition of one's nerves after hearing them take off on the SW runway past the hangar every three to five minutes. Anyways, noise or not, more power to 'em and here's hoping they turn out lots of air observers. The presence of the above 16 machines, plus eight club machines and a fleet of trucks, cars, steam rollers, graders and 30 ton Letourneaus engaged in resurfacing the runways makes quite a problem in getting our trips in and out without turning them into hurdle jumpers. We don't envy Jimmy Bell, the airport manager, his job of keeping everybody out of everybody else's way. One TCA pilot on Trip 23 reported seeing vivid lightning flashes close by to NNE, but since taking Carter's Little Liver Pills, is all right.

Telegrams

Messages will be transmitted by radio free of charge, as a convenience to passengers for transmission by commercial telegraph services at regular rates from ground stations. Ask the stewardess for this service.

— TCA brochure, June 1941

On April 15, 1941, while Gordon McGregor, the Webster trophy winner who was now an RCAF wing commander, was leading the first RCAF offensive patrol above Boulogne, Trans Canada Airlines was extending its service to Dartmouth Airport near Halifax, finally covering the length of the Canadian mainland from sea to sea. Malton cargo clerk Ross Smyth remembered that on his familiarization flight to Halifax, blackout curtains were pulled over the air-craft's windows twenty minutes before they landed. He did not appreciate why this precaution was taken until he rode the ferry from Dartmouth to the city and saw the "multitude of ships" at anchor in the harbour.

That month, in compliance with the agreement on bilateral air routes hammered out the previous September, the United States Civil Aeronautics Board gave TCA permission to operate two daily flights between Toronto's Malton Airport and New York's LaGuardia Airport. A contract for servicing its aircraft was entered into with American Airlines, and the first flight into the still neutral US took place on May 10, 1941. Demand was so great that by June there were three daily round trips. Max Church, pleased to be posted to his hometown of Toronto, worked the New York run. "Our schedule called for six one-way flights over three days. On the fourth day the pilot was on call or 'reserve,' the fifth day was his day off, and on the sixth the cycle started all over again. We used to see the network of rotating airway beacons between Buffalo and New York that the U.S. government had built for their airmail pilots to follow at night and always wondered about them in their single-engined biplanes 'pushing the weather' in order to get the mail through. We felt rather proud of our twin-engined Lockheeds and our superior instrument training."

With the war, passengers on TCA flights to New York were faced with more stringent immigration and currency regulations. Counter staff were taught to make sure that Canadians travelling to the United States possessed valid Canadian passports and US visa or border permit cards, and had completed their Canadian Travel Permit forms "H," obtainable through any bank.

Joe Fontaine was the airline's New York publicity representative. "Every now and then a true incident occurred that put to shame the best comic stories dealing with delightful old ladies. When a truly delightful old lady made her first air trip from Toronto aboard a Trans Canada Airlines flight to New York in 1942 she told the stewardess Margaret Dickson that she had ear trouble. Margaret gave her a package of gum and assured her that if she chewed it she would be fine. As the plane reached cruising altitude, the passenger called Miss Dickson and 'bellowed' that she was now 'stone deaf.' Margaret was worried and frantically pointed to the gum. The old lady pointed to her ears. She had chewed the gum and plugged her ears with it. A minor operation with a hairpin ensued, the gum was brought out, and the passenger's hearing restored—somewhat."

New York was the only foreign station the airline had, and as expected, TCA's city office there was like no other. An employee described a typical day thus:

> We at NYX start the day in the middle of the night. The office opens at 6:00 a.m. as you collide with refuse cans and policemen in the New York dim-out. Today Trip 21 is delayed two and a half hours. On this particular morning all the passengers

have left their homes at five-thirty. Breakfasts on the plane are cancelled because of the delay. Naturally, the passengers turn up at the airport ravenous. Employee-in-charge Janet Mitchell arrives to get everyone off in the right spirit. Concentration is a simple matter since the only outside disturbances are the testing of the air raid sirens, the chimes of the clock across the street, the shrieking whistle of the doorman at the Stork Club (which is below the office) as he impatiently signals for taxi-cabs and the Fifth Avenue busses starting up like Lodestars with bronchitis. Little incidents occur to break up the monot-ony such as Mr. Geddes coming up from Washington and expecting to continue on to Toronto and Ottawa only to find that the space has been cancelled because Mr. Geddes went to Toronto the night before. This sort of thing has been happen-ing every time Mr. Geddes travels, until a great light dawns. It develops that Mr. Geddes is two passengers! At 2300 a slight-ly dazed operator signs off the "tely" (teleprinter) and wan-ders down the seven flights of stairs of the Eighth Avenue subway station.

Things were hardly better at New York's new airport, named for its mayor Fiorello LaGuardia. William Munroe, the TCA agent there, complained that "in the largest airport of the largest city in the world" he was one of only two rep-resentatives of the airline. "Here Trans Canada is announced as Transcontinental and not Trans Canada, if it is announced at all."

S.J. Hungerford resigned from the board of the CNR in July 1941, and R.C. Vaughan, a railway and steamship authority, was elected to take his place. But this time it did not automatically follow that he would be appointed president of the airline as well, as TCA was now judged stable enough to have a presi-dent of its own. That post went instead to Herbert Symington, K.C., on July 24, 1941. Symington, a Winnipeg lawyer, had begun his career in the trans-portation industry in 1906 as a solicitor for the Grand Trunk Railway. Appointed to the board of directors for the CNR in 1936, he accompanied Howe on his "Dawn to Dusk" flight the next year. "Canada's energies," the new president wrote to his employees, "are now directed to Victory, and the largest proportion of TCA business must be war business." With Howe and Mackenzie King, he believed that TCA could negotiate an independent course in post-war international civil aviation, away from British imperial schemes and American domination.

One of Symington's first priorities was dealing with a proposal from Sir Edward Beatty received on August 15 via Howe. Beatty was suggesting the cre-ation of a single airline in Canada, jointly owned by the federal government and the Canadian Pacific Railway. He pointed out that it would eliminate wasteful competition domestically and allow the country to field a strong

Top: The Liberator LB-30A (at top) in which Prime Minister W.L. Mackenzie King flew to Britain and Scotland in August 1941. NAC 132639
Bottom: King preparing to reboard the aircraft at Gander with G/C K.M. Guthrie (at left).
NAC 116995

national team with which to conduct international negotiations. Howe replied that while the war was on, no permanent solutions to Canadian commercial aviation could be worked out practicably. However, as the minister of munitions and supply, he did not object to the CPR buying up more than 50 percent of the shares of Canadian Airways.

On August 19, 1941, after a seance in which he consulted his long-departed mother and former Prime Minister Wilfrid Laurier, Mackenzie King took the first aircraft flight of his life. A Consolidated Liberator had been outfitted with a bunk and two reclining chairs for his personal use, and he left St. Hubert airport in Montreal in midmorning, touched down at Gander at sunset, and then slept soundly all the way across the Atlantic to Prestwick, Scotland. From there he took a train to London to confer with Churchill and visit with Canadian troops in England. He returned on September 7, becoming the first VIP to use the new airport at Dorval. He was met by Howe but refused the minister's offer to avail himself of the TCA flight to Ottawa; he took the train instead. Mackenzie King never did display any enthusiasm for flying on the airline that he had helped set up. He disliked the mode of transport altogether and explained that he would only take an aircraft if absolutely necessary. Vincent Massey, the Canadian high commissioner with whom King had met in London, knew many Canadians in Britain who envied the prime minister's power to get a seat on an aircraft home.

The Consolidated Liberator that King used was part of the Return Ferry Service (RFS), which brought ferry pilots back to Montreal. Next to the B-17 "Flying Fortress," the Liberator was the United States's most famous World War II strategic bomber. It had first flown on December 29, 1939, and almost immediately the desperate French government had placed an order with its manufacturer, Consolidated Vultee, for the export version, the LB- (for Land Bomber) 30A. However, France surrendered before the aircraft could be delivered, and they were passed instead to the British as part of the Lend-Lease program. The RAF had great misgivings about the value of an "altitude-limited" bomber that had neither armour nor self-sealing fuel tanks, and they adapted it instead for transport and maritime operations. In the meantime, in order to avoid giving offence to American isolationists, the British had ensured that the RFS would be entirely a civil operation by charging their new government airline, British Overseas Airways Corporation (BOAC), with the job of running it. At Lord Beaverbrook's insistence, the British Air Ministry had then handed over six of the French LB-30As to what was ostensibly the Atlantic division of BOAC.

With the bomb bay doors sealed, a wooden floor fitted up to the tail and benches along each side, the "Libs" were devoid of comforts such as cabin heat or windows, and they were hardly competition for Pan American's luxurious flying boats, which still flew to Lisbon in neutral Portugal. To George Lothian, the Liberator "flew like a great water-soaked log with none of the gracefulness usually found at that time only in British aircraft."[7] But because of its Pratt & Whitney R-1830 Twin Wasp engines and revolutionary Davis airfoil wing, it had the longest range of any aircraft at that time and was able to cruise steadily though slowly across the ocean.

Vital to the war effort though the BOAC flights were, they made a mockery of the terms of the Joint Operating Company of 1935. While it had never been formalized, that agreement required that any commercial transatlantic service have the participation of the Canadians and the Irish, and although aware that the JOC had been negotiated under peacetime circumstances and before the birth of TCA, Howe, Symington and Massey saw this legal breach as an opportunity to initiate Canada's own transatlantic service. The British were not unaware of Canadian ambitions, either. When the Royal Air Force Ferry Command took over ATFERO's duties on July 20, 1941, putting CPAS and Beaverbrook out of the picture, the British Air Ministry approached Howe to ask if Trans Canada Airlines would like to run the RFS. It was—as the British well knew—a rhetorical question. Having lost both aircraft and trained employees to the armed forces and committed to doing maintenance for the RCAF, TCA was hardly in a position to run ATFERO. Besides, with Pan American Airways forced to terminate its flights at Lisbon, both governments understood the ramifications of Canadians operating American Lend-Lease aircraft between North America and Britain. The United States, Howe was warned, might protest the use of the Liberators to benefit a civilian airline, particularly a publicly owned one like TCA.[8]

At this point, however, Harold Balfour, the British parliamentary undersecretary in the Air Ministry, held out the carrot that TCA could maintain the BOAC aircraft in Montreal, and perhaps when there were sufficient Liberators available, one or two could be given to the Canadians to operate under TCA's own markings. Until such time, to gain transatlantic experience, a pair of the BOAC aircraft might be loaned to TCA to operate and its maple leaf insignia painted on them. They would remain British aircraft in the meantime and the RFS would bear the cost of operating them and pay the salaries of the Canadian crews.

Jim Bain attended one of the BOAC/TCA meetings in Montreal and wrote about it in his memoirs. "After discussion it seemed to me that this was an excellent opportunity for TCA to get started on the Atlantic run. I somewhat exceeded my terms of reference and committed the company to taking on the maintenance of the Liberator fleet. When I got back to Winnipeg and said I had promised to maintain the Return Ferry Service, I was *fired* by Ron George, the Acting Operations Manager."[9]

Bain refused to withdraw his commitment and was on the point of leaving TCA to take a job with BOAC when Symington and Howe decided to profit from the opportunity, and Charlie Palaisy, Dorval's maintenance supervisor, was put in charge of the Liberator program. Because these were the first scheduled oceanic flights and the great, lumbering four-engined aircraft were in constant use shuttling back and forth over the ocean, maintenance of their Pratt

& Whitney Twin Row R-1830 engines was critical. Added to the problem was the engine manufacturer's warning that the carburetor heat of the R-1830 was inadequate for the severe icing encountered over the Atlantic. With time to do only the simplest inspections in Britain, the maintenance contract was awarded to TCA at Dorval. The airline had access to Pratt & Whitney expertise at its plants at Longueuil, Quebec, and Hartford, Connecticut, and the engine manufacturer also assigned permanent staff to Dorval. So too did the aircraft's manufacturers, Consolidated Vultee and Canadian Car & Foundry, the latter sharing part of Hangar 6 with TCA, where the company's employees recognized the fact that besides helping the war effort, the BOAC contract was preparation for the day when the airline would have its own multi-engined aircraft. By December 1943, 300 TCA employees were engaged in servicing the BOAC aircraft, performing three checks on the Liberators—"two check" (every 30–40 flying hours), "three check" (every 100 hours) and the major "four check" (every 200 hours).

Sammy Reid, chief mechanic on the BOAC program, had been one of the Canadian Airways Vancouver Airport staff on that historic September day in 1937 when the Seattle route was taken over by TCA. For much of his youth Reid had fixed aircraft in the bush and started his career in aviation in 1928 with Pacific Airways in Vancouver and then with Canadian Airways when they bought Pacific out. In 1940 TCA loaned him to the BCATP in Windsor as chief mechanic. Sammy went on to use his engine experience on the "Libs" and later the TCA Lancastrians, and he returned to Vancouver in 1949 as maintenance training assistant. Many years later, remembering all the aircraft he had worked on, he said, "Each new aircraft type was a favourite with the mechanics. After a few years we would perfect maintenance and overhaul procedures. Then the aircraft would become obsolete and we'd start all over again, ironing the bugs out of a new model."

"The bulk of our personnel at BOAC are locally hired—Montreal and the region," *Between Ourselves* reported. "At least 50 percent are French Canadian and if ever there was a superstition that they are not a technically inclined race it has been dispelled by the quality of work they have done and are doing."[10] That this comment was published in the newsletter of the national airline, a company with its head office in the province of Quebec, is deplorable but indicative of a culture in which bilingualism, along with equal opportunity, employment of visible minorities and gender equality was a long way off. On the other hand, from the very first, the annual reports of Trans Canada Airlines were published in both languages, although except for the rare article in French, *Between Ourselves*, all brochures, timetables and forms remained in English—that is, until TCA flew to Paris.

Once Ferry Command had become part of the RAF, aircrew could be drawn from the graduating classes of the BCATP, where promising pupils destined for long-range operations such as coastal and bomber commands were selected. Trans Canada Airlines could also be tapped for experienced pilots, and in

September 1941 Ron George ordered George Lothian and "Jock" Barclay to report to the ATFERO office at Dorval. TCA's expansion into the BOAC program having come when pilots were already in short supply, Lothian and Barclay's secondment to fly Hudsons to Prestwick via Gander was limited to three

Top: Machinist at work at TCA's Winnipeg facility, c.1940. Hugh Reid photo
Bottom: Planning a flight. A weatherman goes over charts with Captain H. W. Seagrim (two stripes), First Officer W.E. Barnes (one stripe) and the dispatcher (right).

months. "We went to the ramp on the day before our flights for a look at our aircraft," Lothian wrote. "There they were, true enough versions of the Lockheed 14s, but somehow we had envisioned a shiny new aircraft straight from the factory... What did we find? Two Hudsons in drab camouflage war paint which had obviously seen a good deal of life... We were standing there a little dismayed when who should join us but Adolph Merta, who had for years been the Lockheed representative in Winnipeg. He followed our gaze and must have read our minds. 'Those are your two. When I heard you were going out on them I gave them a real going over. I even put in a new set of controls. They are in good shape.'"[11]

Another difference between TCA aircraft and these Hudsons was the complicated fuel system on the military craft. Besides the usual wing tanks, because of dangers of the Atlantic there were also auxiliary fuel tanks, one in the passenger cabin and a second in the bomb bay. After takeoff, the cabin tank was opened while the wing tanks were shut off. In TCA service shutting the wing tanks down would mean both engines quitting instantly.

In 1978, in the 50th anniversary issue of *Canadian Aviation*, Lothian wrote of his first flight across the Atlantic that "we had no fixes or lines of position since we had left the coast of Newfoundland, so the moon was welcomed when it began to show dimly through the haze ahead of the aircraft. It stayed in view long enough for the navigator to get a shot, which when plotted across our track showed us at 35 degrees West. Not much in the way of information as it gave no indication of our track, but some consolation that we were making headway toward Ireland... or somewhere."

When he and Barclay had ferried the Hudsons over to Prestwick, Lothian was struck by the history of the moment. "Neither of us thought of it at the time, but ours were the first crossings by TCA pilots." Lothian returned to St. John's on the tiny ship *Mosdale Castle*, feeling he was the target of every U-boat in the Atlantic. On later flights he came back with eighteen other pilots on an RFS Liberator, a windowless metal cocoon in which all of them suffered the twenty-four-hour flight in a cabin temperature of –30 degrees F. Describing these RFS flights home, he recalled that "all talking ceased the instant the engines were started... When they were opened up for the endless takeoff, it was not uncommon to see people crossing themselves; and there was always some sadist aboard who would start to intone a countdown." What must have made it worse for all the pilots on board was the knowledge that three of the RFS "Libs" had recently crashed, killing all twenty-two crew on each plane—almost a third of the total number of the available ferry pilots.

It was these three crashes that forced the issue of direct Canadian participation for both the British Air Ministry and Ottawa. On December 6, 1941, Vincent Massey wrote to Howe not only about the impossibility of obtaining passage from London to Ottawa but about the volume of diplomatic mail, machine parts and blueprints for the armament plants in Canada—to say nothing of armed forces mail—that threatened to overwhelm his high commission.

His suggestion that Canada should disregard the British and Americans and establish its own transatlantic air service received wide circulation and much approval in senior government circles. It was certainly more attractive than operating RFS Liberators on behalf of BOAC, a potential post-war rival. Howe decided that TCA would continue to train its crews for the ferry service, while at the same time pursuing the establishment of a separate service. American entry into the war in December 1941 ended the chance of any protest that might have been expected from that quarter as now two US airlines, TWA and American Export Airlines, were flying regularly across the Atlantic.

Afraid that the Canadian connection would jeopardize the relationship they had negotiated with the Americans concerning Atlantic flights, the British government vacillated about giving TCA control over the Liberators that its pilots would fly. At the same time, Massey's dispatches calling for an independent air service flowed unabated from London to Ottawa, prompting Howe at last to fly to Britain himself to discuss the matter with the Air Ministry. But seeing the problems at Canada House at first hand, he became thoroughly dissatisfied with Balfour's long-promised loan of the two Liberators and in characteristic fashion acted immediately. Sensing Canada's potential as a future world aviation power, in May 1942 the government set up the Interdepartmental Committee on International Aviation (ICIA) to formulate Canada's post-war policy on transatlantic air service. On September 26 the British, Newfoundland and Irish governments were told that the Canadian government, on the advice of its legal department, was not about to abrogate the 1935 agreement but would circumvent it. A month later Howe announced to the Cabinet War Committee that it was time to take unilateral action and establish a government air service for the purpose of taking mail and personnel to and from England. He estimated that it would be necessary to build fifty suitable airliners for this and, until they entered service, thought he could count on the Americans to loan Canada three aircraft.[12] No one in the CWC dared argue with Howe and the Canadian Government Trans Atlantic Air Service (CGTAS) was born.

That same month Lothian, Barclay and Lindsay Rood were told to attend flight school in Dorval on the Liberator. Dave Tennant, TCA's engineer at Dorval, was already flying in Liberators to gain mechanical experience. In all, three complete TCA crews were slated to be trained for the RFS. They were:

Captains	**First Officers**	**Radio Officers**
George Lothian	W.R. Bell	G. Nettleton
M.B. Barclay	H.I. Hayes	A.J. Blackwood
J.L. Rood	A.H. Palmer	J.A. Webster

Flight Engineers	**Navigators**
F.D. Burgess	J. Gilmore (RCAF)
J. Wilson	D. Florence (RCAF)
R.R. Spafford	H. Thomae (RCAF)

Without the navigators from the RCAF, it is safe to say that CGTAS could never have been established. Flying across the Atlantic Ocean beyond the safety of a radio range network had put a premium on this ancient brotherhood of stargazers and sextant users whom electronics had supposedly made obsolete. Providentially, navigators were still necessary to the air force. Observing this, the journalist Ross Wilmot predicted that "gadgets had their limitations but human skill was still essential in following the pathways of the air. The best navigators in the RCAF," he wrote, "were being chosen for ferrying and some of them held pilot's licences as well." No matter what their ability, all had to take a three-week course in navigation followed by a check trip to Bermuda, done entirely by astro-navigation. It was from this air force elite that the navigators for the Canadian Government Trans Atlantic Air Service came.

Gilmore and Florence were RCAF veterans decorated from tours of duty and Thomae was an American who had enlisted in the RCAF early in the war, then loaned to Ferry Command and BOAC before transferring to CGTAS. Many of his flights were with Lothian, who later wrote: "Harold was a professed agnostic who knew more about the Bible...than most people. On one occasion we had been pushing our way for hours through a deluge of sleet and rain...We had been buried in cloud for three hours and there was no way of getting a fix. I looked over my shoulder for a glance at the chart to update our estimated position. In the dim reading light...Harold was hunched at the navigating table reading the Bible. A little startled, I continued to watch as he paused every few lines to make margin notes, 'nonsense,' 'poppycock,' and so on. Unable to stand it any longer, I finally exploded, 'For Pete's sake, if you want to do that at least wait until we are over land.'"[13] Howe, Symington and Massey were pleased that the TCA crews were flying the BOAC "Libs" but less pleased that the British still would not promise that the Canadian-piloted aircraft would be used exclusively for Canadian passengers and mail. The most they would concede was that if a Canadian VIP such as Mackenzie King were to fly the Atlantic, Ferry Command would try to get him on board one of the TCA-manned Liberators. As for Canadian forces mail piling up on either side of the Atlantic, it would continue to be transported on a space-available basis.

By the end of 1941 Trans Canada Airlines had been in existence for five years. It operated only 18 of the 214 commercial aircraft registered in Canada, but accounted for more than 50 percent of the miles flown, more than 40 percent of the passengers and not quite 40 percent of the mail carried. A divisional headquarters had now been set up in Moncton, and encouraged by the very modern airport terminal building that the city of Edmonton constructed in 1942 for TCA and CPA, the airline was looking north, planning to expand between Edmonton and Whitehorse as soon as the airway to Alaska was complete, though it was a plan that was bound to cause competition with the Canadian Pacific Airlines.

In signing the annual report in December 1941, Symington must have wondered how his personnel were able to do it. Over a route of 4,857 miles the air-

Wake-up call on a blustery day at Dorval airport as ground crew scramble to remove the wing covers from Liberator II AL507. A return ferry service aircraft in late war markings, it sports the BOAC Speedbird on the nose and looks little worse for wear after being out in the cold overnight. British Airways.

craft now flew 22,670 miles daily, more than 8.4 million miles annually. Between 1940 and 1941, the number of passengers carried had increased by 60 percent, airmail by 50 percent and air express by 64 percent. But as of December 1941 the airline had only 12 Lockheed 14Hs and 6 Lodestars, and to help Grant McConachie's airline, Yukon Southern Air Transport, adequately service the Alaskan supply line, the government had requisitioned TCA's *CF-TCR* and *CF-TCS* for that route. (*CF-TCS*, re-registered as *CF-CPD*, crashed into Mt. Cheam in the Fraser Valley of BC on December 20, 1942.) In addition, TCA had lost *CF-TCP* in February when it crashed at Armstrong, Ontario, killing all aboard. Further expansion was also hampered by the airline's difficulty in purchasing more aircraft because it was no longer the manufacturers but the Office of Production Management in Washington that allocated planes.

RESULTS OF OPERATIONS

	1941	1940	Differences
Operating Revenues	$5,807,794.03	$4,592,383.39	$1,215,410.64
Operating Expenses	5,306,136.00	3,855,934.04	1,450,201.96
	$ 501,658.03	$ 736,449.35	($ 234,791.32)

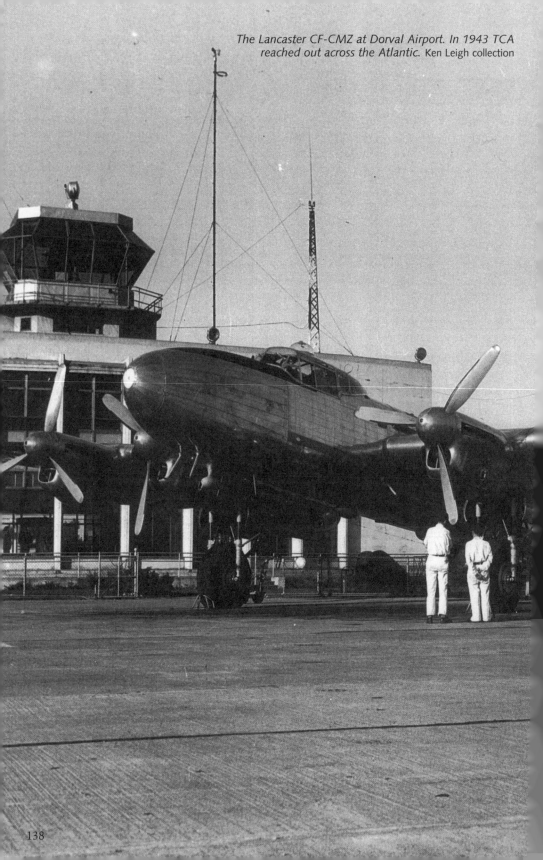

The Lancaster CF-CMZ at Dorval Airport. In 1943 TCA reached out across the Atlantic. Ken Leigh collection

CHAPTER 6

I Am Resolved

As the Sun comes up on 1942, this world is wracked with deadly anguish. A Canadian mother tearfully eyes a vacant chair; a young wife anxiously scans the news; a little girl lies bleeding in Russia; a hunted youth in Serbia slinks through the night; an English woman shudders at the shadow in the sky; an old man in Poland wonders if release will come in his time.

- I am resolved to undertake vigorously the work which lies before me.
- I am resolved to be cheerful and uncomplaining at all times.
- I am resolved to be tolerant of the shortcomings of others, realising that to make an effort is commendable, to attempt nothing is deadly.
- I am resolved gladly to do without some of those things that I am accustomed to enjoy—for it is good to deny oneself—even to suffer in a noble cause.
- I am resolved that if I am fitted to serve my country best in the fighting forces, I shall take my place proudly beside my comrades.

BRAVE MEN SHALL NOT DIE BECAUSE I FALTERED.

Issued by the Department of Munitions and Supply for display on TCA premises

Trans Canada Airlines' continuing financial deficit in 1941 had been due to expansion of services, high turnover in staff and increased labour and material costs due to the war. Although the Post Office had taken the mail contract in the Maritimes away from Canadian Airways and awarded it to TCA on April 15, the importance of mail as revenue continued to decline from 1939 when it was 70 percent, to 1940 (62 percent) and 1941 (53 percent). It would decline even further in 1942 (44 percent) and in 1943, when it amounted to only 37 percent of the total revenue. This was partly because of the increase in passenger business and because airmail payments were reduced as a wartime measure from 60 cents to 45 cents a mile. Speaking before the Standing Committee on Railway and Shipping on April 30, 1942, Herbert Symington objected to the rate change: while it saved the Post Office money, it was causing a loss for the airline. Uncharacteristically, he got no support from Howe, who believed TCA could afford the loss while the government, in the midst of a global war, could not. Airmail was paid for on the basis of the number of miles flown, not the poundage carried, so when the TCA Act was drawn up in 1937 it had been anticipated that the cost to the Post Office would decrease steadily and the volume of airmail increase as the airline's operations were extended. This had been to the airline's advantage in pre-passenger days as revenue had been assured whether the mail was light or heavy. The amount of mail certainly grew over the years, so much so that sometimes passenger seating could not be sold to capacity on transcontinental night flights because of the heavy mail load. By 1943 it is estimated that TCA was carrying approximately 200,000,000 letters annually—apart from the transatlantic mail service—but although this was a volume increase of 61 percent, it brought an increase of only 9 percent in mail revenue. As the annual report for that year noted rather pointedly: "It did, however, result in a substantial increase in the revenue of the Post Office."

Year	Airmail (lbs)	Rate per mile (cents)	Rate per mile (lbs)	Average load per mile (lbs)
1939	523,906	60	2.7	221
1940	927,037	60	3.2	187
1941	1,389,614	48	2.1	230
1942	2,308,812	46	1.4	321
1943 (9 months)	2,689,747	43	1.1	443

The bitterness toward the Post Office that surfaced in the annual report for 1943 was keenly felt throughout the airline's administration. This prompted Bill English to remind his staff in a memo that the Post Office was still the airline's best customer, "and more important, it is by association with the Post Office that TCA is able to render its greatest service to the people of Canada.

Not everyone is able to take a trip by air these days, but there are few people in Canada today who do not buy an airmail stamp to speed their own and the nation's business."

Aware of the growing hostility, officials at the Post Office felt their department was becoming the weaker partner in the arrangement, especially because of the proposed transatlantic services. Since the postmaster general was also a TCA director, the issue was certain to be a future source of trouble, and as he had been accustomed to dictating terms to Canadian Airways, he was prepared to cross swords with the minister to improve the situation in relation to TCA.

New and Improved Wartime Schedules!

Above the Weather! Up above, where TCA planes fly, there's bright sunshine. It is crisp and clear; there's a brilliance to familiar landscapes. It may be very different on the ground but with up to the minute flight information disclosing good conditions aloft, TCA planes take off and in a few minutes you are above it all.

— TCA advertisement, January 1942

Scotten, Jack Clarence SGT(WAG) R101980. From St. James Manitoba. Killed In Action Sep. 11/42 age 20. #405 City of Vancouver Squadron (Ducimus). Halifax aircraft #BB 212 was damaged over the target. Sgt.s J.C. Scotten and V.R. French were ordered to bail out over enemy territory and were both killed. The aircraft returned to England but the flaps were not lowered fully during the landing at Topcliffe, Yorkshire and the aircraft swung off the runway and hit a parked aircraft. F.S. Drennan was killed in the crash. Sergeant Wireless Operator Air Gunner Scotten was buried at Monchen Gladbach, Germany, exhumed, and reburied in the War Cemetery at Rheinberg, Germany.

The war also affected what the stewardesses had to be proficient in when making conversation with their passengers. The January 1942 class was taught subjects that three years before would have been considered unfit for female ears. Because of the military personnel that increasingly made up the passenger list, along with topographical details of the Canada that they would be flying over, they were briefed on such subjects as meteorology, aircraft types and communications as well as how to recognize military ranks.

Margaret Dickson, supervisory stewardess for the trainees, was aware that the airline was losing its stewardesses almost as fast as she could train them.

Hanbury, Bruce Alexander SAL(P) C1329. From Vancouver, BC. Killed Dec. 31/42 age 21. #409 Nighthawk Squadron (Media Nox Meridies Noster). S/L. Hanbury was demonstrating the flying characteristics of a Beaufighter aircraft to P/O P.M. Sweet and WO. J.W. Dickson when their Beaufighter #T3142 went into a flat spin at 10,000 feet. Hanbury, Sweet and Dickson were all killed when they crashed at Lexeton, Dutgate, Lincolnshire. Squadron Leader Pilot Hanbury is buried in the Scopwick Church Burial Ground, Lincolnshire, England.

In February 1942 the TCA staff at Malton coped with "the Great Snowstorm" that befell their city. Maintenance worker Ross Smyth's diary tells part of the story.

Feb. 7. To work in the afternoon with Al Brown and Dave Mathias. Snows heavily and windy. Our relief does not arrive at midnight. We are stranded at the airport. Some passengers en route to city get stuck and almost freeze to death during night in cars.

Feb. 8. Continue working through having had only half hour's sleep last night. Trips operate through Toronto but unable to load any mail or passengers here account roads. Start ferry service flying between Malton and de Havilland Airport on Dufferin Street. Relief Ozzie Candy and Jack Fletcher arrive by plane at dark. Have worked 27 hours. Too tired to sleep. Eat with pilots Herb Hopson, Don Barnett and stewardess Delia Murphy. Unable to operate ferry service after dark as D.H. field has no lights. Finally go to sleep at midnight on some empty mail bags.

Feb. 9. Roads finally opened in the morning but we operate ferry service to D.H. field to be certain of getting flight crews in. Fly to D.H. airport with Captain Barney Rawson and other employees."[1]

The following December, Smyth was promoted to radio operator and posted to Dorval, perhaps as a reward for remaining at his post—although his diary says the promotion was only the result of a wartime shortage of trained personnel.

In the winter of 1942–43 the airline flew RAF pilot officer George Frederick "Buzz" Beurling across Canada on a Victory Bond tour. As the highest scoring Canadian-born air ace of World War II, Beurling was feted everywhere as "the Knight of Malta." Ironically, Beurling's secondary mission on this trip was to encourage Canadians to enlist in the RCAF—the service that had twice refused him entry in 1939.

By 1942 the number of women on TCA's payroll had climbed dramatically, but the changes were most noticeable at the TCA hangar in Winnipeg. "To see a pretty head bending over an ignition harness would have caused a commotion in a pre-war machine shop," wrote Gudrun Bjerring in the Winnipeg *Free Press*, "but not so today at the Trans Canada Airlines maintenance and overhaul division. There women are doing men's work which only proves that women's place is not necessarily in the home, but where she is needed." And she quoted Jim Bain, TCA's superintendent of maintenance, as saying: "Training girls to do productive machine work was a radical development, but it proved worthwhile. In repetitive work we have found them generally much more efficient than men." He added that once they had been taught a job, they could be counted on to do it well. Mrs. May MacMaster, for instance, had been adjusting and calibrating indicators in the instrument shop and it "was just the type of work she had been looking for." She told Bjerring, "I find it exceptionally interesting and hope I never have to go back to office work." In the accessory shop where the work was heavier and dirtier, Mary Goshlak echoed MacMaster's sentiments. An indication that the airline planned to utilize more women in its new propeller overhaul shop was that there were as many women's toilets as men's in this building. When the war ended, however, women's futures in the TCA shops were uncertain. Bain reassured the reporter that "in some departments, such as upholstery, we have no intention of replacing them." But he expected that all other jobs would be given to returning soldiers.

TCA Lodestar pilot and stewardess with RAF Spitfire pilot George Frederick "Buzz" Beurling (centre), in 1942–43 during his cross-Canada Victory Bond tour. CNR Archives 19901

Meanwhile the airline's maintenance, baggage handlers and ground personnel, all members of the International Association of Machinists (IAM), were unnerved by the increasing number of females on the shop floor, and William Cook, chairman of Airline Union Lodge 714, wrote what many of them were asking. "Are the girls holding their own?" Then he answered his own question.

> They are a little slower in picking things up because they haven't the same mechanical aptitude as men, and are also handicapped physically. Yet, on their behalf, it can be said that some of them are fully as good as males and at certain jobs demonstrably more than holding their own—with greater patience and a lighter touch, especially with the delicate weld-

ing of aluminium and its alloys. Does all this suggest a moral? The next time any of us feel inclined to disparage the ability of the girls, let's ask ourselves these questions: Could TCA carry on its present operations without them? Could the Company have expanded and performed its work for the RCAF without them? We think not. A year and a half ago the girls forced us to recognize them and invite them into Lodge 714 by demanding that they be admitted as members with full privileges. They did this, aware that their stay as employees of TCA was limited to the duration of the war. As one girl so wisely said, "Who knows? I may be holding open my future husband's job for him when he returns."

Widespread use of credit cards for air travel was still three decades away, but as early as 1933, to attract the "frequent fliers" of the day, US airlines had been using an "Air Travel Plan" card, introduced to TCA by W.J. "Jack" Dalby, the system traffic manager, on May 1, 1943. Dalby had become familiar with this system while working on the west coast, first while employed by Thomas Cook as a traffic representative for Seattle–Juneau flights, and later for Canadian Airways and United Airlines. Under this plan, the airline issued Air Travel Cards to the officers and employees of subscribing companies or, if the subscriber was an individual, to members of his immediate family. To obtain a card, a subscriber with an approved credit rating made a deposit of $425. His card was honoured by seventeen of the major airlines in North America, which would issue air tickets and carry the passenger's excess baggage without the immediate payment of cash. Besides the convenience of not having to carry large amounts of cash, the customer was also given a 15 percent discount on fares and billed at the end of the month.

As part of the revenue accounting division, the Air Travel Card department was shoehorned into Room 705 of the Lombard building in downtown Winnipeg, where the airline had moved its administration departments in December 1941 after outgrowing its space at the airport. Under the direction of George Featherstone of accounting, desks, typewriters, files and accounting staff had disappeared into the empty reaches of the huge building so thoroughly that the night watchman would hear bloodcurdling screams of lost employees echoing down its corridors years later—or so it was said.

On May 26, 1943, Queen Wilhelmina of the Netherlands, seeking temporary refuge in Canada, travelled on a special TCA flight from Montreal to Ottawa, where she was met by the prime minister. The TCA crew were Captain Art Hollinsworth, First Officer Bob Smuck and Stewardess Ina

Molyneaux. In July the Queen took another TCA flight from Ottawa to a certain east coast airport (the name was censored) to board ship for Britain. In recognition of the part they played in the Queen's travels, on January 20, 1944, W.G. Boissevain, chargé d'affaires of the Netherlands Legation in Ottawa, presented the TCA crew with a gold pin in the form of a "W." The recipients were Captain W.W. Fowler, First Officer Art Tomkin and Stewardess M.L. Clinch.

Despite repeated representations from the Newfoundland government, TCA's president, Herbert Symington, had no interest in extending TCA's routes past Halifax, and it was out of the question, in Symington's view, to land TCA Lodestars at the half-built airport at the fishing village of Torbay outside St. John's. Designed to provide air coverage for the Atlantic convoys, the Torbay airport was not far from Lester's Field, where in 1919 Captain J. Alcock and Lt. A. Whitten Brown had taken off to make the first successful transatlantic crossing. When the RCAF moved coastal reconnaissance squadrons to Torbay, the Department of National Defence (DND) added its voice to that of the Newfoundland government, pointing out that if TCA could supply transport for DND personnel, they would not have to do so. But Symington still resisted; TCA had too few Lodestars to extend service to the island colony, and there was too little commercial traffic generated there to warrant it. Then in October 1941, Leonard Earle of Harvey and Company (general shipping agents and importers) of St. John's went to Ottawa to meet with Symington and present him with requests from both the Newfoundland government and the RCAF commanding officer at Torbay for air service. Seeing Symington's reluctance, Earle pointedly asked what TCA's reaction would be to an American airline providing passenger, mail and freight connections between Torbay and the Maritimes. The Newfoundland government had, in fact, opened negotiations with Northeast Airlines—the same airline that would soon be flying to Goose Bay—to connect Torbay with the mainland. The implications of what such a service would mean to relations between Newfoundland and Canada, plus subsequent pressure exerted by London and by a concerned Department of External Affairs in Ottawa gave Symington no choice but to comply. On May 1, 1942, at 4:15 p.m., a TCA Lodestar landed at Torbay and regular service to Canada was begun via Moncton and Sydney, continuing on to the air base at Gander the same day. With the heavy military presence in Newfoundland, the load factor was higher than estimated and reservations had to be made months in advance, so a second flight was added in November and a third in 1943. When Torbay was closed in by weather, the military air base at Argentia was designated as the alternate field.

To no one's surprise, Harvey and Company became the airline's representatives in Newfoundland. The firm's origins predated Canada's: it was the

Gander airport. Under wartime pressures, TCA was at first reluctant to expand its overseas services to include Gander. When the company initiated Lodestar flights on May 1, 1942, under pressure from the British and Canadian governments and the RCAF, it was rewarded by full loads and expansion of services to the "busiest little airport in the world."

direct descendant of the Bermuda Trading Company of 1667. Besides owning cod fishing and cold storage plants, baking bread and making furniture, Harvey and Co. would take advantage of the Air Age by becoming agents in Newfoundland for TCA, BOAC, Northeast Airlines and Pan American Airways. They maintained two offices for TCA, one in the business area of St. John's and the other in the Newfoundland Hotel for passenger traffic, and the airline staff at both were native Newfoundlanders.

Within the first year TCA carried 31,681 passengers to and from the colony. So packed were the flights to Torbay that in March 1943 the officer commanding Eastern Air Command sent an urgent communiqué to the secretary of air, DND, Ottawa. There were no civilian facilities at the airport, he wrote, and to use the toilets, which belonged to the RCAF, passengers were forced to walk through an operational hangar. He requested that due to the intensification of submarine warfare off the Newfoundland coast, high priority be given to constructing a TCA toilet, preferably in a building of its own. A two-storey clapboard building was quickly erected, and it was in use by the airline until 1958.

On January 24, 1943, Captain Gil McLaren and First Officer J.A. Collett in *CF-TCY*, with thirteen passengers on board, were attempting a night landing at

Newfoundland's more famous airport at Gander. Visibility was "blowing snow," and McLaren was already flying on instruments. He made several approach attempts on the east–west runway before spotting what he thought were the approach lights and lined up for landing. They proved to be the boundary lights for the southeast–northwest runway, and *CF-TCY* ran off the far side of the runway into a snowbank. No one was hurt but the damage to the Lodestar was substantial. The undercarriage was crushed along with the bottom of the fuselage, nose and pilot masts, and the propeller blades were bent, but the aircraft was patched up and flown back to Winnipeg for repairs. The cause of the crash was determined to be inadequate runway lighting and pilot error, and the airline lodged a complaint with the RCAF to improve approach lighting. (A year later Captain McLaren became one of the first TCA pilots to complete 10,000 hours in the air, equivalent to sixty times around the world. *CF-TCY* eventually found a home at the Canadian Museum of Flight and Technology in Langley, BC, but sans engines, propellers, instruments and interior furnishings.)

Being on the front line of the Atlantic naval campaign, Gander was not without its problems. Though maintained by the RCAF, its runways were used by the USAF, the RAF Ferry Command, the RFS, three American civil airlines and TCA, making it one of the busiest airports in the world. At first everyone not in the military—TCA personnel, Customs and Immigration, passengers and their baggage—were housed under one roof, and not a very big roof at that. TCA staff boarded at the Gander Inn, which had been made famous by RAF Transport Command pilots, but by the fall of 1943 TCA's expansion had forced the company to find more spacious quarters for them in Number 2 Administration building, where they were given the whole east wing's ground floor. Staff at that time included station manager Dave Weir, radio operator Art Balfour, operators Mike Thomey and Bruce Bettinson, passenger agents Ralph Wilcox, Ian Edwards, Brian Kemp and Harris Bowering, cargo handler Steve Glavine, and mechanics Cec Burton and Frank Lukeman. Despite access to the RCAF officers' messes and the American military bowling alley, TCA personnel found Gander an isolated posting: it had no road access, although a train came through three times a week that could take personnel suffering from cabin fever to the docks, where they could catch the ferry to the mainland. Fishing was a popular local pastime, but TCA staff griped that it was impossible to find worms for bait—there was too much muskeg and rock and not enough soil to support them.

Offshore, the Battle of the Atlantic was by then at its height, and without air coverage for the convoys, its outcome was very much in doubt. To bridge the mid-ocean gap between British and Canadian coverage, the British asked the RCAF to extend their anti-submarine patrols to some 800 miles off Newfoundland, far beyond the range of Number 10 (BR) Squadron's Digbys stationed at Gander. The only aircraft that could do this job were Liberators, and as Howe had discovered, neither the Americans nor the British were willing to

George Lothian.   *J.L. "Lindy" Rood.*

give them up. It irked many Canadians that at a time when their own coasts were in danger, they could see these precious long-range bombers lined up at Dorval Airport to be ferried to distant parts of the Empire. It took unacceptably heavy shipping losses in March 1943 to force the British to part with fifteen Liberators from their own allocation to supply Number 10 (BR) Squadron.

However, the jump from the docile Digbys to the four-engined giants was beyond the RCAF's training capability, and once again TCA was called on to tutor their crews. Ron George sent for captains Lothian and Rood; the latter went to Gander on April 9 and Lothian followed on May 3. They began a relentless training with the air force pilots: seven days a week from dawn to dusk and sometimes well into the night. They flew within a 20- or 30-mile radius of Gander Airport, which Lothian described as "like an area surrounding some treacherous ocean reef for it was dotted with the wrecks of aircraft."

When the RCAF's 10(BR) squadron at Gander got their Liberators, they called on George Lothian and Lindy Rood of TCA to train their pilots. DND photo

One of the wrecks was an RFS Liberator that had made it safely across the Atlantic, but when the area's infamous fogs had shut it out of Gander, its pilots had performed three instrument approaches before tragically running out of fuel and crashing into the bog.

Lothian and Rood quickly discovered that on a military base their civilian clothes were out of place, so the pair adopted air force battle dress with their TCA uniform caps. While their RCAF trainees knew who they were, their uniforms mystified new recruits, who didn't know if the airline captains warranted a salute or not. By May the first Liberator patrols were flying over the Atlantic, and the U-boat threat began to recede. To the TCA pilots' satisfaction, on July 3 while they were training the crews, one of Number 10 Squadron's Liberators, very early into its patrol, depth-charged and damaged the German submarine *U-420*. Lothian and Rood racked up 720 hours before leaving Gander on July 27, having completed the training of all the RCAF pilots, many of whom they would meet again as TCA pilots after the war.

The airline also began a temporary service to Goose Bay, Labrador, in March 1943, using the ex-RAF Lancaster bomber *R5727*. The airport's location—150 miles inland and on the extreme western tip of Goose Bay on the end of Lake Melville—and the process by which TCA came to be using such an aircraft is a story typical of the times. To the American Air Transport Command (ATC), Goose Bay was unimaginatively labelled Station 685, but their crews said that anyone who was posted there deserved a medal. Even before the United States' entry into the war it had been necessary to ferry whole fighter squadrons across the Atlantic, and because of their shorter range, more staging bases had been needed in Greenland and Labrador. Therefore, in June 1941 an RCAF

Stranraer flying boat took a survey party from Dartmouth, Nova Scotia, into Labrador to look for potential landing fields. When it landed at Northwest River, a trading post near the head of Lake Melville, surveyor Eric Fry had taken a powerboat and set out alone. One evening he noticed an elevated terrace set against the sunset sky and returned to base to report it. Two days later the whole party climbed the terrace to find that it was not only higher than the surrounding area but flat as a billiard table. By the spring of 1942 the gravel runways were ready for the ferry flights and in July the first detachment of fighter planes were landed at Goose Bay for an onward flight to Thule, Greenland.

But as Goose Bay was accessible in winter only by air, the Canadian government tried to interest an American airline in flying supplies to it between November and April. When there were no takers, the RCAF was given the responsibility of getting all construction material to the airport, even though the air force had no heavy transport aircraft in that area, and flying thousands of pounds of construction material to Goose Bay was well beyond its capabilities. In spite of this, in January 1943 Wing Commander Zebulon Lewis Leigh, a former TCA pilot, was ordered to begin service to Goose Bay, using Number 164 Transport Squadron's Lodestars. Although they served valiantly, much of the required material could only be flown in a heavy, four-engined transport. The only source of these was the Americans, and the chances of Washington's Munitions Priority Board agreeing to release Douglas DC-4s or Lockheed C-69s were slim.

It was said that Mackenzie King always believed the worst of the British and the best of the Americans, but this time it was the former who came through. At the start of the war the National Steel Car Company at Malton had been awarded a contract to build Halifax bombers, but when this was abruptly changed in December 1941 to the manufacture of Lancasters instead, Ottawa attached such a high priority to the program that the company was nationalized the following year and renamed Victory Aircraft Ltd. A.V. Roe Ltd., manufacturer of the Lancaster, had sent over a pattern aircraft, *R5727*, to speed up production tooling. A TCA crew with Jock Barclay as captain took it to Malton, where its weaponry was removed; by using it as a template, Victory Aircraft rolled out the first Canadian-built Lancaster on August 1, 1943. Once the engineers at Victory Aircraft had no further use for it, in March 1943 with British consent and on Howe's authority the Lancaster was sent to Goose Bay for the supply run.

On the CGTAS account books *R5727*, or "Aircraft #100," is valued at $324,000 minus engines but including propellers, radio and miscellaneous. In Canadian aviation history it ranks slightly below that of J.A.D. McCurdy's *Silver Dart*, Punch Dickins' Fokker *C-CASK* and the first Canadair North Star, *CF-TEN-X*. One of the batch within the serial range R5482 and R5763, it was a Lancaster Mark I, built in early 1942 at A.V. Roe's Manchester factory and fitted with four Rolls Royce Merlin 20 series engines with single-stage, two-speed superchargers. (These were supplied by the Packard Company in the US, which had been

Two views of the same aircraft. Above: shown on a demonstration trip to Ferry Command Facilities at Dorval Airport after arriving in August 1942. An early production Lancaster Mk 1, R5727 was provided as the pattern aircraft for Canadian production. Later, demilitarized, it flew transport flights with TCA to supply construction material for the new Goose Bay Airport, then to England for conversion to passenger/transport configuration for use by TCA on the CGTAS flights. Below: Registered CF-CMS at Dorval on its return in July 1943.

licensed to build them in 1940.) Manned by a crew of seven (pilot, flight engineer, navigator, bomb aimer/front turret gunner, radio operator, dorsal turret gunner and rear turret gunner), it had three hydraulically operated Frazer Nash gun turrets, six fuel tanks that carried 2,154 Imperial gallons (there was also a provision for an overload fuel tank of 400 Imperial gallons in the bomb bay), a wingspan of 102 feet, length 69 feet 10 inches, height to the top of the fin of 20 feet 6 inches. Its maximum speed was 271 miles per hour at 6,250 feet, or 281 miles per hour at 11,000 feet, with the most economical cruising speed at 216 miles per hour at 20,000 feet. When empty, the Lancaster weighed 41,000 pounds, with a maximum takeoff weight of 72,000 pounds "all up" weight. The simple and sole reason for the Lancaster's existence was its 33-foot-long bomb bay, which could fit in a maximum load of 22,000 pounds of explosives, thus fulfilling the aim of A.V. Roe's chief designer, Roy Chadwick, to make the aircraft the best deliverer of bombs to Germany in its day.

At some point between February and July 1942, the Lancaster *R5727* had been delivered to Number 44 (Rhodesia) Squadron at RAF Station Waddington in Lincolnshire, under the aegis of Number 5 Group, Bomber Command. Although 44 was the first squadron to be equipped with the Lancaster, there is no evidence that *R5727* was ever used operationally by it, and the aircraft's earlier history remains a mystery. Because of the heavy casualties incurred by 44 Squadron from December 1941 onward, replacement Lancasters were no longer recorded individually in the monthly summaries as they were delivered. On the other hand, according to the squadron's historian, Henry Horscroft, it may have been fed into 44 Squadron but deliberately kept "pristine," a requirement for a pattern aircraft.

The Merlin engine that powered *R5727* was to figure in much of the drama surrounding Trans Canada Airlines in the 1940s and 1950s. Configured by Rolls Royce as a high-performance military engine, it had powered the British Schneider Trophy entries to victory in the 1930s and during the war allowed Spitfires, Hurricanes, Mustangs and Lancasters to triumph over the Luftwaffe. It was a four-stroke V-12 type of petrol (gasoline) engine, with a two-stage, two-speed supercharger and a pressurized liquid cooling system. Constructed in a two-piece aluminium alloy crankcase with two aluminium alloy cylinder blocks with a detachable head for each block, it had two inlet valves and two exhaust valves per cylinder actuated by the overhead camshaft. The carburetion was a Rolls Royce SU variable stroke fuel injection pump with injection through one nozzle into the eye of the supercharger impeller. Ignition was by two magnetos, two 14 mm short-reach spark plugs per cylinder. What made the Merlin simple to interchange and repair was Chadwick's "power egg" concept. Everything—the engine, the cooling system, all electrical, hydraulic and pneumatic lines—was contained in a single unit that could be removed from its cradle for quick servicing or replacement. More than anything else it was this advantage that impressed Jim Bain when it came time for TCA to select an engine for its post-war airliner.

In a fighter or a bomber the whole Merlin series had no equal, and a generation of British schoolboys were taught that if the Battle of Waterloo had been won on the playing fields of Eton, the Battle of Britain had been won at the Rolls Royce factory at Derby. But in fighting a war the Royal Air Force did not have to take into account the cost of replacing Merlins or their pistons and rings, and during the bombing offensive, when a Lancaster that had accumulated 200 flying hours was considered old, few Merlins ever made it to their full lifespan. But with the York, a civil version of the Lancaster, on the way, A.V. Roe was very interested in discovering the bomber's potential as a transport and welcomed the demonstration of its capabilities on the Goose Bay run, and they took a keen interest as a TCA crew, led once more by Jock Barclay, took over *R5727* on March 19, 1942, to shuttle between Moncton and Goose Bay on behalf of the Department of Munitions and Supply. Then in May, when the RCAF replaced their Lodestars with the larger C-47s, TCA's Lancaster was declared surplus once more. TCA did not return to Labrador until 1946.

On May 15, 1943, when Howe flew to Britain, he was the first civilian VIP to be a passenger on *R5727*. Using a TCA crew and RCAF navigator, the Lancaster was returned to the A.V. Roe factory at Manchester to undergo a complete civil conversion. New Merlin engines and larger fuel tanks were added and the forward gun turret was faired over, changes that would allow it to carry cargo and passengers and expand its range to 4,000 miles. Just as the Electra *CF-AZY* had introduced the modern airliner to Canada, the Lancaster *R5727*, now re-registered as *CF-CMS*, became the country's first four-engined transoceanic commercial aircraft. That it was never designed for the monotony or economies of commercial aviation (long transoceanic flights at reduced power), that its Rolls Royce engines had been built without regard for financial restraint, and that it had none of the creature comforts that passengers expected—such as heating—had no impact on Howe. Trans Canada Airlines had its first transatlantic aircraft.

By 1943, everyone at TCA knew a former colleague now serving in the armed forces. At the Royal York Hotel city office they remembered Harold Smith, now a gunner with the artillery overseas, Bill McCarthy with the Lanark and Renfrew Scottish regiment, Don Jones with the RCAF in Souris, Manitoba, Harry Cooper with RAF Ferry Command, former eastern traffic manager Don Wood now an artillery captain, the former station manager Bob Williamson now in the RCAF. And when a colleague was decorated, the whole airline felt great pride. By 1942 three former TCA pilots now in the RCAF had been awarded the Air Force Cross. Marlowe Kennedy, now a wing commander, was decorated by the governor general on December 3, 1942, for flying the Duke of Kent on his Canadian tour. At the same investiture another former TCA first officer, Andrew Madore, also received the Air Force Cross for organizing elementary flying training schools. Decorated too was another of the early TCA pilots, Wing Commander Bruce Middleton of Number 168 RCAF Heavy Transport Squadron, for rescuing nine airmen stranded on a northern Quebec lake.

The company made a point of keeping in touch with former staff who were serving in the armed forces, particularly those overseas. The various Trans Canada Airlines Recreation Associations across the country wrote to the servicemen with news of home, sending parcels of food and clothing, and the airline's magazine. Seeing photos of familiar faces and reading of the airline's expansion in *Between Ourselves* brought something of Canada and the company to former and seconded employees, some 90 percent of whom had never been abroad before. In turn, they wrote back from bases in North Africa, India, France and England.

> Everything here [England] is much better than I expected but fresh fruit, eggs and milk are what I miss the most. The English "cigs" are not too bad and I have mastered the English money.
>
> Sgmn Al Patton (formerly passenger service, Toronto) No. 2 Coy, 1st Canadian L. of C. Signals.

> I've seen quite a lot of England and Scotland and the country is swell. TCA is coming to light in England now and there have been several articles in the London papers about them starting the Trans-Atlantic operation. I was spending my leave with my relatives and my uncle said he was going to fly to Canada for a weekend after the war. I thought I saw a lot of flying around Malton, now I know that was a mere nothing. Boy... when the "Spits" hedge-hop and hundreds of "Forts" fly over, there is no doubt in your mind as to the home of all this.
>
> Sgmn Vern Bentley (formerly cargo services, Toronto) No. 2 Coy, No. 1 CSRU

> I have been receiving *Between Ourselves* quite regularly and enjoy it thoroughly. The new developments in the airline game are pretty exciting. Lots of action in Jerry's territory these days—hope he will quit soon.
>
> F/O Jack Jackman (formerly communications, Toronto) RCAF Overseas

> As you will note from the heading, I am now in France. We are living on a beautiful old French estate that has been knocked about. Shells keep whizzing over your head, sounding like express trains going by. You just keep hoping they don't decide to stop where you happen to be at the moment.

The Canadians have put up a magnificent battle. They really had just about the toughest opposition the Germans could put up...Everyone is optimistic about the war being over soon. Sure hope they are right. It can't be over too soon to suit me or anyone else over here.

Sgt. Bill McCarthy (formerly traffic, Toronto)

Editor's note: Sergeant McCarthy was killed in action shortly after writing this letter.

Two letters arrived from Sgt. Jim Olding, a former cargo clerk at Malton, now serving with the RCAF in England. His first letter, published in *Between Ourselves*, was sent to Harry Scholfield, supervisor at Winnipeg: "I'm with a swell crew who really ought to get places in this racket. I wonder if you see Fred Wright or any of the old gang, they were a good bunch of fellas...I have about three weeks leave coming up soon and expect to get down to London again and maybe up to Edinburgh and Glasgow. This time I will try to get to the Tower and St. Paul's. We have lost a few crews here, but it doesn't do to think too much of this, as it is liable to give a guy cold feet. My best to your wife and TCA. Hope to see you in the future. Action for now."

When the next issue of *Between Ourselves* came out, there was another message from Jim Olding, this time on a little heavily stamped card addressed to D.R. MacLaren, superintendent of passenger services in Winnipeg.

As you can deduce, I am now a prisoner in Germany. Before meeting my Waterloo in the form of an ME 110, I had heard of your association with the RCAF which pleased me very much. I have now read of your experiences in the last war. They are available here along with Collishaw's, Brown's, and Ball's. I have been recommended for my commission by the RAF and it should soon arrive but the mail is slow. If it's convenient to write to me, I would appreciate it.

Jim Olding
Gefangennummer:220
Lager Bezeichnung,
Kreigagefangenenlager der Lu(undecipherable) Nr. 3
Deutschland (Allemagne)

The war was already over for some other TCA staff members. Passenger agent Alan Frome had returned from serving in the army overseas and after convalescing at Vancouver General Hospital joined the company in March 1942. Working with him as a counter clerk was Gwen Colvin, who had also served with the military. Moncton radio operator Edward M. "Mac" Wilson had tried to join the air force in 1939 but had been turned down because of his poor eyesight. He then took a nine-month radio course and joined the merchant marine. On January 13, 1941, his ship was torpedoed in the Atlantic. "The torpedo struck at 4 a.m. and the crew was very calm," he recalled. "There was less excitement than when the men were going ashore. We weren't going anyplace, so there was no hurry." Two boats were launched with eighteen men in one and nineteen in Mac's boat. The first boat was never heard of again. "We never lost hope. Twelve men went to sleep and froze to death and we put them overboard." Through four days and nights they were tossed on a heavy sea in a driving snowstorm. "We ate corned beef and sea biscuit and when the water froze, sucked the ice. "It was just luck," Wilson says, "that we were picked up by a British destroyer on the fourth morning. It was nothing but a big grey shape in the snow and how they ever saw us, I don't know. We were 250 miles from land and couldn't have lasted another hour." Wilson was discharged from hospital in July 1942 and joined TCA. The company gave him a refresher course at Winnipeg before assigning him to Moncton.

Radio technician Dudley Taylor had decided to stay on at TCA.

> The airline was an essential service and had taken on a lot of maintenance work for the RCAF. I was involved quite deeply as their radio equipment was different from ours, and a lot of study was required. They did their own test flying after certain maintenance checks, and I was often called to go up with them. One pilot was all they used for such flights, and on one trip I recall, the pilot was so young I was sure that he had just obtained his "wings" the day before. I sat in the co-pilot's seat. The young man did the routine cockpit check prior to take off and was given clearance. Of course, I was quite experienced with takeoffs by this time and watched the cockpit checks very carefully. As we swung onto the runway, I leaned over and said, "Fuel tank check?" He quickly switched the fuel gauge across the four tanks—the first three were dry and number four was a quarter full. This is not a criticism of the RCAF. They were a fantastic bunch but so young and mostly inexperienced. It just paid to keep one's eyes open!

Frank Smith, who would soon be flying for the airline himself, had the good fortune while in the RCAF to be taught instrument flying regulations (IFR) by two former TCA captains. "In May 1941 I started the course being given at Number 13 OTU at Pat Bay and was held on at the squadron as an instructor." It was commanded by Z. Lewis Leigh, and the second-in-command was Harry Winnie, the pilot who had left Canadian Airways just before TCA bought its Vancouver operations, thus giving George Lothian his big chance. Smith grew tired of instructing and tried for an overseas posting but instead was sent to

Number 12 Communications Squadron in Ottawa, where Marlowe Kennedy was the CO. "My job, Leigh told me, was to teach service pilots how to fly the way TCA pilots did. Fine. I knew nothing about it. But they taught me the rudiments of IFR operation, and eventually I became at least marginally competent to teach it. The aim of Lewis Leigh and Kennedy was to make Transport Command fully IFR like TCA, and the first thing they did was organize a scheduled run between Ottawa and Halifax, calling en route at Montreal and Moncton—the 'Blueberry Bullet.' The squadron even used two of TCA's original Lockheed 10A aircraft that were pretty limited, but they were IFR equipped. TCA ran its dispatch service, counter ticket service, all communications and ground handling. The run operated to TCA limits of 300 feet and three-quarters of a mile visibility." The name "Blueberry Bullet" had actually been coined by TCA Captain Bert Trerice in May 1941. The way Trerice remembered it, he was "hustling out of the Dorval dispatch room when someone stopped him to enquire, "Where ya going Bert?" Bert replied in his lightning-like drawl, "I'm flying the Blueberry Bullet to the Island." With Captain Jack Holly and F/O Jack Collett, Trerice had been operating one of the two TCA Electras (now with the RCAF), *CF-TCA* and *CF-TCB* to Charlottetown and Summerside. But it was ever after known as the Blueberry Bullet.[2]

Later in the war Frank Smith was made detachment commander in Edmonton in charge of the northwest staging route to Alaska. "We were very proud of our scheduled services. The TCA motto was Safety first, passenger comfort second and schedule third. Ours, I am afraid, tended to be Schedule first, safety second and passenger comfort third."[3] TCA was also contemplating moving north at this time. Already a sea-to-sea operation, the company looked to extend its services from Edmonton to the Yukon and Alaska. As this was not part of the original Act, on August 6, 1943, Orders-in-Council PC 6256 and PC 6255 were drawn up to authorize this future extension to the main line route.

As with most station managers, T.C. "Tommy" Cunningham had served time in Armstrong, Ontario, before being appointed Edmonton station manager in 1941. The "Gateway to the North" had always considered itself in the forefront of aviation, gaining worldwide attention when the great aviation pioneers of the 1930s like Jimmy Maltern, Wiley Post, J. Ryan and Matt Berry had flown through on their way to Siberia or Alaska. But the city was at the farthest end of the TCA network, and the airline had only begun to move into the new administration building by the start of the war. The Japanese attack on Pearl Harbor changed Edmonton Airport forever, by causing "the Great American Invasion," a continuous flow of US military aircraft on their way to only-the-censor-knows-where. The "Big Snow of 1942" enveloped the airport for weeks, and Cunningham had to drag himself to work in full ski equipment, using "protruding telephone poles as guides, as the passenger agents beat time behind the counter with their snowshoes." Tommy was a Montrealer who at age fifteen had his own ham radio operator's licence; in 1937 he worked for

Newfoundland Skyways in Labrador, identifying himself with his famous V06D, "The Voice of the Six Ducks."

Lightheart, Alvin Ernest SGT(AG) R180436. From Toronto, Ontario. Killed Apr. 19/43. #22 Operational Training Unit. Wellington aircraft #DF 743 crashed at the Staple Farm, one and one half miles west of Withington, England. Sergeant Air Gunner Lightheart is buried in the Cirencester Cemetery, Gloucestershire, England.

With the Americans in the war, both the US State Department and Canada's Department of External Affairs were eager for an air connection between Ottawa and Washington. Howe and Symington knew that an air service between the two capitals would be more symbolic than profitable, and once the war had ended, the traffic would not warrant tying up a TCA aircraft and crew. Besides, if diplomats like Lester Pearson, then Canada's ambassador to the US, wanted to scurry back and forth on official business, let the RCAF fly them. Canada had been allocated only two air routes from the 1940 agreement and Howe made it clear that "the government would be better off letting an American airline operate the route in exchange for a really valuable service— Toronto–Chicago was what he had in mind." Speaking for the Opposition in the House, Howard Green (Vancouver Quadra) asked, "In effect, this makes the minister a dictator in respect of all the airways in Canada, does it not?" Howe replied, "Perhaps so. But who would you suggest be dictator?" There was no more debate on an Ottawa–Washington service.

The minister was also battling for his airline on the home front and this brought him into conflict with the ever-expanding empire of the Canadian Pacific Railway. When under the name of Canadian Pacific Airlines (CPA)—the CPR's air branch commenced operations on July 1, 1942—it had twenty-nine aircraft, making it the country's largest airline. For all of that, when compared with Trans Canada Airlines, CPA was still a bush airline—by and large a disconnected patchwork of local services, its pilots flying obsolete float and ski aircraft in VFR conditions. Its strength lay in the forty-eight air licences it now owned with routes that stretched from Victoria to eastern Quebec and from Whitehorse to southern Ontario, but in January 1943 the Board of Transport Commissioners ruled that the licences were non-transferable. CPA immediately applied for fifteen new licences that would cover all the routes that the forty-eight had covered. This was agreeable to the commissioners, and they recommended to the Governor-in-Council that the new licences be issued, creating what would in effect be a second coast-to-coast national airline.

At the same time, TCA applied to the board for a licence to service the Vancouver–Victoria route. Victoria had not been included in its original mandate because in 1938 Victoria had only a grass airfield. TCA passengers continuing from Vancouver had changed to a float plane owned by Ginger Coote Airways. On February 1, 1941, this air company was bought by the Canadian Pacific Railway for the sum of $62,743—hardly a bargain for two ragged de Havilland float planes but a steal for its Vancouver–Victoria licence. Under the Transport Act of 1938, CPA was entitled to keep the licence as long as it provided reasonable service, and it did this with five flights daily shuttling back and forth between the harbours. Then the Japanese bombed Pearl Harbor, and with the Pacific coast in peril the DND constructed a vast military airfield at Patricia Bay on Vancouver Island for the use of the RCAF, the BCATP and the RAF.

TCA now had a strong case for extending their routes to Victoria: the "Ginger Coote" licence owned by CPA was inadequate to meet wartime demands and inconvenient for passengers and airmail that had come off the transcontinental route. Besides, when Parliament had set up the Trans Canada Airlines Act, it intended that the whole of Canada should be serviced by the government-owned airline, not just the mainland. The Board of Commissioners was in an unenviable bind. It had been established to implement a policy of impartiality between the Canadian National and the Canadian Pacific railways. Their airlines were a different matter. The new owners of the "Ginger Coote" licence may be entitled to the route, but by setting up TCA as a monopoly the government itself could hardly be thought of as impartial.

With the wisdom of Solomon, the commissioners agreed that CPA had every right to continue to fly the route to the new airport at Patricia Bay. They also granted TCA the right to fly between Vancouver and Victoria, but only to carry passengers and airmail from its transcontinental service. The CPA head office at Windsor Station, Montreal, must have greeted this with joy: compared with the busy local traffic there were few transcontinental passengers continuing on to Victoria.

The Vancouver–Victoria dispute boiled over into the House, and on April 2, 1943, Mackenzie King was forced to state the government's aviation policy. "Competition between air services over the same route will not be permitted whether between a publicly owned service and a privately owned service or two privately owned services. There will remain a large field for the development of air transport in which private Canadian companies may participate, and while preventing duplication of services, the government will continue to encourage private companies to develop services as traffic possibilities may indicate." The thrust of the prime minister's speech was that TCA was to be the country's sole transcontinental and international carrier, and the wisdom of his government's policy gave Canada "a freedom of action in international relations because it wasn't limited by the existence of private interests in international air services." Although Canadian Pacific Airlines was not mentioned by name, it was clear who the warning was aimed at.

The Governor-in-Council, aware of the minefield that the commissioner's recommendations had dropped them into and fearing Howe's wrath, on June 28 wisely turned down the CPR's request for new licences. Beatty died that May but his dream of challenging the federal government in commercial aviation had gathered momentum. The Vancouver–Victoria *casus belli* was a harbinger of decades of squabbles. In November 1943 CPA not only issued its first national timetable, but its annual report brazenly alluded to post-war international expansion. However Mackenzie King and Howe had tried to prevent it, the rivalry between the railways that had crippled the country for so long now intruded into aviation as well. Both railways now had their proxies in the air, foreshadowing sixty years of punishing competition, duplication of services, and the polarization of the parts of Canada that each airline served.

Trying to put a brave face on it, Trans Canada Airlines proclaimed its first flight to Victoria with suitable fanfare. At 11:25 p.m. on Sunday, June 6, 1943, a TCA Lodestar flown by Captain Don Brady and First Officer Norman Ramsay arrived at Patricia Bay airport. The passengers were members of chambers of commerce from various cities along the route, all carrying messages to the mayor of Victoria from their own city halls. The airline publicity made much of the fact that also on board was R.W. Mayhew, the MP for Victoria, who at 8:00 that very morning had eaten breakfast at Ottawa's Chateau Laurier hotel! Trans Canada Airlines now operated the longest air service in North America: 3,911 miles from St. John's, Newfoundland, to Victoria.

The company took up quarters in an old farmhouse convenient to Pat Bay airport and, as at Malton, crowded in its radio equipment, passenger counter and waiting room. There was no teletype circuit to Vancouver, but with just two daily flights—arrivals 11:25 a.m. and 11:25 p.m., departures at 1:30 a.m. and 4:15 p.m.—it was hardly necessary, as there were few passengers. However, to no one's surprise, in 1945 the Air Transport Board allowed TCA to pick up the local traffic between Vancouver and Victoria. (By coincidence, the RCAF commanding officer at Pat Bay was one Group Captain Gordon McGregor, newly arrived from commanding the Canadian squadrons in Alaska, and in March 1943 the governor general, the Earl of Athlone, and Princess Alice visited Pat Bay to inspect the base and award McGregor the Order of the British Empire.)

Although Vancouver unselfishly yielded up its title as the western terminus of Trans Canada Airlines and accepted its fate as a "through station," Sea Island was still a unique airport. Able to handle both land and seaplanes, it was home to Catalina flying boats as well as Lodestars, and sometimes to four-engined DC-4s and Boeing Stratocruisers on their way to Alaska. In 1943 W.P. "Wally" Rowan, who had been Well's radio operator in 1938, became Vancouver station manager.

The summer of 1943 was a memorable one for Canadian airmen, both military and civilian. The nation accomplished feats that three years before would have been impossible. For its bombing offensive on July 28, No. 6 RCAF Group

The Lodestar, a wartime arrival of TCA, at Patricia Bay Airport, Victoria. Postal flights between Vancouver and Victoria began on June 6, 1943. Ron George, station manager (left), looks on as G.H. Clarke, postal director, hands over mail personally to the MP for Victoria, R.W. Mayhew. A sign of the wartime conditions prevailing even on the West Coast at the time: all the curtains on the cabin windows are closed.

amassed 200 aircraft—almost the total number of aircraft in the whole RCAF just four years earlier. On the home front that month, the first licence-produced Curtiss Helldiver dive bombers were being test-flown at Canadian Car & Foundry, Fort William, Ontario, and on August 1 Victory Aircraft Ltd. at Malton rolled out its first production Lancaster (*KB700*).

For Trans Canada Airlines, it was their transatlantic summer. The first hint of an auspicious season for the airline came on April 2, when the prime minister reminded the House that TCA had by its charter the right to operate international air transport services and had been designated as the instrument of the Canadian government in flying across the north Atlantic. Then on May 5 the British, Newfoundland and Irish governments were informed that a

Canadian Atlantic air service was about to begin. It would be operated by Trans Canada Airlines on behalf of the federal government for as long as the war lasted and, in keeping with its non-commercial character, would accept no airfare.

At this time Howe must have been completely occupied with the setting up of the Polymer Corporation, the Export Credits Insurance Corporation and the Industrial Development Bank, all immense public enterprises related to the war effort. But this was his airline, and like an anxious father watching his daughter go off to college, he felt a mixture of concern and pride. However, when he stood up in the House on June 16 to announce the inauguration of the service, the nation was already aware of it: someone had leaked the story to the Montreal newspapers the day before.

> Arrangements have been completed for the immediate establishment of a Canadian government wartime transatlantic air service to carry mail to and from the Canadian armed forces in the British isles and to transport members of the Canadian armed forces and of Canadian government departments and technicians engaged in the production of war material. The new war service is not commercial or a permanent one. It will carry no fare-paying passengers. Space on the aircraft from Canada will be allocated by the deputy minister of transport in Ottawa, space on aircraft westward by the Canadian high commissioner in London. The growing strength of the Canadian armed forces overseas and their increasing activities have made it necessary to establish this quick and effective means of communication with the United Kingdom for men and materials. The need for a speedy and regular troops' airmail service is particularly pressing. Over a quarter of a million members of the Canadian armed forces are now in the United Kingdom. During the past year, due to lack of space on aircraft, they have unfortunately not been receiving mail regularly and quickly. It is expected that the initial flight of the new service will occur in July."[4]

When questioned by the Opposition, the Minister corrected himself. Only "aerograph" mail and all armed forces letters would be accommodated on the new service—not parcels.

As Howe had guessed, American objections to the service did not materialize. There was no reason they should. The United States was not providing the aircraft and three American airlines were already flying the Atlantic. The British could say even less. With BOAC crews manning the Return Ferry Service Liberators for the last two years, it would have been akin to the pot calling the kettle black. On July 15, in an exchange of diplomatic notes with

All ready to board Lancaster CF-CMS *on the first eastbound CGTAS flight from Dorval to Prestwick, July 22, 1943. Note the TCA civil registration over the camouflage scheme and faired-over mid-upper turret. Twelve hours, twenty-six minutes after takeoff, they arrived, setting a speed record.*

the British and Irish governments, landing rights at Gander and at the ferry airport in Prestwick and overflying rights for Ireland were granted. The terms agreed to by the British for a "Canadian Government Trans-Atlantic Air Service (CGTAS)" were:

- The arrangements would apply for the duration of the war and six months thereafter.

- The service would neither be commercial nor permanent. Only service or other official traffic (passengers, mail and freight) would be carried, including troop mail. The service would primarily be for Canadian traffic directly connected with the Canadian war effort. In London a committee at Canada House would decide who would qualify to fly as would a DOT committee in Ottawa.

- The service would be operated by Trans Canada Airlines as agents of the Canadian government. The aircraft used initially would be a Lancaster, to be replaced at a later date by Canadian aircraft.

- A Canadian liaison officer would be stationed with Transport Command at the terminal in the United Kingdom.

On July 19, under the authority of Order-in-Council PC 5742, the government provided the aircraft that TCA agreed to operate, billing the Department of Civil Aviation for operating costs. The postmaster general and the minister of transport (civil aviation) had to agree on the rates for the carriage of mail, but as all passengers would be on government business, no carriage charges would be assessed for them. The stage was finally set on July 22, 1943, for the first eastbound CGTAS flight between Montreal and Prestwick to take place. The former RAF bomber, now registered as *CF-CMS*, was crewed by Captain R.F. George, First Officer A. Rankin, Radio Officer G. Nettleton and Navigator (RCAF) J. Gilmore. Twelve hours and twenty-six minutes after takeoff from Dorval Airport, the Lancaster landed at Prestwick. It was a record for a non-stop flight, breaking the previous mark set by a BOAC Liberator by twenty-five minutes.

Stan Hewitt, who was to be the CGTAS liaison officer at Prestwick, was one of the three official passengers who arrived with the first 2,600 pounds of mail. Dubbed by the company "TCA's first ambassador overseas," he was eminently suited for the job as he had been born and educated in Surrey, England, and served in the Royal Navy and merchant marine in World War I. After coming to Canada in 1926, he had worked for the Canadian government Coastal Radio Service in British Columbia until joining TCA in 1938 as a radio operator. Hewitt was impressed by the tight security at the ATFERO terminus. All load information had to be passed to the High Commission by "scrambled" telephone and the whole Prestwick airport was under blackout, which meant that hangar doors could not be opened until the lights were extinguished. For obvious reasons, to taxi an aircraft at night was to invite catastrophe.

Few of the CGTAS crews at Prestwick Airport had time to pause to appreciate the history around them, but the place fairly reeked of history. Robbie Burns, who had described the area as "a pleasant spot near sandy wilds," had come here as a guest of the Baillie family on whose estate the airport had been built. The Laird of Orangefield, whose ancestor had been Burns' patron, had sold the estate in 1930. The mansion itself, which dated from 1720, had then become the Orangefield Hotel, but after the Scottish Aviation College had opened the grounds in 1935 as an aerodrome, its students were housed in it. Now a glass control tower sat atop the old mansion and ferry pilots partied in the Terminal Mess below. The airport's runways, built in 1940 to accommodate the Tiger Moths of the Royal Air Force Volunteer Reserve, were hardly adequate for the Liberators and Lancasters that it now saw, and when the ferry flights began, a main highway had intersected them and road traffic had to be halted by swing gates every time an aircraft came in for a landing.

The first westbound flight Prestwick–Montreal took place on July 24, crewed by Captain M.B. "Jock" Barclay, First Officer R.M. Smith, Radio Officer A.J. Blackwood and Navigator (RCAF) H. Thomae; they brought back 3,000 pounds of Canadian forces mail. After such a good start, the service faltered on August 9, when *CF-CMS* was involved in a mysterious accident at Gander, which cost CGTAS $53,3221.36 to repair.

The CGTAS liaison engineer at Prestwick was Alan P. Stewart, who married a girl from Dundee the following July. Because it was a formal wedding at St. Paul's Church, Dundee, Stewart had to rent a cutaway coat, top hat and striped trousers for the occasion. Though known for its cakes, Dundee could not supply a wedding cake because of wartime rationing, so one was flown (unofficially) in a CGTAS Lancaster from Montreal. Then, proving that TCA engineers put the airline above all else, Stewart cut short his honeymoon to rush back to Prestwick to change an engine.

The CGTAS aircraft displayed its British parentage as it sat on the Dorval Airport apron, a thin, angular "tail-dragger" reared up on its doughnut wheels among the chunky BOAC "Libs" squatting on their tricycle undercarriages. It did not fit into TCA hangars easily, and its forward compartments were difficult to reach, let alone load. In contrast to CPA, the official policy of Trans Canada Airlines has always been to discourage christening its aircraft, but TCA personnel could not resist unofficially nicknaming *CF-CMS* "Lanky the Lancaster." The former British bomber was to be joined by eight Canadian-built Lancasters (pulled off the Malton production line and modified to carry ten passengers) to become Canada's first transoceanic aircraft.

Registration	C/N	F/N	In Service	
CF-CMS	R5727	100	3/43	crashed 1/6/45
CF-CMT	KB702	101	5/43	sold 5/47
CF-CMU	KB703	102	5/43	lost 28/12/44
CF-CMV	KB729	103	6/43	sold 5/47
CF-CMW	KB730	104	6/43	sold 5/47
CF-CMX	FM184	105	7/45	sold 5/47
CF-CMY	FM185	106	7/45	sold 5/47
CF-CMZ	FM186	107	8/45	sold 5/47
CF-CNA	FM187	108	8/45	sold 5/47

The second aircraft, *CF-CMT*, was the third Lancaster built at Malton and for Victory Aircraft Ltd. to redesign a bomber to carry passengers and cargo required many hundreds of modifications. As TCA was to fly them, its own engineering department was actively involved, and this became radioman Dud Taylor's next big project.

Passengers aboard the Lancaster. Two-abreast seating five rows deep was all this pioneering aircraft could accommodate on its early flights across the Atlantic. Headroom was also at a premium on the early flights, which took twelve to thirteen hours. The new Boeing 747s, which make the trip in six hours, seat 365 people and have nine-abreast seating.

I spent many hours at Victory Aircraft specifying the radio equipment to be used on the Atlantic flights. On delivery at Dorval even more modifications were planned, and I must have been among the first of the "jet setters" although no jets were involved. I commuted between Winnipeg and Dorval almost every week, and although I had been given a non-contingent pass to expedite air travel, many trips were made by train due to the heavy air passenger loads. We all worked long hours at Dorval, and I recall one flight home to Winnipeg on a Friday night. I fell asleep shortly after takeoff and the next thing I knew the stewardess was shaking me, saying it was time to wake up. "Ottawa already?" I muttered. "No," she said. "You slept through landings at Ottawa, North Bay, Kapuskasing and here we are in Winnipeg." That was a first for me. I've never slept well on an aircraft since then.

The Lancaster had never been designed for the mundane routines of airline service and many unforeseen problems developed. There were no tail or wing de-icers. Parts fell off after prolonged use—a blade tip from a propeller sliced through the astrodome, casings disappeared from engines, the coolant system leaked, a dinghy ejected in midair, its cover hitting the tail planes. This was no reflection on Roy Chadwick's design and should be taken in the context of the day. Apart from its heavily ribbed, double-skinned floor, which carried the bomb load and was firmly bolted to the wing spars, the remainder of the Lancaster was only rivetted together to make it easier for an untrained work force to build and maintain it. But while some of its shortcomings were annoying, others were lethal. TCA pilots discovered that on takeoff for a long flight, with fuel tanks filled to the brim, fuel escaped out of the overflow pipes and ran along the length of the fuselage, transforming the whole aircraft into a potential fireball. When pipes were inserted into the overflow holes to carry the fuel off to the wings, they caused suction, which collapsed the tanks as the fuel left them.

The liquid-cooled Rolls Royce Merlin engines had been designed for high speeds, and running them at lower speeds, despite additives to the fuel, clogged the spark plugs with lead deposits. When that occurred, the engines banged, sparked and almost shook off their mounts. Their carburetor intakes had wire screen meshes in front of them that iced over on the slightest pretext, causing first the power and then the speed to drop. With multiple engine failure assured, the only evasive action that the pilot could take was "feathering" the Merlins and making for the nearest airport, praying he could accomplish this before the last one quit. A successful flight in a Lanc, according to George Lothian, who suffered through a few near-disasters, was one where they got home in one piece with two of the four engines still operating. Rose Lothian was once waiting at the airport fence for his arrival and as the flight taxied in, she saw one of the mechanics clap his colleague on the back, point to the engines and shout, "Look! They're all running. They're all running!"

The "stepping stone" airports across the Atlantic that CGTAS used when the winds were against the aircraft were Reykjavik in Iceland and Lagens in the Azores. The crews naturally preferred the sunny, peaceful RAF base at Lagens to the cramped one at Reykjavik, where the runway had been built up a hill and went over the top and down to the bay. When landing at speed, the

CGTAS Lancaster crested the hill and the crew saw the bay coming up to meet them with no runway below them. Then, as if on a roller coaster, the aircraft dipped down, using the remainder of the runway to stop. It was a frightening process, giving everyone in the aircraft the illusion they were sliding helplessly into the bay, particularly when the downslope was wet. Taking off was even more harrowing. Charlie Mackie, a CGTAS radio operator, recalled taking off from Reykjavik in the spring of 1945 in a heavily loaded Lanc. The flight cleared the hill but hit the top of a cross on a tombstone in the little graveyard beside the runway's end, tearing a strip of metal off the underside of the fuselage. Said Mackie, "A few inches more and we would have been history."

When the Americans opened their "Station 720" (Meeks Field) at Keflavik, it became a welcome alternate field, not only because of its bountiful PX and hotel, but because, being on the southwest tip of the island, it had been built on a lava field, which allowed for long runways. Many TCA personnel were rotated through Keflavik, especially during the early North Star flights, including Slim Munson, Pete Diorsonens, Al Johnston, Bob Tribe, George Anthony, Ernie Hand, Davy Davidson, Bill Russel, Gordy Aitchison, Gus Campbell, Clarence Oliver, Al Gallacher, Ken Cronkley, Johnny Lessard, Gerry Kiely, Ian Edwards, Ray Farmer, Stew Abrams, Dusty Miller, George Weller, Jim Allen and Tony Savatonio.

Apart from the crews, few TCA employees actually flew in the CGTAS aircraft. One who did, however, was W. "Al" Loke, supervisor of radio, who made four familiarization flights in "Lanky" and took careful notes.

> Twenty-four hours before departure the crew checks in with the meteorological office at Dorval Airport to determine the approximate departure time. Two hours before take-off, the crew are picked up by the RAFTC station wagon from their homes and brought to the Airport. Their first briefing is once more at "Met" where particular attention is paid to what the weather will be like on the British coast. On the basis of the latest weather reports the Captain makes his decision as to which route they shall follow. Then the weather office compiles the complete weather data for that route. Signatures are given for coded weather sheets that cover the whole ocean—and all possible alternate airports in between. Watches are then checked and the pilots and navigator hold a "bull session" that involves dexterous use of fancy-looking flight calculators (i.e. they work on the flight plan). The radio operator is given the "colours of the day." A plan is worked out showing altitudes, expected drifts and necessary course changes at various longitudes en route. Side bets are placed on the indicated elapsed time. (I couldn't find this in the Company Regs.)

When the crew climbs on board, TCA 101 is already loaded with the armed forces mail, priority cargo and VIP passengers. The crew go through the "checks" and ask for taxi clearance from the control tower. "TCA 101 from Montreal Tower, you are cleared to go." This is the signal for throttles to be pushed forward and the Rolls Royce Merlins to pull "Lanky" down a mile of runway before the thirty tons of metal become airborne.

The aircraft heads east, but as there are thunderstorms ahead that can't be circumvented, the pilot turns west and slowly circles to gain height. Prevailing westerly winds make eastbound flights nonstop, and flights are timed so that full advantage may be taken of celestial navigation and better radio reception. At 10,000 feet the oxygen masks are put on, and the climb continues, culminating at 22,000 feet to the top of the thunder-heads. Then there is a descent to a more comfortable altitude. Because of the climb over the storms, there is now not enough fuel to fly nonstop and a brief stop is made at Gander. Flying eastbound from the Great Island, the night comes on quickly. You reach the PNR [point of no return], and this is the time for the captain to call his shot. Is everything in order, destination weather OK etc? We still have fuel sufficient to return to the coast hundreds of miles behind. But we head eastwards and Lanky's engines drone steadily on, the glowing red exhaust stacks emitting a long, blue flame. What a wonderful picture that makes! (Publicity Dept. take note.)

The navigator passes back a note asking for a QTE [bearing by means of a radio direction finder from stations in Iceland and the British Isles]. The information is passed back and compared on the chart with the celestial fix taken by the navigator through a break in the overcast. The weather forecast for the next three Atlantic zones and our destination is amended by a closely guarded coded message. Lanky's heading is changed to compensate for additional drift so that our course can be maintained.

Land Ho! The weather clears and dawn comes rushing up. The sun is well above the horizon and the navigator waves his hand and points downwards. Looking out past the first officer, we can see out first landfall. It's the Irish coast and soon we are flying over breakers dashing against it 10,000 feet below. Over the patchwork quilt of the Emerald Isle, its numerous small farms and neat landscaped hedges. Then more water below and finally the distant shore of Scotland can be seen. Radio Approach Control takes us in hand. We've been on their plotting board for the last several hours and now we're cleared to the Control Tower. We line up with the mile and quarter runway and receive a landing clearance. The wheels touch down on Scottish soil just twelve and half hours after becoming airborne at Montreal. I've earned the right to become a 'Short Snorter.'

Met by Stan Hewitt, Al accepted an invitation to fly south on a troop transport and visit London. "A truck filled with 'GI Joes' finally set me down in Oxford Street in the heart of the Empire's metropolis...I had a few bad moments when a double decker bus bore down on me on the 'wrong side' of the street." Al struggled with the English phone system—"never did get it to work"—and ate dinner with a newly found friend in the Canadian army. Next morning he discovered that what he thought had been German V1 rockets roaring throughout the night had actually been buses dashing through the blackout. Loke managed to meet with former TCA station manager Jack Ross before catching a train back to Scotland. "Half the [railway] car wanted to know about Canada, and as an ambassador at large I hope I did our fair country justice." He discovered the odd thing about British railways was that there was a First Class and a Third Class and nothing in between. Scotland Yard, he thought, should look into what had happened to the missing Second Class.

Humphrys, Peter Robert FS(P) R140397. From Vancouver, British Columbia. Killed Dec. 19/43 age 22. #433 Porcupine Squadron (Qui S'y Frotte S'y Pique). Halifax aircraft #HX 345 crashed into another Halifax on take-off from Skipton on Swale, Yorkshire. FS Humphrys, Sgt.s K.N. Lake, L.D. Griese, FS. H.L. Miller, and one of the crew, not Canadian, were all killed in aircraft HX345. Flight Sergeant Pilot Humphrys is buried in the Stonefall Cemetery, Wetherby Road, Harrogate, Yorkshire, England.

Harry Cooper, a former traffic clerk at the TCA Royal York office, now serving with the RAF's Transport Command (RAFTC), had flown east across the Atlantic in a RAFTC Liberator but returned to Canada on December 3, 1943, in *CF-CMS*. Cooper later wrote:

The captains on the flight were Jock Barclay and Kelly Edmison, and it was "chocks away" at 12:00 noon British

Standard Time. A few minutes after takeoff we're over the sea and shoreline is falling away in the distance behind us. A few small islands just north of Ireland are soon below us and then a large convoy is sighted, steaming for a British port. Now we are out of sight of land and settling down to a 10-hour flight over the sea.

Our weather map indicates that in the first two zones we can remain at 8,000 feet, then we will have to climb high over a frontal condition, perhaps to an altitude of over 20,000 feet. Spread below us is a magic carpet of fluffy clouds. The sea is completely blotted out from our sight by this solid cumulus cloud bank. As we go up and up, the oxygen comes on and passengers adjust their oxygen masks. At 15,000 feet Jack Frost artistically decorates the outside of the windows with crystal-like designs and the temperature in the cabin drops considerably. We can see our breath now and the warm flying suit is appreciated. The clouds rise up like white mountains ahead of us and we are now at 20,000 feet. But still that cloud bank encroaches and our pilots gradually climb higher—now it is 22,000, then 24,000 and finally we have conquered the cloud formations at 26,500. The Lancaster's four mighty power plants still drive us forward and at this great speed we have soon crossed over the weather and are descending on the other side. Gradually we drop down to 8,000 feet.

All day we have been racing the sun, but now we are falling behind for it is sinking beneath the horizon and the sky is a mass of brilliant colour. Soon it is dark and with the frost gone from the cabin windows, the stars stand out in the cold clear night. Presently there are lights ahead, and we are over a huge airport. We are circling the field, making our letdown and Captain Barclay "three-points" the aircraft perfectly. We are at Labrador. The westbound Trans Atlantic flight is complete. We are four hours from Dorval and home. The final leg is uneventful and service No. CMW-8 has been completed. Several hundred pounds of freight, 3,800 pounds of mail and 8 passengers have been delivered without incident across the North Atlantic. And so it goes—day after day—making history and a better world tomorrow.

On August 30, 1943, the prime minister invited Howe and several of the Cabinet to dinner at his home. The first Quebec Conference at the Chateau Frontenac had ended the week before and, buoyed by the inter-Allied discussions on the conflict's outcome, talk around the table turned to what the post-war world and especially aviation would be like. Howe and Symington were scheduled to attend the upcoming Commonwealth civil aviation conference in London that October and both men knew of the British agenda to internationalize air routes. They knew too that the British expected that the Commonwealth's airlines would support them in this. There were many Canadians who also held this to be preferable to seeing the country engulfed by the American air empire expected by all after the war. Among them were certain members of Parliament, Conservative Premier George Drew of Ontario and John Baldwin, of the Privy Council, who was the air transport adviser on the ICICA. But with CGTAS now a reality, no one around the dining table wanted to return to the precepts of the 1935 Joint Operating Company, and the consensus among King's guests was that with a strong post-war TCA, Canada could pursue an air policy independent of both the Americans and the British.

Prime Minister Mackenzie King and Ontario Premier George Drew held each other in disdain. Not that King ever believed that Drew's patriotism was in doubt—he had fought and been a casualty on the Western Front in 1916—but Drew opposed TCA and that was enough for King. When, as an anglophile and former soldier, Drew wanted to go over to England and visit Canadian Army regiments from his province, King took great delight in making sure that he never got a seat on a CGTAS flight. The prime minister was therefore furious when he heard that Drew had wangled a flight over on an RAF Dakota, though it was given quite innocently to him by Harold Balfour. But to King's glee, at an airport stopover where Drew got out of the plane to stretch his legs, he accidentally fell into a river. "He was forced to carry on pantless, with only a rug around his legs for protection from the cold."[6]

By this time TCA's ambitions were no longer confined to crossing the Atlantic. Howe had already met with officials from the British West Indies to discuss the possibility of TCA reaching into the Caribbean and on to South America. However, to operate on these routes required British permission and once more American sensitivities had to be taken into account. Therefore, in planning to steer an independent course between the two powers, on September 28 Howe and Symington drew up their own agenda for the conference: TCA would have an equal share with BOAC of the transatlantic service; TCA would participate in a Pacific service to Australia, with or without the British; and TCA wanted exclusive rights to fly from Canada to the British West Indies and later South America.

The pair took the CGTAS flight on October 8, surrounded by 4,700 pounds of mail. Accompanying them was Baldwin, who, because of his "internationalist" views, had been warned not to participate in any discussions. The crew were Captain M.B. Barclay, co-pilot K. Edmison, radio officer A.J. Blackwood and navigator Squadron Leader J.R. Gilmore. They flew non-stop Montreal–Prestwick, breaking a transatlantic record, arriving in 11 hours and 56 minutes.

Although Lord Beaverbrook, no friend of TCA, was chairman at the conference, the Canadians need not have worried: the British globe-girdling scheme had had its day. Post-war aviation was to be regulated by international organizations, not run by them. The Americans favoured multilateral and bilateral negotiations for reciprocal rights. With the importance of Shannon Airport to transatlantic flights, the Irish had no need of the JOC's protection and withdrew from it officially in 1945; like the Empire, the "all-red route around the world" faded into history.

By December 1943 there were 272 personnel working for CGTAS and a year later this had doubled to 553. ATFERO and BOAC had been able to scrounge their navigators from Imperial Airways and for its transatlantic flights CGTAS was blessed with trained navigators from the RCAF and the Air Training Plan, many of whom remained with TCA after the war. One was Ronald Peel, who had already seen active service overseas. Born in Leeds, Yorkshire, Peel had immigrated to Canada and qualified as a navigator in 1941. "I was nineteen," he recalls, "and a bunch of us had finished our RCAF training and were waiting at Halifax to go overseas, when some of us were suddenly told to report back to Montreal. When they told me to climb into a twin-engined Hudson and navigate it to Prestwick, my jaw dropped. The longest trip I had ever made until then was from Montreal to Toronto." But he reached Scotland safely and in the course of a prolonged tour with Bomber Command, Peel completed thirty operations, survived a near-fatal crash, and was awarded the Distinguished Flying Cross. The role of navigators was relatively new then, both in the military and in the airlines, and though most of the glory went to the pilots, it was the navigator who through his fixes and calculations kept track of each flight, getting it on target and home. (In some RCAF bombers the navigator was in command if he outranked the pilot.) Before its transatlantic crossings TCA did not use navigators, so no one was quite sure where the profession fitted in the rigid hierarchy of the flight deck. As a result, in the "Trans-At" division, Peel discovered that navigators were not accorded flight crew badges and rightly felt unappreciated.

All TCA flight crews seconded to CGTAS attended courses given by the medical officer on the use of oxygen and were tested in the airline's decompression chamber in Dorval. Noel Humphrys told of the training and the experiences that went with it.

> Mindful of what was told to them at the lecture, six or eight timid men enter the chamber with the M.O. The operator, after locking the door, decompresses the chamber and "up they go" very rapidly to 25,000 feet while others wait their turn outside, watching their comrades with keen interest. Upon reaching 25,000 feet, the M.O. gives each a pad and pencil, requesting they do simple problems such as multiplying "1234" by the same number or writing out their names

and addresses. Then the fun begins. Anoxia affects one much the same as alcoholism with much the same symptoms: sluggish inertia, hilarity, pugnacity, etc. Some crew members immediately show sluggish inertia combined with a to-hell-with-it attitude. Others become hilarious and giddy (you've seen them in a tavern), quite willing to render a song and dance at the slightest pretext, and even though it is against their principles, they would gladly give all they own in a fit of generosity. Then there are those who show signs of pugnacity and get fighting mad at themselves and everybody else. For example, one of our husky captains got the twitches in his right hand when trying to write his name. This annoyed him intensely, but a seemingly logical counter-measure seeped into his groggy mind, so with grimaced face, he slowly lifted his left hand high above his head and suddenly literally pounced upon his misbehaving limb which he had watched cat-like during the process.

The Lancs may have sported roundels rather than TCA maple leaf crests, but the whole airline took pride in the CGTAS and in the Summer 1943 issue of *Between Ourselves*, the editor could not help but crow. "We hadn't broken a record since someone sat on 'Begin the Beguine,' but Lindy Rood has crossed the Atlantic from East to West in twelve hours and fifty-six minutes! That shaved three minutes off Captain Bob Smith's old time. The crew were 'first tripper' Barney Rawson in the right seat, Flt. Lieut. Gordon Stringer navigating and Bill Tritter keying. All were accompanied by Lancaster 101 and an unlimited supply of tail winds. Ironically, they passed Captain Barclay bound for the United Kingdom in Lancaster 103. Captain B was buffeting those same winds which makes us think of the old proverb, 'It's an ill wind...'"[6]

But Jock Barclay would have his day. In October he claimed the Dorval–Prestwick record with a flight time of 11 hours and 56 minutes. The next month a BOAC Liberator brought it down to 11 hours and 25 minutes. But the Canadians were getting faster. On January 12, 1944, two Lancasters weighed down with mail and freight left Montreal four minutes apart—the first at 6:05 p.m. with Captain George Lothian, co-pilot A. Rankin, navigator F/Lt Harold Thomae and radio officer G. Nettleton. It landed at Prestwick at 5:21 a.m.—11 hours and 16 minutes later. The second with Captain M.B. Barclay, co-pilot K. Edmison, navigator F/Lt R. Peel and radio officer A. Blackwood left at 6:09 p.m. and landed at 5:23 am—11 hours and 14 minutes. "Harold had the honour of holding the speed record for a whole two minutes," wrote Peel. The Post Office estimated that the dual flights carried nearly half a million letters for the men and women in the Canadian forces overseas.

Good Cheer for
Our Fighting Men

or A Very Useful Nose is "Lanky's"

Drop into Dorval Airport and you will see, almost every second day of the week, a Great Illusion, worth any man's money in the nearest palace of Wonders. We all remember photographs of snakes distended in the midriff by swallowed articles of greater bulk than themselves, and, of course, the poor ostrich with an orange destroying the symmetry of his neckline.

Well, you look out on the ramp at Dorval and there is "Lanky"—slim and graceful. Not a spare ounce. Fit and trim. All muscle. And there beside him is a truck-load or a great heap of mail bags and freight. In comparison it is amorphous and misshapen. Lumpy. Like boiled potatoes in the peck beside a ballet dancer—although "Lanky" probably wouldn't appreciate the simile. He's really very masculine.

Then they start putting the lumps inside. They are crammed in the nose. They are pounded into the nether cargo compartment where once were the bomb bays. And they keep putting them in, putting them in. Surely "Lanky" is satiated! You know he can't take another mouthful. Yet the mail goes on and on. 1,000—2,000—3,000—4,000—5,000—yes, even 6,000 pounds of it. You wait for the fuselage to split. Sweat dropping from the propeller blades wouldn't surprise you. But "Lanky" goes on looking lithe and sleek and unperturbed. The fact that he has consumed what appears to be the equivalent of his own bulk without even releasing a notch in his belt leaves him unexcited. In fact, he contemplates an immediate 3,000 mile sprint at about 250 miles an hour.

Pity the poor snake and the ostrich who lack the physique of "Lanky" and have to show their bulges. The truth of the matter is that he is a war-baby conditioned to the rigours of a tough world. Such loads are a pushover for him. He does the seemingly difficult with contemptuous ease. The proud fact, too, that he is the personal messenger between the boys and girls of Canada overseas and the folks at home seems to lend lift to his wings and power to his already stupendous digestion.

Between Ourselves, Summer 1944

That was how it looked to anyone who didn't have to fly in it. In reality the fuselage was crammed to the roof with mailbags, making it impossible for the crew to reach the Elsan (chemical toilet) in the rear. To provide for their relief during twelve-hour flights, a rubber pipe was available, and to the discomfort of the poor navigator, the rubber cup that opened into the pipe for the crew to use was right beside his table. Smokers also discovered that the pipe made a good ashtray. As airline personnel, the CGTAS crews wore their uniforms throughout the flight, but by the time they had crawled their way forward from the entry door in the rear over thirty feet of dirty mailbags, they were filthy. Art Rankin once suggested that the bags be loaded in the form of a spiral. That way the crew could get in and roll their way forward—as Lothian put it, "like nuts on a screw." Sometimes the Lanc was so full that the only way for the crew to get in was by climbing a ladder and stepping through the cockpit windows.

The speed and complexity of mechanized warfare meant that TCA Air Express came into its own during these years. If in 1939 the airline had prided itself on its ability to transport bouquets of flowers through three time zones before they lost their bloom, in 1943 the packages in the Lodestar's compartments were of a more warlike character: urgently needed tires, telephones and radio tubes for the Alaska Highway, instruments for fighter aircraft squadrons on Canada's rim, tanks at a munitions factory, machinery that would allow a bulldozer to crash through the forest on the CANOL route, blueprints, maps, blood plasma—anything that the Allied war machine had to have. And it wasn't just hardware that was being flown in the Lodestars. How many soldiers overseas or at isolated bases on the North American continent realized that it was TCA Air Express that was responsible for the quick distribution of first-run films, morale-boosting newsreels and transcripts of radio interviews? A government Victory Loan campaign meant that hundreds of pounds of pamphlets, posters and bonds were loaded for nationwide distribution the next day "to spread the gospel of safe and sane war finance."

There was also the lighter (if no less important) side to TCA Air Express. In June 1943, at the request of thirsty GIs stationed at the US Army base at St. John's, Newfoundland, thousands of pounds of Coca-Cola in pure syrup form were flown to them from the bottlers in Montreal. Then there was the day the airline was asked to fly 200 live pigs from Sydney, Nova Scotia, to Newfoundland, in the cabin. The airline declined this one "with the olfactory sensibilities of its two-legged passengers clearly in mind."

Growth of TCA Air Express

Year	Total Shipments	Total Weights (lbs)
1939	11,076	51,408
1940	18,363	106,896
1941	26,936	176,648
1942	40,501	387,318
Jan–July 1943	32,437	406,972

ANNUAL REPORT OF TRANS CANADA AIRLINES FOR 1943

In the annual report for 1943, Symington praised the airline for proving in the six years of its operation to be "a dependable and valuable public servant." Then, in a direct attack on Canadian Pacific Airlines, he echoed his prime minister's voice. "Trans Canada Airlines is the sole Canadian agency designated by the government to operate international air services and awaits with interest the results of conferences between governments affecting world air policy and the completion of international agreements with regard to these services. In co-operation with the Department of Trade and Commerce and the other departments of the Dominion Government it has been studying fields in which Canada would expect to participate and has already surveyed routes to the West Indies and South America."

Results of Operations

	1943	1942
Operating Revenues	$9,379,501	$7,337,318
Operating Expenses	8,974,902	6,628,399
Difference	404,599	708,919
Income Charged and		
Interest on Capital Invested	256,710	214,004
Surplus	147,889	494,915

Passenger Service

Revenue passengers carried in 1943, apart from the transatlantic service, totalled 140,276 as compared with 104,446 in 1942, an increase of 35,830 or 34 percent revenue per passenger averaged at $30.04.

Air Express Service

The growing use of air transportation for the rapid movement of materials essential to the military forces and to the war industry, was reflected in the 126 percent increase in the volume of air express handled: 821,606 pounds in 1943 as compared with 362,837 pounds in 1942.

Property and Equipment

As of December 31, 1943, there were 12 Lockheed 14-08 aircraft and 11 Lockheed Lodestars, both types equipped with twin Pratt & Whitney Twin-row Wasp engines.

To handle the overhaul of military aircraft a new hangar, service building and annex were completed on TCA property in Winnipeg with badly needed office accommodation in a two-storey brick annex. For the same reason the hangar at Toronto was extended and work begun in August on a similar extension to the hangar at Moncton.

Cargo agent Hugh Long handing a special air shipment to Jean Hodgins, a stewardess, at Vancouver. The box of apples was a gift from Lt. Gov. Pearkes.

Personnel

The personnel of the company numbered 2,343. The proportion of women employees increased to 35 percent from 30 percent and the loss of experienced male personnel to the armed forces continues to be serious. An understanding has been reached with the RCAF as a result of which a supply of Air Force personnel will be made available to the company. This marks the beginning of a policy of rehabilitation of returned airmen. There were 215 men and 12 women from the airline who had enlisted in the armed forces.

A contributory pension plan was put into effect on July 1, 1943. Employee contributions together with the Company's matching contributions are paid monthly into a separate trust fund which is invested in Dominion Government securities. The trust fund is administered by the Company as trustee but is not an asset of the Company and not included in its balance sheet. The amount of the fund at December 31, 1943, was $187,743.05.

C H A P T E R 7

By the fall of 1943 TCA's management was narrowing the search for the aircraft that would fulfill the company's post-war aviation needs. The most obvious candidate was the Avro 685 York, which Victory Aircraft Ltd. had been licensed to build for A.V. Roe. Its distinguishing feature was a high wing, rather than the mid-wing fuselage of the Lancaster and Lancastrian, and a central tail fin. In Britain A.V. Roe built 250 of them, two of which achieved fame as the personal aircraft of General Montgomery and Lord Louis Mountbatten. But Jim Bain, TCA's superintendent of engineering, doubted the suitability of the Avro York or of Victory Aircraft's capability to produce an airliner equal in standard to anything the Americans had. This left the company with three options: the Lockheed 049, the Boeing 307 Stratoliner and the Douglas Commercial 4. The idea for the Lockheed 049 had originated in 1938 from a requirement by TWA's Howard Hughes and Jack Frye for an airliner that would compete with the Douglas DC-4E. The result was Lockheed's first four-engined aircraft—code-named Excalibur—which was given to Hall Hibbard and Kelly Johnson in 1940 to refine as the Model 049. It was test flown on January 9, 1943, although it was 1946 before it entered commercial service with TWA and Pan American. However, given TCA's unhappy experiences with Lockheed's Electras and Lodestars, the management was reluctant to return to Burbank for its future requirements, especially for flying the Atlantic. As for the Boeing 307 Stratoliner, it had gone out of production, and in any case TCA wanted a larger and faster aircraft. That left the DC-4, and those used by American Overseas Airlines and Pan American Airways that had refuelled in Gander on their way across the Atlantic or in Edmonton heading for Alaska had been a good advertisement for their manufacturer. Reasoning that Douglas now had ten years to overcome the model's teething problems, the company opted for the Douglas Commercial 4, and in February 1944 Douglas licensed Canadian Vickers to build DC-4s for TCA as well as their newly designed DC-6, which was to be pressurized.

From the Diary of Ross Smyth

radio operator at Kapuskasing, Ontario:

> Jan 21, 1944: See about 200 German air force prisoners in their smart uniforms get off train to work in the lumber camps on the honour system. Few Guards. The prisoners' arrival creates a problem for the airline by engaging all the taxis for miles around, and René Baudru cannot get to the airport in time for the flight's arrival. Radio operator Gordon Hennigar and Capt. René Giguère thus take some thirty minutes to find all the right switches and nozzles on the fuel tender, considerably exceeding the schedule stopover.

> Jan 22, 1944: All operators were given a short course in flight refuelling.

Meanwhile, the Canadian Pacific Railway's successful challenge in 1943 to Trans Canada Airlines' Vancouver–Victoria route had emboldened its board of directors, and they began to press for a post-war monopoly for their airline to fly onward to Alaska and eventually to the Orient. At the same time they hoped to prevent TCA from expanding north of Edmonton. To discuss both, Beatty's successor, D.C. Coleman, came to see Mackenzie King personally on February 23, 1944. Only a year before Coleman had proposed that the government merge both airlines into one, but this had been rejected out of hand. Now he asked King to clarify the government's policy on the future of private commercial aviation, especially with regard to continental and international routes.

King's diary entry about the interview reads: "I replied that the statement which I had given to Parliament early last year set forth the Government's policy and that there had been no departure from it of which I was aware, that the matter had not been discussed recently, but I would see that it was brought before Cabinet anew without delay."[1] The prime minister was as good as his word, and when Cabinet took up Coleman's request on March 2, he ensured that he had its full support for the maintenance of the Trans Canada Airlines' continuing monopoly, especially in international aviation.

The war years had not lessened his abiding mistrust for the CPR, and once more his diary revealed his intentions: "I am sure that what is now proposed by the CPR would give them the best for the future of the Canadian north-west and of what will be the most important air route around the world. I intend to use my influence more strongly than ever in the Cabinet to see that these areas do not fall to private monopoly which has been doing all it can to destroy the present Government and myself in particular and which is wholly indifferent to the trend of public demand."² His anti-CPR feeling aside, King had another reason for digging in his heels. He knew that nothing attracted criticism quicker than monopolies, and he was determined to make his position clear to the Opposition, especially the increasingly vocal Co-operative Commonwealth Federation (CCF), which, according to a recent Gallup poll, had forged ahead of both the other parties in popular support. As a result, King formulated a new major air policy statement and tested it before Cabinet on March 9. In it he made a convincing case for preventing the CCF from having "exactly what they had always wanted: the two old parties standing for private interests against the people's right to control national monopolies." He said that he did not wish to exclude private air companies completely, and he acknowledged the pioneering work they had done in the north, but the basic tenet that his government had espoused in 1936 was unchanged: private enterprise was to be confined to bush flying and feeding passengers into the Airway, where TCA would continue to have the monopoly.

Calder, Robert George P/O(P) J19340. From Kenora, Ontario. Killed Mar. 3/44 age 26. #1666 Heavy Conversion Unit. Lancaster aircraft #650 crashed near Rochester, Northumberland, England. Pilot Officer Pilot Calder is buried in the Morningside Cemetery, Edinburgh, Scotland.

Tindall, Charles Edward F/O(P) J20618. From Winnipeg, Manitoba. Killed In Action Mar. 22/44 age 22. #425 Alouette Squadron (Je Te Plumerai). Halifax aircraft #LW 417 missing during night operations against Frankfurt, Germany. F/O K.V. Duffield, P/O.s C.W. Hay, and D.W. Pulham were also killed. Two Canadians, Sgt.s Brine and Quinlan were either Evaders or were taken Prisoners of War, one of the crew, not Canadian, missing believed killed. Flying Officer Pilot Tindall is buried in the South Cemetery at Cologne, Germany.

As with other St. Patrick's Days in the House of Commons, March 17, 1944, began with the usual speech from an Irish-born MP to "celebrate the passing of that great missionary, St. Patrick." Once this rite had been performed, Howe, in his role as minister of munitions and supply, stood up to report on the war estimates of the air services branch, but instead of dealing with the air force, he chose the occasion to deliver a major policy statement on the future of civil aviation in Canada. It was the longest speech in his entire career. He began with a summary of the development of civil aviation in Canada, leading up to why his government had ensured with the passage of the Trans Canada Air Lines Act that TCA would monopolize the principal routes parallel to the international boundary.

"Service to the public had to be of paramount consideration and it seemed obvious that the cost of a non-competitive and non-profit service was the lowest that could be offered to the public." He reminded the House that in 1937 the CPR had declined the government's invitation to participate in the founding of the airline "at a time when it alone was able to afford new and modern equipment [and had] challenged the non-competitive position of Trans Canada Airlines." Since then, he continued, even the prime minister's statement on domestic and international aviation policy in the House on April 2, 1943, had failed to end attempts at intervention of private interests in the international field.

> It has become obvious that ownership of airways by our two competing railway systems implies extension of railway competition into transport by air, regardless of the government's desire to avoid competition between air services. In the old days, competitive railway building developed pressure methods for obtaining new franchises. Such methods must not have a place in the development of our airways... Accordingly, after full consideration, the government has decided that the railways shall not exercise any monopoly of the air services. Steps will be taken to require our railways to divest themselves of ownership of airlines, to the end that, within the period of one year from the ending of the European war, transport by air will be entirely separate from surface transportation. In the meantime, no new air routes other than the government operated routes will be allocated to the airlines owned by any railway or other operator of surface transportation.

Later in his speech he explained that his "paramount reason for halting expansion at this time is that the young men who should a have a prominent part in any such expansion are overseas on combat duty. We can all picture the resentment of these men if, on their return to Canada, they found that all profitable air routes had been preempted in their absence." He reminded his listeners that during the debate on the Trans Canada Airlines bill in 1937 he had stated his reasons for making TCA a subsidiary of the CNR, and "while I have had no cause to regret the step taken at the time, the entry of a privately owned railway into the field of air transport has made it apparent that the advantage of government ownership without the obligation of direct government operation does not compensate for the disadvantage of introducing into air transport the competitive methods of the railways. Therefore, it will be necessary to divorce Trans Canada Airlines from Canadian National Railways and operate the former as a government company. Canadian National Railways have given splendid administration to Trans Canada Airlines, and personally I regret the necessity for the separation." He then went on to talk of a four-engined aircraft to be constructed in Canada and the establishment of an air transport board that would be concerned solely with matters of aviation. The minister concluded by tabling a draft for an international air convention that would be held in Montreal.[3]

It was a policy statement unique in Canadian transportation history. Had the government acted on it, the policy would have transformed commercial aviation for the remainder of the century. Mackenzie King expressed his belief that the speech and policy were "as fine as anything the Government of Canada has done at any time." Although directed at the CPR, it was generally well received in the House, both among the CCF and, Howe noted, the younger Progressive Conservatives. Who, after all, could argue with giving employment to returning war veterans and building the country's own transport aircraft?

To everyone except CPA employees, divorcing the airline companies, public and private, from their railways also made sense. The Roosevelt administration had legislated exactly this in 1938, allowing the airlines in the United States to develop and expand under their own power. Having the Dominion's two airlines owned by the two railways, in particular the privately owned, profit-seeking CPR, was sure to beget a transportation monopoly, and there was even less need for cutthroat competition in the air than there was on the rails. Of course, the CNR would have to sell its shares in Trans Canada Airlines, but these would be simply transferred to the Treasury. As well, the airline would now have to pay for the services that the railway had provided, but this would only mean moving the figures in government ledgers from one column to another. For the CPR, on the other hand, being deprived of its air companies would bring considerable financial loss. For CPA, it was a disaster. The recently acquired collection of air companies could not survive a financial quarter if the umbilical cord from Windsor Station was cut; the inevitable outcome would be another "Canadian Airways" bankruptcy. And with the government's obvious bias toward TCA, no one was going to buy the collection of antiquated bush planes or take on their routes.

The CCF not only supported Howe, Stanley Knowles (CCF–Winnipeg North Centre), its most vocal member, went further and advocated that rather than allow it to die, the government should nationalize Canadian Pacific Airlines and merge it with the government airline. On March 31 the Cabinet War Committee (CWC) received a delegation led by Coleman, who condemned

Howe's speech as "a death sentence" for CPA. The prime minister was unsympathetic and took the opportunity in his capacity as minister of external affairs to remind Coleman that the routes to Alaska and the Orient that CPA wanted were (like all international routes) the exclusive jurisdiction of the federal government—and Trans Canada Airlines.

On the same day that Coleman met with the CWC there was an exchange in the House that had all the ingredients of a scandal: corruption by a hitherto unassailable person close to the minister, impending job losses in Toronto and, for good measure, a little xenophobia. Howe was, however, prepared for the charges: only a week before in the *Globe and Mail*, Ontario Premier George Drew had been quoted as saying that he knew why the Department of Munitions and Supply had given "the very generous contract" to manufacture DC-4s destined for TCA to Canadian Vickers, the Montreal shipbuilder, rather than to the government-owned Victory Aircraft Ltd., which employed 9,000 men and had been turning out Lancasters for the past year. According to Drew, it was because the Montreal investment firm Royal Securities Corporation was heavily committed to financing the expansion of Canadian Vickers into the aviation field, and the president of TCA, H.J. Symington, was an officer on Royal Securities' board. Furthermore, he said, Canadian Vickers was no longer a Canadian or British or even American firm; it was controlled by Belgians and Swiss—and who knows who else.[4]

When Howe stood up to answer the ensuing howls from the Opposition benches, he demolished each of Drew's accusations in his usual style. The DC-4 contract, he said, could not be awarded to Victory Aircraft Ltd. precisely because it was engaged in the building of Lancasters, vital war work to defeat Germany. On the other hand, Canadian Vickers was then completing its contract to build Canso flying boats, and it was essential to keep its workforce together. In dollar value the DC-4 contract was hardly generous—only $15 million compared with the Lancaster program expenditure of $200 million. The Royal Securities Corporation was only one of the investment houses that distributed Canadian Vickers bonds, and its officer, H.J. Symington, had never been consulted in the choice of one plant over another. Finally, the charge that Drew had made about Canadian Vickers being controlled by citizens other than Anglo-Americans was untrue. British and Americans held 78 percent of its stock, while the remaining 22 percent was controlled by a Belgian bank, Solvay & Cie, which had no connection with Switzerland—or, as had been implied, Germany. The bank's other investments were in such solidly Canadian firms as Hollinger Mines and Dominion Steel. Howe's rebuttal was well researched, but unfortunately enough mud had been thrown to affect the future of Trans Canada Airlines and the unborn DC-4M—and quite possibly Canadian Vickers, because just eight months later that company opted out of the aviation industry to return to its traditional business of shipbuilding. The company's airplane assembly plant at Cartierville in the Montreal suburb of St. Laurent was bestowed upon the federal government.

Its new federally appointed president, Ben Franklin, in an inspired moment chose to name it "Canadair," and the DC-4 that it was to build the "North Star."

Although the Liberals had the upper hand in the House for now and could protect TCA from all rivals, to ensure that there would be no further attempts at incursions by CPA, Howe ordered the Board of Transport Commissioners not to consider any more applications for route licences until the war had ended. Then through passage of an Aeronautics Act, he created an Air Transport Board (ATB) which was empowered by the Governor-in-Council to license air companies to operate commercial air services "subject to the approval of the minister." This board could also cancel a licence for what it or the minister considered a violation of that licence. The Act also compelled the ATB to issue whatever licences TCA required to enable it to carry out its obligations under the Trans Canada Airlines Act. To further ensure that TCA's interests were looked after on the Board, the company's station manager in Montreal, Romeo Vachon, was appointed to it later that year (he held the post until his death ten years later). Howe had got what he wanted—a more compliant administrative body than the Board of Transport Commissioners.

Bill 133, an act to amend the Aeronautics Act, was introduced later in the parliamentary session of 1944 and passed without difficulty. It contained two relevant sections. Section 12, subsection 2 read: "No such licence shall be issued in respect of a commercial air service, owned, leased, controlled or operated by any person who is engaged in the transport of goods or passengers for hire or reward by means other than aircraft unless the Governor-in-Council is of the opinion that it is in the public interest that such licence be issued." Section 14 was more specific: "every such licence, if not cancelled or suspended by the board under section 13 of this act, shall cease to be valid one year after the termination, as fixed by Order-in-Council, of the war in Europe."[5] With this, Mackenzie King and Howe were confident they had mortally wounded the CPR dragon, at least in Canada's post-war skies. They could not know then that St. Patrick's Day 1944 was to be the zenith of the Liberal government's patronage of the airline it had created.

But while they fought off enemies from without, the Liberal government also faced insurrection from within. Despite most labour activity being banned in the aviation industry during the war, in the spring of 1944 CALPA, the pilots' association, attempted to get a contract for the TCA pilots working at CGTAS. Both government and airline opposed this, arguing that the pilots were prohibited from bargaining while the nation was at war. But Canada had already suffered through serious industrial unrest in 1943 among steelworkers in Sydney, Nova Scotia, and Ford assembly line workers in Windsor, Ontario, who wanted parity in wages and working conditions with their brothers in the United States. Mackenzie King, aware that a substantial part of the CCF's strength lay in the factory workers' militancy, decided to turn the tables and in February 1944 he enacted Privy Council Order Number 1003 which allowed the

Wartime Labour Relations Board to certify professions as unions. The aviation industry, its ranks already swelling with returning veterans, took King at his word, and all the occupations within it applied for certification. On May 11, 1944, the Department of Labour certified CALPA as the bargaining unit for TCA and CPA pilots, and a month later they signed their first collective agreement, formalizing work rules and establishing a seniority system for pilots. With CPA's future in question, its pilots hoped that membership in CALPA might ensure them some sort of permanence. The CGTAS pilots' problem was not resolved until the federal government ended CGTAS in 1947 and absorbed its pilots into TCA.

Moffat, Archibald Douglas P/O(P) J88479//R786738. From Winnipeg, Manitoba. Killed Jul. 24/44 age 21. #1666 Heavy Conversion Unit. Halifax aircraft #JD 3 72 had suffered battle damage during the operation, was returning home and flying at 7,000 feet when the starboard outer engine caught fire. The aircraft spiralled down in flames and crashed one half mile southeast of Slingsby, Yorkshire. Pilot Officer Pilot Moffat is buried in the Stonefall Cemetery, Wetherby Road, Harrogate, Yorkshire, England.

In March 1944, following an agreement between the company and the RCAF, the first group of sixty air force pilot "re-pats" attended the instructional school at Winnipeg for their conversions on Lodestars. Entry qualifications were a minimum of one tour of operations and 1,000 flying hours, and many were far beyond these basic requirements. Among the first group were Squadron Leader Ian March, DFC; F/O R.S. Joe White from Orillia, Ontario, who had taken part in forty operations in Egypt, Libya and Malta; F/O H.H. Bolton of Stettler, Alberta, who had served in Coastal Command; F/Lt. E.L. Howey, DFC, from the "Demon" Squadron; and F/O J.C. Morden, of Fleming, Saskatchewan, who had flown Wellington bombers. White was one of the first of the repatriated RCAF pilots to receive their captaincies in 1946. The others were D. Holland, C.N. Campbell, J.B. Higham and R.R. Stevenson.

As the company's pilot requirements included an age limit of twenty-eight years and a minimum of 1,500 hours' flying time, preferably on aircraft heavier than fighters, only eight former fighter pilots would make the grade. They were also handicapped by having far fewer flying hours than the pilots who flew for Bomber or Coastal Command or the BCATP. Fairly typical of the war veterans who were recruited by TCA were the following three. James Henry Foy was hired from the RCAF in August 1944. Educated at Vaughan Road

Collegiate, Toronto, where he had been a classmate of Bob Fowler, who was now assistant general manager at Winnipeg, Foy enlisted in the air force in 1940. Within two years he had completed thirty-one operational flights in Wellington bombers—once flying his aircraft home on a single engine—and had been awarded the Distinguished Flying Cross. Foy's Halifax bomber was shot down on July 16, 1943, and he and his crew parachuted into Nazi-held France, where, with the aid of the Resistance, he escaped through the Pyrenees to Spain and Gibraltar.

Gordon Jones and Mike Fugala each had a total of 1,310 hours before coming to TCA. Jones had flown for 233 Squadron RAF and 436 and 437 RCAF transport squadrons. His flying time was on aircraft that ranged from Tiger Moths to a "liberated" Luftwaffe Fieseler Storch. He had also dropped the paratroopers of the 2nd Airborne Division in operation "Market Garden" at Arnhem. He remembered them as "the bravest men I ever met." Fugala had come from RCAF Training Command and flown Tiger Moths, Fairchild Cornells, Avro Ansons and Airspeed Oxfords.[6]

The company check pilot who put the former RCAF personnel through their paces at Winnipeg was "Doc" Lowell Dunsmore; he had replaced Herbert Hopson, who was now chief pilot for the airline. At the average age of twenty-five, Dunsmore's charges had just spent three or more years taking chances with their lives to reign death and destruction upon the enemy. Now they had the difficult task of stepping from their Spitfires, Mosquitos and Lancasters into the Lodestar's cockpit and making the psychological transition from flying officers into first officers. In classes of six to eight, they were taught that the pilot's job was to fly methodically and with infinite precision, keeping the safety of his passengers and care of his aircraft paramount in his mind. When one of them was asked what he had learned in the program, he commented, "For one thing we have to learn now how to set down our aircraft gently. We can't land as we like to."

The CGTAS also attracted its share of first officers from the RCAF, the last to serve on the Lancasters:

R.H. Richardson

A.L. Quickfall

T.J. Harrison

J.R. Shaw

H. Tilson

C.M. Harper

A.W. Pavey

H.W. Holland

R.W. Chadwick

J.G. Turner

J.L. Little

B.G. Hughes

D.W. Lamont

S.G. Matheson

G.S. Quinn

R.W. Dick

R.K. Walker

J. Jones

C.S. Buchanan

A. McCabe

Jack Jones remembers that the Lancaster was "a great aircraft to fly. However, to endure the uncomfortable, noisy, short stack exhaust of the Merlin engines on those long flights was a recipe for fatigue. A long time afterwards one's acoustics would be at an all time low. To be young was a prerequisite."[7]

Wilcox, George John F/O(P) 151803— Royal Air Force. From Vancouver, British Columbia. Killed May 21/44 age 22. #5 Operational Training Unit. Ventura aircraft #FP 659 crashed at Turnberry, Scotland after the port engine failed during take-off. Flying Officer Pilot Wilcox is buried in the Dunure Cemetery, Ayrshire County, Scotland.

Meanwhile, by mid-1944 the CGTAS flights had taken a heavy toll on the Lanc's Merlin engines. Jim Bain was not surprised by this. "The Rolls Merlins were designed for short, full-power flights. We were using them for long-range, low-power flights, and the engines couldn't keep themselves burned free of carbon."[8] However, through close communications with Jim Pearson, the Rolls Royce representative, and some previous work at the University of Glasgow, Bain was just able to keep them running.

But the frequent engine failures had near-disastrous consequences. Radio officer Charlie Mackie recalled a particularly hair-raising ordeal that June. On a westbound flight, pilots Lindy Rood and George Lothian had just cleared the Irish coast when Mackie noticed oil pouring out of the No. 2 engine. It was "feathered" and they returned to Prestwick. The next day they tried again, but when just past the mid-ocean point of no return the same engine failed. With a frontal weather system ahead and no radio contact, Rood and Lothian made for the nearest land, which was Cape Farewell at the southern tip of Greenland.

They flew up Greenland's west coast, aiming for the US military airfield called Bluie West One, which was at the end of a long, narrow fjord. None of them had been there before but all knew that on an island at the mouth of the fjord there was a radio range that could guide them in. Unfortunately, they could not raise its operator, who, not expecting any arrivals, was probably off duty.

Aiming for the island, they ran into heavy cloud and moved away from the land, descending to about 700 feet. Mackie remembers that it was quite dramatic—the cold black water and the surly icebergs bobbing just below the speeding Lanc. Passing directly over the island with its silent radio station, they then entered the fjord, flying under the cloud base with walls of rock almost at their wing tips, and Mackie desperately trying to raise anyone on the Bluie West One radio. Suddenly, in front of them the fjord forked left and right. A mad scramble for the charts ensued and the crew confirmed that the left one was correct. After that, everything happened quickly. Mackie got the control tower operator, who told them they had only one chance to land on the single runway—it ended in a glacier. Abruptly they saw it at two o'clock and nose-dived right down onto it.

The CGTAS crew were well looked after by the US military at "Bluie" for the next two days and they left for Goose Bay on a bright "CAVU" day. But no sooner had they reached 9,000 feet than it happened again. Oil, fire and smoke poured out of No. 2 engine. This time, rather than risk a return, they feathered it and made for Goose on three engines. Four and half hours later they landed there—after a transatlantic flight to remember.

The converted bombers continued to trundle off into the air, staggering under the mail loads, and although there were more close calls, there were no crashes until December 28, 1944. That day, while George Lothian was delayed from taking off "because the weather in mid-Atlantic was blowing 80-knot gales," he learned that the flight before him had disappeared somewhere over the ocean between Gander and Prestwick. The crew was Captain Maurice Gauthier, First Officer Bob Jankiewicz, Radio Officer Dick Smith and Navigator F/L L.B. Gregory (RCAF) flying in *CF-CMU*. The only trace was a last garbled radio transmission that might or might not have originated with the Lanc. When it was pronounced an emergency, Lindy Rood took Lothian's aircraft to search for survivors. There was salt spray plastered to his wings when he returned. "It was a token effort," he wrote later. "With 30 to 50 foot waves and horrible weather, there wasn't a hope for survivors."[9] When a full search did get underway later, retracing Gauthier's route proved fruitless. The weather in the Atlantic was still blowing gale force winds and the chances of finding a dinghy, let alone anyone surviving in one for all that time, were nil. (The prevailing wisdom is that the aircraft simply exploded. There is speculation that the pilot was transferring fuel from the bomb bay tanks to the wing tanks using a wobble pump and the aircraft filled with fumes while the radio operator was sending a morse code message using the key system. The spark from the radio ignited the fumes.)

From the Pioneers

Why should a bird so gifted be,
With wings to explore infinity,
While man, God's noblest and most dear,
Must plod the weary earth? O hear
Our daring cry:
"We, too, shall fly!"
So we dreamed our dream, and we made it real,
With brain and courage, prayer and zeal.
Now the blue, blue heavens our pathways are.
We have brushed the clouds, we have touched a star,
And the rivers flow,
Far, far below.
And if some of us died in the doing—what!
Pity us, you of the common lot?
Life's sweeter if short to us of the brave.
You stumble your way to a well-planned grave,
But sudden and true,
To ours we flew.

Mary Wright, stewardess

With the advent of four-engined aircraft and transcontinental flights, it became important to find the best cruising speed to obtain maximum efficiency from the aircraft's engines and save gas. Two American airlines had already conducted studies on the relationship between speed, power and fuel consumption, and in July 1944 TCA embarked on its own cruise control studies, bringing three Pratt & Whitney engineers to Winnipeg to work with Hugh Reid, TCA's performance and operations engineer. After thirty hours of intensive flight tests, a new set of calculations emerged that brought joy to management because of fuel savings and the need for less frequent engine maintenance. These cruise control guidelines would also benefit passengers because they meant less engine noise and vibrations. The entire program was put in the hands of Captain Ron Baker, a test pilot in the engineering and research division. Educated at the University of Saskatchewan in mechanical engineering, Baker had worked as an engineer and pilot for M & C Aviation Company at Prince Albert before joining TCA in June 1939 as a first officer. In his thirty-three years of service with the airline he would be involved in the certification of the North Star's crossover exhausts, the cold weather proving trials of the Viscount, and finally the flight deck layout of the DC-8.

Everyone in TCA knew that the Lancasters were interim airliners for transatlantic service until the DC-4s became available, and by mid-1944 this day was rumoured to be close at hand. So when a shiny DC-4 landed at Dorval on July 11, many at the company's offices thought that it was theirs. An honour guard snapping to attention and an RCAF band breaking out into "La Marseillaise" cast the first doubts among the onlookers. Alas, the DC-4 belonged to the towering figure who strode off the plane. With nary a glance at the TCA staff, General Charles de Gaulle and his entourage walked through the administration building to the fleet of cars that waited to take them to Ottawa.

However, progress was being made on TCA's own DC-4s. In the airline's Winnipeg carpentry shop a strange skeleton was arising—a mock-up of the cockpit of a DC-4M (the "M" was for its Merlin engines) built by the engineering division to exact Douglas specifications. The reason for it, explained Jim Bain, was to experiment with possible arrangements of cockpit equipment. At the operations meeting, "the Shape" received much attention from the superintendents of all the divisions, especially transatlantic, who learned that the DC-4M would have a fully retractable tricycle landing gear—the first airliner in Canada to do so. The cabin would be pressurized, ending the need for oxygen masks at high altitudes. Passenger seats would be arranged in rows of two on either side of a central aisle, and there would be separate men's and women's dressing rooms and toilets. The crowning touch would be a buffet with facilities for hot and cold food.

This last would bring a welcome change from the cold meals then served on the Lodestars, where at 14,000 feet the TCA sponge cake fell flat, its whipped cream ballooned and coffee tasted like dishwater. Since May 1, 1943, Aero Caterers, a subsidiary of Canada Railway News, had served on-board food for TCA from their kitchens in Moncton, Montreal, Toronto, Winnipeg, Edmonton and Vancouver. Food on flights out of New York were provided by the New Yorker Hotel and those out of Lethbridge by the Marquis Hotel. All meals had to be prepared no more than two hours before the flight, and to prevent spoilage each container was covered with wax paper; in summer a piece of dry ice was added. Although the airline claimed that seven bills of fare were rotated through the whole system annually so that no two points could have the same meal on the same day, the choice, it seemed to some passengers, was invariably fried chicken, potato salad, fruit cocktail, tart, roll and coffee for dinner and cereal, cream, roll, a muffin, jam and coffee for breakfast. However, the caterers did make an extra effort during the holidays, varying the chicken and potato salad with roast beef (cold), mince pies, nuts and olives—but no alcohol. But whatever the shortcomings of these meals by modern standards, they were a nutritious improvement over the sandwich, apple and coffee served on the Vancouver–Seattle run in 1937 and owed much to wartime advances in technology. The "fibre food box," which sat flush upon the passenger's knee, had replaced the old, unsteady box lunch containers. Prepared by the caterers, they would arrive at the aircraft in sets of seven on portable steel racks that were anchored at the rear of the aircraft's cabin on the starboard side. A full load of fourteen passengers needed two racks, which weighed about 40 pounds. Each food box contained a cardboard insert punched with standardized holes for the various cups and dishes. Unsanitary wooden knives and forks had been replaced by TCA engraved lightweight silverware specially designed with short blades and prongs to allow for their use at close quarters. Tiny salt and pepper shakers, plastic plates and Dixie cups—a product of the ice cream industry—also made their appearance at this time. With all these improvements it was said that all the stewardess would have to do was pour the coffee!

While the Lethbridge commissary did not prepare meals, because of its location in the western region, it was one of the company's busiest in-flight operations. This was where all the catering equipment—plasticware, silverware, thermos bottles—as well as oxygen masks, were washed and sterilized before they were sent on to the caterers at Vancouver, Winnipeg and Edmonton. It was here too that the fibre food containers were loaded on board, laundry checked, stewardess satchels made up and magazines collected for the next flight.

Lonie, Jack Maurice P/O(N) J85164//Rl 66140. From Regina, Saskatchewan. Killed In Action Jul. 30/44 age 21. #115 Squadron (Despite the Elements), Witchford, England. Lancaster aircraft #PB 130 was shot down, crashed and burned south of Bretteville-Sur-Laize during an operation against Amay-Sur-Seulles, France. P/Os C.A. Thompson, W.M. Conly, G.J. Imrie, R.W. Carey and two of the crew, not Canadians, were also killed. Pilot Officer Navigator Lonie is buried in the Bretteville-Sur-Laize Canadian War Cemetery, France.

In March 1944 the twentieth edition of the airline's timetable had rolled off Bulman Brothers' press. No longer a single sheet with calendar-type photos, it was now a multi-page book that folded like a road map with a print run of 170,000. Like all airline timetables, it was a complex entity that few outside the business could appreciate. National co-ordination was required: the traffic division in Winnipeg was responsible for proposing basic schedules on the basis of projected passenger convenience and traffic flows but it was still the Post Office in Ottawa that decided, on the basis of its own agenda, whether they could be implemented. When these adjustments had been made, Winnipeg's operations division assigned fleet utilization and servicing schedules. Because the timetable had to be distributed to the offices, hotels and homes of its customers a month in advance, the instant the final schedules were agreed upon all the preparation of the actual brochure had to be completed within a fortnight. This meant that three other divisions in TCA then went to work on it, usually in all-night sessions. Advertising (Montreal) prepared ads appropriate for the season and the target audience and laid out the brochure. Various front covers were tried—from photographs and drawings of Lockheeds to a stylized Speedbird—before the Maple Leaf crest was made standard. The communications department (Winnipeg) verified all phone numbers. Passenger service (Winnipeg) provided the data on limousines, meals, accommodation and immigration regulations. Fares were calculated, connecting airline schedules consulted and flight crews assigned before it went to printing. As with all the other timetables, this one—number twenty—told of the airline's current history: the new service to Blissville, New Brunswick, which had been temporary from May 10, 1941, to June 16, 1941, but was returning again in July 1944; the third transcontinental flight that had just been inaugurated; and the new Lethbridge–Calgary–Edmonton service. No longer a travel brochure, the 1944 Trans Canada Airlines timetable had through its nineteen predecessors evolved into a masterpiece of calculation, history and sales stimulant.

Wilmot, Brian Edmund SAL(P) J23777 D.F.C. & Bar. From Winnipeg, Manitoba. Killed Aug. 21/44 age 21. #415 Swordfish Squadron (Ad Metam). Halifax aircraft #MZ 633 was in a mid-air collision with Halifax aircraft #ND 609. MZ 633 crashed five miles southwest of Selby, Yorkshire, on the Doncaster Road between Birkin and West Haddlesey. SAL Wilmot, Sgt. E. Henley, P/O. T.E. Wiltse, F/O.s J.H. Hudson, W.R. Eaglestone, Cpl. W.R. Dickson, and Sgt. N.M. Malpass (RAF) were all killed in #MZ 633. There were six airmen, not Canadians, killed in aircraft #ND 609. Squadron Leader Pilot Wilmot is buried in the Stonefall Cemetery, Wetherby Road, Harrogate, Yorkshire, England.

On September 14, 1944, the company learned that P.G. Johnson, TCA's first vice-president of operations, had died at the age of fifty. There was shock at the suddenness of his passing, and the November edition of *Between Ourselves* paid tribute thus: "When Philip G. Johnson departed Canada after the organization of Trans Canada Airlines he was a young man. When he shouldered the massive responsibilities of a Boeing Company dedicated to mass weapon production for civilization's survival, he seemed at the height of his powers. So it is that his sudden death seems incredible. The news of it fell as a shock upon the entire aviation industry, but with greater intensity upon those of our employees who remember Phil Johnson personally and worked with him in the monumental task of flinging a modern airline together within twelve months across the immensity that is Canada. *Let us now praise famous men . . . their bodies are buried in peace and their names liveth evermore . . . Ecclesiastes."*

The US media had it right the first time: P.G. Johnson was "King of the Air"—at least in Canada.

Emery, Sydney James (FW) J22394. From Lethbridge, Alberta. Killed Oct. 17/44 age 28. #177 Squadron (Silenter in Medias Res). Beaufighter aircraft #RP 709 crashed into a hill, after take-off, eight miles east of the aerodrome at Chuinga. F/Lt. Emery's brother-in-law, the RAF navigator, was also killed. Flight Lieutenant Pilot Emery has no known grave, his name is inscribed on the Singapore War Memorial, Malaya.

TCA employees were entitled to one air pass annually to anywhere on the TCA network, but given that the fourteen seats on the Lodestar were already too few for those travelling on official government duties, when even businessmen had to obtain a priority pass to fly, for a TCA employee to complete a flight across the country must have been equivalent to a lottery win. Staff attempting such a feat in 1944 remember their joy on hearing the agent say, "You're in luck. Central ticket office had a 'Latcan'," or "We've had a no-show, and I think we'll be able to board you as the mail and baggage are lighter than expected." But more often than not they heard, "Get ready to leave us now. You'll be deplaned in Armstrong," or, in a stage whisper from the counter staff, "It's that man again. Who's going to tell him that we're deplaning all baggage to clear the flight? He's going to be stuck here in Kap until next week." One weary employee remembers that after having spent most of his vacation being bumped and sitting in airport lounges, he was ready "to blackjack the entire population of Kap or Armstrong if they showed the slightest desire for that solitary seat." However, one of the perks of being part of the mighty CNR was that TCA employees and their families also received a rail pass annually, and this method of transport must have been far more accessible. (Sadly for the railway employees, very senior CNR staff excepted, this privilege was not reciprocal.)

As with all airlines, the priority for boarding was based on length of service, and then as now "deadheading" flight crews took priority over all, including revenue passengers. Company employees travelling on TCA business were given special air and rail passes with "jump seat authority" to travel in the cockpit if necessary, although until the transatlantic operation formally became part of TCA, the employees of CGTAS, including flight crews, had no pass privileges on the airline and vice versa.

For those employees who hoped to make it onto a flight, the company put out the following rules:

- Be sure to request your pass in plenty of time.
- Let the passenger agent know that you are travelling on a pass.
- Be at the airport 20 minutes ahead of the departure time.
- Do not boast about your pass to other passengers.
- Board the plane last.
- Take at least $20.00 with you for a journey of 1,000 miles. Take more for more. Do not depend upon the hospitality of staff at other stations.
- If your flight is interrupted, ask for your pass back.
- Allow one day more for the return journey.

What every "bumpee" dreaded was being marooned at Armstrong, Ontario. By the beginning of 1945 there were twelve TCA staff "studying" at the "Armstrong College of Airline Knowledge," and perhaps because indoor plumbing had just been installed in the airline's boarding house, they took vigorous exception to their station's poor reputation. This was in part due to the company's policy of misinformation: in best Orwellian tradition, the stopover did not officially exist. Although it was essential for refuelling the transcontinental flights, it was deliberately left off all TCA timetables and advertisements. The first the passengers knew of its existence was when they were shaken awake and told they were about to land there. TCA's resident radio operators, passenger agents and control tower operators, and CNR's brakemen, defended their station. They pointed out that they lived 50 yards away from where the flights landed, so there were no bus woes as in Toronto. And speaking of that city, they were sure that the Royal York Hotel did not serve pemmican or fresh game (sometimes shot by the TCA employees themselves) as did their hostel in Armstrong. Unlike at Gander, travel to the "outside" was no problem for Armstrong employees: the CNR line ran behind the airport and a passing train could be flagged down, or they could take the "jigger," the fondly remembered "Silver Louse," to the town of Armstrong itself. In his description of the town, the local *Between Ourselves* correspondent said, "There is a voting population of 250, exclusive of Canada's brown natives. There is no municipal governing body as Armstrong comes under the jurisdiction of Port Arthur. The only law is one policeman with a six shooter. The only brick building is the CNR station, the only licensed establishment the hotel (known as Ye Olde Leaky Roof). There are also two bootleggers (one at present incarcerated)."

(Armstrong's days as a TCA station were numbered. This was partly due to the ever-increasing range of modern aircraft, but its value diminished even more after the "Great Lakes Airway" was negotiated with the United States in

1945, and transcontinental TCA flights were allowed to overfly US territory and thus could refuel at Lakehead (now Thunder Bay), Ontario. Having played so essential a role in the nation's history, the unloved and much-storied station at Armstrong was closed on Dominion Day, 1947.)

"They are dropping out of the skies with every flight these days—men who only months ago were piloting their aircraft over a blazing beachhead in Normandy, fighting the Luftwaffe over Europe, crumbling the cities of Germany and hounding the enemy's submarines from the Atlantic," announced the editor of *Between Ourselves*. "Home again! And are we glad to greet them!" With the war winding down, seconded employees were returning home to reclaim their jobs, and familiar faces reappeared in the airline's offices, hangars and shops. Employees were warned to "limber up your good right arms for a campaign of earnest hand-shaking." In the traffic department Bill Dalby greeted some of those who had left early in the war on a military leave of absence. Graeme Gibson, who had gone overseas with the First Canadian Division, had risen to the rank of lieutenant-colonel, Crawford Burns had served in an anti-aircraft unit with the Royal Canadian Artillery, Max Eagles had been an RCAF flying officer, and Murray Law a navigation instructor and then pilot officer. All were awarded five-year-service pins.

In December 1944, Major Gus Sivertz, Army Public Relations, accompanied Private "Smokey" Smith, the young winner of the Victoria Cross, as he flew across Canada to his family home in New Westminster, BC. As the aircraft sped westward through the night, the Major realized that it was Christmas Eve, and looking at his fellow travellers, he was struck by the wealth of human sorrow, joy and consolation within the Lodestar cabin. The country had, after all, been at war for five years, and in a surge of emotion the Major composed the following essay. He gave it to airline personnel on arrival at Winnipeg and it is reprinted here in its entirety.

Flight By Night

Inside the warm cabin of the Trans Canada airliner the quiet was broken only by the rhythmic beat of the powerful motors. And the passengers, now knit into a family of fellow travellers, were silent. Many slept, tucked under wool blankets and pillowed against back-tilted seats.

Only one small light glowed above the stewardess's seat as she prepared hot coffee for the pilots. Far below a few lights glimmered as late revellers carried Christmas Eve into the chill hours of Christmas morning. Fields and lakes showed white where they lay blanketed in snow—sheeted up for the long Ontario winter.

Over the starboard wingtip, throwing gleams of cold light on silvered metal, played the weird spectacle of the Northern

Lights—the Aurora Borealis. Like a huge hand it covered the northern horizon, now pale and chill, now brilliant as it reached to the zenith. Like fingers of ectoplasm from a million heroic dead reaching toward heaven.

And steady as a ship upon a placid sea the airliner knifed through the night sky, winging its way westward with a human cargo as mixed in emotion as the cargoes of the great Atlantic convoys.

The passengers were not all asleep. The tall, quiet Air Force corporal still sat bolt upright and smoked one cigarette after another as he stared straight ahead. It was a race against time and only the speed of flight could help him win and see his mother alive.

It was a heavy burden and one that he alone could bear, but sympathy flowed out to him from those few who knew his mission. That's why the stewardess came quietly with a cup of hot coffee and sat on the arm of his chair to talk to him about other things—little things, impersonal things.

And the little old woman who sat forward near the pilot's door was awake. It was her first flight and her spirit was far from the peaceful fields of Canada. It was roaring over Germany with her son, a tail gunner in a Lancaster bomber. Never had she been so close to him as in this aircraft. The steady beat of the motors, the swift flight through the keen winter night, the feeling of being above the earth brought a new kinship with her fighter son. A smile played on her tired face—a face lined and tanned by prairie winds and suns.

On two opposite seats, bundled up to their chins, slept two little dynamos of energy, children of a naval officer whose wife now slept the sleep of exhaustion. And of course, it was their first Christmas aloft, flying above the roof of Canada.

There was still no hint of dawn in the sky but the Northern Lights had paled a little as the plane held its steady course for Winnipeg. The stewardess opened the door to the pilot's cabin and the sudden light made an aureole of her hair. As she came back, she smiled at the young soldier in battle dress on whose breast was a new scarlet ribbon with a single small bronze Maltese cross in the centre.

He also slept. But there was little sleep in a humble New Westminster home where a proud Father and Mother waited to meet a hero son.

Morning came and the fabulous sunrise of the West filled the plane with gold and flame-coloured light. Passengers stirred as the rich smell of coffee pervaded the small home—a metal cabin speeding them on their several errands.

Breakfast trays appeared, each adorned with a sprig of holly, and each accompanied with a bright "Merry Christmas."

Yes, it was Christmas morning and faces brightened as the age-old lively greeting passed from one to another. Each individual burden seemed lighter, each heart sprang with new hope.

The miracle of flight had brought together this diverse group of humans for the space of a few hours and left on each an indelible impression, a happy memory.

Fulton, Stanley Joseph SAL(P) J7537. From Vancouver, British Columbia. Killed Dec. 21/44 age 26. #410 Cougar Squadron (Noctivaga). Oxford aircraft #R 6329 was flying in fog when it struck Wrotham Hill, England. Squadron Leader Pilot Fulton is buried in the Brookwood Military Cemetery, Woking, Surrey, England.

The unsung and unknown heroes of TCA were undoubtedly the telephone operators who doubled as counter staff. It was said that the women (and they were always women) who manned the airline switchboard lost their youthful laughter and good dispositions very early into the job. One of them was Marie La Zary who told a journalist that she "daily harnessed and tamed the Winnipeg switchboard" along with Lorna Beauchamp, Gladys Armstrong, Eileen Bowman and Grace Campbell. Her interviewer, in explaining why the job had such a high level of stress, wrote:

> The unfortunate girl looks around at the blaring lights—dazed! She clutches one phone, sometimes two phones, answering call after call, soothing the nerves of busy executives, putting through long distance calls, relaying and taking messages, and at the same time trying her utmost to please the visitor at the counter. Her fingers fly! Her head spins! Yet all the time that little voice within her goes on saying, "Smile, sister, smile and keep calm and cool!" For our young lady behind the counter and the switchboard knows she must keep her head high, as her manner and voice represent Trans Canada Airlines. She witnesses hundreds of little everyday

The TCA telephone switchboard, Winnipeg, 1944.

dramas. She listens to the problems of everyone from office boys to executives, salesmen waiting for appointments, and the entire cross section of the world's aviation travelling public with its foibles and fun. Here are just a few of the queer incidents that have added spice to our Winnipeg operations switchboard:

- A passenger got off one of the flights and, approaching the counter, said, "I want to see someone." A pause. "I forget his name." "What department does he work in?" "Oh my goodness, I don't know. I don't work for your airline!" "Can you describe him?" "No, but he told me to visit him when I got into town. I know he works in an office here. Could you rattle off some names?" "Well sir, we have 1,200 employees here in Winnipeg." "That's okay, go ahead. I'll know his name when you come to it."

- One woman phoned on a Wednesday and asked the TCA operator if it was going to rain on Saturday as she was taking several children to a picnic.

- Then a brilliant person phoned and asked the operator what was the exact distance from England to India and the travelling time by air. The TCA operator, caught unawares, replied that she was unable to give her that information at the moment but would call her back. "My oh my," sighed the voice. "Very stupid of you not to know and be able to answer promptly, especially working for an airline." The operator after one big gulp replied, "I'm sorry, Madam."

- One evening a quiet, meek voice whispered over the phone, "May I please speak to Willie?" "Willie who and what department does he work in?" "I really couldn't say. I met him last night at a dance and he told me he worked at Stevenson Field." "You know, my dear, Stevenson Field covers a lot of territory." "Does it? I didn't know. Oh well, forget about it."

TCA Suggestion Awards for 1944 (Winnipeg):

- William Westwood and "Bud" Allen of Revenue Accounting won $100 each. Every month they were inundated with ticket sales reports from all the traffic offices. They suggested staggering the submission of the reports and so relieved the congestion.

- Eddie Blake of the Winnipeg shops was awarded $5 for eliminating erosion in the aircraft intensifier tubes. By placing a small baffle inside the ring immediately where the gasses come in contact with the tube under high pressure, he discovered that the eroded portion was eliminated.

- Harry Walberg reclaimed 30,000 aircraft batteries and 20,000 insulators in two years. Harry discovered that they could be reclaimed by drying them individually on a perfectly flat surface. The idea got him $166.

- Loretta Havorka was awarded $5 for her proposal that fitted wooden blocks be used for spray painting nose sections and crank cases. The parts not to be painted were masked with large quantities of tape, which because of the war was impossible to buy. The blocks were made in the carpentry shop.

- John Easveld, TCA agent in charge at Winnipeg, was awarded $10 for his suggestion. Passenger agents in the rush of flight departure sometimes forgot to endorse excess baggage on flight coupons. John suggested that the words "Did you endorse excess on flight coupon?" be stamped on the back of the envelope where they could not be missed.

Christie, Harry Dean F/O(BA) J3623 1//R176577. From Raymore, Saskatchewan. Killed In Action Jan. 12/45 age 27. #424 Tiger Squadron (Castigandos Castigamus). Halifax aircraft #MZ 805 failed to return from a night mine-laying operation in the Harbour at Flensburg, Germany. Flying Officer Bomb Aimer Christie has no known grave, his name is inscribed on the Runnymede War Memorial, Englefield Green, Egham, Surrey, England.

When Vice-President O.T. Larson returned to United Airlines on January 12, 1945, he was the last of the Americans from P.G. Johnson's original group who had come to Canada to set up the airline. Over 300 staff crowded into Winnipeg's Fort Garry Hotel that evening to wish him well. The mayor of the city, Bill English and Captain R.E. Hadfield, representing the pilots, gathered at the podium to present him with the painting *Winter in the Laurentians* by Frank Hennessey, RCA. Larson said he had seen the company "come of age in his seven and a half years to assume its place in the global picture."

But Trans Canada Airlines staff had not seen the last of their American foster parents. At 15:50 on January 21, 1945, a Boeing B-29 Super Fortress landed on Vancouver Airport's Runway 25, causing the worst traffic jam of onlookers that airport employees had ever seen. At the B-29's controls was none other than "Slim" Lewis, and one of the passengers was Oliver West. Both had risen to become executive vice-presidents at Boeing, and with Johnson's death, it was reckoned that West was slated to become the next president of that company. When this did not occur, he returned to Canada in 1947, this time as president of Canadair.

Scorer, Jackson Carlyle F/O(P) J26770//R122266. From Winnipeg, Manitoba. Died Mar. 31/45 age 22. #148 Squadron (Trusty). F/O. Scorer died while in #133 General Hospital as a result of injuries sustained in an off duty collision between a truck and a brick wall one mile southeast of Brindisi, Italy. Flying Officer Pilot Scorer is buried in the Bari War Cemetery at Bari, Italy.

In the final months of the war there were two more CGTAS crashes. On February 27, 1945, Captain James H. Hattie and First Officer Kenneth Moreland were killed on a training flight in the Lockheed 14-H2 *CF-TCF* at Moncton. Shortly afterwards, with the end of hostilities in Europe imminent and CGTAS set to evolve into a full commercial operation, four more Lancasters were added, bringing the total to six aircraft. When a number of pilots volunteered to fly them, conversion flights were scheduled for the summer at Dorval, using the original Lancaster, *CF-CMS*. On June 1, 1945, when Captain Bob Smith, who had been appointed check pilot for CGTAS, was taking Bill Barnes on one such flight, almost immediately after takeoff, the old war horse's number three engine burst into flames. When fire extinguishers failed to extinguish it, the wing started to burn off. Rather than make a full circuit, Smith turned the blazing Lanc back toward the runway, but by this time the wing's upper skin had burned off along with the aileron controls, and the aircraft started to roll over. Then, as they neared the runway, they knifed through the tops of the trees surrounding a small farm on the airport's edge and the flaming aircraft levelled off before hitting the ground and scraping along the field until it was stopped by a large manure heap. An appropriate place for the Lanc, wrote Lothian, but a sad ending for the company's (and Canada's) first four-engined airliner.

While hundreds of people witnessed the fire and the crash, for one schoolboy it was a heart-stopper. John Wright, son of senior CGTAS pilot Jack Wright, was in the schoolyard in Pointe Claire, the Montreal suburb next to Dorval Airport, when the stricken *CF-CMS* lurched overhead. Now a retired Air Canada pilot, he recalled the incident. "I was at school recess when a Lancaster flew over very low with its number four engine on fire. As I knew that my dad was at Dorval Airport to do a test flight, I assumed it was him and ran to the crash site. But by the time I had got there, the crew had left. The pilots were Bob Smith and Bill Barnes. But what a terrible feeling to see what I thought was my dad crashing."

The company paid out $1,168 in property damage, but no one thought to commemorate aircraft #100's demise with a photograph or keep a part of it for future generations.

Lancaster R5727, soon to be CF-CMS, possibly at Ottawa. The aircraft has guns and a unique ventral turret, which was discarded on all the Lancs. The German-made Junkers W-34 in the background provides a historical contrast. Ken Leigh collection

CF-CMS at Dorval Airport, a half hour before it crashed. This was the first installation of the power egg for the North Star. The wooden nose has been refitted with alclad and the Merlins are wearing North Star cowls, their exhausts blasting noise into the open cockpit window. Ken Leigh collection

When the company's Victory Loan canvassers came around for the ninth time in April 1945, it was a far cry from the Gold Star drive of 1941. Now the American and Russian armies were in the suburbs of Berlin and the RCAF was assembling its "Tiger Force" bombers for service in the Far East. Persuading employees to buy more bonds just as the war was drawing to a close might have seemed like a hard sell, but of the 3,121 employees that were canvassed, 2,833 subscribed, and the 9th Victory Loan campaign yielded $662,250 in bonds, exceeding the airline's quota by $140,150. For the final time, the V-Flag Award hung above 63 company offices that had exceeded their quota; the traffic division topped the list at 149 percent, followed by the Western Division at 136 percent, and overall the employees at Winnipeg with 131 percent. All purchasers were advised to hold onto their bonds as nest eggs as long as they could—at least until the far-off year of 1957. Although the canvassers carried them about the Winnipeg Shop as a joke, they insisted that their baseball bats and brass knuckles were not used to sell the bonds, "just good old-fashioned patriotism and enlightened self-interest. No wonder we are building a great airline."

And then it was over. At nine o'clock in the evening of May 4, 1945, Gordon McGregor, Commanding Officer at 126 Wing, Uetersen, North Germany, received a signal: PERSONAL FOR COMMANDERS FROM AOC. ALL HOSTILITIES ON 2ND ARMY FRONT WILL CEASE AT 0800 HOURS TOMORROW 5TH MAY.

While some of his pilots thought of volunteering for action against the Japanese, McGregor, who had once applied to TCA for a job, looked forward to returning to his desk at Bell Telephone Company and once more becoming a "Sunday pilot."

On June 19, 1945, Joseph W. "Windy" Reid's training as a TCA first officer, flying between Winnipeg and Toronto, was interrupted by a summons to Ottawa to be decorated with the Distinguished Flying Cross by the US Ambassador to Canada. The citation was signed by Lt. General Carl Spaatz himself. "For extraordinary achievement while participating in many patrols over the Normandy beach head area. As a result of his outstanding leadership, Wing Commander Reid's squadron has destroyed at least 20 enemy aeroplanes since D-Day. His courage, skill and devotion reflects the highest credit upon himself and the armed forces of his country." Having joined RAF Ferry Command in 1941, Reid was one of the youngest wing commanders in the British Empire. The Sydney, Nova Scotia, native had flown supplies into and wounded out of Malta and also served as personal pilot to Prime Minister Winston Churchill on his historic mission to Moscow. Later he would fly Churchill and Sir Anthony Eden to meet with President Roosevelt in Washington.

On August 14, 1945, Japan surrendered, and the world was no longer at war. Canada prepared to welcome back its veterans. Of the thousands of homecomings that took place in the days and weeks that followed, the greatest for the nation undoubtedly began on October 26. In the early dawn that day, the liner *Queen Elizabeth* majestically entered Halifax harbour, carrying the largest number of Canadian servicemen in any single ship movement. Waiting for them at the Halifax railway station were twenty-two special trains that would deposit them at their homes across the country. But before the first soldier had even disembarked, TCA Flight 19 took off from Dartmouth Airport with fifty packages of photos. The Canadian Army Public Relations Bureau had called on the company's Air Express to perform one more vital service. With notice of the ship's arrival spread by the wire services, the whole country was savouring the event, and the army wanted every community in the Dominion, whatever its size, to awake the next morning to a front-page photo in the local newspaper of the *Queen* with her decks lined with "our boys." That was how many a soldier stepped off the train to be greeted with the ship's and in some cases his own photo in his hometown newspaper.

But that wasn't Trans Canada Airlines's last service of the war. Two of those special trains were heading toward Vancouver carrying the city's own Seaforth Highlanders, covered in glory after the Italian campaign, and the city fathers planned to march the Seaforths down the city's main street from the station. Tradition demanded that the Highlanders be led by their own pipe band in full regalia, but somewhere over the prairies it was discovered that the band members' gaiters and stockings were missing. Without these, the heroes who had thrown back the best of the German Army would not be able to march. A frantic exchange of phone calls located the stockings and gaiters at headquarters in Ottawa, and once more TCA Express was called on. Could they get the 54-pound box out to the Seaforths before their train pulled into Vancouver?

By this time the "specials" were hurtling past Winnipeg, and in Vancouver the streets were already being decorated with bunting and school children were preparing to line the route. The precious cargo was put aboard Flight 7 at Ottawa Airport with the hope that it would make Regina before the train stopped there. It did: the Lodestar touched down in the wee hours, and airline personnel rushed the box over to the train conducting officer at Regina station. Two days later the skirl of the pipes and swing of the kilts brought tears of joy and pride to the thousands of Vancouverites as their own came marching home. The airline wasn't there to take a bow. For TCA Express, it had been one more job well done.

"We of TCA expect much of the coming world of peace," wrote the editor of *Between Ourselves* on VE Day. "We see ourselves loading giant airliners, lacing this country with schedule upon schedule, and reaching out across the oceans to many lands. These are our great days of testing. Thus far we have measured up. Only if we can continue to do so can we claim our future honestly."

By that same summer George Lothian, Harold Thomae and Alan Blackwood had all completed their 100th Atlantic crossings, and on August 25 Symington honoured them with a presentation. Lothian was given a silver coffee urn, Thomae an illuminated globe of the world, and Blackwood a Longine wristwatch. Lothian recalls that Thomae expressed all of the CGTAS veterans' thoughts when he stood up at the presentation dinner to say, "Thank you for

serving Canadians

TCA Captain J. Wendell Reid, D.F.C.

A native of Sydney, N.S., he has, like all TCA Captains, flown over a million miles with the Skyliners. He has six years' service with the R.C.A.F., seven years with TCA, and over 10,000 flying hours to his credit.

TCA company esteem was shown to its pilots and personnel with a series of post-war ads featuring various personalities, routes and equipment. This colour ad appeared c. 1948.

the gift and the friends that I have gained in TCA. As a matter of fact, the happiest days of my life have been spent here, outside the doors of a Lancaster." That September Captain George Lothian was made check pilot of the CGTAS. Thomae, an American who had joined the RCAF and flown for Ferry Command and BOAC before coming to CGTAS, was discharged from the air force and put on TCA payroll. Alan Blackwood had joined the airline in 1939 as a ground radio operator and began Atlantic flying in 1942 on loan to BOAC.

WELCOME HOME !

The following TCA employees have returned from leave of absence on account of Military Service to resume their work with the Company.

J.J. Sandusky, Cargo Handler, Lethbridge. P.D. Roy, Navigating Officer, Trans Atlantic Service, Montreal, E.L. Brook, Passenger Agent, Winnipeg, W.J. Burden, Cargo Handler, Windsor. Miss A.E. Jonason, Clerk, Winnipeg. J.W. Singer, Cargo Handler, Toronto, F.A. Bennet, Assistant Stockkeeper, Winnipeg.

Company policy in hiring veterans was guided by the federal Reinstatement in Civil Employment Act, and Billy Wells, now in the personnel department, was put in charge of explaining to "employees in His Majesty's Forces on Leave of Absence" their rights and opportunities in TCA.

As the British Commonwealth Air Training Plan was now winding down, almost all of the overhaul of military aircraft, engines and propellers had been completed at the maintenance shops in Winnipeg, and with the incoming veterans training on the new power plants and hydraulic brake systems, it was a convenient time for the company to let its wartime female staff go. The role of women in society now did a complete reversal—and not only in TCA. As the gods of war were supplanted by household gods, the women went from "Rosie the Riveter" to "Happy Homemaker." They had always known that their jobs were not careers, and it was now expected that, having had their "adventure," they would be pleased to return home and raise families. The airline itself saw no contradiction in letting go trained female machinists who had proven their adaptability.

There was not a little sadness at their passing out of the TCA ranks. At Lethbridge, for instance, where in 1944 there had been eleven single women at the TCA Airport and City office, there were three by September a year later. The loss to the Lethbridge TCA ladies' fastball team was keenly felt by its manager, Flight Control Officer Orv. Knight. Gone were Jean Brodie, Hazel Ellis, Hazel Matheson and Molly Andersen. At the TCA Lethbridge Commissary, the exodus was almost frantic: Sally Erickson married to become Sally Aschin and was then replaced by Vi Miller who, having been "also shot up by Dan Cupid," was replaced by Elda Lizzi.

However, many of the female staff who were made redundant didn't marry and were forced to look for other jobs. Jack Dyment related that for years after the war whenever he and his wife went shopping at Eaton's or The Bay, they'd get on an elevator and the female operator—elevator doors did not open or close automatically in those days—would say, "Hello, Jack, how's TCA?" When they got off, Mrs. Dyment would inquire, "And who is she?" Jack would have to explain that she had worked for him in maintenance during the war. Then they would go to a counter and another sales lady would say, "Hello Jack! How's everybody?" And again Jack would have to explain.

Several of the original employees who had joined the airline before or early in the war were promoted in 1945–46. Captain Barney Rawson was appointed director of flight development. Captain Herb Seagrim was made superintendent of flight operations. W.S. "Bill" Harvey became assistant auditor, replacing Henry Keil, who had been chief clerk. Captain René Giguère was appointed flight instructor, Winnipeg; Miss P.E. Harding was made stewardess supervisor of the Central Division; and Herb Harling became supervisor of the convention and meeting bureau, Winnipeg. Jack Crosby was named assistant chief pilot (Eastern Division) at Toronto, allowing him (he said) more time to play with his son John Jr.'s electric train set. Ted Allan, who reckoned that in the last seven years he had completed 5,981 hours and 45 minutes in the air in TCA aircraft, turned in his headphones to become flight assistant in the operations department. Jim Storie became assistant chief pilot (Western Division) and was moved from Toronto to Winnipeg. When asked what he was looking forward to, he said, "Pressurized aircraft" and the day he could trade in his old Hudson on a Cadillac Sport Eight. Some who had flown into war zones, like Lindy Rood and George Lothian, were awarded the "Atlantic Star."

In November 1944, representatives of fifty-four nations met in Chicago to establish an international civil air organization for the post-war world. In Canadian fashion, TCA President H.J. Symington played the mediator between the British and American negotiators, causing Canada to be courted by both camps. The fruits of the Chicago Convention were not only the eventual establishment of the International Civil Aviation Organization and its headquarters in Montreal, but for TCA the cross-border route monopolies that were to become the airline's future money spinners: Halifax–Boston, Toronto–Cleveland, Toronto–Chicago, Port Arthur–Duluth, Victoria–Seattle, Whitehorse–Fairbanks. To the company's relief, the Americans did not take back the lucrative Toronto–New York service but granted it Toronto–Chicago as well. In an about-face, having championed multilateralism at Chicago, the Americans then

TCA officers meeting in preparation at the Windsor Hotel, Montreal, 1944. The officers were prominent participants at the Chicago Convention that set up ICAO and the later Havana Conference that created IATA. Photo courtesy Janet Proudfoot

embarked on a series of bilateral air agreements, each seemingly designed to detour around the British and their scattered colonies. A final benefit from the Chicago convention was that the International Air Transport Association (IATA), which had been created in Havana in April 1945, would now be headquartered in Montreal. In October Symington was elected its first president. On December 27, 1945, Canadian delegates chartered Lancaster *CF-CMY* to fly to Havana to join thirty other nations in expanding worldwide the International Air Transport Association, which until then had been limited to Europe.

In one month—December 1945—CGTAS operated 12 flights eastbound and 13 westbound carrying 148,831 pounds of mail, 4,356 pounds of express freight and 71 official passengers. In a signal that passenger revenue rather than mail was poised to become the airline's greatest source of income, as it would for airlines everywhere, TCA's traffic department reported that fifty-four people had already requested that their names be placed on the waiting list for the first "peacetime" crossings. In the United States passenger revenue already accounted for 70 percent of the combined transportation revenue of all airlines, and it was becoming difficult to remember when there had been a time when mail had been in that position. The statistical record for the last five years plus first six months of 1945 told the story at TCA:

Year	Total Transport Revenue	TCA Passenger Revenue	Passenger Revenue as % of Total
1940	$4,483,006	$1,574,217	35.0
1941	5,503,830	2,348,428	42.7
1942	6,479,856	3,065,453	47.3
1943	8,119,570	4,213,599	51.9
1944	8,635,678	4,456,767	51.6
1945 (6 months)	–	–	54.4

With the troops returning home, mail revenue fell to less than 40 percent, although the weight of the mail increased. This was beneficial to the Post Office because the TCA Act of 1937 had set the rate on a miles-flown basis, regardless of weight, and every time the airline showed a profit or a loss the rate was accordingly reset by the government. By 1945, when TCA posted annual profits, subsequent reductions in the rate combined with the more than doubled weight of the mail hurt the airline's finances. For its part, the Post Office wanted to rein in the airline's route expansion because for every extra mile flown, its payments to TCA increased proportionately. TCA, on the other hand, with its ambitions to fly far beyond Canada's borders after the war, blamed the postmaster general for exerting his influence to inhibit the company's post-war expansion. Now there were no magazine advertisements in the "Air Mail Gives Wings to Business" theme, and when TCA employees expressed resentment toward the Post Office, Vice-President Bill English did not write a memo in defence of carrying the mail, as he had in 1943. The Trans

An almost tranquil setting at Montreal's Dorval Airport as CF-CMZ sets out on yet another transatlantic flight. Now featuring the long slender nose, the Lanc XPP could carry ten passengers and crew and 4,524 pounds of mail to Europe.

Canada Airlines Act with its sliding-scale formula, which in 1937 had provided for a guarantee against losses, was now too inflexible.

However, with the end of the war the Act was amended and the mail contract renegotiated so that the Cabinet could arbitrate between the postmaster general and the minister. The Post Office would now pay TCA to transport the mail on a ton-per-mile basis, wherever it flew. This meant, of course, that the airline had no incentive to extend its airmail routes into parts of the Dominion where the loads would be too light to pay the costs—something that was certain to inspire citizens in isolated communities to write to their members of parliament.

There were other amendments to the Act that year. The airline's authorized capital was raised from $5 million to $25 million, allowing for the purchase of the DC-3s and North Stars. Most important, the 1945 amendments allowed TCA to petition the Governor-in-Council to incorporate subsidiary companies. As long as it retained 51 percent of the shares of any subsidiary, the corporation could buy, hold and sell shares in them. With the war drawing to a close, the government was moving to put CGTAS onto a civil footing and Trans Canada Airlines (Atlantic) Ltd. was established. Financially separate from TCA—which was to service North America only—this second division would be responsible for all over-ocean routes, in particular to Britain, but later to Bermuda and the Caribbean. This corporate distinction stayed on the books until 1952, when the Atlantic division was absorbed into the airline.

TCA employees Peggy Edwards (left), a draftsman for Airways, and Edee Wickberg, a steno in engineering, Winnipeg, 1944.
Photo courtesy Janet Proudfoot

In what might be viewed as a minor victory by the Opposition, the airline was for the first time made accountable to Parliament. Its board of directors now had to report annually to MPs with "the results of their operations and any such information as appears to them to be of public interest." More mystifying from a political vantage point, there were no guidelines, principles or standards laid out for them to follow, and in the years to come the directors could have used their reports to subject the government to criticism—something that they chose not to do. However, Howe still retained complete control as Section 15 of the original Act was also amended with the following subsection: "The Governor-in-Council may from time to time authorize the minister to enter into a contract amending the Trans Canada contract and containing such terms as the Governor-in-Council may order."[10]

Since passengers were to be the company's post-war elixir, to cope with the number expected, especially when the DC-4Ms were to be put in service, the training programs for passenger and traffic agents were accelerated. As the company's policy was to give preference to war veterans, there was a predominance of RCAF personnel in both occupations. Instructed by Al Godbold, the graduates of the second traffic training school were F/O Bob Slessor, F/O Bill Dickinson, P/O Hugh McElligott, F/L Phil Baby and P/O Kel Turner. Of the 11 graduates of the 13th passenger agent class, 9 were RCAF veterans, bringing to

136 the number of repatriated RCAF men assigned to TCA stations as agents since 1942. They were B. Blight (Moncton), F/O George Mitchell (Winnipeg), Flt-Sgt Ed Mann (Winnipeg), F/O Frank McDonald (Glace Bay), Eric Stull (Sudbury), F/O Bob Livingston (Edmonton), Flt-Sgt Jack Cooke (Edmonton), F/O Barry Kerr (Winnipeg), F/O Howard Barber (Toronto), P/O B.W. Foggo (Winnipeg) and Flt-Sgt A. MacDonald (Moncton).

ANNUAL REPORT OF TRANS CANADA AIRLINES

For the year ending December 31, 1945

Elected by Shareholders:

H.J. Symington CMG KC		
Director, Canadian National Railways	Montreal	
Wilfrid Gagnon CBE		
Director Canadian National Railways	Montreal	
J.A. Northey		
Director, Canadian National Railways	Montreal	
R.C. Vaughan		
President, Canadian National Railways	Montreal	

Appointed by Governor-in-Council:

C.P. Edwards OBE
Deputy Minister of Transport — Ottawa
J.A. Wilson — Ottawa
George Herring
Chief Superintendent of Air
and Mail Services (Post Office) — Ottawa

Officers

President . . . . H.J. Symington, CMG, KC, Montreal
Vice President . . . . W.F. English, Winnipeg
General Manager, Operations . . . . J.H. Tudhope, Winnipeg
General Traffic Manager. . . . . G.R. McGregor, Winnipeg
Operations Manager, Central Region . . F.I. Young, Toronto
Traffic Manager, Central Region . . . . . W.R. Campbell, Toronto
Operations Manager, Western Region. . . . . F.W. Stull, Lethbridge
Traffic Manager, Western Region. . . . . W.J. Dalby, Vancouver
Operations Manager, Eastern Region . . . . T.F.K. Edmison, Moncton
Traffic Manager, Eastern Region . . . . . J.G. Maxwell, Montreal
Operations Manager, Canadian Government Trans-Atlantic Air Service. . . . . F.M. McGregor

Director of Research &
Economic Control . . . . H.C. Cotterell, Winnipeg
Director of Facilities and
Supply Control . . . . F.T. Wood, Winnipeg
Director of Personnel. . . . . E.H. Moncrieff, Winnipeg
Director of Maintenance
and Engineering . . . . J.T. Bain, Winnipeg
Director of Maintenance
and Overhaul . . . . A.M. Sutherland, Winnipeg
Director of Engineering . . . . J.T. Dyment, Winnipeg
Director of Flight Development. . . . . . B.A. Rawson, Winnipeg
Director of Flight Operations . . . . H.W. Seagrim, Winnipeg
Director of Passenger Service . . . . D.R. MacLaren, Winnipeg
Director of Communications
and Electronic Development. . . . . S.S. Stevens, Winnipeg
Director of Training. . . . . J.H. Sandgathe, Winnipeg
Director of Cargo Services . . . . E.T. Howe, Winnipeg
General Auditor . . . . P.W. Baldwin, Winnipeg

To the Shareholders:
The Board of Directors submit the Annual Report of Trans Canada Air Lines for the calendar year of 1944. (The following are the highlights of the Report.)

Passenger, mail and express was close to the capacity of the Air Line. In July, flights were rerouted in the Maritime provinces to bring main line operations closer to the New Brunswick cities of Fredericton and Saint John. A direct service was also provided between Halifax and Sydney, Nova Scotia. A direct operation between Winnipeg and Edmonton waits only upon the installation of airport and airway facilities along this route. The shortening of the transcontinental line by flight across the Great Lakes awaits equipment and airways facilities. Plans for international flight, other than the present trans-Atlantic service are still tentative, but the West Indies, South America and the Pacific are areas of admitted interest to the Company. The newly agreed on TCA operated routes between Canada and the United States will be serviced as soon as wartime conditions permit, these lines being: Halifax–Boston, Toronto–Cleveland, Toronto–Chicago, Port Arthur–Duluth, Victoria–Seattle and Whitehorse, YT–Fairbanks, Alaska. Following a decision of the Canadian Government to undertake the manufacture in Canada of a Douglas DC-4 type of four-engined aircraft engineered to meet special requirements, Trans Canada Air Lines, as the intended user of the equipment, has maintained close liaison with the manufacturer and its designers.

In 1944 the number of passengers carried increased by 12%, air express volume by 4% and air mail volume by .3%. The growth was not as great as in former years but had the Company possessed the equipment and personnel, more traffic could have been handled.

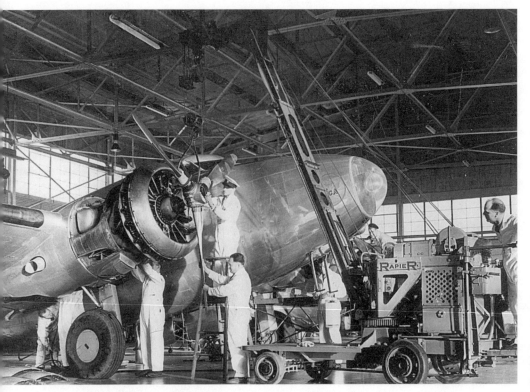

A crane in place at the Winnipeg shop, ready to remove the aircraft's power plant.
Hugh Reid photo

Personnel

As of December 31, 1945, staff at Trans Canada Air Lines numbered 3,272 as compared with 2,790 at the end of 1944. Of these 865 were engaged in the Trans Atlantic Service and on BOAC maintenance at Dorval. In engaging personnel, it is the policy of the Company to employ only those who have seen military service. At the end of the year the number of employees who have served in the Armed Forces was 1,161. Instruction of former RCAF pilots in the techniques of civil air transport was accelerated and eight classes were completed, comprising seventy-six men. Training was similarly given to new radio operator, passenger agent and traffic personnel. The return of former male staff was reflected in further decline in the proportion of female employees. At December 31, women comprised 23% of all TCA personnel, as compared with 29% in 1944 and 35% in 1943.

During the war, three hundred and twenty five TCA employees enlisted in Canada's Armed Forces. At December 31, 1945, one thousand, one hundred and sixty-one members of the airline had seen military service.

Year	Aircraft	Total Seating Capacity
1937	5 Lockheed Electras	50
1938	5 Lockheed Electras 9 Lockheed 14s	140
1939	15 Lockheed 14s	150—16 daily flights
1940	15 Lockheed 14s	150—18 daily flights
1941	6 Lockheed Lodestars 12 Lockheed 14s	204—22 daily flights
1942	12 Lockheed Lodestars 12 Lockheed 14s	288—26 daily flights
1943	11 Lockheed Lodestars 12 Lockheed 14s	274—29 daily flights
1944	14 Lockheed Lodestars 12 Lockheed 14s	316—29 daily flights
1945	3 Douglas DC-3s 14 Lockheed Lodestars 11 Lockheed 14s	369—37 daily flights

Projected Purchases for 1946: 12 Douglas DC-4s, 21 Douglas DC-3s.
Estimated seating capacity: 1117

CANADA'S
National Air Service

The DC-3 in TCA service. Almos
maintenance-free, it was a bargain at $20,00

TRANS-CANADA Air Lines

"London is licking a million wounds." So began the first dispatch from TCA's ticket offices at 17–19 Cockspur Street, London SW1. "No words or pictures can adequately describe the appalling damage that has been wrought upon this city by the Nazi bombs. Everywhere you can see vast open spaces where large building blocks once stood," reported the office manager, Crawford Burns.

The TCA ticket office had opened in November 1945 as part of the CNR office just off Trafalgar Square and across the street from the Canadian High Commission at Canada House. Directly opposite it stood the shell of the Carlton Hotel. A Luftwaffe bomb had penetrated the roof, gone down the elevator shaft and then blown the insides out, leaving only the outer walls. Other TCA divisions were scattered throughout the city with some as far away as Sackville House in Piccadilly.

The British capital was hardly a choice posting for TCA personnel in 1945. Accommodation was impossible to find, most office buildings and stores were still boarded up and food was still rationed. None of this had deterred a stream of TCA visitors to the station. In anticipation of the first Montreal–London flights in September, Stan Hewitt came down from Prestwick to negotiate landing facilities for the airline. W.S. Thompson, director of public relations, was in London to help set up TCA and Canadian National Railway city offices. As welcome as they were, all visitors depleted the city's food supplies further, so much so that Burns's dispatch concluded with: "If you are thinking of having steak or some bacon and eggs on your trip to London, you'd better bring them with you because there ain't no such animal around these parts."

The company wanted to move out of its CNR premises and bring together all of its staff under one roof because of rationing, a shortage of building materials and manpower and the difficulty of obtaining licences to refurbish old buildings, but it would be another four years before this was possible. In the meantime TCA's chief architect, John Schofield, flew back and forth across the Atlantic, touring sites before settling on 27 Pall Mall, another bombed-out building. In late October 1949 it was ready for TCA staff, who moved out of their CNR premises to their own street-level office. It was fronted by a smart picture window that displayed the passenger waiting room, sales and reservations desk, and a wall map with the airline's routes. The company soon outgrew Pall Mall, however, and in 1953 Ed Sellors, the airline's new chief architect, designed new quarters on New Bond Street to which the staff moved in November of that year.

The London ticket office opened to prepare for implementation of the bilateral air agreement that C.D. Howe signed for Canada with the British government in Bermuda on December 21, 1945. By its terms, both Trans Canada Airlines and British Overseas Airways Corporation were to fly between the two countries, with each airline entitled to two destinations. As TCA already had Prestwick and London, BOAC, which already flew to Montreal, chose The Pas, Manitoba. Each airline was also restricted to as many flights as it took for a total capacity of up to 350 passengers per week travelling in each direction, including mails and freight. It was a signal that the honeymoon of wartime cooperation had ended and that the era of commercial rivalry was about to commence.

With its route mileage and personnel soon to triple, the company needed senior managerial skills urgently. Fortunately the war allowed H.J. Symington the luxury of being able to choose men who had proven their leadership under hardship conditions. "In Canada's armed forces," explained Symington in 1945, "was enlisted much of the finest ability of our country and in tapping it, we do both ourselves and the nation a service." Typical of the calibre of man hired then was Group Captain C.J. "Cammie" Campbell, MBE, who was appointed assistant superintendent of TCA communications. Campbell had sited and supervised the building of the RCAF radar stations on the east and west coasts and was loaned for similar duties to the US Army Signal Corps in the Panama Canal Zone. In 1942 he had done microwave technology research at MIT that would lead to the widespread use of Long Range Navigation, or loran. Appointed RCAF director of signals in 1944, he retired from the air force a year later for a job at the Department of Reconstruction. When S.S. Stevens resigned in 1946, Campbell replaced him as director of communications.

If the RCAF aircrew provided TCA with pilots and navigators, then the company looked to the service's senior commands for executive talent. Three such men were hired, all group captains with organizational experience, having commanded wings overseas. Paul Davoud, Ernest Moncrieff and Gordon McGregor were personally chosen by Symington to lead the airline in its postwar expansion.

Appointed operations assistant to "Tuddy" Tudhope, Group Captain Paul Davoud, DSO, DFC, OBE, had entered the RAF as a pilot officer in 1933, but two years later James Richardson invited him to return home and fly for Canadian Airways. Two years after that he became transportation manager for the Hudson's Bay Company transport facilities, which included everything from aircraft to sternwheelers to dog teams. With the outbreak of war, Davoud served in the RCAF as chief instructor at Trenton before being posted to England as commander of 410 Squadron of night fighters; later he was promoted to wing commander of 409 Squadron of Beaufighters. In June 1943, after recovering from serious burns from an air crash, he took over 418 "City of Edmonton" Squadron of Mosquito night fighters. Promoted in 1944 to group captain, he commanded 143 Fighter Bomber Wing made up of three squadrons of Hawker Typhoons that would provide close air support for the Allied armies in Normandy.

Assigned special duties and reporting to the vice-president was Group Captain E.H.G. Moncrieff, OBE, AFC, who had joined the RCAF in 1933, and at the outbreak of war was commanding officer at the RCAF recruiting centre in Sudbury. He was awarded the AFC for his work at No. 12 SFTS at Brandon, Manitoba. In September 1942 he commanded an army co-operation squadron in England and, a year later two RCAF fighter reconnaissance squadrons.

Trans Canada Airlines was too small a canvas for such men; Davoud left in 1948 to accept a job with the air rescue program of Canadian Breweries/Argus Corporation. In 1959 the federal government appointed him chairman of the Air Transport Board. Moncrieff also resigned soon after to become president of Standard Aero Engine Ltd., Winnipeg. Providentially for Trans Canada Airlines, Gordon McGregor stayed for twenty-three more years.

It is the last day in June 1910. On a farmer's field in Montreal's west island, spectators marvel at the spectacle of so many heavier-than-air machines in one place. Balloons and dirigibles, Bleriot monoplanes and Wright Flyers strained to become airborne, and the *Baddeck No. 2*, the aircraft of the Canadian hopeful J.A.D. McCurdy, met with disaster. The country's first aerial meet attracted Edwardian aviation enthusiasts from Europe, the United States and Canada. Two days later Jacques de Lesseps, the son of the engineer who built the Suez Canal, would keep his Bleriot *Le Scarabee* in the air for a full forty-nine minutes and circle the city of Montreal.

Scurrying among the adults at that meet was a nine-year-old boy. The son of Thomas McGregor, a Montreal dentist who had a summer home nearby, Gordon Roy McGregor thought that he "supervised the preparation of the ground, the erection of small grandstands and the arrival and assembly of aircraft," though it was just that the aviation enthusiasts recognized a kindred spirit. Born on September 26, 1901, and educated at St. Andrew's College (as was J.A.D. McCurdy) and McGill University, McGregor kept up his interest in aviation by building balsa wood models, using the construction skills he had inherited from his grandfather, a piano maker. Twenty-two years later, when he was Bell Telephone manager for Kingston, Ontario, McGregor made his first solo at the local flying club in the D.H. Tiger Moth *G-CAKE*. Once he had earned his commercial licence, he wrote to Hungerford to ask for an interview to join TCA. Inexplicably, although he was now a three-time winner of the Webster trophy for best amateur pilot (1935, 1936 and 1938), McGregor received nothing more than a polite acknowledgement.

On October 1, 1938, after being transferred back to Montreal by Bell Telephone, he joined the Non-Permanent Air Force as a weekend pilot, training with 115 Squadron at St. Hubert. With war imminent, in 1939 the squadron's personnel were absorbed into No.1 Fighter squadron and re-equipped with Hurricanes. McGregor soloed in one on October 31, 1939. He took a leave of absence from Bell Telephone to go overseas with the squadron on June 11, 1940. In the middle of the Atlantic he learned that France had capitulated. His squadron's Hurricanes were already obsolescent, and although "half of the squadron had not flown solo in an operational aircraft," the Canadians were thrown into the Battle of Britain, and F/L McGregor distinguished himself as one of "The Few."

Typically McGregor was reticent about his Battle exploits, but among his personal papers he kept a newspaper clipping of the Battle that someone had sent him. The author of the article, written about the same time as Winston Churchill's "Never before in the field of human conflict . . . ," was British Lord Chancellor Sir John Simon, who had been sitting in the House of Commons as the Battle of Britain raged overhead. He wrote these lines in Greek; the British papers published the translation.

> They met up there with "Death"
> And nonchalantly passed the time of day.
> "Immortals these," he said beneath his breath,
> And put his scythe away.

To his dismay, McGregor's administrative experience with Bell Telephone got him transferred to a desk at RCAF headquarters in London, and it was only by entreating his superiors that in 1942 he was posted to Alaska to command a Canadian wing of Kittyhawk fighters. Here he showed what his trademarks would be when president of TCA: the willingness to speak his mind and a direct approach to his job. Remembered as having fought to get his pilots dinghies in case they had to ditch their aircraft, he told "the brass" that in local weather conditions, hand signals were more reliable than radio. He was awarded an OBE in January 1943 and brought back to England as a group captain to prepare for D-Day. Commanding 83 Group in the 2nd Tactical Air Force, he was responsible for eighteen squadrons of fighters—fifteen of them Canadian—that landed in France on June 12, 1944. Later he said handling the logistics of moving across the Channel was the first big administrative job he had ever tackled.

There are so many stories about "GRM" that they almost border on the apocryphal . . . His personal aircraft was a "liberated " Luftwaffe Me. 108 with his initials painted on its fuselage, and for the rest of his life he was very proud to include it on the list of aircraft he was endorsed to fly. When his Wing was using forward landing fields in the Netherlands, and Prince Bernhard asked the mud-encrusted Spitfire pilots if he could get them anything, did McGregor really say

"A hot bath"? (A pilot himself, Bernhard appreciated the answer and later made him a Commander of the Order of Orange Nassau with Swords.) Was it true that whenever the "brass" inspected his airfields, McGregor hid under his caravan in case they transferred him back to headquarters and out of the action?

What was true (his staff witnessed it) was the following story: On December 21, 1962, an old British rabbi came to Montreal and asked to meet the president of Air Canada. He was ushered into McGregor's office on the thirty-ninth floor of Place Ville Marie, the airline's head office at the time. Rabbi Leslie Hardman said he wanted to personally thank "the young RCAF officer" who in the spring of 1945 had saved many lives at the liberation of Belsen concentration camp. Hardman had been attached to the first British Army unit to enter the camp and when the Canadians arrived he saw their commanding officer, Gordon McGregor, passing out food, medicine and cigarettes from his RCAF supplies to the emaciated former inmates. McGregor's initial comment was that he was surprised Hardman recognized him as he had been in uniform then. Then (and his eyes must have lit up) he asked: Did the rabbi perhaps remember his squadron's Spitfire Mk 1Xs? Gordon McGregor was the consummate pilot.

In the closing weeks of the war Symington had cabled Group Captain McGregor, inviting him to an interview on his return to Canada. GRM came back to his home on Grey Avenue, Montreal, and after his discharge on November 27, 1945, he met with Symington. On hearing that McGregor was going to use his leave to travel across Canada, Symington asked him to stop over in Winnipeg and meet Bill English, the vice-president of operations. He was offered a position on December 1, 1945, as a special representative in the traffic department in Winnipeg. "It will not be long," prophesied the editor of *Between Ourselves* in 1945, "before his presence is strongly and effectively felt among us." Bell Telephone Co. was very accommodating and gave him a six-month leave of absence to "undertake a personal adventure with the TCA" until he "would come to his senses."

McGregor reported for work in the airline's traffic department in the very

Gordon R. McGregor, RCAF, 1945.

TCA's Clayton Glenn, Beth Buchanan (McGregor's personal secretary) and a museum curator (right) examine remains of a German Jumo engine. In 1977 a research group excavated a known Junkers Ju.88 crash site in England, confirming that a "probable" credited to McGregor in 1940 had actually been shot down. So, thirty-seven years after the fact, McGregor officially received RCAF "ace" status. Photo courtesy Clayton Glenn

heart of downtown Winnipeg, four storeys above the intersection of Portage and Main. He was introduced to the boss, W.J. "Jack" Dalby, and Vic Fulcher, his assistant, and all the others in the office: Ted Deyman, Bill Myers, Al Godbold, Bruce Hay, Clyde Banfield, Helen Atkinson (Dalby's secretary), Edith McDowell, Laura Shebeski, Kay Ogston and Hildegarde Cameron. Beth Buchanan, who had worked for Canadian Airways and was now the stenographer for Dalby and Fulcher, would transfer to Montreal when McGregor became president to become his private secretary. On his retirement, she became the company's first archivist.

Two months later, after McGregor had familiarized himself with all aspects of the job, he became general traffic manager and discovered that the situation in the department was considerably worse than he had imagined. The airline had been used as a political tool during the war; its personnel had spent company time working for other government departments such as airways and airports; it had been forced to take on uneconomical routes, use aircraft that had been built to keep a Montreal plant in operation, and even had two kinds of engines in its DC-3s—an uneconomical maintenance situation. Worse, the CNR, who served as the airline's bankers, was pessimistic about its chances of ever breaking even.

In 1947 McGregor and several of the TCA staff attended the first joint traffic conference of IATA at Petropolis outside Rio de Janeiro. Always understated, McGregor described what occurred at the conference in these words: "Due to...a mixup, coupled with the fact that the major participants, the US representatives and the Europeans, did not trust each other very much, I was elected chairman of that joint conference." This resulted in publicity that brought him to the attention of the TCA board of directors, and in February 1948 he was elected to the presidency of TCA, replacing Symington, who was retiring. Shortly after, he was taken on a tour of CNR headquarters in Montreal and was introduced to the railway's officers, some of whom were responsible for TCA's fortunes. "When I was introduced to the joint comptroller, his opening remark was, 'I certainly hope you don't have any silly ideas like Mr. Vaughan [the CNR president] that a Canadian transportation enterprise can be operated at a profit.'" McGregor replied that he did not think that any of the airline's personnel, least of all himself, would want to work for the company if it could not be lifted out of a chronic deficit position. Considering the potential for rivalry between the two organizations, he thought it amazing that the airline had survived its infancy at all and surmised that it could not have done so without the protection of Howe.

The relationship between the men, both of whom were passionate about TCA to the point of political shortsightedness, was always one of mutual respect. At their first encounter, the minister set the stage with McGregor with the warning, "You keep out of the taxpayer's pocket and I'll keep out of your hair." McGregor didn't always agree with Howe but he admired him tremendously—even when he wasn't getting what he wanted out of him. "Very early on, he firmly cut down on my pretensions by saying, 'You can't claim one day that TCA is an independent company under its own board of directors and the next a ward of the government entitled to special treatment.'"[1]

Forty-six-year-old Gordon R. McGregor, at the time of his appointment as president of TCA.

The war's end signalled the withdrawal of military units, foreign and domestic, from certain TCA stations. This had advantages and disadvantages. The departure of the RAF at Dorval led the airline to open its own elementary navigation school at the airport, where they could give all transatlantic crews a six-week course. Besides the RAFTC Link training facilities, the company also took over all communications, including the RAF-operated switchboard. Unfortunately for many TCA staff, it did not continue the RAF's bus service from downtown Montreal. With no pilots to ferry back to Canada, the wartime agreement to service the BOAC Liberators was terminated on November 30, 1946, but there were now other airlines to work with. In Vancouver, in preparation for its own Pacific service, TCA looked after the DC-4s of Australian National Airlines, and in Winnipeg the company provided radio coverage for Northwest Airlines' Boeing Stratocruisers on their way to Alaska and the Orient.

When the RCAF and the US navy left the airport at Sydney, Nova Scotia, on December 31, 1945, the local TCA staff were affected on a more personal level. Field maintenance through the remainder of the winter became a TCA problem, especially runway lighting. Until the Department of Transport took over the airport in March 1946, the airline had to provide and maintain the "lily pad" replacements. All eating facilities at the airport had been closed, the loss of the "wet canteen" and American coffee being the most difficult for TCA staff to bear. They also mourned the destruction of two old friends, the Marconi Radio Towers five miles southeast of the airport, which were taken down in January 1946. Convenient for estimating ceilings and visibility (they stuck up through low cloud), they had been an unforgettable—if unnerving— sight for TCA flight crews.

Sydney was designated the alternate for CGTAS flights whenever Gander shut down because of fog, and it later became a regular stop. As Lancs dropped in more frequently, the lack of sufficient airport refuelling trucks became serious. The only two left after the RCAF's departure belonged to Imperial Oil, and they were responsible for the entire island of Cape Breton. One thing the airlines had in abundance, as Sydney Airport's sole tenants, were packs of unwanted cats and dogs that had been abandoned by servicemen. These were not especially popular with the TCA station cat—a large striped tom called Molson.

The TCA Station at Torbay, St. John's, lost its RCAF neighbours overnight—and unexpectedly. On March 16, 1946, number one hangar, aided by 27,276 litres of stored gasoline, burned to the ground. The conflagration consumed the RCAF Control Tower, four aircraft (one of which was the new DC-3 belonging to the US commanding general at Fort Pepperell), four Link trainers and assorted jeeps and tools. The fire brigade from St. John's and the US military from the fort arrived in time to prevent it from spreading to the TCA offices and the DOT took over the airport on April 1. Although TCA continued to fly into Torbay, it would be without a permanent control tower until

December 1952 when the RCAF returned. Perhaps to cheer everyone up, when TCA captain Bill Loftus landed he took the staff at the airport and city ticket offices on a "fam" flight over Argentia. For many it was their first flight.

The Trials of a Stewardess, or Anything for TCA

In civilian air circles a "short" is a non-priority passenger who must be removed from a flight if a priority passenger comes along. If possible, what is known as "protection" is given him. Arrangements are made to continue the journey by a later flight, by train, pony cart or whatever is available.

Recently a young stewardess, unfamiliar with flight vernacular, went to work for TCA. An hour out of Winnipeg she received by radio the following instructions: "Prepare to remove shorts at Toronto. No protection." For a while she wondered how much she really wanted this job.

From *Between Ourselves*

TCA stewardesses in Winnipeg, wasting no time in demonstrating that nylons were back. Left to right: Monica Gillis, Eileen Howard, Helen Sainsbury and Betty Hemingson.

The first TCA flight from Scotland to Vancouver, July 14, 1946. Wartime pressures gave way to the lighter things in life on TCA's domestic and overseas services. The 6,000-mile hop to celebrate Aviation Day in the the city's Diamond Jubilee celebration was made in 28 hours—about 18 hours from the United Kingdom to Montreal and 10 hours 8 minutes on the Lanc's first trip across the Rockies to western Canada.

It was fortunate for TCA that in 1945 only BOAC directly paralleled its Montreal–London route because, except for BOAC's London–New York route where its few Lockheed Constellations were allocated, the British company relied for all its other services on pre-war flying boats until March 1947 and on converted bombers until as late as 1949. These last, known as "Lancastrians" in BOAC service, were Lancaster bombers modified by A.V. Roe and put on the airline's London–Montreal run. The British also unashamedly used their imperial clout to sell them to BOAC's sister airlines, British South American Airways (BSAA) and QANTAS. By the time BOAC could assign Constellations to its Montreal route on April 15, 1947, TCA had its North Stars in use, albeit unpressurized.

While concentrating on building combat aircraft during the war, the British had been aware that American supremacy in transport production was going to leave them far behind after it. Therefore, even before the hostilities ended, London had appointed the Brabazon Committee to search out national aeronautical designs of such technical superiority that in one fell swoop the country would leap ahead of the Americans. The nation that gave the world the steam engine might be impoverished and on the verge of losing its empire, but it still had a flair for innovation. As a result, Rolls Royce adapted jet engine technology to power commercial transports, and the British aircraft manufacturers de Havilland and Vickers Armstrong produced a turboprop and a jet airliner: in production they looked capable of challenging United States products.

In the face of such American and British competition, TCA could not afford to be complacent about its transatlantic service, and until the Canadair DC-4Ms came on line, the final four CGTAS Lancasters were rebuilt as interim Atlantic aircraft. The last four of these, delivered to Dorval in 1945 from Victory Aircraft Ltd., were dubbed the "deluxe" Lancs, for compared with the previous ones, they were just that. Coming into use as the amount of armed forces mail was declining and passenger traffic was about to increase, the four were the true predecessors to all the transoceanic airliners that TCA would ever use.

The government wasted no time in reorganizing CGTAS on the cessation of hostilities in Europe. By the authority of Order-in-Council P.C. 5499 of May 15, 1945, the relationship between the Department of Civil Aviation and Trans Canada Airlines took on a commercial form. It would put into effect:

- the transfer of any cash balances from the previous agreement from the Department to the company,
- the assessment of fares on passengers and cargo,
- an agreement between the Post Office and the company for the carriage of mail.

For all their historical significance, the Lancs 101 to 104 from 1943 had been basic wartime mail carriers and assessed for insurance purposes by CGTAS at $300,000 each. Numbers 105 to 108, assessed at $400,000 each, were not just "new" in the sense of recently being rolled out of Victory Aircraft, but new in their design as well. In an article in the company newsletter entitled "Swelling the Trans Atlantic Fleet," the company introduced to its employees the last four additions to the transatlantic air service. "These deluxe Lancasters are, of course, basically of military design and will serve only until the time when we secure four-engined aircraft built for purely commercial purposes. But of their kind they are distinctive, by no means taking second place to similar British Lancastrians. They are tributes to Canadian workmanship and to the excellence of Canadian aircraft manufacture."[2]

"Flown to the Rolls Royce plant in Hucknell, Derby, to be fitted with the latest in Merlin engines, they were then returned to Malton for TCA interiors to be installed. Reducing cargo space and eliminating the bomb bay accommodated a "stand-up" cabin in which ten passengers could be seated in two rows. The flight crew compartment was enlarged to provide for additional room for the navigating and radio officers. There was a galley for the serving of hot meals and beside it a cabin attendant's chair and desk. The entire aircraft was insulated against the cold with fibreglass and rather than extracting heat from the glycol coolant in the engines, the cabin was heated by gasoline-operated combustion heaters. Individual reading lights, call buttons, ashtrays and oxygen outlets were provided for each passenger. The upholstery and interior colour design were chosen by an interior decorator. Ceilings and walls were yellow with the lower side-wall panels in rust. A mahogany-coloured carpet covered the entire cabin floor and the standard TCA seats were finished in a light green.

To foster a gentleman's club-like atmosphere in their flying boats, both Pan American Airways and BOAC used male flight attendants and retained them after the war in their land planes, especially for flights over water. With the very real possibility of a ditching at sea, training in air-sea rescue was strenuous, as it included competence in the use of aircraft dinghies. Trans Canada Airlines called its first male flight attendants "purser-stewards" and chose seven former servicemen from the current training course for passenger agents on the basis of "their initiative, tact and knowledge of flying." The seven—D.V.

State-of-the-art kitchen facilities, available on later TCA Lancastrian conversions. They were manned exclusively by male purser-stewards on transatlantic flights, in the event that, in a ditching situation, they could physically handle the inflatable dinghies and get passengers aboard.

Miller, G.B. Kerr, T.D. Philip, A.W. MacDonald, M.A. Southern, A.E. Mann and B.W. Foggo—were then trained to be "hosts" on the CGTAS flights. They were first posted to various TCA stations around the country for six months to obtain actual working experience as passenger agents, then assembled in Montreal. There the airline's chief medical officer, Dr. K. Dowd, gave them a two-week course on first aid, followed by training in the use of oxygen at high altitudes, the serving hot meals and, most complicated of all, helping passengers to understand and fill out customs and immigration forms and to unravel the mysteries of the dreaded Form H on currency restrictions.

Besides handing out magazines, newspapers and cribbage boards and conducting a bar service, the purser-stewards were responsible for serving the first hot meals on TCA. The menu was filet mignon, roast chicken or lamb chops with vegetables or salad, afternoon teas and coffee. As the noise of the Merlin engines prevented general announcements from being heard, the pursers distributed a "flight log" or "captain's bulletin" every two hours, giving the speed and position of the aircraft. More onerously, they had to make all travel arrangements at both ends of the trip, and this included the impossible task of finding hotel reservations in bombed-out London. "Everything you did, you had ten pairs of eyes on you because the passengers had nothing better to do," said CGTAS steward Alex Stebner. "In front of the purser-steward's station was a spar with a couple of little swinging doors which led to the baggage area, then the flight deck. The cargo compartment had netting on either side to hold the baggage. It was a dead air space so you had to keep close tabs on anyone in that area; they could pass out there. We only flew eight to nine thousand feet and the aircraft was not pressurized.[3]

With the troops now home, what were the CGTAS loads? In the winter of 1945 when the French government feared a national epidemic among its undernourished and poorly clothed population, 100,000 vials of penicillin were packed into the CGTAS Lancs and rushed over in what became the company's first charter flights. The editor of *Between Ourselves* wrote of the "penicillin flights": "It's not every day that we carry such blessed cargo."

Eastbound, the passengers were still VIPs. VJ Day had passed, but restrictions on obtaining passage on the Lancasters were not relaxed and passengers still had to secure official authorization from the Canadian High Commission in London or the Department of Transport in Ottawa to prove that their mission was of vital importance. With the many post-war international conferences being held in connection with the United Nations, European reconstruction, refugee assistance and the establishment of the Provisional International Civil Aviation Association in Montreal, the passengers were usually Canadian diplomats, general staff officers and senior politicians. Rather than the menace of the U-boats or the Luftwaffe, difficulties in obtaining passage were now caused by the post-war resettlement crisis, the lack of food in London, and British foreign exchange limitations. Conditions were so critical that the cynical joke at the time was that the initials "BOAC" stood for "Bring Over American Cash." Currency regulations at that time permitted Canadians travelling to Britain a maximum of $50 in notes plus traveller's cheques.

On the westbound flights, as there was little mail from the British Post Office (which naturally used BOAC), much of the CGTAS load consisted of war brides. One pilot recalls that when they overnighted at the RAF base at Lagens in the Azores, there were four women among the ten passengers on board. They spent the night in the hospital while the males were put up in the RAF huts. Because the heating on the Lanc did not work that day, Angus Campbell, the TCA representative at Lagens, borrowed RAF flying boots to keep the female passengers' feet warm until they reached Montreal. On January 22, 1946, Lindy Rood and Jack Wright made an unscheduled stopover at Sydney, Nova Scotia, in "Lanky" 106, bringing with them a passenger complement of seven British war brides. It was an overnight delay, so TCA staff took the women out to dinner at the local hotel. Steak was on the menu that night, and when the first one arrived at the table, one of the women began to cut it in equal portions to share it with the other six. Told that there was a steak that size for each, she broke into tears and explained that they hadn't seen anything like that for the last six years.

Then in February 1946 came the first hint of normalcy: cameras could once more be taken and used on board. On March 18 prohibitions on the carriage of children on CGTAS were lifted, and children under two years of age and not occupying a seat were carried at 10 percent of the fare, those between two and twelve at half the adult fare. There was no "UM " (Unaccompanied Minor) policy then: all children had to be accompanied by an adult passenger. More significant, in April the DOT authorized the abolition of the wartime passenger priority system and commercial reservation practices began.

For TCA, the war truly ended on April 1, 1946. Ownership of CGTAS was still vested in the federal government, but with the fiscal new year a financial agreement was worked out with the government whereby all revenues from the operation were to be credited to TCA, as were all expenditures. This differed from the previous practice of the government collecting all revenues— during the war they were only postal—and paying TCA its operating expenses. Although the chances were slim, from now on if the airline earned a surplus on the Atlantic run, half of it was to be retained as a reserve to fund research and development expenses and the other half was to be given to His Majesty as a return of capital. As a result, more staff would be assigned to the Atlantic services, going from twenty-nine in 1945, to sixty-six by May 1946, to a hundred by the year's end.

1945 Stewardess "Casualty" [the airline's designation] List

Stewardess Helen McLean (Winnipeg) to Captain Jerry Lloyd (Toronto) on September 22.

Stewardess Kay Dennis (Moncton) to Flying Officer Joe De Boupre.

Stewardess Betty Walsh (Toronto) has deserted the East for the West and "nest" in sunny Vancouver.

Stewardess Myrtle Hunter (Sweetheart of the Mountains) to Jack Ledger (local Coca Cola rep.) on September 7.

Formally adopting CGTAS was hardly beneficial for the company, which was preoccupied with expanding into the United States, absorbing war veterans and equipping itself with DC-3s. The Lancaster's capacity of ten passengers translated into a maximum revenue of only $3,750 for a single flight, not including Air Express (at $2.00 per lb) and mail. In 1945 the operating costs for a one-way flight from Montreal to Prestwick was $12,900, including services that the military performed for TCA without charge—such as communications and hangar facilities—and not including landing fees. With demobilization, this arrangement was not going to continue. The International Air Transport Association (IATA) had fixed the passenger tariff for crossing the Atlantic at $375 one way (Pan American had wanted it set at $275), and while this assured airlines using Constellations and DC-4s some profit, it meant that TCA's Lancaster flights were going to run at a deficit until a more commodious aircraft could be put into service. As Gordon McGregor drily observed, "Obviously no organization other than a government could have afforded to operate ten-seater aircraft on the transatlantic route."[4]

On May 1, 1946, the frequency of Atlantic flights was increased from three to four per week, with departures from Dorval at 1:00 p.m. Eastern Time on Mondays, Wednesdays, Fridays and Saturdays and at 9:00 a.m. Greenwich Mean Time from Prestwick on Sundays, Mondays, Wednesdays and Fridays. This meant a weekly carrying potential of forty passengers each way. Passengers for London had to report to the Montreal TCA city traffic office at 1478 Peel Street not less than four hours prior to takeoff.

On behalf of Mrs ___, I am writing to express her gratitude and that of her relatives for the remarkable service. To hear a lady in her seventy-ninth year define an Atlantic crossing in February as 'a delightful experience' is in itself a high tribute to the general efficiency of your aircraft and staff. Mrs ___ highly esteems the personal service of your Purser Steward on the flight. Please convey our deepest thanks to this young man and assure him that if ever circumstances bring him to Birmingham he will receive a warm welcome from Mrs ___ and her family."

——————————— A letter received from Birmingham, England, summer 1946

While waiting for the runways at London's airport to be made ready, TCA approached the British government about stationing an aircraft at Prestwick and conducting some sort of shuttle service between it and one of the other London airports such as Croydon or Northolt. However, this smacked of a "Eighth Freedom" privilege and was a precedent that neither country really wanted to get into. Instead, the British offered to fly TCA passengers in transit to Northolt, the domestic airport near the capital. Service to London's new airport (christened "Heathrow" and more of a tent city at that time than an international terminus) began for the Canadians on September 16, 1946. Initially it was via Prestwick, TCA's United Kingdom maintenance centre, but later it would be through Shannon, Ireland. By December this was a daily service with Flight 200 leaving Montreal at 11:30 a.m., arriving at Glasgow Airport (as Prestwick was now called) at 7:00 a.m. GMT, leaving Prestwick for Heathrow Airport at 8:00 a.m. GMT, arriving at 9:50 a.m. The Canadian government did make enquiries about Fifth Freedom rights onward into continental Europe, but the precedent that this would set with BOAC in Canada was such that the idea was dropped.

John Ross, TCA's first station manager at Heathrow Airport, was aware of the history beneath his feet and wrote: "The grim row of gibbets have gone from Hounslow Heath as have the red-coated soldiers that protected the stage coaches from the local highway man Dick Turpin. During excavations for Number One runway, remains of a Celtic temple were found and where the marshalling apron stands was once Caesar's camp grounds. The site of Runway Number Five is where [the woods of] Perry Parks were. Here it was that England's last wolf was killed. A brass plate let into the taxiway parallel to Number One runway marks one of the triangular points of the first survey of Britain."

With predictions that passenger traffic would be 3.5 million annually and that aircraft movement rate would be fifty-five to sixty per hour, Heathrow Airport was being developed in three stages. This involved an "airport first"—the construction of a tunnel under the runways. There were also to be four hangar "pens" and permanent maintenance facilities for BOAC, which was contracted to service TCA aircraft at Heathrow until 1948 when TCA would assume full responsibility for all its own aircraft maintenance in the United Kingdom. As Croydon airport was closed down on November 1, 1947, Heathrow Airport was restricted to international flights, and the British domestic (and continental) airline British European Airways (BEA) was based at Northolt Airport.

What made the frequency of transatlantic flights possible was the installation of loran equipment in the Lancasters. Derived from the first two letters of LOng and RAnge and the first letter of Navigation, loran had been developed by the Radiation Laboratory at MIT; TCA's Communications Department had been assigned to the project since 1944. The basic characteristic of loran was that it utilized pulse transmission rather than the continuous wave transmission of previous radio navigational aids like "Console" and "Sonna." Because pulse systems measure time of travel of the signals, loran gave an accurate fix well over 800 miles from transmitting stations and over 1,400 miles at night, with an accuracy better than that of celestial. No transmissions and no calculations were required from the aircraft, and fixes could be obtained in less than a minute. Independent of weather conditions and limited visibility, except for extreme precipitation static, loran owed much to the Royal Canadian Navy and its isolated ground stations in the North Atlantic during the war and to the RCAF's testing of the receivers on-board its aircraft. It was the loan of those receivers from the RCAF by Group Captain Campbell and Wing Commander S. Kendall and their installation by Dave Tennant in the Lancs that allowed TCA to become the first commercial airline to use loran.

The letter from the appreciative relatives of the seventy-eight-year-old passenger from Birmingham had concerned the Atlantic flight only. More frequent

TCA technician checking Loran navigational equipment at the Dorval base, November 1945.

were letters directed to management about the remainder of the TCA system. A Toronto passenger complained: "When we made out our customs declaration forms during the flight, the stewardess informed me only one declaration was necessary for my wife and self, since our purchases were well under $100. Upon checking at Toronto, the customs officer stated we each needed a form. An annoying delay which could have been avoided by the stewardess thus came about." A Montreal passenger wrote: "I don't usually write letters such as this, but I feel impelled to express my appreciation of the unknown individual or individuals who handle the selection of those members of TCA who come in contact with the public. I didn't know that there were so many nice Canadians." From a New York passenger came this note: "The airline cab leaving the hotel pulled out without picking me up. I came from my room as soon as I received the call, but only to find the car gone. Needless to say, this gave me a poor introduction to TCA." A Toronto passenger wrote: "This disinclination to advise as to delays and departures seems to be universal with TCA... and is one of the most irritating things to travellers... the young lady behind the counter disappeared and it was nearly 30 minutes before we were advised by a very unprepossessing man (certainly not TCA style) that the flight was cancelled." A passenger from southern Alberta enthused: "I was more than delighted with my first flight. The stewardess going in was very considerate and I wondered where you had found a girl who could be so courteous and friendly, and then, on the return, I found that there was another one equally as courteous and this one had beautiful red hair."

The stewardess in question might have graduated from the first post-war class in April 1946, held in Winnipeg under the guidance of Supervisor Betty Hemingson. There were eighteen graduates (all registered nurses), and they represented six of the Canadian provinces. One graduate recalls that they were just in time for the reappearance of nylon stockings as part of their uniform.

Another sign that the war had ended was the new colour scheme on the aircraft. They retained their all-silver finish, but there was now a red cheat line running the length of the plane, covering above and below the windows with two white lines running through the window area. The TCA symbol, also in a flying logo style, appeared under the cockpit side window and on the tail where the Lockheed star had been. "Trans-Canada Air Lines" was in red on the upper fuselage.

The US Civil Aeronautics Board (CAB) issued an unparalleled number of "foreign carrier permits" in June 1946, allowing TCA to begin its Toronto–Chicago service on July 1, Toronto–Cleveland August 1, and Fort William–Duluth on September 16. By the time the Halifax–Yarmouth–St. John–Boston service was inaugurated in April 1947, the airline's whole transcontinental pattern had changed. Bilateral air negotiations with the United States and increased range of the DC-3s allowed the company to shorten their Winnipeg–Toronto route; to do so, in 1946 Frank Young and Barney Rawson completed the aerial survey across the state of Michigan and the Great Lakes. From July 1 that year Trans Canada Airlines no longer flew between Toronto and Winnipeg via North Bay, Kapuskasing and Armstrong, but more directly across the Great Lakes, via Sault Ste. Marie and Fort William. Between Winnipeg and Calgary it now stopped at Saskatoon on the way to Edmonton, while Swift Current and Medicine Hat were added to the Winnipeg–Lethbridge route. The DC-3s also allowed TCA to navigate the Rockies from Calgary instead of Lethbridge, which lost its status on the transcontinental route.

The only impediment to further domestic and cross-border expansion was that TCA did not have enough DC-3s. With Howe's predilection for Lockheeds, Trans Canada Airlines might just have been the last western airline to bring the ubiquitous "Douglas Commercial 3" into airline use. The first aircraft built by Donald Douglas Sr. to land in Canada were the celebrated four Douglas World Cruisers of the US Army Air Service, which on April 6, 1924, had refuelled at Prince Rupert, BC, on their way to circumnavigate the globe. The first Douglas Commercial aircraft with any Canadian connection was a DC-2 purchased in November 1934 by Great Northern Airways. That it had the Japanese registration *J-BBOI* and never actually touched down in this country was because it was part of a subterfuge by the Japanese government. Great Northern was merely a Canadian subsidiary created as a "front" for the express purpose of buying a complete aircraft before applying for a licence to manufacture it as the "Showa L2D-3." Canadians were to see their first Douglas Commercial aircraft on a scheduled service in August 1939 when the American Airlines-owned Colonial Airways operated the Canadian-registered DC-2 *CF-BPP* on their New York–Montreal–Ottawa service, replacing it with a DC-3 in September 1942.

(Canadian Colonial deserves some recognition of its history in bilateral air services. It had the Montreal–New York route to itself until 1950, when TCA put North Stars and later Viscounts against its DC-4s. American Airlines then put Canadian Colonial up for sale and Eastern Airlines and National Airlines battled for possession of it, its value lying in the fact that it had the only licence to fly between Washington and Bermuda. After Eastern won and took it over, the company adopted Colonial's falcon logo, stylized it and used it as the "Golden Falcon" on their Miami run.)

By 1936 the Douglas company had been churning out one DC-3 every three days—and still couldn't keep up with the demand. Though it flew as the Dakota, the C-47, the Skytrain, the Skytrooper, the Pionair, the Gooney Bird and many other names, it was unique. No other flying machine would ever become part of commercial aviation for such a long time, in every sky and climate, and be so admired and loved. Without question, it is the most successful aircraft ever built. To quote C.R. Smith, the president of American Airlines, "The DC-3 freed the airlines from complete dependence upon government mail pay. It was the first airplane that could make money by just hauling passengers."

DC-3 Dimensions and Performance Data

Span: 95'0"/Length 64'6"/Height 16'11"
Cruising Speed: 160 mph
Range: 1,600 miles (2,575 km)
Wing Area: 987 sq ft

Wings: cantilever, multi-cellular construction in three sections. Ailerons metal with fabric cover, right hand one with trim tab. Rudder and elevator also fabric covered. Landing lights inserted in leading edges.

Engines: forward of fireproof bulkhead easily detached for repair with oil from supply tanks behind firewall. Engine nacelles differed according to engine type. Wright Cyclones had narrow cord cowlings like Russian built Li-2s. P & W "Twin Wasp" had broad ones. Propellers were three-blade 11'6³/8" Hamilton Standard.

Fuel system: main fuel tanks in centre section up to 684 gallons in the TCA DC-3.

Fuselage: semi-monocoque construction with smooth, mushroom-rivetted "Alclad" sheet. Large forward baggage hold of 150 cu ft and another at rear of 156 cu ft, each with external door.

Crew complement: normally three with two pilots and radio operator. Passenger seating: initially 21, and although the typical TCA cargo load was 1,217 lbs including baggage, up to 2,150 lbs cargo could be carried. Seating in pairs to allow for two on either side of aisle.

Cruising speed: 173 mph
Maximum speed: 219 mph
An average TCA flight using a DC-3 was to be $4^1/2$ hours.

Locked into Howe's Lockheed purchases before the war and prevented from buying during it, Trans Canada Airlines did not acquire its first Douglas aircraft until September 1945. By then 11,000 DC-3s had been built in various civil and military versions. They had been in service with every major airline and air force in North America (including the RCAF), Europe (including Nazi Germany), Australia and Japan, and, like the Lockheed Lodestar, they had fought for both the Allied and Axis causes. When in January 1945 TCA set up a committee to study its future fleet requirements, the DC-3's design was more than a decade old and committee members were understandably hesitant about acquiring it. The same problem faced American and British airlines, and how each coped explains the TCA decision. Vickers-Armstrong adapted their pre-war Wellington bomber design to a civil aircraft, named it the Viking and sold it until their turboprop aircraft—tentatively called the Viceroy—was in production. When the original "DC-3 airline," American Airlines, asked Convair to build it a replacement, that company turned out the Model 240, which flew on March 16, 1947, but only 176 of the civil version were built before production was discontinued. There was no real choice in the market for a modern short-haul transport, and it was not difficult to guess why: as long as there was a glut of war surplus DC-3s, no manufacturer was inclined to compete. Without an alternative, the TCA committee recommended that the company acquire thirty DC-3s as a stopgap measure for all but its long-haul services.

At the conclusion of the European war, TCA must have awaited the flood of ex-military DC-3s like children on Christmas Eve. It might be assumed that the RCAF would be an abundant supply as its three transport squadrons, 435, 436 and 437, were using Dakota IVs (the RAF name for the DC-3/C-47). But in the summer of 1945 all three squadrons were still heavily employed in the war, either in devastated Europe (437) or serving in Burma (435 and 436), and none of their aircraft would be available for another year. What was plentiful were DC-3s from the Reconstruction Finance Corporation (RFC), the US aircraft disposal board. Across the United States there were whole parking lots of well-used C-49Js—military versions of the DC-3 with a different engine and a 12-volt electrical system—and many a future airline giant, such as Cathay Pacific Airlines, got its start by raiding the collection points, especially at Busch Field, Georgia. Anticipating a doubling in demand for air travel as soon as the war had ended, TCA decided to seize three of whatever DC-3 variant was readily available. Designated DC-3Ws because they had 1,200 hp Wright Cyclone R-1820-71 G202A engines, the first three were less than satisfactory purchases, but the plan was to trade them in for the RCAF Dakotas when they came on the market. Not as smooth running as the Pratt & Whitney 1830s that TCA used in the Lodestars, the Wright Cyclones leaked oil and would be the cause of future tribulations.

Each of the original three, like most DC-3s then, had checkered pasts. The first, ordered by the Netherlands East Indies Air Force in 1940, had been orphaned by the Japanese invasion and taken over by the USAAF. Converted to US military specifications as a C-49J, it had twenty-eight seats and a left-hand door had been fitted for troop carrying. Fortunately for TCA, this aircraft was not sent to a war zone or the tropics but flew within the United States. In 1945 the RFC put it up for sale and on April 24 Trans Canada Airlines purchased it, registering it as *CF-TDJ*. The second, registered as *CF-TDK*, had been built for American Airlines but in 1943 was impressed into USAAF service as a C-49J and sent to the Air Transport Wing in Alaska. The third, an order from Delta Airlines, did see service with the USAAF in the Panama Canal Zone before being sold in October 1945 to TCA, where it was registered as *CF-TDL*. All were inspected by TCA personnel, and the first two bought for $60,000 US each, while the Panamanian veteran was in such poor condition that it was only accepted until a substitute could be found.

Canadian Pacific Airlines also got its first four DC-3s in June 1946 but, without TCA's government clout, took aircraft that had seen more action. Three (*CF-CPW, CF-CUC,* and *CF-CUA*) had served with the US 8th Air Force in the North African campaign, and the fourth (*CF-CPY*) with the US 10th Air Force in India. *CF-CUA* was destroyed by a bomb in midair on September 9, 1949, but *CF-CPY* can still be seen in CPA colours at the airport at Whitehorse, Yukon, where it is used as a weathervane.

It should be noted that TCA's three DC-3s, like the company's last purchase of Lodestars, were all financed by funds generated from within the company. The airline did not go to the CNR or the federal government for an increase in capital but collected the money from profits, disposal of equipment and depreciation provisions. In preparation for post-war expansion and the necessary shopping spree the company had set up an inventory reserve of $218,000 in 1943. Two years later, anticipating the North Star purchases, the authorized capital had been increased from $5 million to $25 million.

The first DC-3, *CF-TDJ*, was accepted at Cartierville Airport on September 22, 1945. The official welcoming party was led by Howe, now the minister for reconstruction; the airline's president, H.J. Symington; TCA's director of public relations, W.S. Thompson; and Miss Diana Dudley, who would design the DC-3 interior. The first DC-3 crew was Captain R.F. McGregor, First Officer R.B. McWilliam and Stewardess Mary Aitkin. It was the beginning of a historic season in Canadian aviation. A week later the country entered the jet age as the RCAF flew its first jet aircraft, a Gloster Meteor Mk III. And at Malton the 694 Lincoln XV prototype had its first flight on October 25, 1945, its manufacturer Victory Aircraft becoming Avro Canada Ltd. that December.

Wonders of Modern Travel

"Graceful as a puff of dandelion, the silver-tipped plane circled above Vancouver Airport, dipped its wings in the Wednesday afternoon sunshine and swooped down lightly to a perfect landing." So reported the Vancouver *Sun* on July 12, 1946. "The door of the big Lancaster flew open. A passageway was shot down to the ground. Then out ran the first passenger—a pert, five-foot blonde Welsh girl—into the arms of her Vancouver boy friend. Thus the first TCA flight from Scotland to Vancouver, made in about 28 hours, reunited Anne Williams, 28, of Bridgend, South Wales, with George Milne, 35, a Vancouver *Sun* classified salesman. The 6000-mile hop was arranged to celebrate 'Aviation Day' in the city's Diamond Jubilee celebration. With a crowd of 400 looking on, flashbulbs popping and announcers from CBR, CKWX and CKNW orating adjectives, the Lancaster swooped down at 3:15 pm. Captain George Lothian and First Officer C.M. Harper, both of Vancouver, agreed it had been a smooth flight—about 18 hours from the United Kingdom to Montreal and 10 hours 8 minutes to zip across the Dominion. Crowds lined up to examine the plane which is a peacetime version of the famed four-engined Lancaster bomber. Its precious cargo included copies of Tuesday afternoon's London papers and a dozen suitcases containing some of the latest Paris and London fashions. In its mailbag were several congratulatory messages which Mayor J.W. Cornett read aloud. "

———————————————————— The Vancouver *Sun*, July 13, 1946

In the spring of 1946 it wasn't only Canadair that the company was dealing with concerning its future DC-3 replacements. Having lost heart attempting to market its York transport, Avro had designed Canada's first jet fighter, the CF-100, and was now building it for the RCAF. But it also had another project on the drawing boards, a civil airliner that would be powered with jet engines. In 1946 jet engines were barely out of the realm of science fiction and had only been tried out in a few jet fighters and German bombers. The original jet aircraft, the Messerschmitt 262 and the Gloster Meteor, were now three years old, but it would be two years before the first flight of the turbo-prop Viscount and three before the de Havilland Comet airliner would fly. The Americans were reluctant to enter the field; not until 1948 would Pratt & Whitney have a jet engine running, and that was a copy of the Rolls Royce "Nene." The first American jet transport, the Boeing 707, was still eight years into the future.

For TCA the jet age began when Ernest Hives, chairman of Rolls Royce, threw the cat among the pigeons by telling Jim Bain that his company had developed the AJ-65 Avon, a jet engine with an axial-flow turbine. Although it was on the British air ministry's classified list, Hives said that it could be built in Canada for the proposed Avro aircraft, the C-102 Jetliner. He also intimated that because TCA was a good customer of Rolls, the company could be the "launch airline" for North America of the world's first jet transport.

With the company's ongoing Merlin engine problems, Symington and Howe were not prepared to commit themselves to anything that Rolls Royce built, let alone an untried commercial jet engine. However, both knew that TCA would soon be looking for a DC-3 replacement for its transcontinental and domestic service, and "it was a matter of coming up with a specification for an airplane they thought would fit the power plants that were going to be available." Jack Dyment, Bill deHart and Fred Ades were sent to Malton to consider the AJ-65 Avon engine being proposed. "Probably at the insistence of Jim Bain, I was selected to be the liaison engineer between TCA and Avro," remembered Clayton Glenn, who was given an office at Avro and commuted on the weekends between Canadair in Cartierville and Malton.

TCA wasn't the only airline interested in the Jetliner. Jim Bain would write, "I might mention that to verify our own analysis, Jack Dyment and I went down to Eastern Airlines to see what they thought of the project. After a couple of days Eddie Rickenbacker [the president of Eastern Airlines] said, "Build that aircraft and I'll place an order for ten of them." American Airlines and National Airlines were also interested, and the latter put a tentative bid in for six of them.[5]

For TCA's purposes, the aircraft had to seat between thirty and forty passengers and cruise between 350 and 400 mph at an altitude of over 30,000 feet. The range capability was to be such that a full passenger payload could be carried from Toronto to Winnipeg against headwinds, with Rivers, Manitoba, as an alternate. When the Avons were taken off the secret list by the British government, the Jetliner was ready to be built. Approval was given by Ottawa in April 1946 for TCA to purchase the Avro C-102 with its two AJ-65 Rolls Avon engines at a price of $350,000. At this point the British government put the Avons back on the secret list. There is a suspicion among Jetliner supporters that the British government was afraid that the Canadian-built Jetliner would affect the export possibilities of its own de Havilland Comet, which was seen as the great hope for British aviation. The Comet had four centrifugal "Ghost" jet engines, but they were inferior to the axial-flow Avons. But putting the AJ-65 back on the secret list was really a case of closing the stable door after the horse was gone because Britain's Labour government, holding that jet technology should be available to all, had already sent examples of Nene and Derwent engines to Hispano-Suiza in France, Pratt & Whitney in the United States, and to aircraft manufacturers in the Soviet Union.

As a result of the British putting the Avons back on the secret list, the Jetliner had to be redesigned around four other Rolls Royce engines, the Derwents. Bain explained what happened next: "The power output of the four engines was about the same as the two axial-flow AJ-65s but there all similarity ended. The increased weight and balance, payloads, fuel consumption, take-off performance, altitude performance and cruise speed all deteriorated." With the four Derwents, the aircraft's gross weight increased from 45,000 to 55,000 pounds, and the range was reduced so that it could no longer fly between Toronto and Winnipeg with a reasonable payload against a headwind. This, along with a critical centre of gravity problem—one check pilot commented that it made a difference on which side you parted your hair—made the Jetliner incapable of meeting TCA's requirements, and the company withdrew from participation. Desperate for a sale, Avro proposed other specifications and redesigned the aircraft, offering it once more to TCA but at the higher price of $750,000. The prototype (and only) Jetliner did fly on August 10, 1949, but by then TCA had its North Stars, and they were priced at $660,000 each. "This did not stop the manufacturer," wrote Gordon McGregor, "from periodically intimating that TCA was buying the Jetliner, in its efforts to make sales elsewhere."[6]

To wrap up this lamentable story, Bain concluded that TCA's forecast of performance proved to be accurate. "All other airlines who examined the aircraft came to the same conclusion. The Avon AJ-65 engine was a complete success and would have been available in lots of time for the Avro C-102."[7] The Avon engine did go on to an illustrious career and later versions were used in the British bombers, the Canberra and Valiant. The Jetliner did not, and all that remains of a promising project is the cockpit section on display at the National Aviation Museum in Ottawa. Like Avro's other product, the famed Arrow, it was perhaps too ambitious for a second-tier aviation power like Canada.

With the DC-3s in service, the company started to sell off its Lockheed 14H-2s and Lodestars, reserving a few for the transcontinental service, especially over the Rockies. Whether it was intentional or not, none of the Lockheeds went to Canadian Pacific Airlines or air companies that might threaten TCA commercially. The first one, *CF-TCK*, was sold in late 1946 to a Montreal photographic survey company that would also buy *CF-TCE*, *CF-TCO* and *CF-TCG*. Others became executive transports for companies, such as Magnavox and Pacific Petroleum. But the airline couldn't prevent one of its Lockheeds from

The Avro C-102. In April 1946, TCA was given approval to purchase the aircraft, which had two Rolls Royce Avon engines. When four Derwents were substituted, the Jetliner's range was so reduced that it could no longer fly with reasonable payload and the airline did not take up the option. UNN

ending up in the hands of potential competitors. Central Northern Airways, which later became Transair, made its start with TCA's *CF-TCN*.

The Lodestar *CF-TCY* was destined for immortality of a sort. Sold to the DOT for its ice patrols on the St. Lawrence, in 1947, it was refitted to become the personal aircraft for C.D. Howe, whose love for Lockheeds was well known. Other senior Cabinet ministers and two prime ministers, Louis St. Laurent and Lester B. Pearson, also flew in it, and for a while *CF-TCY* was Canada's prime ministerial aircraft. In 1960, when it was retired from government service, it passed through several companies until being abandoned ignominiously at Chicago's Midway Airport. The American aviation enthusiast Earl Reinert bought it in 1967 for his Victory Air Museum in Illinois and cut the wings off at the roots to move it there. When the museum closed in 1985, the Canadian Museum of Flight and Transportation in Langley, BC, bought it for their collection with the help of a $5,000 donation from Air Canada. By 2000 it had been reassembled at the museum, though it still lacked engines, propellers, instruments and interior furnishings.

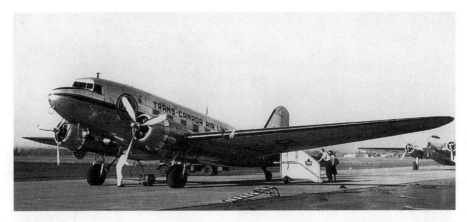

The new Canadair-reconditioned DC-3, available in numbers from 1945. The potential of this aircraft hastened the departure of the Lockheed Electra and Lodestar fleet that had served TCA on domestic routes throughout WWII. Ken Leigh collection

The original TCA "three sisters," the 10As, fared somewhat better. After a fire while in RCAF service, *CF-TCB* was cannibalized for spare parts, but *CF-TCA*—the other "Blueberry Bullet"—and *CF-TCC* survived to be enjoyed today. In 1945 War Assets Disposal sold *CF-TCA* to the Thunder Bay Flying Club, which resold it to Wisconsin Central Airways. Registered as *NC 79237*, it became an executive transport for Bankers Life and Casualty Co., a Florida company. Before being passed on to other enterprises—International Air Services at Lantona, State Airlines of Florida and Great Lakes Airmotive of Willow Run, Michigan—the ailing and by now much abused Electra was finally crash-landed on her belly at Willow Run Airport and sold as scrap for $500 to Lee Koepke. As a mechanic for North Central Airways Koepke understood her value and spent two years refitting her for a round-the-world flight in 1967, with Ann Pellegreno to commemorate Amelia Earhart's earlier attempt. The crew that Pellegreno and Koepke recruited were co-pilot William Payne and navigator William Pohemus, a former Air Canada navigating officer. The Canadian airline loaned them a loran set and sextant. It took thirty-one days with forty-one takeoffs and landings for Pellegreno and her crew to follow the original route. They were caught up in the Six-Day War in the Middle East, which caused a change of route from Earhart's trip. Between Nauru and Howland islands, Pellegreno dropped a wreath over where Earhart's plane was thought to have gone down. Throughout the 256 flying hours, the Electra never once faltered. It was after their return that Pohemus informed Air Canada that the aircraft, now *NC 79237*, had once been *CF-TCA*. The airline purchased it on March 11, 1968, and donated it to the National Aviation Museum at Rockliffe, Ontario. Repainted and re-registered as *CF-TCA*, she was flown to her final resting place by Air Canada Captain A.W. Ross and Herb Seagrim, now company vice-president, who had first piloted her in 1937. The Electra *CF-TCA* took one last curtain call at the Air Canada pavilion at Expo 86.

The other surviving 10A, *CF-TCC*, was transferred to the DOT after the war and later purchased by Matane Air Services of Quebec to fly the Rimouski–Mont Joli–Sept Isles route. In 1965 she was sold in the United States, disappearing from Canada until a former Air Canada pilot saw her in 1975 flying in vintage United States Army Air Corps colours for the Confederate Air Force in Harlingen, Texas. The Electra was purchased by Air Canada in 1983 for restoration and refitted as *CF-TCC* for the airline's Golden Anniversary celebrations in 1986. She is currently to be admired at the Western Canada Aviation Museum, Winnipeg, during the winter but spends her summers on national goodwill tours for the airline.

In the summer of 1946 the first "Miss TCA" made her appearance in the newsletter, complete with a full-length photo. Her name really was "TCA"— that is, Tannis Constance Anne Nicholl. She was six years old, born in Winnipeg and had been deliberately named after the airline. Early in the war, her father, C.W. Nicholl, OBE, had played a crucial part in the organization of flying schools for the British Commonwealth Air Training Plan. On August 7, 1940, he received a telegram at his home in Winnipeg requesting his presence at a meeting in Ottawa, one that would lead to the setting up of No. 14 Elementary Flying Training School at Portage La Prairie. The complications were that the meeting was scheduled for August 8 and so was Tannis. During the battle of the Somme in World War I, Nicholl had served as a dispatch rider and later flown in the Royal Flying Corps. One of the founders of the Manitoba Flying Club, he was an aviation enthusiast and, as his daughter remembers, not one to take no for an answer. Nicholl pleaded his case at the TCA office at Winnipeg. Could the airline get him to Ottawa for the morning of the 8th and back home the same night? If it could—and here he made the grand gesture— his new daughter (this was an assumption on his part) would be named "TCA." Of course the company could, and Nicholl was back in Winnipeg on the night of August 8. Tannis was born in Misericordia Hospital a few minutes behind schedule but of the proper gender, and Trans Canada Airlines became her godparents—or something like that. "I always thought that he had made a deal with the pilots," Tannis says today, "but please don't take my word for that. I don't know where they came up with Tannis and Constance, but Annie was my grandmother's name." As a little girl she heard the story many times from her father. "When I was eight or nine years old, my dad took me out to the airport in Victoria [where the family had moved in 1945], and TCA was celebrating some sort of open house. They had placed on one of the display tables a booklet they had published on bits and pieces of airline memorabilia, including this story and a picture of me. Did I think of the story when TCA was [still called] TCA?" Tannis says today. "You bet I did! I was right bent out of shape when they changed to Air Canada." Tannis's two sons both work in aviation for subsidiaries of American Airlines.

Not until 1946, when Canada's three RCAF squadrons were flown home to be "demobbed," were DC-3s of all varieties plentiful in Canada. As expected, many of the RCAF Dakotas were in poor condition; this was especially true of those that were used in Burma and left in India for relief RAF squadrons. TCA opted to buy only those that had been operated by the air force within Canada. Twenty-seven of them, operated by and large at 32 OTU at Patricia Bay, BC, were acquired by TCA between September 1945 and March 1947 and designated as DC-3Ps because of their Pratt & Whitney 1830 engines and standard 24-volt systems. Compared to those from Busch Field—which, legend had it, came with orange crate packing, bird's nests and snakes in the fuselage—they were in excellent condition, some with only 800 hours. But as the twenty-seven were originally Lend Lease aircraft given to the RAF, their ownership had reverted at the war's end to the US government, which had declared them surplus. The RAF, as the original owners, then had first right of purchase. When they refused, the aircraft were released to the RCAF, which turned them over to the War Assets Corp. In early 1946 TCA paid a bargain price of $20,000 each for them and they were registered *CF-TDJ* to *CF-TEJ*, then *CF-TER* to *CF-TET*.

When in 1913 Gustave Pollien had chosen Montreal's Bois Franc polo grounds at Cartierville to test his Caudron biplane, he could have had no idea that one day the field would be for Canada what Seattle is to the United States

Swords into plowshares. The C-47s returning from the war were extensively renovated to zero-time DC-3s in large numbers, keeping the Canadair workforce in place and ready for the DC-4M to come.

Plant 2 at Canadair, 1946. Here all twenty-seven of the TCA DC-3W fleet went through the mill to come out as virtually new aircraft. The large building at centre is where the work was carried out on the DC-3s; the preflight area is at right. The same building housed the later T-33 Sabre and CF-5 production lines. Canadair photo

and Toulouse to France. It was here that W.T. Reid would start Curtiss-Reid Aircraft to build the Rambler in 1928, and that Bob Noorduyn would design and build the Norseman, the first authentic Canadian bush plane, in the 1930s. In January 1946, setting up for its DC-3 conversion program, Canadair rented the former Noorduyn building across the airfield from their plant, and in May Jack Dyment put together a team of TCA engineers to work with Canadair on converting the DC-3s to TCA specifications. They were flown to Montreal by RCAF pilots—actually coming full circle, as they had been ferried through nearby Dorval during the war. The dull, drab ex-RCAF C-47s were lined up nose to nose outside the building where Norsemen had been turned out, ready to be transformed from ugly ducklings into swans. First all military equipment and certain structural parts like wings and empennage components were taken off. The engines were packed off to Winnipeg for overhaul and testing at the TCA engine shop. The fuselages were put through the paint stripping shop and then rolled onto the tail end of the production line. Inspectors then went through each aircraft, marking down everything that had to be done. The double cargo door was replaced with the standard DC-3 passenger door. A loading door was cut into the rear baggage compartment, which was then separated from the cabin by a new bulkhead containing the lavatory. At this time the wiring for the installation of the Harrington hot meal buffet was also added. The heavy floor beams were removed and replaced with lighter ones. A plywood floor was laid down underneath the seats, and special aisle panels covered with 'Alcad' were installed. Hot air ducts along the floor and cold air ducts above the hat racks were put in along the length of the cabin. The passenger seats were arranged in a single row on one side of the aisle and a double row on the other. The cargo compartment area behind the cockpit was reworked to provide space for a heater on the starboard side and a radio rack on the port.

It also provided space for carrying pets, a first for the airline. Only "domesticated animals" would be allowed and only at the captain's discretion, the airline advised, and they were to be housed in suitable containers and travel as excess baggage. Seeing eye dogs would travel free of charge.

Orders were placed for sufficient sets of SCS-51 and VHF communications units for all DC-3s and DC-4s as ground installation of instrument approach facilities were to begin later in 1946. Flare chutes were put in the tail and fuel dump valves into the two tanks. This was followed by 600-watt, sealed-beam landing lights, engine fire extinguishing systems to the baggage compartment and de-icer shoes. The top of the DC-3s nose was removed for the installation of the TCA-designed instrument panel and the latest in radio equipment.

The entire fuselage was lined with a form of insulation consisting of 1-inch pads of a revolutionary type of lightweight insulation called "fibreglass," and cabin lining and trim were installed over this. Diana Dudley, the TCA interior designer, set out to make the DC-3's interior as unmilitary as possible. Fabric and leather gave way to synthetic materials on the walls, and above the baggage racks the walls and ceilings were cream yellow. The side walls from the windows to the racks were powder blue and the lower walls to the floor were blue-grey. The carpets were a deep blue, the upholstered seats a dull shade of rose clay.

But what the stewardesses who worked on the DC-3s were most impressed with was the galley. Finished in what the airline called "buffed aluminum," the cabinets were fitted with roll-top covers that slid down over the food and utensils. The stewardesses also appreciated the improvements to cabin heating. After the complaints about the heating in the Lockheeds, the company had gone to great pains to make the DC-3s as comfortable as possible. To heat their cabins, the standard military C-47 and C-49 had used water-glycol boilers driven from the engine exhaust—a system totally inadequate for Canadian winters. TCA decided to install a Janitrol gasoline-burning heater "package," which would provide 125,000 BTUs per hour and could be controlled by the stewardess to

Diana Dudley (left) designed the DC-3 interior, and Janet Lowe (right) the Northstar's.
Photo courtesy Janet Proudfoot

keep the cabin at 65 to 70 degrees F. On the ground, the heater could be operated by means of a recirculating fan. Clayton Glenn, who was involved in the design of the heating system, chose a unit and controls identical to those used on the C-54G, which operated on a 24-volt system. Unfortunately, the first three DC-3s, having been C-49s, had 12-volt systems. "Somebody tipped me off that some of the tanks built for the Allies at the Montreal Locomotive Works (MLW) were designed to accommodate 24-volt radios in a 12-volt system. I visited the MLW's surplus stores and found three 12- to 24-volt converter units . . . They did the trick. MLW had only three so there would be no spares. Fortunately, we never had a failure over the life of the airplane."

The test flight to check out the DC-3's heating system was very eventful. "The first problem was with the engines. For the same rpm there were two different manifold pressures and nobody knew which was the faulty engine. Another problem was the electrical system. The generator on one engine was not working and the voltage regulator on the other was not regulating—we flew the airplane on batteries, with no generators. In any event, we had parachutes and knew how to use them. Then the electric fuel pump overheated and caught fire and it was necessary for us to use the CO_2 fire extinguisher, which worked. When we landed we found that the big door at the back could not be opened from the inside and we would have had some difficulty had we been required to jump."

Unlike the Lockheed 14s and 18s, the DC-3s required minimal maintenance, a godsend to the company's accountants. The TCA pilots thought that flying the DC-3 "was a real pleasure. It did not have any bad characteristics and flew readily on one engine."[8] The airline was quick to press its first DC-3Ws into service, basing all three at Toronto for the cross-border and Ottawa–Montreal shuttles. At 1:00 p.m. on November 1, 1945, the inaugural flight (26-1) took off from Malton for New York. The watching TCA staff were aware of the event's significance: the airline's long-awaited post-war expansion had begun.

However, the pattern of air travel had shifted, in part because of the war. While the number of revenue passengers increased between 1945 and 1946 by 67 percent—from 183,121 to 122,321—the average journey shrank in 1946 from 579 to 510 miles. So did revenue—from $29.83 and 5.15 cents per passenger mile in 1945 to $26.41 and 5.18 cents respectively. Airmail continued the downward slide that had begun in 1944, when it was 3,739,105 lbs, to 2,325,977 lbs in 1946. Only air express increased by 10 percent—from 950,323 lbs in 1945 to 1,043,713 lbs in 1946.

North Star CF-TEN-X on its first flight, July 15, 1946. With this aircraft, TCA entered the multi-engined era. Photo courtesy Canadair

C H A P T E R   9

Max Church never forgot one Toronto–New York DC-3 flight.

One blustery night I was called up by Flight Dispatch in the wee hours of the morning to operate a second section they had set up between Toronto and New York. Since I was on reserve duty, I dressed and left the house, driving through the dark to Malton. F/O J.T. Breen had most of the flight plan done when I arrived in the parking lot holding my hat with both hands to keep from losing it to the wind.

We completed the weather briefing, finished the flight plan and headed for the aircraft. The DC-3 was loaded and ready to go, even the passengers were on board. The wind aggressively rocked the plane and the ground crew had placed padded board locks over the ailerons to stop the wind from flapping them to pieces. The control wheel in the cockpit was firmly held by a metal yoke. When Breen and I had completed the standard cockpit check, I asked him to hold the control wheel while I removed the resisting yoke from my side since the two control columns moved as one. At this time the ground crew signalled 'All clear ready to start engines.' I saw a man dragging the board locks away. Holding the brakes on, I started the right engine and then the left. When both were idling smoothly I signalled 'Ready for taxi.' The tower cleared us to runway 31, and releasing the brakes I taxied into the blackness with the winds still buffeting the controls. The runway was dead into the wind and we lined up for takeoff. With full power the DC-3 climbed to 1,000 feet, then we did a gentle turn through the cloud layer to cruise at 7,000 feet ASL southeast toward Buffalo. The lights of Toronto disappeared as we climbed. At this altitude the air was quite smooth, and we flew using our instruments and navigating on the beam. Later on the stewardess brought us some coffee as the sun was beginning to lighten the eastern sky.

Somewhere past Elmira, NY, John Breen said, "Max, you won't believe what I can see on my right side now that it is light." Leaning over to peer out John's window, I was horrified to see the aileron on the right wing still clamped with the wooden board. Yellow strips and all. A quick check showed the left wing was clear. My mind raced at full speed as I planned what to do about this potentially dangerous situation. The rudder and elevator controls were all right during taxi and takeoff. So how about the left turn to set the course? We had no problem making the turn because of differential aileron control—during any turn the down-wing aileron was designed to deflect more than the up-wing aileron—therefore with a lock on the right aileron there was no problem, as long as all our turns were made to the left.

Happy with the thought of almost full control, my attention raced ahead to the safe landing at La Guardia Airport. The Catskill mountains were now behind us, and upon reaching the George Washington bridge spanning the Hudson River, we contacted the tower and advised our situation. They cleared us for a downwind leg of the approach and a left turn for landing on runway 31, and we saw a fire truck was standing by. But we landed without incident and taxied to the gate. While the DC-3 was serviced for the return flight, John Breen and I had a weather briefing at the American Airlines Flight Dispatch Centre. Returning to the aircraft, we chatted with the mechanic, and he assured us that the aileron lock was stowed in the cargo hold. Boarding the plane, we started the pre-flight check when surprise, surprise, the cockpit door opened and TCA's flight operations superintendent, Capt F.M. MacGregor himself was standing there. "Hello," he said. "May I ride home in the jump seat?" I figured that I had better report the locked aileron incident to him as soon as we got squared away. I never got a chance. As soon as we called the tower for taxi clearance, the controller cleared us and then added, "Have you unlocked your controls this time?" Well, the "super" heard this on his headset and spluttered to me, "What's all this about?" So I only had time for a one-liner before we took off. He told me to report to his office after arrival.

My story didn't end on the super's carpet. He said that he knew the early airplanes flew without ailerons but he didn't want me to do it again. But because of this, TCA flight operations immediately revised their flight manuals to include a full movement check of the flight controls prior to takeoff.

TCA's youngest post-war station was Goose Bay, Labrador, three hours and forty-five minutes north east of Montreal—as the Lancaster flies. Like Gander and Torbay, it was a refuelling stop for transatlantic flights, but because of the January 1946 Canada–United Kingdom conference in Bermuda, only TCA was designated to pick up and drop off passengers at all three. No one expected much commercial traffic from Gander or Goose Bay, but in May 1947, at the request of the DOT, the airline was contracted to take over from the RCAF and start a fortnightly service between Goose Bay and Montreal for DOT personnel and the contractors working on the base's infrastructure.

In the twelve months before the TCA opened its station there, 24,000 flights had gone through, making it one of the busiest airports in North America. The first fifteen TCA staff members lived in temporary accommodation in the RCAF officers' mess, while across the field their own quarters, "the Chateau Terrington," were being built. The pioneers were Bob Irwin, acting station manager; Norm Smith, crew chief; Dave Ross, Charlie Cotton and Bill

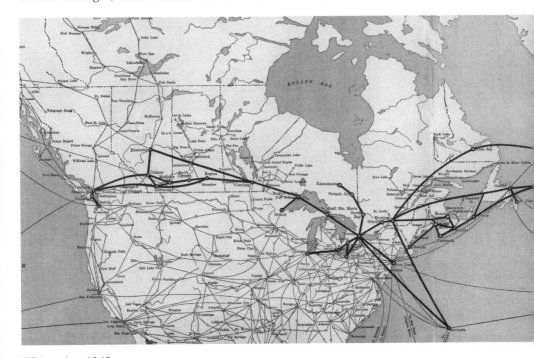

TCA routes, 1948.

Konowalchuk, mechanics; Jack Tufford and Bob Tribe, passenger agents; Roy Hamilton, radio technician; Carl Webusky, Gil Sanson, Don White, Bob Affleck, Charlie Mackie and Mel Brown, radio operators. All radio contacts were then in CW or Morse as compared with the voice circuits used down south, and the TCA operators also gave radio coverage to BOAC, American Overseas, Trans World Airlines, KLM and Pan American flights. Though Goose Bay seemed desolate, Mel Brown reported that it was "quite enjoyable with plenty of fishing, hunting and sports." The United States Air Force base on the other side of the field was then only a transit station and relatively small, but as TCA staff at Gander had discovered, being across from a USAF base, no matter its size, had advantages. When the USO shows visited Goose Bay, they generously gave two performances on the Canadian side. Base personnel operated their own radio station, VOUG, and rather than Armstrong's "Leaky Roof" pub, there was a large, well-equipped gymnasium, free movies at the "Little Theatre," several hobby clubs and a licensed ham radio station, call sign VO6F. With the use of the North Stars, the TCA station at Goose really came into its own, and on April 10, 1947, an RCAF hangar was given over to the company as a passenger terminal and later as a hotel, the forerunner of the "Goose Hilton." In Goose Bay's future would be the rows of Strategic Air Command "tankers," the RCAF suburb of Spruce Park and the radio station CFGB.

The first TCA men at Goose Bay were loath to speak ill of their compatriots at Armstrong, Ontario—for one thing, most of them were Armstrong alumni—who thought themselves isolated, but they would happily have traded places with them in one respect. What the Ontario station did have over Goose was its railway line. Besides the aircraft, Goose staff joked that the only way off the airport was by dog team.

The only hotel in Goose Bay—and Labrador—was the TCA-owned and operated Airlines Inn, a six-wing, 107-room building run by twenty-seven TCA employees, which had been established not for tourists but for inconvenienced passengers on the Atlantic run. Five other airlines—BOAC, Air France, Pan American Airways, SAS and Trans World Airlines—contributed to its maintenance, an indication of how many times their aircraft were grounded there. Each airline paid $25 per day (TCA paid only $20) for a room. Besides stranded passengers and some local contractors, the hotel had also played host to celebrities like Bob Hope, Lord Tweedsmuir and Premier Joey Smallwood, who said he had come to inspect the real estate. It was said that Goose Bay's own television station, CFLA, was never more avidly watched (from the hotel's lounge) than when several flights were grounded simultaneously.

For TCA the DC-3s were the first of its high-density shuttle aircraft. On November 1, 1946, three of them replaced the Lockheeds on the Vancouver–Victoria run, dating from September 1, 1937. Discontinued in May 1941, the run had been revived in June 1943, but not until 1946 did the ATB rule that the airline was allowed to carry local traffic. From the first day the route was a moneyspinner, as the residents of Vancouver Island depended heavily on the flights. In 1950, for example, of the 68,648 passengers on the route, 64,402 lived in Victoria. During the rail strike that year, when all freight and passenger shipping was paralyzed, the three TCA DC-3s were flying 1,350 people daily as well as milk and meat and other perishables. Unlike their twenty-one-seat brothers in the rest of the TCA system, these DC-3s had twenty-eight seats each; when it was discovered that the passengers sat upright to view the scenery on the eighteen-minute flight, the company modified the seats so that they couldn't recline and added seven seats. It took five crews to work the nine daily return flights with a turnaround time of two minutes flat. Operations Manager E.W. Stull calculated that TCA could do the Vancouver–Victoria shuttle every thirty minutes if it had to—twenty-four round trips every twelve hours.

Three years after it entered service, one of the DC-3s starred in the airline's second legal drama, set this time at the Nova Scotia Court of Appeal. On May 25, 1948, the Sydney–Dartmouth flight had passed as usual over Musquodoboit Harbour on the Airway. Within sight of Dartmouth Airport, the pilots deviated from their IFR course to avoid clouds and switched to flying VFR. Preoccupied with landing, they did not look for or see below them a collection of buildings, one of which was a mink ranch—it had the words "Mink Ranch" painted on its roof. The noise of the DC-3 flying at 400 feet above them caused a panic among the mink, and because it was whelping season, many of the females devoured their young. The ranch's owner, Nova Mink Ltd., sued the airline, saying that the noise of the engines was responsible for the financial loss, their lawyer emphasizing that the ranch's location near the Airway was known to the airline through DOT information circulars. The court decided that while the airline could not be exonerated—the crew had failed to keep a proper lookout—the captain had carried out the flight at that altitude with the safety of the passengers foremost in his mind and was thus absolved from blame.

There were now 2,388 company employees between London, England, and Victoria, B.C., and one of them was Joanne Peck. "I joined Trans Canada Airlines in Dorval about January 1946, and although the war had ended, to get on the base we still had to wear security badges with our pictures on them," she remembers.

> My first job was working for J.D. (Dick) Leigh, the supervisor of maintenance inspection and overhaul in number 1 bay of hangar 6. There were four bays in the hangar, and facing east when they opened the large doors to bring the aircraft you could see Montreal. We were in the overseas department [CGTAS] and BOAC was in the same hangar. I used an old Underwood typewriter, which I had learned typing on in business school. My salary, as far as I can remember, was somewhere around $94 per month and in those days that was fine with me.

In the centre of the office was a large bank of yellow Cardex cards pertaining to the shelf life of every component on the aircraft from a doorknob to an engine. When anything became "time expired," it had to be removed and inspected. One of my duties was to take the log books from the incoming aircraft and then type all the "snags" onto a master sheet. This could mean anything from a burnt-out light bulb to a failed engine. One thing that used to puzzle me was the numerous times I used to see that an engine had been "feathered." I never knew what this meant until thankfully my boss, Mr. Leigh, explained that it meant stopping a propeller from turning on a stalled engine since it could create drag with the flat side against the wind. The feathering meant turning the blades so that they were parallel with the airflow. Then it began to dawn on me why the representative for Rolls Royce was in our office a great deal of the time, and I made a mental note to travel across the Atlantic by ship.

There were now two TCA liaison offices at Cartierville. Besides the one at plant no. 2, the former Noorduyn building where the DC-3s were being rebuilt, a second was opened in the main building for the DC-4M or North Star, the transport chosen to equip the post-war fleets of both the RCAF and TCA. Canadair's president, Ben Franklin, had convinced Donald Douglas Sr. to sell him at scrap metal prices—about $200 a ton—surplus C-54 fuselages (the military version of the DC-4) from the Douglas factory at Parkridge, Illinois. Working on both the DC-3s and the North Stars was the TCA team of Jim Bain, Clayton Glenn, Andy Anderson, Art Higham, Al Cargill, Ken Rutledge, Bill de Hart, Grace Stewart, Hal Coverdale, Baldwin "Baldy" Torrell, Frank Rousseau, Jimmie Miller and "Jud" Judson. Glenn remembered, "Jack Dyment worked us like slaves but we loved every minute of it. He was a man who could work all night and after four hours of sleep, be at it again. I recall him calling a meeting in his room at the Mount Royal Hotel at seven in the morning following the VJ Day celebrations. Present were myself, de Hart, Torrell and Rutledge. When Dyment noticed a couple of us dozing off, he gave up and told us to go to bed. The fuselages were rolled into Canadair's property on trucks and were lined up side by side inside the company fence, near the flight test hangar." The 60 C-54 fuselages were more than enough for an initial run of twenty-four aircraft for the RCAF and twenty for TCA. But as TCA had insisted that the aircraft destined for its fleet were to be pressurized, DC-6 fuselages and noses were used for its twenty, shortened by 6 ft. To get the North Star into airline use as soon as possible, the first six North Stars built for the RCAF would be loaned to TCA.

By July 1946 Canadair had assembled the crew to test fly the first DC-4M. Bob Brush was brought in from Douglas Aircraft as captain, with Al Lilly, Canadair's chief pilot, as co-pilot and W.L. "Smokey" Harris as flight engineer.

The crew for the North Star's first flight: Clayton Glenn of TCA, Bob Brush of Douglas, Al Lilly and "Smokey" Harris of Canadair.

Clayton Glenn was not scheduled to be on the first flight but Brush felt uncomfortable about the propeller controls and insisted he fly with them as a second flight engineer—just so he would have somebody along who knew something about the controls. "It was not as if I could do anything about a major problem in the air," Glenn said, "if we had a problem." Insurance was taken out on the flight crew, but Glenn noticed that in case of an accident Canadair would be the beneficiary. "We did a fair amount of taxi tests up and down the runway at high speeds to the liftoff point to check the controls, followed by heavy braking, and burned out a number of sets of brakes in the process."

On the evening of July 15, 1946, they were scheduled to do more taxi tests and Glenn was wearing a new gabardine suit to go out for dinner later with a friend. When the flight crew had boarded and the doors were closed, Brush told everyone to put their parachutes on. The one assigned to Glenn had dirty straps, and he was reluctant to put it on over his new suit. He remembers thinking that Brush did not appear to have much confidence in the aircraft, and when someone inquired as to the purpose of the rope that ran from the cockpit to the rear cabin door, Brush said something like, "When this thing goes into a dive, I want to be able to climb up the slippery cabin floor to get out of the rear door." Brush, Harris and Glenn stood up in the cockpit while the two pilots had their seat belts fastened.

The North Star lifted off the runway and the landing gear was raised. Then the cockpit filled with smoke and a heavy smell of burning rubber. There was no change in Brush's expression. "Don't panic. It's just the nosewheel spinning against the 'up' brake," he said. The flight lasted an hour as they checked all systems and controls, checked for wing flutter and vibration. Apart from the excessive engine noise, no problems were discovered. As there were no lights at Cartierville, they landed just before dark but, before doing so, "shot up" the field. Other than the fire crew, no one else knew of the DC-4M's first flight, and Ben Franklin was put out because nobody had told him in time to alert the media. Jim Bain, on the other hand, was so delighted with the positive results that he took all of them off for a celebration dinner at Ruby Foo's restaurant. There, Glenn remembers, they were served the largest steaks he had ever seen.

Bain had good reason to be relieved, as he had been so closely involved with the choice of the Rolls Royce Merlin engine for the North Star. The aero engines available in 1944 had been the Pratt & Whitney Double Wasp R-2800-C,

The prototype Canadair North Star, July 20, 1946, landing at Canadair's Cartierville Airport.
Photo courtesy Canadair

the Pratt & Whitney Twin Wasp R-2000, the Bristol HE-10 Hercules and the Rolls Royce Merlins, RM-14-SM and RM-20-SM. After a detailed analysis of the engines' power, weight, fuel consumption, operating cost and interchangeability of parts, the final cut had come down to the Pratt & Whitney R-2800-C and the Merlin RM-14-SM. (The Hercules was never a serious contender, and the P & W R-2000 was said to have insufficient cruise power at high altitudes. It also had higher installed weight, higher engine drag and higher operating costs.) Bain and Dyment knew that the Pratt & Whitney engine had been designed for commercial use and that several American airlines were already using it in their airliners. The Merlins, on the other hand, were derived from military engines, but what gave them the edge was the British manufacturer's desperation to break into the post-war North American market. Rolls Royce had even agreed to a never-be-sorry clause in their warranty, specifying that the cost for replacement parts for the Merlins would not exceed those established by airlines that used air-cooled engines of comparable power. TCA's choice of the Rolls Royce engine was also coloured by sympathy for the war-devastated British. As Howe told the House on July 8, 1947, "The Rolls Royce was chosen, first, because it is of British make. It did not represent a drain on Canadian dollars, and we believed it was the engine most suitable for aircraft to perform the services we had in mind in the North Star planes."[1] (In 1946 the Canadians, like the Australians, lacked sufficient foreign exchange to buy anything American.) The choice of the Merlin for its DC-4s was to marry the company to Rolls Royce for better or worse for the next thirty years.

"With the North Star Jim Bain recognized the opportunity to build an aircraft to TCA specifications, and...since maintenance is a very high proportion of operating costs...to overcome the difficulties of an M & O [maintenance and overhaul] system which required lengthy [twenty-four to twenty-six hours] engine changes." Bain's first reason for choosing the Merlin was its "easily dismountable engine units." His other reasons for choosing it were:

- fuel consumption of the Merlins was superior to the available air-cooled engines
- the engine was liquid-cooled which would maintain high efficiency in Canada's extremes of climate
- the drag of the Merlin power plants was actually slightly less than that of air-cooled engines of equivalent horsepower
- the Merlin power plants were built as self-contained units that could be quickly and simply exchanged with serviceable units
- the installation of accessories was greatly simplified by the introduction of an accessory gearbox. This was for ease of maintenance.[2]

Because the Merlin engine blocks were overhauled in Winnipeg, the airline ran a DC-3 freight shuttle between Stevenson Airport and Dorval, where the engine changes were carried out. Although no one realized it then, this was TCA's first

The North Star line at Canadair plant 1. TCA DC-4M-2 CF-TFA, at left, is nearing completion. This is the same production line where later RCAF Argus, Yukon and CF-104 aircraft came together. Canadair photo

all-cargo venture. Gordon McGregor remembers his reaction when he saw a Merlin engine delivered to the TCA workshop in Winnipeg. "Filled with fond recollections of these engines in Hurricanes and Spitfires, I received a man-size shock. The power plant which was to be installed in the soon-to-be delivered North Stars to my eye had more built-in head wind resistance than seemed possible." Having sat behind Merlins in his fighter aircraft, McGregor knew about their noise, but as he wrote: "In fighter aircraft our ears were covered with radio-telephone receivers mounted in thick pads." In commercial use, the famed Merlins were a poor advertisement for Rolls Royce and Trans Canada Airlines. The exhaust gases from the liquid-cooled, in-line engine were thrust outward from the firing chambers on both sides of the engine, one set blasting toward the cabin and the other into the slipstream. Trapped between four Merlins over a lengthy flight was guaranteed to drive the most enthusiastic supporter senseless, and the airline received several letters attesting to that. Besides the "boiler factory" noise, the exhausts also gave off discreet displays of sparks and orange flame. This was a normal condition of the Merlin, occurring when a change in engine speed or power loosened carbon or lead deposits in the cylinders and then exhausted them, but there was little use in the TCA stewardess comforting passengers with this information when they were sure that the engine was on fire.

TCA's Canadair DC-4M North Stars

Model Designation:
In all, Canadair built 71 DC-4Ms or North Stars: 20 M-2s for TCA, 22 C-4s for BOAC (called Argonauts), 24 DC-4M1s for the RCAF, 4 C-4-1s or "Canadair Fours" for Canadian Pacific Airlines, and one C-5 for the RCAF VIP transport wing. The cost per aircraft varied according to the customer's requirements. The RCAF paid $630,000 per plane, TCA $660,000, CPA $800,000 and BOAC a bargain $671,107 with flight training provided by TCA crews. In July 1950, when Canadair built the last North Star (designated the C-5) for Prime Minister Louis St. Laurent's travels, it provided the Opposition with complimentary

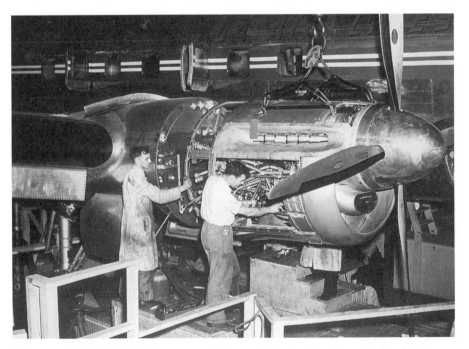

The concept of the Merlin "power egg," demonstrated on the Canadair line being installed on a TCA DC-4M-2 North Star. Seen at right, the engine, cowling and propeller have only three attachments to the firewall on the aircraft left. The "power egg" can be fitted in any of the engine positions and on any aircraft in the fleet. The engine could be pre-positioned in the route system or be easily flown in if the occasion called for a replacement. Canadair photo

ammunition. Not only did the VIP aircraft come equipped with quieter Pratt & Whitney engines instead of Merlins, but it cost the taxpayer $1,226,000, and three spare engines had to be built as well.

All TCA North Stars were designated by different numbers according to the types of engines and propellers fitted, and whether the aircraft was for passenger or all-cargo use.

- DC-4M1: the six RCAF non-pressurized aircraft on loan to TCA

- North Star M2-3: a pressurized DC-4M-2 with the type 722 engines and four-bladed propellers

- North Star M2-4: the pressurized DC-4M-2 with the type 724 engines and three-bladed propellers

- North Star M2-4C: the stripped cargo version of the DC-4M-2 with type 724 engines and three-bladed propellers

- North Star C4-1C: the stripped cargo version of the Canadian Pacific Airlines North Stars C4-1 with the type 724 engines and three-bladed propellers. The airline converted two C-4-1s and one M2 for cargo operation by removing seats, galley and front left cabin bulkheads, all windows and cabin lining. A plywood floor was installed with tie-down rings.

Main Dimensions:

Overall wing span: 117 ft 6 inches
Overall length (M-2): 93 ft 10.5 inches; (C4-1): 93 ft 7.5 inches
Overall height (empennage): 27 ft 6.3 inches
Height, ground to top of fuselage: 17 ft 7 inches
Fuselage height: 11 ft 6 inches
Fuselage width: 10 ft 6 inches
Horizontal stabilizer span: 39 ft 6 inches

Main Areas:

Wings: 1,457 sq ft
Ailerons (aft of hinge line including tab): 92.5 sq ft
Aileron tab (starboard): 3.2 sq ft
Wing flaps (total): 214 sq ft
Horizontal tail surface (total): 324.9 sq ft
Elevators (aft of hinge including tabs): 86.5 sq ft
Elevator tabs (total): 6.84 sq ft
Vertical tail surface (including dorsal fin): 179.3 sq ft
Rudder (aft of hinge line including tab) 47.6 sq ft
Rudder tab: 4.75 sq ft

Tank Capacities:

maximum fuel (8 tanks)	3,226 imp gals	22,582 lbs
6 tanks	2,358 imp gals	16,506 lbs
oil 4 tanks	100 imp gals	900 lbs
Anti-icing alcohol:	13.5 imp gals	
Hydraulic reservoir:	4.5 imp gals	
Galley water supply:	14 imp gals	
Centre washroom and drinking water:	14 imp gals	
Aft washroom and drinking water:	14 imp gals	

Cabin Dimensions:

Length of main cabin: 46 ft 6 inches
Width of main cabin floor: 8 ft 8 inches
Height of cabin: 7 ft
Number of windows: (48 and 57 seats) 24; (52 and 62 seats) 26
Size of windows: 17.5 x 15 inches
Height of main cabin door: 6 ft 2 inches
Width of main cabin door: 3 ft

Number of passenger seats: from the original 36/40 the seating would be expanded to tourist domestic class of 62

Pressurization differential: 4.16 psi

Cabin altitude at	10,000 ft: 1,000 ft	15,000 ft: 4,600 ft
	20,000 ft: 8,000 ft	25,000 ft: 11,300 ft

Performance:

Cruise speed: 383 km/h (238 mph)
Range: 4,924 km (3,060 miles)
Ceiling: 8,138 m (26,700 ft)

The first six unpressurized DC-4 M-1s loaned to TCA until their pressurized versions were ready had their cargo doors removed and passenger doors installed and a DC-6 main undercarriage added to allow for an increase in weight. The nose gear stayed as the standard DC-4 type for the M-1, the North Stars not being fitted with the DC-6 type of nose gear until the M-2s. The airline set up a reserve of $296,500 to pay Canadair for refitting them. To allow for cabin pressurization and a differential of 4.16 psi, the airline's own M-2s would have thicker skin and DC-6 windows.

The airline took delivery of its first M-1 North Star on November 16, 1946, the RCAF its first on September 12, 1947. In service, TCA lost three North Stars, CPA one, the RCAF nine and BOAC three. The first TCA North Star crash occurred on August 12, 1948, at Sydney, when *CF-TEL*, coming in to land, hit a pile of earth on the edge of the runway. The undercarriage punctured the fuel tanks and the aircraft burnt, but all eleven passengers and six crew escaped injury. *CF-TEL* was one of the borrowed RCAF North Stars and rather than replacing it with another, DND ordered the C-5 from Canadair. On April 10, 1957, *CF-TFB* slid off the icy runway on landing at Sydney, ending up on its nose, and on October 24, 1960, when the North Stars were about to retire, *CF-TKF*'s nose wheel was accidentally retracted; the aircraft ended its career in an embarrassing position.

Registration	In service	Model	Withdrawn from TCA use	Notes
CF-TEK	11/46	M-1	4/49	RCAF
CF-TEL	6/47	M-1	8/48	not returned to RCAF (crashed at Sydney, NS)
CF-TEM	2/47	M-1	3/49	RCAF
CF-TEO	2/47	M-1	10/49	RCAF
CF-TEP	3/47	M-1	8/49	RCAF
CF-TEQ	3/47	M-1	6/49	RCAF
CF-TFA	10/47	M-2	8/61	"Cartier"
CF-TFB	10/47	M-2	10/61	"Cornwallis"; accident at Sydney—cargo conversion
CF-TFC	10/47	M-2	5/61	"Champlain"
CF-TFD	1/48	M-2	12/56	"Selkirk"; crashed, Hope BC
CF-TFE	12/47	M-2	7/61	
CF-TFF	12/47	M-2	11/61	
CF-TFG	12/47	M-2	11/61	
CF-TFH	1/48	M-2	10/61	cargo conversion
CF-TFI	1/48	M-2	10/61	
CF-TFJ	2/48	M-2	7/61	cargo conversion
CF-TFK	2/48	M-2	7/61	accident at Sydney, NS
CF-TFL	2/48	M-2	7/61	
CF-TFM	2/48	M-2	7/61	
CF-TFN	3/48	M-2	7/61	
CF-TFO	3/48	M-2	7/61	
CF-TFP	4/48	M-2	11/61	
CF-TFQ	4/48	M-2	1/61	
CF-TFR	5/48	M-2	12/61	
CF-TFS	5/48	M-2	12/61	
CF-TFT	6/48	M-2	12/61	
CF-TFU	11/51	C-4	7/61*	CPA's *CF-CPI*
CF-TFV	2/52	C-4	7/618	CPA's *CF-CPJ*
CF-TFW	12/51	C-4	4/54	CPA's *CF-CPP*; crashed over Moose Jaw, SK

* cargo conversion

Unlike other airlines, Trans Canada Airlines had never subscribed to the nam-
ing of individual aircraft. There were Pan American Airways' "Clippers,"
KLM's "Flying Dutchman" and American Airlines' "Flagships." The QANTAS
Constellations would be named after Australian aviation pioneers Ross Smith,
Bert Hinkler and Charles Kingsford Smith. James Richardson baptized his first
Fokkers with the names of cities—Winnipeg, Fort Churchill and Toronto— and
Grant McConachie crowned his fleet of unpaid-for Barkley-Grows as "Queens."
During the war every RCAF bomber, it seemed, had an individual motif paint-
ed on its fuselage; 427 (Lion) squadron's Lancasters were named after movie
stars in the Metro Goldwyn Mayer stable, thus entitling all squadron members
to two free seats at any cinema showing an MGM movie. Canadian Pacific
Airlines evoked the grandeur of the great Canadian Pacific ships and launched
their C-4-1s as "Empresses." BOAC relied on the "As" from Greek mythology
for their Argonauts (Atlas, Amazon, Artemis, etc.) and on the stars (Astra,
Aurora, Antares).

Until the arrival of its pressurized North Stars, Trans Canada Airlines did
not succumb to such affectations. Even when it did, the practice was adopted only for the first four. Typically for a government airline, the names chosen—Cartier, Cornwallis, Champlain and Selkirk—were non-controversial
and covered all bases, linguistically and geographically. In retrospect, perhaps
the names were too parochial. While the two French explorers' names
required little explanation, Alexander Selkirk, the founder of the Red River
Settlement, was sometimes confused with the man who was Daniel Defoe's
inspiration for his character Robinson Crusoe. "Cornwallis" might have
caused some consternation on May 1, 1948, when it was used on the inaugural North Star flight between Toronto and New York. The airline's public
relations staff were at pains to emphasize that the aircraft's name was *not*
commemorating the British general who had devastated the American
colonies during the Revolutionary War but Edward Cornwallis, a British governor of Nova Scotia who in 1749 had led a fleet of immigrant ships into
Halifax harbour.

On October 14, 1947, Steve Albulet, who was destined to become the airline's most famous, most colourful transatlantic pilot, was piloting a North Star
out of Prestwick when a radio distress call was picked up. The *Bermuda Sky
Queen*, a Boeing flying boat out of Foynes, Ireland, had been making for
Newfoundland when gale-force winds hindered it to the point that it had neither enough fuel to return to Ireland nor enough to go on. It had sixty-two passengers and seven crew on-board, the most ever carried on a flying boat.
Albulet not only located the stricken aircraft but guided it to the weather ship
USS *Bib* at Ocean Station Charlie. The flying boat landed as close as it could
to the cutter and, in spite of treacherous seas, transferred its passengers to it.
In his quarter-century with TCA, Albulet, who had joined the company in
1939, served in Lancs, North Stars, Constellations and eventually DC-8s across
the ocean.

When Diana Dudley, the interior designer who had decorated the DC-3 cabins, left to marry, a new designer was needed for the North Stars. "Winnipeg Girl Decorates Canada's Latest Plane," the Winnipeg *Free Press* article was headed. "Passengers sitting back in comfortable seats in the tastefully decorated cabin of the North Star, Canada's newest and fastest plane, will be enjoying the work of a Winnipeg girl. She is Miss Janet Lowe, ste 8, Sandhurst Apts." Janet Lowe remembers:

> It was a fascinating job, including a number of buying trips to New York. In those days, before all the wonderful plastics were invented, the interior walls of an aircraft were covered with material to cut down on the noise. I wanted the cabins to look Canadian, so looked up Madame Bulow, who was famous for her woven ties and hangings. Together we designed curtains and drapes with the Canadian maple leaf motif. Commuting between Winnipeg and Montreal, it was a wonderful time as usually four or five engineers or head office people were down in Montreal at one time—we all worked hard—and enjoyed our evenings in the great restaurants and night life of Montreal in its heyday. When the aircraft were complete, it was weighed and loud cries—It was too heavy! Every department had to cut back, and even inches were cut off the draperies.

Diana Dudley, designer.

With the North Stars complete, Janet returned to Winnipeg and worked once more in the airways division for Charlie Proudfoot. It was said that Charlie's division could find a map of Tibet, a chart of the approach to Pago Pago, or a report on the clay content of Kapuskasing airport. They could even find some maps of the Iron Curtain countries although, as he commented, "We haven't checked them for some time." But having decorated Canada's first airliner, Janet Lowe was never the same, and like all great artists she longed to put her mark to her work. "I objected to the maps of airports in the handbooks as being too unrealistic so I started to illustrate them in the third dimension. Trees didn't say 'trees,' they now looked like them. One night at a party with some pilots one of them mentioned that the charts now looked so real that there could be rabbits in the woods. That was how the 'Rabbit Club' came into being. I would add one rabbit in the woods for each chart." The rabbits appeared on six charts, "until Charlie got wind of it—that was the last of the rabbits." Charlie did not, as a later newspaper article put it, "storm about and bluster in rage. He was a super boss who knew everything that went on in his department (well, almost)." By then Janet's rabbits were part of the TCA legend and in the post-war uncertainty, perhaps they came to symbolize a brighter future. It certainly was for Charlie Proudfoot, who fell in love with Janet Lowe and married her in October 1947. "Married women didn't work," Mrs. Proudfoot writes, "and that was the end of my great years with TCA. It still is a great airline but I was always glad that I was part of the company when it was just starting out, a vibrant young TCA."[3]

The war had catapulted radio technology into common use and as more ground stations were installed, VHF communications became the norm for domestic navigation. VOR (Visual Omni Range) navigation stations replaced the four fixed legs of the low- and medium-frequency radio ranges with a 360-degree signal. DME (distance measuring equipment) gave pilots continuous readings of their distance from a fixed ground station as ILS (instrument landing systems) guided them through overcast with a radio beam to follow to the airport and a glide path down the runway. Now approach limits could be reduced to half-mile visibility and 300 feet altitude. The North Stars were equipped with the Bendix type PB-10 autopilot, which was integrated to the ILS to allow pilots to make automatic approaches to the airport. The PB-10 featured "throttle control," which automatically adjusted power to maintain position on the glide path. Jack Dyment would write, "It worked like a charm—when it worked. The airline was never able to release the system for line use because the reliability of its electronic tubes could never be trusted."[4] It wasn't an idea, Dud Taylor recalls, that pilots readily accepted either.

Off to the Stockholm Air Conference, 1946. Left to right: Charlie Proudfoot, Jack Dyment, S.S. Stevens.
Photo courtesy Janet Proudfoot

In those days, they weren't about to give up control of the aircraft. Being a progressive bunch that we in engineering were, we decided to buy one set of equipment for test purposes and install it on North Star #214. Bendix was a great help and one of their engineers came out to Winnipeg to help adjust the equipment. The problem was the radio tubes (too many failures) and that the early ILS beams were not that straight. A pilot could readily compensate for a rather uncomfortable ride. One of our test flights was to demonstrate the system to Herb Seagrim at Dorval. Everything went well and on final approach Herb turned on the equipment well out from the airport and it picked up the localizer very nicely and gave us a smooth ride in. We intersected the glide path and started down, again very smoothly. At about 400 feet, the throttles came full back, leaving us with no power. Herb calmly folded his arms and said, "What would you geniuses like me to do now?" Ron Baker, the co-pilot and TCA engineering test pilot, applied power and suggested that we now land. This was fine with Herb. It was not exactly the way to convince top management that we had a good thing going.

The tests continued for another year before the "throttle control" was generally accepted.

With the first six North Stars in use, beginning in November 1946, the Lancasters were gradually retired. But even when no longer the property of TCA, the last two Lancs continued to dog the company, as the new president, Gordon McGregor, discovered. The story as pieced together by McGregor is fascinating. A "glib, ex-used car salesman" (McGregor's words) had been employed by TCA to sell its surplus Lodestars. When he was discharged from the company, he turned up in London, where he met with the British aircraft broker Boyes Segrave & Co. He convinced them that he still represented TCA and offered them the last two CGTAS Lancs. Next he contacted Bill English and told him that he had effected a sale of both aircraft for 11,250 pounds sterling. What he did not mention to English was that because of sterling restrictions, the Bank of England forbade the export of funds.

Both Lancasters were flown over, Lothian in one and Bob Smith in the other. As one who had suffered their inadequacies for three long years, George Lothian deserved the last word on the Lancs: "As though trying to make amends, the old Lanc ran like clockwork all the way to London. When we climbed into the crew car and left her standing on the ramp, there were no nostalgic backward glances. Three years together had been enough, and more."[5]

Boyes Segrave & Co. resold the Lancs to one F. Sidney Cotton of the Aeronautical & Industrial Research Corporation, Curzon St., London, who paid 15,000 pounds for the pair. But while Boyes Segrave & Co. and the former TCA

TCA North Stars at Dorval Airport, 1946. Increasing numbers of them carried out short proving flights in preparation for transatlantic services in 1947. CF-CMT, the second Lancastrian converted, is shown alongside, still fulfilling that role.

employee had made a tidy profit, TCA could not be paid because the money was in a "blocked sterling account." It took McGregor himself going to London with an introduction from the manager of the Bank of Montreal to put TCA's case before the manager of the Bank of England. To his relief, not only was he taken to lunch by the sympathetic bank manager—who pointed out that the regulation had not been drawn up to "make it possible for any Britisher to obtain valuable property without payment"[6]—but soon after McGregor's return a cheque for 11,250 pounds from Boyes Segrave & Co. was received by the airline in Montreal. To McGregor's delight, the "glib ex-used car salesman" was suitably punished, and by then the two ex-CGTAS Lancs were living out their days, it was rumoured, as gun-runners in the Middle East.

With the North Stars, the airline introduced its first round-trip excursion fares to encourage winter travel, basing them on the normal one-way fare plus a third. In March 1947 the schedule read as follows:

TCA now flies the forty passenger "Skyliners"

Flt 200 EASTBOUND

Montreal:	Lv 4:00 pm EST
Sydney:	Arr 8:20 pm
	Lv 9:20 pm
Glasgow:	Arr 11:30 am GMT
	Lv 12:30 am
London:	Arr 2:30 pm

Flt 201 WESTBOUND

London:	Lv 7:30 pm GMT
Glasgow:	Arr 9:30 pm
	Lv 11:00 pm
Sydney:	Arr 7:25 am
	Lv 8:25 am
Montreal:	Arr 11:00 am

On the 1st and 15th of each month, Goose Bay replaced Sydney as a refuelling stop. On June 1, 1947, Shannon, Ireland, was a refuelling point for transatlantic flights. It would not be until May 1, 1947, that Trans Canada Air Lines

(Atlantic) assumed responsibility for the operation. In that first year from May 1 to December 31, 1947, TCA (Atlantic) Ltd.'s operating revenues were $5,483,298, of which $3,912,070 represented passenger traffic, $735,013 air mail and $331,557 air cargo. Operating expenses totalled $5,341,898, leaving a surplus of $141,400, which, after payment of interest, realized a surplus of $136,303. Of the 15,815 passengers who flew the Atlantic in those eight months, 14,393 were on scheduled flights; the remaining 1,422 were immigrants from the United Kingdom carried under a charter agreement with the province of Ontario. In July 1947 George Drew, the premier of Ontario, had contracted with Trans Ocean Airlines, an American charter carrier, to fly thousands of immigrants from the United Kingdom to Toronto at $10,400 US per flight. Mackenzie King was still in office then, and when his government blocked Drew's move, the Ontario government passed the contract to TCA at $9,000 Cdn per flight. Waiting for its North Star M-2s, which were to be delivered in the summer of 1948, the company took what immigrants it could as space became available on its regular flights. However, even after the North Stars' arrival, the company had insufficient capacity to carry the immigrants. "The airline asked the Ontario government to increase the payments to $11,500 per flight, even though its westbound M2s could carry only twenty-nine to thirty-six passengers, according to weather conditions. The province objected strenuously to Howe, and the episode did nothing to modify George Drew's distaste for TCA and all its works."[7] In an embarrassing turn of events, TCA was forced to subcontract the charter flights back to Trans Ocean Airlines.

During the war Muriel Peacock had been a nursing sister in the Canadian Army at home, and when the war ended she had been told by Matron to make way for those colleagues who had served overseas. She was discharged in Winnipeg on January 17, 1947, and caught a train the same day for Toronto to join Trans Canada Airlines. After her training she was assigned to fly out from Malton. Airline stewardesses were called upon to do many odd things in those days, but the most interesting for Peacock was feeding oxygen to goldfish. The episode took place just after the plane took off from Moncton. When the pilot had to climb to get above bad weather, one of the passengers carrying a bowl of prize goldfish noticed his fish gasping and flopping over on their backs. The alert stewardess rescued them from death by carrying the bowl to the nearest oxygen outlet. Although she loved her job, Peacock[8] soon discovered the handicaps of working for a company that had expanded so rapidly. Before the war, when TCA was small enough to be a family (and it was said that everyone knew each other by their first name), employees were expected to work long hours and conform to company regulations without question. As in most industries at that time, the welfare of the company came before its workers' personal lives, and it was a long-standing joke among TCA employees that their wives never called the airport unless they were more than seven days late coming home. If there were grievances toward or disciplinary actions by the airline, they remained on a personal level, went unrecorded and were never subject to public scrutiny. To be fair to the company, those in supervisory jobs had no qualification or training to be the bosses. In many cases they occupied their positions on the strength of their political connections, military decorations or membership in the "old boys club," that is, the too-old-to-fly-any-more club. Most were former bush pilots, self-reliant and brusque, hardly sympathetic toward organized labour or women. CALPA representatives, for instance, thought that their post-war dealings with TCA were repeatedly stymied because of the personality of the company's personnel director, Ernest Moncrieff. "He was a retired senior RCAF officer, whose ideas were definitely hardline. Encounters with him were at best rugged."[9] The company had assigned low priority to personnel relations, expecting few complaints, knowing that airline employees who had suffered through the Depression and innumerable layoffs with Canadian Airways were grateful for a job with TCA.

With post-war demobilization, staff in any occupation were loath to complain—least of all if they were females. But in retrospect, it is clear that airline management, like the Liberal party in power, had misread the common mood. A generation that had defeated fascism had gained so much self-confidence that it was not going to endure the inequities of the labour market as it had been in 1939. In the general election held just after VE Day, Mackenzie King and the Liberal party squeaked in with a narrow majority, proof that Canadians wanted a change.

TCA passenger agent Edward Hill, vice-president of the Canadian Air Line Passenger Agent Association (CALPAA) voiced what thousands of TCA employees were thinking when he went before the Wartime Labour Relations Board (WLRB) on May 21, 1946. "After all, gentlemen," he said, "that is one of the things that we three and all the others who are returned men in the room, have fought for in this war—the right to stand on our own feet and bargain for what we feel is justifiably coming to us."[10] The war had forever changed the labour movement. Through Hill, the passenger agent rank and file were expressing "the need for a fully consolidated working understanding between Trans Canada Air Lines and the agents of the Passenger Service Department of the said company, with special reference to the following conditions, namely: hours of labour, scales of wages, seniority, investigation, and settlement of grievances, and all other working conditions... and the express desire of all passenger agents throughout the Company's entire system to have complete working relationships clearly defined."[11]

TCA's flight dispatchers, no longer called flight control engineers, achieved legitimacy in 1945 when they organized themselves into the Canadian Airline Flight Dispatchers Association (CALDA). Mainly former radio operators, these "backroom boys of ocean flying" owed much of their improved status to TCA's transatlantic services. In 1949 the stationing, provisioning and financing of weather ships across the North Atlantic to provide aircraft with meteorological reports that had been begun on an ad hoc basis in 1946, was formalized. Canada provided one such ship, positioned at 56°30'N 51°W. Combining weather information from these ships with navigational knowledge, they produced the flight plans with which crews were briefed before takeoff. For a transatlantic 3:30 p.m. flight, the dispatchers started checking passenger, weather and freight elements twelve hours earlier. Supervised by A.P. Brown, in 1949 there were five dispatchers at Dorval, four at Gander and six in London. CALDA's first president was Bill Mills; Al Took was secretary-treasurer. The association immediately affiliated itself with the American Air Line Dispatchers Association and received an American Federation of Labour (AFL) charter. Perhaps the ultimate sign of the dispatchers' acceptance came in April 1951, when the president of CALDA, E.G. Ashton, figured on the airline's timetable brochure. Joining TCA in 1938 as a radio operator, Ashton (who in the photo was a Bob Hope look-alike) had been appointed dispatcher in 1941.

Ross Smyth, now a dispatcher, was elected council chairman representing "those near the bottom of the seniority list in Montreal. I was duly impressed at a meeting when our fiery president, Bill Mills, bravely waved his finger at the company's representative, Herb Seagrim, and said, 'Wait a minute, Herb. You know that's not true!' Seagrim used to refer humorously to Mills as 'Mr. John L' after a renowned American labour leader, John L. Lewis. All negotiations in this era were conducted quickly and on a first-name basis, much different from the present time."[12]

Unlike the other employee associations, the pilot's union, CALPA, had a permanent office staff in Winnipeg by 1945, with an assistant to the president, a constitution and local executive councils at the major stations, so that it was possible for them to coordinate their first convention on November 12 that year. The pilots were more sophisticated in labour relations not only because of their head start but because of their liaison with pilot unions of other airlines. Having flown across the border during the war or met with the BOAC Liberator pilots, they had consulted with the British Air Line Pilots Association (BALPA) and the American Air Line Pilots Association (ALPA). As a result, two years after the war ended, the TCA pilots had felt themselves strong enough to negotiate for a new contract for better pay comparable with pilots in the United States, and for the creation of "reserve captains," the last a thorny issue dating back to 1937. The airline accepted the need for reserve captains but stood firm on salaries, especially those of first officers, causing C.R. Robinson, president of CALPA, to resign in disgust. At this, the remainder of the negotiating committee accepted the airline's terms, and a contract deemed less than satisfactory by a majority of the pilots was signed on January 13, 1949. But rather than promoting first officers to reserve captains, the airline reduced junior captains. This had the effect of making the pilots increasingly disillusioned with TCA and their union and looking enviously at the contracts that ALPA was negotiating for its members in the United States.

Actual Pay Scales in the Original and 1949 Contracts

	Captains				First Officers		Reserve Captains			
	Mountainous		Flat terrain		4 engine					
					Dom.	OS	Dom.		OS	
	1945	1949	1945	1949	1945	1949	1945	1949	1945	1949
Start	$419	$450	$419	$450	$550	$900	$269	$200	$400	$430
After 3 yrs	$769	$800	$719	$750	$850			$400		
After 18 months						1,000	$369		$480[13]	

Dom. = Domestic. OS = Overseas.

There had traditionally been a distinction between passenger agents stationed at the airport and those at the city office—being at the airport, especially during the war, was seen as more prestigious—and this division had hindered the employees of both groups from organizing. But in February 1946 all ninety-eight passenger agents in TCA (of whom forty-one were women) circulated ballots to form the Canadian Air Line Passenger Agent Association (CALPAA) and applied to the WLRB to do so. TCA management was less than pleased with this. "It is our intention to oppose this application... We have intimated to the officers of the association," wrote Bill English to Symington, "that we do not take kindly to such an attitude on their part."[14]

Nevertheless, on May 21 the agents' representatives met with the WLRB and the airline's representative, "Tuddy" Tudhope, an aviation pioneer and now the general manager of operations. The company's position was that certification should be deferred because "organizing would hinder the passenger agents' chances for promotion" and also because the new traffic department manager, G.R. McGregor, was in the process of reorganizing the department. This only strengthened the passenger agents' resolve to bargain collectively, and CALPAA was officially certified on August 13, 1946. But to help bring the telephone agents into the fold, H.W. "Bert" Young was given a pass to travel the circuit, meeting with both groups. On November 1, 1946, this was accomplished and the broadened association was renamed the Trans Canada Airline Traffic Employees Association (TCA/TEA). Young was elected president and served in that capacity until he was promoted to passenger agent-in-charge in 1948, and G.C. McCardy of Halifax was elected in his place. The first agreement remains a testimony to Young's achievement.

TCA Traffic Employees Association 1946–47
Collective Agreement Wage Scale

Period	Passenger & Reservations agents	Telephone/teletype operators: local reservation
First 6 months	$145.00	$125.00
Second 6 months	150.00	130.00
Third 6 months	155.00	135.00
Fourth 6 months	160.00	140.00
Fifth 6 months	165.00	145.00
Sixth 6 months	170.00	150.00 maximum
Seventh 6 months	185.00 maximum[15]	

With the return of men from the armed forces, the ratio of males to females was affected, with men dominant, and the women quickly discovered that the "old boys' club" was not confined to management. In 1949 the TEA pushed to have the company install only male passenger agents at airports, explaining that women were suddenly not suited to the work as they had difficulty handling baggage. "We do not agree with the Company's contention that an irate person will be pacified by a girl's pretty smile. The average passenger is a man of middle age, likely old enough to be the young lady's father… and his time is worth too much money to be shrugged off with a flash of teeth."[16] Until the 1960s, when more women entered the profession, the union would be male-dominated.

Although the 1949–50 TCA/TEA contract changed the classifications to passenger agent (counter) and passenger agent (telephone), subsequent agreements were not as sweeping as the agents had hoped. Bill Mills's brave words notwithstanding, the agents lacked assurance in dealing with management. Revealing its members' insecurity and fear of reprisals from the personnel department, the association always censored the TCA/TEA magazine *Airscoop* so as not to give offence to senior staff. The one issue that did unite association members was their opposition to the wearing of uniforms that were introduced in 1946, as they held that "a businessman will not treat as an equal a man who is wearing a uniform." The airline gave in and the standard dress of the day, blue jacket and grey trousers, continued.

At the Chateau Laurier office, "On no two consecutive days was work ever the same," passenger agent Joan (Keogh) Rankin remembers. "One day I might work at the Chateau and make out tickets for people travelling the following day. The second day I could be sent to the airport to work my shift. There I would take passengers' tickets or issue them if they didn't have one, check their names on the manifest and weigh their baggage. After announcing the flight departure, I would follow the passengers on-board. It was my job to count to make sure the correct number of people were there. If all was fine, I told the stewardess that all the passengers were accounted for, then would step back out on the ramp, close and lock the passenger door, walk down the steps and wave to the pilot." Though passenger agents had a variety of duties then, Rankin thought her work better than a nine-to-five office job. "At the airport I would be the only woman on duty among a group of male baggage and cargo handlers, mechanics and the weatherman. If we weren't busy, they were sure to play some practical joke on me."[17]

In contrast to pilots, passenger agents and radio operators, a stewardess wasn't considered to have a career, and if she was dissatisfied about her working conditions, management was not seriously concerned. As the "height restriction" incident illustrated, there was no dearth of applicants. To walk comfortably within the Electra and Lodestar, stewardesses had been restricted to 5 feet 6 inches in height, but with the arrival of the DC-3s and soon North Stars, prospective stewardesses of 5 feet 7 inches and more hoped that the height restrictions would be relaxed. In 1946–47, so many wrote to their members of parliament about this that the question was brought up in the House. Howe replied that he had not heard any of the airline's customers complaining about the height of TCA stewardesses and that it was to the aircraft's advantage to carry less weight in the air.

To justify its perspective on stewardesses, the company could produce statistics showing that they only worked an average of twenty-six months before leaving to marry. It was a temporary job, they said, well suited to young, healthy women before they settled down to get married. And at a time when there were few such interesting career alternatives available, stewardessing was seen by the public as a glamorous interlude between homework and housework. In fact, there was great speculation in the media as to who the women married when they left.

For stewardess Marguerite Brezenski, who was featured in the airline's advertisements, the popular belief that stewardesses married their passengers was untrue. A nurse at the Ottawa Civic Hospital before joining TCA in 1941, Brezenski was by then a ten-year airline veteran, having served first as station stewardess in Moncton and, once the North Stars were launched, in TCA's transatlantic division. She had seen many a stewardess trade in her trim blue uniform for dishes and diapers. "Stewardesses work with an aura of glamour surrounding them, and when they leave the company to marry, most people seem to assume that they have picked for a husband a maharajah they met on a flight out of London or Paris. The fact is they have probably left to marry either someone from their hometown or someone they met during their nurse's training in a hospital. It is only occasionally that a stewardess marries one of her passengers." Marguerite proved her point when she left TCA to marry William Sirola from her hometown of Cobalt, Ontario, although her travelling days were not over—they moved to Liberia before settling down in Port Henry, NY. But the Danish-born stewardess Lisa Eriksen—a runner-up in the International Airline Stewardess of 1958 contest—did marry one of her passengers. It was love at first sight when she leaned over to check Bob Kellogg's seat belt on the

Vancouver–Victoria run one February day in 1958. And when Kellogg, a millionaire, took her dancing on their first date, her shoe slipped off in Cinderella fashion. They were married in the Cathedral of Aarhus, Jutland, Denmark.

Whatever the cause of the high turnover among stewardesses, because of it there were no codified rules or policies on their duties, rates of pay or working conditions. Management also counted on the certainty that the stewardesses really loved the job, as it was more romantic than the nursing profession they had all come from. Because of this, the women endured working conditions that were unhealthy (the smoke-filled, unpressurized cabins led to continuous colds and sinusitis), undignified (stewardesses were regarded as "easy" and open to sexual harassment from passengers), underpaid (pay scales were not equal to those for purser-stewards), and overworked (there was no standard for maximum hours of duty).

"I guess they [TCA's first stewardesses] were like the rest of us in the company," said Bill Fabro, the former director of Air Canada in-flight service.[18] "You were hired, you were paid a salary, and you were told 'to get on with it and don't make mistakes.' And that was it." But what irked the women most of all was their automatic dismissal on marriage—or even the intention of marriage. It was a foolish stewardess who flashed her engagement ring at work. The stewards on the CGTAS Lancs might be husbands and fathers, but they had no fear of their employment being terminated. On the contrary, considered the sole breadwinners of their families, they were employed indefinitely. And they had no weight and height restrictions, either.

Heavy as all the injustices were, the fuse that lit the stewardess revolt was the interminable commute from Toronto out to Malton. Earning $150 a month—$30 less than the pursers—and having to pay for their uniforms, they couldn't afford the taxi fare to and from Toronto's airport, let alone the price of a car. The wartime Malton bus service had ended, and as TCA did not pay commuting costs for its other employees, it saw no reason to do so for stewardesses. The problem had existed since 1939 when TCA first began flying from Malton, and the original stewardesses had long ago worked out an ingenious system. They caught the streetcar down Yonge Street to the Royal York Hotel, crossed the street to the post office terminal and cadged a ride in the mail truck cab going out to Malton. There was no charge, and all one had to do was call the post office and make a reservation. Or they could hitch a ride with the captain or first officer of their flight, if they lived close by. On return they again had to beg rides with mail truck drivers or pilots to be dropped off at a street corner near public transport. If it was late at night they sat near the streetcar driver to fend off unwanted attention: for stewardesses, commuting was not only uncomfortable but unsafe.

By the time Muriel Peacock joined in 1943, the commute had become even worse. "As the company grew quickly, soon we found three or four stewardesses wanting the same mail truck. We could squeeze two of us in the one available seat beside the driver; the latest 'calling in' had to sit on the mailbags or the spare tire. These same young ladies were used to advertise 'the pride of TCA'!"[19] At her insistence, a number of stewardesses met in the summer of 1946 at one of their parents' homes. They discussed how to request from the company a transportation allowance and a guaranteed seat in an airport limousine from Malton. Then they approached management.

When meetings with the company supervisors proved inconclusive, on April 10, 1947, Peacock and another stewardess, Victoria Stewart, applied for certification on behalf of all the stewardesses at Toronto. As former nurses, many of the stewardesses were leery of the word "union," with its underworld connotations, and settled for "association." The airline was now sufficiently concerned to give Peacock a pass to travel between Moncton and Vancouver and the use of vacant crew rooms to hold meetings with stewardesses in at other stations. In July she flew across the country and at each base attracted great interest from the stewardesses who attended the meetings. Peacock then called on a Winnipeg lawyer, Edward J. Kirby; after studying the CALPA constitution, he drew up a model for the stewardesses. At the same time Alex Stebner, one of the first CGTAS purser-stewards, was applying for certification for the twenty-one male flight attendants, and on November 5, 1947, the Canadian Air Line Purser Stewards Association (CALPSA) came into being. Six days later, the Canadian Air Line Stewardess Association (CALSA), representing the 124 TCA stewardesses, was born with Peacock as president and Stewart as vice-president. At first, members of the two organizations thought that they had little in common because of the generally held perception that the men were in a lifetime career and the women only temporarily employed, and the women worried that the men would be given seniority over them. But when the Labour Relations Board ruled that it would not accept two separate bargaining units from a common employer, they were forced to combine. The resulting organization, the Canadian Air Line Flight Attendants' Association (CALFAA), came into being on July 26, 1948, with Peacock as president, and soon afterwards commenced negotiations with TCA. There were years of hard fighting ahead but at least it would be done collectively. Victoria Stewart was not part of this battle because "very shortly after the formation of CALFAA, I was promoted to a supervisory position—which at that time was a normal procedure for companies wishing to quiet a raucous voice in their midst. My time and energies were thus directed on company policies."[20]

Despite the labour upheavals, all employees—pilots, stewardesses and passenger agents—had a grudging respect for those who ran the airline. CALPA's F.E.W. Smith wrote that TCA had proved itself a hard-fisted team, consistent and not easily bested. They had to be. The company was no longer enjoying its wartime economic boom. Set up to move military mail, TCA (Atlantic) was now coping with money-losing flights to Europe and the Caribbean, and the chances of TCA (North America) breaking even had been hampered by the disappointing performance of the North Star. Employee euphoria of the war years had worn off, and TCA was now in deficit, struggling to come to terms with labour contracts while suffering public criticisms: in the House from the new Opposition leader, George Drew; in the media led by the owner of the *Globe and Mail*, George McCullough; and from taxpayers who wanted airline expansion, preferably to their hometowns, but did not want to pay for it.

With the war's end, every small town in Canada, it seemed, had its own airfield, courtesy of the Commonwealth Air Training Plan, and with the "Yellow Peril" now gone, the locals waited for all the benefits that the Air Age was supposed to bring them, such as airmail and scheduled air services to their provincial capitals. In 1948 there were, besides Canadian Pacific Airlines, five other air companies in Canada: Maritimes Central Airways operating from PEI; Leavens Brothers Air Services at Leamington and Pelee Island, Ontario; Central Northern Airways in Manitoba; Queen Charlotte Airways on the British Columbia coast; and the Saskatchewan Government Airways at Prince Albert. All were monopolies themselves, feeding off the TCA Halifax–Victoria main line at various points. For obvious reasons they scorned routes that were sure money-losers. As a result, having granted it a monopoly on the transcontinental route, the government expected TCA to cover the scorned routes itself.

Two of these were the "prairie milk run" of Brandon–Regina–Swift Current–Medicine Hat–Lethbridge and the Ontario hinterland run of North Bay–Porquois Junction–Kapuskasing. Cynics saw these post-war additions as having been purposely inserted by the Liberals into CCF and Conservative strongholds, especially after their dismal 1948 election results, while regions that needed air service more—such as British Columbia and the North—were ignored. Whatever the reason, the "milk runs" made gratuitous use of DC-3s: loads rarely averaged more than $1^1/_2$ passengers per flight. These runs had a personality all their own. The cargo manifest of one flight out of Regina included live birds, licence plates, newspapers, one dog's head (frozen), machine parts and feed. Some routes were seasonal, as in June 1953 when TCA began a daily summertime flight between Toronto and the Muskoka resorts. When the milk runs inevitably lost money, TCA's critics were quick to find fault: the airline was obviously using the wrong equipment, wrong timetable and/or wrong fare structure. These money-losing routes, along with the increased competition on the Atlantic from BOAC and soon Air France and KLM, made TCA's transcontinental monopoly even more indispensable.

Without doubt the most versatile employees in the company were the station managers of the two-man stations at Brandon (Russell Alexander), Yorkton (G.A. Saunders), Swift Current (J.F. Ames), and Medicine Hat (J.J. O'Flynn). There were two flights daily through each of these airports and since all lacked any DOT presence, the station managers doubled as weathermen, as well as air traffic controllers, flight dispatch, baggage handlers, air cargo clerks and wing de-icers. They issued tickets and load clearances, "worked" the company pouch and heated water twice daily for the stewardesses to make lunches. As the airline operated out of these airports seven days a week, for two days

The new fleet of TCA DC-3Ws. The aircraft were proving capable on high-density routes such as Toronto–Montreal–Ottawa, as expected. But there were demands that TCA fulfill its role as Canada's national air service and offer flights on low-traffic routes not served by private concerns.

every week the station managers were entirely on their own—not a happy situation, especially when the temperature on the Prairies dropped to –45°F.

After World War II, the combination of cheap military surplus aircraft and enthusiastic "de-mobbed" pilots meant that local airlines sprang up daily—just as they had in 1919. But as James Richardson had understood then, in order to start up, aviation entrepreneurs needed the security of airmail subsidies from the Post Office. Several times the House heated up in debate on precisely this subject. On August 17, 1946, Opposition members from British Columbia pointed out that while TCA flew between Victoria and Vancouver, there were no air services (and thus no airmail) in the Interior of the province. Penticton, Trail and Kimberley were all population centres large enough to warrant scheduled air services. If the government airline wasn't willing to provide these, why wouldn't the Air Transport Board and the postmaster general encourage local air companies, in this instance Capilano Airways, to do so?

At that time Mackenzie King was in France laying the cornerstone for the memorial at Dieppe, and the acting prime minister, Louis St. Laurent, did not enter into the debate. Therefore, as the questions concerned TCA, C.D. Howe rose to answer them. At first this looked like another skirmish that the old

politician would win. His own constituency of over 100,000 people, he pointed out, had no airmail service, proving that even he had no influence over the
postmaster general's decisions. (Howe was being economical with the truth:
exactly a month later on September 17, 1946, TCA began a service between his
constituency at Fort William and Duluth.) As to Capilano Airways, Howe continued, its president, Leigh Stevenson, was a personal friend, and he had
already interceded with the board to reconsider his plight.

Then Stanley Knowles stood up. In the recent election his CCF party had
carried twenty-eight seats in the House and was at the height of its national
power.

> The minister knows that we in this group welcomed and gave
> strong support to the general statement of policy which he
> made on March 17, 1944...but he made one pronouncement
> which does not seem to be carried out. "Steps will be taken to
> require our railways to divest themselves of ownership of air
> lines to the end that, within a period of one year from the end-
> ing of the European war, transport by air will be entirely sep-
> arate from surface transportation"...So far as I can learn, the
> many subsidiary companies which were bought by the
> Canadian Pacific Railway are still operated by that company. I
> suppose there might be some argument as to when the war in
> Europe ended, but I think it ended in May 1945 and more than
> a year has since elapsed. I should like to hear from the minis-
> ter with respect to the whole question of policy relating to the
> ownership of air lines by railway companies, with particular
> in reference to Canadian Pacific Air Lines.

Howe rose to reply.

> At the time I made the announcement I was very sure I was
> right. A good section of the house was very sure I was wrong
> but that gave me no pause whatsoever. At that time the pub-
> lic was not getting the service to which I believed it was enti-
> tled, and I think the public in that area believed it too...The
> position is that we explored the possibilities of carrying out
> the announced government policy. It seemed easy when it
> was announced. We thought it would be easy to divide up the
> system and return it to small operations, but when we under-
> took to do so we were faced with a great expansion of air
> activity in the north which required additional air services.
> Obviously Canadian Pacific Air Lines was not in a position to
> buy extra equipment until it had some security of service. We
> then explored as to how we could break the system down into

individual routes, each serving a particular territory as was proposed at the time the discussion took place. But we could find no group strong enough to take over any of these services. The value of the equipment owned by the Canadian Pacific Air Lines was in the vicinity of seven or eight million dollars. The additional equipment required ran into several more millions . . . It is not a business which can be entered into lightly.

The air transport board was established when that policy was announced. There was a change of management in Canadian Pacific Air Lines and a change in the directorate, from the president down. The closest co-operation was obtained between management and the air transport board in working out policy matters. Those honourable members who are familiar with the territory served by Canadian Pacific Air Lines will agree that the service has improved tremendously. All sources of friction have been removed as between the government authority and Canadian Pacific Air Lines and between Canadian Pacific Air Lines and Trans Canada Air Lines. Today the two systems are working as an integrated system. At the time Canadian Pacific Air Lines was ambitious to extend its territory in other parts of Canada. Today it finds it has a sufficient task to develop the parts of Canada for which it was then and is now responsible for giving service, with the result that any new airlines that care to enter their operation can find scope for their activities in parts of Canada at present not served. Today I have come to the conclusion that, while the policy when it was announced may then have been the correct policy . . . the public interest, which I say again must be the paramount consideration of all air line activities, is better served by the present combination of services than it could be served by any plan which can now be devised as an alternative to the present arrangement.

Knowles warned darkly that "the day will come when we will have to undo the harm done to the Canadian economy by the monopoly which we are building in transportation." Another Opposition member, who was a Latin scholar, said that the minister's motto should be: *Tempora mutantur, nos et mutamur in illis* (I change whenever I find myself in error),[21] a sentiment that Howe would have agreed with.

It was a subtle turning of the page in aviation history. The decision had to have been taken at Cabinet level and this was no off-the-cuff reply. But how much Mackenzie King's absence had to do with the reprieve of Canadian Pacific Airlines can only be guessed at. On his return, as the first step toward retirement in 1948, the prime minister gave up the office of secretary of state for external affairs to St. Laurent. Relaxed, urbane, and travel-loving, "Uncle Louie" would bring to power with him a new breed of politician, men like Lester B. Pearson and Jack Pickersgill, both of whom exerted a vigorous influence on commercial aviation in Canada. In 1948 Howe would become minister of reconstruction and supply in addition to minister of trade and commerce, but the minister of transport was now Lionel Chevrier (1945–54).

In October 1948 Pickersgill accompanied acting Prime Minister St. Laurent on his first visit to London, the pair catching a regular TCA flight over. On their way home, the Merlin curse asserted itself. Pickersgill described it thus:

Prime Minister Louis St. Laurent. He loved flying, and travelling in general. He made several transatlantic flights, usually on TCA North Stars, even before becoming prime minister.

The first leg from London to Prestwick was uneventful and we took off…in the late evening. I had fallen asleep and was woken up by hearing St. Laurent exclaim, "This is a pretty pass! We have been ordered to fasten our seat belts preparatory to landing again at Prestwick!"…We were told that the plane would not take off again until noon the following day. There was only one hotel at Prestwick airport and it had no room until after midnight…[When Pickersgill explained to the night staff who St. Laurent was, they found a room that the two men had to share.] Next morning all the passengers were cooped up for more than an hour before the plane was ready. We had stops in Reykjavik in Iceland and at Sydney and finally reached Montreal at two o'clock in the morning. There was no complaint from St. Laurent, but I felt it was hardly an appropriate way for our next prime minister to travel abroad. When I told Claxton [Brooke Claxton, the minister of defence] about our journey, he ordered the first VIP plane, which was called the C-5.[22]

But TCA would have the last laugh. In January 1951, when Prime Minister St. Laurent and his party were returning from an official visit to London and Paris, the same RCAF VIP C-5 "lost" one of its Pratt & Whitney engines and had to land at Keflavik. This time poor St. Laurent and Pickersgill were marooned in Iceland for three days, waiting for the RCAF to fly an engine over. While Claxton phoned Gordon McGregor to arrange for a passing TCA North Star to pick up the pair (it only had three seats available), the prime minister took the opportunity to visit the surprised Icelandic ministry of foreign affairs and open diplomatic relations with that nation.

Where Mackenzie King had been suspicious of foreign entanglements, St. Laurent, Chevrier and Pearson seized opportunities now and in the future to involve Canada with the world—whether at the United Nations or NATO or by way of its airlines. More pertinent for CPA, neither of the future prime ministers regarded the Canadian Pacific Railway, as King had, as the Great Satan, bent on fulfilling Downing Street's agenda in Canada. From this point on Chevrier and the ATB began to view CPA and other airlines' route applications more favourably. Officially the government's "two airline policy" was years away, but its tolerance for airlines other than TCA had increased.

In practical terms, they recognized that to force the Canadian Pacific Railway to abandon its airline would be a repeat of the collapse of the Canadian Northern and Grand Trunk Railways earlier in the century. The patchwork of bush routes that comprised CPA extended from Whitehorse and Fort Liard, NWT, to the Saguenay and Magdalen Islands in Quebec, encompassing not only isolated villages like Senneterre, Quebec, and Pickle Lake, Ontario, but provincial capitals like Regina, Edmonton and Quebec City. As

The Canadair DC-4M-2 Cornwallis overflying Dorval Airport, early 1948.

in 1922, the federal government would have had to buy up every little bankrupt company and hook them to a perpetual life-support system, and inevitably TCA would then be forced to assume services to those cities, to say nothing of the bush communities where aircraft was the only means of travel. In the meantime the Canadian Pacific Railway's air operations were losing heavily, particularly in the bush, but it suited Ottawa just fine if the railway chose to keep CPA within its fold. The successful route integration of both airlines that Howe had spoken of meant that CPA "knew its place." Howe's ATB had even thrown CPA a couple of new routes: Vancouver–Prince Rupert (August 1, 1947) and Vancouver–Penticton–Castlegar–Cranbrook–Calgary (December 15, 1947). As long as CPA did not attempt to infringe on TCA's mandate by competing on the country's main arteries or outside Canada, it was to be tolerated.

Trans Canada Airlines was hardly in a position to cut the umbilical cord from the CNR either. The airline that Howe had talked of in his St. Patrick's Day speech in 1944 was not in the same state of health two years later and would not be for the remainder of the decade.

Year	TCA Domestic & Cross-Border		TCA Atlantic	
1946	Loss	$1,269,624	—	—
1947	Loss	1,761,043	Profit	$136,303
1948	Loss	1,183,022	Loss	1,750,218
1949	Loss	1,419,444	Loss	2,898,149
1950	Profit	201,206	Loss	1,526,412

TCA's net loss for the next five years was to be $11,470,403; capital advances from the CNR between 1945 and 1948 to meet those losses totalled $9,945,717. The causes of TCA's shortfall were not difficult to deduce. In 1946 it was the purchase and reconditioning of twenty-four DC-3s, the refitting of the first RCAF North Star, and the opening of offices in Chicago, Cleveland, Seattle and Duluth, not to mention taking over the Goose Bay service. In 1947 three more DC-3s and four RCAF North Stars were added, offices at Boston and Sault Ste. Marie were opened, and the DOT raised its landing fees. Emergency flights during the British Columbia floods, while laudable, did not help TCA's bottom line. In 1948 the company acquired thirteen North Stars (and lost one at Sydney, NS), started the money-losing Caribbean services and faced increased competition on the Montreal–London route from BOAC. In 1949 the company's financial plight caught up with it and TCA hit the bottom.

While the company had little competition internally, the low-overhead US carriers were still flying into Montreal, Toronto and Vancouver, offering more extensive connections throughout the United States. The original American "windows" to the south were still operating—Colonial Airlines from Ottawa and Montreal to New York and Washington and United Airlines between Vancouver and Seattle—but now there was also Northeast Airlines flying Montreal–Boston–New York and Western Air Lines connecting Lethbridge with Great Falls, Montana.

It was Symington who now pointed out to the minister the benefits of TCA remaining within the protective fold of the CNR. For one thing, leaving it would mean appointing a new president and board of directors, all of whom would require payment (he and the present board were on CNR salaries) and whose loyalties to the Liberals might be questionable. The CCF's Stanley Knowles, on the other hand, was aware that all the TCA directors were based in Montreal or Ottawa so that no other region in Canada had any representation on the board, and he began lobbying—though unsuccessfully—on October 24, 1949, to get two members of the Winnipeg Chamber of Commerce onto it. On a lower level, separating from the CNR would mean that whole departments of employees—legal, accounting, sales, medical and purchasing—would have to be hired and given office accommodation and furnishings.

In April 1947 Blissville was closed and all operations moved permanently to Pennfield Ridge. The first direct Halifax–Montreal flight, which took place on June 1, 1948, was called the "Silver Dart" service, and some of the mail that was carried was signed by J.A.D. McCurdy himself. As more of the public flew, it was becoming apparent to them that the airlines' schedules had been written to accommodate the Post Office. The DC-3s were delayed at interim airports for the convenience of last mail deliveries, and Howe fielded constant complaints in the House from MPs who had travelled on flights between Halifax and Ottawa that had been held overnight in Montreal or Blissville to collect last mails.

What Others Think of Us

Letters from TCA Passengers

Window Seat Problem:
I enjoyed very much my trip to Winnipeg but I'm wondering if anything could be done regarding the window seat situation. I would have liked a window seat but they were all taken. During the flight however, several window seat occupants were reclined in their seats fast asleep while we who wanted went without. Would a system of an extra charge for these window seats be workable?

Sheepish Passenger:
This is a grouse. Don't you serve anything but lamb? Had it on my trip to Vancouver, ditto return to Edmonton. Lamb is my pet peeve. Can't eat it. Period. Would suggest at least have extra buns. Asked for another instead of meat. No buns. Wonderful service! Think I'll try CPA next time.

Weighing-in:
About five years ago at the Vancouver Airport a customer could stand on the baggage scales and weigh himself. The scales are now so placed that this is not possible, and I miss the opportunity of checking my weight.

Crow's Wing:
Could the upper surface of each wing be painted a drab black? My first flight was very uncomfortable as far as looking out of the window was concerned, due to the sunshine being reflected through my window from the wing.

Warm-Blooded:
Okay you asked for it. Today's flight from Edmonton to Vancouver was so blame cold. I speak for the two Americans and one Canadian who was educated in the US. 62 degrees is not fit for man or beast. On the other hand, it was okay for the Canadians (no slur intended). Had I known, I would have worn woollen sox, heavy underwear and a sweater. The least you could do would be to warn us San Franciscans and Los Angelinos your frigid intentions

so we could prepare for the ordeal. Other than that the flight was fine. You have excellent pilots and capable stewardesses (but latter probably cold-hearted).

Don't Bolt Your Food:
I unfortunately found a large one and one-half inch bolt in my bran muffin. It gave my teeth quite a jar. Suggest you pass my censored comments on to your supplier out of Calgary.

Poetical Passenger:
God willing and weather permitting,
Again with TCA you'll find me sitting.

The Bristol Freighter on tour—after the TCA engineering crew at Dorval rebuilt its entire electrical system.
Photo courtesy Joanne Peck

CHAPTER 10

T he revised transcontinental route that came into effect on July 1, 1947, almost on the tenth anniversary of the company's birth, was as much symbolic as it was technical. The airline no longer flew directly along the Airway between Toronto and Winnipeg but over the Great Lakes via Sault Ste. Marie and the Lakehead. Its childhood had ended and, as with most adolescents, the years ahead for TCA would be ones of growing pains, of multiplying insecurities punctuated with moments of intensity.

Thunder Bay Airport, winter 1947–48. A Canada–US Agreement in 1945 allowed free passage over US territory for TCA flights between Sault Ste. Marie and Thunder Bay, Ontario.

Because the new Toronto–Winnipeg airway was via the Lakehead (Fort William and Fort Arthur) and Thunder Bay, Sault Ste. Marie became one of the new services to be inaugurated on July 1, though poor weather prevented the first flight from taking off until the following day. It was a unique service because, while the town of Sault Ste. Marie could trace its origin to 1668, when the Jesuits built a mission on the Canadian side of the St. Mary's River, in 1947 the town still had no airport. Its namesake on the Michigan side of the river had a small one at Kinross, and this was where TCA's flights landed. But although the TCA DC-3 and its passengers had physically entered the United States, technically they were still in Canada. In fact, the very tarmac they stepped on had been paid for by the Canadian government along with the entire nearby airports and radio range at Grand Marais and Houghton, Michigan. Under the DOT requirements there had to be "alternates" at 100-mile intervals, and on the Canadian side DOT airports were built at Gore Bay on Manitoulin Island and Wiarton near Owen Sound. But at Kinross the airport was managed by TCA, the airline being reimbursed by the DOT, and its tenant was Capital Air Lines. TCA passengers were taken to and from the Canadian side by a bonded convoyed limousine service. If they deplaned at Kinross, they did not have to submit to US Customs, but a Canadian Customs officer examined their baggage and non-residents checked in with Canadian Immigration at Fort William or Toronto. TCA staff from other stations were amazed that there was no bridge over the St. Mary's between the two "Soos." During the winter the ferry service that carried the limousine depended on an old Liberty ship belonging to the US Coast Guard to keep the channel ice-free. Until Kinross became a USAF airbase in 1952, most TCA passengers were not aware that they had landed in a US airport, but after that TCA became the airport's

Passengers making for the Nissen hut at Sault Ste. Marie.

tenant rather than the manager. TCA moved out on August 1, 1961, after a temporary terminal was built at Sault Ste. Marie.

Other revisions to transcontinental routes in 1947 were more modest. On the Winnipeg–Calgary service the airline now flew via Saskatoon and Edmonton and between Regina and Lethbridge via Swift Current and Medicine Hat.

Hired in time for the arrival of the North Stars was a new batch of stewardesses. Kathleen Stewart joined in October 1947 as her sister Victoria was already one "and a stewardess's pay cheque was more than I was getting in nursing." At this time classes were taught by Flo Perkins and Gordie Thompson. "Our classes were very interesting," wrote Stewart, "not only because we were learning something new but because they also included men—and as there were more men than women we didn't have to worry about getting a date for any of the dances." After her training ended, she opted to be posted back in Toronto where she shared an apartment with her sister. "Most of the passengers were quite appreciative of the service we gave them. One man decided that he should tip me and when I refused the tip he threw the money at me. I gently put it back in his suit pocket." Stewart married in July 1949. "At that time any stewardess who got married no longer had a job. The stewards could be married and it seemed very unfair."[1]

Noreen Searson joined in 1952, when "they did not expect anyone older to be around so there were no regulations about when you had to retire. Later they decided that anybody newly hired would have to sign a release form saying that they would leave voluntarily at thirty-two. There was a great outcry about this...New stewardesses were being asked to sign this form and of course when you are twenty-one you never think you will ever be thirty-two."[2] Though marriage meant an end to a stewardess's career, common-law relationships were tolerated by both TCA and CPA, and for years many a stewardess's husband found himself being referred to as the "boyfriend" or "fiancé." To its credit, TCA did not hunt down suspected offenders, but there was a rumour that CPA sent a detective to Victoria to look up the marriage registers. Perhaps it didn't need to. "One of the biggest problems we had was that the flight attendants would tell on themselves," said Bill Fabro, the former director of in-flight service with Air Canada, "and then we had to do something about it."[3]

It was not only stewardesses who were penalized by the airlines for marrying. Wilse Jessee, elected president of the TEA (traffic employees association) in 1952, reported that upon marriage, TCA female employees—whether typists, passenger agents or switchboard operators—were automatically reduced to casual status because they were sure to become pregnant soon. This was such a widely accepted practice that ten years later the union was still fighting it. "In August 1962 at a meeting between management and the TEA, when inquiries were made as to the possibility of employing more than one permanent switchboard operator in Calgary, Jessee (who was now in management as a personnel and services manager) had to explain that married women were employed on a temporary or casual basis only, and that as two of the three Calgary switchboard operators were married women, they could never expect to be reclassified as permanent employees."[4]

During the war, while Bermuda and the Caribbean were isolated from

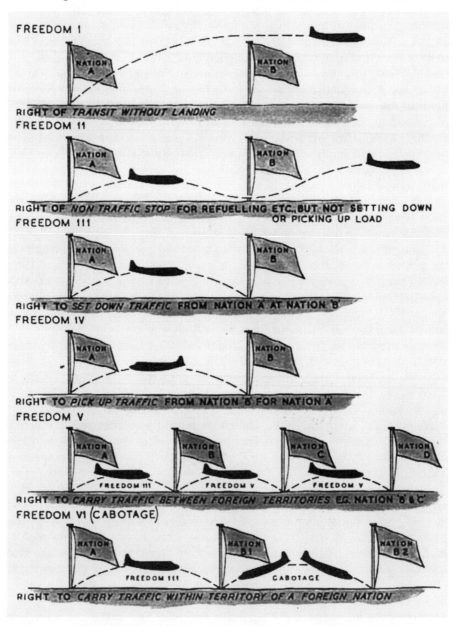

Diagram showing 5th Freedoms and cabotage. Illustration by Peter Masefield

Britain, Howe had been encouraged by colonial authorities to extend TCA's routes to those regions. Now that it was finally feasible with the North Stars, there was both potential for trade and tourism between Canada and the islands and an opportunity to counter growing American influence in that area. Howe, who had been a frequent visitor to the Caribbean, was enthusiastic, but Gordon McGregor, the new TCA president, did not think that the sparse winter traffic warranted the use of resources from an airline already in deficit or that the time was right for expansion to Bermuda and the Caribbean. When he was overruled by Howe, nothing demonstrated to McGregor more clearly TCA's use as the government's chosen instrument in international matters than the minister's reply. "I have been well aware that profitable business does not exist at the moment, and that the hope for the route is that tourist business from Canada can be built up to a profitable level, particularly during the winter months. Canada desires to offer an outlet for Canadian tourists in sterling areas, and, for that reason, I think that the route should be operated in the national interest."[5]

At war's end, however, the British opposed a Canadian service there as BOAC was in the process of starting up British West Indian Airlines (BWIA) to service that area. To generate sufficient traffic to and from Canada, the logical solution would have been for TCA to use Bermuda and Jamaica as staging posts for Fifth Freedom rights to South America. Unfortunately, as they were both British colonies, any flights between them would be considered cabotage (that is, air transport within a country—in this case, the United Kingdom—by domestic aircraft). In the end, a compromise was effected at the 1946 Bermuda conference by Howe, Symington and Baldwin: TCA was given the route to Bermuda and Fifth Freedom rights from Bermuda to Nassau (Bahamas), Kingston (Jamaica), Bridgetown (Barbados) and Port of Spain (Trinidad), but still prevented from flying onward to South America from the West Indies.

On May 1, 1948, TCA inaugurated services from Toronto and Montreal to Bermuda, and on December 2 to Nassau, Bridgetown and Trinidad. It was 1,372 miles from Bermuda to Barbados, or 5 hours and 50 minutes by North Star, and then on to Trinidad, another 231 miles away, in 1 hour and 20 minutes. Bill Stuart, the first TCA station manager in Barbados, was impatient for the runways at Seawell Airport to be lengthened as northbound passengers were forced to first go south to Trinidad. In Port of Spain, TCA's local agents were Gordon Grant & Co., who also handled KLM—and, it seemed, everything else on the island from sugar cane, coconut and cocoa plantations to shipping, insurance, automobiles and hardware as well as the bottling of beer, Pepsi Cola and Canada Dry. The Caribbean flights also inaugurated the airline's first promotional "Flite Pac," a collection of items distributed to passengers that it was thought they would find useful in the tropics—from Yardley's night cream to a bottle of Bromo-Seltzer.

With its Atlantic routes functioning, the government airline was expected

A superb view of the DC-4M-2 CF-TFF, which has made landfall over Hamilton, Bermuda. In 1948, TCA began regular services to the Caribbean Islands, appropriately using the new North Stars

to turn next toward the Pacific, but while Mackenzie King and Howe had been willing back in 1943 to disregard British and American sensibilities in the Atlantic and strike out independently with CGTAS, their attitude concerning Canada's other ocean was quite the opposite. And although at the Commonwealth air conference that year, Howe and Symington had indicated TCA's ambitions in that region, Trans Canada Airlines management had very little interest in venturing across the Pacific at that time. The minister, who had heeded calls from the British colonies in the Caribbean for a Canadian service, was deaf to similar cries from the Australian and New Zealand dominions for a Pacific one. When both of those governments joined with Britain to apply diplomatic pressure to Ottawa, even offering to co-operate in a joint air service linking the three senior members of the Commonwealth, the most that King and Howe would do was sign a bilateral air agreement with the Australians on June 11, 1946, that agreed to a service between Sydney and Vancouver by an airline of each country. Believing this meant imminent action on the part of the Canadians, in April 1948 British Commonwealth Pacific Airlines (BCPA), an Australian/British/New Zealand venture, bought two DC-4s and began flying what was then the longest route in the world: Auckland–Sydney–Vancouver–Nandi (Fiji)–Honolulu–San Francisco.

When TCA did not reciprocate, BOAC offered to co-operate with a joint service to Sydney from Montreal via The Pas, Vancouver and Tokyo. Howe said that he was waiting for the results from a route study expected in the summer of 1948. Paul Davoud was asked to assess the commercial potential of flights from Vancouver to Sydney via Honolulu and Nandi; he concluded that TCA would lose between $25,000 and $50,000 a month on it.[6] Jack Dyment estimated that the subsidies required from the public purse to keep such a money-losing route in operation would be in the range of $1.25 million annually, and McGregor, as a pilot, did not trust the North Star's Merlin engines over such vast expanses of ocean. He also knew that unlike the BCPA DC-4s, the TCA North Stars could not fly the westbound trip without more than a 25 percent load factor. Nor could he help but notice that Hudson Fysh, the managing director of the nationalized Australian airline QANTAS and as hard-nosed a businessman as himself, had no interest in extending his network to Vancouver.

Enter Grant McConachie, who had become president of Canadian Pacific Airlines on February 7, 1947. Prevented by the Liberal government's air policy from flying across the US border or over the Atlantic, CPA's only avenues for expansion were the Pacific, the Orient and South America. As a young man McConachie had dreamed of flying to China, convinced that a Shanghai–Vancouver route had great economic potential, and if CPA would first have to run a service to Australia and New Zealand via Fiji, it was the price he was willing to pay. He not only offered to placate the Australians and everyone else with a Canadian airline in the Pacific but said he would do it without a subsidy from the federal government. Fortunately for him, the CPR had deep pockets. But Howe was not finished with him yet. He coerced Canadian Pacific Airlines into buying four North Stars for their proposed Pacific service.

Grant McConachie and Gordon McGregor were a study in contrasts, similar only in their devotion to their airlines. The two men, both of Scottish Presbyterian stock, would be pitted against each other through the next decade. Eight years younger than McGregor, the son of a CNR chief master mechanic in Calder, Alberta, Grant McConachie lived his life in opposition to the strict Presbyterian upbringing that his father had tried to instill. His education had ended at grade ten when he realized his considerable charm could get him further than books. Ebullient and shrewd, McConachie loved wheeling and dealing—and flying. While McGregor was working his way through the ranks

Canada's two airline and railway executives—adversaries in the airline business and good friends personally. Left to right: Donald Gordon of CPR, Grant McConachie of CP Air, Gordon McGregor of TCA and W.A. Mather of the CNR. NAC 121814

to becoming Bell Telephone's youngest manager, McConachie's youth had been filled with tipsy snake dancers, a Jewish cowboy called "Two Gun Cohen," a cabin at Takla Lake, BC, and, along with Art Rankin (who would later join TCA), flying airmail routes to the Yukon. McGregor, on the other hand, was never ostentatious and even as president of TCA lived in an unpretentious house in lower Westmount, preferring to entertain at the Field and Stream Club. McConachie partied incessantly, owned a huge home in the Shaughnessy district of Vancouver and a ranch near Merritt, BC. McGregor drove an old American car—the only TCA (and for many years Air Canada) president not to have a chauffeur. Both men were synonymous with their airlines, both fought the federal government all the way for their own purposes. Decades before it was fashionable, McConachie believed in the "open skies" doctrine; decades after it became unfashionable to do so, McGregor still believed in the "chosen instrument" policy. But strangely enough, they were friends, and McConachie explained that "the only flaw in our friendship is the fact that I envy him. I would envy anyone who can eliminate his competition by the simple device of losing money, and the more money he loses, the more secure his monopoly." (At McConachie's funeral on July 3, 1965, the pall bearers were Ian Sinclair, John Gilmer—McConachie's successor, John Baldwin and Gordon McGregor.)

Transport Minister Lionel Chevrier placed CPA's case on the Cabinet agenda for discussion on May 11, 1948, and although the minutes of the meeting were confidential, by early summer rumours were circulating through the House that TCA was to be cuckolded by the Liberals and the Pacific franchise was going to its rival. But each time Stanley Knowles or other CCF MPs asked in the House for confirmation of this rumour, Howe vigorously denied it.[8] As a public enterprise, TCA and its Winnipeg staff were close to Knowles's heart, and he suspected that the government was playing for time, correctly surmising that the Liberals did not want to be subjected to the parliamentary scrutiny of both their own party and the CCF. Knowles remembered later, "I had heard rumours that it was going to change its clearly stated policy, namely that TCA was to fly the Pacific. So I asked question after question, in one form or another, and was given the assurance that there was no change in that item of clearly stated government policy. The session ended, and we went home. Within a week or so, an announcement was made of a change in government policy, to the effect that flying the Pacific for Canada was being turned over to CPAL." CPA had actually been informed in confidence of the ruling on July 13, 1948, but it was not until July 21, a week after Parliament had adjourned for the summer and the members had gone home to their ridings, that it was made public. Trans Canada Airlines had been shut out of the Orient and Pacific.

Although it was unusual for a president so close to the minister, McGregor forever claimed that he had not known that the Australian licence had been lumped together with that of operating to the Orient. As the official instrument of the Canadian government, TCA had planned, he said, to expand to Australia in 1951. McGregor had always wanted to fly to the Orient, but he had known that TCA was too deep in deficit in 1949 to fly a show-the-flag exercise to Australia; such a long, unprofitable route without a subsidy would have required a much higher domestic fare structure to compensate. He had irrefutable logic on his side at the time but the loss of the Pacific would haunt him throughout his career.

Meanwhile, the Liberals, with a general election in the offing, could not afford another political defence of TCA's transcontinental monopoly. They were fielding the unknown Louis St. Laurent against the Opposition's "Gorgeous George" Drew, who in one of his most memorable phrases had called the government's monopolies "socialism in a silk hat," knowing that so soon after the war the word "socialism" carried with it the baggage of national socialism and communism. "We have contended that the government is more and more monopolistic...The Prime Minister has now dotted the 'i's' and crossed the 't's' of a policy which means the end of free competition where the government has entered any business." With heavyweight accusations like that, giving CPA permission to serve Japan and China was a political bargain for the Liberals. Howe and McGregor were both aware that with both those countries suffering the after-effects of the war, for the foreseeable future there would be no market in the Orient for a Canadian airline. If all went as they hoped, McConachie would lose his shirt on the whole enterprise.

On July 13, 1949, CPA inaugurated its South Pacific service, flying Vancouver–San Francisco (a refuelling stop only)–Honolulu–Nandi–Sydney. It is safe to surmise that former prime minister Mackenzie King would never have approved of Canadian Pacific Airlines representing Canada overseas, and as expected the Australian and New Zealand governments were not pleased either. They were expecting Canada's national airline, not the air branch of a private Canadian railway. This was hardly Commonwealth solidarity. On September 19, CPA began the Vancouver–Tokyo–Hong Kong portion. Unlike the Australians and New Zealanders, the British colonial government in Hong Kong was ecstatic about CPA's arrival, and the tiny island was pleased to fill McConachie's Canadair-Fours bound for Vancouver. McGregor could take some solace in the fact that because only TCA flew across Canada, the passengers that CPA brought to Vancouver at great expense from Australia and the Orient were all funnelled into the TCA network.

With Mackenzie King's departure from the political scene, the last of the 1937 doctrine, reinforced in 1944, had been removed. The country was to have two international airlines now, one public and one private, each dependent on a mother railroad company for its existence, each with its own designated area of the globe. Mackenzie King and Howe had mistrusted Canadian Airways because it was a private enterprise, and the Liberals had entered the field of

The Empress of Sydney *on a refuelling stop at Honolulu, Hawaii, on its first trip from Vancouver to Sydney, Australia. Canadian Pacific Airways inaugurated South Pacific services on July 13, 1949, using four new Canadair DC-4M aircraft.* Canadair photo

commercial aviation to prevent a repeat of the insanity of the railway boom era, where over-expansion had led to cutthroat competition and widespread bankruptcy. But by allocating the Pacific routes to Canadian Pacific Airlines, the Liberals gave it credibility as an international airline, and that is what it primarily became. From 1949 to 1957 under Grant McConachie, CPA withdrew from its old domestic bush pilot networks, exchanging them either with TCA in Quebec or with upstart Pacific Western Airlines on the prairies. At the same time, with its European and Caribbean forays, TCA was expanding within Canada and across the US border. The historical irony was that having sanctioned all of this, the Liberals shut their eyes to the ensuing TCA/CPA wars—a modern replay of the CNR and CPR rivalry that they had planned to avoid.

Permitted to fly the Pacific, McConachie not only bought the four North Stars but supplemented them with a pair of de Havilland Comet 1As. He then turned his back on eastern Canada and moved his airline as far from the CPR's Windsor Station as he could, buying from War Assets Disposal the empty Boeing hangar at Vancouver Airport for CPA's headquarters. Giving up eastern Canada—especially Montreal—for the uncertain and underpopulated Pacific was a strategic error that would cost McConachie and his successors dearly.

As directors of the CNR, both Hungerford and then Symington had kept their offices near that of the railway in Montreal, at that time the largest city in Canada. It was home to both ICAO and IATA, and its proximity to Toronto's financial and commercial interests and to Ottawa's corridors of power didn't hurt either. (One of the reasons why James Richardson had failed with Canadian Airways was that he had lacked a continuous political base in the national capital, where aviation policy was made.) With the inauguration of transatlantic flights, Montreal had grown even more in importance to TCA so that it overshadowed Winnipeg, the airline's official headquarters. Now the airline's vision was spreading south to New York, Boston and the Caribbean—all this from its eastern bases.

From the time Gordon McGregor had been appointed general traffic manager and had found himself commuting between Montreal and Winnipeg, he had considered it illogical to base the airline in Winnipeg—and not just because he was a native Montrealer. As a result, early in 1949, president McGregor decided to move TCA's operational headquarters from Winnipeg to Montreal, leaving behind only the accounting department, part of the public relations department and a line maintenance and overhaul unit. As TCA already had a large engineering component in Montreal from its CGTAS days, there would be considerable duplication if all the Winnipeg staff were moved, and some were therefore scheduled to be let go. "Although both engineering departments, Winnipeg and Montreal, fell under the responsibility of Jack Dyment," wrote Clayton Glenn (who moved to Montreal), "the unpleasant job of telling people was given to Fred Ades in Winnipeg and Dave Tennant in Montreal. Jack was just too soft-hearted to fire anybody himself. The Winnipeg staff quickly became aware of the situation and there was a lot of uneasiness.

The following question rumbled through the Winnipeg halls, 'Are you ready for Freddie?' This was taken from the then current episode in the life of 'Li'l Abner,' the Al Capp comic strip. Once it was decided who was to be relocated, the air-line generously moved everybody's personal effects—cars, boats and just about everything except fishing camps."[9] With expansion into the Pacific out of bounds, in October 1949 TCA also began reallocating its Vancouver mainte-nance staff to Montreal, cross-posting 37 with seniority and laying off 111, many of whom immediately protested to the local MP, Angus MacInnis (CCF, Vancouver East). When questioned in the House, Howe said that he hoped the two airlines would come to some informal arrangement and take over each other's laid-off employees in Vancouver and Montreal. Overall consolidation in Montreal was an unpopular decision and lost the Liberals political support in British Columbia and on the prairies for years to come, but guided by Howe, Prime Minister Louis St. Laurent did not interfere. However, "behind his back, the prime minister's eager and devoted secretary, Jack Pickersgill, let it be known that the move must not be allowed to take place," wrote McGregor. "With supreme confidence we regarded this as, while unfortunate, irrelevant and stuck to our guns. This was never forgiven." MPs tried to reverse the deci-sion at the next parliamentary sessional committee meeting, and it was only Howe's contention that the committee could not interfere with a TCA man-agement decision that ensured the move was not postponed. (The construction in Montreal of the International Aviation building on the corner of University Avenue and Dorchester Street for ICAO and IATA was a further incentive to move the TCA staff there.)

With the North Stars and DC-3s now overhauled at Montreal, TCA's Hangar No. 1 at Stevenson Field, Winnipeg, looked decidedly forlorn, and in January 1951 the DND asked the company if it would take on maintenance work on RCAF training aircraft. As Macdonald Brothers, a local firm, had held the contract for this work during the war, giving the contract to those TCA employees left in Winnipeg was seen to be politically motivated. In fact, the loss of the RCAF contract was probably the main reason why three years later Macdonald Brothers sold out to a British firm, Bristol Aeroplane Co. Whatever the reason for handing off the contract to TCA, on June 1, 1951, the pilots of Central Northern Airways began to ferry RCAF Harvards, Dakotas and Expeditors to and from training schools at Gimli and Macdonald. Key TCA line maintenance men—Doug Clifford, Bob Critchley, Jack Dahlgren, Stan Denning, Bert Fennessy, Bob Petersen and Bill Ross—were borrowed from permanent staff to head up the crews, and laid-off TCA employees were recalled. During September it took four and half days to complete a mainte-nance check on one of these aircraft; by October this had been cut to three and a half days.

The most interesting job in the RCAF contract was held by the "mobile crew" under Bob Petersen. Equipped with a station wagon, they drove to what the air force termed "C, D or E crashes." A or B crashes were write-offs or too seriously damaged for only maintenance work, but the Cs, Ds and Es could be repaired. Petersen's mobile crew carried its own tools, and when necessary they could dismantle the stricken machine and load it onto a truck for transport to Stevenson Field. The overhaul contract ended in July 1955 following an RCAF decision to assume responsibility for the work. Of the 666 employees who had been hired by TCA on a temporary basis for the job, 352 were then absorbed into the Winnipeg base for the Viscount operations.

One who was forced to move from Winnipeg to Montreal was Dud Taylor. "From my point of view, things seemed to start changing after we all moved to Montreal in 1949. I can't explain exactly what it was but we were now split in two—headquarters in downtown Montreal and engineering and maintenance at the airport. The airline was also now very big with thousands of employees, and the usual problems of big organizations were being felt. Also that old feeling of who controlled the aircraft radio—communications or engineering—was still there and, in fact, increased in Montreal. I felt that I had two loyalties and often wasn't sure which way to turn. So when Aviation Electric in Montreal approached me with a good offer, I decided it was time to move on. I left on January 31, 1952. It was a very sad departure, believe me—I did love the airline business." When Dud retired from Aviation Electric (by then Bendix Avelex) in 1976, he was the president of the company.

Put Wings on Things—Ship Air Cargo
Phone your nearest TCA office.

————————————————————— TCA advertisement, January 1, 1949

"There seems to be a good chance that the sun is about to break through the financial clouds that have darkened the past four years," wrote McGregor in late 1949, the year when the ledger figures began to increase. Compared with 1948 there had been a 27 percent increase in revenue, a 22 percent increase in revenue passengers flown, a 50 percent increase in cargo, a 25 percent increase in air express and a 48 percent increase in mail revenue. No new aircraft had been added, and he put the financial improvement down to better budgeting and more aggressive sales. "This was primarily because the commercial side of the organization had been translated from an order-taking department to a sales organization actively stimulating business."[10]

In 1950 TCA (Atlantic) Ltd. still brought in a deficit of $1.5 million, but North American services recorded a surplus of $201,000. Employee morale, McGregor said, was an intangible, but if it had a dollar value, it would be close to that $201,000. He acknowledged this turning point in the airline's fortunes in a letter to Howe on February 28, 1951. "It is gratifying to report a surplus for North American operations and a reduced deficit overseas, approximately half that of 1949. The total revenue mileage flown by the company increased by 6% over 1949 with 5% fewer employees and with a fleet [20 North Stars and 27 DC-3s] that remained unchanged in size." While he had little chance of success, he then asked Howe to have Parliament authorize payment of the $1.5 million deficit that year. Howe's reply was: "Do you seriously think I would ask the government for $1,500,000 while you retain the $200,000 surplus that you managed to make on North American operations?"

It was not until June 1952, with Walt Fowler as co-pilot, that McGregor toured his empire, piloting a de Havilland Dove himself through the western region and the next year the eastern region. There were luncheons, dinners, press conferences and meetings with local civic leaders at all of TCA's stations.

On July 27, 1953, the Canadian and Mexican governments exchanged diplomatic notes that allowed each other's airlines to fly between their respective countries. It was a landmark bilateral negotiation as both TCA and CPA were given permission to fly to Mexico City from their respective sides of the country and either could continue on to Lima, Peru, and Sao Paulo, Brazil. Both Toronto and Vancouver were designated as terminals, with Tampa and San Francisco as intermediate points. All this had come about because of McConachie's maverick tactics. Knowing that it was unlikely that the Department of Foreign Affairs would negotiate on his behalf with the Mexican government, he by-passed official channels and flew down to Mexico City himself to secure the proper permits personally—as he had done in Japan, China and Australia.

McGregor held little hope of a Mexican or even a South American service ever being profitable, but he knew that McConachie wanted TCA's Toronto–Mexico City route desperately in order to start a South American service. McConachie had suffered a grievous setback on his Pacific service that March when his first Comet 1A had crashed at Karachi on its way to Australia, but never one to look back, he got off the mark first on October 24, 1953, with a CPA DC-6B, christened the *Empress of Lima*, inaugurating not only CPA's Vancouver–Mexico City service but continuing on to Lima, Peru. Within four years CPA had completely encircled the Pacific—from Sydney to Hong Kong to Tokyo to Vancouver to Mexico City and Lima—except that without a domestic network, none of the routes were ever going to break even.

Meanwhile, TCA was still mired in US bureaucracy. Its North Star flights were to begin October 31, 1953, but the US Civil Aeronautics Board (CAB) objected on the grounds that TCA would be carrying traffic to Tampa under the Canada–United States Bilateral Agreement but using the same aircraft to continue on to Mexico City under the Canada–Mexico Bilateral Agreement. It was not about to grant TCA landing rights for a technical non-traffic stop at Tampa. In vain did TCA protest, pointing out that the CAB had not objected to Air France carrying traffic between Paris and Chicago by way of Montreal and BOAC using the same aircraft to fly London–New York via Montreal. Although the CAB's action was in opposition to the State Department's wishes, there was little that the Department of External Affairs could do. It was the Dutch airline KLM that proposed a solution: if it was allowed to operate between Montreal and Mexico City, it would pick up and drop off passengers in both cities until a Canadian airline could take over. Although McGregor warned of the consequences of trying to dislodge KLM later, this was accepted as a temporary solution, and KLM flights between Montreal and Mexico began on September 9, 1953. In the meantime, Howe pressed McGregor to ignore Tampa completely and have the North Stars overfly US territory by refuelling at Windsor; not for the first time, the minister believed that the benefits of trade and goodwill outweighed the company's financial loss. However, the company calculated that this alternate route would cause a loss of $200,000 in the first year of operations.

It was only when Transport Minister Lionel Chevrier directed the ATB to issue "show cause" orders to two US airlines flying into Canada (Pan American Airways and Colonial Airways) that TCA's request was expedited, and the Mexicans and Dutch were told on December 21, 1953, that TCA could now begin the service. Weekly Saturday night flights began on January 16, 1954, Montreal–Toronto–Tampa–Mexico City—"Las Rutas Hoja De Arce" ($259 Toronto return, $304.60 Montreal return) with a return flight on Sunday morning. Although defeated, the CAB forbade TCA the right to deplane passengers on the northbound Mexico City–Tampa–Montreal flight. As a result, no company passes were allowed to Mexico—in case it was necessary to deplane pass holders at Tampa.

"If it can fit into an aircraft, the shipment is halfway there" was the motto for the Montreal sales office run by M.J. "Mike" Scullion, George Miller and Tod Laflamme. With the DC-3 and North Star in use, TCA could earn additional revenue flying cargo, and that service had been introduced at Dorval Airport in 1948 when 2 million pounds were carried. Such was the service's success that four years later business from this station alone amounted to 20 percent of the airline's cargo revenue, and McGregor dedicated a DC-3 to hauling freight.

The two men who ran the Dorval station were Harvey Lesage, domestic station manager, and Roy Lockhart, international station manager, but it was the chief cargo agent, Bob Wilson, who was the operational force behind it all. Besides carrying standard air cargo, the airline took the unprecedented step of actually touting for business. For example, when the Caribbean flights began, the TCA sales staff realized that there was a market for fresh fruit and vegetables there and personally canvassed the local supermarkets to ship produce there. This sometimes brought TCA into conflict with the traditional freight handlers—the two railways and their shipping companies—and Scullion told of once being bodily ejected from a certain railway's premises for attempting to canvass its tenants to ship via air.

This apparently did not faze Scullion. In 1942 Able Seaman Mike Scullion had been aboard the destroyer HMCS *Assiniboine* on escort duty in the North Atlantic when it encountered a U-boat that was trying to escape them by diving.

The *Assiniboine* resorted to quarter firing—each gun working independently as it began a criss-cross pattern to close in on the submarine. Scullion made his way to a silent gun, loaded and fired it, putting a shell through the U-boat's bow. His action delayed her dive long enough for the destroyer to get into position and ram her. The story made news in wartime Canada, and the mayor of the city of Verdun visited Scullion's parents and asked that on their son's return he sign the city's "Golden Book." A full eighteen years later, Mike did so.

What "dogged" the air cargo office at Dorval were, literally, dogs. Freighting canines between Britain and North America was a profitable business, and as long as they were in their Tuttle kennels, the pets were less trouble than many of the passengers. On the ground in the care of TCA air cargo staff, they were another matter. In June 1952 one such animal was being aired by a kindly ramp attendant on the midnight shift when it escaped. A frantic search party failed to produce results. In the morning the new shift combed the airport area with a greater sense of urgency as the dog was to be put on a flight to New York, where its owner waited for it at Idlewild. It was the supervisor himself who spotted the animal mooching around the ramp. "The animal nipped in and out of buildings and hangars pursued by the entire station staff before he was cornered and housed in a kennel." The dog was put aboard the New York flight and, confident that he had seen the last of its canine guest, the supervisor resumed his duties. Two hours later, he got a phone call from Idlewild, his counterpart there screaming that he had sent the wrong dog! The bewildered animal was returned on the next flight, with the distinction of having visited the Big Apple, and the genuine article was picked up by the local police and flown to its now frantic owner in New York. But the story didn't end there. What were the cargo staff to do with the other dog? Canada Customs staff were not amused as it had no licence or entry health certificate and technically was "without a country." Before the whole embarrassing incident went any further, station manager Lockhart assigned the luckless ramp attendants to walk the dog up and down nearby Dorval streets until it found its home.

If the TCA air cargo division at Dorval was embarrassed about losing a dog, their counterparts at Malton would gladly have changed places with them. On September 24, 1952, the airline was transporting a 500-pound shipment of processed gold bullion valued at $215,000 from Malton to Dorval. The ten boxes were to be placed on the flight to Montreal and from there flown overseas. But when the aircraft arrived in Dorval, the boxes had disappeared. The RCMP and CNR police investigation were able to establish only that they had been taken from the cargo cart after it had left the warehouse. The consignor had a "nil" valuation on the shipment, which meant that it was not covered by TCA's bullion insurance policy. The embarrassing publicity could not have come at a worse time for the airline, which was then defending its commitment to air cargo.

Ode to our C.S.R.

Our Cargo Rep is getting thin
And here's the reason why:
There's tons of freight still on the ground
When it should be in the sky.

Four little words, "There is no space,"
Plague him by night and day.
His sleepless nights are filled with thoughts
Of freight left along the way.

Chrysanthemums for eastern trade,
A cat for gay Peru,
And next a dog from New Orleans,
And birds from Timbuktu.

To settle things once and for all,
To help you, Mr. Main,
To aid equipment, though it's small,
Here's your own private plane!

— By YJ (Traffic), *Between Ourselves*

"The logical pattern of development of air cargo service in Canada...was to use residual space in passenger aircraft until they were fully depreciated... and could be converted to cargo use," wrote McGregor. "This was the only way the economics of operation made sense... and in the meantime rates were set high enough to hold the increase in the carriage of air cargo which could be comfortably handled by an aircraft primarily providing passenger service." When the passenger-carrying TCA DC-3s and North Stars were replaced by Viscounts and Constellations, the older aircraft still had a valuable role to play as freighters. In the meantime, anything that could not be fitted into their holds was subcontracted to small air cargo companies—with clapped-out Avro Yorks and C-46s—which had sprung up to serve the DEW Line. What broke McGregor's pattern were two unforeseen difficulties. First, he was expecting that by 1953 TCA would be carrying in excess of 18 million pounds across its system, but its DC-3s and North Stars were so heavily utilized carrying passengers that they could not be converted into freighters, and the company had to subcontract the work to Dorval Air Transport. Second, and more worrying, were the encroaching ambitions of Canadian Pacific Airlines. In one of his most ingenious schemes to expand CPA's network, in November 1951 Grant McConachie announced that there was a critical need for a transcontinental air freight service and applied to the ATB to allow CPA to begin one. A fish hauler in his early days, McConachie claimed that the lakes around The Pas, Manitoba, were a source of vast quantities of fish that if flown in bulk to cities in the east could make a national freight carrier a profit. To his knowledge, he said, a minimum of 21,000 pounds of fish was available each week, and he visualized a freight-carrying aircraft plying the route Vancouver–Edmonton–The Pas–Toronto–Montreal—north of the Airway—which would in no way compete with TCA's passenger-carrying monopoly. He would, he told the ATB, be purchasing a pair of DC-6A freighters to do the job. McGregor recognized this as a "foot-in-the-door tactic . . . If it got a cargo licence, CPA would operate for a while and then scream loudly that it was operating transcontinentally with an aircraft partially loaded in one direction and empty in the other, and since its costs would not be increased thereby, please could it not carry passengers in the otherwise unused space?"[11]

Duncan Dingwall MacLaren, president of Pacific Western Airlines (PWA), supported McConachie's bid to break into the transcontinental air freight market. Hired by PWA in 1952 to expand the company out of its coastal origins, MacLaren was a former TCA engineer who had taken the airline's instrument flying course on the side. He then worked for Queen Charlotte Airways (QCA) and to get "the bush pilot mentality" out of that Pacific coast company, had begun writing its operations manuals. It was while doing this that MacLaren realized that QCA and now PWA were always going to be "fair weather," resource-based outfits—not far removed from the airlines of James Richardson's day. After McConachie applied for a freight service, MacLaren—without permission of his PWA board—applied to the ATB to fly an "air coach" service from Vancouver to Winnipeg, stopping at Calgary, Edmonton, Saskatoon and Regina. Fares would be 30 percent less than TCA's first (and only) class fare and $2 less than the price of a railway ticket. Publicly attacking TCA as "a luxury line that left a large mass market untapped, MacLaren said it set fares that could appeal only to upper income groups."[12] The attention this pronouncement brought PWA in the Vancouver media added fuel to McConachie's fire to launch his own service. But in 1954 MacLaren would go one better. He proposed an "air bus" service between Vancouver and Halifax with stops at all major cities along the way. TCA's monopoly across the length of the country, he told the press, was depriving Canadians of benefits that Americans enjoyed. Fares were high in Canada and the obsolete North Stars were still in use because TCA had no competition. In the United States free enterprise and competition were giving working class families the benefits of air travel.

Parliament had just strengthened the powers of the Air Transport Board (ATB) in 1953, allowing it to initiate its own inquiries, instead of waiting for complaints to be made, and it was now chaired by John Baldwin, the same man who in 1943 had taken a CGTAS flight with Howe to the London conference on aviation. Baldwin had been under pressure from regional carriers to open up the transcontinental route to them, and to McGregor's disgust (he considered it a waste of taxpayers' money) announced that he would conduct hearings across the country. But while the TCA president saw through Baldwin's tactics, no one else did. McGregor might plead shortage of equipment, but he knew that unless something was done to stop Baldwin, the ATB would bow to public pressure and allow either CPA's freight service or sometime in the future PWA's "air bus." The cross-Canada hearings began on February 17, 1952, and ran for three weeks. Through it all Howe continued to reassure McGregor that TCA's transcontinental monopoly was safe, but the president chafed under what he suspected was the ATB's growing bias against his airline.

The hearings were played out between the airlines' corporate lawyers and public relations departments. TCA's legal counsel, Hugh O'Donnell, proved more adept at airline phraseology than CPA's Philip Brais, who had very little to work with. CPA's case began to look doubtful after McGregor personally informed the minister of transport that CPA already had a licence to operate between The Pas and Winnipeg (the minister had been unaware of this). Next, an unexpected ally suddenly emerged in Carl Burke, the respected founder of Maritime Central Airways, who argued that if McConachie got in, "the door would be shut for other operators." What clinched it for TCA was when one of the witnesses called by Brais stated that while there was fish at The Pas to be transported, the volume was not enough for rail transport and barely filled the refrigerated trucks that handled it now. After that, McConachie was shown to have deflated his estimates of the expense involved just as he had inflated the estimated revenue.

McGregor continued to worry that the ATB would recommend that CPA's transcontinental cargo licence be granted, but Baldwin knew that to do so would mean a major change in government policy, and he wisely passed the ATB report on to Cabinet without any recommendation. As Howe had said it would, Cabinet rejected McConachie's plan on the grounds that dividing the transcontinental air cargo market could only lead to overexpansion among competing carriers and a heavier burden on shippers and taxpayers alike. Still, McGregor was left with a foreboding sense that the minister had been "horrified" having to turn down CPA. Years later, McConachie admitted that he would have "lost his shirt" on such an operation. But if TCA won in the courtroom, it lost out in the media. Not for the last time was it portrayed as a dog in the manger.

On November 10, 1952, Lionel Chevrier made a speech at the Seigniory Club, Montebello, Quebec, on "Government Policy in the Regulation of Competition," in which he stated that "transcontinental air services of the type presently provided by TCA will continue to be reserved for TCA. However, it is no longer necessary to insist on monopoly conditions with regard to regional scheduled services, and government policy will not forbid . . . a reasonable amount of competition between scheduled air services." For the government to allow competition on its regional routes was a minor setback for TCA as, except for the Montreal–Toronto and Vancouver–Victoria shuttles, none were moneyspinners. McGregor could take comfort in the fact that the transcontinental route remained protected.

The CPA air cargo hearings and the media attention they had generated influenced the TCA board of directors sufficiently that on December 16, 1952, to better safeguard its passenger monopoly, they agreed that the company should demonstrate its commitment to air cargo by immediately operating a fleet of all-cargo aircraft, a temporary solution until the Constellations arrived. To accomplish this the airline had four choices: pull some of the North Stars off the passenger flights and convert them into freighters, purchase second-hand DC-3s, lease C-119 Fairchilds from the RCAF or, with an eye toward resale, buy Bristol 170 Freighters. Jim Bain was given the task of doing the cost study on these options, and he established that per ton mile the Bristol 170s' operational costs would be 11 cents, those of the converted North Stars would be 13 cents, and those of the DC-3s, 20 cents. Leasing RCAF C-119s was not seriously considered because, if available, they would need commercial certificates of airworthiness and would have to be test flown for at least a year before entering service with TCA.

The board approved expenditure of $1.1 million for the purchase of three Bristol 170s with spares in February 1953. The Bristol Aeroplane Company of Filton, UK, owed its beginning to the farsighted managers of the Bristol Tramways Co., who in 1910 had talked their shareholders into putting up money to build flying machines. With the Bristol 170 Freighter, it looked as though the trams got their revenge. The Freighter configuration resembled the earlier troop-carrying Bristol 130 Bombay of 1935. It had been intended for use as a military vehicle transport, hence its clamshell nose doors. Powered by two Bristol twin-row Hercules sleeve-valve engines of just under 2,000 hp, the Freighter could lift up to three vehicles or 12,000 pounds of freight at minimum speed and cost. But even for Bristol, with its tradition of building ugly, purposeful aircraft like the Bombay, the Blenheim, and the Brigand, the 170 was homely. The cargo deck ran the length of the fuselage with the flight deck located above it. The cockpit was reached by a vertical ladder, which led up through a hatch behind the first officer's seat, reminding George Lothian of a submarine's conning tower, and younger crew members couldn't resist "piping all hands on deck. The result was an aircraft that looked like a giant pollywog."[13] It was little wonder that the TCA nickname for the Bristols was "The Frighteners."

Americans were perplexed by the homeliness of TCA's new Bristol Freighters. As Lothian tells it, "The Freighter is circling Idlewild on its first inbound flight to New York, loaded with 10,000 pounds of cargo. The voice from the control tower pauses in its continuous roar of instructions to ask, 'What is it?' The crew replies, 'It's a Bristol Freighter.' Another pause, then from the Idlewild Tower, 'Did you make it yourselves?' (Wallace Murray swears that this exchange took place at Bradley Field, Windsor Locks, Connecticut, but who would contradict a Canadian aviation icon like Lothian?)

Top: The Bristol Freighter in all its glory—or the "Blunt Instrument," as Ron Peel used to call it. Appearance notwithstanding, it was pleasant to fly and light on the controls.
Bottom: The redeeming feature of the Bristol Freighter was the relative ease of access, through large clamshell doors, for large, bulky loads weighing up to 6.5 tons.

Daddy's Riddle

"Child, take note of all these data;
Most resembles a potater,
Fat and round at its equator,
Nailed beneath a nutmeg-grater,
Yawns just like an alligator
Or some vast volcanic crater,
Doubtless, boy, its perpetrator
Is some brilliant innovator
Who has managed to create a
Flying Cargo Elevator."
"What the devil is it, pater?"
Child, observe, the Bristol Freighter!"

———————— by G.B.S. (LONT), *Between Ourselves* (November 1953)

Pilots of the British airline Silver City Airways flew the Freighters over, the first arriving at Dorval in October 1953 with Bristol test pilot P.O. Falconner to train TCA crews. Though they were the first addition to the TCA fleet since the North Stars had arrived in 1947, they would be the last piston-engined aircraft in the TCA inventory, and it seemed at first as if the three (*CF-TFX, TFY* and *TFZ*) were a step in the wrong direction. But they would allow a five-times-a-week service between Montreal–Toronto–Lakehead–Winnipeg and Montreal–New York–Toronto with a third in reserve.

TCA's engineering department had asked for fifty-five modifications as the aircraft were being built, and Bristol had incorporated thirty-three of these into the final version with the remainder to be done in-house at Hangar No. 2, Dorval. Some of the modifications were as elementary as the inclusion of an on-board ladder to help in refuelling. The board of directors approved an extra $165,925 for the substitution of TCA radio equipment and flight instruments, the installation of ice protector plates on the fuselage sides, restraining gates in the cargo hold, a loading winch, floodlights to allow for checking the ice on the wings at night. But as Hugh Reid of TCA engineering discovered, each adaptation led to another. The substitution of a 200,000 BTU heating system instead of the standard 50,000 BTU unit with 200 amp generators instead of 100 amp ones led to a whole new insulation program in the cargo hold with fibreglass blankets encased in moisture-resistant plastic film.

To move the expected large and heavy loads in and out of the Freighter, TCA invested in its first deck loaders at Dorval and Toronto and positioned electrically operated forklifts at these and other posts. Then Hugh Johnston, director of cargo sales, sent the Freighter on a road show, inviting shippers in Montreal, Toronto, the Lakehead and Winnipeg to see it in operation. At every stop the media recorded its doors opening majestically on a thousand-pound engine box. The local TCA ground crew would then smartly assemble on one side of the ramp, and a forklift would on signal demonstrate the ease at which such a shipment could be taken off the aircraft. The shippers then inspected the remainder of the freight on board. Tod Laflamme, Mike Scullion and Bruce Miller had put together a collection of chicken boxes, Tuttle kennels, flowers, medicine and clothes—all neatly stowed and lashed down with the new nylon nets. At Malton the TCA station manager even drove his car onto the Freighter. In Toronto chief cargo clerk Don Wilkes contracted Air Terminal Transport to operate five distinctive pickup and delivery trucks to move the freight shipments, their drivers wearing TCA uniforms. According to Lothian, none of the crew ever forgot a demonstration of the opening of the great cargo doors: "All the pilots are standing in the cabin as the tarmac and hangar became visible through the nose. There was a minute of silence, followed by Captain Merv Harper's 'On stage, everyone. Take your places.'"

Air freight service began on December 21, 1953. Captain I.K. "Bing" Davis was designated chief pilot for the Freighters in Montreal and Kent Davis the check pilot in Toronto; the flight crews were split between the two bases. The Montreal base was a very small entity, with the DC-3 crews flying east coming under the administrative wing of Eric Jokinen and Cliff Seddon's Eastern Region in Moncton, while the North Star and now the Bristol crews were den-mothered from the Central Region operated by Al Edwards and Rube Hadfield in Toronto.

Captain Murray Wallace remembered why he got into the freight service. "We were still on a flat-salary pay scale at that time, and as the Bristol paid about $50 a month more than the DC-3, when it became operational it looked like a good deal and went to fairly senior captains who couldn't quite reach the North Star. However, a year of the operation (the time they had signed up for) became a little much for the original group, and they resigned at the end of their tenure. Lindy Rood, fearful that the same thing would keep happening, decided to force-move the three most junior Montreal-based DC-3 captains to the Bristol, and at the same time replace the F/Os with senior co-pilots with a view to promoting them on the equipment."

So began Wallace's personal involvement in the spring of 1954.

> My fellow captains were Roy Cartwright and Garth Dundas, with Gord Jones, Ron Walker, Ron George and Buzz Gauthier as F/Os. The extra F/O provided holiday relief, etc., while Bing Davis did the same for the captains. We took the usual "nuts and bolts" ground school of that era in the old number five hangar at Dorval. If my memory serves me, the instructors were Dal Woodward, Ron Peel and Tom Truscott from maintenance. By the time it was over, we could build a Bristol Freighter and a sleeve-valve Hercules, but had yet to see

either, as they were all out flying somewhere! Flight training followed. No simulator, of course—Bing took Roy, Garth and myself together. We were profoundly impressed by the performance of the Bristol. On one engine, despite the hard-wired landing gear, it ran rings around the DC-3.

Although a staunch performer, the Bristol had a few weak points. One of the strangest was the tail-wheel lock, which was operated electrically and failed in the "locked" position if it overheated, which it did after about ten minutes. Switching it off was part of the after takeoff check, but everyone forgot it at least once. I managed to do it on a flight to IDL and couldn't turn off runway 31L! The ATC people were not amused. It was also blessed with pneumatic brakes operated by rubber expander tubes inside the drums on each wheel, a standard British feature of the day. If you used the brakes too much while taxiing, the tubes would overheat and blow out, leaving you brakeless at a most inopportune moment.

Despite its shortcomings, it was a very pleasant aircraft to fly, light on the controls, lots of power and basically very reliable. In a little over a year of flying it, I only had one engine shutdown, and that precautionary because of a fuel leak. Its biggest Achilles heel was operating in icing conditions, which was most of the time in eastern Canada. The anti-icing system consisted of porous leading edge strips (they looked like unbaked ceramic) on the wings and tail, which oozed glycol from a 55-gallon tank in the right wing. The same glycol went to the props through the usual slinger ring. The problem was that you could run out of glycol long before you ran out of fuel. The designers had also artfully placed two little air scoops about halfway down each undercarriage leg to cool the generators. These, of course, were the first things to ice and had no protection, resulting in dual generator failures on more than one occasion. To crown it all, the leading edge of each tire would ice up, the unbalanced wheels would begin to rotate faster and faster, and it didn't matter if the generators failed because you couldn't see the instruments anyway due to the vibration!

The crews became very independent compared to our normal TCA operation. We wore a distinctive battle-dress style uniform jacket—Bing Davis modelled it for the newsletter as the "Eisenhower jacket"—as it was hard to crawl out on the wing and refuel at an off-line station in a double-breasted suit. We also learned to carry a screwdriver, pliers, etc., in our flight bags. On one memorable flight, the TCA people at Goose Bay loaded a GMC van to return it to Montreal for servicing. About halfway between Seven Islands and Mont Joli, Gord Jones and I tried to fly under a line of cumulonimbus clouds [thunderheads]. In the turbulence we heard a lot of thumping going on down below. Fearing that the van was breaking loose, I waited for a calm spell and went down the ladder to investigate. The van was secure but loose on the tie-down cables, allowing it to move about a foot in all directions, which was all the clearance it had. While I was there, I squeezed past it to visit the chemical toilet by the rear door, and while I was in the act, Gord Jones flew under another thunderhead! Aside from peeing all over myself, I couldn't get past the van, which was thrashing all over the place. There was a phone by the rear door, so I called Gord to tell him I was still alive. He advised me that right at the moment he didn't care—he had more to do than talk to me on the phone!

The cargo we carried varied depending on the route. Between Montreal and Goose we were normally loaded heavily with such things as trucks and trailers for Bell Telephone, and, believe it or not, telephone poles! In a part of Canada consisting of nothing but trees, none of them were big enough for this purpose. This generally required an en route stop at Seven Islands, as we were too heavy to carry a full fuel load. As there was no TCA ground crew there, we had to refuel the aircraft ourselves—the first and only situation where I ever got my hands dirty as a captain. I finally managed to escape the "Blunt Instrument," as Ron Peel called it, by bidding back to YYZ in the spring of 1955, to return to the DC-3 and soon the Viscount.

Now "Flying Merchant" Freighter Service

TCA's Air Freight 5 Nights a Week—Monday through Friday. Freighters operate between Montreal and Vancouver. All TCA's 125 daily passenger flights as well as TCA's Bristol Freighters carry Air Freight—at an amazingly low cost !

—————————————————— TCA advertisement, June 1955

Tampa, Florida, had been added to the Caribbean route in 1950, but it was unappreciated by Canadians then as TCA would have preferred to serve the tourist playground of Miami instead: the overland flight to Tampa was a more direct way for intended services to Mexico City and South America. Tampa's only claim to aviation fame at the time was that the world's first scheduled airline flight had ended on a beach there on January 1, 1914, when Tony Jannus landed in a Benoist Airboat with paying passengers from St. Petersburg, Florida. During World War II, when it became a USAF base, three 7,000-foot runways had been constructed, but after the war it was Eddie Rickenbacker, the president of Eastern Airlines, who realized its promise. Through his lobbying, the old wooden wartime terminal that TCA shared with Eastern and National Air Lines was replaced in 1952 with an $850,000 fawn-coloured, two-storey creation with walls of pastel blue, green and pink.

New York was the other American point on the TCA system that in 1952 got a new terminal plus a whole new airport. After Britain, New York had the

An unusual turnout at Tampa/St. Petersburg, Florida, to greet the first of TCA North Star services on April 2, 1950. TCA needed a stopover to carry out its planned services to South America.

second largest number of TCA-appointed travel agents, and except for the Vancouver–Victoria shuttle, the city had the highest volume of traffic as it was responsible for traffic to and from Washington, DC, as well. In response to complaints from passengers and crew, Howe admitted that the facilities TCA had been allotted in 1941 at La Guardia had been barely suited to the company's two daily Lodestar flights from Toronto, but as this had jumped to three daily DC-3 services in 1945 and the DC-3s had been replaced by North Stars in May 1948, the facilities were now totally inadequate. The space problem was complicated by the fact that when it opened in 1939, La Guardia had not been designed for international travel and had reached saturation within three years. In 1948 the Canadian government had increased the pressure on its New York facilities when it negotiated two bilateral agreements with the United States for flights from Montreal to Florida and Montreal to New York, hoping that more north–south traffic in winter would alleviate the low periods on the east–west routes. The Civil Aeronautics Board (CAB) had at first balked at both agreements. The Montreal–New York service had been a Canadian Colonial Airways monopoly for two decades and that airline took legal action to block TCA's access. TCA then found itself in the unaccustomed position of fighting to break a monopoly rather than defending its own. But by good fortune the British colony of Newfoundland, with its strategically important transatlantic Gander and Goose Bay airports, had passed into Canadian hands that year, and CAB

North Star at New York's La Guardia Airport, 1950. TCA had broken the Colonial Airways monopoly on the Montreal–New York service.

acquiesced in March 1950. A month later the New York–Toronto service was supplemented with three daily North Star flights from Montreal, and as a result the daily passenger accommodation on the TCA flights to New York jumped in a matter of nine years from 28 to 336 passengers.

Even before the war it had been generally recognized that New York needed another airport, and in 1942 the marshy wetlands around the city's Jamaica Bay had been dredged and filled in to make the nation's largest airport. Named after the golf course that it was built on, Idlewild Airport opened on July 1, 1948. Four years later, when it was ready for TCA to move in, the company was given just two days' notice to transfer staff and equipment to "temporary accommodation" there. The year would prove to be a trying one for TCA's district manager Don Richardson and station manager Bill Munroe because many local employees did not want to make the move and there was a serious staff turnover. That same year also saw the expansion of the traffic department, and the sales office on 58th Street was renovated. The new reservations office that opened at 730 Fifth Avenue was not only more spacious but it had two innovations: a "rotary reservations memorandum filing table" and a multikey telephone system designed to overcome the need for a switchboard operator to answer every incoming call.

At least TCA staff at Idlewild did not have to cope with the 140 mph hurricanes that devastated the Palisados Airport at Kingston, Jamaica, in September 1950. Bob Cowan, the station manager, remained on duty throughout, rounding up passengers from outlying resorts by car when the phone lines went down. When Dick Tritt, the stores inspector, flew down with replacement parts and donated medicine, the only thing still defiantly upright among the twisted wreckage of hangars was a TCA passenger ramp. Although Palisados would continue to be battered by hurricanes, it remained in use until the service was transferred to Montego Bay on December 17, 1953.

TCA now offers "SKY TOURS"—
All Expense Paid to Bermuda

Ranging from $239.25 for 7 days from Toronto
To $244.90 for 9 days from Montreal

Obtain description folder from your travel agent or nearest TCA office.

———————————————————— TCA advertisement, 1950

In the Caribbean, TCA was better known as "Bowker's Airline." Gil Minorgan, the airline's first station manager in Bermuda, didn't know when the label first appeared but it stayed in their region until Bob Bowker, TCA captain, retired years later. The only company pilot based outside Canada then, Bowker lived in Bermuda and took over at the controls of the incoming North Star from Montreal, flying it south to Trinidad and back. How he got the plum post was not difficult to understand: in 1949 he was eighth on the seniority list and second among pilots on line duty. According to Lindy Rood, "Not many people were going to bid him out of his Bermuda job as long as he wanted it. When the run originated, we were faced with a problem in the pilot group. The layover was eight days and the pilots didn't like being away from home so long. They decided to take turns at spending longer times at Bermuda, and eventually Ken Main went down on a temporary basis with his family. Then Bob volunteered to take it on on a permanent basis, and this was mutually agreed to by the company and the pilots." A navigator, a first officer and a purser-steward were also based at Bermuda, but they came in for six-month stretches.

A tall man with close-cropped hair, Bowker dressed uniquely for a TCA captain. In place of the regulation heavy hat, he wore one with a perforated ventilation strip to cool it. His shirts were short-sleeved with the "most ancient tarnished four-strip epaulettes in TCA." He would drive up to Kindley Field in his Austin convertible and meet Flight 600 from Montreal. Then he would be away for a minimum of eighteen hours flying the 3,158 miles round trip to Trinidad, with a couple hours' rest at Piarco Airport, Port of Spain. With his famous wicker seat on board, he would tell friends, "I travel in comfort."

The Bermuda–Trinidad run gave Bowker his share of strange cargo. On one flight to Trinidad it was a four-foot cougar and on the return to Bermuda he took four monkeys—all in the cockpit. "Talk about personalized service," he said. "Once I was getting ready for my two-hour sleep at the hotel in Trinidad when a woman who had been on the flight down phoned me. She had travelled with a small dog, and the Trinidad airport authorities wouldn't let the animal in. She wanted to know what I was going to do about it."

CANADA IN ONLY A DAY! BY TCA.
GOOD NEWS FOR DOLLAR EARNERS!

Fly TCA to the Canadian dollar market for only pounds sterling 94.13.0
London–Montreal. And as low as pounds sterling 170.8.0 Return.

Other bargains: London to Toronto 103.12.0,
Winnipeg 127.7.0, Vancouver 154.0.0

Baggage Allowance 40 lbs North American routes,
44 lbs on Atlantic, 66 lbs on Bermuda, Caribbean.

Meals: Free on Atlantic. At nominal cost on domestic.

———————————————————————— British advertisement, May 1, 1952

When TCA had first taken delivery of its twenty North Stars from Canadair back in the early months of 1948, the company hadn't really known how to fill them. "It was a number far exceeding the traffic requirement to say nothing of the cost at the same time of learning to operate and maintain a much larger aircraft than it previously had experience with," wrote McGregor, reckoning that the reason for that year's deficit was the oversupply of seats combined with the uneconomical routes that had been foisted on the airline.[14] Moving from ten-passenger Lancasters to thirty-six- to forty-two-passenger aircraft was more than the post-war market could accommodate, but with the airline overequipped for the first time in its existence, McGregor had seen it as an opportunity to restructure the company's organization, especially its sales department. Eastbound transatlantic traffic was soon close to fleet capacity in the summer and this included freight (with the heavy volume of food parcels that were sent to the United Kingdom). In addition, well-off Canadians were now travelling to Europe in the summer, and the airline promoted the Holy Year in Rome (1949) and the Festival of Britain (1951) in co-operation with British European Airways and Alitalia. Domestically, the North Stars allowed TCA a 45 percent increase in passenger capacity between 1947 and 1948 and were put on a twice-daily transcontinental service on June 1, 1948. Initially they were confined to Montreal, Toronto, Winnipeg, Calgary and Vancouver because those were the only airports that could accommodate the aircraft, and it wasn't until April 27, 1952, that North Stars were available for the Maritime routes. But until passenger demand grew in the early 1950s, what made use of the North Stars' capacity were immigration flights, natural disasters in British Columbia and Manitoba, and the effects of the "All up" mail Act.

During the Depression, Mackenzie King had reduced immigration to Canada to a trickle—as a young labour negotiator he had earned a reputation for Asian exclusion schemes—so his retirement had signalled a tentative opening of the doors. While ship was the preferred method of travel, so soon after the war there was little low-fare shipping accommodation available for passengers and non-priority cargo. Through the Canadian Government Immigration Plan, subsidized airfares were used to bring 10,648 immigrants to Toronto, 70 percent of them originating in the United Kingdom. TCA was "also faced with moral obligations to bring as many New Canadians to this country as space permitted," wrote G.B. Duhamel, supervisor of group sales, and he praised the flight attendants for adapting to people with language difficulties. Except for Canadian military personnel they had met during the war, few of the immigrants had any previous contact with Canadians, and the airline was the first impression that many would have of their new home.

Moral obligation apart, the company stood to gain enormously from the flights: except for charters, only seats not sold to regular passengers were made available to immigrants, and these were subsidized by the federal government. The immigrant fare from London in 1947 was set at $160, with Ottawa making up the difference in cost of a one-way flight, and by its last month—May 1952—it had been increased to $195. Once the immigration flights went into full operation in 1948, 6,000 more people were brought over in 175 charters, and between January and March 1949 TCA North Stars were also chartered to transport 1,200 European refugees from Munich. Westbound the airline was quite pleased to fill its regular North Star flights with immigrants for the seventeen months the plan was in effect.

In January 1948 British Columbia was virtually isolated by severe snowstorms. Slides closed the CNR track at Hope in the Fraser Canyon and plough trains were unable to clear their way through. Besides RCAF aircraft, TCA North Stars and DC-3s were called into use, and between January 20 and 26, 183 railway passengers were flown out of Penticton. In addition to the normal load, 1,350 passengers were carried in and out of Vancouver with 48,000 pounds of mail, 60,000 pounds of cargo and 140,000 pounds of baggage. The airline gained much good publicity for being able to respond to a natural disaster, and Herb Seagrim flew Howe up the Fraser Valley in one of the North Stars to show him the extent of the flooding.

When Winnipeg was threatened with flooding in May 1950, TCA was enlisted again as part of the relief effort. This time, company North Stars were chartered by the Ontario provincial government to airlift equipment and sandbags from Montreal to Winnipeg.

But more significant than either immigration flights or disaster relief, what the North Stars accomplished was to change forever the relationship between the Post Office and the airline. With the introduction of the North Star, Trans Canada Airlines had beaten its cost for carrying mail down to 15 cents a mile, but with its history of grievances against the Post Office, the company no longer wanted to tie itself down to carrying the mail, especially when there were so many regional carriers willing to do so. (The ATC had routinely rejected applications from start-up airlines such as Capilano Airways, and with good reason: launching any service of five passengers or more would require an airmail subsidy of at least 50 cents a mile.) TCA's reluctance and the need for a more equitable distribution of mail contracts finally compelled the federal government on July 1, 1948, to initiate an "All up service," a North American first. From now on all first class mail weighing up to an ounce and originating in Canada for delivery within the country would be carried by any available air service—commercial, RCAF or even United States Air Force flights.

The large increase in mail that resulted from this policy immediately spawned several regional airlines. Though it also filled the holds of the North Stars, TCA was not satisfied because the company's mail revenue was still fixed at $450,000 a month regardless of weight and mileage. The airline complained that it received a lower return per ton-mile than was received by airlines of comparable size in the United States. However, that monthly payment of $450,000 remained in force until the end of 1950.

"Divided by the plastic curtains from the 36 passengers aboard North Star Flight 210/08 leaving Gander Airport early on the morning of December 9, 1950," wrote Bill Stevenson in the Montreal *Star Weekly*, "was a cool young navigator called Gerry Chesley who, given a ruff, a rapier and a goblet of canary would be accepted among Elizabethan adventurers."[15] Practising an art familiar to sailors before the Age of Steam, Chesley was navigating the North Star across the ocean by taking advantage of the winds. According to Ron Peel, now TCA's chief navigator, and Peter Powell, a former RCAF wing commander from the elite bomber group "Pathfinders," the quickest way across the Atlantic was not necessarily the shortest way. Proponents of the pressure pattern formula, they were getting the North Stars to the opposite side of the Atlantic by making use of tailwinds and dodging headwinds. Because of the prevailing westerly winds, eastbound TCA flights were now made at 17,000 feet and westbound at a lower altitude, where the headwinds were reduced. In coordination with the company's meteorologists and dispatchers, the Peel–Powell team of navigators plotted the strength and the direction of winds in order to draw upper air contour charts and select the best route across the Atlantic for fuel economy. While speed records were not always broken, Peel estimated that he had saved an average of twenty minutes on each of the 998 crossings made in 1949. The North Stars were not equipped with radio altimeters that gave the navigator a pressure profile, so en route analysis and revision had to be continuous. On Chesley's flight his revisions brought Flight 210 into Shannon Airport thirty-five minutes ahead of schedule. Stevenson concluded: "It cost TCA nothing more than the enthusiasm of the airline's 21 navigators and saved the Canadian taxpayer at least $25,000 last year."

The inaugural TCA flight between Montreal and Paris took place on April 1, 1951, the result of an air services agreement signed with France by Transport Minister Lionel Chevrier the previous August. Since the end of the war Air France had refuelled at Gander on its Paris–New York run, though it did not land in Canada until August 31, 1948, when a Constellation had arrived at Halifax on its way to the French colonies of St. Pierre and Miquelon. However, with the new agreement in effect, Air France rushed to inaugurate a Paris–Montreal service on October 5, 1950. TCA's service came six months later and, known as the Aerobus North Star, operated via London, leaving there at 3:50 p.m. and arriving in Paris (Orly) at 5:55 p.m. The company opened a city office at 24 Boul des Capucines in Paris, which was manned by G.H. Lesage (soon to be replaced by Guy Perodeau from the recently opened Quebec city office), Lucille St. Jacques, also from Quebec City, Howard Whitehead, Danny Gnesko and Kurt E. Hass.

The service set new precedents for the airline. The timetable—while not always correct in language or meaning—was in French. "La Route la Feuille d'erable—Un Nouveau Service liaison directe Montreal–Paris par avions TCA." In fact, there was nothing "directe" about the route; it was Montreal–Gander (or Goose)–Glasgow (Prestwick)–London–Paris. But what was truly historic about the brochure was that for the first time instead of the literal translation of "the Maple Leaf Route" printed under the maple leaf insignia, the words "Air Canada" appeared above it. It was two more years before the company received permission to use "Air Canada" as a trade name where it thought fit, but this authorization did not even consider the supplanting of "Trans Canada Airlines" with "Air Canada" as a corporate trademark. It was merely an adaptation for sales and publicity reasons in European markets. But it wasn't just in France that "Trans Canada Airlines" had little meaning. McGregor held that "Nine out of ten Englishmen insisted on calling it 'Trans Canada Airways'." Then again, he added, some Canadians were wont to call the Vickers Viscount (TCA's next purchase) the "Vicar's Viscount."

The province of Quebec had traditionally been Canadian Airway's and now CPA's territory, so although based in Montreal, TCA did not land anywhere else in the province. However, both the prime minister and transport minister were French Canadian; it was only a matter of time before the government's airline was constrained to fly there, and TCA opened a sales office in Quebec City in 1950 with André Gauthier as manager. This service, along with the Paris flights, marked the start of TCA brochures destined for those offices being published in French, but the airline was still staunchly unilingual. The fact that the emergency exit signs on its aircraft were in both English and French was only because of an ICAO requirement. As with other large companies and federal government institutions in Montreal, no attempt was made to compel staff dealing with the public to explain or repeat instructions in French, whether at the counter or in flight. Only the stewardesses who actually encountered the public in flight on the Quebec or Paris routes were required to speak French. Edward Kirby, the labour relations lawyer hired by them later, wrote: "I remember the girls operating out of the Montreal base agreed that they should be bilingual, but as most of their flights were Montreal–New York, the second language should be Jewish not French. That used to be the gag back then."[16]

The following letter to the editor of *Between Ourselves* was received in May 1950.

Dear Sir,

My first idea in planning a trip to New York was to go TCA but return via a US line. But after receiving propaganda material from your employee Bill Glass, I decided to fly TCA both ways. He then took over and did all my planning, made reservations and smoothed out the wrinkles. First evidence of his handiwork was on the flight from Seattle to Victoria when I was invited forward to view my favourite local fishing area from the nose. I hit the jackpot in personalized travel when I stopped off for several hours at Fort William–Port Arthur on my return where I was met by Harold Smith and Alexander Mackay of TCA. After viewing the Twin Cities by private auto transportation, I was introduced to Don Johnson, TCA radio operator, amateur bush pilot and professional wolf hunter.

He quickly organized a wolf hunt for me in his little grasshopper plane, and we took off to a nearby frozen lake. He should have had a shotgun with buckshot, but I had to make the 10.05 plane to Winnipeg that night, so he just grabbed the first available gun—a 22 caliber automatic pistol. We reached the lake, saw a wolf, swooped down on him, and at 15 feet altitude Don let him have it. The wolf dropped, apparently dead.

Don landed the ski-equipped plane nearby, kicked the wolf a couple of times, elicited no signs of life, picked him up, tossed him into the luggage compartment just behind our seats and took off for the Twin Cities. But when we had reached an altitude of about 1,000 feet the damned wolf came to life, started taking the plane apart by mouthfuls, working his way rapidly forward towards Don and me. For a few anxious minutes, Don had his hands full handling the plane and firing back at the wolf while I ducked for cover. However, the battle was soon over, order restored, and the wolf subsided. Don made a perfect landing—as cool as a cucumber.

Ground crew men (all TCA) skinned the wolf, rushed him to the Prince Arthur Hotel where the cook processed him in a pressure cooker and we enjoyed wolf meat at the Rotary Club banquet at 6:30 that evening at which I was the personal guest of Alexander Mackay. Following that, Alex took me out to Plug-of-Tobacco Falls and safely returned me to the airport for the night flight to Winnipeg.

If there is anyone who questions the wolf story, I have as proof a visitor's key chain presented to me by the Rotary Club. You may rest assured when I go back to the Nipigon to ride "squaretails" bareback, my guides will be Smith and Mackay and chief fish wrangler Don Johnson, and I will fly by Trans Canada Airlines.

All Hail to TCA!

Respectfully submitted,
Wm. G. Long
Judge of the Superior Court
Seattle, King County
Washington, USA.

Hard on the heels of brochures printed in French came ones in German. In 1951, an operations team of Charlie Proudfoot, C.S. Hewitt and Gordon Wood conducted preliminary surveys for flying into Germany. As the besieged city of Berlin was off-limits to all airlines except those of the four occupying powers, and the city of Frankfurt was in the American military zone, it was easier to negotiate for landing rights to Dusseldorf, both because it was in the British military zone and because the service would be an extension of flights to the United Kingdom. Dusseldorf also had the double advantage of being on the fringe of the industrial Ruhr and being close to Bonn, the new capital of West Germany. Although Dusseldorf had not been levelled like nearby Cologne, the scars of the nightly Allied bombing raids were evident on the city, and the Canadians could not help but notice that its streets were full of "begging urchins doing cartwheels for money." In fact, the city had just chosen the figure of a cartwheeling child as its unofficial emblem. On November 1, 1952, TCA was given full traffic rights by the Allied High Commission for service from Montreal to Dusseldorf and Hamburg with BEA looking after maintenance at Dusseldorf's Lohausen Airport, where the TCA manager was H. Ralph Weller.

CANADA - LANDER GOLDEN MOGLICHKEITEN!
VON DUSSELDORF NACH MONTREAL FUR NUR DM 1260
DIE FLUGROUTEN DER 'AHORNBLATT' LINIE

———————————————— TCA advertisement in German media, 1952

To publicize the new services, with the co-operation of the Canadian Embassy in Bonn, the airline held an essay competition in which thirty German high schools were to write on the theme of "What Canada means to me." The judge was T.C. "Tom" Davis, the new Canadian ambassador to West Germany, previously ambassador to China. By coincidence, in that post he had also been involved with a Canadian airline—CPA. While based in Shanghai in January 1949, Davis had arranged for Grant McConachie to meet Madame Chiang Kai Shek at a party, and she had approved CPA's landing rights to China—just before fleeing to Taiwan with her husband. "It was the easiest permit I ever got," said McConachie, "but the least fruitful." The city surrendered to the Communists soon after and China was closed off to all foreign airlines.[17]

On October 27, 1952, the sound of Merlin engines was once more heard over Dusseldorf, but not this time from Lancaster bombers. The inaugural North Star flight carried a group of ministers, airline employees and media, all of whom were met at the Lohausen Airport by Tom Davis and the Canadian Army 27th Brigade Pipe Band. Weekly service began November 5, 1952, at $246 each way and $442 return. The two teenagers who had won the essay contest, Rita Steiner and Rhinehard Dolgnar, were sent to Canada courtesy of the airline. Both had recently fled from Communist East Germany and in Canada they told their "hair-raising stories of escape, of long, cold months in camps and the terrors of totalitarian indoctrination against Western imperialists."

Passengers' opinions of the North Star can be seen in these excerpts from their letters, which appeared in the company newsletter feature "What Others Think of Us."

> Probably a dependable workhorse but noisy as hell. Came back from Seattle to New York to Toronto on a Boeing Stratoliner to get away from noise. Seems to me common complaint of all your passengers. Even DC-3s are better.
>
> Everything first class except the noise of the engines, which prevents conversation.
>
> Could use better sound proofing. Rather noisy at take-offs especially.
>
> Very pleasant trip, right on time. Splendid breakfast with ham and eggs, perfectly cooked. Coffee served deliciously hot. My only suggestion for improvement would be to provide noiseless motors. Perhaps that will come with atom power. When they come I presume you will have them.
>
> Having just completed my first flight in a "boiler factory," the experience suggests that the time has arrived for TCA to give serious thought to...the purchase of second-hand aircraft from Lower Slobovia. If the "Skyliner" is the pride of the fleet, I don't hold much hope for TCA's continued success in commercial aviation.

The TCA North Star's raucous Merlin engines were a perfect target for the air-line's detractors, chief among thcm George Drew. As leader of the Opposition in the House in 1949, Drew had a platform from which to attack what he always called "the noisy North Stars," which he said had been "foisted" on the airline. He was aided by George McCullough, publisher of the *Globe and Mail*, and the reporters of *The Vancouver Sun*, both of which newspapers were viru-lently anti-TCA. (With local jobs at stake, the two Montreal newspapers, the *Star* and the *Gazette*, were equally enthusiastic TCA boosters.) The announce-ment of the airline's annual deficits played right into the hands of Drew and his friends, and when in March 1950 the government was asked to cover TCA's losses for the fiscal year 1949–50, Drew was prepared with the figures.

"In 1946 there was a deficit for the year of $1,269,624. In 1947 there was a deficit for the year of $1,624,739. In 1948 there was a deficit for the year of $2,933,240. Now we are asked to provide for a deficit of $4,317,594 for the year of 1949. On the domestic services of Trans Canada Air Lines for last year there was a deficit of $1,419,444, and on the transatlantic operation there is a deficit of $2,898,150. That represents an increased deficit of $236,422 on the domes-tic services...and an increased deficit of $1,147,932 on the overseas service. That large increase follows an assurance last year by the general manager of Trans Canada Air Lines that there was every reason to believe that the over-seas services would improve."[18]

Time and again, the airline's press office pointed out that the North Star had not been "foisted" on TCA but had been chosen after exhaustive research and that the model of Merlin engine used in the North Star was not that used in the Lancaster but had been designed purely for commercial use. However, never allowing truth to get in the way of a good story, the *Globe and Mail*, the *Sun* and the Conservatives continued their tirade. (Fortunately for George Drew, by the time the Conservatives came to power and Prime Minister Diefenbaker appointed him high commissioner for Canada to the United Kingdom, Trans Canada Airlines was phasing out the North Stars on its transat-lantic route, and he could enjoy the quiet of its Lockheed Constellations and DC-8s instead.)

The North Star's noise problems were partially overcome in the end by the company's supervisor of job methods and development, Merlin "Mac" MacLeod. While all things mechanical at Trans Canada Airlines were under the jurisdiction of the two "J.T.s"—J.T. "Jim" Bain, director of maintenance, and J.T. "Jack" Dyment, director of engineering—both men deferred to MacLeod. Just as the world is indebted to Thomas Edison and Henry Ford for making life easier, so TCA and anyone who ever flew in a North Star is indebted to MacLeod—although before the crossover exhaust controversy of 1950 few out-side his immediate circle knew of this genius. MacLeod's modifications and inventions for the airline numbered in the hundreds—from his radio tube "tor-ture rack," which fatigued tubes in 200 hours to permit structural deterioration, to improved battery carts, socket joints, aircraft cowling flaps and aircraft door locks, so that by the time the Merlin engine problem was handed to him, Macleod had been named an Associate Fellow of the Canadian Aeronautics and Space Institute. To all in the company he was better known for his motto: "If it's good, let's make it better."

When the problem of modifying the Merlin engines' exhaust arose, Ben Franklin had been replaced as Canadair's president by Oliver Wells, former TCA vice-president, who was well aware of MacLeod's ability to resolve aircraft design problems, but instead he turned to Canadair's own engineers. Only when they had tried and failed to solve the problem did he turn to MacLeod. To contain the Merlin's exhaust gases, MacLeod thought of connecting both sets of exhaust outlets to one crossover manifold and then dumping the gas (and noise) away from the cabin. Initially he funnelled them across the side and over the top of the engine and then dumped into the slipstream. However, after several hours of testing, when the exhaust temperatures hit 1,600°F, the walls of the manifold above the exhaust outlet cracked. Convinced that the basic concept was correct, he and his team began again. This time the converging

The crossover exhaust exposed here on number one engine gives a clear view of the principle involved in diverting hot gases away from the fuselage. Ken Leigh collection

streams of hot gas, travelling at great speed, were colliding and applying their full thrust against the wall of the manifold, causing it to break. The solution came to him "one bright and early morning": the answer lay in where these hot gases met over the engine. The outlet or exhaust dump would have to be placed so as to allow those gases to escape directly opposite the outboard exhaust stacks. His tests showed that the slip joint socket between the cylinder stacks functioned without problems, and this proved that a flanged pickup joint was the answer to controlling the blast. The new crossover ducts he designed reduced the noise level by about 50 percent. This, the company warned its staff, did not mean that the North Star's Merlins would be half as quiet as the engines of a Lockheed Constellation or DC-4. Rather, they were to tell passengers that the noise level had been "reduced to a comfortable frequency. The change in noise level can be compared with a radio set pitched at a high frequency with resulting excitation and nervous strain. The new crossover exhaust deepens the note, providing a more comfortable ear level range of sound." On being congratulated, MacLeod is supposed to have said, "It certainly is a good way of choking off a lot of hot air."[18] The crossover exhausts were fitted on the Merlins by Canadair between April 1953 and March 1954, the same year that Merlin MacLeod was honoured with the McCurdy Award.

A cabin window view showing the location of the engine exhaust stacks. They are still there, under the streamlined bulge, where the gases are diverted across the top of the engine to the outboard side. Ken Leigh collection

Merlin "Mac" MacLeod. With such a name, it was only to be expected he would have some interest in an aircraft engine of the same name. His innovations were legendary at TCA and his solutions to the noise problems on the North Star were magical.
Photo courtesy Janet Proudfoot

McGregor would later write about the exhaust problem with some humour. "Orange exhaust flame, fresh out of cylinder ports, is completely invisible in sunshine," he wrote. "At the time TCA was operating a transcontinental flight that, at one season of the year, arrived in Winnipeg at about sunset. It stayed on the ground about half an hour and many 'through' passengers stayed on board. It would then start up, taxi out and take off at full throttle, with all four engines apparently enveloped in flame, now completely visible due to the advancing dusk. The alarmed passengers knew perfectly well that the flame had not been there before and were convinced that the stop in Winnipeg had done the poor North Star no good whatever. When the cross-over exhaust system was installed in 1953 and relieved passengers of a substantial portion of exhaust noise, it also deprived them of the thrill of suspected multiple engine fire."[20]

But it wasn't only engine problems that plagued the first North Stars in TCA service. When its Lockheed 14s had suffered from lightning strikes, the cause was thought to be their 30-foot trailing antenna, but in 1948, within a ten-month period, five North Stars were similarly damaged, causing delays for repairs and the expense of ferrying passengers. This time there was no antenna involved.

A/C No.	Type	Date	Altitude	Location	Remarks
189	DC-4M1	29/1/48	8,000 ft	Irish coast	Strike on No. 1 engine. Elevator, ailerons burnt off
185	DC-4M1	30/1/48	4,000 ft	over Ireland	HF damaged, aileron and wing tips burned
184	DC-41	3/2/48	8,500 ft	Between London and Iceland	Strike No. 3 engine, burns in ailerons and wingtips
212	DC-4M2	21/8/48	13,000 ft	Cowley, BC	wingtip, ailerons burned
208	DC-4M2	9/10/48	19,000 ft	Sterling, ON	discharge from nose: no damage[21]

Along with the engine noise and sparks, and the lightning strikes, there were numerous, lesser known problems associated with the Merlin engine. Its overly sensitive fire warning system reacted to sudden changes in temperature at low altitudes and would send lights flashing in the cockpit. This even happened when the aircraft flew over a factory's smokestack or, as happened at Winnipeg Airport, when a mail truck was left idling near the aircraft. Spark plug fouling forced the pilots to maintain higher charge temperatures during run-up and ignition checks in cold weather. The tendency if the aircraft was standing for a while in cold air was for the oil to congeal in the small line running from the pressure regulator to the fuel pump. This made the engine run "rich," a situation that would not be noticed until the throttles were advanced for takeoff, when the engine would abruptly shut down.

All of these problems were plaguing the airline and forcing the replacement of engines at a time when McGregor was trying to get TCA into the black. Rather bitterly, he would write, "Canadair, whose contractual responsibility it was, had long since given up on the problems, and therefore it was particularly galling that for economic reasons that the company should get the contract for the manufacture of the cross-over exhaust manifolds to the MacLeod design."[22] In the meantime, to be competitive McGregor realized that the airline would have to standardize its fleet around as few types of aircraft and engines as possible. The first three DC-3s with their Curtiss Wright engines were already disposed of, the Lodestars were being sold, and the unpressurized North Stars returned to the RCAF. But getting rid of the Merlin engines on the North Stars was more complicated. Howe, who was as interested as McGregor in getting the airline out of debt, refused to allow him to repower the North Stars with Pratt & Whitney engines or even use the threat of this as leverage with Rolls Royce. Instead, he sent McGregor away, telling him to concentrate on reducing maintenance costs—something, the airline president grumbled, that everyone in the company had been "growing grey-headed over for months."

Obviously the airline could not afford to re-engine the whole North Star fleet without help from Rolls Royce, so McGregor went off to Derby armed with the never-be-sorry warranty on the North Star contract and comparisons of what it was costing the airline in replacement parts for the Merlins with what it cost US airlines for their radial engines. He explained to Lord Hives of Rolls Royce that with the company in a constant deficit position, he could not continue with the burden of operating costs that the Merlins were responsible for. To his astonishment, Hives readily agreed that Rolls Royce should make good any money TCA had spent on Merlin replacement parts. The company's reputation was at stake, Hives said, and Rolls Royce engines should not cost more to operate than the best produced by any other firm. Not only was the contract honoured in full, but after that Rolls Royce kept a liaison staff in Canada to make sure that, in McGregor's words, the airline "was not mistreating the engines in operation." The cordiality of the meeting set the tone for a relationship between McGregor and Hives, TCA and Rolls Royce (and Vickers) that lasted for the next three decades.

In retrospect, it was clear that the North Star was a stable aircraft with the wrong engines, and though it may have been a mongrel of mixed parentage, it got TCA out of its Lancaster bombers on the Atlantic service. Had it never been built, the airline would have been faced with a Hobson's choice: buying either the British built Avro Tudor or the Handley Page Hermes IV, both of which were inferior to the North Star, or waiting a few years while Douglas and Lockheed turned out enough of their DC-6s and Constellations. But as Howe and Franklin hoped, assembling the North Star kept Canadair functioning until it received the Korean War/Cold War military contracts for the F-86 and T-33. To McGregor, the Merlin was a good engine, "manufactured by a great and completely ethical company, but basically a racehorse called upon to pull a heavy cart when it fell into the hands of the airlines." It must also be noted that the Merlin engine for all its complexities did not require TCA to employ flight engineers as its next purchase, the Lockheed Constellation, would nor was it ever proved that the airline ever lost a North Star because of the lack of a flight engineer.

If the airline's president, its pilots and passengers had little affection for the North Star's engines, it took a national poet to appreciate their majesty. In 1951 Earle Birney, a professor of English at the University of British Columbia, twice awarded the Governor General's Award for Poetry, wrote "North Star West," a poem about a TCA flight from Montreal to Vancouver. It appeared in the *Canadian Home Journal* and included this description of the North Star's takeoff:

> Snorts through four great nostrils Bellerophon's stallion
> roars him seven thousand strong
> trembles moves like a cloud on the runway. Wheels—
> charges the night.[23]

The distinctively shaped Lockheed Super Constellation,
probably the most beautiful airliner ever built.
TCA would use 14 "Connies" between 1954 and 1963.

CHAPTER 11

The tensions of the Cold War gave Canadians more discomfort than the sound of Merlin engines. Although reassuring articles appeared in *Between Ourselves* discussing atomic energy and promising that it would soon be heating "vast new cities or powering TCA's future spaceliners to the moon," the reality was that North Americans lived in fear of nuclear attack by the Soviet Union. "Daily we seem to teeter-totter on the brink of disaster, as the international scene grows hot, hotter then cold," a TCA employee directive announced. "The dictator strikes in a world devoid of sentiment, a world where personal power is prized above the lives of little children, therefore it is better to be prepared rather than prostrated by a sneak atomic attack." In the United States, the federal government had long since made all airlines part of the Civil Reserve Air Fleet. The Canadian government did not go that far but, presuming that TCA's aircraft—especially those at outlying airports—would survive a nuclear strike, the company was tasked with aiding civil evacuation from the cities. In 1951 the company became so concerned about the danger to its employees of an atomic attack on Montreal and Toronto that under the title "Panic kills. Calmness saves," it issued the following instructions to all personnel:

To Do during the Blast:

The blinding flash is your first warning.

- Crouch behind a tree or cover yourself with an overcoat or briefcase—whatever comes to hand.
- Dash into a doorway. If wheeling a carriage, cover yourself and the baby with a blanket.
- Fall flat on the sidewalk, close to a wall to avoid falling rubble. Cover your head.

If At Home after Blast:

- Close door and windows to prevent draft.
- Use sand or foam to quench oil fires.

- Don't try to use the telephone.
- Don't try to drive your car.
- A good scrubbing after the blast will remove radioactive particles clinging to the skin.
- Don't eat or drink or touch metal. It may be contaminated.

Finally if an A-bomb should fall on your city, remember the idiomatic advice of Cockney civil defence workers during the London blitz: "If you hear the bomb, don't worry, you'll live. If you don't hear it, don't worry, you're dead!" Remember, a moment prepared is a life spared.

It is our fervent hope that everyone of our employees is now enlightened in case of atomic attack.

The tense international situation led to the reactivation of a number of RCAF airports and the establishment of jet fighter bases around Canada's main cities immediately adjacent to designated airways and air routes with fully loaded interceptors standing by on "Ready Alert." Typical of this was the decision to base jet fighters at St. Hubert, Montreal, with RCAF aircraft practising instrument procedures for landings and departures right next to Dorval Airport. While the airline recognized the air force's role in the difficult times, its flight operations superintendents knew that it was only a matter of time before an accident occurred involving one of its airliners. Airports and airliners were often "buzzed" by exuberant military jet pilots who flew alarmingly close to airliners on the airways. Because "getting numbers for identification purposes was an impossibility," in October 1951 the pilots took the matter up with the chief pilot, Captain R.E. Hadfield, who brought it to the attention of management to little purpose.

On January 5, 1952, while over the Stirling, Ontario, radio range and climbing to 9,000 feet, TCA Flight 6-4 was "buzzed" by an RCAF Vampire jet. The aircraft came from below and behind, approached at 45 degrees from the port side and cut across Flight 6-4's track with—in TCA's language—"a lateral separation of 300 feet at the point of interception." The weather was overcast, but visibility at that altitude was unlimited. When flight 6-4's radio operator contacted Malton and asked that ATC be notified of the violation, he was shocked to be told that the RCAF base at Downsview admitted that there were three Vampires aloft at that time practising interceptions on civil aircraft!

Whatever the menace, from the Soviet Union or the RCAF, bouquets and brickbats from the passengers flowed unabated in the "What Others Think Of Us" column of *Between Ourselves*:

- In regard to excess luggage with all of the commotion about having extra days on your vacation by flying, what encouragement is there for a person to fly when the equipment he would normally carry on a vacation—golf clubs, for instance—run his total baggage over the prescribed limit and his excess baggage charges into figures not unlike the national budget? How about an extra weight allowance for sporting equipment? Naturally, I don't want to take my car along, but if I'm going to fly to my vacation destination, I'd like something of my own for use when I get there without having to equal the original investment with excess baggage charges.

- Competition is very healthy and TCA doesn't have any.

- To get the morning flight from Toronto to Montreal, I rise at 5:30 to get the airline bus at 6:30 to catch the 7:30 flight. By this time I am fairly hungry and to my usual amazement and dismay when the breakfast hour finally rolls around, the pilot and co-pilot are served first. I believe this is bad sales psychology. I am a paying passenger, they are simply employees. Most employees eat before or after they go to work and not when they are working. If you are so kind as to feed them when they are working, I believe they should be fed after the other passengers.

- My young son, aged five, said tonight, "They do have a nice mummy for each plane!"

- To a non smoker, the smell of stale tobacco that seems to pervade some planes is disgusting. Could not some sort of air freshener be used to counter the smell of stale tobacco?

- I suggest that the national airline of a Christian country make non-meat meals available on Ash Wednesday and other Wednesdays in Lent.

- I enjoyed the trip very much, however there was one fellow who radiated very numerous odours. I would think there would be a system where a passenger such as this could be politely informed by the captain of his need for a bath. The ventilation system didn't help, by the way.

- The seats have all the restful qualities of a church pew. Sleep is impossible unless one were able to do so sitting bolt upright.

These are just a few of the 4,460 suggestions for improvements and complaints that the airline received in 1952. If 2,007 of them were negative (mainly comments on the Merlin engines), happily 2,453 were commendations for good service. Almost from its first flight the company had made available to its passengers green and white Comment and Suggestions cards, and these were collected and sent on to the sales division. "There has rarely been a suggestion received which hasn't been thought of before and discarded as impractical or too costly," said Nora Masson, one of the four "Complaints and Claims" women who handled the replies, using the only electric typewriters in the office because of the volume of mail. "If the company could supply all the things that passengers ask for in the aircraft—from hot water bottles to soft drinks and television sets—there would be no space left for passengers and the aircraft would be too heavy to get off the ground." The more seriously critical letters, calling for an investigation, were answered immediately by phone, telegram or a letter asking for more facts. Besides reproaches for things like the butter served on TCA being too hard to spread, the two most common complaints concerned lost baggage and reservations. The airline accepted that in moving millions of suitcases around, some were sure to be lost or damaged, but in 1952, 818 baggage claims were paid out after consultation with the CNR's legal department.

Years later, Alan Godbold, manager of passenger relations, wrote to Beth Buchanan, secretary to Gordon McGregor, pondering why the number of complaints had grown each year. The company's early years were by comparison "horrific," he recalled, with delays lasting days and the airline forced to use hotel and railway vouchers on almost every flight, but there had been few complaints because "systems were simple." There was little that could go wrong with a box lunch and the passengers understood local weather delays or personally witnessed mechanical failures. Most of the complaint letters that the Complaints and Claims people answered fell into two categories: the "prestige" complaint of one-upmanship sent to impress friends, and the twice-told tales that grew worse with each telling. Barb Whitehouse remembered that it was no use telling a passenger who had "misconnected" that the airline had to dispatch a flight earlier or later because of mail commitments, as the retort would invariably be "Aren't I as important as a bag of mail?"

The following chart was published by the company under the title "Where Does the Money Go? A Distribution of Revenues for 1951 (All Services)":

Revenue used for:	% of Total Revenue	Days Required to Work For
Salaries and Wages	37.9	154
Gasoline and Oil	13.4	43
Depreciation	7.8	26
Aircraft Maintenance	6.5	21
Traffic and Sales	6.6	20
General Administrative	2.8	9
All other Operating Expenses	15.3	55
Total Operating Expenses	90.3	328
Non-Operating Charges	1.6	6
Surplus	8.1	31

The company published the chart to point out that it took all of the months from January 1 to June 1 just to pay employee salaries, and only in the month of December could the company make any surplus—if all went well.

With the introduction of the forty-eight-passenger version of the North Star, a "hot/cold" meal service was established, but since it was impossible to serve forty-eight meals with the existing kitchen and food stowage system, the passenger and station service section (P & SSS) developed a more efficient system. The main courses would still be frozen, but part of the meal was heated on the ground before takeoff, allowing the flight attendants to begin serving as soon as the seat belt sign was turned off. The trays, now plastic instead of the compartmentalized metal ones, were boarded with the cutlery, salad and bread already in place. The meat, potatoes and vegetables were heated separately (previously, the potatoes and vegetables had absorbed the meat's juices) and the steward portioned them out onto each passenger's plastic plate in the galley. Another time-saver was a new container for serving coffee, so that the flight attendant no longer needed to rush back and forth to the galley to fill each cup. In tests it was found that forty passengers could be served complete meals in forty minutes, and the P& SSS were sure that with experience the time would be bettered.

"Your attention please. Will passengers on Trans Canada Airlines Flight No. 302 for Chicago who have claimed their reservations and had their baggage checked proceed to the outbound waiting room for Canada Customs (Foreign Exchange Control) examination and final United States Immigration inspection, please." This announcement, made by a TCA agent over the public address system at Malton Airport on April 1, 1950, proclaimed the first pre-flight inspection service in the Western Hemisphere. From now on passengers on TCA's flights destined for New York, Cleveland, Chicago, Buffalo and Tampa could be inspected by US immigration officers before they left Toronto. Previously they were examined on their arrival at those cities, and any who were found inadmissible were detained at immigration centres like Ellis Island pending a hearing or until they could be deported back to Canada. The airline had been responsible for all expenses, including returning them to Canada, while they languished in the United States. The same type of Customs clearance was planned for baggage as well as express and cargo—and would soon be introduced in Montreal as well.

In 1950, when TCA began looking for a replacement for its North Stars, Canadair offered a concept based on the conventional Douglas DC-6, and designated the C-7. Although its performance would have been better than the North Star, it would still not have been able to fly the Atlantic non-stop with a full passenger load. When Canadair's president was unsuccessful in selling TCA on it, McGregor knew that he would go crying to Howe, but the minister dismissed his complaints. "Any decisions of that nature," he said, "lie entirely with TCA management," and that even the threat of discontinuing an existing aircraft manufacturing industry would not cause him to deal with the manufacturer's approach in any other manner.[1]

The airline then looked south for its North Star replacement. Here the two Californian rivals, Lockheed and Douglas, were engrossed in a battle for a larger share of the commercial market. The goal was to be the first to build an aircraft that could fly non-stop across the Atlantic, or as near as possible. In response to Douglas's stranglehold on the commercial market with its DC-3, in 1939 Lockheed had left the twin-engined field altogether and begun work on a four-engined, pressurized transport. First flown at Burbank, California, on January 9, 1943, the Model L49 was then wearing the military transport guise of the C-69—as military transports, not airliners, were the priority in a nation at war. At war's end design and production were well in hand, and soon both Pan American and TWA were flying the elegant civil version, the 649 or Constellation either across the Atlantic or the United States, and on the latter route were three hours faster than the DC-4s of American Airlines.

The later L749 Constellation allowed Lockheed a temporary lead over Douglas, but when it became a race to extend the series, in 1946 Douglas moved far out in front with its DC-6/DC-6B. Three years later Lockheed countered with a stretch version of its 749: the 1049 or Super Constellation, which first flew on October 13, 1950. This four-engined, low-wing monoplane was designed for high speed and very long-range transportation, but every time it was redesigned it got heavier, its power plants more powerful and much more complex.

When TCA's board of directors met on August 10, 1951, the North Star replacement was at the head of its agenda. Whatever aircraft was selected would have to fly the Atlantic non-stop, be capable of ready conversion from luxury to high-density seating, and be able to earn revenues in excess of all forecasted expenses. The choice boiled down to either eight Douglas DC-6Bs or eight Lockheed 1049 Super Constellations. The DC-6B was powered by the Pratt & Whitney R2800, an engine that was at the end of its development life, and TCA's engineering staff reported that it had to be used at cruise powers at a higher percentage of maximum power; that is, the engine was less than required of the DC-6 airframe. The mechanical difficulties of the Lockheed 1049's Wright 3350s were known, but the power plant was widely used by the military. The RCAF, for example, had just placed an order for thirty-five of them for its Fairchild C-119 freighters. Finally, engineering thought that the 1049 had a higher potential resale value than the DC-6B.

However, what appears to have clinched the deal for Lockheed was the Douglas company's indifference to TCA's business, with replies giving vague delivery dates and prices. To add to the insult, Douglas only fielded their aerodynamicists and "back-room" boys, who knew the theory behind the "Connie" but not what cabin interiors it came in. But having just rid itself of its Lockheed Lodestars, an aircraft that it had found wanting in many ways and one that had been re-engined at great expense, TCA was hesitant to be involved once more with Lockheed. That company, on the other hand, anxious to keep TCA's loyalty, launched an aggressive sales campaign led by their main salesman, Kirk Yost, who promised TCA the first Super Constellation delivery by November 1953 and all eight by February 1954. The airline therefore chose

The simple elegance of line in the basic model L-1049G, without the optional tip tanks or later radar nose. The aircraft is on a pre-delivery flight over the Mojave Desert. Ken Leigh collection

Lockheed and opened an office at Burbank. Don Benson and Shirley Robinson were sent there in October 1952, followed by two inspectors, Frank Lukeman (mechanical) and Norm Surridge (electrical). Clayton Glenn, Dick Tritt, Howard Cotterell, Jack McGee and George Lothian were among those who would follow on a temporary basis.

Without doubt the most distinctive design of its day, the 1049 had a dolphin-like shape and three fins that made it a classic even then. But because the L1049 had been outperformed by the DC-6B, the Model L1049 "C" had been developed with the controversial Wright Cyclone R-3350 Turbo-Cyclone engines. These were the climax of piston engines, stretching the technology to the limit to gain every ounce of power. Each R-3350 18-cylinder radial engine had three power recovery turbines (PRT), which were driven by exhaust gases through an 11-inch turbine wheel, boosting the engine to a rating of 3,250 BHP (brake horse power) and thus 20 percent more power. The concept was hardly new—exhaust-driven engines had powered the B-24 Liberator and the P-38 Lightning during the war—but like the Rolls Royce Merlin, this was the first time that they were to be used in commercial aviation. The turbo-compound engines had increased the Connie's cruising speed to 330 mph, outpacing the DC-6B. The engines were coupled to three-bladed, 15-foot Curtiss Electric propellers that provided constant speed control, full feathering and reversing.

Then on September 8, 1952, Lockheed suffered a labour strike. Although it lasted a mere twenty days, the delay was enough for Robert Gross to inform Gordon McGregor that the 1049Cs could not be delivered on the agreed-upon

A TCA postcard view of the first Super Constellation delivered, CF-TGA—a model 1049C. On February 26, 1954, Captain George Lothian flew it in eight hours from Burbank, California to Montreal Dorval, where it was put on public display to admiring crowds. Canada's first truly transcontinental airliner had arrived.

dates. With the ongoing Korean War, Lockheed's energies and talent were being poured into a variety of military aircraft that took precedence over the Connies. TCA was also told that it was now behind Eastern Air Lines, KLM, Air France and Iberia in 1049 allocation and that the revised delivery schedule was three by April 1954 and the remainder by September 1954. In fact, TCA received its first L1049, *CF-TGA*, on February 26, 1954. When it was shown off to the public, someone was heard to comment about the distinctive tail, "That's typical for a government company. Everything has to be in triplicate."

The airline acquired five Model 1049C (*CF-TGA* to *CF-TGE*), three Model 1049E (*CF-TGF* to *CF-TGH*)—which were identical to the Cs except for increased weights—four 1049G (*CF-TEU* to *CF-TEX*), which were distinguishable for their optional wingtip fuel tanks, each carrying 600 US gallons, and two of the final version, the Model 1049H (*CF-TEY, CF-TEZ*). With the jet age looming, Lockheed was hedging its bets with the "H" series, and they had been built as heavier cargo aircraft though with the same dimensions as the "G" series. As a result, in *CF-TEY* and *CF-TEZ* the floor line sloped downward to the rear, and the galley was aft of the main door and all seating forward of it. Externally on the left of the "H" aircraft were two cargo doors visible in outline, one forward of the wing and the other aft of it. The semi-monocoque, circular fuselage was sealed for pressurization with two doors on the left of the fuselage for boarding and deplaning. Crew recall that the main rear door moved inward and slid aft, the front passenger door swung out and forward, while the crew door was on the right and slid upward. The two cargo compartments below the cabin floor of the 1049 were adequate and, as they were pressurized, could be entered from access hatches in the cabin floor.

Those TCA veterans who had bad memories of the leaking cockpits of the Electras were pleased to note that Lockheed had improved the flight station "glass" dramatically. The shatterproof panels were equipped with anti-icing, de-icing, and de-fogging devices as well as windshield wipers. For a clearer vision, the second panels could be opened without bringing in the rain when the aircraft was not pressurized. TCA had also asked that plastic tubing be used in the water system to prevent freezing.

The Connies brought with them a new group of flying personnel: flight engineers. The captain was still in command, but the flight engineer kept the engines, cabin air conditioning system, pressurization and hydraulics running. The F/E replaced the radio operator in the cockpit and sat sidesaddle at a complex instrument panel before a set of power plant controls. There were throttles, propeller control switches, cowl flap controls for each engine and the main item: an ignition analyzer. Through its oscilloscope all of the 36 spark plugs on each engine were monitored for fuel injection, mixture, spark timing, exhaust valves and intake airflow. Two wide-angle lens windows, one in the crew door and one in the left side of the flight station behind the captain's seat, were focussed directly on the propellers so that they could be monitored from the flight engineer's position. The first DOT flight engineer licences were issued by Captain Lindy Rood, director of flight operations, to Boyd Moore, Maurice Fellows, Aubrey Cooke, Joe Held, Eric Grimmet and Tom Woodhouse. Graduating in the summer of 1953 from the Wright Aeronautical school, Woodbridge, NJ, and the Lockheed Burbank plant, they were to be the instructors of the first thirty-five candidates chosen from the ranks of the maintenance and overhaul department.

On May 14, 1954, TCA inaugurated its first Constellation flight on the Toronto–Montreal–London run, piloted by Capt. S.S. Albulet and F/O A. Snyder. Five days later the Connie was first used on the Montreal–Dusseldorf route. During the summer the Super Constellations would be operated across the Atlantic eight times a week; in winter this would be reduced to six times weekly as service to Florida, Bermuda and the Caribbean was stepped up. A year later the Super Constellations would be providing an "express" service between Vancouver and the East with an intermediate stop at Winnipeg. The Connies were fast. On December 21, 1955, aided by a tailwind at 23,000 feet, Captain S.F. Found would pilot one 2,691 nautical miles (about 3,027 statute miles) from Montreal to Prestwick in 8 hours and 1 minute—seven minutes faster than the record set by Captain Steve Albulet on October 19 the year before.

Dimensions	1049E	1049G
Span (ft/m)	123.0/37.49	123.5/37.62
Length (ft/m)	113.7/34.62	113.7/34.62
Height (ft/m)	24.9/7.54	24.9/7.54
Wing area (sq ft / sq m)	1650/152.291	1654/153.662
Cruising speed (mph / km/h)	255/410	305/491
Rate of climb (ft/min / m/min)	960/293	1100/335
Ceiling (ft/m)	25,000/7,620	22,300/6,795
Payload range (lbs/mi / kg/km)	18,800/2,880	18,300/4,140

The Super Constellation allowed TCA to compete with the luxury of the BOAC and Air France on the Atlantic run. Bill Fabro, the director of passenger services, had been so impressed with the Dutch Constellation galleys that the company had ordered its galleys made by KLM in Amsterdam. Each was 56 square feet but with ovens, automatic coffee makers and a 10.8 cubic foot refrigerator, it was a "super kitchen," according to TCA supervisor of catering, Pete Colato. "We're planning to have three basic nine-course meals, and for the first time in airline history, we'll be serving proper coffee." All this on individual tables with real English china and linen, only two decades after the box lunches on the Lockheed 10s.

TCA's interior designer, Henry Dreyfuss, had planned the interior of the Super Constellation for privacy. It had four separate cabins with fifteen tourist class passengers in the forward compartment, thirty-nine tourist class in the main compartment, two first class passengers in the lounge and seven in first class aft. By putting the first class seats just inside the entry vestibule before the tail and using cabin partitions, a mid-plane lounge and toilets and several wooden walls, Dreyfuss successfully cut down on through traffic and had baffled noise. Cabin configuration could be quickly changed as each set of chairs (three abreast on one side and two on the other and two in a semicircle in the rear) rested on concealed tracks. Ceilings and wall linings were seamless, decorated with antique maps of the world. For the first time too each passenger's cluster of service facilities—light, air vent, call button and oxygen—was located not on the wall but under the baggage rack. Later configurations for Atlantic, Southern (Caribbean) and Domestic services would vary the cabin layout.

With the introduction of the Super Constellations, the airline brought out its "TCA blue" uniform—a standard shade of dark blue for all personnel with the exception of stewardesses, who in summer wore sky-blue uniforms. While the traffic branch had changed uniforms in 1950, this was the first major change in uniform for the flight operations department since the company had begun in 1937. Flight crews, flight attendants and station personnel would wear the all-year-round gabardine. Ground personnel would wear a double-breasted two-button jacket with TCA gilt buttons and the newly designed insignia. The hat would continue to be standard RCAF officer style with maple leaf hat badge. The uniform to be worn by women in the traffic division was

The Super Connie, carrying more passengers, needed an expanded flight crew. The new "TCA Blue" uniform made its first appearance in 1954: dark blue garb, with an optional lighter blue for summer wear for stewardesses.

a straight skirt with two side pleats and a collarless, tailored jacket with three gilt TCA buttons and the new ground staff brevet. It was topped off by a small felt cap on which were two parallel white ribbons linked to a maple leaf badge. For stewardesses it was their first change in five years. The tunic was cardigan style with bone buttons and two small wing lapels set on either shoulder line, the skirt straight with a pleat back and front. The head-hugging hat made of the same fabric as the uniform had an all-over stitched design.

Your Wonderful New Way to the Old World...

For the most Luxurious and Exclusive First Class Service to Europe.
Fly TCA Super Constellation
Luxury Plus At Five Miles a Minute

- Only Nine Passengers in First Class
- Special fully-reclining foam soft "Siesta Seats" at no extra charge.
- Exclusive club lounge for occasional and delightful "change of scene."
- Tourist Season Too! New High in Low Fares

——————————————— TCA Brochure, July 1954

When Lockheed had begun flight testing its 1049C, Douglas was still working on the similarly powered DC-7, and Lockheed thought it had a coup that would allow it to capture the very tail end of the piston airliner market before jet aircraft took over. However, the R-3350 engine had problems, and TCA was in for another North Star/Merlin experience. The 18 cylinders in two rows of nine had forged aluminium heads and forged steel barrels, and each accommodated an intake valve, an exhaust valve, valve springs, rocker arms, two Champion R-103 spark plugs and the fuel injection nozzle. But they were so highly stressed that they cracked around the fuel injection insert, the spark plug inserts and the exhaust valve inserts, and they leaked telltale oil. Changing cracked cylinders was tedious, painful and even dangerous work. What the mechanics hated most was having to be under lower cylinders: as they pulled each one out, they were soaked in dirty "120" oil. With so many injection lines, exhaust stacks, manifold intake pipes and leads, reassembling a R-3350 engine was an emotionally and physically daunting task, and to have to do it so soon after the Merlin controversy seemed somehow unfair. The maintenance required to keep the Wrights functioning consumed time and finances, and like all the airlines that used them, TCA tried to stretch out the overhaul times as much as possible.

In the Constellations' nine years of service with the airline, only one was lost. It happened on December 17, 1954, when the L1049E *CF-TGG*, inbound from Tampa with sixteen passengers on board, was on an instrument approach to Malton's Runway 10 in poor weather. It crash-landed in a field at Brampton, skidding and catching fire. There were no fatalities but the airline settled insurance claims amounting to $57,626. The airline ruled that Captain Doug Holland had descended below acceptable limits until hitting a tree, and he was removed from flying. Holland, supported by his first officer, maintained that he had not broken limits, that they were at 200 feet by their altimeters and on the glide path when they had hit the tree. CALPA supported Holland but could not force TCA to hold a board of arbitration. The new CALPA director, Captain R.R. Stevenson, put forward the argument that the Connie's altimeters were not registering accurately and that the glide path to the runway was scalloped and low on the point of impact. Though the Holland case went to court in an attempt to force a systems board of arbitration, the airline held firm and Holland left the company. "Not long after," wrote Captain F.E.W. Smith in the association's history, "the aircraft that Holland had piloted crashed in California under circumstances that indicated altimeter error."[2]

In the early 1950s airlines operating DC-3s were looking for a replacement type, and TCA was no exception. Acquired at very low post-war capital costs, it was the solid reliability of the DC-3s on short and medium haul domestic flights that ironically kept replacement a low priority. The company's dilemma was how long the decision could be stalled.

If six years before there had been few alternatives to the Merlin, in 1950 there was a surplus of Pratt & Whitney engines, and American Airlines, Eastern

Air Lines and TWA were busy replacing their DC-3s with larger aircraft like the Convair Liner and the Martin 404. On the other side of the Atlantic, myriad types came on the scene but they barely satisfied local traffic. All, however, had similar passenger-freight capacity and performance, all were powered by piston engines, and though some had tricycle gear, all looked like the DC-3. The one possible exception was an aircraft being offered by Vickers Armstrong in Britain.

As with most European aircraft manufacturers then re-emerging from wartime production, in 1945 the Vickers organization had been quick off the mark with their VC-1 Vickers Viking short haul airliner. Designed as an airliner from the outset, it had been based on the Vickers Wellington, the only British bomber produced throughout World War II, and powered by twin Hercules radial engines. This chubby DC-3 look-alike made its mark on aviation history when the 107th Viking to come off the production line was fitted with two new Rolls Royce Nene turbo-jets. It flew successfully on April 6, 1948, and four months later made the trip from London's Northolt Airport to Paris's Le Bourget carrying twenty-four passengers.

However, Vickers was pinning the company's main hopes on a second design, the four-engined VC-2, which had been in the works since 1944 and had been based on the recommendations of the Brabazon Committee. Britain had some five distinctive turboprop engines in development at the time, and after testing three of them the company chose the new Rolls Royce Dart turboprop because the sturdy centrifugal-compressor type of engine would attain the full operational reliability quicker on medium-range operations than the others, which were axial flow units. The new aircraft was pressurized as Vickers already had considerable expertise in that field, having built about 100 pressurized Wellington bombers during the war.

The prototype emerged as the Vickers V-630 Viceroy to honour Lord Louis Mountbatten, then Viceroy of India. Registered as *G-AHRF*, it first flew on July 16, 1949. Then, as India had obtained its independence the previous year, the aircraft was renamed Viscount and shown off at the 1949 Farnborough Air Show, followed by a media jaunt to Paris on September 20. Gordon McGregor, who attended that show, was offered a demonstration flight. "Never having flown other than piston-engined aircraft, I was tremendously impressed with the smoothness of the four Dart turboprop engines. I was given the full treatment. As I sat in the cabin, a coin was balanced on its edge on the table in front of me, and a mechanical pencil stood on its non-business end."[3] McGregor was then put in the left-hand seat to fly the Viscount himself. That day he also met George Edwards, who equally impressed him. More than anyone else, Edwards, who had just moved from the Vickers' experimental design to its sales department, would be responsible for North American airlines buying the Viscount.

But TCA wisely bided its time, watching events unfold at Vickers prior to its production run. The Viscount airframe was enlarged to accommodate more

The V630 prototype Viscount on its flawless first flight July 16, 1949. Its outstanding performance offered growing airlines a viable replacement for the DC-3.

passengers and more powerful Dart turboprop engines, and Vickers began canvassing European airline operations and conducting sales demonstration flights. On a series of test flights between London and Paris in 1950, Dickie Rymer, a Vickers test pilot, invited TCA Captain "Gath" Edwards on board.

During this period between the completion of the enlarged prototype V-700 and the beginning of the production run, the prototype V-630 continued to perform flawlessly. But suddenly in December 1950 British European Airways (BEA), which had been designated the lead customer for the new aircraft, announced that it would purchase twenty Airspeed Ambassador aircraft, which seated forty-nine passengers (compared to thirty-three in the Viscount prototype). BEA was hedging its bets with the Ambassador because, although it was designed to the same Brabazon Committee recommendations as the Viscount, it was powered by the more conventional Bristol Centaurus piston-radial engines. (As it turned out, BEA was the only customer for the Ambassador.) But BEA continued to be the lead customer for the Viscount, and when the first production model V-701, *G-ALWE*, flew on August 20, 1952, it was decked out in the latest BEA colour scheme. BEA ordered twenty-six and ended up with a fleet of sixty-seven Viscounts. Orders from other airlines followed: Air France (twelve), Aer Lingus (four) and Trans Australian Airlines (four) .

For the airline customer looking to replace its wartime DC-3s, the Viscount appealed to company personnel and passengers alike. By building the cockpit canopy as a slight bulge on the main fuselage and fitting it with large windscreen panels, Vickers had provided the captain with a clear view. The F/O's seat slid back and his control column disengaged, so he could assist with the radio and navigation. The four engines were almost noiseless and vibration-free, but every airline's public relations people played up the Viscount's huge windows—the largest ever installed in a commercial aircraft—which could be used as emergency exits. At a time when the safety record of British airliners like the de Havilland Comet 1A was being questioned, the Viscount proved to be an unusually "safe" British aircraft. Extensive high-pressure tests were carried out to ensure that the double-skinned Perspex of the large windows did not shatter. "For the first time our wing icing problems were behind us," wrote George Lothian. "Its designers had incorporated an inner layer behind the leading edge of the wing into which hot air could be directed."[4] The propellers and engine cowlings were protected from ice by electrically heated rubber shoes, though Captain Lowell Dunsmore discovered that it was not wise to let the ice build up on its engines before turning the de-icing shoes on because the high concentration of water that the ice carried affected the running of the engines. The use of kerosene instead of aviation gasoline, double-slotted flaps and tail de-icers, plus the minimizing of tire-burst risk by fitting twin wheels to each undercarriage unit, were all safety factors in the Viscount.

What accounted for the Viscount's lack of vibration and noise was that the Dart gas turbine engine had no reciprocating parts such as pistons and valves. (In promoting the Viscount's turboprop engines, McGregor used to delight in quoting Sir Frank Whittle, the inventor of the jet engine, who said, "Reciprocating motion might be all right biologically, but mechanically it stinks!") However, Rolls Royce—having suffered in its commercial applications of the Merlin engine—continued to put the Dart through exhaustive testing. As a result, Rolls Royce was able to supply the more powerful Type R Da.3 Darts for the later Viscounts, allowing them to cruise at speeds in excess of 300 miles an hour. Another selling point as far as TCA was concerned was the reworking of the production model of the Viscount early on—largely due to the insistence of Edwards—which increased the fuselage length by 6 feet 8 inches and removed the central pantry so that forty to fifty-four seats could be fitted in.

On October 17, 1952, McGregor phoned Howe to tell him that he planned to recommend to the board the purchase of seventeen Viscount 724s the following month. He began by saying, "While expressing worries about the maintenance of British equipment in this country..." and concluded with, "I suppose it's the right thing. Let me know what the board's decision is." Later the minister expressed the opinion that the airline could have done better in North America. "Your blood be on your own head!" he warned McGregor. "You'll never get them on time."

Elegant and sleek, the Viscount was a European sports car when compared with the rugged truck-like North Star, a well-bred aristocrat to the plebian DC-3. By the time it was introduced into the TCA fleet, it had three years of airline experience so that any deficiencies—and these were few—had been worked out. Despite this, many in TCA's engineering department were openly hostile to it, favouring instead the Convair Liner 340 with its reliable, conventional Pratt & Whitney R2800 engines. "We found the Viscount systems extremely complicated and poorly designed," wrote Clayton Glenn, "and forecast difficult maintenance problems ahead." Jack Dyment, director of engineering, drew up a list of its deficiencies, recommending to the board of directors that the aircraft not be considered until they were corrected. He and his staff distrusted the aircraft's unconventional wing structure. American-built aircraft had three main spars—at the root or centre spar and one for each wing. The Viscount had a single spar "with ribs more or less hanging from it like a Christmas tree." Then there was a taxiing hazard; clearance between the inboard propellers and the runway was very small, sometimes as little as 7 inches. Pilots were warned that extreme caution had to be exercised when taxiing over snowbanks and runway lights. So strong were the negative feelings toward this British aircraft with its unproven turboprop engines that when Dyment wrote up a comparison of it and the Convair Liner, copies of his study were published and distributed by the company:

- Although the Viscount consumes considerably more fuel than the Convair, the cost of the fuel burned, assuming JP-4 in Canada, is almost identical for both planes over the entire band of ranges from 300 to 1,100 miles.

- The Viscount could fly a 500-mile trip with a 11,000 lb payload at an average block speed of 257 mph at a cost of $510. To break even it would have to carry 34 passengers assuming zero revenue from cargo. Under the same conditions the Convair could carry the 11,000 lb payload at an average speed of 228 mph at a cost of $495. To break even the Convair would have to carry 33 passengers. According to TCA cost estimates the Convair was .05 cents per seat mile cheaper to operate.

However, in spite of pessimism from the engineering department, the combined force of McGregor's popularity and the enthusiasm of pilots like George Lothian seems to have carried the purchase through, though even when the decision was made to purchase, with the Merlin and Comet traumas still fresh in their minds, TCA engineering called for so many modifications that another manufacturer would have balked. They complained that the fuel system was seriously deficient—a single failure could cause the engines on the same side to shut down—so Dyment had Vickers design a system similar to that on all other four-engined aircraft: four independent fuel systems. The Viscount's heating system, vital in Canadian winters, did not allow the aircraft to be heated while on the ground with the engines stopped; cabin heat in-flight was from the heat of compression of the cabin superchargers. The aircraft was to be delivered without radar, and only after CALPA researched the time that was lost when pilots avoided all cloudy weather that might contain violent thunderstorms did TCA retrofit weather radar to the Viscounts, the first in the airline's history. The airline installed its own fuel-burning Janitrol heater, which in the early days did not work well. Also installed was an American radio system, American instruments, an engine lubricating oil suited to the Canadian climate, a fire crash system that would not cut the fuel on all four engines—the list went on.

When the TCA team inspected Vickers at Weybridge in November 1952, they not only had to cope with the worst fog in London's history but, used to the modern Lockheed plant at Burbank, they found the Vickers facilities antiquated and untidy, and they joked that James Watt's steam engine was still running a punch press there. Edwards promised to modernize, and W.H. Bird of TCA's engineering department was stationed at the Vickers plant at Weybridge to ensure that all of the modifications were done as Bain and Dyment specified. To everyone's surprise, George Edwards was most amenable to Vickers correcting all perceived deficiencies in the Viscount and making any design changes required by the Canadians at an added cost of only $25,000 per aircraft. The final aircraft was so different that it had to be re-certified, but Edwards knew that any improvement to "North Americanize" the Viscount could only help sell it in the United States. He was proved right. Capital Airlines placed the largest order—for sixty Viscounts, all of them incorporating the modifications initially made for TCA.

Before delivery of its first Viscount, TCA's engineering department insisted on severe cold weather tests because the Dart engine had not yet been cleared for starting at temperatures below 10°F. In February 1953 the prototype Viscount V-700, *G-AMAV*, loaded down with test equipment, made the first turboprop flight across the Atlantic and collected the TCA team of Ron Baker, Jim McLean, Bun Moore, Norm Stoddart and Clayton Glenn from Dorval. They then flew to Winnipeg and on to Churchill, Manitoba, to be put through cold weather and icing tests. To the disappointment of the engineering division, the Dart engines started in temperatures of forty below, but the Viscount's door seals froze enough that the aircraft could not be pressurized. Vickers obligingly changed the material of the seals so that cabin pressure held them in place and the aircraft passed the test. Tongue in cheek, Gordon McGregor would write, "Unfortunately, the worst we could produce that winter at Churchill on Hudson's Bay was 27 degrees below zero, but since there was a 25-knot wind at the time, while the aircraft did not suffer the pilots and technical crews did. However, all the modifications... were considered highly satisfactory."[5]

George Lothian was part of the TCA team sent to Weybridge in the fall of 1954 while the Viscounts were being modified for the Canadian market, and he flew as an observer when Vickers test pilots Jock Bryce (who would go on to test the Vanguard, VC10 and BAC 111) and Brian Trubshaw (one day to be

The TCA engineering team hamming it up in Churchill, Manitoba, for the Viscount's cold weather tests. Photo courtesy Clayton Glenn

the chief test pilot for the Concorde) put the first TCA Viscount through its paces. There were a few hair-raising flights. Of one of them he wrote, "it seemed as if the wings clapped hands over the top of the cockpit," but by December 1954 the TCA Viscount was ready for delivery.

McGregor had been phoning Edwards daily to ask where his new aircraft was, so on December 6, 1954, everyone was relieved when pilots Jock Bryce of Vickers and TCA's own George Lothian took off from Wisley in *CF-TGI*. Stephen Anderson, a regional public relations officer who was one of the twelve passengers on-board, wrote of the flight: "Within minutes after their take-off, Wisely was struck by a tornado, but at 20,500 feet they knew nothing of it. Held prisoner in Iceland for two days because of the weather, on a bright clear day *CF-TGI* pressed on to Bluie West One, Greenland. They let down off the coast and entered 'Tuna' or Tununggassdg Fjord, the only way in. For 48 miles the little Viscount flew down the twisting fjord with icy mountains towering on either side, and then ahead they saw the tiny plateau with the runway." Anderson was amazed at the small American hamlet complete with church and the large sign that said: Narsarssuak—the Miami of the North. Two

TCA's first Viscount engines, still shrouded, receiving last-minute attention from ground crew at Weybridge, just prior to a delivery flight. Vickers representative George Edwards (centre) looks on. Ken Leigh collection

hours and forty minutes after takeoff from Bluie they dipped down into Goose Bay, Labrador. Anderson knew it was home because cut out in the snow was a clump of pines in the shape of a (TCA) Maple Leaf. The only untoward incident on the Viscount's first flight across the Atlantic was when the centre cockpit window cracked. When word came that it had landed in Goose Bay, Gordon McGregor could not resist telegraphing the news to Howe, who had doubted that he would ever get them on time. "I suppose you are saying, 'I told you so,'" Howe replied. McGregor later wrote, "How could anyone not delight in working with and for a man who could so prettily acknowledge an error in judgement?"[6]

On the final leg between Goose Bay and Montreal, Lindy Rood and Herb Hopson came out in a North Star filled with newsmen to greet them. Visual contact was made over Quebec City, and both aircraft went into a series of manoeuvres to give the photographers the best shots possible. "When we were requested to do a shoot up before landing [at Dorval], Jock [Bryce] complied with gusto, skimming over the hangars at about five feet and executing a vertical bank inside the perimeter with the wing tip...about three feet off the ground." It was a cold, wet overcast Sunday morning when the Viscount landed at Dorval Airport but there was a crowd of some 200 at the terminal. McGregor, Bill English and Gordon Wood were on hand to greet them, accompanied by Jean Drapeau, mayor of Montreal. "That night," wrote Lothian, "the Vickers boys gathered in our home for a celebration and a sing-a-long around Rose's white piano."[7]

North Star CF-TFT *loaded with news photographers, greeting Viscount-TG1 on the last leg of the trip to Montreal. To say that TCA anxiously awaited the arrival of the Viscount is an understatement.*

On a personal note, in June 1954 Jack Dyment had been awarded a fellowship in the Royal Aeronautical Society for his many contributions to aircraft engineering, and when IATA then asked him to chair a committee to study fuels for jet and turboprop aircraft, Aer Lingus Captain J.C. Kelly-Rogers penned the following poem.

Dyment Poetized

There is quite a tough problem with fuel
In conditions hot, humid or cool;
It imposes a strain on the chap at Bahrain
And the poor lonely hermit at Thule.
When it's light it increases the drag;
When it's heavy the line flow will lag;
But the task's on the back of Canadian Jack
And the answer is now in the bag.

Viscount supporters at TCA were counting on its low engine noise—"a point on which we were inclined to be a little bit tender" wrote McGregor—to win over the company's skeptics. But even its shortcomings were gently "British"— more Agatha Christie than Stephen King. There was the "ghost" problem. In humid conditions, the ventilation system created heavy condensation, which came up from under the passengers' seats like steam. Some passengers thought the aircraft was on fire, others that a psychic phenomenon was manifesting itself from under them. The "stroboscope effect" was even spookier. One night an elderly lady in a window seat asked the stewardess if they were in any danger because the two propellers on the wing outside were no longer turning. The stewardess saw that she was correct and ran to the flight deck to report that the starboard engines had stopped. The crew laughed and pointed to the instruments to assure her that all four engines were indeed working, but she stuck to her contention that they had stopped. Eventually, for the sake of peace, the captain had the first officer return with her "to see what all the fuss was about." When he returned, he reported, "They sure appear to be stopped, but of course they are not." Subsequent investigation determined that the anti-collision lights were illuminating the propeller blades at the instant they were in the same radial position. With all engine speeds synchronized, the blades actually appeared to be stationary.[8]

He insists on Service...
He insists on Speed...
He insists on TCA Viscount to Canada.
The World's Most Modern Air Liner introduced
to America by TCA.
Four Rolls Royce, propeller-turbine engines wing
you effortlessly and quietly to your destination.
Arrive Relaxed and Refreshed.

——————— TCA advertisement in a US magazine, 1956

In Canada, advertising emphasized the Rolls Royce name at a time when the Dominion still had strong British ties. The Viscount proved itself marginally faster than the Convair 340, and the public did hold that four engines were safer than two. The Dart turboprop was at the beginning of its long development cycle, in contrast to piston engines like those of Pratt & Whitney that were nearing the end of their development cycles. In fact, TCA discovered that Rolls Royce had been conservative in its assessment of the Dart's durability, thinking that it would achieve 1,000 hours of operation before a major overhaul; TCA demonstrated that it was capable, and approved by the DOT, to go 9,000 hours—an industry record.

TCA's initial Viscount order was later reduced by two, and fifteen Viscount Model V-724s were delivered for a total cost of $11.5 million; with the addition

An ad for TCA, published in 1955 by Vickers and Rolls Royce. The companies often ran feature ads in British trade journals in conjunction with new sales or deliveries made.

of spare parts and tools the bill came to $15 million. After the first arrived in December 1954, they were delivered on the average of one a month through 1955 with the last coming in February 1956. They were registered *CF-TGI* to *CF-TGW*. In what was the first scheduled turboprop airliner flight in North America, on April 1, 1955, the TCA Viscount entered service on the Montreal–Toronto–Fort William–Winnipeg route, flown by Captain D.F. Tribe and F/O W.H. Kent. Three days later the Viscounts were used on the Toronto–New York route and by November 1 they were flying transcontinentally. In March 1956, the company bought thirty-six of the improved Model V-757s, registering them as *CF-TGX* to *TGZ*, then *CF-THA* to *THZ* and *CF-TIA* to *TIG*. This brought to fifty-one the number of Viscounts in TCA service. To make sure company employees could answer questions about the Viscounts, the airline published a brochure packed with information.

FACTS AND FIGURES: THINGS YOU WILL WANT TO KNOW ABOUT THE NEW VISCOUNT

Weights

Maximum takeoff weight	58,000 lbs
Maximum landing weight	52,000 lbs
Maximum zero fuel weight	48,000 lbs

Dimensions

Wing span	93.7 ft
Overall length	81.2 ft
Overall height	26.8 ft
Wing area	963 sq ft
Propeller diameter	10.0 ft

Wing loading

Take-off	58.2 lbs per sq ft
Landing	54.0 lbs per sq ft
Fuel capacity	1.720 imp gals
Fuel type	Kerosene

Payload

Total passenger seats	40–54
Cargo space available	550 cu ft
Average flight altitudes	10,000–30,000 ft
Average cruising speed	310–330 mph
Engine	Rolls Royce Dart RDa 3-506
Power (static, sea level)	1,400 BHP and 356 lbs thrust
Maximum speed	340 mph

Average fuel consumption

15,000 ft	320 gals/hr
20,000 ft	282 gals/hr
25,000 ft	240 gals/hr

Pressurization

At 25,000 feet a cabin altitude of 5,500 ft is maintained.

For the Viscounts' interior design, instead of using an in-house interior designer as it had for the North Star and DC-3, the company went to the New York design firm of Butler-Zimmermann. The initial passenger configuration was to be all first class with forty-four seats arranged with two seats on either side of the aisle, each pair spaced 39 1/2 inches apart. Beth Buchanan, McGregor's secretary, recalled that this had not matched up with the panoramic windows and caused "much grumbling."[9] Fortunately for the airline, the facilities—reading lights, air vents, etc.—were based on a forty-eight-seat plan that could be expanded to fifty-three. The galley and coatroom were in the rear and two lavatories up front. The Viscount had three cargo compartments, the largest one in the floor, with smaller ones behind the cockpit and at the rear of the cabin. The huge elliptical windows were dressed with handwoven "Dominion plaid" drapes by Karen Bulow, a Montreal decorator. The predominant colours of the Viscount interior were brown and grey, with the floor a deep umber and the front of the cabin grey-green. The final Bulow touch was in the grey-beige coatroom curtain decorated with a large green maple leaf pattern.

Max Church's flight training instructor on the Viscount was a senior pilot, Captain Arthur H. Hollinsworth. "Once on a routine check from Winnipeg we had the chief test pilot from Vickers, Dick Rymer, on the flight deck with us. Our nighttime instrument approach to Toronto Airport was in moderate to heavy snowfall and visibility one half mile. The leading runway to the north was not equipped with ILS [Instrument Landing System]. No problem, I thought, the Toronto VOR navigation station was located one mile west of the runway. Over the station I noted the time and steered the reciprocal runway heading while descending to 1,000 feet above ground. After twenty-five seconds I started a left-hand rate one turn to the runway heading and descended to 500 feet. Although the tower advised that all approach lights and runway lights were turned up full, we did not see them immediately. Suddenly the approach lights came into view and straight ahead. I flicked on the wing lights, but the streaking snow was too mesmerizing so we landed using the runway lights for depth perception. It worked well. As we taxied through the snow, the English pilot said he had heard about Canadian winter operations, but now had something to talk about."

In 1958, four years after the delivery of the first one, TCA embarked on a major modification program on its Viscounts. George Edward's reassurances notwithstanding, the airline was concerned about the lower spar boom on all its aircraft. This spar ran span-wise from one wing tip through the fuselage below the cabin floor to the opposite wing tip and resembled a girder beam used on road bridges. It was the centre of strength around which the entire structure of the wings was built, and because of this a "safe life" limitation had been specified. Engineering had calculated the time expiry date for each Viscount in the fleet and established a modification program to change all affected spars. Rather than return the aircraft to Vickers, the company decided to perform the work at the Winnipeg overhaul base, and a "Spar Mod" group was sent to be trained in Britain instead. They knew that the big problem was not only replacing the spar but reaching it. The whole aircraft first had to be supported on a specially designed trestle, and then the engines, fuel tanks, undercarriage, etc., removed. When the program began in 1958 it took five weeks to complete the replacement of a spar; by 1969 it was twenty days. Then in July 1969, when Vickers lowered the "life" of the inner spar boom by 10 percent, TCA intensified the program in order to avoid grounding their whole Viscount fleet, and the Winnipeg overhaul base met the challenge admirably, going from a turnaround in fourteen days to seven days.

Trans Canada Airlines lost three Viscounts in service. On November 10, 1958, a Seaboard & Western Airlines Super Constellation on takeoff at Idlewild

Airport suffered a propeller reversal, went out of control and hit the empty TCA Viscount *CF-TGL* that passengers were about to board. Both aircraft burned. The second accident occurred at Malton on October 3, 1959, when the crew of *CF-TGY* was carrying out an ILS approach in heavy rain. In the poor visibility the pilot misjudged the height, and the Viscount hit a water tower, landing 900 feet short of Runway 23. The aircraft was damaged beyond repair, but none of the thirty-four passengers were injured. The next accident was at Bagotville, Quebec, when on October 10, 1962, *CF-THA*, having touched down, was nearing the end of its landing run when it was hit by an RCAF Voodoo CF-101B taking off. The fuselage of the Viscount was torn open and two cabin occupants were fatally injured, but the Viscount did not catch fire. The Voodoo, however, did, although it climbed to 12,000 feet before the crew ejected safely. On June 13, 1964, on final approach at Malton, *CF-THT* lost power in engines number one and two and swung into the trees. The left wing was torn off at the root and a vast quantity of fuel spilled, but all occupants were rescued; the aircraft was written off. A bizarre incident took place over Windsor on a flight from Toronto to Chicago when one of the Viscount's engines suffered a runaway propeller, and Captain Bob Smuck diverted in order to land at Windsor. But before he could do so, the prop blades separated from the shaft and "walked" across the top of the fuselage, ripping through the metal and killing a passenger. Captain Smuck landed the Viscount without further damage, but at the inquest it was ruled that he had diverted too quickly, exerting too much pressure on the runaway prop and causing it to come loose. The verdict was pilot error.

The Viscount proved to be a public relations coup for TCA and for Vickers. No other airline in North America—not TWA, Eastern or United—flew jet-powered (or propjet as they were then called) airliners at that time. There was, however, great curiosity about the aircraft in the United States, and even the reclusive Howard Hughes showed up at Dorval to be checked out on it by George Lothian. But Lothian's daughter, Heather Chetwynd, remembers her father arriving home each night exasperated that all Hughes wanted to do was circuits around the airport. She admits that her father was "probably driving Hughes nuts, too. George was very attached to his ever-constant pipe." While at Dorval, Hughes lived on board a TWA 1649 Constellation parked nearby, and she points out that "the eccentric Hughes was taping up the windows of the cockpit to keep out the dust. Imagine the horror the man felt when George needed a smoke!" The Hughes Tool Co. eventually bought a Viscount in order to study turboprop airliners.

When Capital and Continental Airlines in the United States both ordered the Viscount in quantity they soon realized what TCA had learned before them—the Viscount was losing out on seat economics. Washington-based Capital Airlines bought seventy-five Viscounts for its high-density Washington–Chicago–New York–Atlanta routes, and although it achieved an 84 percent load factor, it could not compete against Eastern Airlines' larger, slower Constellations or faster Lockheed Electras, and the company went bankrupt on June 1, 1961. As many of its Viscounts were not paid for, seven were returned to Vickers and the others flew in United Airlines colours after that.

With the arrival of the first jets, airlines had a surplus of DC-6s and L1049s that they could now economically assign to their "shuttle" routes. As exceptional an aircraft as it was—and the Viscount was known in the US as "the pilot's plane"—by the mid-1960s time had caught up with it. The growing high density on inter-city routes overwhelmed its passenger-carrying capacity, and it didn't have the range for the medium-length routes. To pack more passengers in, TCA reconfigured its Viscount several times. In 1961, as it was assigned secondary city routes, it converted them to all economy with fifty-four seats, five abreast. After complaints from its premium passengers, in 1962 the company reintroduced twelve first class seats, leaving thirty-nine economy in a fifty-one-seat configuration. Three years later the Viscount became a forty-eight-seat "classless" aircraft with seats four abreast.

The concept of tourist or coach class had been pioneered by American Airlines in an effort to sell off at reduced prices any empty seats on imminently departing flights. It was an innovative way to get rid of seats that were hard to sell because of inconvenient departure or arrival times or because the aircraft was on a "milk run." Between 1949 and 1952 the coach market in the US grew by nine times and soon airlines were devoting whole aircraft to cheap fares. Advertised as a means for the ordinary person to avail himself of a mode of transport normally affordable only by the wealthy, tourist fares owed their birth in part to a rising economy and a surplus of obsolescent aircraft. Paying 30 percent less than the standard, passengers who flew tourist cheerfully put up with dense seating, old aircraft, no free food, no advance reservations and inconvenient flight departures. TCA, however, with its equipment shortage, could not indulge in tourist class and, on its monopoly routes, had no need to. But such was the demand for seats that in September 1953 the North Stars were converted from forty to forty-eight seats, and in January 1954 an exclusively tourist class version began service with fifty-seven to sixty-seven seats.

Suffering from overcrowding on its Viscounts as well, in the spring of 1953 British European Airways approached Vickers with its specifications for a Super Viscount, an aircraft that would be as popular with passengers as the Viscount but could also operate on high-density routes between the major British cities and internationally to the Mediterranean resorts. Trans Canada Airlines too wanted a "big brother" to the Viscount that could carry passengers on its Toronto–Montreal–New York routes and also carry more freight and mail. By a coincidence both airlines' specifications arrived at Vickers together. The first proposal that the manufacturer came up with was a wooden mock-up called the Model V-870, which then went through several changes as Vickers tried to satisfy each airline. BEA wanted a high-wing aircraft like the Fokker F-27 or Handley Page Herald, which would give it greater passenger appeal. TCA didn't want a high wing because of de-icing problems. Vickers then revised the design, giving the mock-up a low wing. When TCA signed a letter of intent with Vickers on December 12, 1956, both the manufacturer and the airlines were conscious of the imminent arrival of jet aircraft, and both knew that, whatever aircraft was designed, it would have a very tight "window" to prove itself.

TCA Facts and Figures: Personnel and Payroll Statistics

	1948	**1949**	**1950**	**1951**
Employees	5,084	5,137	4,904	5,512
% change	N/A	+ 0.01	–4.5	+ 12.4
Payroll	$13,426,610	$16,187,062	$15,864,796	$18,462,734
% change	N/A	+ 20.6	–2.0	+ 16.4
Average monthly wage	$237	$258	$262	$292
% salaries of operating expenses	38.7	39.1	38.6	42.0
Average no. of aircraft	N/A	46.5	46.0	46.0
Average TCA employees per aircraft	N/A	113	110	115
Average miles per employee	14,310	16,077	18,747	20,608

	1952	**1953**	**1954**
Employees	6,224	7,072	7,991
% change	+ 12.9	+ 13.6	+ 13.0
Payroll	$23,240,007	$26,810,644	$30,932,284
% change	+ 25.9	+ 15.4	+ 15.4
Average monthly wage	$324	$330	$340
% salaries of operating expenses	43.9	43.6	45.5
Average no. of aircraft	48.7	48.8	55.1
Average TCA employees per aircraft	123	139	137
Average miles per employee	22,285	22,030	20,884

As director of flight standards, Lothian initiated a safety awareness program for the flight crews that was considered the most advanced in the aviation community. In liaison with the DOT, TCA's engineering department printed up-to-date navigational and instrument approach charts, and the pilots would commit to memory the salient features and the approach, knowing that the co-pilot had the chart at hand. But Lothian thought this procedure much too informal and initiated a review of this vital phase of the flight. TCA's Instrument Approach Verbal Review became a landmark in the industry and went like this:

> **Captain**: This will be an ILS [Instrument Landing System] approach to Runway 23L at Toronto. I will intercept the glide path at 2,500 feet and cross over the outer marker at 1,500 feet. You [the F/O] will report over the outer marker and call me at 100 feet above the Minimum Descent Altitude [MDA] of 300 feet and also call at the MDA, and I will answer "Landing or Go Around." In the event of a go-around, I will apply full power, call for gear up and climb to 2,500 feet, proceeding to the holding pattern at Guelph intersection.

> **First Officer**: I will report over the outer marker. I will call out when 100 feet above and 300 feet MDA.

As this standard review was adaptable to any approach chart, it was a valuable tool for flight deck management. A pilot contemplating an instrument approach uses available weather reports, which by nature can be variable. Hence the descent to a predetermined altitude above the ground. It is at this height that the captain must decide to land or execute a missed approach. At the MDA, the main concern is visibility. Anything less than half a mile can seriously affect orientation during the touchdown and roll-out.

> Aviation celebrated its fiftieth birthday on December 17, 1953, and to commemorate the Wright brothers' flight on that date in 1903, every TCA passenger travelling that day was presented with a special "Golden Anniversary" certificate. The Wright brothers' wing warping/aileron legal battles with the Aerial Experiment Association had almost strangled aviation at its birth, but inadvertently they had created Canada's first aviation manufacturing venture, which was run by J.A.D. McCurdy, the first man to fly in Canada.

In fifty years of advancement, what was still constant about commercial aviation in Canada was winter and the de-icing of aircraft. With DC-3s and even Viscounts, this had not improved since the 1930s, and George Brien, Stephenville operation agent, remembers that all TCA stations had a good supply of brooms and mops to brush clean the wings and mop them down with standard de-icing fluid (SDF). The only modern feature at a small post might be the use of a backpack sprayer, which held about 3 gallons of fluid. With the right tailwind the operator could hand-pump a tiny spray about 4 or 5 feet; with a headwind most of the spray would end up in his face and clothes.

> One snowy day in the mid-fifties at YFC we were having a problem keeping ahead of the falling snow on the wings of a DC-3 so the captain suggested that we try the wing covers. These were canvas covers that we slipped over the wings on an overnight layover to protect the surfaces from freezing rain accumulations. How this was going to get the flight airborne was a little vague to us at the time, but the covers were slipped on and tied down and the passengers loaded on board. The captain requested a startup and slowly taxied out for takeoff followed by the ground crew. When we got the nod, the covers were quickly pulled off, takeoff power was applied and away it went. When the Viscount arrived, spraying and mopping from the ground was a poor option. The use of a forklift and basket made it easier, but a spray job meant you were wet all over. The only way the SDF fluid could be recycled in those days was to wring out your clothes after you came in from a spraying.

In spite of all the politics surrounding the marriage of airlines and railways, TCA's divorce from the CNR was actually a quiet, gradual process that provoked only fleeting media comment. And it began not in the boardroom but in the public relations department. Beginning in 1949, the airline had taken over its own advertising, featuring its own employees in many newspaper layouts. The next department to leave the CNR fold was stores. When the airline was established in 1937, it did not buy in sufficient quantity to warrant placing orders independently of the CNR, and all purchasing had been done by the railway's employees. But in 1952, with its requirements ranging to 25 million gallons of gas, 118,000 pencils, 3,900 Benzedrex inhalers and 3.5 million paper cups, TCA's board of directors approved the formation of the airline's own department of purchases and stores. Howard C. Cotterell, the company's former director of research, was made general manager; K.E. Olson became manager of purchases and R.J. Needham manager of stores. The airline also wisely took two men from the CNR's purchasing department who had been working on its affairs: W.H. Payne in Montreal and E.G. Richardson in Winnipeg. In 1952, for the first time, all TCA purchases appeared on the company's own ledgers. Revenue accounting and insurance followed quite naturally in 1958, and on June 24 of the next year TCA retained its own legal counsel. By 1963 the only positions that the railway and airline shared were the senior medical officer and corporate secretary.

But other changes were being imposed by Parliament on the airline's management. Another series of amendments to the Trans Canada Air Lines Act had been passed in 1953, the most critical one being that which regulated the company's board of directors. The number of directors was increased from seven to nine, with five to be elected by shareholders and four appointed by the Governor-in-Council, though these would no longer come from the ranks of the CNR or senior civil servants. Both changes were the result of criticism levelled at C.P. Edwards, who had been serving as a TCA director while employed as deputy minister of transport.

The old question of regional representation on the TCA board had also come up too often in the House—especially during the CCF's ascendancy. Howe had argued that members should be based in Montreal or Ottawa because of the difficulty of directors attending meetings from distant cities, but with restrictions on air travel gone after the war, this was no longer valid. To counter this, when McGregor was made a director he was listed as being from both Winnipeg and Montreal. The first effects of the 1953 amendments were seen when Symington retired five years later and his place was taken not by a CNR director but by E.W. Bickle, a Toronto stockbroker. The following year when W.G. Parker left, W.G. Stewart, a Moncton barrister, replaced him, and when C.P. Edwards (one of the original "Dawn to Dusk" gang, along with Symington) retired, C.P. McEwen, a retired RCAF air vice-marshal from Toronto, was appointed in his place.

The company's capital was also reorganized during the 1950s, with the CNR surrendering capital stock in exchange for a $20 million bond, and the airline was allowed to deduct from its income for tax purposes the interest payable on this bond. Now the airline was also permitted to own, lease or operate motor vehicles and hotels. The 1953 amendment also repealed two of the original TCA clauses: first, that the company's contract could be amended by the Governor-in-Council on the joint recommendation of the minister and postmaster general, and second, that a subsidy should be paid to the airline equal to the annual deficit, although this clause had not been utilized since March 31, 1942.

While a 1945 amendment to the TCA Act had called for the board of directors to "make a report annually to Parliament [concerning] the results of their operations and such other information as appears to them to be of public interest," under the Financial Administration Act of 1951, TCA, as with all publicly owned enterprises, had to submit its estimates of capital expenditure for approval—in its case to the ministers of transport and finance and the Governor-in-Council. The procedure was for the capital budget to be approved by the minister of transport, who then laid it before Parliament for its edification. The airline also received some attention when the Canadian National Railways Financing and Guarantee Act came before the House. How all these myriad acts and amendments evolved into the necessity for Gordon McGregor to make an annual appearance before the House of Commons Sessional Committee on Railways, Airlines and Shipping, he didn't quite know, but it became a source of some bemusement to him. This committee was drawn from MPs in numbers roughly proportional to the parties' representation in the House, and it met to consider the annual report of the preceding year, then later (if the report was satisfactory) to recommend it to Parliament for adoption. This was regardless of the fact that Cabinet had long since approved of the report, the budget and the operating expenditures and that many of its items were already in progress.

TCA North Star flying over post-war Ottawa: The airline took delivery of its first M-1 North Star on November 16, 1946.

In the bad old days of deficit operations, these sessions were often long and acrimonious, and McGregor was quite relieved that he could count on Howe to make an appearance in these "Donnybrooks," defending the airline's right to make its own decisions—especially in the case of the headquarters' move from Winnipeg. But McGregor himself had little fear of MPs, especially as they wasted the opportunity to question him on policy by busying themselves on trivia like the reasons why pipe smoking was banned on TCA flights and why the washrooms at the airport (usually the one in their constituency) were so dirty. (In answer to the latter question he enjoyed pointing out that airports were the responsibility of the DOT and not TCA.) A typical session of the committee went like this:

> **Mr. Smith** (Calgary South): I do not suppose you are considering any improvements to the Constellation's kitchens, for example?
>
> **Mr. McGregor**: We are installing radar on the Constellations as the Report suggested. We have installed wingtip tanks on all but one of them.
>
> **Mr. Smith** (Calgary South): You are not improving the kitchens of the Constellations. I have heard that the kitchens are substandard.
>
> **Mr. McGregor**: I have not heard that they are substandard.
>
> **Mr. Smith** (Calgary South): You have only one heating unit for coffee.
>
> **Mr. McGregor**: We have only one heating unit?
>
> **Mr. Smith** (Calgary South): You have only one heating element.
>
> **Mr. McGregor**: I have not heard that the coffee-making capacity was inadequate.[10]

To save everyone embarrassment, McGregor later asked that the questions be restricted to policy matters and not operational details. But being Gordon McGregor, he left nothing to chance: with the help of Bill Harvey he had the staff prepare detailed reports and kept voluminous statistics for every question that might be asked. He was amused to know that what commanded the most attention from the members was their lobbying—in public and private—for passes on TCA to enable them to visit their constituencies more frequently.

It was to McGregor's advantage that the mercurial Donald Gordon, president of the CNR, had to undergo this trial just before the airline did, and he could be counted on for "lively debate," so that the committee members had less energy when it came time for the TCA's turn. While McGregor liked the publicity that the hearings brought, apparently he felt that it was a cross between farce and inquisition, especially since some of the committee members also expressed doubts as to the usefulness of the exercise. On several occasions after the morning session was over, the airline would take the MPs on a 1¹/2 hour flight over the then new St. Lawrence Seaway, depositing them back at the House at 3:30 to be in time to approve the Annual Report. All in all, parliamentary scrutiny of TCA was a depressing record of trivialities, hardly auspicious in a constitutional democracy. But given the Liberal dominance in the House and Howe's fearsome reputation, it could hardly have been otherwise.

The year 1954 began well for the airline. The Bristol Freighters were in service, the first of the Constellations and Viscounts were expected and the fleet shortage crisis would soon abate. Service to Mexico City had been taken over from KLM; flights to Montego Bay (Jamaica) and Sudbury, Ontario, were about to begin. The airline had sought diligently to accommodate all that was required of it. Two new directors on the board were far removed from Montreal or Ottawa—W.J. Parker was from Winnipeg and Frank M. Ross was the lieutenant governor of faraway British Columbia. On February 1, 1954, TCA proved that it could change, that it was sensitive to public opinion, by reducing its cargo rates by 10 percent in some cases and 30 percent in others, and by introducing the first tourist class fares, set at 20 percent less than first class. That summer two-daily all-tourist class flights using fifty-seven-seat North Stars were scheduled to join the four first class daily transcontinentals. Then, as the

Until the ReserVec computer system, TCA "Space Control" handled all seat sales manually.

summer traffic on the Atlantic was expected to slacken and the last of the Connies were delivered, more North Stars could be reconfigured to provide either a fifty-two-seat or sixty-two-seat service. Other North Stars were to be stripped as pure freighters, allowing the airline to sell off the Bristol 170s. Meanwhile, the ATB had rejected applications by PWA and CPA to operate out of their geographic regions, though having tasted blood it was expected that both MacLaren and McConachie would return.

Of more immediate concern was the rising number of military flights in commercial airspace. On March 29, 1954, Bill English wrote to Major R. Dodds, the controller of civil aviation in Ottawa, to report that on March 21, at 1724 EST, TCA's Captain W.C. Boyes in Flight 300 had been "buzzed" by two RCAF CF-100 fighters over the Hudson Radio beacon. Visibility had been less than a mile in light snow, and both fighters came within 100 feet of the aircraft before peeling off and climbing out of sight. When Captain Boyes checked with ATC, he was told that there were two RCAF B-25 bombers in the TCA position but at a higher altitude, waiting to be intercepted by the fighters. Apparently the radar had got the TCA flight mixed up with them and the fighters were vectored in on the passenger plane. English reminded Dodds that the DOT had specified that this sort of exercise was only to be carried out in Visual Flight Rule (VFR) conditions and that these certainly weren't.

CALPA, in the meantime, was fighting to change VFR conditions, along with rates of pay and augmentation of the pension plan with an equity retirement fund. Unlike their American colleagues, TCA pilots were paid under a flat pay agreement as five-day-a-week employees, an agreement that did not differentiate between a workday that was five hours long and one that was eighteen hours long. "The management felt entitled," wrote F.E.W. Smith, "to the full contract hours and accepted little responsibility for the amount of time it took to get them...waiting at airports or in hotels for the next leg of the flight."[11] Already unhappy with their salaries in comparison with those earned in the United States, led by Captain Jim Foy in 1955, the union liaised with ALPA on formula pay. The subsequent negotiations with TCA management proved easier than with its own members, many of whom remembered the old days in bush operations before flat pay.

In 1956 TCA signed a contract to "formula pay" its pilots, and Foy was elected president of CALPA just as pilot dissatisfaction boiled over. The first formula pay contract barely raised pilot salaries by 3 percent, and while the senior pilots on North Stars now "could make more money, they had to fly 120 hours more annually for it, and if they lost trips along the way, actually took a pay cut." There were also rumblings about the seniority issue at bases like Vancouver, where there were concentrations of senior pilots who took the best flying blocks and left "the dogs for the juniors."[12] The pension equity plan, however, was more successful, and on May 12, 1958, TCA management agreed to CALPA's proposal for an equity fund, the first set up in Canada.

Comparison between United Airlines and TCA Captain Rates, 85 hrs 1949–54

Year	United Airlines	TCA	Wage Gap %
1949	$1,260	$850	48.2
1950	$1,260	$930	35.5
1951	$1,434	$1,005	42.3
1952	$1,434	$1,030	39.2
1953	$1,527	$1,050	45.4
1954	$1,635	$1,160	41.0

F.E.W. Smith, *The First Thirty Years: A History of the Canadian Air Lines Pilot's Association* (1970), p. 33.

Seventeen years after the company had begun with 2 Electras and 71 employees, there were 81 aircraft and 8,737 employees. Of these employees 6,977 were male and 1,760 female. The largest group were mechanics (2,483) followed by clerical staff (1,069) and ramp service (798). The 226 first officers and 221 captains flew the 27 DC-3s, 22 North Stars, 7 Super Constellations, 22 Viscounts and 3 Bristol Freighters.

TCA's guardian angel, C.D. Howe. He left
public office on June 21, 1957.

CHAPTER 12

April 8, 1954, was a bright, sunny day in Moose Jaw. Mrs. F. Anderson was standing outside the front door of her home at 1036 - 6th Avenue, shaking out the rugs, when she saw a passenger plane approaching and stopped to watch it "because you don't see one like that at that hour of the morning. While watching, I noticed a yellow plane approaching from the southeast, and it seemed to be flying in a straight flight and would pass over the top of the passenger plane."

Harold Braaten, the foreman of Bird Construction, Moose Jaw, had just stepped out of his office on 7th Avenue at 10:00 that morning. "I happened to glance up in the sky and saw a big North Star flying west. I guessed it was around 5,000 feet. I also saw a Harvard plane about 200 to 300 feet southwest and it was flying in a northeast direction."

The aircraft was TCA C-4-1 *CF-TFW*, formerly CPA's *CF-CPP*, *Empress of Hong Kong*, on scheduled Flight 9 on the Montreal–Toronto–Winnipeg–Calgary–Vancouver route. It had left Winnipeg at 8:58 CST that day, already 7 hours and 33 minutes late as a result of thunderstorms in Toronto. On board were thirty-one passengers, including five company employees or dependants. The crew were Captain I.A. Bell, F/O D. Guthrie and steward L. Penner and stewardess M. Quinney. The flight plan specified IFR, and Flight 9 had been cleared via Airway Green 1 to Swift Current and then direct to Calgary at 6,000 feet altitude. It was to cross Portage at 4,000 feet or higher as traffic flight control air space reservation covered a five-mile radius around Portage from 3,000 feet altitude and below.

At 9:26 CST, TCA Winnipeg radio received the message, "Over Portage at 6,000 feet. Visual." At 9:54 TCA Winnipeg and Regina radio simultaneously received the message, "Over Rivers at 9:54 CST at 6,000 feet. Visual. Estimate Broadview at 10:24 CST." At 10:25 CST Regina radio heard, "Over Broadview at 10:24 CST at 6,000 feet. Visual. Estimate Regina at 10:52 CST." At 10:52 CST Regina radio received—and Winnipeg, Calgary and Vancouver radio checked— "Over Regina at 10:50 CST at 6,000 feet. Visual. Estimate Swift Current at 11:30 CST." That was the last transmission from TCA Flight 9.

At 10:57 CST an RCAF Harvard No. 3309 took off from Runway 13 at Moose Jaw Airport. The sole occupant of the aircraft, Acting Pilot Officer T.A. Thorrat, was on a navigational training flight from Moose Jaw return via Raymore, Hanley and Beachy. His flight plan specified VFR and called for an altitude of 9,000 feet at Raymore, 8,500 feet at Hanley, 8,000 feet over Beachy and back over Moose Jaw at 7,500 feet. His course crossed Airway Green 1 at the northeast side of the city of Moose Jaw.

Mrs. Anderson: "I looked down, bent over to pick something up and then looked back up and it was just as I looked up that I saw them come together. The yellow plane seemed to hit the tip of the left wing of the passenger plane."

Harold Braaten: "I could not tell if the Harvard was higher than the North Star. I turned away and about a second or so later I heard a loud noise and then saw a flash. I glanced up at the sky again and the Harvard looked as though it had torn the far motor off the left wing of the North Star."

Mrs. Anderson: "The wing came off the passenger plane after the collision, and after the wing dropped off there was an explosion. At the same time the tail fell off. It seemed to take the tail a long time to come down—it just drifted slowly down. The passenger plane continued in straight flight until after the first explosion and then it burst into flames. After the tail fell off, it nosed up—not right vertical—but the rear portion was lower than the front. I could see things dropping from the rear of the plane where the tail had been knocked off."

Harold Braaten: "The right wing then fell off and the plane tipped over on its left side and fell to the ground. I did not see the Harvard after it struck the ground. I was too busy watching the North Star."

Mrs. Anderson: "It seemed to me as though the passenger plane was steered for a time following the collision—even following the explosion it seemed to be steered for a while—as though the pilot was trying to steer it north of the city."

At 11:29 CST, Winnipeg TCA radio was informed by air traffic control that a North Star had crashed at Moose Jaw at 11:03 CST, and that they had no other North Star in that vicinity other than Flight 9. Winnipeg TCA radio then advised air traffic control that Flight 9 was now overdue at Swift Current. At 11:52 CST, air traffic control advised Winnipeg TCA radio the location of the crash was 1324 - 3rd Avenue NE in Moose Jaw and that one house was burning but that a nearby school had not been hit. At 11:55 CST, passing TCA Flight 802 was requested to contact Flight 9 but the crew were unable to do so. At 12:03 CST Winnipeg radio was advised that an RCAF Harvard was involved in the crash, and Canadian Press announced that the two aircraft had collided and that there were no survivors. A Moose Jaw woman also died when the wreckage from the crash landed on the house where she was working.

Within ten hours of the accident, the company announced that all next-of-kin had been located and personally told of the tragedy by a TCA staff member accompanied by someone from the Red Cross. The investigation into the crash was led by Baldwin "Baldy" Torrell, who was dispatched by Vice-President Bill English to the crash site along with Jim McLean, Tommy Gilmour and Stan MacDonald. The probable cause of the crash, ruled the Accident Investigation Board, was the failure on the part of pilots of both aircraft to maintain a proper lookout. But the responsibility for keeping out of the way lay with the RCAF pilot officer, who had the North Star on his own right side. Further, he had crossed the Airway and climbed through altitudes normally reserved for commercial aircraft. However, the board was unable to determine whether the window post on the left side of the TCA aircraft would have hidden the Harvard trainer from view.[1]

In Remembrance of

Ian Bell, Captain, Vancouver

Allan Craig, Passenger Service Supervisor, Vancouver

James Crossen, Budget Assistant Vancouver

Douglas Guthrie, First Officer, Vancouver

Mr. Carol Nelson, Passenger Agent, Toronto

Louis Penner, Steward, Vancouver

Majorie Quinney, Stewardess, Vancouver

Andrew Smart, Lead Stock keeper, Winnipeg

Trans Canada Air Lines personnel who lost their lives in the tragic accident at Moose Jaw on April 8th.

The Company extends its sincere sympathy to the families of these men and women in their sad bereavement.

Between Ourselves

Bill English later wrote to Jim Bain, "At Moose Jaw, Baldy, Jim and Stan worked night and day on the examination of the wreckage, the photographing of it and assembling the report. They would be out as long as there was daylight and longer, and I would drop into their room before I went to bed, sometime after midnight, only to find them reviewing the work of the day and planning their tomorrow. Baldy made an excellent witness at the DOT and RCAF Hearings. He was asked two or three technical questions... and I think rather confounded his questioners. Tommy Gilmour looked after the disposal of the wreckage, and before I left, the mayor and the chief of police complimented me on the way that Tommy had cleaned up. Looking back over the

A view of Canadian Pacific's Empress of Hong Kong *before it was sold to TCA to become* CF-TFW *in 1952. In spite of a series of protests to the RCAF, airliners still underwent close intercepts by enthusiastic fighter pilots and trainees. The inevitable happened: this aircraft fell victim to a Harvard collision in 1954, with the loss of all on board.* Canadair photo

whole affair, what pleased me most was the fact that our people who were sent to Moose Jaw seemed to know exactly what to do and how to do it. We in TCA are proud of our engineering and maintenance department, and it lived up to its reputation in the handling of the tragic circumstances of the Moose Jaw accident."

What didn't please Gordon McGregor was the grudging attitude of the Department of National Defence (DND). The airline was prepared to absorb the loss of the North Star and its earning power but would not pay the third-party claims involved. When it became clear that some of these would be in large amounts, the minister of defence objected to the payments being charged to the defence vote and suggested that the Department of Finance cover it in a separate vote. When finance refused, the matter came back full circle to TCA. Howe promised to bring the matter to Cabinet, but what settled it was McGregor's warning that if litigation was brought against the Crown, airline personnel would be subpoenaed as witnesses. The Department of Defence then settled the claims in aggregate payments of $951,331.

A sign of the company's maturity was the first retirement on its pension plan. On March 1, 1955, after seventeen years service, John Roy Douglass, chief inspector at aircraft overhaul, Dorval, retired. He had joined TCA in Winnipeg on April 4, 1938, as one of the "metal bashers." On August 6, the first member in the engineering department retired. Francis Slaney Smith had begun his apprenticeship in engineering in Edwardian England, been a soldier in World War I and joined TCA on February 4, 1938, as a draftsman.

Many TCA employees had fought in World War II but none had given service quite like that of Rodney Dove, a Vancouver passenger agent. In September 1955 the thirty-four-year-old suddenly received a cheque for $700 from the British Admiralty, courtesy of the recent book and movie called *Above Us the Waves*. A Royal Naval lieutenant during the war, Dove had been a pilot on a two-man "Chariot" torpedo. Launched from a submarine, the two frogmen would ride the torpedo into an enemy harbour and fasten the warhead to the hull of the ship. Then they would set the fuse and attempt to ride the Chariot back to the submarine before the warhead exploded. Dove was captured on operations off Palermo, Sicily, and spent two and a half years "behind the wire." For some reason his operational pay stopped while he was "in the bag" (his words); after the movie prompted an investigation, the cheque had been sent to cover his back pay. The Doves said they planned to spend the windfall on their two-year-old son.

Grant McConachie of CPA must have watched the introduction of the Viscount to North America with some rancour because his fabled good fortune seemed to have run out. One of CPA's Comets crashed at Karachi on its way to Australia on March 3, 1953, and the other was cancelled. The South Pacific flights were draining the CPR coffers so that on May 15, 1954, CPA closed down its Auckland service. The transcontinental route was still off limits to CPA, as were the major European capitals served by TCA: London, Paris and Dusseldorf. But Amsterdam, Lisbon, Madrid and Rome were not, and flights to the first two would require no government intervention as Canada had signed bilateral air agreements with the Portuguese in 1947 and the Dutch in 1948, and a Canadian carrier had not been designated to either of them. Canada had also signed with the Swedish government on June 27, 1947, and after November 15, 1954, when Scandinavian Airline System inaugurated a service over the North Pole from Copenhagen to Los Angeles through Winnipeg, it came as no surprise that McConachie was able to convince the new minister of transport, George Marler, to designate CPA to fly Vancouver–Yellowknife–Amsterdam on January 21, 1955. Flying the Great Circle route from western Canada to Europe had been another boyhood dream for McConachie, but he made very clear that "the polar route would bypass TCA's Atlantic preserve." Marler too reassured McGregor that in its application CPA had indicated that Vancouver would be the only point in Canada that it chose to serve. Both the minister and McConachie, it seemed, had forgotten that this move contravened the policy announced by Lionel Chevrier in 1952 when the airlines were given spheres of influence: TCA's was to be the United States and the Atlantic, and CPA's the Pacific and South America. Soon, McGregor predicted, McConachie would say that as there were so few passengers to be picked up at Yellowknife, could he use Edmonton instead?

But McGregor had always known that McConachie desperately wanted TCA's Toronto–Mexico City service—a route that he himself could see no future in—while he coveted CPA's Quebec services. Allowing CPA into Toronto, however, was hardly a threat to TCA as that city was still isolated from CPA's western network. That is why one September morning in 1955 the TCA DC-3 *CF-TEF* was making a survey flight from Montreal northeast over the province of Quebec—traditional Canadian Pacific Airlines terrain; in charge was operations manager Frank Young. At the same time another TCA DC-3 carried Herb Seagrim, general manager of operations, over Quebec City, Bagotville and Sept Iles. Both aircraft were filled with regional representatives, flight dispatch, telecommunications staff, and a CPA district superintendent. Afterwards, the ATB arranged an amicable trade in which CPA would give up its Quebec City–North Shore network for TCA's Toronto–Mexico City route. Effective November 1, the route exchange would mean that Quebec City, Saguenay, Sept Iles, Val d'Or, Rouyn/Noranda and Earlton would become part of the national route pattern.

TCA's all-cargo transcontinental service began on May 2, 1955, with five flights weekly between Montreal and Vancouver, using three cargo-converted North Stars, the first flight in *CF-TFV* flown by Capt. J.R. Fisher. As a result, that December the Bristol Freighters were put up for sale. All three, along with the DC-3 freighter *CF-TET*, went for $825,000 to Central Northern Airways, a company that would soon merge with Arctic Wings to form Transair. Two of the Freighters were written off within a year of leaving TCA: *CF-TFZ* broke through the ice at Beaver Lodge Lake, NWT, on May 30, 1956, falling on its port wing and crushing its side. On June 18, 1956, while waiting to be unloaded at Povungnituk, NWT, *CF-TFY* also broke through the ice, sank in 40 feet of water, and had to be abandoned. *CF-TFX* went on to fame and to make Max Ward's fortune. Resold to Wardair, it became the first aircraft to land on Melville Island beach with a D4 Caterpillar and at the North Pole in 1958. "Its very versatility caused its demise," wrote a pilot who flew *CF-TFX* in Wardair service, "as operators and pilots would on occasion push it to extremes." Designed to fly military vehicles across the English Channel, it gamely took heavy mining equipment into remote areas, and when the ice roads were closed and ferries icebound, *CF-TFX* was Yellowknife's lifeline, airlifting food from Hay River across Great Slave Lake. Reminiscent of the Canadian Airways Ju.52 "Flying Boxcar" in the 1930s, *CF-TFX* plodded on until 1968, when its main spar became too expensive to replace. The ex-TCA "ugly duckling" was retired at Yellowknife Airport, having accomplished more in adverse conditions in the Canadian North than any swan.

The year 1956 promised to be more prosperous for TCA: in late December 1955 its rival was denied rights to fly to Paris, and in January 1956 McConachie's campaign for an Edmonton–Winnipeg–Amsterdam service was squashed. Both McConachie and McGregor wanted to get into the eternal city of Rome as much as Hannibal had, and on February 28, 1956, TCA asked the

*Top: DC-4M-2 CF-TFF at Dorval Airport, Montreal, with passengers disembarking,
1956. It was the end of the heyday of the North Stars.* Peter Marshall photo.
*Bottom: The same aircraft, assigned to all-freight services. Note the crossover exhausts
have been installed earlier, the freight designation added to the TCA logos and the
windows blanked out. The aircraft served in this function until sold to World Wide
Airways in November 1961.*

A Wardair Bristol Freighter, mounted on a pylon as a monument to northern flyers in Yellowknife, NWT. This was a TCA aircraft acquired by Wardair and reputed actually to have landed at the North Pole. Graham Wragg photo

ATB for a service to that city. This provided the opportunity for Marler to lay out the government's newest policy. "Competition is only useful for what it achieves. If it achieves greater efficiency, lower costs and charges and better service, it is an admirable principle to insist upon. But if it achieves overexpansion of expensive facilities with a division of the market among competing carriers, it will lead to heavy burdens on carriers, shippers and taxpayers alike." Proving that little had changed, the minister had quoted from the Duff Royal Commission Report on Railways in Canada written in 1932 to mediate between the CNR and CPR.

In August 1956 CPA was refused permission to carry the passengers to London that it had brought from Canada to Amsterdam. McConachie then complained—with what McGregor called Alice-in-Wonderland logic—that his Vancouver–Amsterdam traffic was being encroached upon by TCA because it was licensed to serve London, and that CPA needed to be "saved from its ruinous competition." Refused permission for flights across Canada, the CPA president then hoped to operate around TCA with a Vancouver–Los Angeles–Chicago–New York flight, but his lobbying for a revision of the US bilateral air agreement was blocked in November 1956. The Americans had always doubted the true nationality of CPA, as defined by the Chicago Convention of 1944, because it was a subsidiary of the CPR, much of which was owned by shareholders who were not Canadian. Using the ownership clause, the US government had earlier recorded its right to object to CPA operating an international service between Whitehorse and Fairbanks. This was music to McGregor's ears. Even if the Canadian government had no backbone as far as CPA was concerned, the Americans had proved that they had.

The Avro Jetliner apart, the commercial jet age began in North America on July 15, 1954, when test pilot "Tex" Johnson took Boeing's prototype of the famous 707 series, the Dash 80 on a successful ninety-minute flight. TCA's choice for its first jet airliner lay between the Boeing 707 and the Douglas DC-8, the latter handicapped by its lack of jet experience and still working on its jet design with lengthy wind-tunnel testing. Boeing, on the other hand, had taken the lead in jet technology with their military aircraft, some of which had served as a test bed for the Dash 80. Boeing was better known as a builder of military aircraft, and its reputation with the airlines had not been improved by the unsuccessful Stratocruiser. They were also aware that while Boeing might have experience in swept-wing technology, both the B-47 and B-52 were, unlike the Dash 80, high-wing aircraft. However, such was the prestige of Pan American Airways that in 1955, when Juan Trippe ordered twenty-five of the first jet aircraft to come off both manufacturers' production lines, many other airlines followed suit, and the race to select an engine for their choice of air frame began.

Because of the Cold War, all US jet engine technology was still secret: the US government was not about to make the same mistake that the British had. This hindered sales at Pratt & Whitney, as it could not be very forthcoming to potential buyers about the characteristics of its J-57, a civilian version of the military JT3, eight of which powered Strategic Air Command's B-52. Rolls Royce, on the other hand, had no such restrictions. The British critically needed to get into supplying jet engines for the new era in transportation, and Rolls Royce had developed the Conway "by-pass" or turbo-fan engine. It differs from the straight jet in that low-velocity air is forced through a duct, by-passing the main jet stream and rejoining it at the exhaust nozzle beyond the combustion chamber and turbines. The velocity of gas emitted from the main jet nozzle is slowed by mixing with the by-pass air, and the entire propulsive exhaust—including the by-pass air—leaves the engine at a slower speed but from a larger nozzle than it would in a straight jet. This results in greater propulsive efficiency and less noise. Rolls Royce had built its first by-pass jet engine in 1950, and its Conways had powered the Handley Page Victor bomber. By 1955 it was ready to offer this engine on the commercial market.

Early in 1956 TCA sent a team to tour both the Boeing and Douglas plants. Because of their purchase of DC-3s, the Canadians were warmly welcomed at Long Beach, meeting old friends. The reception at Boeing, with which TCA had not dealt before, was less hospitable, possibly because precisely at that moment the company was in the process of moving its facilities from Boeing Field to Renton. Interestingly, Vickers also sent its observers, George Edwards (who had been awarded the Daniel Guggenheim medal for "the introduction into commercial service of the first turbine powered aircraft) and Jock Bryce. When it came down to choosing Boeing or Douglas, it was Edwards who advised McGregor that Boeing was further ahead in jet technology than Douglas. Given the same engines, there was really little difference between the Douglas and Boeing entries in speed, performance, payload and seating, but TCA considered the DC-8 more structurally sound and knew that it could be stretched. The Boeing 707 could not. Clayton Glenn recalls that at a dinner hosted by Boeing at the Montreal Forest and Stream Club, McGregor met him in the men's washroom and said, "Which aircraft should we buy, Clayt?" Glenn told him that Boeing, with an aircraft already flying, was less of a risk. At the same time Douglas's order book wasn't as backed up and they had a good after-sales service program. After months of comparative analysis between the Boeing 707 and the Douglas DC-8 equipped with alternatively the Pratt & Whitney J57, the J75 or the Rolls Royce Conway by-pass engine, on April 28, 1956, the airline placed a "wire" of intent for four DC-8s to be powered by the Rolls Royce Conway engine. This was followed up on May 9 with a public announcement of the purchase of four jet airliners plus an option for two more. On July 18, 1956, Douglas received a firm order for delivery in 1960. The price was $5,976,000 for each aircraft, the whole investment with associated spare parts amounting to $28 million. Capable of carrying 120 passengers and three tons of cargo, the DC-8 cruised at 550 mph at about 35,000 feet. The inevitable press release stated it was capable of flying from Vancouver to Toronto in 4 hours and 10 minutes and from Montreal to London in 6 hours and 10 minutes. Thankfully for TCA, the combination of Rolls Royce engines with a Douglas airframe for the second time passed unnoticed by the press, the travails of the North Stars still being a sensitive point.

The decision to choose DC-8s had been made by Jim Bain and Jack Dyment on the carefully considered opinion that the Conway-powered DC-8 would better meet TCA's long-range pattern, and in spite of the knowledge that the Boeing 707 would be available ahead of the DC-8. The Conway had a current rating of 17,500 lbs thrust, which could be increased by modifications later to 18,500 lbs with improved fuel consumption. Eventually TCA as Air Canada would operate eleven Conway powered DC-8s, beginning with *CF-TJA* to *CF-TJK*, before switching to the Pratt & Whitney JT3D turbo-fan engines for the DC-8-53s in 1963.

The engine order disappointed Pratt & Whitney Canada, still hurting that TCA had opted for the Rolls Royce Merlin engine and now having to deal with CPA and its DC-6Bs. With a branch plant at Longueuil, outside Montreal, they employed several hundred Canadians and had provided TCA with years of engine maintenance during its Liberator and DC-3 programs. But the reason for the combination that TCA (and CPA and Alitalia) chose was that the Conway

Conway-powered DC-8, characterized by a lack of visible exhaust on takeoff and always an unimpressive sight as the wheels come up. Note the sound-suppressor rings slid back on the engine nacelles: they were usually moved forward during flight.

was considered superior to the J75 pure jet in engine fuel, oil and anti-icing systems, weight, direct operating costs, and development potential. Though Douglas initially doubted that Rolls Royce would have the Conway operational in time, the British came through, and as with the Merlin, provided TCA with a never-be-sorry clause, guaranteeing that the cost of the Conway engine would be no greater than the equivalent cost of an engine made in the United States. All overhaul work on the engines was guaranteed to be done at TCA's new overhaul base in Montreal. By 1961 McGregor's dream of the world's first all-turbine air fleet would be a reality. All TCA aircraft—the DC-8 with the Conway, the Vanguard with the Tyne and the Viscount with the Dart—would be using Rolls Royce engines.

The rental of five floors of office space in the International Aviation building (IAB) was costing the company $128,291 per annum, and with the agreement scheduled to expire in September 1954, the company began looking for suitable accommodation. The airline was, however, still tied to the CNR, which had ambitious plans for its Montreal headquarters. In 1927, when Sir Henry Thornton had been president of the CNR, he had planned to build a business complex directly above the company's main Montreal station, and the site had been marked for almost thirty years by a cavernous pit, known to Montrealers as the "Dorchester Street Hole." In 1956 Donald Gordon, president of the CNR, took the first step toward making Thornton's dream a reality by hiring William Zeckendorf, an architect and head of the New York firm Webb & Knapp, to submit a plan for the Hole. He came up with a smaller version of New York's Rockefeller Center, and the railway board approved it a year later. The heart of Place Ville Marie was to be a forty-two-storey cruciform skyscraper, two floors of which would house TCA's entire head office, and moving day from the company's present location at the IAB nearby was slated for October 1961.

News that company headquarters was to move so close to the IAB must have come as a relief to TCA's six mail boys, employed to deliver and pick up 27,000 pieces of mail daily in the surrounding area. Cogs in the TCA wheel that few knew about, eight times every day they took the mail from the 175-slot sorting rack in the mail room and delivered it on foot to twenty-seven downtown addresses. Collectively they walked about 10,000 miles annually or about 10 miles daily; the exception was the teletype runner (they took turns in this job), who walked/ran 15 miles daily, handling an average of 12,000 teletypes during an eight-hour shift.

After the euphoria of planning for Place Ville Marie, of choosing the DC-8 and of beating back CPA's encroachments, the year 1956 ended badly for the airline. On December 9, 1956, North Star *CF-TFD*, Flight 810-9, headed out of Vancouver for Toronto at 6:10 p.m. PST with a crew of three and fifty-nine passengers. A cruising altitude of 19,000 feet was selected, and because of icing and turbulence, permission was granted by ATC to maintain at 21,000 feet. At 6:52 p.m. the captain reported a fire in number two engine and said that he was shutting it down and returning to Vancouver. At 6:53 he reported that he was turning southwest and losing altitude fast, and he requested immediate clearance to get down. This was given and at 7:01, ATC asked Flight 810 if they would be able to hold at 14,000 feet and the reply was affirmative. At this time the captain on Flight 4, which was also in the vicinity, advised 810 that conditions were poor at lower altitudes and that they were encountering strong downdrafts and icing at 11,000 to 13,000 feet. At 7:10, Flight 810 stated that he was near Hope, BC, and requested permission to descend to 10,000 feet, and ATC cleared him to cross Vancouver at 8,000 feet. The acknowledgement of this clearance was the last transmission of Flight 810. The TCA tape showed that the tone of voice on the radio did not suggest undue concern. The final radar plot indicated that the North Star was 21 miles southeast of the Hope beacon. Nothing more was seen or heard of Flight 810 for months.

Speculation mounted that the aircraft had disappeared into the ocean. Then on May 12, 1957, a party of mountaineers climbing Mount Slesse discovered part of an aircraft at the 7,600 foot level. The coroner and an RCMP party reached the crash site on September 11, 1957, to remove the remains of twenty-eight bodies. The impact had reduced the North Star to small pieces with many nuts, bolts and washers embedded in the crevices in the cliff face. Only one seat belt was fastened, indicating that whatever happened, had happened suddenly. The cause of the aircraft being at that altitude—that is, low enough to strike Mount Slesse—remains unknown, but while flying on three engines it may have encountered either severe icing, turbulence, downdrafts or a combination of all three.[2]

In the spring of 1957 George Brien's transfer to Yarmouth, NS, came through. The RCAF had abandoned the airport there after the war, and when the municipal authorities refused to accept it, the DOT had been forced to take it over. "This was a small town with the airport within walking distance along an unpaved road," Brien recalled. Staff were station manager Jimmy Ames, operations agents Jim Moore, Fred Boddington, "Scotty" Stewart and Jim Greig. The mechanic was Ed Morrison and load agent "Les" Falle. With the tourist traffic from Boston in the summer there were two DC-3 flights in daily. "Many of the TCA pilots in those days had done bush flying and so were pretty laid back," remembers Brien. The station was known for its "sawmill dog approach." On good weather days, when an aircraft was a mile away on its "final" for Runway 24, the pilots would see the dog run out of the sawmill and hear it barking. On marginal weather days they would say that they knew they were lined up to the runway although they couldn't see it because they could hear the dog barking. "Not much chance of really hearing the barking in the cockpit, of course," said George, "but I can vouch that the sawmill and the dog were there."

Back in June 1951, Gordon McGregor, president of TCA, had received a letter from a little Calgary girl named Ruth applying for a job as a stewardess when she was old enough. McGregor answered her letter himself, telling her that she would have to work hard in the next few years to first become a nurse. Ruth did take up nursing, but in the course of her training she changed her mind about becoming a stewardess and found her career in a hospital. In the interval between her letter and her decision not to become a stewardess, McGregor kept her informed about the changes in air travel, including the fact that it was no longer necessary for a stewardess be a nurse. As airlines had expanded, the supply of registered nurses willing to fly for a living could not keep up with the demand, and by the war's end most North American airlines had waived medical training qualifications. As well, since aircraft were pressurized now and flew above the weather, there were fewer cases of airsickness, and the war had seen to it that there were fewer first-timers. Besides, stewardess training courses had progressed to such a degree that the medical knowledge of a nurse had become superfluous. Nevertheless, when TCA did drop the nursing qualification in 1957, it was the last major airline in North America to do so.

This was not the end of the Calgary girl's story. On February 25, 1962, McGregor received a letter from another little Calgary girl. "Dear Sir," it read, "you may wonder who I am. Well, I am Patsy. If you remember Ruth, well, she's my sister. Ruth doesn't want to be a TCA stewardess, but I sure do..."

Although the majority of TCA stewardesses eventually chose to leave the airline and marry, by 1959 the age limit had become a major problem. Stewardesses who had joined after World War II and were still with the company were now in their thirties, and as with all airlines, TCA's marketing strategy depended on a continuous flow of fresh-faced young women. The company, therefore, announced that all stewardesses hired after January 1, 1960, would be released on reaching age thirty-two. A press statement from Gordon McGregor's office rather callously condemned the veterans as "often the ones *least able* to meet the standards of appearance and personality which the public expects of a stewardess."[3]

This battle would take CALFAA five years to win, but in the meantime it had ground other victories out of the airline for its membership. Duty day limitations, guaranteed days off and block rules had all been successfully negotiated. The fight over revised hours of work on the DC-8s and the question of the pay scale for acting pursers on the Vanguards would lead to a strike vote in 1961. As there were too few male pursers on the payroll when the Vanguards came on line that year, the company had created the designation of "acting purser" for the stewardesses, who had to take on the purser's responsibilities, but the salary for the position was less than that of the men who held down that job. Under its president, Bob Smeal, CALFAA was organized and militant enough to picket the company at a time when it was about to experience its worst deficit in its history. Almost at the deadline, TCA, which had called in strikebreakers, gave in and agreed to a seventy-five-hour monthly flight time on DC-8s—a first in North America. As CPA, PWA and Transair stewardesses looked to their more numerous TCA colleagues to set the trend, it became the TCA stewardesses' responsibility to crusade constantly for additional rights from management. Ahead were the struggles for a wage indemnity plan, statutory holidays and the elimination of marriage and maternity as a cause for discharge, the last won on December 2, 1965.

Both British European Airways and TCA had specified that their next aircraft should have a large cargo hold, and to accommodate them Vickers built its model V.900 with a double-bubble fuselage. Rolls Royce was then looking for a vehicle for its twin-spool RB109 turboprop engine called the Tyne, and it seemed a perfect fit for the Vickers V.900. But even this double-bubble cargo capacity did not satisfy either airline, and not until the designers came back with the V.952, which could offer a payload of some 6,000 lbs, was TCA pleased. On January 31, 1957, it signed an order for twenty V.952 Vanguards or "VGs" at a total cost of $67.1 million for delivery in 1960, with three additional aircraft to be delivered through 1962. These were registered as *CF-TKA* to *CF-TKW*. Dave Tennant, vice-president of operations, helped choose the Vanguard and summed that decision up with: "The Vanguard was the best for the mission; when we looked at the cost projections, it was a winner. The belly compartment with its great cargo capacity just added to that."

The only other contender in the field of medium-sized propjets had been the Lockheed L-188. The creators of the graceful Constellation had turned out a tubby, four-engined turboprop with wings that seemed too short and propeller blades too long, characteristics that might be explained by the fact that its designers were still high on their phenomenally successful C-130 Hercules and had spun off from it a number of its assets, including its Allison engines. The L-188 first flew on December 6, 1957, and Lockheed's president, Robert Gross, hoped to evoke customer loyalty by naming it after his and TCA's first aircraft, the Electra. It lost out with TCA because its circular fuselage allowed it only a third of the cargo volume of the Vanguard. The few airlines that bought the Electra lost heavily when it developed structural failures and the

FAA grounded them because of aero-elasticity, structural failures associated with vibrations between the engine installation and the wing. While the fault was not with the Allison engine itself, its total mass did contribute to the problem. The modifications cost Lockheed $25 million, and by the time the FAA lifted the restriction in December 1960, turboprops like the Electra had lost their markets to the pure jets, and Robert Gross had died under the strain. Ironically, Lockheed was saved once more, just as it had been in 1939 when it introduced its Hudson. The Soviet Navy was just beginning to exert itself on the high seas, and Western navies required an off-the-shelf successor to the Lockheed Neptune, so the Electra was converted into a maritime patrol aircraft—the winning P3V-1 Orion.

The US government's refusal to approve CPA's Vancouver–Los Angeles–Chicago–New York route failed to slow down the irrepressible Grant McConachie, and to his delight by 1956 it looked as though the Canadian political administration seemed to be tilting in his direction. On November 12 of that year no less a person than C.D. Howe asked McGregor if he had any objections to CPA applying to extend its Mexico–Toronto route to Lisbon and Madrid. If this was granted, McGregor knew that it would be the only direct flight to Europe from Toronto, TCA being required to stop at Montreal en route, and he estimated that it would damage TCA's Atlantic revenue by $228,000 annually. It was obvious too that McConachie saw Lisbon as opening up an entry to Rome, but he promised that all traffic carried to Lisbon and Madrid would originate or terminate in Mexico City and not Toronto. This swayed the Air Transport Board to grant CPA's request in February 1957. The loss of two more European destinations was the last straw for McGregor, who had just been refused permission by the ATB to serve Amsterdam from Halifax. He predicted that, as with the air cargo escapade, CPA would lose so much revenue on this venture that McConachie would soon be asking for the continuation to Rome. Therefore, McGregor was determined to ensure that TCA was designated the sole Canadian carrier from Montreal and Toronto to Brussels, Copenhagen, Oslo, Stockholm, Geneva—and Rome—as well as all other cities in Europe except Lisbon, Madrid and Amsterdam. This he accomplished on February 14, 1957, when the government issued Order-in-Council PC 1957-228.

The logic of the ATB (and the Liberal government behind it) never failed to astound Gordon McGregor. The "one carrier policy" for the operation of mainline domestic and international routes had been clearly reiterated in the House on April 2, 1943, by Mackenzie King, but there had been numerous deviations from it since then, beginning in 1949 with the South Pacific routes, a service that TCA had warned could not be operated other than at a deficit. It was followed by the South American and Mexican route in 1952, the polar flight to Amsterdam in 1955, and now Lisbon and Madrid. Each time the plea from McConachie was that these additional routes were required to improve the company's financial position. As McGregor pointed out, if the rapid expansion of CPA had brought about increasing deficits, that was its own fault. The government had no responsibility to remedy its financial position—least of all at the expense of the publicly owned airline. Throughout his presidency he remained mystified as to why the government gave in to CPA at all; in 1964, after the company had suffered three years of deficits, he wrote: "I would think that the government would move heaven and earth to protect the interest of the airline which is its property, providing, of course, that the airline is doing a satisfactory job serving the needs of the country. It does not feel able politically to fend off the demands of the so-called private enterprise carriers demanding pieces of the flag carrier's route pattern—always, of course, the most profitable ones. The politicians show a strange tendency to grant these requests even though it would appear to be their duty to protect the public purse against these diversions of revenue."

That Canadian Pacific Airlines inaugurated its DC-6B Toronto–Lisbon service on May 30, 1957, was bad enough for TCA, but infinitely worse was to follow that summer. On June 10 the political arena changed for both airlines when almost unexpectedly the Progressive Conservatives were elected, and after twenty years in power the Liberals were resoundingly defeated. As McGregor had said when the Korean War broke out and CPA got a contract to fly US troops to Japan, "Jesus Christ, only McConachie could be that lucky!" If anyone could have read them, there had been bad omens for TCA that spring in the unusually lively Sessional Committee. Gearing up for the general election, the Conservatives had used the occasion to cross-examine TCA more thoroughly, with its members interested this time not in trivia but in the effects on TCA's revenues of CPA's competition. The Tories did not win the 1957 election, Jack Pickersgill once said, the Liberals just lost it.

When McGregor called on Howe to express sympathy about the rout, the minister only shrugged and said, "The roof fell in." The Liberal party, he commented, had just run out of ideas. McGregor didn't need to remind Howe that he had lost his own Lakehead riding in part because TCA had cut off its money-losing flights from there to Duluth. Soon after, John Baldwin found the old man sitting on the steps of Parliament and asked if he could do anything for him. Howe, who at the height of his powers during the war had once proclaimed that all he really wanted to be was president of "his" airline, is reported to have said, "John, whatever you do, take care of TCA." On June 21, 1957, C.D. Howe left office forever, and although the Conservative government grudgingly allowed him to keep his Trans Canada Airlines Pass "No. 1" until his death, the only involvement he had with his creation after that was as a passenger. Without his sheltering arm, well might Gordon McGregor look to the future with trepidation. When Symington retired from TCA's board in February 1959, McGregor must have felt really alone.

Symington moved to California after he retired, but in 1963 he became very ill and his son asked McGregor's help in flying him home to Montreal. TCA did not fly to Los Angeles then, but McGregor sent a DC-8 to collect him, his wife and a doctor. At Montreal, before he was rushed to hospital, Symington asked for the bill. McGregor refused to give it to him, citing all the years of unpaid service that Symington had given not just to TCA but to the country through his work with ICAO. Unfortunately, the Toronto *Star* got word of this gesture and published an exposé on public funds being wasted on flying a sick old man home. McGregor was saddened by this but reluctantly sent Symington the invoice for the flight. When word of this leaked out, TCA employees offered to set up a fund to help thank and repay, in effect, the two men—Symington and McGregor—who had done so much for the company.

Prime Minister John Diefenbaker had campaign promises to fulfill that stretched all the way back to 1926 and his first unsuccessful bid to be elected to Parliament. As the only Conservative elected from Saskatchewan in 1945, 1949 and 1953, and always overshadowed by party leader George Drew, he had appeared to have little chance of ever becoming prime minister. To accept the office from the governor general, John and Olive Diefenbaker caught the regular TCA "red eye" overnight flight on June 13 from Saskatoon to Ottawa. Unfortunately the airline lost one of their suitcases at Prince Albert and, in the words of an aide who witnessed the incident, "he had a temper tantrum and jumped up and down like a little kid...'Don't you know who I am?' he shouted at the TCA counter. 'I'm the new prime minister!'"[4] When the TCA flight landed at Toronto, Diefenbaker's mood worsened. News of his tantrum was spread across the front page of the *Globe and Mail*, as a reporter at the Prince Albert airport had phoned in the story. After such an inauspicious start, there was little that TCA could look forward to throughout his time in office.

Two days after being sworn in, the new prime minister rushed off to the Commonwealth Leaders Conference in London, but before doing so he appointed a Toronto businessman as his minister of transport. Thought to be a lightweight in politics, just "a voice in a suit," as he called himself, George Hees had no idea of the Augean stables given him to clean out, and perhaps that was why John Baldwin was retained as his deputy minister. McGregor, meanwhile, could take some small consolation that the new chairman of the ATB was Paul Davoud, but inexplicably, given what was about to unfold, McGregor's impression of Hees was that he was "very agreeable, very reasonable and approachable but failed completely to defend the airline." Hees, on the other hand, thought TCA "a spoiled child."

Having campaigned on the benefits of competition, Diefenbaker was expected to deliver, and both McConachie and Russ Baker of PWA were counting on him. CPA's application to the ATB to fly across Canada and onward to London was expected, but Baker took the industry by surprise when in September he filed an application with the ATB for a Vancouver–Windsor service, hinting that if it was granted he would use de Havilland's latest Comet IVs on it. The second route he wanted was closer to home—the Vancouver–Victoria–Seattle shuttle. TCA had just begun its daily non-stop Toronto–Vancouver service with Super Constellations that June and McGregor

TCA "Connies"—sleek, elegant and full of life. They would pale in comparison to jet airliners coming into use, and were strangely inappropriate in the space age after 1957.

knew that for the public flying a pure jet like the Comet instead of a piston-engined Connie would be overwhelming. As well, McConachie and Baker were striking at the routes that TCA counted on to make money: the transcontinental, the Atlantic, the Caribbean and the shuttles serving Toronto–Montreal–Ottawa and Vancouver–Victoria. Its remaining services—transborder, Maritimes and Pacific coast—broke even in the good years. Its social routes, the prairie milk runs and the northern Ontario circuits, were the price it had to pay for being a government airline, and they would always lose money. However, that October the indigenously built Avro Arrow was rolled out to great fanfare, and Canadians were wildly optimistic about the jet age. That Baker's spunky little airline, which had just emerged from the bush, was going to operate jet aircraft before either the stodgy TCA or the hopeful CPA, seized their imagination.

Russ Baker hadn't understudied Grant McConachie for nothing, and he and McGregor had tangled once before. On February 8, 1956, he had written to McGregor with an offer not to appeal the ATB's rejection of Duncan MacLaren's "airbus" idea to the Cabinet if TCA would transfer to him the

Edmonton–Calgary shuttle and the Prairie "milk run." McGregor, however, knew that Marler had already firmly rejected the airbus idea. Now, a year and a half later, when Baker applied for the Vancouver–Windsor and Vancouver–Victoria–Seattle routes, McGregor saw Russ's swagger for what it was, as he knew that PWA was struggling to maintain its war surplus Avro Ansons, let alone buy Comet IVs. Furthermore, Baker did not have the political and financial clout of the Canadian Pacific Railway behind him, and when McGregor called Baker's bluff about taking over the Vancouver–Victoria shuttle, "in the outcry from [the people of] Victoria we found . . . just how excellent the TCA service, how reliable . . . how altogether desirable it was that it should continue."[5] As far as the Vancouver–Windsor route was concerned, however, McGregor reasoned that if the ATB was inclined to grant one request for a transcontinental route, PWA was the lesser of two evils.

On November 13, 1957, W.A. Mather, the chairman of the CPR and one of the most influential men in the country, stated that his airline would apply to the ATB for the right to provide a competitive air service on a main line route between Vancouver and Montreal. Then, before Hees could make a decision to open up the transcontinental market to CPA, John Baldwin persuaded him to look into the economics of airline competition. Hees mistrusted the experts in the DOT—which, after all, was a Howe creation—and hired Stephen F. Wheatcroft, a British airline economist, to study competition in Canada and make recommendations. To explain what he wanted from Wheatcroft, he wrote, "I am of the view that the time has come for the introduction of some measure of competition on our transcontinental lines. The rapid growth in airline traffic would seem to indicate that competition can be introduced gradually, without major detrimental effects to existing operations, providing that the changes are made with caution and on a gradual basis."[6] Hees then asked him to report on the implications of such a policy. Before Wheatcroft's report was released, however, on February 7, 1958, at Timmins, Ontario, the transport minister made his first policy statement with respect to both airlines. "It is not intended to place TCA, CPA or other Canadian airlines in competition with each other in the international field. International routes are set up by reciprocal arrangement with other foreign countries and provide rights for foreign airlines to operate over the same or equivalent routes. Therefore, plenty of competition already exists in the international field without duplication which would result if Canadian airlines were made directly competitive over the same international routes." This statement should be seen in the context of the times. Prime Minister Diefenbaker had just obtained a dissolution of Parliament in an effort to transform his party's minority into a majority and the voters were going to the polls on March 31, 1958, so Hees had been sent to campaign in the Liberal strongholds of northern Ontario. The statement he made on airline policy, therefore, was calculated to offend no one: it avoided the thorny issue of domestic competition but promised a continuation of the "spheres of influence" overseas.

McGregor could only hope that Hees's policy statement would not soon be contravened as Marler's had. But taking the minister at his word, he made a pre-emptive strike by augmenting TCA's European network with Constellations, which were used to inaugurate a service to Brussels (April 2, 1958), then Zurich (May 18, 1958) and Vienna (May 1, 1959). These were hardly money-makers but did serve to block CPA from seeking the same locations. McGregor was very aware that there was a price to pay for these European flights: as the arrangements were reciprocal, very soon Sabena, Scandinavian Airlines System, Lufthansa, Alitalia and Swissair would be flying in to Montreal, further depleting TCA's Atlantic revenue.

The airline also pioneered its own version of a polar route. Called the Hudson's Bay service, this was Vancouver–Winnipeg–Gander–London, with the first flight on May 28, 1958, being flown in 1049G *CF-TEW* by Captain E.E. Jokinen and F/O R.T. Whitman. Four days later CPA matched this by replacing its DC-6Bs on its Vancouver–Amsterdam service with Britannias—which, although not quite capable of non-stop flights (they had to refuel at Frobisher Bay), were faster. Ross Smyth, who had been transferred to TCA's public relations section, toured the chambers of commerce and Rotary clubs across the country to press the airline's case and in his speeches used this story of what happened on one of the first Hudson Bay flights to use DC-8s: "A bishop was nervously making his very first jet flight, so he ordered a double whisky after takeoff. When the captain announced that they were climbing to 39,000 feet, the bishop mumbled the altitude out loud and summoned the stewardess. 'My dear,' he said, 'you had better make it a weak lemonade. We're getting awfully close to my headquarters.'" While Smyth got a laugh with the joke, spreading the good word about the company was an uphill battle. The chambers of commerce had substantial political influence and were adamantly pro-competition. It took all of Smyth's persuasive skills to convince businessmen in rural areas that the reason they had an air service at all was because of TCA's cross-subsidization: that is, profits from the transcontinental monopoly enabled the airline to run such money-losing, short-haul routes.

Wheatcroft, meanwhile, had investigated both airlines and concluded what most Canadians already knew. He praised McGregor for an efficiently run public company but saw that a major reason for the undue degree of public criticism to which TCA was subjected was that passengers with small grievances had magnified them into major complaints because they did not have "the normal redress of taking their custom elsewhere." Competition might, in fact, make the public more appreciative of the service provided by TCA."[7] But, he said, "The strongest argument in favour of airline competition is that the travelling public unquestionably wants the right, wherever possible, to have the satisfaction of choosing which carrier it will use."[8]

However, the economist warned that competition came with a price tag. Introduced on all routes, competition would so reduce the traffic density for TCA that the company's operating costs would rise to the point of a continuous deficit. Only three routes in Canada could stand competition: Toronto–Montreal, Vancouver–Victoria and Toronto–Winnipeg. The report concluded that, in the immediate future with larger aircraft, the potential for airline competition in Canada was not likely to change because the larger aircraft required higher route traffic densities to operate profitably. "By 1966, however, the traffic growth will be significantly greater than the increase in aircraft size... This would appear to indicate that, for example, a transcontinental route Vancouver–Calgary–Regina–Winnipeg–Toronto–Montreal might be reasonably considered as having adequate potential to make competition worthwhile in 1966." Finally, the Wheatcroft report suggested limited competition that would not bankrupt the government airline, that CPA be allowed to provide services between the cities from which its international routes radiated—Vancouver, Toronto and Montreal, that other private carriers be allowed to take over some of TCA's routes at peak periods, and finally that private companies operate charters over routes that TCA had scheduled flights on. It was a modest endorsement for competition, but one that the Conservatives would seize upon for their own agenda.

With the report in hand, on October 6, 1958, the ATB began public hearings on the CPA application, moving them through Vancouver, Edmonton, Regina, Winnipeg and Moncton, with the final hearings commencing at the Chateau Laurier in Ottawa on October 20 and terminating December 3. How each of the three airline presidents prepared to conduct his case defined the man. McGregor not only brought with him J.D. Edison, QC, TCA's legal counsel, but he had commissioned his own economist, W.C. Gilman, a New York financial consultant, to make a study of the probable effects of competition on TCA if it commenced on January 1, 1959, on the transcontinental routes. Baker arrived with the bearing of a man who was fully prepared to win. After planting some enticing publicity in the media about his phantom Comets, he hired a legal team headed by John B. Hamilton, QC, with close connections to the Conservatives. McConachie, on the other hand, filled one of CPA's Convairs with company personnel and supporters and flew them all down to Ottawa.

On October 6 the only good news for TCA came when Hamilton informed the ATB that Russ Baker had instructed him to withdraw the PWA application. It seems that McConachie had bought him off with what he had wanted all along: the promise that if CPA was granted the Montreal–Toronto–London route, it would turn over all of its Mackenzie District network to PWA. The deal would take PWA inland from the Pacific coast and into northern Canada, in reality putting it on the first step toward one day buying CPA. The *Financial Post* recognized this as collusion on a major scale but the revelation failed to make an impression on Hees. When the hearings began, having had experience before parliamentary committees, McGregor spoke well, making out that TCA was the public's champion against the sort of sleazy big business dealings that CPA and PWA were then engaged in. He stated that a monopoly of essential services such as transcontinental routes was better for Canadians than the

Some of the myriad specialized ground handling equipment required to manage the transfer of freight to various aircraft in the fleet. All had to be able to operate in the clearance spaces under the aircraft.

duplication, and that competition only increased the end cost to the consumer. The supporting example he gave was that no municipality had two competing fire departments. TCA, he said, would have an all-turbine fleet in operation by 1961 that would allow a reduction on fares—unless CPA was allowed to compete. "Any diversion of the forecast traffic...would eliminate the possibility of achieving fare reductions. TCA is not defending monopoly as such but is concerned that the introduction of uneconomic competition on this route may have serious results on the quality of air service being provided to the Canadian public."[9] The findings of Gilman, the economist, were that the minimum diversion of traffic from TCA to the competing carrier that could be expected in 1959 would be 20 percent, but in 1960 and 1961 it would have increased to 25 and 30 percent. He then calculated the financial losses for TCA:

	Prior to Competition	After Competition
1957	$405,000 surplus	$6,238,000 deficit
1959	470,000 surplus	8,142,000 deficit
1960	500,000 surplus	12,665,000 deficit

TCA's counsel, J.D. Edison, then attacked McConachie's flimsy speculations. Calculating that CPA would have to keep all of its DC-6Bs in the air all of the time in order to achieve what McConachie wanted, he said that it was obvious to all that "CPA's expense estimates were computed on an unreasonable added-cost basis without any traffic study."[10] What saved the day for McConachie was that as part of his deal with PWA, Baker had turned over his expensive legal team to CPA's defence, and it was Hamilton along with the CPR legal counsel Ian Sinclair who stemmed the rout. He cited the precedent case of Colonial Airlines vs TCA, in which the latter had challenged the monopoly that Colonial had enjoyed on its Montreal–New York route. Although Colonial had cried foul when TCA started on the same route in 1950, claiming that this would undermine its traffic revenue, Hamilton pointed out that in 1954 despite—or perhaps because of—TCA's competition, Colonial's traffic had actually increased by 76 percent. Sinclair's final argument struck a popular chord. He suggested that after more than two decades on the most lucrative routes in the country, TCA should by now be in a position to cope with some degree of competition.

The ATB handed down its findings at the end of December, and on January 21, 1959, Hees announced the government's decision. The ATB found that additional transcontinental air services could not be introduced at this time without major detrimental effect to existing operations. It also denied the CPA application because its expenses were computed on an unreasonable added-cost basis, its revenues were estimated without any traffic study and its schedules for the proposed service appeared to have been based on optimistic block speeds. However, the board found that the position of CPA as an international carrier needed strengthening, and it recommended issuing CPA a licence to operate a single domestic scheduled service from Vancouver to Winnipeg–Toronto–Montreal to connect with its existing international operations. This new service would be limited to one return flight a day on which domestic as well as international passengers could be carried. It further recommended that the adequacy of this arrangement be reviewed again in two years to see whether additional services would be warranted. The board also recommended that where limited controlled competition would result in improving the position of regional carriers, this be authorized, and indicated that an intensive investigation of the position of regional carriers in this connection was warranted. The single flight would allow the Conservatives to honour their pledge to introduce competition but not enough of it to bankrupt TCA, as Wheatcroft and Gilman had warned.

The minister endorsed the findings, privately disappointed that CPA had only won a single flight out of the long, drawn-out exercise. But the Diefenbaker government was then struggling to maintain the Avro Arrow program, and the impact on the national economy—to say nothing of the party's chances at re-election—if an essential service such as TCA was plunged back into its post-war deficits, would have wide ranging social and political repercussions. Donald Fleming, the finance minister, thought the decision to break the TCA monopoly and license a CPA flight "right in principle." However, he warned his Cabinet colleagues that they would have to pay the piper. TCA's deficit, which he would have to meet, came when unemployment was rising, and the unemployment insurance fund was so depleted that the government would have to borrow $550 million and liquidate government securities to cover its cash needs.[11] The country couldn't afford much more airline competition.

For McGregor the ATB decisions were the thin edge of the wedge. In February 1959, in his column "From the President" in the company newsletter, he wrote that TCA had won every battle but lost the war. "TCA's board of directors are certainly not opposed in principle to competition. Indeed, it is recognized that some of TCA's problems might be simplified if competition existed. But it is the opinion of the board that mainline competition at this stage of Canada's national development would bring in its train a deterioration of the company's financial position, a deterioration of standards of service due to the inability to acquire the most modern and efficient equipment available, and higher costs due to reduction in volume of transportation performed."[12] He knew that with a single daily flight McConachie had no intention of using his sixty-one-passenger DC-6Bs because on April 1, 1958, CPA had taken delivery of the first of six turboprop Bristol Britannias. This aircraft carried 89 passengers although, as BOAC had already demonstrated, it could be reconfigured to take 139, and was so quiet that it was advertised as "the Whispering Giant." McGregor wrote to the minister, bitterly predicting that when the travelling public took to these new aircraft, which were faster and quieter than the TCA Constellations, and if McConachie introduced a bar service on board as he threatened, there would be such a demand for seats that he would soon ask for a second transcontinental service. Again he proved prescient: on May 4, 1959, CPA deployed their Britannias on their daily Vancouver–Winnipeg–Toronto–Montreal service.

Whatever sympathy Hees felt for TCA's plight did not prevent him from dropping another bombshell on McGregor. Using Comet IVs, the British airline BOAC had already launched its scheduled jet service from London to Montreal on December 19, 1958, though they had now given up on their globe-girdling plan that would have used The Pas, Manitoba. As BOAC was therefore entitled to another Canadian point of entry (TCA had Prestwick and London), Hees announced on January 29, 1959, that he proposed to allow BOAC access to Toronto as well. Baffled by Hees's latest move, McGregor protested that TCA already expected to lose between $2 and $3 million in transcontinental revenue in 1959, depending on whether McConachie used DC-6Bs or Britannias, but with the BOAC entry into Toronto's rich anglophile market it would lose a further $2.9 million in domestic and Atlantic revenue—all this at a time when the airline had to pay for its Vanguards. He even offered to pull TCA out of Prestwick, but Hees had made up his mind, although he did ask that the TCA president propose a list of air rights that Canada might expect to get in return for Toronto. McGregor submitted the requests, chief among them granting Fifth Freedom rights from London onward into Europe and allowing a second Canadian carrier to serve the British colony of Hong Kong. Not surprisingly, the British refused the first—though they did condescend to a pooling arrangement on the Atlantic run—then surprisingly gave in to the second, giving TCA access to Hong Kong. After twelve years of being shut out of the Orient, McGregor could now look forward to his DC-8s landing at Kai Tak Airport.

This would be some compensation for the government's giveaways to CPA and BOAC, and traffic from the developing Oriental market would help to offset the deficits that the company was about to incur. To encourage Hees to accept the British concession of a second Canadian carrier entering Hong Kong, McGregor pointed out that just as the CPA Montreal–Lisbon service did not parallel TCA's Montreal–London and Montreal–Paris services, so TCA's Hong Kong flight would in no way parallel CPA's Vancouver–Hong Kong flight. Instead, it would be taking traffic from TCA's New York–Toronto service and flying through Alaska and Japan to Hong Kong. Hees conceded the point and on June 2, 1959, he wrote McGregor that he had designated TCA as the second Canadian carrier to Hong Kong, though suspiciously the minister asked him to keep this confidential. Then, emboldened by what he had done, on June 13 Hees formally turned down McConachie's request to fly Vancouver–Calgary–Gander–London, as it would parallel TCA's route. As McGregor had so recently reminded Hees, that proposal was in direct contravention of the policy he had announced at Timmins during the election campaign and of his most famous line, that "granting traffic privileges to CPA is like paying hush money to a blackmailer."

At TCA's board of directors' meeting that June, it was agreed that the company would adopt "Air Canada" as its trade name within North America, since it already used that name in Europe and had been unofficially using it in advertisements in francophone communities at home. As well, having laid plans to change the colour of the aircraft to an all-white fuselage, though keeping the same red cheat lines, the board decided that adding a new name at the same time made sense, especially as the French equivalent of "Trans Canada Air Lines"—"Lignes aériennes Trans Canada"—would be more difficult to add to each aircraft than "Air Canada." The airline had also been warned that if the French name were added to the fuselages along with a new colour scheme, air traffic controllers could be hopelessly and dangerously confused. Therefore, it would not only be safer but also cheaper—given that advertising, stationery and tickets would have to be altered and cutlery, linens and signs replaced—to introduce a wholly new name. Conscious of the fierce pride that its employees and most Canadians had in "Trans Canada Airlines," public relations staff planned a careful campaign to introduce the name gradually. Then, as this change would require an amendment to the Trans Canada Airlines Act, the minister of transport was duly informed.

All might have worked had not the prime minister heard of the board's decision to change the name and recognized it for the political dynamite it was. He called in the minister. "Who," he demanded of Hees, "does this fellow McGregor think he is? And what is he up to? At any rate, McGregor had no right to make such a major decision; it was a political matter and it should have been submitted for the government's approval in advance."[13] Parliament had adjourned for the summer, and the minister and his family were about to take a ship to Europe. McGregor wrote of what occurred next. "I got a call from the minister asking me to come and see him at his hotel. At this meeting he insisted in giving me back my letters on the subject and, despite the considerations which had led to the board's decision, stated that the change of name was unthinkable. He kept repeating the new name with progressively increasing disparagement, although I got the impression that he had no personal quarrel with the name but had been instructed to make sure that it was not introduced."[14] The TCA board were aware that changing the airline's name fell within their jurisdiction but given what else was taking place, McGregor thought that "it would have been a particularly inopportune time to antagonize the minister." The new colour scheme was implemented anyway with "Trans Canada Air Lines" across an upper white fuselage with the type of aircraft—Viscount or Vanguard—added to the tail. Never again would McGregor attempt to bring about the change in the company's name by himself.

On his return in August, Hees lunched with Norris "Buck" Crump, the new president of the CPR, who casually suggested that he intended to personally bring to Prime Minister Diefenbaker's attention the fact that the minister had refused to grant CPA its British service. That Crump knew of the letter that Hees had given to McGregor in June agreeing to a Hong Kong route for TCA can be assumed, since the letter had been discussed at TCA board meetings and could have been leaked inadvertently by one of the board members. At this point the minister must also have remembered the letter as he asked McGregor to return it, and TCA's Hong Kong flights were cancelled. Crump did bring up the CPA request with the prime minister later that month, but little came of it.

The news from Vickers wasn't encouraging either. When Jock Bryce and Brian Trubshaw flew the Vanguard prototype on its maiden flight at Weybridge on January 20, 1959, the program was already several weeks late, thanks to problems with its Tyne engines. However, while these were being worked out at Wisley, Vickers sent a Vanguard to Canada in the summer of 1959 to reassure the Canadians and allow them to evaluate the aircraft. At 3:15 p.m. on June 29, Bryce put the Vanguard down at Dorval's International terminal in humid, hot weather. Its unique "air stairs" unfolded, and Sir George Edwards (he had been knighted in 1957) stepped out to be greeted by McGregor and Dave Tennant. Edwards pronounced the transatlantic flight "a jolly fine test." He also brought the welcome news that the program was back on schedule— although few knew that there was a spare Tyne engine on board the Vanguard in case of failure.

CF-TET was sold to Transair in 1955, becoming the first of the TCA DC-3s to be sold (the three with Curtiss Wright engines had been disposed of in 1948). Then in 1956 Quebecair, formerly Rimouski Aviation, bought two, and

The second TCA Vanguard, CF-TKB. The aircraft made its first test flight at the Vickers Weybridge (Wisley) airfield in July 1960 and went on to its public debut at Farnborough later in the year. Vickers/Ken Leigh collection

a year later one went to the DOT, which was in the process of selling off its previously TCA-owned Lodestars. As more Viscounts came into service in 1958, the company sold off 13 DC-3s, mainly to Frontier Airlines in the United States. The last DC-3 flight at Patricia Bay Airport on May 1, 1959, marked not only the inauguration of the first Viscount flight but the change in name to Victoria Airport. Over 3,000 Victoria residents came to bid farewell to the DC-3 and to guest of honour Captain Art Rankin, who had flown the first one into Pat Bay on November 1, 1946. For the occasion Captain Lowell Dunsmore and a passenger agent, Bert Chapman, dressed up as "Father Time," while stewardesses Carol Gaetz and Anne Watson helped with the courtesy flights.

The first DC-8 with J57 engines flew on May 30, 1958, with Donald Douglas and his son Donald Jr. on board. Without the massive military orders that Boeing had got for their 707-120, which had flown a year earlier, the DC-8 was facing an uphill battle. Gordon McGregor saw his first DC-8 on February 5, 1959, when he was invited by Donald Douglas to fly in number four off the assembly line. The TCA president was accompanied by Herb Seagrim, vice-president operations; H.C. Cotterell, general manager, purchases and stores; J.E. Nickson, general sales director; J.T. Dyment, chief engineer; and Lindy Rood, director of flight operations. All of them travelled to California on an American Airlines 707 from New York, allowing them to

Senior management overview of proceedings at the TCA maintenance base at Dorval Airport. Here close scrutiny is being given to Pratt & Whitney J57 engine checks on a DC-8 by Ralph Misener, Gordon McGregor and Herb Seagrim.

compare both aircraft—except for Dyment, it was also their first time in a 707 as well. Each TCA member spent time in DC-8's left-hand seat after takeoff and pronounced himself satisfied that TCA had made the right choice. The DC-8 had more passenger appeal and was quieter. Lindy Rood's impressions were that the aircraft was very easy to handle, the control response was immediate, yet the airplane was not "touchy." Lindy thought that this was going to be a real "pilot's plane." McGregor wrote later: "While one must never decry the other man's product, we agreed that none of us, given the chance, would have considered for a moment changing the decision which had been taken 18 months ago." After their test flight, McGregor's party went to the assembly plant, where they saw the ninth DC-8—the first to carry TCA markings—under construction.

During a driving snowstorm almost exactly a year later, on January 20, 1960, after a 4-hour and 14-minute flight from Long Beach, the company's first DC-8 landed in Montreal. This was the first appearance in Canada of a

An early-delivery DC-8 in southern climes, featuring the new white fuselage tops and flash markings on each of the Rolls Royce Conway engine pods.

commercial jet ordered by a Canadian airline. It had just returned from a sales tour of Mexico City, Bogota and Port of Spain and George Lothian, superintendent of flying, was one of those on board. He announced that the aircraft had performed "magnificently" on the non-stop flight, achieving speeds of almost 600 miles an hour. It taxied directly to the company's new maintenance and overhaul base, where it underwent seventy-two hours of training and familiarization before returning to Long Beach. TCA took official delivery of its first DC-8 on February 5, 1960, and began transcontinental jet service Montreal–Toronto–Vancouver on April 1, 1960. It would be almost another full year (February 23, 1961) before CPA's first DC-8 arrived at Vancouver, but it was a faster model and carried 159 passengers compared with TCA's 127.

With TCA's regular transatlantic service due to begin on June 1 with DC-8 *CF-TJC*, on May 28 George Lothian and Captain R.M. Smith—with observers on board from the Federation Aéronautique Internationale—set two official

Prestwick Airport, built around the famous Orangefield Hotel known to Robbie Burns but without the control tower mounted above it. The location evoked many memories for TCA and RCAF crew well into the 1960s, usually after long, exhausting transatlantic flights.

records with *CF-TJC*: Ottawa–London (3,341 statute miles) at 562.9 mph in 5 hours, 55 minutes and 22 seconds, and Montreal–London, (3,247 statute miles) at 565.3 mph in 5 hours, 44 minutes and 2 seconds. The previous record had been held by an RAF Canberra bomber at 6 hours, 46 minutes, at an average speed of 496.8 mph. The following day when they landed at Prestwick, the old ATFERO airport must have brought back memories for Lothian of the time almost twenty years earlier when he and Jock Barclay had guided their Hudsons down onto that same field.

On September 11, 1961, exactly twenty years to the day that he had flown a Hudson over, Captain J.W. "Windy" Reid was piloting a DC-8 on the same route. With a sense of history Reid brought back the "Short Snorter" by signing several dollar bills to take on the DC-8 flight with him. On hand to witness the "Short Snorter" ceremony at the flight dispatch office were other owners of such mementos: Capt. W.R. Bill Bell, chief pilot, domestic base; Sir William Hildred, director general of IATA and one time manager of the Atlantic Ferry Service; and C.S. Hewett, the regional operations manager.

When he had returned home from inspecting the DC-8 at Long Beach, one of the first things that Dyment did was join Jim Bain in hosting a farewell dinner for Merlin "Mac" MacLeod at the Queen's Hotel, Winnipeg. On February 25, 1959, MacLeod, the inventor of the crossover exhaust system, had retired, ending a chapter in Canadian aviation history. Don MacLaren, who had himself retired the year earlier, told how he had first met MacLeod in 1927.

At the foot of Bute Street at the mouth of False Creek [Vancouver], Western Canada Airways had taken over a waterfront dock and warehouse, once a rum-runner's stronghold, and built a seaplane base there complete with slipway. The future looked bright—aviation always looks bright, excepting to the bookkeeper. We had visitors to our seaplane base—wide-eyed youngsters, curious and keen on learning—and almost every weekend a stocky, firmed-jawed chap would drive down the ramp and without being asked, pitch in and help with whatever was going on. He was always asking questions about engines and how could a man get experience to help get him an engineer's licence. This was Mac MacLeod. He had an automobile repair business up on Broadway known as the Motordrome. Our chief mechanic, I think to frighten him off, gave him some low-carbon steel tubing and told him to weld a complicated joint. When Mac brought it back completed, the chief seemed disappointed when he could find no fault with it. Tommy Siers at Winnipeg needed a man that could keep up with fractured engine mounts, chronic in the Fokker F14 mail planes. When Stan MacMillan tore the undercart off the Junkers "BK" at Aitlin in the Yukon, Siers sent for MacLeod. Mac was there for three months, taking with him the complete landing gear, Junkers corrugated skin and rivets. Some new tools and techniques were invented, the damaged wing built up—all this in an unheated shed behind Louis Schulz's store. Louis was a '98 trader, known as 50-50 Louis Schulz (50 for Louis and 50 for Schulz). Stan MacMillan flew the Junkers out to Carcross, the department inspector approved the repairs and Mac MacLeod had made history.

Herb Seagrim, vice-president of operations. He was responsible for selecting the DC-8 and DC-9.

TCA's annual report for 1959 showed the company still making a profit. Gross revenue had risen by 12 percent, passenger

Two children, Normand and Evangeline Perras, flying from Montreal to Rome in the care of stewardess Madelaine Boucher.

revenue by 13 percent, mail was up by 1 percent and express freight by 11 percent. But the airline had a smaller surplus than the year before, thanks to what McGregor called "sizeable down payments" on DC-8s and Vanguards and expenses for breaking in four more Viscounts and two more Constellations. For McGregor, the New Year began with a bombshell. On January 7, 1960, powerful industrialist Frank Ross informed the board that he was resigning. He then wrote to the prime minister and Hees on January 25 with a list of reasons why he was doing so. It wasn't a fit of pique, he explained, "but a definite feeling over a long period of time that the future development of Trans Canada Airlines, as it is now set, is not in my opinion in the best interests of Canada." He had long been gravely disturbed, he said, by the fact that the board had been asked to approve enormous sums of money for aircraft and the new maintenance plant in Montreal. He thought both were unnecessary and had twice asked McGregor to arrange a meeting with the Cabinet "with a view to having a policy outlined which would give guidance to the directors. This has not been done." What finally determined him to resign was that the airline was contemplating a route from New York by way of Toronto to Tokyo and Hong Kong. That part of the world was already well served, he said. "My belief . . . has been that Trans Canada Airlines should be the exclusive main line carrier from Victoria to Newfoundland, retain its West Indies service and if possible a prestige run to London . . . and no more." This time the prime minister and McGregor did meet for a discussion. Unfortunately there is no record of what was said.

At the House of Commons Sessional Committee meeting in April 1960, McGregor showed that in the eight months that CPA had operated its transcontinental service, at least $3.49 million worth of business had been diverted from TCA. If this continued, he warned, the airline would have no choice but to abandon some of its unprofitable social routes, that is, the prairie milk runs. This was more than an idle threat. As in the days of James Richardson, small airlines could not maintain even a minimum network locally without some form of government subsidy. When the TCA main line was routed over the Lakehead, making the pre-war stops by TCA at Kapuskasing and Armstrong unnecessary, the government had forced it to maintain a daily DC-3 service to "Kap," a route some of whose passenger loads were conspicuously lonely. In 1958, as more DC-3s were taken out of service, TCA had begged off the route and the ATB had awarded it to a local carrier, Austin Airways. After ten months of incurring losses, this company had discontinued the run, leaving the region without a scheduled air service.

New name, new logo, new aircraft—all in TCA's future.

C H A P T E R   1 3

A fter the first TCA Vanguard, *CF-TKA*, made its inaugural flight at Wisley on May 21, 1960, it looked as if the aircraft would be in service in time to match CPA's Britannias. Then on a proving flight from London to Athens, the compressors of a BEA Vanguard's Tyne engines failed and were shut down. As a result the whole fleet was grounded, and it was only after extensive testing of the engines by Rolls Royce that the aircraft received its certificate of airworthiness in late 1960. As its first three Vanguards, *CF-TKA, CF-TKB* and *CF-TKC*, had already been test flown at Wisley in May, July, and October 1960, TCA had sent over five pilots—George Lothian, Ron Baker, Bill Benson, Ed Marriott and Al Wilton—to train on them at the end of October. All were to be pilot instructors on the Vanguard and later the check pilots. The Vickers instructors were Dick Rymer and Denis Hailey-Bell. With Vickers and Rolls Royce working out the modifications, training was carried on through the winter without pressurization and cabin heat. On December 7, 1960, the airline took delivery of what was actually its fourth aircraft, *CF-TKD*, which was flown to Montreal by Lothian and Al Wilton, with Benson and Marriott in *CF-TKC* joining them a week later. TCA commercial operations with the Vanguard didn't begin in Canada until February 1, 1961, with *CF-TKD* flying Montreal–Toronto–Winnipeg–Regina–Calgary–Vancouver and *CF-TKC* flying the reciprocal service on the same day. Now the airline had an almost all-turbine fleet.

With a wingspan of 118 feet and a length of about 123 feet, the Vanguards were more than "just big Viscounts." Each of the Tynes put out 5050 shp plus a static thrust of 1,265 lbs, and the whole grossed 146,500 lbs. The Vanguards carried 108 passengers and could hold 5,100 imperial gallons of fuel. There was also a cargo capacity of more than 1,500 cubic feet, a very important factor. They cruised about 85 knots faster than the Viscount, and normally operated between 15,000 and 20,000 feet.

For all its good points, however, the Vanguards had problems that commenced immediately. The Tynes required a lot of maintenance, and hydraulic leaks were legion. At one point most of the fleet sat on the ramp at the Dorval base bleeding hydraulic fluid until it was discovered that the seals in the system

TCA Vanguard CF-TKB *touches down at the Farnborough Airshow, with flaps down and propellers in fine pitch, 1960.* TKB *was on static exhibition and a BEA* Vanguard *was on show to demonstrate the flying qualities.* Aeroplane magazine

didn't like "Skydrol," which TCA had specified. Then the Vanguard windshields started to crack, and when the British manufacturer couldn't replace them fast enough, there was a delay before an American firm was able to come up with a better design. At another point several Vanguards sat on the ramp with aluminum panels installed where the windshields should have been (to keep out the weather and birds) while waiting for new screens.

Passenger response was also less than enthusiastic. Known as the "Mudguard," the aircraft was noisier than the Viscount, and despite efforts to eliminate vibration it continued over the years. (It was said that a few minutes seated on the forward toilet, right between the engines, gave one a great prostate massage.) By the time Captain Murray Wallace flew the Vanguard in early 1962, many of the problems had been overcome.

> Ground school at our brand new training centre at Dorval was the usual four-week nuts-and-bolts course of that era. The instructors were Jerry Quinn, Glen Cawker and Scotty Stewart. It immediately became apparent that this [the Vanguard] was in some ways a very strange bird. It fell to Glen Cawker to teach the electrical system, which seemed incredibly complicated. Each engine had a frequency-wild alternator (to avoid the complication of a constant-speed drive, according to the manual!) The resultant AC was fed to 4 transformer-

rectifiers which converted it to DC. This in turn was fed to inverters, which converted it back to AC of a frequency that the instruments and radios could use. As if this wasn't enough, there were 2 more alternators on the outboards used for tail and windshield de-icing. The hydraulic system had a pump on each engine and operated the landing gear, flaps, brakes and nose-wheel steering. The system had the usual pressure gauges, and also, by the Captain's left knee, four mysterious "Hydraulic Low Flow" lights which nobody really understood. In desperation, maintenance finally removed the bulbs from the lights and painted the gauges matte black! From then on we had few problems in flight with hydraulics!

Pressurization was handled by two huge Rootes-type blowers mounted on the inboards rather than the now familiar bleed air system, and these too were a constant source of trouble. There was also a strange resonance in the ducts, which usually became apparent while reducing power at the top of the climb. The result was an enormous rumble, known to all as "the Elephant's Fart," emerging from the duct immediately behind the right pilot seat. It was fun to wait for the F/O's reaction to this the first time it happened, followed immediately by a terrified scream from the stewardesses in the forward galley!

The engines were equipped with enormous electric starters rather than the familiar pneumatics and needed a hefty ground power unit to get them wound up. Nose wheel steering was heavy but positive, and also had its own peculiarity. If you managed to get it beyond 70 degrees (or if the towing crew left it that way), it turned into a giant caster with no control whatsoever. It was possible to get it through 180 degrees, and if you didn't have room to jiggle around until it got back into the steering range, it was necessary to get a tractor and tow bar to straighten it up.

By the time the aircraft had settled in, strange things were still happening. Pilots Gary Anderson and Murray Wallace were on a Montreal–Toronto flight when their Vanguard started slowly losing cabin pressure. "A few seconds later an excited flight attendant arrived to tell us that there was a loud howl coming from one of the rear washrooms. I went back to investigate and had a hard time getting the door opened. When I finally did, I discovered our cabin pressure (and all the towels, toilet paper and my tie) disappearing down the toilet! It turned out that the cap had come off the holding tank and the check valve had failed. As near as I can guess, we dumped the entire contents somewhere around Perth, Ontario. Thank the Lord no one was seated on the contrivance at the time!"

> A TCA passenger sent this note to Bob Todd, the associate editor of *Between Ourselves*. He claimed to have found it in the galley of one of the DC-8s, written on a piece of masking tape and stuck on the fridge door.
>
> Captain—Coffee black (Left Hand).
>
> Captain—Coffee and cream (Right Hand).
>
> Second Officer—Coffee and a small kiss.
>
> Navigator—Coffee, cream and sugar.
>
> Todd commented, "Who said captains had the best of everything?"

Like most aircraft, the Vanguard had its own peculiarities. For example it had both forward and rear air stairs, but for some strange reason it was impossible to operate the rear stairs unless the left prop brakes were on (the aircraft actually required these to stop the huge 15-foot paddles after shutdown). There was a red warning light by the switch to warn the cabin crew when the brakes were not on, but faithful to Murphy's Law it could happen. However, even worse was the fact that the front stairs could operate with the engines running! One day at O'Hare Airport, Murray Wallace was sent by ground control to hold in the famous "Penalty Box" while awaiting a gate. "After being stopped for a minute or two, I was astounded to look out and see several of our passengers wandering around in front of the running engines about two miles from the terminal!"

"The Vanguard was probably the most difficult airplane to introduce into service," wrote Clayton Glenn. "The systems were extremely poor, particularly the hydraulics . . . we had problems with instability in the empennage, and it was necessary to bolt down massive weights to cut the flutter down. The Tyne engine was too long and too lightweight for the power it developed and really not suited for TCA's short stage lengths because of the high turbine inlet temperatures on takeoff." The aircraft also suffered from high noise level, caused this time not by the engine but by vibration. The length of the fuselage and position and rpm of the props gave rise to a natural vibration like a tuning fork; this would slowly work its way back to the tail and forward to the wings and back again! A temporary solution was for the pilot to climb with 5 degrees of flap. Later with the addition of weights to the tail plane the vibrations stopped. Murray Wallace later instructed on the Vanguard. "Much to my surprise, I enjoyed it immensely, took it on permanently, and continued doing it on various aircraft for the next seventeen years. Actually, most of us learned to love the Vanguard, and the airline flew it for ten years without a major incident.

A staged Vickers promotional shot featuring the self-contained air stairs on the front and rear door positions. In this view they appear to make sense, but with props turning and hot gases being emitted from the engines, they were decidedly disconcerting.
Photo courtesy Vickers

With only a 16,000-pound gap between Max T/O and Max LDG, it was very versatile. It was possible to fly from Montreal to Torbay making all the stops without refuelling if you only needed adjacent alternates. It was a very stable instrument platform, once you learned to keep that big rudder trimmed, and a joy to handle on slippery runways due to the ground fine and reverse features."

All transport aircraft are certified with a maximum takeoff weight and a maximum landing weight, the latter generally being much lower. The difference is the weight of the fuel burned off during the flight. The closer these weights are together, the shorter the flight leg before the aircraft can be landed. In the case of the Vanguard, these weights were very close together, so a lot of fuel could be carried and the aircraft could be landed in a relatively short time, meaning the flight could have several short legs without having to be refuelled—an important feature on short flights. This is why pilots think in fuel weight (pounds or kilos) rather than volume (gallons or litres).

When the Vanguard was introduced on its cross-border routes from Malton, the airline was still not sure about the reliability of its engines and

Vickers Vanguards approaching final assembly on the Weybridge line, 1960. A TCA aircraft already completed and being touched up is shown outside. Vickers photo

took no chances. In what became unofficially known as Operation Conguard, a Constellation was parked beside the Vanguard on the ramp, so that if the Vanguard's engines failed, the passengers could be transferred to the Constellation. As there were no Connies in Toronto, a Montreal crew was kept at a nearby motel and brought to the airport. If all went well, they returned to the motel and were replaced in a week by another Montreal crew.

The cockpit—the biggest, most spacious cockpit ever—was a pilot's dream, and they could thank Brian Trubshaw, the chief test pilot at Vickers, for it. Better known as the test pilot for the Concorde, Trubshaw later said that he knew from experience that the cockpit dimensions he originally asked for in the Vanguard would be cut back and confessed that he had overcompensated when he put in his request.

> This was the last aircraft where TCA had the final say in flight-deck design, and it really was great. Everything was right where you expected it to be. The nose section was so large

that you entered your seat by walking erect around the outboard side of the seat and just sitting down! A large space beside the seats accommodated your flight bag, and there was a fold-down table for charts. Everything was adjustable, including the control wheels, which could be moved up and down. Each pilot had his own set of interlinked throttles, weather radar scope and nose-wheel steering. The central pedestal looked very much as it would today, with all the radios, autopilot, cabin intercom and trim tab controls close to hand. Flight instruments were state of the art for 1960, with split needle ADIs and HSIs and RMIs on both panels. The autopilot could be operated in both NAV and Approach modes, and did quite acceptable auto approaches. The flight deck featured our first built-in mechanical checklist, folding up from the centre of the glare shield. Feathering and fire controls were grouped along the edge of the shield.

Vickers and BEA had designed the Vanguard to be a three-crew operation. Lindy Rood didn't think three pilots were necessary, but as a result of the British requirement, there was a second overhead panel out of reach of the pilot's seats that consisted mainly of "set them and forget them" switches and indicators. After lengthy negotiation with CALPA and the DOT, it was agreed that TCA would fly with two pilots, and this panel was covered up by a hinged aluminum hatch. Officially termed the maintenance panel, it became known as the Lindy panel. Over the years little holes appeared whenever it was decided that some warning light or switch had to be accessible. By the time the Vanguard was retired, there were more holes than panel!

Aeroquay terminal at Malton in the 1960s. It was a far cry from what it was when TCA began service to the airport in 1938. Photo courtesy DOT

Sometimes derided as "a collection of aircraft parts flying in close formation," the Vanguard proved to be a hard worker for both airlines and pilots, who came to know that it was built like a dreadnaught battleship. (In fact, the aircraft had been named after the last British battleship, HMS *Vanguard*, and BEA had christened each of theirs after other famous Royal Navy ships—the frigate *Amethyst*, the cruiser *Swiftsure* and the destroyer *Dauntless*.) On one memorable flight in 1963 Captain George Smith encountered downdraft over the east slope of the Rockies and dropped over a thousand feet in a split second. Some seats came loose, several passengers and flight attendants were injured, and one passenger died of a heart attack, the only fatality in the ten years and more than 400,000 hours of the Vanguard operation. The aircraft never even popped a rivet.

However, because the Vanguard had been so precisely configured to the requirements of the two airlines, even after an extensive sales campaign, Vickers failed to interest other customers in it. US and European airlines knew that the first medium-sized jet airliners were very near and would be immeasurably

A cover illustration for Horizons Unlimited, TCA's in-flight magazine.

more attractive to passengers. The agent of the demise of propjets like the Vanguard and Lockheed Electra came in the form of the Sud Aviation's Caravelle in Europe and the DC-9 and Boeing 727 in the United States, and even BEA was quick to replace its Vanguards with Comet 4Bs and the Trident 1s. No one, it seemed, wanted any longer to fly in an aircraft that had propellers.

With the delivery of TCA's final Vanguard, *CF-TKW*, on April 3, 1964, the Weybridge production line was shut down permanently. In all, only forty-four Vanguards were built. Vickers kept the prototype and eventually scrapped it. Twenty had gone to BEA, and the remaining twenty-three were all TCA Series 952s. One of them, *CF-TJK*, was converted to a cargo liner by Air Canada in 1966, but without the addition of a wide door. It had a payload of 42,000 lbs and flew in that configuration until it was retired in 1972.

Reservations

a poem by Betty Gordon, Vancouver

Reservations. Yes sir, and the name?
S. Fugwig, did you say?
I'm sorry sir, we do not show
S. Fugwig on that day.

Your uncle booked it? Oh, I see,
H. Smith's the name you mean,
And he booked your reservation
Last Wednesday in Moline?

No, nothing's wrong, sir.
Not at all. What does your ticket show?
Vancouver–Calgary is OKAY
And Calgary–Lethbridge NO?

You say the space was all confirmed
Before leaving for the West?
And that you intend to travel,
That we'd better do our best?

Why, it's a pleasure, sir,
To deal with passengers like you,
If we didn't have the odd old grump,
I don't know what we'd do!

On March 2, 1960, Alitalia's maiden flight touched down at Montreal; after picking up Canadian passengers, it continued to the United States. This was the culmination of a series of misfortunes that began for TCA in 1957 when the previous Liberal government had designated it the sole Canadian carrier to Rome. The airline would have continued its Paris flights on to Rome had not the Italians demanded (in Gordon McGregor's opinion) "quite ridiculous proposals" that on a Rome–Montreal service they be given Fifth Freedom rights from London to Montreal. At that time 30 percent of Italian aviation was owned by British interests, and this would have given the British a second carrier entering Canada. However, as Air France had been given Fifth Freedom rights to pick up passengers in Montreal and fly them on to Chicago, TCA was allowed to do the same between Paris and another European city, a privilege that McGregor planned to use for Rome. Then on August 13, 1957, McConachie, very depressed about CPA's loads to Lisbon, had gone to see McGregor. What they needed, he said, was "beefing up." Then, once again bypassing the Department of Foreign Affairs, McConachie had flown to Rome and met with representatives from Alitalia directly. By the time Hees got Crump to recall him, the damage had been done. The Italians now understood how desperately Rome was needed and used this to their advantage. Unable to grant CPA its London service, and fearful that his letter to McGregor about Hong Kong would be leaked to the Opposition, Hees (according to McGregor) "felt that he would have to get Rome for CPA at any cost." That was why on February 2, 1960, in its most shameful agreement in bilateral air negotiations with any country, Canada signed a treaty with Italy. It was done in such haste that it came provisionally in force on signature with the instruments of ratification not exchanged until 1962, although McGregor badgered both Hees and Baldwin to prevent it from being implemented. By the terms of the agreement, as compensation for not being allowed to fly to London, CPA was given rights to Montreal–Rome–Bangkok and points beyond. Alitalia was not only allowed to fly to Montreal but hit the jackpot by being permitted to pick up passengers there and continue on to either Mexico City or Chicago and Los Angeles, the last one being a destination to which neither TCA or CPA flew. The appendix to the treaty stated that neither contracting country could designate more than one carrier to operate the agreed services, thus preventing TCA from ever being able to use its Fifth Freedom rights from Paris to Rome. Then, as though Rome were CPA's to trade, and in complete disregard of the fact that it was McConachie's mishandling that had got Canada into this, Crump had the effrontery to propose that if the Italian negotiations were to be suspended, CPA had to be given its Vancouver–London route as compensation! It must have taken all of McGregor's self-discipline and sense of duty to keep his opinion of this out of the press.

The losses that both TCA and CPA incurred in 1960 brought calls from the Opposition to amalgamate them, especially as it had become so difficult to nominate one or the other for international routes. When questioned in the House, the minister said that an interdepartmental committee was studying the situation. As both airlines now competed on the transcontinental route, it made sense to co-operate in a fare adjustment, and McConachie and McGregor held a joint press conference in November 1960 to announce a proposed domestic tariff revision, to be effective January 2, 1961. The TCA board approved the revision, relating fares to a "cost curve" that generally lowered long-haul rates per mile but increased short-haul rates.

Bill English, one of the architects of the airline and its former vice-president of operations, died on May 12, 1960. "Mr. TCA" to everyone who knew him, he had seen the need for the company newsletter *Between Ourselves* in 1941 and overseen the first two issues himself. Herb Seagrim said that when English travelled "the line," it was like old home week wherever he went. He never forgot names or faces. Gordon Wood remembered him as "a man with an open door and an open heart." A measure of the man, wrote the present newsletter editor, was that employees thought of him first as Bill and second as the vice-president of operations.

In 1960 all the world's airlines should have been planning something special in the way of a celebration of the thirtieth anniversary of the profession of stewardess. However, at TCA recruitment was becoming a big problem. The average stewardess—never called air hostess in TCA—now left after about twenty-six months of service, forcing the company to recruit more than 250 new stewardesses that year. Each had to measure up to these qualifications:

- The applicant must be a secondary school graduate or have experience, background and knowledge such as would be acquired in obtaining a business education.

- The applicant must be under twenty-seven years of age but not under twenty years of age.

- Her height must be at least 5'2" but not over 5'7".

- Her weight must be between 100 and 130 pounds.

- The applicant must pass a medical examination given by the company's medical officer.

- Applicants who are obliged to wear glasses or dentures will not be considered.

- An applicant must possess a good moral character and a pleasing personality and appearance.

- TCA stewardesses travelling on flights in Quebec are required to speak both English and French.

- All TCA stewardesses assigned to overseas routes must be bilingual.

TCA provided a training salary during the ground school course. Following satisfactory completion of the course, line service commenced and with it entrance into a pay scale that provided a starting salary of "over $200 a month." As a point of contrast, the airline published a comparative pay scale for teachers and secretaries. The most recent year that figures were available was 1957–58, when secretarial stenographers earned a monthly salary of $280 to $325 and teachers in Ontario earned $3,738 per year.

Little had changed in the qualifications or the salaries since Ellen Church had pioneered the profession back in 1930, taking home $150 a month. While stewardesses still had duties like assisting in the birth of babies in flight—one transcontinental flight having been forced to set down at Fort William after an in-flight encounter with the stork—in Canada the profession of stewardess did not legally exist and would not until the drafting of Air Navigation Order, Series VII, No. 2, 1965. This was the year that ICAO recognized stewardesses as essential members of the flight crew and required that they receive training in emergency evacuation and flight safety. In contrast, in the US as early as 1952, civil air regulations required that there be at least one stewardess on any aircraft with a passenger capacity of ten or more. On the plus side for TCA stewardesses, what had improved—apart from no longer having to look after their passengers on the ground or carry railway schedules on flights—was the attitude of the pilots toward them. Captains who had once put stewardesses in the same category as engine failure and still played jokes on them—such as the TCA pilot who got on the public address system at La Guardia to broadcast the news that stewardess Jones was loaded and ready for immediate departure— now had a healthy respect for their female crew members. This was because both they and the stewardesses knew that the general public had become more demanding. Blame it, they said in 1960, on the democratization of a once-exclusive means of travel, on longer flights, on a breakdown in social manners.

In April 1960, when Marion Hedd, a stewardess working Flight 701, went to remove Alistair McKaye's suitcase from the overhead rack to store it elsewhere, McKaye said that he had a bomb in it. This was the first recorded instance in TCA's history of a bomb threat. The airline took McKaye to court, where he was found guilty of public mischief, ordered to pay a personal bond of $500 and put on a peace bond for two years. The judge said that he hoped this behaviour would not be repeated in the future. Unfortunately the next one wasn't long in coming. Colleen Christian, a passenger agent at the Toronto office, received a call at 3:05 p.m. on June 20, 1961, in which a man told her that there was a bomb on board Flight 3, which was about to take off from Malton. John Lauman, a golf ball manufacturer from Kitchener, Ontario, was later convicted of making the call; in his defence he said that he had missed the flight by a few minutes and swore that he would get it back to the ramp.

Cabin crews served hot meals on economy class flights for the first time on the transatlantic run in December 1961. Until then hot meals had been available only on DC-8 flights, first class Viscount flights and economy class North Star flights. With the exception of the Constellations, whose galleys could not accommodate the necessary equipment, hot meals would be served to all passengers on all flights. Breakfast in 1961 was juice, bacon and omelet, rolls, jam and beverages. For lunch and dinner they served filet mignon, chicken or veal, vegetables, rolls, dessert and beverages. On Fridays there was always an added choice of fish: sole, salmon, Arctic char or halibut.

Until 1958, all in-flight meals at Dorval had been prepared by Aero Caterers from their quarters in the cafeteria building on the "Atlantic" side of the airport near the domestic terminal. Construction began on new kitchens in 1956, and two years later the company—which was then operating nine other kitchens from Vancouver to Sydney—moved in, along with TCA's commissary. Alex Jarvis, general manager, remembered that at first the idea was to install one continuous "assembly line," but this would have resulted in a very long, narrow building. Aero Caterers produced some 3,000 meals for the TCA and eight other airlines each day.

Stewardess uniforms through the ages (clockwise from top left): Victoria Stewart in 1940 (photo courtesy Kathleen [Stewart] Torrell), 1948, 1953, 1964.

Top: TCA staff with Ronald Reagan, who was on tour for "King's Row" in 1942.
Bottom left: A TCA stewardess being entertained by Bob Hope aboard a North Star.
Bottom right: Victoria Stewart (bottom) and other stewardesses pose with Frank
Sinatra, who flew TCA in 1950.

"I HAVE A QUESTION"

by Fred T. Wood, Administrative Assistant to the President.

Questions to this column must be directed to the Editor, *Between Ourselves*, Trans Canada Airlines, 1080 University Street, Montreal. All questions should be signed, but all signatures will be considered confidential with the editor.

Q. (a) Why with all the unemployment in our country today, does TCA employ married women? (b) Also why do we hire female passenger agents in preference to men at downtown locations?

A. (a) The fact must be recognized that the employment of married women in industry is here to stay, and TCA can be no exception to that rule. It must further be admitted that the employment of married women in industry has been and is a factor in raising the general economic level of the country. (b) The answer is a simple one. Female passenger agents are equally as efficient in this particular assignment, and our Company is merely following a natural principle that there should be equal opportunity for all. I stress the point of equality rather than preference because no discrimination is shown as between the employment of males and females for passenger agent assignment.

Q. As a baggage handler I notice more and more stickers used on baggage by other airlines and none by TCA. This seems like a good way to get some free advertising and I wondered why our advertising department does not design a distinctive sticker similar to the three aircraft shown on the company lighters and put one on each piece of baggage?

A. Baggage stickers are a mixed blessing. Some passengers like them while others do not and in recent years the latter have been in the majority. However, stickers are available at the company sales office for distribution to those desiring them, but it would be my opinion that to arbitrarily put one on each piece of luggage would result in an adverse reaction.

Q. Would it not be better to issue employees a yearly permanent pass as the railroads do, have it punched and initialled as it is used, and still allow the correct number of passes according to seniority. I feel this would eliminate a lot of bookwork. Something else I would like cleared up; as a TCA wife I have heard it said that these passes are part of one's wages. Is this correct or is it a courtesy on the part of the company to grant this privilege?

A. (a) From the point of view of work reduction the proposal would seem to have merit until a closer look is taken at it. It would require the application for and issuance of the annual passes. Secondly, it would require a form to be completed by the passenger agent each time it is presented for use. But apart from this, the proposal is at variance with the regulations of the ATB and cannot be considered. (b) The granting of free or reduced rate transportation is a privilege rather than a right.

Trans Canada Airlines had long been dissatisfied with flying into the airport at Dartmouth for its Halifax traffic because Dartmouth Airport was also the naval base HMCS *Shearwater*, and the situation there had become more difficult in 1955 when an anti-submarine helicopter squadron was based there. The airline recommended to the DOT that a more suitable site for a municipal airport would be near Kelley Lake, and construction began in November of that year. The new Halifax Airport was operational by June 1960, and on July 31, 1960, as TCA Viscount Flight 426 departed Dartmouth on schedule at 11:45 pm, Halifax station manager "Hec" MacKenzie and his crew of fifty-two men began moving out to the new airport 30 miles away. Ramp equipment, vehicles and office furnishings all had to be in place by the next morning when Flight 400 from Toronto touched down to disgorge its passengers. But it was not until September 10 that Transport Minister Hees donned a kilt of Nova Scotia tartan and, escorted by Ann Standish, a TCA stewardess, officially opened Halifax's new airport. For Hees this must have been one of the brighter moments in his ministry as he had gamely attempted to untangle the airline rivalries that the Liberals had left him. A month later Prime Minister Diefenbaker would reward the Spadina MP by making him minister responsible for trade and commerce, a role in which he excelled. At the same time the prime minister got to punish Leon Balcer, the Quebec MP who had led a protest against him at the national convention, by making him the new minister of transport. (Balcer was also a good friend of Quebec premier Maurice Duplessis.)

In his first public appearance as minister on the morning of December 15, 1960, Balcer officially opened the company's Dorval engineering and maintenance base, and in the afternoon he did the same for the new $30 million Montreal Airport terminal. An "honour guard" of pilots from the fifteen airlines that flew into Dorval—eleven of them international—led by TCA Captain George Laing, met Balcer's Viscount on arrival. On the dais with ministers and local mayors (Jean Drapeau of Montreal and John Pratt of Dorval) were the presidents of the three main airlines that were to use the airport—Gordon McGregor of TCA, Grant McConachie of CPA and Eddie Rickenbacker of Eastern Airlines. Before more than 2,000 guests, Paul Emile Cardinal Leger, resplendent in his ecclesiastical robes, blessed both of the buildings. Enjoying his new portfolio, Trade Minister Hees introduced the fifteen stewardesses representing the airlines that used Dorval, and as André d'Argis of TCA was introduced, the band struck up "The Maple Leaf For Ever." Balcer unveiled a plaque of what he had just said in both official languages, and it was later cast in bronze.

What the employees at the new overhaul base would have liked at this point, however, was for the various levels of government present to settle the problem of the closed road. The base straddled both Montreal suburbs of Dorval and Ville St. Laurent, but Côte Vertu—the only access road to it—ran through Ville St. Laurent. A country road, it was now overused, especially at rush hour, and after several accidents the airline had made representations to that municipality to have it widened. Instead, St. Laurent officials brought in a bulldozer, cut a ditch through the road and put up a fence. It would cost at least $150,000 to widen the road and, because there was a provincial election in the works, they used this as a means of getting attention. While every TCA commuter bounced over a hastily built road that ran around the fence and accessed a busy four-lane highway, the airline's 226 employees who lived in Ville St. Laurent harassed their city council; within a week politicians at all levels sat down to find the $150,000 to widen Côte Vertu.

"Family Day," established for the employees' families to visit the new base, was February 4, 1961. They lined up at the door at 7:45 a.m. and the last one left at 10:30 p.m. Each type of aircraft was "walked through," engines and cargo bays were inspected, 3,100 pints of chocolate milk were drunk, Mae West jackets were tried on in front of closed-circuit television—this was, after all, where Dad (and in some instances Mum) worked. Each child received a pin in the form of captain's wings engraved with the letters MDHMTCAFOTA (My Dad Helps Maintain TCA's Fleet of Turbine Aircraft).

In December 1960, when TCA had just suffered its first deficit in ten years—to the tune of $2,607,350—the man who had once said that he didn't care if TCA ever made any money, C.D. Howe, wrote from his retirement home in Montreal to McGregor, wishing him and the airline the compliments of the season and telling him about a recent flight he had taken on a TCA plane to London. He died on New Year's Eve, and at the funeral services at Christ Church Cathedral, Montreal, on January 4, 1961, enemies and friends alike crowded in to pay their respects to the man who had once said proudly that he was American by birth but Canadian by choice. McGregor was convinced that of all the Crown Corporations Howe had been responsible for, he had a deeper interest in TCA than in any other. It was known that on Symington's retirement, the minister had planned on assuming its presidency, but the new prime minister, Louis St. Laurent, asked that he stay on in the House.

Early in 1961 CPA again sought to gain additional flights on the transcontinental route, despite the fact that it was now flying Britannias and soon would be using 153-passenger DC-8s on it. McGregor suffered a stroke on June 18, 1961; confined to hospital, he missed the parliamentary sessional committee meeting, but while in bed he was told by Balcer that Cabinet was going to designate CPA to operate a Vancouver–Calgary–Gander–London service, contrary to Hees's statement in Timmins. This time it was the British government that came to TCA's rescue by blocking McConachie on the grounds that such a flight was "contrary to the spirit and intent of the bilateral air agreement between the two countries," coupled with the fact that the volume of traffic was insufficient to warrant the introduction of a second Canadian carrier on the Canada–United Kingdom route. The British government had created the Air Transport Licensing Board in 1960 with the object of encouraging private air companies to compete with the state-owned BOAC and BEA. When this board bravely permitted Cunard-Eagle to fly the Atlantic in 1961, its timing was poor. BOAC was then undergoing financial indigestion following the purchase of its new jets, and it took the British minister of aviation to step in and overturn the decision. At least the state-owned BOAC could count on being protected by its own minister. But two years later, when the British government tried to merge the Atlantic services of BOAC and Cunard-Eagle—an interesting experiment in public/private merging that Ottawa watched closely—it was the Americans who blocked them, pointing out that the bilateral air treaties did not allow the licences to be merged. Meanwhile, back in Canada, although CPA could not operate the Vancouver–Calgary–Gander–London route, McGregor noted that Ottawa did not rescind its designation. McConachie, however, never lived to fulfill his ambition of flying to London, nor did McGregor fulfill his to fly to Hong Kong.

It had been planned that the company would withdraw the last of its Super Constellations from scheduled service on January 31, 1962, with a final flight from Trinidad, Barbados, Antigua and Bermuda to Montreal. But because the Vanguards had performed so successfully they were substituted on the southern service by January 15 and the Connies were taken off early to be maintained at Dorval as substitute aircraft. Two of them were returned to Lockheed under a buy-back scheme, while four were taken by Douglas Aircraft in an arrangement connected with the purchase of four DC-8F Jet Traders. The era that had begun with so many expectations on February 26, 1954, came to an end almost without notice, and the last two 1049s, watched appropriately only by the TCA mechanics who had laboured on their Curtiss Wright engines, left Dorval in the fall of 1963, sold to Capitol Airways to be used on their intercity shuttles.

But TCA wasn't quite an all-turbine airline yet. As some of the smaller prairie airports had neither the runway length nor weight-bearing strength required for the Viscount, the company's last two DC-3s, *CF-TEA* and *CF-TES*, still called at Brandon, Yorkton, Swift Current, Medicine Hat and Winnipeg, Regina, Saskatoon, Prince Albert and Lethbridge. These milk runs, it was said, carried everything from chickens to passengers, but no one could ever remember them actually carrying a single milk can. Transair, the regional airline, really wanted these routes and gave out statements explaining that TCA was losing money on them because their fare structure was wrong and scheduling ill-conceived. Confident that they could do a better job, they appealed to the ATB for them. Simultaneously, on July 14, 1961, McGregor had applied to the ATB to be

The "Conguard," an elegant lady in waiting. The aircraft was a regular feature at Dorval in the early '60s as standby in case the Tyne Vanguards had startup problems. L-1049C, now fitted with radar nose and tip tanks, featured the white fuselage top that was standard on TCA aircraft of the period.

allowed to relinquish the milk runs on the grounds that it was not sound business practice to operate two DC-3s in an all-turbine fleet. Certain of the outcome, the DOT delayed the proceedings while hoping to upgrade all of these small-town airports to a standard that TCA's Viscounts could use. As a result, it took until February 16, 1963, for an Order-in-Council to bless the transfer of these routes to Transair; as an incentive, Transair was also given both DC-3s and the Viscount *CF-TGI* for the sum of $1. There was relief all round until Transair discovered that, even with these gifts, without a subsidy they could not make a profit either, and they threatened to pull out. In the summer of 1964 a new Liberal transport minister, J.W. Pickersgill, asked if TCA would take up the milk runs once more "to prove that it was uneconomic." He was surprised when McGregor refused.

The last two TCA DC-3s had accumulated 40,000 hours of flying time each—equivalent, someone calculated, to flying twenty-four hours a day for four and a half years. Their departures marked the airline's farewell to its most worry-free, cheaply maintained, reliable servant. In the seventeen years since September 22, 1945, the thirty TCA DC-3s had flown more than 875,000 hours in service—not a bad return on an investment of just over $162,000 per aircraft!

Running an airline wasn't cheap and Jim Bain, director of engineering and maintenance, J.L. McLellan, director of station services, and K.E. Olson, director of purchases and stores, issued this comparison of DC-8s and North Stars in September 1962.

- Cost of a wing flap on a North Star was $8,600. Cost of a wing flap on a DC 8 was $74,000.

- A pair of first class seats on a North Star cost the company $600. On the DC-8 they were $2,600.

- A set of tires on the North Star was $824. On the DC-8 they were $3,130.

- When on takeoff a bird was sucked into an engine of a DC-8, the value of parts scrapped was $142,138, an amount equal to the cost of 10 North Star Merlins.

- A North Star cost $1.71 per landing while the cost of landing a DC-8 was $16.14.

The last transcontinental, passenger-carrying North Star Flight 702 left Vancouver at 3:30 p.m. on October 29 and flew via Edmonton, Saskatoon, Winnipeg and Toronto, arriving at Montreal at 10:00 a.m. on October 30. In the East, the aircraft had one more historic moment when Flight 722 (crewed by Captain Bick Neill, F/O Joe Gulyes and stewardesses Betty Jean Rybka and Valerie Cleworth), on the Toronto–Montreal service, was the first to arrive at the new Montreal International terminal on the morning of December 1, 1960. The last North Star flight to the West Indies, once called "Bowker's Airline," took place on January 28, 1961, and at Nassau Captains Johnny Poulain and Peter Bartman posed on its stabilizer while the photographer recorded the occasion. But the final passenger flight took place on April 30, 1961, when Flight 7751 flew Sydney–Montreal. There were no passengers on board but this was the turnaround for Flight 762 Montreal–Halifax on April 29, which had carried fifty-two passengers, the last revenue load on the North Star. The last all-cargo transcontinental North Star touched down at Montreal on July 1, 1961, with Captain Don Orr and F/O Ord Johnson, the ultimate TCA crew to operate the aircraft.

The beginning of the end of the North Stars had come in late 1960, but unlike the DC-3s and Constellations, North Stars were impossible to shift. The British had managed to unload some of their Argonauts onto the Royal Rhodesian Air Force, East African Airways and Kuwait Airways. But without dependant colonies and after its experience selling its last two Lancastrians, TCA's management was forced to search for a private buyer. As a result, Captain Rube

Something not seen any more, a dedicated cargo TCA DC-3 loading and TV sets made in Canada. The small crew hatch takes the load on a wet day in 1952.

Hadfield, manager of aircraft sales, and his assistant Roger Morawski, an engineer, tramped the world looking for customers. Hadfield had been a line pilot from 1940 to 1946 and then was made chief pilot in the Central Region until grounded because of visual requirements. He had then been recruited by Vice-President H.C. Cotterell in 1959 for his new position. "Rube was a natural," Cotterell recalled. "He knew the product inside out, since he had flown, instructed and trained on the aircraft." Equipped with air travel cards and strong stomachs, Hadfield and Morawski worked sixteen countries in three months, covering a total, they estimated, of 28,000 miles. They rode camels in Egypt, met a lion at close quarters at a Kenyan national park, sought an audience at the emperor's court in Addis Ababa, and almost went into the Persian carpet business in Teheran. "The problem was not finding the people who wanted the aircraft, but finding those who could afford to pay for them," Hadfield said. When they stopped at Karachi, the scene of a fatal CPA Comet crash in 1953, Rube visited the graves of his old friends, Captain C.H. Pentland and Pat Roy, a navigator who had at one time worked for TCA. Hadfield even tried bartering the North Stars in the Caribbean or South America. "The anticipated sight around the office at one time," he said, "was to see me looking toward the harbour, scratching my head and wondering what I was going to do with the tons of coconut and sugar coming up the river from South America." Bombay, New Delhi, Beirut and Berlin followed, and then it was back to Montreal and the Canadian winter. The pair had to report that no one wanted the North Stars because, at a time when the jets were about to make hundreds of DC-6s and Constellations surplus, the cost of converting them to Pratt & Whitney engines was prohibitive. Not only had there not been a single sale, but on the way home from the airport Roger got stuck in snowdrifts and "was sorry for having left the camel in Cairo."

The entire fleet of TCA North Stars sat forlornly at Dorval Airport until the summer of 1961, when two of Hadfield's leads came through. Eleven were bought by the British aircraft brokers Overseas Aviation, and the Mexican freight carriers Lineas Aereas Unidas bought five. Overseas paid a total of $100,000 for theirs and another $65,000 for spares. Having hit the market at a time when many companies were dumping their old piston-engined planes, Rube Hadfield had done very well indeed. Cotterell concluded admiringly, "I would have been satisfied to have received next to nothing for the aircraft; we had questioned whether we could even get scrap prices for the aircraft." Rube Hadfield resumed flying when the DOT adjusted the visual requirements for pilots. Out of Canada, most of the North Stars ended their days scrapped in Mexico or in Britain, sometimes at the same time and place as their Argonaut brothers. Others were destroyed by tropical hurricanes or abandoned after engine failures off Venezuela or in African jungles.

From 1948 the TCA North Stars had logged more than 700,000 hours, and by 1960 some had accumulated 40,000 hours flying time. Even in 1959 after they were removed from long-haul service, they had an average daily utilization of eight and a half hours, phenomenal in light of their age and proof of a sound design in both aircraft and engines. The sole example of a North Star remaining in this country is a single RCAF C-54M at the National Aviation Museum at Rockcliffe, Ottawa, the only monument to a lot of rueful memories.

To A Merlin Engine

There you purr full of triumphant pow'r
Sitting on the test-stand like a Queen—
Five-hour test completed and this hour your final one.
They say you have been officially retired—poor old "V."
Hallmark of dependability!
Farewell, old friend, whose valiant heart
Pulsed Mosquitoes, Spitfires, Hurricanes,
Droned over continents, played your part
In Britain's bravest battle; these the planes
You helped to make immortal, and then
In the North Star rose in peace again
Somewhere your strong pulse will carry on,
There must still be work for you to do—
What matter if Dart or Tyne or "Con"
In this new jet age outdistance you!
When they are outdated, may we say
That they, too, were great Queens in their day!

— Mary E. Davis, Winnipeg

Even before the departure of the North Stars, officials at Canadair had decided that it was an opportune time to re-enter the commercial aviation market. Having licence-built Sabres and T-33s, in 1956 the company had then licence-built a Canadian version of the Bristol Britannia as the maritime patrol aircraft, the "Argus." Three years later it brought out the "Yukon," a long-range transport, for the RCAF, basing it on the Argus. Not surprisingly, since jets were so close to coming off assembly lines, no passenger-carrying airline was interested in its civil version, the CL-44, and it was only by giving it the novelty of a "swing tail" that Canadair was able to sell off a few as freighters. The first swing-tail freighter, *CF-MKP-X*, flew on November 16, 1960; the company then went on to build five CL-44s powered by the Rolls Royce Tyne engine that TCA had used on its Vanguards and CPA on its Britannias in the hope that one or other of the airlines would buy them. Naturally, the government-owned TCA was seen as the prime customer.

The company had been considering both the CL-44 and the Lockheed C-130 for its next freighter, but after its experience with the Bristol 170 McGregor was reluctant to burden the company with a dedicated freight aircraft again. Canadair assured him that the CL-44 could be used for cargo one way and passengers the other, but with the jet era almost upon them, how many passengers would want to fly in a turboprop aircraft? As the only minister from Quebec in Diefenbaker's Cabinet, Balcer's responsibility was to keep Canadair in business, and he pressured McGregor to purchase the CL-44 to keep the Canadair line open. Meanwhile, the company's technical team had recommended to the board that instead TCA purchase four DC-8 freighters for delivery in 1963. This presented McGregor with an unpopular decision: both the airline and the manufacturer were Montreal-based and he knew that many of his employees' friends would be out of work if TCA did not buy the CL-44. However, memories of the expensive crossover exhaust system for the Merlin had not died at TCA, and he was not going to be pulled into another politically motivated project. Privately he also believed that Canada had little to gain from attempting to force an entry into the expensive aircraft manufacturing business and that duplicating manufacturing facilities here only drove the price of the product beyond acceptable limits.

On December 1, 1961, Geoffrey Notman, president of Canadair, who had been to McGill University with McGregor, called on him and appealed to his patriotism. The argument that ensued is unrecorded, but as Notman sent a précis of it to the prime minister, it is not difficult to guess what was said. State airlines were, after all, expected to buy their countries' aircraft, and TCA was in the market for freighters to replace its North Stars. However, TCA had not spent a penny on re-equipping its fleet in Canada, since that aircraft had been turned out at Cartierville. Instead, by buying the Viscount and Vanguard and fitting the DC-8 with the Conway engine, McGregor had kept the British aviation industry in business at the expense of Canadair. As well, TCA had wasted millions of dollars on the Dorval maintenance base when Canadair could have done the work just as well. In his diatribe Notman did not mention that the state-owned BOAC had bought Canadair's North Stars and would go on to buy Boeing Stratocruisers, Lockheed Constellations and Boeing 707s. In fact, BOAC's most unfortunate purchases had been the British-built Avro Tudors and de Havilland Comet 1s.

McGregor, on the other hand, was wary of TCA being stuck with what he called "the millstone of owning a small type of all-cargo aircraft which would become the orphans of the fleet." Clayton Glenn wrote, "Perhaps one of the main reasons for us selecting the DC-8F over the CL-44 was the fear of something happening to the cargo market. If we found that the aircraft could not be profitable as freighters, we had the possibility of putting them into a passenger configuration, similar to the rest of our DC-8s."

The company went back to Long Beach for its freighters and bought four DC-8-54Fs for delivery in 1963, registered as *C-FTJL* to *C-FTJO*. In 1961 Douglas designed a turbofan version of the DC-8 that could be used in configurations that were either all-cargo or all-passenger or a mixture of both. Although its exterior was like the regular DC-8, structurally the "Jet Trader" was very different. It was heavier and stronger, and had an improved wing, strengthened floor beams and a large cargo door. Its average payload was 60,000 lbs from London to Montreal and it would be available in 1963 for $6.6 million. The 117-seat passenger configuration was different in that all facilities like reading lights and cold air ducts were in the baggage rack—not the seats—and these

The first of three DC-8-54 CF "Jet Trader" models, with beefed-up airframe, engines and cargo door, delivered to TCA in 1963. Douglas demonstrated its flexibility and understanding of airline needs for mixed passenger/freight jet aircraft with this model.

racks could be folded up when the aircraft was in complete cargo mode. The only thing that did not sit well with McGregor about the Jet Traders was that they were powered by Pratt & Whitney JTD-3 engines and not Rolls Royce engines. This, a significant break from Rolls Royce hegemony, might be seen as a sign of changing attitudes from those with British leanings at TCA to those with North American leanings.

The year 1961 brought the largest deficit in TCA's history—$6,450,000. This was attributed to a deterioration in average revenue per passenger miles flown—79 percent of all TCA passengers had travelled economy class compared with 44 percent the previous year, so that average revenue per passenger mile had declined from 6.25 cents in 1960 to 5.81 cents in 1961. However, this was in part a miscalculation of the airline's own making—it had voluntarily lowered fares on its domestic routes in an effort to compete with CPA's prices. With the shift in Canadian travel habits, the result was record traffic volume: the number of revenue passengers carried increased by 300,000 to a high of 3,712,068. The fleet had been adjusted to this by changing the seating configuration of each aircraft—in the DC-8 to 111 economy and 20 first class, in the Vanguard 90 economy and 18 first class, and on the Viscount 39 economy and 12 first class. But even this did not counterbalance the lower fares, and McGregor began considering a fare increase.

Then, on February 14, 1962, McGregor reported to the minister of transport that McConachie had promised to propose to his board of directors that CPA match TCA's fares on the transcontinental route in the new fiscal year. Confident that McConachie would follow suit, McGregor announced his fare increase on February 24, something that no other airline in Canada, neither CPA nor Nordair, matched. Six weeks later McConachie wired McGregor to say that he had changed his mind, that CPA would not match TCA's fare increase, and that the public would pay two prices for the same flight. The minister suggested that the airlines come together and discuss a mid-way tariff, but McConachie refused on the grounds that CPA's frequency restrictions entitled it to a fare advantage. To McGregor, it was obvious that what McConachie was angling for was a second transcontinental flight.

After the election of June 1962—which the Conservatives won, although they lost their majority in the House—it was announced that there would be no changes in policy concerning the merger of the two airlines but that "new fields of co-operation between the two airlines were to be investigated." Given that the Conservatives' election platform had favoured competition, they could not now reverse and force co-operation. By late 1962 the relationship between Balcer and Diefenbaker had deteriorated to the point that they were no longer on speaking terms, so that TCA lost its ministerial conduit to the prime minister. Meanwhile, the Conservatives had justified CPA's single transcontinental flight as a logical link between its eastern and western international terminals, and now, equipped with the findings of the 1961 Royal Commission on Transportation (the MacPherson commission), they wanted outright competition between TCA and privately owned airlines on parallel routes. Therefore, in his "Statement on Eastern Air Services" on May 26, 1961, Balcer said that TCA would lose its special status under the new Trans Canada Airlines Act, and that from now on its applications would be considered by the ATB on an equal footing with any other airline. Second, he was granting Montreal-based Nordair a licence to operate a Montreal–Kingston–Toronto service with traffic rights to Oshawa, Windsor and Sarnia. This was the first time that a regional airline had been able to challenge Trans Canada Air Lines, but Nordair had been itching to expand into Ontario. In 1957 Nordair had acquired Mont Laurier Aviation, a Roberval, Quebec, company with routes outside the province; in 1960 it had purchased Wheeler Airlines, which had a Montreal–Val d'Or route. McGregor could take some comfort in the fact that when Nordair was unable to get a subsidy, its Ontario flights were discontinued in August 1962. Another Montreal-based airline, Quebecair, was given an extension to Chicoutimi, which was then served exclusively by TCA. The third route Balcer bestowed connected Trois Rivières with Montreal and Quebec City. This was Balcer's home riding, and as the present local airport of Cap de la Madeleine was outside it, in 1959 the minister arranged for the DOT to begin construction of an airport at Trois Rivières, which he officially opened on October 22, 1961. McGregor agreed that the passing Montreal–Quebec City flight would land there—this was a small price to pay—but pointed out that Trois Rivières' 6,000-foot runway would have to be upgraded for it to do so. A federal subsidy was arranged for the airport and TCA inaugurated its Viscount service on September 2, 1963. But by then, Balcer and the Conservatives were out of office, and Trois Rivières' brief moment of glory ended in 1967 when the subsidy and TCA flights did.

The 1960s had begun with a worldwide slump in commercial aviation, and the financial losses that both airlines endured (CPA lost $4.7 million in 1960 and $7.6 million in 1961) finally led McGregor to advocate a merger between the two. It would reduce costs as "competition meant dollars spent on duplication of effort [and] in this business competition isn't funny," he told the *Globe and Mail* on July 14, 1962. "It's expensive and it's not efficient." It was only a matter of time, he predicted, before the stockholders at the CPR got fed up with bailing out CPA. "The present situation has created the silly predicament where every taxpayer is subsidizing the air traveller."[1]

But while the early 1960s saw a slump in commercial aviation, it also saw the beginning of computerized services. As traffic had grown during the 1950s, the sale of seats via teletype and telephone had not kept up with the volume of traffic being generated. Messages selling seats were being received by Space Control up to six hours after the "Stop Sale" message had been sent out. To circumvent this problem, it became the practice to withhold some seats from sale, and while this helped with cancellations and last-minute requests, it was hardly ideal. With the advent of jets, it became apparent that the manual system was going to break down completely, and in October 1958 TCA rented an

IBM 650 computer system for $14,000 a month and installed Joe B. Reid on the second floor of the Timmins Aviation building at Dorval to manage an electronic data processing centre. A Rhodes scholar and former senior scientific officer at the Royal Aircraft Establishment, he had already set up India's computer documentation centre as part of a UNESCO program. Reid found the TCA computers too slow, and as a result the company ordered the 1401, which arrived in July 1962. This meant that the initial task of TCA's first computer operators—who had been trained by Ferranti-Packard Electric Ltd. and Harvey Gilman Management consultants—was to convert all the existing 650 programs to 1401 language. TCA invested $3.5 million in the ReserVec system, as it was called, to process passenger reservations. Its heart lay in the central registry, which largely replaced the old payload control centre, where paper records had been kept of each flight. Now in a fraction of a second the computers could record the entire schedule for storage on magnetic drums and tape. The ReserVec system went into operation on all direct services to and from New York on June 17, 1962, and on October 15 the airline began selling space on all even numbered flights in North America. By that fall all of the company's reservations centres were on the ReserVec system, with the exception of Tampa (because of the distances involved) and the milk run towns because of their light loads.

To the delight of Gordon McGregor and all TCA employees who had fought in the war, the airline was entrusted on June 7, 1962, with the honour of flying the Queen Mother to Canada. The royal family usually travelled by either RAF or BOAC aircraft, although in 1955 the Princess Royal had taken a TCA flight from Toronto to Victoria return. So impressed had the Princess been that she remembered the name of the senior stewardess on the flight and seven years later, on Sunday, June 24, 1962, "Billie" Houseman, now the flight service training supervisor, received an invitation to dine with her at the Park Plaza Hotel in Toronto. The closest the old "mudguard" ever came to royalty was at the Vickers plant at Weybridge in June 1962, when Princess Margaret and Lord Snowden were shown around a TCA aircraft by Sir George Edwards.

When Her Majesty the Queen Mother had gone to Australia by QANTAS, to the embarrassment of the Australians the aircraft had broken down, but this did not deter her from consenting to travel on a scheduled TCA flight from London to Montreal to present new colours to the Black Watch regiment of which she was colonel-in-chief. High Commissioner George Drew escorted her to the stairs of the DC-8 that was TCA Flight 857, and for the first time in the airline's history, the royal standard fluttered from its cockpit window. The crew for the royal flight were captains R.M. Smith, A.B. Freeman and J.F. Crosby, navigator W. Bridgeford, chief purser F. St. Hilaire, pursers G.C. Smith and C.K. Day, and stewardesses B. Forbes, O. Bowley, M. Paulin and S. Cooper. It took off at 2:45 p.m. with arrival in Montreal expected to be 5:00 p.m. local time.

Naturally, the Queen Mother and her retinue occupied all of the first class section, but the passengers in economy were agog when in mid-flight Her

A DC-9 showing what might have been. The selection of the DC-9 for short-haul domestic flights provoked student protest outside Gordon McGregor's office in Montreal, but the decision was made before the name change to Air Canada.

Majesty, curious to see what an "economy section" looked like, walked down the aisle and chatted with them. Encountering a crying baby among the passengers, Her Majesty leaned down to speak to the mother and gave the baby a gentle poke in the ribs. The baby stopped crying but grabbed the royal finger and wouldn't let go. The Queen Mother was put in a quandary of either continuing the rest of the flight like this or, by removing the royal digit, subjecting the rest of the aircraft to the screams. In the end she risked the screams.

Gordon McGregor had been presented to Her Majesty the Queen Mother during the Battle of Britain, but her arrival in Canada that day complicated his schedule, as he was acting chairman of the executive committee of the International Air Transport Association, then meeting at St. Jovite in the Laurentians. At 3:30 p.m., dressed in a morning suit, he drove to the local airfield, crawled into the tiny cockpit of a Cessna 310 and was flown directly to Dorval Airport, where he joined the welcoming committee of Prime Minister Diefenbaker, and Governor General and Mrs. George Vanier. The TCA base had held a full dress rehearsal on June 3, complete with the Black Watch regiment and band and Joyce Potruff, assistant chief stewardess, standing in for the Queen and reviewing the ranks. Now as McGregor stood waiting, he noted beside the red carpet three very small white rectangles painted on the apron and behind them the mobile stairs. "At four minutes to five," he wrote later, "the tenth or fifteenth quick look over my shoulder revealed a DC-8 low on approach to Runway 24L. Precisely on the hour, the aircraft stopped at the edge of the carpet, the mobile steps squarely lined up with the first class door. Later examination determined that no part of the main undercarriage bogies or the nose wheel overflowed any part of the small painted rectangles. It was a 3,000-mile shot which had precisely hit the bullseye, both as to time and place."

The Dominion Day weekend of 1962 brought the long-awaited move into the company's new headquarters on the 38th, 39th and 40th floors of Place Ville Marie at 777 Dorchester Street West in Montreal. Credit for the smoothness of the move went to John Ferguson, Jim Jackson and Bob Todd of corporate services, Doug Cayford of architectural and Glen Adams of telecommunications, as well as King's Transfer Van Lines. They made it possible for everyone to leave their work stations on June 29 and return to work on July 3 in the new offices. The only part the public would see was the new ticket office on the ground floor of the east wing, which was opened for business on April 22, 1963. Behind the 275 square-foot display window with its DC-8 first class section cutaway were twelve counter positions and a new concept in sales—four desk-sit-down positions within a rotunda for tour planning.

No sooner was the company ensconced in its new headquarters than its choice of a new medium-haul aircraft became a political football. Competition had been growing on short-haul cross-border with US airlines, which were re-equipping with medium jets of British and French design, and in 1960 TCA had begun the process of selecting its next generation of medium-haul aircraft. Its Viscounts were now either too small or too slow, and the Vanguard was not as popular as had been hoped, so the airline was looking for a small jet airliner to replace both of them. A technical-economic analysis included the study of five aircraft: two tri-jets—the Boeing 727 and the British de Havilland Trident—and three twin jets—the British BAC I-11, the French Super B Caravelle and the Douglas DC-9. All except Douglas's product were already in use. That company had begun design work on its Model 2086 in 1962, and fabrication on what was to be the DC-9 started in July of the following year, but it was not destined to fly until February 25, 1965. All five contenders were powered by fan jet engines and all had their engines installed in the rear of the aircraft, the current design vogue. The tri-jets were substantially larger than the twins and their size was a handicap for integration into the TCA fleet. Of the twin jets, the BAC 1-11 with sixty-six seats and the DC-9 with seventy-two seats were very nearly the same size and speed. The Super B Caravelle at eighty-one seats was larger, slower and older in design, having first flown in 1955. It also carried a higher estimated operating cost than either of the other twins. As was to be expected, Gordon McGregor and Sir George Edwards supported the BAC 1-11, but this time they faced a palace revolt led by Herb Seagrim. The maintenance and purchasing divisions, which had experienced unsatisfactory parts service from Britain, preferred Douglas over BAC and de Havilland. Boeing and Sud Aviation were unknown quantities, the company never having dealt with either before, although the pilots considered the Boeing 727 safer because of

The first Air Canada DC-9 is rolled out at Long Beach, July, 1965. As early as 1959 Gordon McGregor had wanted to change the company's name to Air Canada and implement the new colour scheme. Photo courtesy Douglas

its three engines.

What should have been an internal matter became public because of the impact TCA's choice would have on the Canadian aviation industry. In the summer of 1962, before TCA had made its selection, an agreement had been entered into by the Douglas company and de Havilland of Canada, which provided for a Canadian material and labour content of $540,000 in each DC-9 built. Parts were to be built at the old Avro plant in Toronto, largely disused since the cancellation of the Arrow. At the same time there had been discussions between Notman of Canadair and Edwards of BAC (Vickers had become part of the British Aircraft Corporation) which would provide for $400,000 worth of Canadian labour and material content in every second BAC 1-11 built after BAC had made its first sixty aircraft, but this offer was contingent upon TCA ordering the BAC 1-11. Then to add a Gallic accent to it all, reports surfaced that Sud Aviation was prepared to enter into some sort of manufacturing agreement with a Canadian company contingent upon TCA ordering its aircraft. There was no evidence which company in Canada was to share in this, and it seems unlikely that the militant French labour unions would have allowed work to be taken out of France. In the meantime, TCA's technical team had come out solidly in favour of the DC-9 and then was forced to go through a painful session explaining their reasons to McGregor and Edwards—and the government in Ottawa.

There was trouble also in the matter of maintenance and overhaul services. In 1959 the board had decided to postpone transfer of the overhaul work on the Viscount from its Winnipeg base to Dorval, and thereafter the existence of the Winnipeg base became tied to the operational life of that aircraft. By the fall of 1962 the number of Viscounts had dwindled to forty, while continued deliveries of Vanguards and DC-8s to Dorval increased the workload there. On November 14 McGregor wrote to base personnel at Winnipeg, stating that as the Viscount fleet would start to disappear by 1966, so would the reason for the existence of the base. Closure of the base would mean that 860 of the 1,813 workers there would be affected; by 1966 retirements would pare the remainder to 650, who could then be transferred to Dorval.

The city of Winnipeg had, because of James Richardson, once been the pre-eminent aviation centre in Canada, but through the years that the Liberals were in office its citizens had seen this fade away, first with the TCA consolidation in 1949, then the MacDonald Brothers sale to Bristol Aerospace in 1954, and now the impending closure of the Viscount maintenance base. TCA had given contracts to Bristol Aerospace over the years, specifically in May 1961, when the company needed to return the 1049s to service due to delays in getting the Vanguards, and then again when its Connies required an urgent 3,000-hour inspection, but there was nothing like an imminent federal election to bring western alienation fears to the boil. Persuaded by Stephen Juba, mayor of Winnipeg, several Manitoba MPs and citizens groups pressed Balcer to keep the base open. The minister then announced that he had put a halt to any more transfers but had to retract his statement when McGregor pointed out that by halting transfers, he was penalizing the very men whose jobs were at stake as they lost the right to bid for vacancies at Dorval. The Conservatives had then commissioned an independent consulting firm, Dixon Speas Associates of Canada, to analyze the issue.

By the time their report had appeared and affirmed McGregor's position that the base should be closed, the Liberals had been re-elected. To McGregor's consternation, the new prime minister, Lester Pearson, then countermanded the report and promised that the base would not be closed. It was left to Minister of Transport Paul Hellyer in 1967 to work out a compromise solution, but it was not until April 3, 1969, after lengthy negotiations with the International Association of Machinists and Aerospace Workers, that the base was sold to CAE Industries Ltd., to be operated by its North West Industries (NWI) division. The new owner would continue the Viscount overhaul program, and permanent TCA (by then Air Canada) employees were given the option of remaining in Winnipeg and working for them, leaving with a special termination pay package or transferring to Montreal with a moving allowance, a $5000 interest-free loan to set up house, and no loss of seniority or pension rights. On May 6, 1970, when Viscount 651 was pulled out of the Winnipeg maintenance hangar, it ended the "spar mod" program. All former TCA employees were scheduled to move by September 1, 1971, when the facilities were to be taken over by CAE.

September 1, 1962, was the twenty-fifth anniversary of TCA's first flight, but as this date coincided with the Labour Day weekend the company decided not to celebrate the occasion on that day. Instead, on August 22, McGregor was filmed talking about the birthday and the twenty-five years that preceded it, and this was to be shown at all station celebrations whenever they were to be held. From his new office at the top of Place Ville Marie, the president said that he could see two transatlantic liners at their piers in Montreal harbour. He was glad, he said, that there were still people who could afford the better part of a week to get to England, but that transatlantic air travellers now outnumbered ship travellers three to one, and this was partially due to airlines like TCA. The company's statistics experts had provided him with a few numbers to quote. Since 1937, he told his audience, TCA had carried a total of 27 million passengers. It had flown its aircraft an aggregate distance of 650 million miles. It had paid salaries and wages to its personnel of over $500 million. From a route of 122 miles between Vancouver and Seattle it now served fifteen countries on routes of over 40,000 miles.

Of the original seventy-one employees who had joined in its first year, twenty-five were still with the airline. "These men represent, in many respects, the history of commercial aviation in Canada," wrote Edward Thackrey, editor of *Between Ourselves*, in August 1962. "With a helpful boost from friends in the United States in the early days, they set the basic patterns from which has emerged one of the world's great airlines."

To commemorate the twenty-fifth anniversary of TCA's first scheduled passenger flight, Fred Fraser, supervisor of press services in Montreal, came up with the idea of recreating TCA's flight over the original 122 miles between Vancouver and Seattle, and he had located one of the first aircraft, a Lockheed 10A. *CF-TCC* was still in regular service with Matane Air Services Ltd., which operated in central and eastern Quebec, and it was chartered by TCA for this historic re-creation. George Lothian, superintendent of flying, and his son Bruce went to Matane to check out the twin-engined aircraft before flying it to Montreal. "A lot of memories flooded back when I first saw the little ten-passenger Electra," Lothian wrote. As the plan changed to flying the Electra across Canada, leaving Halifax on August 22 and arriving in Vancouver on August 29, and using the original crews—including seven of the first pilots—Lothian phoned his wife Rose (nee Crispin) at their summer home in Perth, Ontario. "Lady, you had better set about getting a uniform. You're going to work again." All along the line, old-timers who had gone on to other things were sorting out uniforms, dieting and preparing to relive the past.[2] George and

Al Hunt of maintenance ferried the aircraft to the Dorval base on August 14, 1962. As it was not possible to repaint the Electra in complete TCA livery in the time available, she was painted white and the names of the cities where she was to stop were listed on one side.

The editors of *Between Ourselves* asked Fred Fraser to record the trip in log style, as he and Al Hunt were to be the only ones to complete the whole flight. Here are some excerpts from the log:

August 22

CF-TCC lifted off the Montreal runway at 0921 EDT bound for Halifax. She was 21 minutes behind schedule because of an improperly functioning master switch which was temporarily repaired to last until Halifax. This was the only problem encountered during the whole trip. Lindy Rood was flying with Walt Fowler in the right hand seat and Mrs. James (Marcelle) Follett as stewardess in the back. The passengers were Al Hunt, Jack Watson of Station Services and Fred Fraser. The cabin noise was thought to be no greater than that of a North Star, although the racket in the cockpit was considerably higher because it lay in the plane of the propellers.

[Lindy Rood would later write, "While the aircraft was mechanically sound, the radio was usable only close to the station, and the compass pointed South at all times. Thank God for Al Hunt . . . Al got a box compass and kept it between his feet in the first seat of the cabin. We would line up on the runway heading, set the directional gyro and hope that it would not precess too much. Al would give us a check on his box compass, although we did not know the deviation on it. We managed."][3]

When it touched down at Halifax at 1409 EDT after 3 hours and 48 minutes' flying time, Rood commented, "Another successful landing, made with a series of graceful bird-like hops."

August 23

They departed Halifax at 0955 EDT for Moncton arriving there at 1051 EDT. Departure was delayed while *CF-TCC* was photographed on the ramp with a Vanguard but at 1240 EDT it was wheels off—making up for lost time due to absence of headwinds. Far above they saw the contrails of a big jet. As they arrived over Montreal a half hour ahead of schedule, Rood did a couple of turns over Place Ville Marie before touching down at Dorval at 1600 EDT.

August 24

The next day with Rood as Captain and Herb Seagrim in the right hand seat the aircraft left for Ottawa. The new passengers were President McGregor and TCA's first stewardess, Mrs. J.A. (Lucille) Grant. At 11:57 it landed at Ottawa to be met by Leon Balcer, the minister of transport, Ellen Fairclough, the postmistress general, Paul Davoud, John Baldwin, and T.C. "Tommy" Douglas. When it took off from Ottawa at 1414 EDT, Mrs. Paul (Kilby) Davoud replaced Mrs. Grant as stewardess. Toronto was right on schedule at 1600 EDT in hot and humid weather. Out of North Bay at 1023 EDT two hours behind schedule because of thunderstorms, *CF-TCC* ran into heavy weather at 5,000 ft, forcing them to turn back to North Bay. A DC-8 far overhead reported clear smooth sailing—at 34,000 ft. Back to the Bay at 1150 EDT.

August 25

Took off again with a 400 ft ceiling and made it off the Sault at 1243 EDT, just an hour behind schedule. By now they

G.R. McGregor, Lucille Garner (Grant) and Lindy Rood, director of flight operations and senior pilot with the Lockheed 10A on the 25th anniversary Cross-Canada Flight.
Photo courtesy Lindy Rood

were out of radio contact and someone remarked that the spare tire in the back of the cabin would make a great life raft. Into the Lakehead at 1342 EDT and out again by 1539.

[Off Kenora, Fraser would write, "Looking at the ground below it's hard to say whether it's lakes dotted with land or land interspersed with lakes." The country, he decides, looks and feels a whole lot bigger and wilder.]

August 26

They touched down at Winnipeg at 1819 CDT, 19 minutes and a full day behind schedule. At 1804 CDT when they left Winnipeg, *CF-TCC* had a new crew. George Lothian and Rene Giguere were now flying with Rose Lothian as the new stewardess and Charles McLellan handling the station services. They were hit by rain squalls south of Brandon before touching down at Regina at 1031 EDT. "Putting this aircraft on the ground is like landing in a hole," said Lothian. When they took off from Regina at 1106 heavy rain crackled off the hull like hail. The ceiling at Saskatoon was 400 feet, but when they came out of the cloud, Lothian had lined them up perfectly with the runway, and the Electra was on the ground at 1223 CDT. They were at Edmonton by 1511 MDT, just before the skies opened and dumped a lakeload of water on the airport.

August 28

CF-TCC left Edmonton at 0913 in cloudy weather, and Rene Giguere was replaced by Art Rankin. Flying at 5,000 feet between layers of cloud, arrived at Calgary 1015 MDT where all spares were removed to lighten the aircraft for the mountain leg. They landed at Lethbridge at 1155 MST.

On August 29 they left at 610 MST in clear skies in case there was a weather buildup during the day. Everyone was cheerful not expecting to have such perfect weather to cross the Rockies.

[Lothian wrote:] During the whole of the operation across the Prairies I was pondering the problem of how to get the under-powered 10A across the Rockies if the weather were bad. Her single-engined performance did not permit facing any severe weather and we had the twenty-fifth anniversary date to meet in Vancouver. We could have diverted over the lower route between Spokane and Seattle which would not make many yards for Fred Fraser and his PR aspirations. Wonder of wonders, I got word in Lethbridge that the weather was forecasted to be clear over the Rockies

TCA's anniversary flight into Vancouver. The on-time, on-schedule arrival of the flight was guaranteed by good weather and veteran Captain George Lothian at the controls. Ken Leigh collection

in the morning. Taking no chances I herded everyone to bed early.

On the horizon were mountains up to 9,000 feet as the aircraft approached the massive ramparts at 0645. They were to fly below the peaks, between the granite walls. The view turned out to be magnificent, with Lothian saying that he had never seen a better day for crossing the mountains. By 0800 PDT the last of the peaks had been crossed—one of the pilots had stayed on oxygen at all times, but no one needed it in the cabin.

[Lothian:] There was only one snag. A reception was planned for our arrival in Vancouver precisely at twelve noon. We would look pretty silly if we got there hours before the guests arrived. Flying in a crystal clear sky, we headed for Abbotsford Airport, a few miles east of Vancouver. There we polished the fuselage and sunned ourselves until twenty minutes before our scheduled arrival time.

Hit Abbotsford at 0855 PDT had a picnic lunch and cleaned up the aircraft. Left at 1129 PDT flying at 1,200 feet for Vancouver. Pulled up at the terminal at 1156 PDT—door opened at 1200 right on schedule.

[Lothian:] We felt something like the Wright Brothers when people cheered as the little 10A pulled up at the ramp.

September 1

There was now a one-day layover while the aircraft was readied for the re-creation of the first flight to Seattle. Off Vancouver in clear bright skies at 1044 PDT with Captain E.P. Billy Wells in the right hand seat and George Lothian in the left. Mrs. Lothian and Mrs. Pat Maxwell were the stewardesses, and in the cabin were Philip Gaglardi, the minister for highways of British Columbia, Mayor Tom Alsbury of Vancouver, Reeve W.H. Anderson of Richmond, Don MacLaren, Al Hunt, George Roper and Ken Fraser.

[Lothian:] There were a lot of memories...under the clear sky the coast was fogged in but the familiar San Juan Gulf Islands were standing out above the mist. When San Juan passed below, I glanced across at Billy Wells who did not look a day older than he had twenty-five years before.

Over Seattle at 1130 PDT but holding due to ground fog. Started descent at 1245 PDT and on runway by 1258. Met by passengers off the special Vanguard which had just landed minutes ahead.

[Lothian:] And a grand excursion into the past was over.

Off Seattle at 1739 PDT bound for Vancouver. Landed in Vancouver at 1843. The odyssey had ended.

—Fred Fraser

The pre-TCA aviation world that those twenty-five original employees came from hadn't vanished completely. It was still there—though just barely. Even as late as 1962 it was said that above the desk of a few TCA employees was a photo of an old friend of their youth—one of the corrugated aluminum Junkers W-34s, either *ABK, ARI, AMZ, ATF, AQB, ASN* or *ARM.* It was in their cockpits that some of the most senior of the company's pilots and supervisors had learned to fly—"like real men do," as one of them said—and it was underneath their engines that cursing, frozen-fingered mechanics hoped that someone would invent a better means to propel aircraft. Gordon Haslett (now chief pilot, Vancouver) could tell of the time he and Art Rankin (now flight operations manager, Vancouver) loaded 75 tons of perishables into a Junkers from a Hudson's Bay barge that was frozen into the Athabasca River delta and flew it all to Goldfields, Saskatchewan. "Mickey" Found, now a TCA captain, was entrusted to keep the fires going to prevent the cargo from freezing. Haslett and Rankin repaired a broken strut on the Junkers with metal from a bear trap found in a nearby trapper's cabin and, fingers crossed, got as far as Fort McMurray with it.

It was James Richardson, owner of Canadian Airways, who had imported the Junkers from Dessau, Germany, in 1933. Fittingly, it was his widow who in 1962 donated the last surviving one, *CF-ATF,* to the National Aviation Museum in Ottawa. The aircraft was made airworthy in Vancouver by TCA mechanics John Hutchinson and Greg Hoban, a Wasp engine having long since replaced the original Junkers in-line liquid-cooled L-5, and the sturdy Winnipeg-made Edo floats the original wooden Junkers ones. It made stops at Kamloops, Edmonton (Cooking Lake), Winnipeg, Fort William, Sault Ste. Marie and Pembroke, Ontario, everywhere evoking the great glory days of bush aviation. On September 17, 1962, Walter Dinsdale, national resources minister, greeted *CF-ATF* at Rockcliffe as the old Junkers came in for her final landing. Where the great bush pilots "Con" Farrell, "Wop" May, Matt Berry and Vic Horner had sat was now thirty-four-year-old F/O John Racey, a Vanguard pilot who donated his time to fly *ATF* to its last home. Racey reported that there had been no difficulties in flight and described the trip as "tremendous." It seemed only fitting, given how many of the first TCA employees were trained by Canadian Airways, that the company should participate in its last aircraft's flight.

Dear Mr. Thackrey,

Thank you very, very much indeed for your kind and generous gift of copies of the Silver Anniversary issue of TCA's *Between Ourselves*. My husband, always I think, was prouder of TCA than of any other single development during his years in the government, and took immense pleasure and satisfaction in following its progress. Some of his happiest moments were spent on TCA flights—certainly the most carefree!

With my warmest thanks and best wishes,
Sincerely yours,
Alice Howe

The question of a change of name for TCA came up in Parliament once more on November 5, 1962, when the Liberal member for Niagara Falls, Judy V. La Marsh, introduced Bill No. C-72, "Trans Canada Air Lines Act: Amendment to change English Name of Air Lines." As with most backbencher bills, it never got a second reading. McGregor did send his comments on the Bill to the deputy minister, however, and continued to discuss the name change at sessional committees, thereby ensuring that the members who attended knew that he was not opposed to the change, but his experience with Dienfenbaker had taught him that change should be brought in slowly. Parliament was dissolved on February 4, 1963, and on Monday, April 29, Gordon McGregor travelled to Ottawa, no doubt smiling. The Liberals had been returned to power, and he was off to meet the new minister of transport, George J. McIlraith, who had assumed office the week before. In the course of their three-and-a-half-hour meeting McGregor was "delighted to be subjected to a detailed, searching and well-informed questioning of the affairs of

Trans Canada Airlines. In spite of his obvious familiarity with the background of TCA, the minister took pains to point out that he was out of touch with the company... and this constituted a gap in his knowledge." And—music to McGregor's ears—McIlraith also said that he looked to McGregor for guidance. The president left the meeting with "the firm conviction that the minister is a man with whom it will be a pleasure to work." But McIlraith remained in the portfolio for less than a year before being moved on to the Privy Council. He was replaced on February 2, 1964, by John Pickersgill, who, although a Liberal brought up on the prairies with an inbred distrust of the Canadian Pacific monster and its airline, earnestly sought to recognize the existence of both CPA and TCA.

At 5:00 p.m. on November 6, 1963, word was received in Montreal that the first of the DC-8-54Fs that the company had received, *CF-TJM*, on Flight 861 out of London Airport, had abandoned takeoff in the fog and overshot the end of the runway, skidding into Long Breakfast Field among rows of cabbages. There were no fatalities but the aircraft was extensively damaged. It was stripped of its seats, engines and fuel tanks and lifted on industrial balloons while track bogeys were put under the wings and tail. A road was laid through the cabbage patch by the Royal Engineers to give the bogeys better gripping power, and the aircraft was hauled to the BOAC hangar. There riggers and fitters from BOAC and a team of fifty Douglas engineers rebuilt *TJM*, with Douglas airlifting the new lower fuselage sections from Long Beach using a USAF Globemaster. The aircraft was back in service by July 1964, but three years later, on May 19, 1967, it crashed as it approached Ottawa Airport on a training flight, killing all three crew.

Pickersgill's "division of the world" policy, announced on April 24, 1964, designated both airlines as the country's chosen instruments in their own spheres—something that Gordon McGregor had long lobbied for. He was also pleased to hear that, while competition was not rejected out of hand, it would not be the kind that would put TCA in deficit. Finally, regional carriers were recognized as having a role to play, and the government would make sure that both major airlines assumed some responsibility for their success.

Pickersgill then summoned to his office the four presidents—Donald Gordon of the CNR, "Buck" Crump of the CPR and their airline presidents, McGregor and McConachie—on April 27 to negotiate some sort of balance of power. However, apart from giving members a chance to pose for a historic photo, the meeting was unproductive, and each side adjourned to continue the armed truce. It would be 1965 before the airlines became engaged in any sort of dialogue. The TCA board gave its opinion of co-operation in a letter to Pickersgill on November 24, 1964: "On at least three occasions Mr. McConachie has agreed to fare equalization, each time he failed to implement it. Each time this violation of a commitment is mentioned, he attempts to start bargaining fare equalization for an increase in transcontinental frequency."

What CPA and TCA were agreed upon was increased access to the United States—especially on the west coast. Diefenbaker had alienated the US government with his refusal to allow it to station nuclear weapons on Canadian soil and by repeatedly telling Canadians "to forge a country independent of the United States." Liberal historians would write the Diefenbaker years off as an embarrassing, incompetent disaster when it came to bilateral air relations with the Americans, but the inescapable fact was that Canada had little to offer in return for cross-border flights, jets having made airports like Goose Bay and Gander unnecessary. Pickersgill, however, began pushing for a conclusion to bilateral negotiations with the US, but when it appeared they would be drawn out indefinitely, Lester Pearson personally raised the issue with President John F. Kennedy, who appointed the Canadian expatriate John Kenneth Galbraith to study the issue. Negotiations began in earnest in April 1964, concluding with CPA getting its first transborder route, Vancouver–San Francisco, on January 15, 1966, and TCA (Air Canada by this time) the much more lucrative Montreal–Miami and Montreal–Toronto–Los Angeles routes.

Thomas Watt was outside his home at Ste. Rose, Quebec at about 6:30 p.m. on November 29, 1963, when he heard a jet aircraft near the new "autoroute" and thought that it was climbing because "the engine noise was strong and then there was an abrupt cessation of power or this engine noise, then a whistling noise that you could attribute to empennage or flying wires." As a former bush pilot, Watt told himself that the pilot was doing an "expedited letdown." The seismograph at College Brebeuf in Montreal recorded a disturbance roughly north of the village of Ste. Therese de Blainville, Quebec, at about 6:33 p.m.

TCA Flight 831, a DC-8, *CF-TGN*, was on a regular scheduled Montreal–Toronto flight scheduled to leave Dorval at 6:10 p.m. ESR. But because of the overcast, light rain and fog, many of the 111 passengers had been delayed getting to the airport, and the flight was departing ten minutes late, finally rolling onto Runway 6 at 6:28 p.m. It took off normally, climbed to 3,000 feet and acknowledged a clearance for a left turn at St. Eustache. Air traffic control radar at Dorval monitored it to about 8 nautical miles from the airport, at which point the aircraft was in a left turn and surrounded by rain clutter on the radar. After that they were unable to see it again. The flight did not report through 7,000 feet as instructed. At 6:50 p.m., St. Hubert Airport called Dorval, saying that someone had seen an aircraft go down at Ste. Therese de Blainville.

In Toronto, the destination of the 111 passengers, it was a Friday night with most of the TCA staff already at home. The sales department was hosting a reception for a group of travel agents at the Park Plaza Hotel when the following message came across the wires: "URGENT FOR DSMS STP CONFIDENTIAL NOT FOR PUBLIC RELEASE STP FLT 831/29 CATEGORY A RPT CATEGORY A EX YUL RPT EX YUL STP BODGSTNS FON PASGR INFO YMLSX STP OTHER STNS ALSO CK RSVN RECS AND FON PSGR INFO 874-4724." Eddie May, the district commercial manager, and Dennis Barclay, area manager public relations, rushed to the airport with Elwood Patton, the airport passenger office manager. Earl Goddard, the counter supervisor, had already arranged for the seventy-five relatives and friends of the passengers on Flight 831 to be taken into a room that Canadian Immigration had placed at their disposal. At the airline office at 130 Bloor, Jack Campbell, reservations manager, and Dick Sellors, assistant district commercial manager, coordinated the names of the passengers as they were received from Montreal, and sales representatives Don Morrison, Jack Smith, Bill Burd, Ron Reed and Vince Zamora tackled the sad task of phoning the next-of-kin. The TCA switchboard stayed open for the next forty-eight hours, handling hundreds of calls from anxious relatives and friends of passengers. At the airport, assisting those who were waiting, were ground hostesses and passenger agents who had been assigned to that duty—Earl Goddard and his assistants, Irene Karrandjas, Peggy Stevenson, Sylvia Westheuser, Pat Heenan, Barbara Cosway, Fran McCarville, Rosemary Karner, Mary Selwyn and Florence Stevenson.

Eight members, seven of them crew and one employee, were killed when Flight 831 plunged into the ground near Ste. Therese, Quebec, on November 29, 1963.

Captain J.D. Snider DFC

Captain H.J. Dyck

Second Officer E.D. Baxter

Purser I.E. Zirnis

Stewardess K.P. Creighton

Stewardess L.C.A. Wallington

Stewardess L.J. Slaght

Joan Grace, a clerk typist at the Montreal Engineering Department

---

Between Ourselves

At dawn the next day the crash scene was photographed from the air by TCA personnel and by noon an access road was completed to the site. Army personnel raked the mud taken from the mangled remains, heavy excavation equipment was brought in, power cables, drainage pipes and roads soon appeared around the perimeter of the crater, and a bunkhouse was built for those who were on duty. The entire area was marked off in grid fashion and plywood boxes were correspondingly marked so that when parts of the aircraft were recovered they could be properly located in the task of reassembling the wreckage. Ian Macdonald, who headed the flight safety analysis group, said that among the dozens of unsung heroes "it was impossible to give praise to one person or group more than the other. It has been a great team effort and will continue to be such until the investigation is finally completed."

The commission of inquiry concluded that the most probable cause of the crash was the pilot applying the near maximum available "aircraft nose down trim" to the horizontal stabilizer. "The DC-8 then began a diving descent building up speed at such a rate that any attempted recovery was ineffective because the stabilizer hydraulic motor was stalled."[4] Reasons for this action were thought to be icing of the pitot system, failure of a vertical gyro, or an unprogrammed extension of the pitch trim compensator. The commission recommended that a flight data recorder should be installed on all commercial aircraft in Canada, that an improved vertical gyro warning system be installed on DC-8s, that the pitot heat circuit be modified to provide for warning the pilot if the heat has failed, and finally that DC-8 pilots be made aware of the stability characteristics of the aircraft with the full extension of the pitch trim compensator and with the stabilizer trimmed to counteract this effect.

While still coping with the Ste. Therese crash, McGregor went before a sessional parliamentary committee on December 3, 1963, and spoke his mind about the company's selection of the DC-9. Unfortunately, he also made disparaging remarks about the Caravelle into a microphone that he didn't know was live. It was this that the press and Quebec politicians like Jean Lesage took up and that caused the Montreal University students to riot the next day outside Place Ville Marie, shouting "Hang McGregor!" and throwing eggs at the new office windows. Never one to shirk his responsibility, as he had all those years ago with Maurice Duplessis, McGregor met with the students. Through an interpreter, he discussed with them the issues of bilingualism, the choice of aircraft and mentioned that the bilingual sounding "Air Canada" might soon be the airline's official name, but that it was up to the government to decide, not the airline.

Thirty-six of the Ste. Therese victims were identified and buried individually in private funerals, but for the airline the ordeal only ended on December 20, 1963, when in sub-zero weather a common burial service was held on a plot adjacent to the old cemetery at Ste. Therese. The 420 mourners arrived by special train from Montreal and eight religious leaders recited prayers at the service for the remaining 82 victims. As tears froze on cheeks in the bitter cold, the mourners gathered around a 15x30-foot sodded mound containing the caskets. Two rows of Quebec Provincial Police lined one side of the rectangle, facing uniformed TCA captains and crews on the other. Later a memorial stone quarried in Vermont was to be erected on the site, 4 miles from where the aircraft went down.

For the president of TCA, the year of 1963 could not end quickly enough. The air crashes at Ste. Therese and London, the Winnipeg base phase-out, the selection of the small jet and the reaction it provoked in the media and among the students had all taken their toll on him. "Perhaps," he wrote, "the best thing about 1963 is that we have now reached the end of it."

On the positive side, on July 22, 1963, TCA marked the twentieth anniversary of the inauguration of transatlantic service when H.R. Weller, station operations manager, greeted the DC-8 piloted by Captain R.W. Welsh and F/O R.K. Walker at London's new airport terminal. A flight that had taken twelve and a half hours in 1943 had been made in five hours.

The airline emerged from a three-year deficit to a net profit of $527,875 that year. This was attributed to higher revenue yields per passenger mile and greatly increased Atlantic charter operations, which now accounted for one-third of the total Atlantic traffic. Revenue passenger miles on charter flights jumped 512 percent, from 30,293 in 1962 to 185,340 in 1963. The number of passengers carried on scheduled service remained almost the same—3,837,491 in 1962 to 3,883,590 in 1963, but passengers carried on charters went from 27,917 in 1962 to 82,957 in 1963, a 197 percent increase. System air freight on the Atlantic runs had increased by 22 percent where the DC-8 freighter service had been introduced. The fact that the national economy was experiencing a boom was demonstrated by the dramatic growth in leisure travel, with an increase of 31 percent in the scheduled services to Bermuda and the Caribbean. Operating expenses per available ton-mile dropped from $29.67 to $28.15 and total expenses from $31.52 to $29.75. There were now 11,330 employees, 3 percent less than the previous year, and the company had taken the first steps toward a policy of bilingualism so that from 1965 all domestic flights east of Toronto and flights to continental Europe would be staffed by bilingual flight attendants. The fleet consisted of seventy-five aircraft: thirteen DC-8s, twenty-two Vanguards, and forty Viscounts. The DC-8 lost in the Ste. Therese crash had depleted the reserve by $7,114,000 and the London DC-8 repair was estimated at $7.2 million. The airline was at pains to emphasize that the causes of the two crashes were unrelated. Six Viscounts were declared surplus. An order for six Douglas DC-9 twin jet airliners had also been placed at a total value of $24 million. A total of 3,883,590 passengers were carried on scheduled services over a network of 37,267 miles. Trans Canada Airlines was now rated the ninth largest airline in the free world.

That winter, in the parliamentary session of 1963–64, the Pearson government was fighting off the Opposition's criticism on items that were increasingly nationalistic and potentially inflammatory. They ranged from sharing water resources with the United States in the Columbia River Treaty, the use of French on Canadian postage stamps, and what a truly national flag should look like. The government did not need another contentious issue to deal with, and therefore the outgoing minister of transport, George McIlraith, chose to evade all questions about changing the airline's name, citing the expense involved. In response, Conservative Louis-Joseph Pigeon facetiously said that he and a few other MPs were willing to "pool their pennies" to buy the paint and refurbish the entire TCA fleet with the new name themselves. The minister replied in the same vein that he "would not be put in the position of commenting on the artistic ability of members of parliament."[5] No less a Bay Street institution than the *Financial Post* took up Pigeon's idea, its editor demanding an end to the interminable debate. "Why not call our government airline Air Canada? Why perpetuate a dualism that is clumsy, confusing and wholly unnecessary? Air Canada would be a proud and splendid name in international usage, and if it incidentally recognized the bilingual character of this country that would be a plus of not inconsiderable importance."[6]

But once again it took a backbencher to reintroduce the Bill which would change the airline's name. Twenty-nine-year-old Jean Chrétien's riding in the valley of the St. Maurice River northeast of Montreal had been a Social Credit stronghold, and it was a credit to the young man that he had been able to wrest the voters' allegiance away from a traditional "people's party" for the Liberals, considered in that region of Quebec to be elitist—and English-speaking elitist at that. He had done it by successfully adapting the populist Créditiste appeal of integrating French Canadians into the federal government at all levels. His timing was right. No less a person than the prime minister, Lester B. Pearson, had confided in him that he wanted to develop a national image in which francophones could find a home in Canada. This, along with the contemporary activities of the FLQ (Front de libération du Québec) in Montreal, had given the rookie MP his courage. Chrétien had read the article in "the great financial paper of Toronto" and with his leader's consent entered into history. Ultimately, he was also fortunate in that the incoming minister of transport, J.W. Pickersgill, the ultimate Ottawa mandarin, was happy to let the young man run with what might be an explosive, contentious issue.

At five o'clock on March 3, 1964, the House proceeded to the consideration of private members' bills. Jean Chrétien (St. Maurice–Lafleche) moved the second reading of Bill No. C-2, respecting the Trans Canada Airlines Act (translation):

> Mr. Speaker, I am pleased to have the honour of being the first member to introduce a bill during the second session of the present parliament. I moved the first reading of the Bill during the last session and I am pleased to see that by chance it is the first one to be considered during this session. As it is a bill of national interest I would like to summarize some of the main

factors behind the introduction of Bill No. C-2. First, the name Air Canada is certainly bilingual. It has precisely the same connotation and meaning in English and in French, the two official languages of the country.

The name Air Canada is a shorter appellation which does away with cumbersome translation, as is the case with Trans Canada Air Lines, which in French is Les Lignes Aerinnes Trans Canada. Many countries of the world are already using a designation of this kind to identify their national airlines. This is the case with Air India, Air France, Air Liban, Air Algerie and Swissair, to name but a few. Originally the name Trans Canada Air Lines served to designate an air line which served a domestic network of communications. This designation is no longer acceptable because the airline services routes go beyond the nation's geographical borders, indeed routes that touch many parts of the world.

Chrétien then drew attention to Judy La Marsh's bill and to an editorial in *La Presse* on October 12, 1963, which had said that even Toronto wanted the designation Air Canada. "It is not only French Canada which is requesting that our state owned airline should be designated only by the words Air Canada . . . Mr. Speaker, I have tried to be as objective as possible in presenting a few arguments in favour of the designation Air Canada. I felt that the name is quite acceptable, that its use would be advantageous throughout the world, and that in Canada itself it would correspond to the bicultural nature of the country, not to mention the fact that it would indicate the international character of Trans Canada Air Lines, a corporation which in a few minutes' time, I hope, will see its name changed to Air Canada."[7]

Remi Paul (Berthier–Maskinonge–Delaudiere) was the first to offer his approval and congratulations—he and Chrétien were old school friends and members of the same bar association. He was followed by Guy Marcoux (Quebec–Montmorency) and Real Caouette (Villeneuve). Gordon L. Fairweather (Royal) explained that he supported the Bill to prove that New Brunswick recognized bilingualism. Not entirely unexpected was the encouragement of R.W. Prittie (Burnaby–Richmond). Chrétien had recruited the New Democrat from BC to the cause because he was aware Prittie favoured the campaign for biculturalism. But it was most important to Chrétien's strategy to ensure that no other members talked out the proposal in the precious hour allotted to it and prevented a vote. Douglas M. Fisher (Port Arthur), another NDP member, would later take credit for "running interference" for the future prime minister (although Chrétien has no recollection of this today) by inviting the Opposition members to a discussion in the lobby at that crucial time. Fisher then returned to the House and humorously harangued Pickersgill, asking if "Good old modest Jack" would not "talk the Bill out before we reach six o'clock." The former CBC radio show host, who had once done a program on "Lanky the Lanc" during the war, also threw in some distractions of a rumoured transport air policy change in which TCA and CPA might be merged overseas. Caught off guard, Pickersgill responded that he had not intended to address the Bill at all (to which someone shouted, "That's a change!") and that he was a politician, not a prophet. It was obvious that like Pearson he wanted Chrétien's motion to succeed. Had this not been the case, a word from either would have shot Chrétien down in his first few minutes, but perhaps Pearson and Pickersgill were testing the waters for the Great Flag Debate soon to come.

The second reading of the Bill and the debate ended with Louis-Joseph Pigeon asking that the matter not be referred to a committee "since its coming into force is a matter of urgency." Reported and read the third time, Bill C-2 was approved unanimously and passed. This must have been an enormous relief for the backbencher, the airline and the Liberal government. Of the 298 private members' bills introduced in the 26th (1963–65) session, only four—less than 2 percent—were enacted. When Chrétien wrote his autobiography *Straight from the Heart*, he related the story as his first victory.

Gordon McGregor was in Toronto when he heard that the Bill was in the Senate and he caught a late night flight to Ottawa to appear before a Senate committee the next morning. He convinced its members that the Bill should be returned to the Commons to be amended so that the old name and its abbreviation could be protected from use by any other organization. Thus did the title of "Trans Canada Air Lines" die in the very room in which it had been born on another March day twenty-seven years before. The Act received Royal Assent and became law on January 1, 1965.

The reaction to the change in name was positive and Chrétien reaped the benefits. The Trois Rivières newspaper *Le Nouvelliste*, which had until then given him short shrift, hailed the young man now as "the champion of recognition for the rights of Quebec, of French, and of bilingualism." The following week they did a feature interview on him in which he called the Air Canada bill "an example of a nationalism that is positive without whining." On the other side of the country, a British Columbian who signed himself as "One of the Majority" in the Letters column of the Vancouver *Province* wrote, "Why should the government spend the taxpayers' money on another pacifier for the Quebecois by changing Trans Canada Airlines to Air Canada? I guess the next step the Liberals will take is to change it again, this time to 'Air French-Canada' and adopt the lily in place of the maple leaf as our national symbol." With more wit than both, on Chrétien's assertion that the "words being the same in both languages," a Mrs. Alice Dalziel pointed out in the Montreal *Gazette*: "To be churlish, however, the words do not mean the same. In English, the word 'Air' so positioned is a verb. Its principal meaning is 'to ventilate,' with a secondary rather colloquial one 'to broadcast by radio or TV.'"[8] But "Ventilate Canada" or "Air Canada," the name had arrived.

The company set a deadline of June 1, 1964 for the name change. After that date, all telephone switchboard calls had to be answered in the name of "Air Canada." All flight departure announcements, in-flight announcements, promotional material and business cards were by then to have the new name on them. The change also meant a revision of the old standard maple leaf insignia, and design consultants Stewart & Morrison Ltd. were commissioned to prepare recommendations for a new Air Canada corporate signature and symbol. As expected, many of the older employees asked, "Why change the TCA style and trademark?" After all, it was still the same airline in personnel, tradition and spirit. The company set up a corporate design committee of senior vice-presidents H. Seagrim and F.T. Wood, director of public relations R.C. MacInnes, and director of advertising J.A. McGee to consider a change in the TCA maple leaf and the slanted lettering signature. They concluded that the old corporate signature hampered rapid identification by its ungainly length and decided that "due to the faster tempo, to increased marketing spirit and ingenuity, the requirements of unique identification were more vital than ever." The simple "visual efficiency" of "Air Canada" with the stylized maple leaf, its rondel joining at the stem, was much more "unique, legible, flexible and appropriate for the Jet Era." At a cost somewhere between one-quarter and three-quarters of a million dollars, painting the new company colours of red and black over silver was probably the largest paint job in Canadian history. In a way, it was all a prelude to what was to come: the re-labelling of Canada. Soon, along with a new national flag and a new identity based on bicultural-ism (then multiculturalism), there would come the severing of the CNR's—and Ottawa's—apron strings and ultimately privatization.

It could be argued that the transition from "Trans Canada Air Lines" to "Air Canada" had been set in motion when Gordon McGregor moved the company from Winnipeg to Montreal. Or perhaps it came about the day GRM retired. Long before the normal retirement date, McGregor had offered his resignation twice before, once in 1966 and again in 1967, and twice the board asked that he remain. But on May 31, 1968, after more than twenty years with the company, he stepped down firmly and one of the directors, CNR president M.J. MacMillan, was appointed to temporarily take his place. "I leave with regret," McGregor wrote, "but regret of a special kind. I do not regret the fact of retirement, but I do regret the fact that the board did not now find itself able to select and appoint the appropriate man as replacement chief executive of the company on a permanent footing. Change of identity of a chief executive in industry is healthy and desirable for many reasons...On an occasion such as this, few old men can resist the temptation to offer free and unasked-for advice. To the 'organized' people I say, We have had one short strike in thirty years. This must mean that neither union people nor the company are all that hard to get along with." The directors wished him "long years of health and happiness and of more accomplishment in the future." Symbolizing the passing of the torch from one Canadian political elite to another, in place of the Battle of Britain hero and Westmount anglophile, the government appointed Yves Pratte, a Quebec City lawyer.

On December 21, 1968, His Excellency the Governor General Roland Michener made the retired Gordon McGregor a Companion of the Order of Canada. At the ceremony at Government House, McGregor was in good company with General Charles Foulkes, actor Christopher Plummer and Hans Selye, M.D. But he probably felt a greater affinity to another of the Order's recipients that night—the immortal bush pilot Clennell Hagerston "Punch" Dickins.

In its twenty-seven years of existence, Trans Canada Airlines had been fortunate. It had grown from two aircraft to the world's first all-turbine fleet, a reflection of the men who had made it—C.D. Howe, H.J. Symington, Bill English, Gordon McGregor, Fred Wood, Jim Bain, Jack Dyment and George Lothian. Not only did each earn the loyalty and affection of the employees but it was their stewardship that allowed the company to steer a course through shifting political philosophies. The original intentions of those who had founded Trans Canada Airlines had by 1964 been partially fulfilled. It had become an instrument of national policy that was also run on sound business principles. It wasn't quite self-supporting but it did fly Canadians, the people who owned it, economically, safely and reliably not only abroad but across the country. This was, after all, what it was set up to do.

Conclusion

T races of Imperial Airways can be found at Croydon Airport near London.
One hangar at Fort Worth's Meacham Field still has American Airlines'
"Eagles" on guard and there are shrines to Pan American Airways on
both coasts—at the Marine Air Terminal at La Guardia, Dinner Key in Miami and
Treasure Island in San Francisco. At first it may seem that the only permanent
monuments to TCA were built to commemorate its worst crashes—the memori-
als at Mount Slesse in British Columbia and at St. Thérèse, Quebec. Fortunately,
as befitting a great national enterprise, the airline lives on. The original TCA
hangar at Winnipeg Airport, built in 1937 and completed in 1939, is part of the
present Western Canada Aviation Museum (WCAM). It is a solidly built structure, which, according to George W. Elliott, Executive Director of the Museum,
has seen much of the country's commercial aviation pass under its roof, for the
front of the hangar was the original municipal terminal. The museum painstak-
ingly replicated the 1938 TCA ticket counter, complete with an authentic weigh
scale piled with period luggage. The museum bought the four TCA buildings
from CAE in 1983, and on October 7, 1984, the complex was opened by Her
Majesty the Queen. It contains a treasure trove of TCA artifacts, from baggage
carts, tools, brakes, glasses, cutlery and crew uniforms to a unique Viscount
jack. The original Lockheed Electra *CF-TCC* (*CF-TCB* was destroyed by fire) is on
static display during the winter at the WCAM. In the summer, in its 1937 livery
(but with modern soundproofing, electronics and seats), *CF-TCC* is operated by
Air Canada in its "Dreams Take Flight" fundraising program. The WCAM also
has the TCA Viscount #637, registered as *CF-THS*, as well as the only surviving
Bristol Freighter of the type bought by TCA and the RCAF in the 1950s (although
it is the *CF-WAE*, the former RCAF 9699, not one of the TCA trio).

As to other aircraft that the airline flew, the National Aviation Museum in
Ottawa is blessed with three on static display. The histories of the Lockheed
10A *CF-TCA* and the DC-3 *C-FTDJ* in "Goodyear Tire and Rubber" livery are
covered elsewhere. On November 19, 1969, the airline's first vice-president,
Herb Seagrim, presented the Viscount *CF-THI* to Dr. D.M. Baird, director of the

The original Viscount CF-THI. It was reacquired and completely refurbished to its original condition at Air Canada facilities in Dorval, and has been proudly on display at the National Aviation Museum, Ottawa, since 1969. Ken Allen photo

National Museum of Science and Technology. Retired from service on February 28, 1969, it had logged 27,203 hours flying time, made 27,152 landings, been through 8 major overhauls, 76 engine changes and 128 propeller changes. *CF-THI*, the twenty-seventh Viscount acquired by the airline, had been used for an average of 6.2 hours per day throughout its service life. On its retirement the Winnipeg base restored it to the original forty-seat, two-class configuration and it is now on display in TCA livery at the National Aviation Museum in Ottawa.

Members of the airline fare better: they are commemorated across Canada in street and lake names. Thus there is a Hollick-Kenyon Drive and Hollick-Kenyon Road in Alberta, a Parc Romeo Vachon in Quebec, a Zebulon River and Lake in the Northwest Territories. There is a Lothian Court in Gander, Newfoundland, a Seagrim Lake in Manitoba and a Gordon McGregor street at Dorval Airport in Montreal.

In 1926 the American J. Dalzell McKee and RCAF Squadron Leader Earl Godfrey made the first flight across Canada from Montreal to Vancouver using a Douglas seaplane. In gratitude for the support given them, McKee endowed an award in his name to be given annually for outstanding achievement in the field of Canadian aviation. It has been awarded to Trans Canada Airlines and some of its employees before, during or after their TCA service. They are J.R. Vachon, Z.L. Leigh, F.I. Young and P.Y. Davoud.

In the country's centennial year, 1967, the Order of Icarus was founded "to honour those persons still living whose airborne skills have resulted in outstanding benefits to manned flight." TCA employees who have been awarded it are L. Rood, H. Seagrim, W. Fowler, G. Lothian, Z.L. Leigh and D.R. MacLaren.

With the airline, the TCA employees who were inducted into Canada's Aviation Hall of Fame are R.J. Baker, R.L. Dodds, J.T. Dyment, W.W. Fowler, J.H. Foy, H. Hollick-Kenyon, H. Hopson, C.D. Howe, Z.L. Leigh, G. Lothian, D.R. MacLaren, M.W. MacLeod, G.R. McGregor, R.B. Middleton, R. Peel, P.G. Powell, L. Rood, H.W. Seagrim, F.E.W. Smith, C.I. Taylor, J.P.R. Vachon, F.I. Young and Jim Bain.

Among those who received the country's highest honour, the Order of Canada, were J.T. Dyment, Z.L. Leigh, Gordon McGregor and H. Seagrim.

As to the original seventy-one TCA employees who got the airline off the ground, Bob Todd, editor of *Horizons* (the successor to *Between Ourselves*), with the help of archivist Beth Buchanan, tracked down as many as he could for the company's fortieth anniversary in 1977. Their list is supplemented by others in *Final Approach*:

E.P. "Billy" Wells started the year off right by appearing on the long-running CBC television show *Front Page Challenge* on New Year's Eve 1962, when he was station operations manager for Vancouver. He stumped the panel, who didn't guess that he had flown the first TCA flight between Vancouver and Seattle in 1937. Wells retired in 1966 and moved to a Vancouver suburb to live with his son and daughter-in-law.

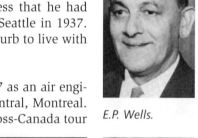

E.P. Wells.

A.R. "Al" Hunt, who was hired in Winnipeg in 1937 as an air engineer, retired in 1974 as manager of maintenance central, Montreal. The highlight of his career, Al said, was the 1962 cross-Canada tour in the Lockheed 10A. "At every stop people came out of the woodwork to meet the flight," he recalled. "It was a wonderful opportunity to renew old acquaintances."

J.D. "Dick" Leigh, who set up the TCA Station at Lethbridge, retired in 1971 as superintendent of shops, Montreal, and went on to be elected mayor of Sidney, BC. "I think I've made a bit of a mistake," he remarked. "You're supposed to take things easy when you retire, I understand."

A.R. Hunt.

J.D. Leigh.

M.B. "Jock" Barclay

C.M. Adams

B.M. Saunders

R.M. Giguere

George B. Lothian

M.B. "Jock" Barclay retired to Oakville, Ontario. He had ferried one of the airline's first Lockheed 14s from California and had taken Hudsons across the Atlantic with George Lothian during the war. Barclay said that he would never forget New Year's Eve 1938, when he encountered severe icing over Grand Forks and the air intakes iced up, making the fuel air mixture overly rich: "the cloud around the aircraft looked as if the whole aircraft was afire."

Charlie Adams retired to St. Catharines, Ontario, in May 1970. At his retirement party he was given a bowler hat because of his close legal associations as manager of agreements and special services. Charlie said that he never regretted giving up a secure job in the CNR to work for Oliver West and "the unknown TCA" in 1937.

Herb Harling retired to Bournemouth, Britain, in September 1963. The company's first sales employee who had worked for the CPR, the Grand Trunk Railway and Canadian Colonial Airlines before joining TCA in 1938, Herb had acquired the nickname "Mr. Exhibition" after many years of looking after the company's display at the Canadian National Exhibition in Toronto.

Bruce Saunders retired to his native Yarmouth, NS, to fish and make ship models. He had been recruited by P.G. Johnson himself from a New Jersey aeronautical school to work as a mechanic with TCA in November 1937.

René Giguère, who started off as a stenographer for TCA in 1937 and went on to become the first pilot to attain 10,000 hours of flying, stepped down as director of flight operations in Winnipeg on January 1, 1969. In retirement he accepted a position as director of the Winnipeg Flying Club.

George Lothian left his position as director of flight standards on January 1, 1969, to take up a flying career in Nepal. As he flew STOL aircraft in that country, he was reminded of his early flying experiences along the Thompson River in the Rockies. When George returned to Canada, he and his wife Rose bought a house near Otty Lake, Perth, Ontario, which housed (almost as famous and beloved as George himself) the Lothian white piano, the scene of many singsongs over the years.

Stan Knight retired in December 1966 as district manager, London, Ontario, where he chose to live. He had started working in aviation on Christmas Day, 1926, had flown for the RCAF as a pilot officer in 1940 and, after a serious illness, had been posted to Nassau as district manager in 1953.

S.N. Knight

Russ Bulger, who was so happy to be with TCA that he "worked for love the first six days before being taken on the payroll," returned to Vancouver to retire. He had moved to Winnipeg to work on the North Star and DC-3, and then to Montreal to join the maintenance and overhaul crew. In retirement Russ looked forward to returning to his first love—ham radio.

Jack Smith, who set up the accounting department for Don Colyer in 1937, retired in May 1970 as manager, statistical bureau. When interviewed, Jack was living in the Transcona area of Winnipeg. There was still not enough time in a day, he said, and he was looking forward to summers at the cottage at Sandy Hook.

R.J. Bulger

Walt Fowler retired as general manager, Eastern Division, in 1971. No one had accumulated more "firsts" in his TCA career than Walt—first Toronto–Montreal airmail, first Montreal–Moncton passenger flight, Toronto–New York and Moncton–St. John's. Walt's staff presented him with a matching set of ship's clock and barometer, and the former captain planned to spend his retirement on his 37-foot diesel-powered cruiser.

W.W. Fowler

Herb Seagrim was named chief pilot of the Western Region in 1943, and vice-president upon Bill English's retirement. McGregor had groomed Seagrim to succeed him as chief executive officer in 1968, but Prime Minister Pierre Trudeau appointed Yves Pratte instead. Herb retired in 1969 to begin a third career running a Florida yacht company. "Every man should have one great adventure in his life," he said, "one major frontier to overcome." He returned to Canada to live out his days on Montreal's lakeshore.

René Baudru retired in May 1970. Norm Garwood, editor of *Between Ourselves*, presented him with a fabricated front page of the newsletter, which Baudru had founded.

Bob Williamson was the company's first flight dispatcher in 1937—with, he said, "nothing to

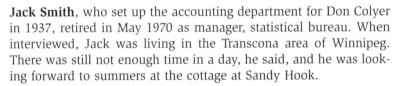

H.W. Seagrim

R.D. Williamson

dispatch." Attached to RCAF 168 Squadron during the war, he used to say its operations manual had been copied from TCA's, "and that's what helped to win the war." Bob retired to Dorval "to be where the action is."

Frank Young retired on August 31, 1971, to take up a position with the Toronto Transit Commission. When interviewed, Young recalled that in 1930 he had written to Sir Henry Thornton, president of the CNR, urging him to form a national airline as part of the railway—so perhaps TCA was all his idea.

Steve Albulet retired on June 15, 1969. Appropriately, for the transatlantic captain, this was also the fiftieth anniversary of Alcock and Brown's non-stop flight over the Atlantic in 1919. Although not yet fifty-seven years old, Steve said that he was taking early retirement to work full time on his own company, Lakeshore Air Services, which flew groups of fishermen to Hudson's Bay—a return to his bush flying days.

Clayton Glenn retired in 1985 to set up his own consulting company, which specialized in resolving fleet and financial problems of small airlines. His contracts with Transport Canada, Treasury Board and the Department of National Defence took him to Asia, Africa and South America. He was also retained by Air Canada for several years after retirement.

Jack Dyment retired on October 1, 1968, to become vice-president of R. Dixon Speas Associates Ltd. At the farewell dinner held at the Ritz Carleton Hotel, Montreal, H.J. Curtis and Bill Bird of engineering presented a pictorial skit of Jack's life from boyhood to the DC-8.

Kelly Edmison retired on August 31, 1971. He had joined TCA on January 15, 1938, during a job ferrying a Norseman from Montreal to Edmonton. Edmison gave up flying in 1945 for a desk job as base manager in Montreal, and during his retirement he said that he hoped to keep up his interest in aviation.

W.S. "Bill" Harvey left Air Canada to become assistant director general, administration and finance, for IATA on March 1, 1971. He remembered that in 1937 the CNR had thought that the airline was "a pesky fly and that it was being run by a bunch of kids who didn't know up from down."

W.S. Harvey

Jack Wright, the company's senior line pilot, retired in 1966. One of the first group of sixteen pilots hired by TCA in 1938, Jack's last flight ended appropriately at Vancouver Airport, where he was greeted by his sons, John and Ken Wright, both Air Canada pilots. In twenty-eight years of flying, Jack estimated that he had logged 24,000 hours flying time.

Ches Rickard, who had apprenticed to be a pharmacist, retired as captain on the DC-8s. A "radio man" when he was station manager at London, Ontario, Ches managed to "beg, borrow and mortgage myself for enough money to pay for flying training." In retirement he and his wife sailed their 37-foot boat from Vancouver across the Pacific to New Zealand.

W.J. "Jack" Dalby, who had begun his career as traffic agent for Canadian Airways in 1932, retired from Air Canada on January 31, 1970. He was "wing three quarter" in the Canadian rugby team that toured Japan in 1932, and he reported that he was now looking forward to lowering his golf handicap.

J.R. "Bob" Bowker had been flying DC-8s on the Atlantic run since 1959 when "Bowker's Airline" had closed. In March 1968, as he brought his final flight in from Zurich, he was greeted by an old friend at Dorval Airport. It was *CF-TCA*, the Lockheed 10A that he had flown in 1938. Wisely, Bowker returned to Bermuda and became a mainstay at the golf club.

Gordon "Gordie" Wood retired on November 1, 1970. He had joined TCA as the traffic representative in Ottawa in 1939 and served for many years as president of the Canadian Tourist Association.

Jim Bain retired on March 31, 1966, and moved to New Seabury, Cape Cod, Massachusetts, where he built a double garage onto the family's rambling new house for his precious Bentley. The car had been made available to him as a retirement gift by Rolls Royce, which had discovered the undelivered car languishing in storage and refurbished it. Jim babied it for a further fifteen years between sailing, curling and consulting with the United Nations. He and his wife Nan returned to Canada in 1979 to live in Morrisburg, Ontario.

Rod MacInnes retired from Public Relations in September 1970. A parliamentary press correspondent before he joined TCA in 1939, he had been one of the guests on the airline's first transcontinental flight on March 19 that year. Rod treasured the press gallery membership card he had from that experience, with the signatures of all the crew members and passengers.

Lowell Dunsmore retired on March 3, 1967. Storytelling, pipe-smoking Dunsmore said that he planned to keep in shape by walking 3 to 12 miles daily and playing badminton, and he was considering taking up an aviation assignment with the Zambian government.

Max Church retired in 1980. On his last flight, on April 30 that year, he had been in command of an Air Canada 747 from London Heathrow to Toronto. After thirty-nine years and a total of 30,657 hours of airline flying, Max built a house on 25 acres near Bolton, Ontario, and developed a Christmas tree farm.

Charlie Palaisy began his aviation career in 1928 as an air engineer and aerial photographer before running the return ferry service and CGTAS for TCA. At his retirement party on January 19, 1967, Rolls Royce presented him with a powerful telescope to commemorate the long-running Rolls Royce vs. Palaisy "feud" over the Merlin engine. "When Charlie gets this telescope set up and examines the rings around Saturn," said D. Boyd, Rolls Royce's representative, "he'll probably claim that they're cracked as well."

Ron Baker retired in March 1972. In thirty-three years of service Ron had probably flown and test-flown every aircraft the company had operated. At his retirement party, aircraft manufacturers Vickers, Douglas and Lockheed presented him with mementos of when he had evaluated their planes: the nameplate from the company's first Viscount *CF-TGU*, the control wheel from its first DC-8 and an emergency beacon transmitter for his own aircraft—from Lockheed.

Lindy Rood retired in 1971 to winter in Florida and play golf and tennis. He spent his summers in Vaudreuil, Quebec, then moved to Delta, BC, in the early 1990s and later to Calgary.

J.W. "Windy" Reid, who once flew Winston Churchill to meet with Stalin in Moscow, retired from Air Canada in 1978. Until his health failed him, Windy continued to fly Boeing 707s for Ontario World Air and sponsored the Canadian Aerobatic team with a Pitts Special. He also built three antique biplanes; one of them, *CF-JLW*, was donated by his son to the Canadian Warplane Heritage.

Soon they will be no more: the collective memory of Trans Canada Airlines will dwindle to those who joined in its last years and served with Air Canada for most of their careers. If airlines like Pan American Airways and Trans World Airlines can vanish so suddenly, what hope is there for TCA, a fraction of their size and scope? As to the company's first employee, Donald Roderick MacLaren, look for his memorial at Grave 3, Lot 435 at Ocean View Memorial Park Cemetery in Burnaby, BC. Perhaps it is the nearest thing to a commemoration Trans Canada Airlines will ever have.

Notes

Chapter 1

1. *Hansard: The Official Debates of the House of Commons* (1944), p. 1573.
2. Government of Canada, Department of National Defence, *Report on Civil Aviation* (Ottawa: Queen's Printer, 1924), p. 12.
3. J.W. Pickersgill, *The Mackenzie King Record*, Vol. 1 (Toronto: University of Toronto Press, 1960), p. 647.
4. *The Canadian Who's Who* (Toronto: Trans Canada Press, 1938), pp. 335–6.
5. Shirley Render, M.A. thesis on Canadian Airways, University of Manitoba (March 1984), p. 69.

Chapter 2

1. *Hansard: The Official Debates of the House of Commons* (March 4, 1937), p. 1468.
2. *Hansard* (March 25, 1937), pp. 2210–11.
3. Ibid., p. 2388.
4. Ibid., p. 2217.
5. B. Reukema, "The Air Canada Acts: The Reason for Change," *McGill University Annals for Air and Space Law*, Vol. VI (1981), pp. 163–64.
6. *Hansard* (March 17, 1944), p. 1572.
7. Frank J. Taylor, *High Horizons: Daredevil Flying Postmen to Modern Magic Carpet, the United Airlines Story* (New York: McGraw-Hill, 1968), p. 57.
8. Philip G. Johnson Jr., letter to the author, March 1, 2000.
9. George Lothian, *Flight Deck: Memoirs of an Airline Pilot* (Toronto: McGraw-Hill Ryerson, 1979), p. 45.
10. *Horizons: Air Canada Employee Communications* (April 10, 1977), p. 15.
11. R. Bothwell, *C.D. Howe: A Biography* (Toronto: McClelland and Stewart, 1979), p. 112.
12. Dennis Duffy and Carol Cane, eds., *The Magnificent Distances: Early Aviation in British Columbia 1910–1940* (Victoria: Sound Heritage Series, 1978), p. 67.
13. Herbert Seagrim's bush flying days are described in detail in Peter Pigott, *Flying Canucks II: Pioneers in Canadian Aviation* (Toronto: Dundurn Press, 1997).
14. J.L. Lindy Rood, "Introducing the Electra," *CAHS Journal* (Spring 1986), pp. 15–33.
15. For all information on CALPA's history I am indebted to Peter Foster of the Air Canada Pilots Association for his loan of F.E.W. Smith, *The First Thirty Years: A History of the Canadian Air Line Pilots Association* (Vancouver: Mitchell Press, 1970).
16. Smith, *The First Thirty Years*, p. 22.

Chapter 3

1. Herb Seagrim, "TCA Acquisition of the Douglas DC-3," *CAHS Journal* (Fall 1990), p. 105.

2. Ibid., p. 106.
3. *Hansard: The Official Debates of the House of Commons* (August 17, 1946), p. 4998.
4. C.H. Glenn, "My 52 Years in Aviation," unpublished memoirs.
5. George Lothian, *Flight Deck: Memoirs of an Airline Pilot* (Toronto: McGraw-Hill Ryerson, 1979), p. 72.
6. Herb Seagrim, "TCA Introduces the Super Electra and Lodestar," *CAHS Journal* (Winter 1991), pp. 124–54.
7. J. Dyment, unpublished memoirs.
8. Ibid.
9. Ibid.
10. Dudley Taylor in conversation with the author.

Chapter 4

1. *Horizons*, special anniversary issue (April 10, 1977), p. 3.
2. F.T. Wood, "Twenty-Fifth Anniversary Recollections," *Between Ourselves* (May 1962).
3. Bruce West wrote "Airline Shrinks Canada" for the *Globe and Mail* (October 1953), when TCA had just carried its 6 millionth passenger and, "scratching his old grey beard," West recalled that he had been one of the party on the company's first east to west flight fourteen years before.
4. *Transcanadanews* (April 1940).
5. Excerpts from interview with Pat (Eccleston) Maxwell by Anthea Bussey, CALFAA research officer, published in *Unity*, Vol. 4, No. 4 (December 1980).
6. John Alexander, "On Duty in the Skies," *Chatelaine* (June 1939), pp. 16, 47–48.
7. Wendy Travis, "On the Wings of a Nightingale," *CAHS Journal* (Spring 1986), p. 33.
8. Jill Newby, "The Sky's the Limit," CALFAA publication, p. 2.
9. Ibid., p. 4.
10. G. McGregor, *The Adolescence of an Airline* (Montreal: Air Canada, 1970), p. 24.
11. Ibid., p. 23.
12. *The Canadian Who's Who* (Toronto: Trans Canada Press, 1939), p. 915.
13. "TCA's First Employees...Then and Now," *Between Ourselves*, 40th anniversary edition (April 10, 1977), p. 13.
14. Jim Bain, unpublished memoirs.
15. F.E.W. Smith, *The First Thirty Years: A History of the Canadian Air Line Pilots Association* (Vancouver: Mitchell Press, 1970), p. 3.

Chapter 5

1. Joan E. Rankin, *Meet me at the Chateau* (Toronto: Natural Heritage), p. 186.
2. Ibid., pp. 183–84.
3. Ibid., pp. 96, 97.
4. C. Christie and Fred Hatch, *Ocean Bridge: The History of RAF Ferry Command* (Toronto: University of Toronto Press, 1995), pp. 87–88.
5. Pierre Vachon, letter to the author, March 5, 2001.

6. *Malone v. Trans Canada Airlines* (1942), 3 D.L.R. 369.
7. George Lothian, *Flight Deck: Memoirs of an Airline Pilot* (Toronto: McGraw-Hill Ryerson, 1979), p. 86.
8. S.F. Wise and W.A.B. Douglas, *The Official History of the Royal Canadian Air Force: The Creation of a National Air Force* (Ottawa: Government of Canada, Ministry of Supply and Services, 1986), p. 649.
9. Jim Bain, unpublished memoirs, p. 5.
10. "Their Coveralls are Uniforms," *Between Ourselves* (March 1943), p. 23.
11. George Lothian, *Flight Deck*, pp. 76–77.
12. George Lothian, "Flying with Ferry Command," *Canadian Aviation*, 50th anniversary issue (1978), p. 101.
13. George Lothian, *Flight Deck*.

Chapter 6

1. Ross Smyth, "The Early War Years," *Between Ourselves* (April 10, 1977), p. 11.
2. *Between Ourselves* (March 1944), p. 29.
3. Frank Smith, letter to the author, December 28, 1995.
4. *Hansard: The Official Debates of the House of Commons* (June16, 1943), pp. 3696–97.
5. David Clark MacKenzie, *Canada and International Civil Aviation, 1932–1948* (Toronto: University of Toronto Press, 1989), pp. 117–18.
6. "Montreal Meridian," *Between Ourselves* (Fall 1944).

Chapter 7

1. J.W. Pickersgill, *The Mackenzie King Record*, Vol. 1,1939–44 (Toronto: University of Toronto Press, 1960), p. 645.
2. Ibid., p. 646.
3. *Hansard: The Official Debates of the House of Commons* (1944), pp. 1570–80.
4. Ibid., pp. 2044–49.
5. *Hansard* (August 17, 1946), p. 5001.
6. "Close of An Era," *Canadian Aviation* (September 1983), pp. 39–41.
7. Jack Jones, letter to the author, December 9, 2000.
8. Jim Bain, unpublished memoirs, p. 6.
9. Lindy Rood, letter to the author, January 16, 2001.
10. Trans Canada Airlines Act, S.C. 1945, c. 31. S. 7.

Chapter 8

1. G. McGregor, *The Adolescence of an Airline* (Montreal: Air Canada, 1970), p. 87.
2. Trans Canada Airlines brochure (Summer 1945), p. 1.
3. Jill Newby, *The Sky's the Limit: The Story of the Canadian Air Line Flight Attendants' Association* (Vancouver: CALFAA, 1986), p. 8.
4. G. McGregor, *The Adolescence of an Airline*, p. 4.
5. Jim Bain, unpublished memoirs, p. 11.
6. G. McGregor, *The Adolescence of an Airline*, p. 39.
7. Jim Bain, unpublished memoirs, p. 11.
8. Max Church, letter to the author, January 23, 2001.

Chapter 9

1. *Hansard: The Official Debates of the House of Commons* (July 8, 1947), p. 5227.
2. Jim Bain, unpublished memoirs, p. 7.
3. Janet Proudfoot, letter to the author, October 1999.
4. J. Dyment, *CAHS Journal* (Spring 1986), p. 37.
5. George Lothian, *Flight Deck: Memoirs of an Airline Pilot* (Toronto: McGraw-Hill Ryerson, 1979).
6. G. McGregor, *The Adolescence of an Airline* (Montreal: Air Canada, 1970), p. 4.
7. P. Smith, *It Seems Like Only Yesterday: Air Canada, The First Fifty Years* (Toronto: McClelland and Stewart, 1986), p. 125.
8. *Ottawa Evening Citizen* (January 20, 1948).
9. F.E.W. Smith, *The First Thirty Years: A History of the Canadian Air Line Pilots Association* (Vancouver: Mitchell Press, 1970), p. 20.
10. Craig Chouinard, *From Dedicated Amateurs to Dynamic Advocates* (Toronto: Canadian Automotive, Aerospace, Transportation and General Workers Union of Canada, Local 2213, 1995), p. 16.
11. Ibid., p. 20.
12. Ross Smyth, letter to the author, October 5, 2000.
13. Smith, *The First Thirty Years*, p. 25.
14. Records of Air Canada: President's Office, 1936–1948, National Archives of Canada, RG 145.
15. Chouinard, *From Dedicated Amateurs*, p. 23.
16. Minutes of the Annual General Meeting, Canadian Automotive, Aerospace, Transportation and General Workers Union of Canada (October 18–19, 1945), CAW Archives, Winnipeg.
17. Joan E. Rankin, *Meet me at the Chateau* (Toronto: Natural Heritage), p. 185.
18. Jill Newby, *The Sky's the Limit: The Story of the Canadian Air Line Flight Attendants' Association* (Vancouver: CALFAA, 1986), p. 10.
19. Ibid., p. 10.
20. Ibid., p. 108.
21. *Hansard* (August 17, 1946), pp. 5000–3.
22. J.W. Pickersgill, *My Years with Louis St. Laurent* (Toronto: University of Toronto Press, 1975), p. 53.

Chapter 10

1. Kathleen (Stewart) Torrell, letter to the author, September 1999.
2. Jill Newby, *The Sky's the Limit: The Story of the Canadian Air Line Flight Attendants' Association* (Vancouver: CALFAA, 1986), p. 108.
3. Ibid., p. 57.
4. Craig Chouinard, *From Dedicated Amateurs to Dynamic Advocates* (Toronto: Canadian Automotive, Aerospace, Transportation and General Workers Union of Canada, Local 2213, 1995), p. 65.
5. David Clark MacKenzie, *Canada and International Civil Aviation, 1932–1948* (Toronto: University of Toronto Press, 1989), pp. 117–18.
6. F.E.W. Smith, *The First Thirty Years: A History of the Canadian Air Line Pilots Association* (Vancouver: Mitchell Press, 1970), p. 26.

7. *Hansard: The Official Debates of the House of Commons* (March 10, 1948), p. 2067.
8. C. Glenn, "Nuts and Bolts," unpublished memoirs, pp. 60–61.
9. G. McGregor, *The Adolescence of an Airline* (Montreal: Air Canada, 1970), p. 36.
10. Ibid., pp. 58–59.
11. John Condt, *Wings Over the West* (Madeira Park, BC: Harbour Publishing, 1984), p. 100.
12. G. McGregor, *The Adolescence of an Airline*, p. 59.
13. Ibid., p. 2.
14. W. Stevenson, "They Hitch their Planes to the Wind," *Star Weekly* (1950).
15. Newby, *The Sky's the Limit*, p. 105.
16. R. Keith, *Bush Pilot with a Briefcase* (Vancouver: Paperjacks, 1972), p. 266.
17. *Hansard* (March 22, 1950), pp. 1026–27.
18. "MacLeod of TCA," *Between Ourselves* (June 1952), pp. 3–7.
19. G. McGregor, *The Adolescence of an Airline*, p. 17.
20. D.R. Taylor, "Lightning Strikes as experienced by Trans Canada Airlines," CIV 25717, CATC (49) 124 (November 3, 1948), pp. 1–4.
21. G. McGregor, *The Adolescence of an Airline*, pp. 16–17.
22. Earle Birney, "North Star West," *Collected Poems*, Vol. I (Toronto: McClelland and Stewart, 1975), p. 156.

Chapter 11

1. G. McGregor, *The Adolescence of an Airline* (Montreal: Air Canada, 1970), p. 88.
2. F.E.W. Smith, *The First Thirty Years: A History of the Canadian Air Line Pilots Association* (Vancouver: Mitchell Press, 1970), p. 139.
3. G. McGregor, *The Adolescence of an Airline*, p. 49.
4. George Lothian, "Enter, The Viscount," *CAHS Journal* (Spring 1986), p. 25.
5. G. McGregor, *The Adolescence of an Airline*, p. 55.
6. Ibid., p. 89.
7. Lothian, "Enter, the Viscount," p. 30.
8. G. McGregor, *The Adolescence of an Airline*, p. 74.
9. Clayton Glenn, letter to Beth Buchanan, November 19, 1971.
10. Government of Canada, House of Commons, Sessional Committee on Railways, Airlines and Shipping Owned and Controlled by the Government, Minutes and Proceedings (1958), pp. 222–23.
11. Smith, *The First Thirty Years*, p. 74.
12. Ibid., p. 89.

Chapter 12

1. *Aircraft Accident Digest*, ICAO Circular 47-AN/42, pp. 93–96.
2. Report by the Department of Transport Canada, Serial No. 56-16, *Aircraft Accident Digest*, ICAO Circular 56-AN/51, pp. 16–25.
3. Jill Newby, *The Sky's the Limit: The Story of the Canadian Air Line Flight Attendants' Association* (Vancouver: CALFAA, 1986), p. 59.
4. Denis Smith, *Rogue Tory: The Life and Legend of John Diefenbaker* (Toronto: MacFarlane, Walter & Ross), 1995, p. 117.

5. G. McGregor, *The Adolescence of an Airline* (Montreal: Air Canada, 1970), p. 112.
6. S.F. Wheatcroft, *Airline Competition in Canada* (Ottawa: Department of Transport, 1958), p. 2.
7. Ibid., p. 23.
8. Ibid., p. 12.
9. John Condt, *Wings Over the West* (Madeira Park, BC: Harbour Publishing, 1984), p. 158.
10. Ibid., p. 158.
11. Donald Fleming, *So Very Near: The Political Memoirs of the Hon. Donald M. Fleming*, Vol. 2: The Summit Years (Toronto: McClelland and Stewart, 1985), p. 25.
12. Wheatcroft, *Airline Competition in Canada*, p. 23.
13. Kevin Christiano, "From TCA to Air Canada: The Political Patterns of a Future Prime Minister," *American Review of Canadian Studies* (Spring 1996), p. 59.
14. G. McGregor, *The Adolescence of an Airline*, p. 141.

Chapter 13

1. Trans Canada Airlines press release, July 17, 1962.
2. George Lothian, *Flight Deck: Memoirs of an Airline Pilot* (Toronto: McGraw-Hill Ryerson, 1979), p. 171.
3. Lindy Rood, "Introducing the Electra," *CAHS Journal* (Spring 1986), p. 18.
4. *Report of the Commission of Inquiry Into the Crash of Trans Canada Airlines DC-8F Aircraft* CF-TJN *at Ste. Therese de Blainville, P.Q. on 29th November 1963*, Order-in-Council (October 8, 1964), P.C. 1964–1544. CA1 EAN605-65. R21.
5. *Hansard: The Official Debates of the House of Commons* (July 31, 1963), p. 2856.
6. "Be Brave, Ottawa, Be Brave," *Financial Post* (October 12, 1963), p. 8.
7. *Hansard* (March 3, 1964), pp. 480–82.
8. Alice Dalziel, "Ventilate Canada," Montreal *Gazette* (March 6, 1964), p. 6.

Index